YOUTH
IN MODERN
SOCIETY

Shirley M. Clark and John P. Clark

University of Minnesota
Editors

YOUTH
IN MODERN
SOCIETY

HOLT, RINEHART AND WINSTON, INC.
New York   Chicago   San Francisco   Atlanta
Dallas   Montreal   Toronto   London   Sydney

To Mary Alison, John David, and Timothy
for Whom This Anthology Is Written
and Who Will Soon Judge Its Merits

Library of Congress Catalog Card Number: 70–186569
ISBN: 0–03–084735–4
Printed in the United States of America
2 3 4 5   090   9 8 7 6 5 4 3 2 1

Preface

Books such as this are usually compiled because there is a need to accumulate the best writing on a specific topic for the convenience of the serious reader who wants a comprehensive exposure to the topic at hand. Therefore, an anthology on the sociology of *Youth in Modern Society* had to wait until there was sufficient material on this topic and until enough people were seriously interested in a sociological analysis of youth status. Although literally volumes upon volumes have been written about the social behavior of youth, it has not been until lately that sociological analyses on a wide range of youth behavior have been available.

There is some danger in attempting a scientific analysis of the condition of youth at a time when societal awareness of youth problems is intense. Under such circumstances, even the scientists' devotion to objectivity may be severely strained. Therefore, we have tried to select those articles which focus upon the more salient social aspects of youth status and which expose their methodology to scrutiny.

Though we have opted for the more rigorous research approach generally and the sociological perspective particularly, these analyses should provide a well-informed general entree to discussions of the current condition of youth. A "groovy" book it is not—unless the reader is "turned on" by the pursuit of principles concerning social behavior. Social science is primarily interested in phenomena which may be understood today, and tomorrow too, with a single explanation.

There is an extraordinary consciousness of youth in modern societies. In part, this awareness of youth may be attributed to the fact that statistically speaking numbers of younger people are increasing. It is more likely, though, that the free-association images of adults when the term "youth" is mentioned are rich with anxious concern about delinquents, student protesters, revolutionaries, draft resisters, drug users, hippies, and so forth. Some feel that today's young people constitute an anti-American generation, a political-social threat to the country. Youthful activism is not exclusively American; it is so universally displayed that it seems safe to assume that the so-called "generation gap" is characteristic of societies on a world-wide basis. In industrial societies everywhere, the young seem to share the sense that there are no adults from whom they can learn.

In her recent book the venerable anthropologist Margaret Mead has focused on the conditions which have brought about the restiveness of youth over the world.[1] She attributes the heightened consciousness and concern for youth to the emergence of a world community wherein, for the first time, human beings have become united by shared knowledge and danger. Wherein the more primitive cultures have skipped whole stages of societal development and have moved into the present via television satellites, tape recorders, jet planes, and the like, we all have moved into an era of accelerated technological and social change. The point is that while adults, who were the prisoners in a new era, moved as immigrants from the recent past into the present, youth were born here; they are at home in all this. As they put it, the future is NOW. Racism, poverty, and war are evils the idealistic young are trying to eliminate now, not with all deliberate speed (which reads "creeping gradualism"). Thus weaves the logic of commentators who argue that the generation gap is really wider today than generational discontinuities have been in the past.

It may seem that our perspective on youth is heavily influenced by societal context and social change. Indeed, it is our intention to contribute to the emerging sociological view of youth which complements the older psychology of adolescence with its emphasis on maturation and personality. We believe that the problems of growth and identity must be combined with the problems of the social structural-functional context in which the youth status is lodged. There is some artificiality in the sectioning of reality, in the presentation of youth in pieces, but we believe that the sociology of adolescence has been neglected.

It has been argued by Musgrove, the British sociologist, that the adolescent was "invented" by the social legislation and social conventions which followed the technological industrial innovations of little more than two centuries ago.[2] The diminishing need for juvenile labor was linked with the enactment of protective legislation, e.g., child labor laws and compulsory education laws which caused an interim status to arise. Musgrove rather pointedly suggests that adults may have had the protection of their own status, rather than protection of the young, in mind when they succeeded in expelling youngsters from the factories and requiring them to be off the streets and in the schools.

American society, like other developing societies, is adolescence-inducing, that is, the conditions under which youth groups tend to arise and age groups layer themselves, are met: the family or kinship unit, by itself, cannot assure full attainment of social status on the part of its members. Thus youth tend to coalesce in peer groups for development of identity, attainment of personal autonomy, and effective transition into the adult world.[3] A sociology of adolescence or youth explores the social, structural, and cultural antecedents

---

[1] For a detailed analysis of this phenomenon see Margaret Mead, *Culture and Commitment: A Study of the Generation Gap*, Garden City, N.Y.: Natural History Press/Doubleday, 1970.

[2] Frank Musgrove, *Youth and the Social Order*, Bloomington, Ind.: University of Indiana Press, 1965.

[3] S. N. Eisenstadt, *From Generation to Generation: Age Groups and the Social Structure* New York: The Free Press, 1956.

of adolescence, the variability in youthful experience, and the social-problem status or deviance vulnerability of adolescents.

Although it may not be necessary or even possible to satisfactorily define the terms "youth" and "adolescence" precisely, some stabs in the direction of establishing referents may be helpful to the reader. We will be using "youth" and "adolescence" synonymously. By these terms we mean age groups extending from the early teens into the early twenties. Actually the upper and lower limits of the age period are variably designated. What, for example, are pre-teens who identify with and share characteristics of teen-agers? Are young people adults if they have matured physiologically and psychologically but have not entered into established society via employment or marriage? Would you accept them as young adults, or would you maintain that they are "youth" as Keniston does?[4] The definitional problem is complicated by the fact that physiological and biological changes which culminate in the physically mature adult usually take many years to evolve in both girls and boys and are typically achieved before an individual's formal education is completed.

The central purpose of this collection of readings is to provide analytical guides and substance for those interested in a large and important social category of population in modern industrial societies. Our purpose will have been achieved if the reader is led to seriously consider the condition of youth from an informed, dispassionate, and sociological perspective.

Minneapolis, Minn. SHIRLEY M. CLARK
February 1972 JOHN P. CLARK

[4] Kenneth Keniston, *Young Radicals*, New York: Harcourt Brace Jovanovich, 1968, Chapter 8.

Contents

CHAPTER 5   YOUTH PREPARES FOR WORK   240

CHAPTER 6   POLITICAL ACTION AND YOUTH   315

CHAPTER 7   YOUTH AND ORGANIZED RELIGION   371

CHAPTER 8   SOCIAL PROBLEM STATUS OF YOUTH   399

CHAPTER I

The Sociological Analysis of Youth

For some curious reason the development of a separate subject matter on the "sociology of youth" has beeen long in gestation. Perhaps the major sociological interests in education, family, and social problems served to meet the early and persistent concern for the condition of youth. Dating patterns, juvenile delinquency, child-rearing practices, and a myriad of youth-related topics have long been scrutinized within these fields of sociology but only within the past two or three decades have sociologists focused upon the several aspects of youth behavior as being sufficiently interrelated and unique to merit separate treatment.

The first two selections of this anthology have been chosen because an appreciation of their content is critical to viewing the analyses which follow from a historical and comparative perspective. Both articles deal in some way with the universal character of the important role played by youth in modern emergent and industrial societies. As with most social phenomena when examined closely, historical antecedents and even equivalents of the character of youth roles in modern society can be found. Further, an understanding of the broad social context often elucidates critical dimensions of the phenomenon being studied. And so it is with the study of youth. To limit oneself to the happenings of "now" would seriously thwart the sociologist's search for the general principles and trends which are the cornerstones of the social scientific endeavor.

Perhaps no other social scientist tailors the sweep of history more expertly to his cause than Eisenstadt. He ranges through time and over the world to muster data upon which to base his observations about the similarities and dissimilarities of youth in modern societies. He provides insights into the universal feature of age grading from which social identities are derived. Perhaps he places excessive emphasis on the transitory character of youth to the exclusion of its being perceived as a static condition by sizable proportions of its participants. However, he erects analytical bridges between the traditional understandings of *rites de passage*

1

in primitive societies and their functional equivalents in modern societies. Our guess is that once steeped in the historical and global perspective which the selection from Eisenstadt represents, current behaviors of youth become much less unique and unfathomable to the observer.

Much of the current adult awareness of youth is prompted by youth's potential and realized political power. Some analysts incorporate the study of population shifts to assist their comparative analysis of the force of youth upon various societies. Musgrove has conducted the most penetrating examination of population changes and the status of youth. He focuses primarily upon his own society, England, but alludes strongly to the applicability of his observations to societies of roughly similar industrial patterns, such as the United States. From his article we learn that the characteristics of youth status may be reflective of such unglamorous and subtle forces as population compositions.

These two articles are admittedly rather "heavy" as an introduction to our very exciting, emotional, and perplexing topic. We hope, however, that the perspective of the articles will provide a backdrop against which to consider the observations which follow. Perhaps, too, it will provide a rudder in the turbulent water which surrounds the analysis of youth behavior in modern societies. This is not to imply that the historical, comparative, and broad picture provides all understanding, but it does provide the social scientist and more serious social observer with threads of insights which have more than fleeting existences.

ARCHETYPAL PATTERNS OF YOUTH*

S. N. EISENSTADT

Youth constitutes a universal phenomenon. It is first of all a biological phenomenon, but one always defined in cultural terms. In this sense it constitutes a part of a wider cultural phenomenon, the varying definitions of age and of the differences between one age and another.[1] Age and age differences are among the basic aspects of life and the determinants of human destiny. Every human being passes through various ages, and at each one he attains and uses different biological and intellectual capacities. At each stage he performs different tasks and roles in relation to the other members of his society: from a child, he becomes a father; from a pupil, a teacher; from a vigorous youth, a mature adult, and then an aging and "old" man.

This gradual unfolding of power and capacity is not merely a universal, biologically conditioned, and inescapable fact. Although the basic biological processes of maturation (within the limits set by such factors as relative longevity) are probably more or less similar in all human societies, their cultural definition varies from society to society, at least in details. In all societies, age serves as a basis for defining the cultural and social characteristic of human beings, for the formation of some of their mutual relations and common activities, and for the differential allocation of social roles.

The cultural definitions of age and age differences contain several different yet complementary elements. First, these definitions often refer to the social division of labor in a society, to the criteria according to which people occupy various social positions and roles within any society. For instance, in many societies certain roles—especially those of married men, full citizens, independent earners—are barred to young people, while others—as certain military roles—are specifically allocated to them. Second, the cultural definition of age is one important constituent of a person's self-identity, his self-perception in terms of his own psychological needs and aspirations, his place in society, and the ultimate meaning of his life.

Within any such definition, the qualities of each age are evaluated according to their relation to some basic, primordial qualities, such as vigor, physical

* Reprinted from S. N. Eisenstadt, "Archetypal Patterns of Youth," by permission from *Daedalus*, Journal of the American Academy of Arts and Sciences, Boston, Massachusetts, Vol. 91, No. 1 (1962), pp, 28–46.
[1] A general sociological analysis of the place of age in social structure has been attempted in S. N. Eisenstadt, *From Generation to Generation* (Chicago: The Free Press of Glencoe, Illinois, 1956).

and sexual prowess, the ability to cope with material, social, and supernatural environment, wisdom, experience, or divine inspiration. Different ages are seen in different societies as the embodiments of such qualities. These various qualities seem to unfold from one age to another, each age emphasizing some out of the whole panorama of such possible qualities. The cultural definition of an age span is always a broad definition of human potentialities, limitations, and obligations at a given stage of life. In terms of these definitions, people map out the broad contours of life, their own expectations and possibilities, and place themselves and their fellow men in social and cultural positions, ascribing to each a given place within these contours.

The various qualities attributed to different ages do not constitute an unconnected series. They are usually interconnected in many ways. The subtle dialectics between the unfolding of some qualities and the waning of others in a person is not a mere registration of his psychological or biological traits; rather, it constitutes the broad framework of his potentialities and their limits throughout his life span. The characteristics of any one "age," therefore, cannot be fully understood except in relation to those of other ages. Whether seen as a gradually unfolding continuum or as a series of sharp contrasts and opposed characteristics, they are fully explicable and understandable only in terms of one another. The boy bears within himself the seeds of the adult man; else, he must as an adult acquire new patterns of behavior, sharply and intentionally opposed to those of his boyhood. The adult either develops naturally into an old man— or decays into one. Only when taken together do these different "ages" constitute the entire map of human possibilities and limitations; and, as every individual usually must pass through them all, their complementariness and continuity (even if defined in discontinuous and contrasting terms) become strongly emphasized and articulated.

The same holds true for the age definitions of the two sexes, although perhaps with a somewhat different meaning. Each age span is defined differently for either sex, and these definitions are usually related and complementary, as the "sexual image" and identity always constitute basic elements of man's image in every society. This close connection between different ages necessarily stresses the problem of transition from one point in a person's life to another as a basic constituent of any cultural definition of an "age." Hence, each definition of age must necessarily cope with the perception of time, and changes in time, of one's own progress in time, one's transition from one period of life to another.

This personal transition, or temporal progress, or change, may become closely linked with what may be called cosmic and societal time.[2] The attempt to find some meaning in personal temporal transition may often lead to identification with the rhythms of nature or history, with the cycles of the seasons,

---

[2] The analysis of personal, cosmic, and societal time (or temporal progression) has constituted a fascinating but not easily dealt with focus of analysis. For some approaches to these problems, see *Man and Time* (papers from the Eranos Yearbooks, edited by Joseph Campbell; London: Routledge & Kegan Paul, 1958), especially the article by Gerardus van der Lecuw. See also Mircea Eliade, *The Myth of the Eternal Return*. Translated by W. R. Trask. New York: Pantheon Books, 1954 (Bollingen Series).

with the unfolding of some cosmic plan (whether cyclical, seasonal, or apocalyptic), or with the destiny and development of society. The nature of this linkage often constitutes the focus round which an individual's personal identity becomes defined in cultural terms and through which personal experience, with its anguish, may be given some meaning in terms of cultural symbols and values.

The whole problem of age definition and the linkage of personal time and transition with cosmic time become especially accentuated in that age span usually designated as youth. However great the differences among various societies, there is one focal point within the life span of an individual which in most known societies is to some extent emphasized: the period of youth, of transition from childhood to full adult status, or full membership in the society. In this period the individual is no longer a child (especially from the physical and sexual point of view) but is ready to undertake many attributes of an adult and to fulfill adult roles. But he is not yet fully acknowledged as an adult, a full member of the society. Rather, he is being "prepared," or is preparing himself for such adulthood.

This image of youth—the cultural definition of youth—contains all the crucial elements of any definition of age, usually in an especially articulated way. This is the stage at which the individual's personality acquires the basic psychological mechanism of self-regulation and self-control, when his self-identity becomes crystalized. It is also the stage at which the young are confronted with some models of the major roles they are supposed to emulate in adult life and with the major symbols and values of their culture and community. Moreover, in this phase the problem of the linkage of the personal temporal transition with cosmic or societal time becomes extremely acute. Any cultural definition of youth describes it as a transitory phase, couched in terms of transition toward something new, something basically different from the past. Hence the acuteness of the problem of linkage.

The very emphasis on the transitory nature of this stage and of its essentially preparatory character, however, may easily create a somewhat paradoxical situation. It may evolve an image of youth as the purest manifestation and repository of ultimate cultural and societal values. Such an image is rooted first in the fact that to some extent youth is always defined as a period of "role moratorium," that is, as a period in which one may play with various roles without definitely choosing any. It does not yet require the various compromises inherent in daily participation in adult life. At the same time, however, since it is also the period when the maximum identification with the values of the society is stressed, under certain conditions it may be viewed as the repository of all the major human virtues and primordial qualities. It may then be regarded as the only age in which full identification with the ultimate values and symbols of the society is attained—facilitated by the flowering of physical vigor, a vigor which may easily become identified with a more general flowering of the cosmos or the society.

The fullest, the most articulate and definitive expression of these archetypal elements of youth is best exemplified in the ritual dramatization of the transition from adolescence to adulthood, such as the various *rites de passage* and ceremonies of initiation in primitive tribes and in ancient civilizations.[3] In these rites the pre-adult youth are transformed into full members of the tribe. This transformation is effected through:

1. a series of rites in which the adolescents are symbolically divested of the characteristics of youth and invested with those of adulthood, from a sexual and social point of view; this investment, which has deep emotional significance, may have various concrete manifestations: bodily mutilation, circumcision, the taking on of a new name or symbolic rebirth;
2. the complete symbolic separation of the male adolescents from the world of their youth, especially from their close attachment to their mothers; in other words, their complete "male" independence and image are fully articulated (the opposite usually holds true of girls' initiations);
3. the dramatization of the encounter between the several generations, a dramatization that may take the form of a fight or a competition, in which the basic complementariness of various age grades—whether of a continuous or discontinuous type—is stressed; quite often the discontinuity between adolescence and adulthood is symbolically expressed, as in the symbolic death of the adolescents as children and their rebirth as adults.
4. the transmission of the tribal lore with its instructions about proper behavior, both through formalized teaching and through various ritual activities; this transmission is combined with:
5. a relaxation of the concrete control of the adults over the erstwhile adolescents and its substitution by self-control and adult responsibility.

Most of these dramatic elements can also be found, although in somewhat more diluted forms, in various traditional folk festivals in peasant communities, especially those such as rural carnivals in which youth and marriage are emphasized. In an even more diluted form, these elements may be found in various spontaneous initiation ceremonies of the fraternities and youth groups in modern societies.[4] Here, however, the full dramatic articulation of these elements is lacking, and their configuration and organization assume different forms.

The transition from childhood and adolescence to adulthood, the development of personal identity, psychological autonomy and self-regulation, the attempt to link personal temporal transition to general cultural images and to cosmic rhythms, and to link psychological maturity to the emulation of definite role models—these constitute the basic elements of any archetypal image of youth. However, the ways in which these various elements become crystallized in concrete configurations differ greatly from society to society and within sectors of the same society. The full dramatic articulation of these elements in the *rites de passage* of primitive societies constitutes only one—perhaps the

[3] For a fuller exposition of the sociological significance of initiation rites, see Mircea Eliade, *Birth and Rebirth* (New York: Harper & Brothers, 1958) and *From Generation to Generation* (ref. 1).
[4] See Bruno Bettelheim, *Symbolic Wounds, Puberty Rites and the Envious Circle* (Chicago: The Free Press of Glencoe, Illinois, 1954).

most extreme and articulate but certainly not the only—configuration of these archetypal elements of youth.

In order to understand other types of such configurations, it is necessary to analyze some conditions that influence their development. Perhaps the best starting point is the nature of the social organization of the period of adolescence: the process of transition from childhood to adulthood, the social context in which the process of growing up is shaped and structured. There are two major criteria that shape the social organization of the period of youth. One is the extent to which age in general and youth in particular form a criterion for the allocation of roles in a society, whether in politics, in economic or cultural activity—aside from the family, of course, in which they always serve as such a criterion. The second is the extent to which any society develops specific age groups, specific corporate organizations, composed of members of the same "age," such as youth movements or old men's clubs. If roles are allocated in a society according to age, this greatly influences the extent to which age constitutes a component of a person's identity. In such cases, youth becomes a definite and meaningful phase of transition in an individual's progress through life, and his budding self-identity acquires content and a relation to role models and cultural values. No less important to the concrete development of identity is the extent to which it is influenced, either by the common participation of different generations in the same group as in the family, or conversely by the organization of members of the same age groups into specific, distinct groups.

The importance of age as a criterion for allocating roles in a society is closely related to several major aspects of social organization and cultural orientation. The first aspect is the relative complexity of the division of labor. In general, the simpler the organization of the society, the more influential age will be as a criterion for allocating roles. Therefore, in primitive or traditional societies (or in the more primitive and traditional sectors of developed societies) age and seniority constitute basic criteria for allocating social, economic, and political roles.

The second aspect consists of the major value orientations and symbols of a society, especially the extent to which they emphasize certain general orientations, qualities, or types of activity (such as physical vigor, the maintenance of cultural tradition, the achievement and maintenance of supernatural prowess) which can be defined in terms of broad human qualities and which become expressed and symbolized in specific ages.

The emphasis on any particular age as a criterion for the allocation of roles is largely related to the concrete application of the major value orientations in a society. For instance, we find that those primitive societies in which military values and orientations prevail emphasize young adulthood as the most important age, while those in which sedentary activities prevail emphasize older age. Similarly, within some traditional societies, a particular period such as old age may be emphasized if it is seen as the most appropriate one for expressing major cultural values and symbols—for instance, the upholding of a given cultural tradition.

The social and cultural conditions that determine the extent to which specific age groups and youth groups develop differ from the conditions that determine the extent to which age serves as a criterion for the allocation of roles. At the same time, the two kinds of conditions may be closely related, as we shall see. Age groups in general and youth groups in particular tend to arise in those societies in which the family or kinship unit cannot ensure (it may even impede) the attainment of full social status on the part of its members. These conditions appear especially (although not uniquely[5]) in societies in which family or kinship groups do not constitute the basic unit of the social division of labor. Several features characterize such societies. First, the membership in the total society (citizenship) is not defined in terms of belonging to any such family, kinship group, or estate, nor is it mediated by such a group.

Second, in these societies the major political, economic, social, and religious functions are performed not by family or kinship units but rather by various specialized groups (political parties, occupational associations, etc.), which individuals may join irrespective of their family, kinship, or caste. In these societies, therefore, the major roles that adults are expected to perform in the wider society differ in orientation from those of the family or kinship group. The children's identification and close interaction with family members of other ages do not assure the attainment of full self-identity and social maturity on the part of the children. In these cases, there arises a tendency for peer groups to form, especially youth groups; these can serve as a transitory phase between the world of childhood and the adult world.

This type of the social division of labor is found in varying degrees in different societies, primitive, historical, or modern. In several primitive tribes such a division of labor has existed,[6] for example, in Africa, among the chiefless (segmentary) tribes of Nandi, Masai, or Kipigis, in the village communities of Yako and Ibo, or in more centralized kingdoms of the Zulu and Swazi, and among some of the Indian tribes of the Plains, as well as among some South American and Indian tribes.

Such a division of labor likewise existed to some extent in several historical societies (especially in city states such as Athens or Rome), although most great historical civilizations were characterized mainly by a more hierarchical and ascriptive system of the division of labor, in which there were greater continuity and harmony between the family and kinship groups and the broader institutional contexts. The fullest development of this type of the social division of labor, however, is to be found in modern industrial societies. Their inclusive membership is usually based on the universal criterion of citizenship and is not conditioned by membership in any kinship group. In these societies the family does not constitute a basic unit of the division of labor, especially not in production and distribution, and even in the sphere of consumption its functions become more limited. Occupations are not transmitted through heredity. Similarly, the family or kinship group does not constitute a basic unit of political or ritual activities. Moreover, the general scope of the activities of the family has been continuously diminishing, while various specialized agencies tend to take over its functions in the fields of education and recreation.

To be sure, the extent to which the family is diminishing in modern soci-

---

[5] A special type of age groups may also develop in familistic societies. See *From Generation to Generation* (ref. 1), ch. 5.
[6] For fuller details, see *From Generation to Generation*, especially chs. 3 and 4.

eties is often exaggerated. In many social spheres (neighborhood, friendship, informal association, some class relations, community relations), family, kinship, and status are still very influential. But the scope of these relations is more limited in modern societies than in many others, even if the prevalent myth of the disappearance of the family has long since been exploded. The major social developments of the nineteenth century (the establishment of national states, the progress of the industrial revolution, the great waves of intercontinental migrations) have greatly contributed to this diminution of scope, and especially in the first phase of modernization there has been a growing discontinuity between the life of the children, whether in the family or the traditional school and in the social world with its new and enlarged perspectives.

Youth groups tend to develop in all societies in which such a division of labor exists. Youth's tendency to coalesce in such groups is rooted in the fact that participation in the family became insufficient for developing full identity or full social maturity, and that the roles learned in the family did not constitute an adequate basis for developing such identity and participation. In the youth groups the adolescent seeks some framework for the development and crystallization of his identity, for the attainment of personal autonomy, and for his effective transition into the adult world.

Various types of youth organizations always tend to appear with the transition from traditional or feudal societies to modern societies, along with the intensified processes of change, especially in periods of rapid mobility, migration, urbanization, and industrialization. This is true of all European societies, and also of non-Western societies. The impact of Western civilization on primitive and historical-traditional peoples is usually connected with the disruption of family life, but beyond this it also involves a change in the mutual evaluation of the different generations. The younger generation usually begin to seek a new self-identification, and in one phase or another this search is expressed in ideological conflict with the older.

Most of the nationalistic movements in the Middle East, Asia, and Africa have consisted of young people, students, or officers who rebelled against their elders and the traditional familistic setting with its stress on the latters' authority. At the same time there usually has developed a specific youth consciousness and ideology that intensifies the nationalistic movement to "rejuvenate" the country.

The emergence of the peer group among immigrant children is a well-known phenomenon that usually appears in the second generation. It occurs mainly because of the relative breakdown of immigrant family life in the new country. The more highly industrialized and urbanized that country (or the sector absorbing the immigrants) is, the sharper the breakdown. Hence, the family of the immigrant or second-generation child has often been an inadequate guide to the new society. The immigrant child's attainment of full identity in the new land is usually related to how much he has been able to detach himself from his older, family setting. Some of these children, therefore, have developed a strong predisposition to join various peer groups. Such an affiliation has sometimes facilitated their transition to the absorbing society by stressing the values and patterns of behavior in that society—or, on the contrary, it may express their rebellion against this society, or against their older setting.

All these modern social developments and movements have given rise to a great variety of youth groups, peer groups, youth movements, and what has been called youth culture. The types and concrete forms of such groups varies widely: spontaneous youth groups, student movements, ideological and semi-political movements, and youth rebellions connected with the Romantic movement in Europe, and, later, with the German youth movements. The various social and national trends of the nineteenth and twentieth centuries have also given impetus to such organizations. At the same time there have appeared many adult-sponsored youth organizations and other agencies springing out of the great extension of educational institutions. In addition to providing recreative facilities, these agencies have also aimed at character molding and the instilling of civic virtues, so as to deepen social consciousness and widen the social and cultural horizon. The chief examples are the YMCA, the Youth Brigades organized in England by William Smith, the Boy Scouts, the Jousters in France, and the many kinds of community organizations, hostels, summer camps, or vocational guidance centers.

Thus we see that there are many parallels between primitive and historical societies and modern societies with regard to the conditions under which the various constellations of youth groups, youth activities, and youth images have developed. But these parallels are only partial. Despite certain similarities, the specific configurations of the basic archetypal elements of the youth image in modern societies differ greatly from those of primitive and traditional societies. The most important differences are rooted in the fact that in the modern, the development of specific youth organizations is paradoxically connected with the weakening of the importance of age in general and youth in particular as definite criteria for the allocation of roles in society.

As we have already said, the extent to which major occupational, cultural, or political roles are allocated today according to the explicit criterion of age is very small. Most such roles are achieved according to wealth, acquired skills, specialization, and knowledge. Family background may be of great importance for the acquisition of these attributes, but very few positions are directly given people by virtue of their family standing. Yet this very weakening of the importance of age is always connected with intensive developments of youth groups and movements. This fact has several interesting repercussions on the organization and structure of such groups. In primitive and traditional societies, youth groups are usually part of a wider organization of age groups that covers a very long period of life, from childhood to late adulthood and even old age. To be sure, it is during youth that most of the dramatic elements of the transition from one age to another are manifest, but this stage constitutes only part of a longer series of continuous, well-defined stages.

From this point of view, primitive or traditional societies do not differ greatly from those in which the transition from youth to adulthood is not organized in specific age groups but is largely effected within the fold of the family and kinship groups. In both primitive and traditional societies we observe a close and comprehensive linkage between personal temporal transition and societal or cosmic time, a linkage most fully expressed in the *rites de passage*. Consequently, the transition from childhood to adulthood in all such societies is given full meaning in terms of ultimate cultural values and symbols borne or symbolized by various adult role models.

In modern societies the above picture greatly changes. The youth group, whatever its composition or organization, usually stands alone. It does not constitute a part of a fully institutionalized and organized series of age groups. It is true that in many of the more traditional sectors of modern societies the more primitive or traditional archetypes of youth still prevail. Moreover, in many modern societies elements of the primitive archetypes of youth still exist. But the full articulation of these elements is lacking, and the social organization and self-expression of youth are not given full legitimation or meaning in terms of cultural values and rituals.

The close linkage between the growth of personality, psychological maturation, and definite role models derived from the adult world has become greatly weakened. Hence the very coalescence of youth into special groups only tends to emphasize their problematic, uncertain standing from the point of view of cultural values and symbols. This has created a new constellation of the basic archetypal elements of youth. This new constellation can most clearly be seen in what has been called the emergence of the problems and stresses of adolescence in modern societies. While some of these stresses are necessarily common to adolescence in all societies, they become especially acute in modern societies.

Among these stresses the most important are the following: first, the bodily development of the adolescent constitutes a constant problem to him (or her). Since social maturity usually lags behind biological maturity, the bodily changes of puberty are not usually given a full cultural, normative meaning, and their evaluation is one of the adolescent's main concerns. The difficulty inherent in attaining legitimate sexual outlets and relations at this period of growth makes these problems even more acute. Second, the adolescent's orientation toward the main values of his society is also beset with difficulties. Owing to the long period of preparation and the relative segregation of the children's world from that of the adults, the main values of the society are necessarily presented to the child and adolescent in a highly selective way, with a strong idealistic emphasis. The relative unreality of these values as presented to the children—which at the same time are not given full ritual and symbolic expression—creates among the adolescents a great potential uncertainty and ambivalence toward the adult world.

This ambivalence is manifest, on the one hand, in a striving to communicate with the adult world and receive its recognition; on the other hand, it appears in certain dispositions to accentuate the differences between them and the adults and to oppose the various roles allocated to them by the adults. While they orient themselves to full participation in the adult world and its values, they usually attempt also to communicate with this world in a distinct, special way.

Parallel developments are to be found in the ideologies of modern youth groups. Most of these tend to create an ideology that emphasizes the discontinuity between youth and adulthood and the uniqueness of the youth period as the purest embodiment of ultimate social and cultural values. Although the explicitness of this ideology varies in extent from one sector of modern society to another, its basic elements are prevalent in almost all modern youth groups.

These processes have been necessarily accentuated in modern societies by the specific developments in cultural orientations in general and in the conception of time that has evolved in particular. The major social developments in modern societies have weakened the importance of broad cultural qualities as criteria for the allocation of roles. Similarly, important changes in the conception of time that is prevalent in modern societies have occurred. Primordial (cosmic-mythical, cyclical, or apocalyptical) conceptions of time have become greatly weakened, especially in their bearing on daily activities. The mechanical conception of time of modern technology has become much more prevalent. Of necessity this has greatly weakened the possibility of the direct ritual links between personal temporal changes and cosmic or societal progression. Therefore, the exploration of the actual meaning of major cultural values in their relation to the reality of the social world becomes one of the adolescent's main problems. This exploration may lead in many directions—cynicism, idealistic youth rebellion, deviant ideology and behavior, or a gradual development of a balanced identity.

Thus we see how all these developments in modern societies have created a new constellation of the basic archetypal elements of youth and the youth image. The two main characteristics of this constellation are the weakened possibility of directly linking the development of personality and the personal temporal transition with cosmic and societal time, on the one hand, and with the clear role models derived from the adult world, on the other.

In terms of personality development, this situation has created a great potential insecurity and the possible lack of a clear definition of personal identity. Yet it has also created the possibility of greater personal autonomy and flexibility in the choice of roles and the commitment to different values and symbols. In general, the individual, in his search for the meaning of his personal transition, has been thrown much more on his own powers.

These processes have provided the framework within which the various attempts to forge youth's identity and activities—both on the part of youth itself and on the part of various educational agencies—have developed. These attempts may take several directions. Youth's own activities and attempts at self-expression may first develop in the direction of considerable autonomy in the choice of roles and in commitment to various values. Conversely, they may develop in the direction of a more complete, fully organized and closed ideology connected with a small extent of personal autonomy. Second, these attempts may differ greatly in their emphasis on the direct linkage of cultural values to a specific social group and their view of these groups as the main bearers of such values.

In a parallel sense, attempts have been made on the part of various educational agencies to create new types of youth organizations within which youth can forge its identity and become linked to adult society. The purpose of such attempts has been two-fold: to provide youth with opportunities to develop a reasonably autonomous personality and a differentiated field of activity; and to encompass youth fully within well-organized groups set up by adult society and to provide them with full, unequivocal role models and symbols of identification. The interaction between these different tendencies of youth and the attempts of adult society to provide various frameworks for youth activities has given rise to the major types of youth organizations, movements, and ideologies manifested in modern societies.

These various trends and tendencies have created a situation in which, so far as we can ascertain, the number of casualties among youth has become very great—probably relatively much greater than in other types of societies. Youth's search for identity, for finding some place of its own in society, and its potential difficulties in coping with the attainment of such identity have given rise to the magnified extent of the casualties observed in the numerous youth delinquents of varying types. These failures, however, are not the only major youth developments in modern societies, although their relatively greater number is endemic in modern conditions. Much more extensive are the more positive attempts of youth to forge its own identity, to find some meaningful way of defining its place in the social and cultural context and of connecting social and political values with personal development in a coherent and significant manner.

The best example in our times of the extreme upsurge of specific youth consciousness is seen in the various revolutionary youth movements. They range from the autonomous free German youth movements to the less spectacular youth movements in Central Europe and also to some extent to the specific youth culture of various more flexible youth groups. Here the attempt has been made to overcome the dislocation between personal transition and societal and cultural time. It is in these movements that the social dynamics of modern youth has found its fullest expression. It is in them that dreams of a new life, a new society, freedom and spontaneity, a new humanity and aspirations to social and cultural change have found utterance. It is in these youth movements that the forging of youth's new social identity has become closely connected with the development of new symbols of collective identity or new social-cultural symbols and meanings.

These movements have aimed at changing many aspects of the social and cultural life of their respective societies. They have depicted the present in a rather shabby form; they have dubbed it with adjectives of materialism, restriction, exploitation, lack of opportunity for self-fulfillment and creativity. At the same time they have held out hope for the future—seemingly, the not very far off future—when both self-fulfillment and collective fulfillment can be achieved and the materialistic civilization of the adult world can be shaken off. They have tried to appeal to youth to forge its own self-identity in terms of these new collective symbols, and this is why they have been so attractive to youth, for whom they have provided a set of symbols, hopes, and aims to which to direct its activities.

Within these movements the emphasis has been on a given social group or collectivity—nation, class, or the youth group itself—as the main, almost exclusive bearer of the "good" cultural value and symbols. Indeed, youth has at times been upheld as the sole and pure bearer of cultural values and social creativity. Through its association with these movements, youth has also been able to connect its aspiration for a different personal future, its anxiety to escape the present through plans and hopes for a different future within its cultural or social setting.

These various manifestations have played a crucial part in the emergence of social movements and parties in modern societies. Student groups have been the nuclei of the most important nationalistic and revolutionary movements in Central and Eastern Europe, in Italy, Germany, Hungary, and Russia. They have also played a significant role in Zionism and in the various waves of immigration to Israel. Their influence has become enormous in various fields, not only political and educational but cultural in general. In a way, education itself has tended to become a social movement. Many schools and universities, many teachers, have been among the most important bearers of collective values. The very spread of education is often seen as a means by which a new epoch might be ushered in.

The search for some connection between the personal situation of youth and social-cultural values has also stimulated the looser youth groups in modern societies, especially in the United States, and to some extent in Europe as well —though here the psychological meaning of the search is somewhat different. The looser youth groups have often shared some of the characteristics of the more defined youth movements, and they too have developed an emphasis on the attainment of social and cultural change. The yearning for a different personal future has likewise become connected with aspirations for changing the cultural setting, but not necessarily through a direct political or organized expression. They are principally important as a strong link with various collective, artistic, and literary aspirations aimed at changing social and cultural life. As such they are affiliated with various cultural values and symbols, not with any exclusive social groups. Thus they have necessarily developed a much greater freedom of choice of roles and commitment to values.

Specific social conditions surround the emergence of all these youth groups. In general, they are associated with a breakdown of traditional settings, the onset of modernization, urbanization, secularization, and industrialization. The less organized, more spontaneous types of youth organization and the more flexible kind of youth consciousness arise when the transition has been relatively smooth and gradual, especially in societies whose basic collective identity and political framework evince a large degree of continuity and a slow process of modernization. On the other hand, the more intensive types of youth movements tend to develop in those societies and periods in which the onset of modernization is connected with great upheavals and sharp cleavages in the social structure and the structure of authority and with the breakdown of symbols of collective identity.

In the latter situation the adult society has made many efforts to organize youth in what may be called totalistic organizations, in which clear role models and values might be set before youth and in which the extent of choice allowed youth is very limited and the manifestations of personal spontaneity and autonomy are restricted. Both types of conditions appeared in various European societies and in the United States in the nineteenth and early twentieth centuries, and in Asian and African societies in the second half of the twentieth century. The relative predominance of each of these conditions varies in different periods in these societies. However, with the progress of modernization and the growing absorption of broad masses within the framework of society, the whole basic setting of youth in modern society has changed—and it is this new framework that is predominant today and in which contemporary youth problems are shaped and played out.

The change this new framework represents is to some extent common both to the fully organized totalistic youth movements and to the looser youth groups. It is connected mainly with the institutionalizing of the aims and values toward the realization of which these movements were oriented, with the acceptance of such youth organizations as part of the structure of the general educational and cultural structure of their societies.

In Russia youth movements became fully institutionalized through the organization of the Komsomol. In many European countries the institutionalizing of youth groups, agencies, and ideologies came through association with political parties, or through acceptance as part of the educational system—an acceptance that sometimes entailed supervision by the official authorities. In the United States, many (such as the Boy Scouts) have become an accepted part of community life and to some extent a symbol of differential social status. In many Asian and African countries, organized youth movements have become part of the nationalistic movements and, independence won, have become part of the official educational organizations.

This institutionalizing of the values of youth movements in education and community life has been part of a wider process of institutionalizing various collective values. In some countries this has come about through revolution; in others, as a result of a long process of political and social evolution.

From the point of view of our analysis, these processes have had several important results. They have introduced a new element into the configuration of the basic archetypal elements of youth. The possibility of linking personal transition both to social groups and to cultural values—so strongly emphasized in the youth movements and noticeable to some extent even in the looser youth culture—has become greatly weakened. The social and sometimes even the cultural dimension of the future may thus become flattened and emptied. The various collective values become transformed. Instead of being remote goals resplendent with romantic dreams, they have become mundane objectives of the present, with its shabby details of daily politics and administration. More often than not they are intimately connected with the processes of bureaucratization.

All these mutations are associated with a notable decline in ideology and in preoccupation with ideology among many of the groups and strata in modern societies, with a general flattening of political-ideological motives and a growing apathy to them. This decline in turn is connected with what has been called the spiritual or cultural shallowness of the new social and economic benefits accruing from the welfare state—an emptiness illustrated by the fact that all these benefits are in the nature of things administered not by spiritual or social leaders but, as Stephen Toulmin has wittily pointed out, "the assistant postmaster." As a consequence, we observe the emptiness and meaninglessness of social relations, so often described by critics of the age of consumption and mass society.

In general, these developments have brought about the flattening of the image of the societal future and have deprived it of its allure. Between present and future there is no ideological discontinuity. The present has become the more important, if not the more meaningful, because the future has lost its characteristic as a dimension different from the present. Out of these conditions has grown what Riesman has called the cult of immediacy. Youth has been robbed, therefore, of the full experience of the dramatic transition from adolescence to adulthood and of the dramatization of the difference between present and future. Their own changing personal future has become dissociated from any changes in the shape of their societies or in cultural activities and values.

Paradoxically enough, these developments have often been connected with a strong adulation of youth—an adulation, however, which was in a way purely instrumental. The necessity of a continuous adjustment to new changing conditions has emphasized the potential value of youth as the bearers of continuous innovation, of noncommitment to any specific conditions and values. But such an emphasis is often couched in terms of a purely instrumental adaptability, beyond which there is only the relative emptiness of the meaningless passage of time—of aging.[7]

Yet the impact on youth of what has been called postindustrial society need not result in such an emptiness and shallowness, although in recent literature these effects appear large indeed. It is as yet too early to make a full and adequate analysis of all these impacts. But it should be emphasized that the changes we have described, together with growing abundance and continuous technological change, have necessarily heightened the possibility of greater personal autonomy and cultural creativity and of the formation of the bases of such autonomy and of a flexible yet stable identity during the period of youth.

These new conditions have enhanced the possibility of flexibility in linking cultural values to social reality; they have enhanced the scope of personal and cultural creativity and the development of different personal culture. They have created the possibility of youth's developing what may be called a nonideological, direct identification with moral values, an awareness of the predicaments of moral choice that exist in any given situation, and individual responsibility for such choices—a responsibility that cannot be shed by relying on overarching ideological solutions oriented to the future.

These new social conditions exist in most industrial and post-industrial societies, sometimes together with the older conditions that gave rise to the more intensive types of youth movements. They constitute the framework within which the new configuration of the archetypal elements of youth and the new possibilities and problems facing youth in contemporary society develop. It is as yet too early to specify all these new possibilities and trends: here we have attempted to indicate some of their general contours.

[7] For an exposition of this view, see Paul Goodman, "Youth in Organized Society," *Commentary*, February 1960, pp. 95–107; and M. R. Stein, *The Eclipse of Community* (Princeton: Princeton University Press, 1960), especially pp. 215 ff.; also, the review of this book by H. Rosenberg, "Community, Values, Comedy," *Commentary*, August 1960, pp. 150–157.

POPULATION CHANGES
AND THE STATUS OF YOUTH*

FRANK MUSGROVE

During the past two hundred years young people in English society have moved through three broad status phases: the first, from the 1780's to the 1860's was a period of high status, the second, from the 1860's to the 1910's, a period of low; the third, from the 1920's up to the present time, a high status phase. "Young people" between the age of ten and twenty, no longer young children, but not yet "adults" chronologically, socially or legally, have enjoyed a status which has varied with population changes and with economic opportunity. The best indices of their status are probably the amount of marriage among them and the extent of their independent income.

The status of the young has often been equated with the extent to which they are protected from adult society. Such an assessment shows increasing status throughout the nineteenth century with every successive Factory and Education Act, culminating in the last thirty years of the century, when the regulation or prohibition of juvenile employment was extended to a wider range of industry (including agriculture), when compulsory education was introduced, and children were finally protected from their parents by Mundella's "Children's Charter" of 1889 and the work of the N.S.P.C.C. This is a proposition which calls for critical re-appraisal. Protective measures are a two-edged device: while they may signify concern for the welfare of the young, they also define them as a separate, non-adult population, inhabiting a less than adult world. The need for protection and distinctive treatment underlines their less than adult status. The young were extensively withheld from the economy and given compulsory schooling after 1870 when the economy no longer required their services on the scale that had prevailed over the previous century. The economy's diminished scope for juvenile labour was already evident in the sixties: not only was the demand decreasing, but it was shifting from the important, central industries like agriculture to employment more marginal to the economy, like domestic service. The statutes of 1870 and 1880 which introduced compulsory education were largely superfluous acts of rescue; they signalized for the young a displacement which had already occurred from a pivotal position in the nation's economic life.[1]

* Reprinted from Frank Musgrove, "Population Changes and the Status of Youth in England since the Eighteenth Century," in *Sociological Review* (March 1963) pp. 69–93, by permission of the author and publisher.
[1] Cf. A. B. Hollingshead: *Elmtown's Youth*, 1949, pp. 149–50: "The establishment of high schools in the late nineteenth and early twentieth centuriies may have been a response to the loss of economic functions of adolescents in American culture. Although

Demographic Influences

The rising status of the young in the Western world, measured by the protective measures and welfare facilities increasingly at their disposal, has been attributed at least in part to their diminishing proportion of the total population. They are held to have acquired a scarcity-value: "The present high status of childhood was not possible until a more economical rate of reproduction and the small-family system came generally to prevail."[2] Their continuing scarcity is held to augur well for their position in the future: "Many interesting consequences are likely to flow from the scarcity of children. They will probably be very much appreciated. Consideration will be given to them in building play space, guarding them from traffic, in providing nurseries for them in department stores."[3] Similar arithmetic of population has been seen to underlie the rise of the child-centred family—particularly the bourgeois family—of Victorian France and England: "La famille, réduit à la famille conjugale, c'est repliée sur les enfants qui constituent son noyau: c'est le triomphe du malthusianisme démographique."[4] With the limitation of family size, of which Malthus would have approved, the child moved to a central, even a dominant, position in family life: "Toute l'énergie du groupe est dispensée pour la promotion des enfants, chacun en particulier, sans aucune ambition collective: les enfants, plutot que la famille."[5]

Even if we take protective legislation and the provision of educational and welfare services as the main criteria of the status of the young, this demographic explanation does not accord with the facts of nineteenth century history. Protection and welfare came when the family was larger, and the proportion of young people in the population greater, than ever before or since. Charles Booth referred to the "remarkable increase" in the number of children under fifteen years of age to every hundred men aged twenty-five to sixty-five, between 1851 and 1881: there were 179 in 1851, 181 in 1861, 185 in 1871, and 190 in 1881.[6] Dependent (unoccupied) children under the age of fifteen years were increasing more rapidly than population: by 12.7 per cent compared with 11.9 per cent between 1851 and 1861, by 15.8 per cent compared with 13.1 per cent between 1861 and 1871, and by no less than 18.7 per cent compared with 14.5 per cent between 1871 and 1881. (In the latter decade, of course, the welfare provisions themselves were causing a greater number to be unoccupied.) The proportion of children (both dependent and occupied) under fifteen years in the total population increased steadily: 35.4 per cent in 1851, 35.7 per cent in 1861, 36.1 per cent in 1871, and 36.6 per cent in 1881. By 1881 the young were never

---

this movement developed under the guise of the need for more training for adult life, the training given has been limited largely to intellectual pursuits; practically it has extended the period of dependency on the family for four or five years in the 'middle classes,' and increasingly in the working class."

[2] J. H. S. Bossard: *The Sociology of Child Development*, 1954, p. 613.
[3] W. F. Ogburn and M. F. Nimkoff: *Handbook of Sociology*, 1953, p. 337.
[4] Philippe Ariès: *L'Enfant et La Vie Familiale sous L'Ancien Régime*, 1960, p. 317.
[5] *Ibid.*, p. 457.
[6] Charles Booth: "Occupations of the People of the United Kingdom 1801–1881," *Journal of the Statistical Society*, June 1886.

so abundant and never so protected. (Never before had they been so richly displayed—in Little Lord Fauntleroy outfits, sailor suits and Eton collars.) The declining birth rate came after extensive measures for child welfare and not before—when the cost of welfare, particularly to the middle class family, proved to be extremely onerous.[7]

The growing concern for the welfare of children is more satisfactorily related to the falling mortality rates at the end of the eighteenth century than to the falling birth rate at the end of the nineteenth.[8] Even the child-centred middle-class family to which Ariès refers can be seen at this earlier period: the seventeen children of the Edgeworth household were not too numerous to constitute the family's central concern, around whom domestic life was organized. (William Cobbett's farm is another good example of the child-centred, educative household, which was by no means uncommon at this time.[9]) Certainly the moralists and the educationists of late eighteenth century England were unanimous that the (middle class) child had never before been treated with such solicitude. "The domestic discipline of our ancestors has been relaxed by the philosophy and softness of the age," maintained Gibbon; "and if my father remembered that he had trembled before a stern parent, it was only to adopt with his son an opposite mode of the behaviour."[10] Clara Reeve[11] and Mrs. Sherwood[12] gave similar testimony; the Rev. William Jones saw the importance given to the young as productive of "a new generation of libertines, some of whom are such monsters of ignorance, insolence and boundless profligacy as never existed before in a Christian country."[13] Both Hannah More and William Barrow attributed the changed standing of children to the pernicious influence of the French Revolution. The former regretted that "not only sons but daughters have adopted something of that spirit of independence, and disdain of control, which characterizes the time . . . The rights of man have been discussed till we are sometimes wearied with the discussion. To these have been opposed, as the next stage in the progress of illumination, and with more presumption than prudence, the rights of women. It follows, according to the actual progression of human things, that the next influx of that irradiation which our enlighteners are pouring in upon us, will illuminate the world with grave descants on the rights of youth, the rights of children, the rights of babies."[14] William Barrow was of the opinion that the new age's solicitude for the young begot all too often "the character known amongst us by the appelation of a Jacobin or a Democratist."[15]

A sensitive awareness of the nature and the needs of childhood, reflected

[7] See A. J. Banks: *Prosperity and Parenthood*, 1954, ch. xi, "The Cost of Children."
[8] Cf. D. E. C. Eversley: *Social Theories of Fertility and the Malthusian Debate*, 1959, p. 80.
[9] See F. Musgrove: "Middle Class Families and Schools 1780–1880," *Sociological Review*, 1959, Vol. 7.
[10] E. Gibbon: *Works* (Vol. 1), *Autobiography*, p. 112.
[11] *Plans of Education* (1792), p. 39.
[12] S. Kelley (ed.): *Life of Mrs. Sherwood*, 1854, p. 40 and 46.
[13] W. Jones: *Letters from a Tutor to his Pupil*, 1775 (1821 ed.), p. 8.
[14] Hannah More: *Strictures on the Modern System of Female Education*, 1801, Vol. 1, pp. 172–3.
[15] See W. Barrow: *Essay on Education*, 1802.

in the literature of the age,[16] long preceded the spread of modern methods of birth control among the middle classes and the reduction of family size. Declining child mortality rates in the later eighteenth century made children worth taking seriously: when they were more likely to survive to manhood, there was more point in taking pains with their early training and education. The serious training for a career provided by apprenticeship had traditionally started only at the age of fourteen; Rousseau in the 1760's had recommended that systematic education was pointless before puberty (the reasons he advanced were partly psychological, but he was fully aware of the likelihood that an early investment in education would be wasted).[17] The considerable resources put into Infant and Preparatory schools after the 1820's make sense only in the light of declining mortality rates among their inmates.

It is probable that in the eighteenth century fewer than half the children born survived to manhood.[18] There is no evidence of marked social class differences: children's stories, which had a wide circulation, written for upper and middle class children prepared parents and children for the latter's probable early death.[19] In these circumstances children were of little account before they reached puberty: Rousseau asked what was the point of a rigorous education "which sacrifices the present to an uncertain future . . . and begins by making the child miserable, in order to prepare him for some far-off happiness which he may never enjoy?" The basis of this advice to upper and middle class parents was the alleged fact that "of all the children who are born, scarcely one half reach adolescence, and it is very likely that your pupil will not live to be a man."[20] (Even a century later Trollope's Dr. Thorne would not have early education made exacting for similar reasons: "Why struggle after future advantage at the expense of present pain, seeing that the results were so very doubtful?"[21])

In the later eighteenth century and throughout the nineteenth child mortality rates declined. While the significance of the eighteenth century decline for population growth may be disputed,[22] no leading demographer would deny that it occurred. The middle and upper classes could avail themselves more easily than the working classes of improved housing, sanitation and medical care;[23] the survival rate among their children up to fifteen years of age was 83 per cent in 1871; in the population at large, while it was much improved on the rough estimate of 50 per cent a century earlier, it was still only

[16] See W. Walsh: *The Use of Imagination: Educational Thought and the Literary Mind*, 1959. Cf. J. Dunbar: *The Early Victorian Woman*, 1953, p. 29.
[17] J. J. Rousseau: *Emile*, 1762, Bk. IV. "The way childhood is spent is no great matter . . . But it is not so in those early years when a youth really begins to live."
[18] *Report of the Royal Commission on Population*, 1949, p. 6.
[19] See James Janeway: *A Token for Children*, 1671; Thomas White: *A Little Book for Little Children*, 1702; Henry Jessey: *A Looking-Glass for Children*, 1672, and James Whitaker: *Comfort for Parents*, 1693.
[20] *Emile*, Bk. II.
[21] A. Trollope: *Dr. Thorne*, 1858, ch. 3.
[22] See H. J. Habakkuk: "English Population in the Eighteenth Century," *The Economic History Review*, 1953, Vol. 4, 2nd Series.
[23] Cf. J. Hole: *Homes of the Working Classes*, 1866, p. 17 for details of social class differences in mortality in 1864.

63 per cent.[24] It seems likely that the social class differential had widened in the course of the nineteenth century. In 1830, 79 per cent of the children of clergymen in the diocese of Canterbury survived their first fifteen years; in 1871, 85 per cent did so.

There is no necessary correspondence between falling mortality rates among young people and the growth of suitable employment opportunities for them. There can be little doubt that the 1870's middle class children, by surviving in greater numbers, constituted a growing burden on their parents while they were growing up and an increasing problem to place in acceptable work when their education was completed. It is probable that a social class differential in fertility existed much earlier in the century—Glass has computed negative correlation coefficients between fertility and status in 28 London boroughs which were not notably smaller in 1851 than in 1911 or 1931,[25] nevertheless, it is from the seventies that the average size of the middle class family began its steep decline. The birth-control movement was a symptom of the superabundance of the young in relation to family resources and to the needs of the economy. "It may be possible to bring ten children into the world, if you only have to rear five, and, while one is 'on the way,' the last is in the grave, not in the nursery. But if the doctor preserves seven or eight of the ten, and other things remain equal, the burden may become intolerable."[26] But other things did not even remain equal: it was unfortunate for the young that they were most abundant when the economy, whether at the level of professional or of manual employment, offered diminishing opportunities for youth and relative inexperience.

The Needs of the Economy

In the later eighteenth century and the first half of the nineteenth, parents valued their children more highly as their chance of survival improved; employers valued them more highly as technological changes gave them a position of pivotal importance in new industries. As the traditional system of apprenticeship broke down because of its irrelevance in the eighteenth century, and the legal requirement to serve an apprenticeship to a trade was repealed in 1814, the young were liberated to find their true level of importance in the changing economy. Debased forms of "apprenticeship"—particularly parish apprenticeship—within industry still often prevented the young worker from achieving his true economic wage and the social independence that went with it; but this

[24] C. Ansell: *Statistics of Families*, 1874. Ansell's inquiry was among 54,635 upper and professional class children. The figure for the general population is from the Carlisle Tables.
[25] D. V. Glass: "Fertility and Economic Status in London," *Eugenics Review*, 1938, Vol. 30. But cf. D. Heron: *On the Relations of Fertility in Man to Social Status*, 1906: "the intensity of the fertility-status relationship doubled between the middle of the nineteenth century and the beginning of the twentieth." T. H. C. Stevenson thought that if analysis could be pushed far enough back, "a period of substantial equality between all classes might have been met with. "The Fertility of Various Social Classes," *Journal of the Royal Statistical Society*, 1920.
[26] T. H. Marshall: "The Population Problem during the Industrial Revolution," *Economic History: Economic Journal Supplement*, 1929.

form of exploitation, often by parents and relatives rather than by plant owners, became less common in the early decades of the nineteenth century. The new industries were heavily dependent on the skills and agility of the young. In remote areas, away from large urban reservoirs of labour, young people were a particularly large proportion of the labour force, partly because the pauper apprentice was the most mobile economic unit; but even where labour was abundant and there was less need to employ parish apprentices, young people were a high proportion of employees. Forty-eight per cent of the 1,020 work-people of M'Connel and Kennedy in Manchester in 1816 were under 18 years of age. The demand was particularly for working class youth; but middle class youth—at least the males—were also needed as commerce expanded even more rapidly than industry and called for a great army of white-collar workers.[27] Only gradually, in the closing decades of the century, were "accountants," for example, distinguished from "book-keepers"—(and Upper Division civil servants from Lower Division[28])—and required to undertake prolonged education and training before receiving the economic rate for the work they did.[29]

In the new industries parents were often appendages to their children, heavily dependent on their earnings. When the farm labourer moved his family to the town, it was commonly for what his children could earn: his own employment might be as a porter, or in subsidiary work such as road-making, at a wage of ten to thirteen shillings a week; his child (and wife) could earn more on the power looms or in throstle-spinning.[30] As Mr. Carey commented in Disraeli's *Sybil* (1845): "Fathers and mothers goes for nothing. 'Tis the children gets the wages, and there it is." The fathers of the poor families imported from Bedfordshire and Buckinghamshire were fit only for labourers. There must have been many a Devilsdust "who had entered life so early that at seventeen he combined the experience of manhood with the divine energy of youth."

Apprenticeship and experience in traditional industries were a handicap in James Keir's chemical works at Tipton, founded in the 1780's,[31] Andrew Ure noted in 1836 that "Mr. Anthony Strutt, who conducts the chemical department of the great cotton factories at Belper and Milford . . . will employ no man who has learned his craft by regular apprenticeship."[32] Samuel Oldknow's spinning mill at Mellor depended on youthful labour; subsidiary industries (lime-kilns, coal-mining, farming) had to be provided for redundant fathers;[33] at Styal the Gregs had to develop an industrial colony to provide employment for the adult dependants of their juvenile and female workers. What shocked middle class commentators on factory life in mid-Victorian England as much

[27] Commercial clerks increased by 61 per cent 1861–71 and by 88 per cent 1871–81 while all occupied males increased by 13 per cent and 32 per cent.
[28] *First Report of the Civil Service Inquiry Commission* (*"The Playfair"*), 1875, recommended an Upper Division recruited from the universities distinct from a Lower Division of routine clerks.
[29] Until the Census of 1891 accountants were not distinguished from book-keepers. In 1880 the Institute of Chartered Accountants, in 1885 the Society of Accountants and Auditors were founded.
[30] See N. J. Smelser: *Social Change in the Industrial Revolution*, 1959, p. 185.
[31] W. H. B. Court: *The Rise of the Midland Industries*, 1938, pp. 230–232.
[32] Andrew Ure: *Philosophy of Manufactures*, 1861, p. 21.
[33] G. Unwin: *Samuel Oldknow and the Arkwrights*, 1924, ch. XI.

as the alleged immorality was the independence of the young. In London girls of fourteen working in the silk or trimming departments earned eight or ten shillings a week; "if they had cause to be dissatisfied with the conduct of their parents, they would leave them."[34] Similar independence was to be found in the Birmingham metal trades: "The going from home and earning money at such a tender age (of seven or thereabouts) has—as might be expected—the effect of making the child early independent of its parents . . ."[35] The Factory Commissioners reported in 1842 that by the age of fourteen young people "frequently pay for their own lodgings, board and clothing. They usually make their own contracts, and are in the proper sense of the word free agents." (Even the Poor Law provisions of the Speenhamland System had a similar effect in the early decades of the century. As Mr. Assistant Commissioner Stuart stated in the *Report* from the Commissioners on the Poor Laws (1834): "Boys of fourteen, when they become entitled to receive parish relief on their own account, no longer make a common fund of their income with their parents, but buy their own loaf and bacon and devour it alone. Disgraceful quarrels arise within the family circle for mutual accusations of theft."[36])

While factory legislation was at least a potential threat to the earnings and power of the young, the Act of 1833 extended their independence by destroying the vestigial authority of parents in the textile—particularly the spinning—mills. Virtually autonomous family units, under the headship of the father, had infiltrated intact into some of the textile factories: Andrew Ure[37] reported in the 1830's that "Nearly the whole of the children of fourteen years of age, and under, who are employed in cotton mills, belong to the mule spinning department, and are, in forty-nine cases out of fifty, the immediate dependents, often the offspring or near relations of the spinner, being hired and dismissed at his option." The spinner paid his piecers and scavengers from his wages. (In the mines outside Northumberland and Durham the young worker in 1840 was often even more completely under his father's authority; in South Wales "the collier boy is, to all intents and purposes, the property of his father (as to wages) until he attains the age of seventeen years, or marries." Butties received "apprentices" at the age of nine for twelve years—a system likened by witnesses to the African slave trade.[38]) The early regulation of the employment of the young, and particularly their shortened and staggered hours of work, had the effect, along with technological change, of removing them from the control of the head of the family who developed a more specialized rôle which "no longer implied co-operation with, training of, and authority over dependent family members."[39]

The importance of the young to the economy is reflected in the high birth

[34] Charles Bray: "The Industrial Employment of Women," *Transactions of the National Association for the Promotion of Social Science*, 1857.
[35] J. S. Wright: "Employment of Women in Factories in Birmingham," *Transactions of the N.A.P.S.Sc.*, 1857.
[36] Vol. 9, p. 54.
[37] Andrew Ure: *op. cit.*, p. 290.
[38] *First Report of the Commissioners (Mines)*, 1842, pp. 40 ff.
[39] N. J. Smelser: *op. cit.*, p. 265. For the administrative complexities which the educational clauses entailed see A. A. Fry: "Report of the Inspectors of Factories on the Effects of the Educational Provisions of the Factories' Act," *Journal of the Statistical Society*, 1839.

rate which was particularly buoyant in the later eighteenth and early nineteenth centuries. This is not simply to say that children were begotten for the benefit of what they could earn whilst still children; in an expanding economy they were valued as a longer term proposition. Talbot Griffith rejected as "scarcely tenable" the theory that the high birth rate of the period[40] was caused by the economic value of children,[41] but conceded that "The feeling that the new industries would provide employment for the children at an early age and enable them possibly to help the family exchequer would tend, undoubtedly, to make parents contemplate a large family with equanimity and may have acted as a sort of encouragement to population without the more definite incentive implied in the theory that it was the value of children's work which led to the increase of the population."[42] Marshall was more inclined to see significance for the birth rate in children's earnings: "By 1831 the birth rate, measured in proportion to women aged 20–40, got back for the first time to the level of 1781 (this is a guess); by 1841 it had slumped far below it (this is a fact). Now it is only fair to older theories to point out how this fall by stages, slow at first and then rapid, reflects the history of child labour and the Poor Law."[43] Glass, on the other hand, found little or no connection between the employment of children aged ten to fifteen and fertility between 1851 and 1911 in the 43 registration counties.[44] The value of children for their earnings *whilst children* is doubtless an inadequate explanation of the changing birth rate; but the value of children more broadly conceived, as likely, in a buoyant economy, to constitute an insurance against misfortune in later life and old age, is an explanation not inconsistent with Arthur Young's argument that population is proportional to employment.[45]

Habakkuk has attributed the growth in population during the Industrial Revolution primarily to "specifically economic changes," and in particular to "an increase in the demand for labour," but has pointed out that the way in which this demand operated (whether directly on the birth rate or indirectly through the lower age of marriage) remains open to question. The experience of Ireland, as Talbot Griffith realized, provides the key to this problem. It was an embarrassment to Griffith's argument that in relatively insanitary Ireland population increased between 1780 and 1840 at almost twice the rate experienced in England; inadequate statistics made it impossible for him to prove or

[40] 34.4 births per 1,000 living in 1780, 35.4 1785–95, 34.2 1796–1806, cf. 31.1 in 1700, 27.5 in 1710 and 30.5 in 1720. See G. Talbot Griffith: *Population Problems of the Age of Malthus*, 1926, Table 5, p. 28.
[41] *Ibid.*, p. 103.
[42] *Ibid.*, p. 105. Talbot Griffith saw economic expansion as having a direct effect on the age of marriage, and hence indirectly on the birth rate (p. 106).
[43] T. H. Marshall: *loc. cit.*, p. 454.
[44] D. V. Glass: "Changes in Fertility in England and Wales 1851 to 1931," L. Hogben (ed.): *Political Arithmetic*, 1938. "Correlations between fertility and child labour yielded coefficients of + 0.489 ± 0.116 for 1851, + 0.29 ± 0.140 for 1871 and + 0.043 ± 0.152 for 1911. Of these coefficients, only that for 1851 is significant."
[45] Arthur Young: *Political Arithmetic*, 1774. "People scarce—labour dear. Would you give a premium for population, could you express it in better terms? The commodity wanted is scarce, and the price raised; what is that but saying that the value of *man* is raised? Away! my boys—get children, they are worth more than ever they were."

disprove his contention that a declining rate of child mortality was the primary reason. On the other hand, the comparative lack of industrial development in Ireland seemed to nullify the argument that the primary reason was increased demand for labour.[46] This latter difficulty is overcome if we regard Ireland-with-England—or at least Ireland-with-Lancashire—as a single field of employment, as the Irish themselves clearly did. The relatively unskilled jobs available in the textile industry were particularly suited to Irish immigrants; and before 1819 movement into Lancashire was easy—easier than moving in from elsewhere in England—since the Irish were regarded as having no place of "settlement" and so could not be removed by the Poor Law authorities if they became a charge upon the rates. But these were not young children seeking employment. Undue concentration on the earnings of *young* children has bedevilled the question of the value of offspring. At this time in Ireland—and in England too—"a large family was regarded less as a strain upon resources than as the promise of comfort and material well being in middle and old age."[47]

Children were of value even and perhaps particularly as they grew up into adult life and work, as an insurance against misfortune, against sickness and old age. They were not an entirely reliable insurance, particularly with increased geographical mobility and the dispersal of the family; their unreliability, at least in London, was commented on by Mayhew in the middle of the nineteenth century[48] and by Booth at the end. Booth was under the impression that this unreliability had become more marked in recent years: "The great loss of the last twenty years is the weakening of the family ties between parents and children. Children don't look after their old people according to their means. The fault lies in the fact that the tie is broken early. As soon as a boy earns ten shillings a week he can obtain board and lodging in some family other than his own, and he goes away because he has in this great liberty."[49]

The importance of children was undermined in the later nineteenth century by the growth of alternative forms of insurance. Indeed, "insurance" in a broad sense—whether paid up premiums, private means or a working wife—has demographic significance as a substitute for children. Children seen as insurance help to explain the apparent paradox, discussed by Stevenson, that in the nineteenth century high mortality appeared to promote large families rather than vice versa. Many were born when comparatively few survived: additional births were necessary to effect replacements. This was particularly the case when there was no other form of insurance against misfortune: amongst miners, whose wives were excluded from employment after the 1840's, child mortality rates were high, but so was fertility. High child mortality rates were also experienced in the families of the textile workers, but fertility was low also; it is arguable that replacements were not so necessary when wives were commonly at work. The low fertility of couples of independent means had perplexed

[46] G. Talbot Griffith: *op. cit.*, p. 66.
[47] K. H. Connell: "Land and Population in Ireland 1780–1840," *The Economic History Review*, 1949, 2nd Series, Vol. 2.
[48] See Peter Quennell: *Mayhew's London*, 1949, pp. 54 and 76.
[49] Charles Booth: *Life and Labour of the People in London*, Final Volume, 1903, p. 43.

nineteenth century demographers. Stevenson considered that their low fertility was the most remarkable case of all: "In their case, presumably those anxieties and difficulties which militate against fertility are at a minimum, but fertility is also at a minimum."[50] Once the rates of infant mortality had fallen, it was safe to assume that even a small family would survive to carry on the family name and estate.

Children were of diminishing value to couples who were covered by insurance. The birth rate at the end of the nineteenth century slumped not only among the professional, middle classes, but among artisans and skilled mechanics, many of them among the infertile textile families, who in large numbers joined Friendly Societies such as the Oddfellows, Manchester Unity (1810), the Foresters (1834), the Rechabites, Salford Unity (1835), the Hearts of Oak (1842), and the National Deposit Friendly Society (1868). By 1872 the Friendly Societies probably had some four million members, compared with one million trade unionists—and the latter had sickness, employment, and sometimes superannuation schemes too.[51] The decline in claims for lying-in benefit by members of the Hearts of Oak gives some indication of their declining fertility: between 1881 and 1904 the proportion of claims to membership declined by 52 per cent.[52] It is likely that they had less need of this benefit precisely because they were members of a provident society.

By the last quarter of the nineteenth century the status of the young was being undermined as a consequence of their earlier importance. Their value had resulted in their super-abundance. As Yule and Habakkuk have observed, the children who are produced in response to favorable economic circumstances may still be there when the circumstances have deteriorated: "the present demand is met only by a delivery of the commodity some twenty years later; by that time the 'commodity' may not be required."[53] Yule speaks of "a very large and quite abnormal increase" in the labour force aged twenty to fifty-five years in the last twenty years of the century; as young workers the "bulge" had entered the labour market in the late sixties and the seventies.[54] This increase was "not produced by any present demands for labour, but in part by the 'demand' of 1863–73 . . .": the birth rate in the sixties and seventies was as high as in the quarter of a century after 1780.[55] Moreover, in the second half of the

[50] T. H. C. Stevenson: "The Fertility of Various Social Classes in England and Wales from the Middle of the Nineteenth Century to 1911," *Journal of the Royal Statistical Society*, 1920, Vol. 83.

[51] See P. H. J. H. Gosden: *The Friendly Societies of England 1815–1875*, 1961. See also Charles Booth: *Life and Labour of the People in London*, 1889, Vol. 1, pp. 106–11. The Hearts of Oak charged a comparatively high subscription of 10 shillings a quarter; they provided £20 on a member's death, £10 on the death of a member's wife, sickness allowances beginning at 18 shillings a week, lying-in benefit of 30 shillings and superannuation of 4 shillings a week.

[52] See Sidney Webb: *The Decline of the Birth Rate*, 1907, pp. 6–7.

[53] G. Udny Yule: "On the Changes in Marriage- and Birth-Rates in England and Wales during the Past Half Century," *Journal of the Royal Statistical Society*, 1906, Vol. 69.

[54] While the population increased by 11.7 per cent in 1881–91 the working population aged 20–55 increased by 14 per cent; the increases 1891–1901 were 12.2 per cent and 19 per cent respectively.

[55] 34.1 1851–60, 35.4 1871–80 cf. 29.9 1891–1900. See G. Talbot Griffith: *op. cit.* Table 5, p. 28.

nineteenth century the survival rates among older children and adolescents improved much more rapidly than among children aged 0 to 4 years. While the annual mortality per thousand declined by 11.3 per cent among boys aged 0 to 4 years (from 71 to 63) between 1841–5 and 1891–1900, the decline among boys aged 5 to 9 declined by 53.2 per cent (from 9.2 to 4.3), and among boys aged 10 to 14 by 53.0 per cent (from 5.1 to 2.4).[56] Thus whilst adolescents were a better "proposition," since they were more likely to live and so justify what was spent on their upbringing and education, the wastage among them was small at the very time that the economy had a diminishing need for their services.

This is the prelude to the introduction of compulsory education between 1870 and 1880. Not only was there a "bulge" in young people, but advances in technology were in any case displacing the young worker. In some industries, too, extended factory legislation greatly diminished his value in the eyes of employers: the administrative complications raised by part-time schooling deterred mine-owners from employing boys under twelve after the Mines Act of 1860;[57] the Factory Acts Extension Act of 1867 and the Workshops Regulation Act of the same year had similar consequences in a wide range of industries including the metal trades, glass and tobacco manufacture, letter-press printing and book-binding.[58] The textile industry on the other hand, which had greatly reduced its child labour force after the Act of 1833, maintained a high proportion of juvenile workers after the Act of 1844 which simplified the administration of part-time work.[59] Agriculture also took the Gang Act of 1867 and the Agricultural Children Act of 1873 in its stride—chiefly by ignoring them.

Technical changes in many industries were in any case breaking the earlier dependence on juvenile labour: steam power in the lace[60] and pottery[61] industries was being substituted for children's energy and dexterity; the dramatic decline in the proportion of young people engaged in agriculture in the second half of the century has been similarly attributed in part to technical development: "A new class connected with the application of science to agriculture has sprung into being . . ."[62] Young people were no longer central to the economy; they were moving ever more on to the periphery, into marginal and relatively trivial occupations: street-trading, fetching and carrying, and particularly indoor domestic service.

The decline in the proportion of young people (under the age of fifteen) had set in before the "slight dose of compulsory education" introduced by the Education Act of 1870[63] and the more effective Education Acts of Sandon

[56] S. Peller: "Mortality, Past and Future," *Population Studies*, 1948, Vol. 1.
[57] 23 and 24 Vict. c 151. See A. H. Robson: *The Education of Children in Industry in England 1833–1876*, 1931, p. 159.
[58] A. H. Robson: *op. cit.*, pp. 204–5.
[59] The Act of 1844 reduced the minimum age of employment from 9 to 8 and limited the daily hours of children to 6½ which could be worked either before or after the dinner hour.
[60] A. H. Robson: *op. cit.*, p. 133.
[61] M. W. Thomas: *Young People in Industry*, 1945, p. 85.
[62] Charles Booth: "Occupations of the People of the United Kingdom 1801–81," *Journal of the Statistical Society*, June 1886.
[63] By 1876 50 per cent of the whole population was under compulsion, but in the boroughs the percentage was as high as 84. See H. C. Barnard: *A Short History of English Education*, 1947, p. 197.

and Mundella in 1876 and 1880. In 1851 young people under fifteen were 6.9 per cent of the occupied population; in 1861 workers of this age were 6.7 per cent of all occupied, in 1871 6.2 per cent, in 1881 they were 4.5 per cent.[64] The following table gives the percentage of workers under fifteen years of age in selected industries between 1861 and 1881:

PERCENTAGE OF UNDER-15S IN SELECTED INDUSTRIES

	1861	1871	1881
Agriculture	7.6	7.2	· 5.5
Mining (males only)	11.9	9.5	5.7
Metal trades	7.9	5.5	3.1
Quarrying and brickmaking (males only)	7.3	5.9	3.8
Bricklayers and labourers (males only)	3.2	2.8	2.2
Textiles and dyeing	15.4	15.7	12.2
Indoor domestic service	8.8	8.9	7.7

Perhaps the most remarkable decline in the proportion of employed young people was in the country's major industry, agriculture. This industry, of course, was experiencing considerable difficulties at this time and its manpower contracting; but while the total number employed in agriculture declined by 24 per cent between 1851 and 1881, the number of young people under fifteen declined by no less than 40 per cent. Under-fifteens in agriculture were 21 per cent of all young workers in 1851, 13.7 per cent in 1881. An opposite trend is marked in the case of indoor domestic service: under-fifteens in this employment were 11.6 per cent of all young workers in 1851, 19.7 per cent in 1881. In spite of compulsory education, while the employed population increased by 38 per cent between 1851 and 1881, young people employed in indoor domestic service increased over the same period by 55 per cent.

But in spite of the growing numbers of young people still employed in certain industries, while the total number of employed people in England and Wales increased by 12.4 per cent between 1861 and 1871, the number of under-fifteens employed increased by only 2.5 per cent. This is not because a greater proportion was attending school. What alarmed investigators in the sixties, and provided powerful arguments in the campaign for compulsory education, was not only the apparent decline in the proportion of children attending school, but a decline in the proportion at work. The consequence was an increasing proportion of young people on the very margin of society, outcast and neglected. "And what are these neglected children doing if they are not at school?" asked James McCosh, after reviewing the evidence relating to Manchester, in a paper to the National Association for the Promotion of Social Science in 1867. "They are idling in the streets and wynds; tumbling about in the gutters; selling matches; running errands; working in tobacco shops, cared for by no man . . ."[65]

Inquiries conducted by the Manchester Statistical Society and by the Edu-

---

[64] All calculations in this section are based on Charles Booth, *loc. cit.*
[65] James McCosh: "On Compulsory Education," *Transactions of the National Association for the Promotion of Social Science*, 1867.

cation Aid Society in the 1860's had produced disquieting statistics. With a decreasing importance to the nation's economy, the young had an exiguous existence in the interstices of adult society. In 1834 there had been in Manchester and Salford 967 day pupils at school for every 10,000 inhabitants; in 1861 there were only 908. The Manchester Statistical Society found in a survey conducted in 1865 that among the children aged three to twelve in their sample, over half were neither at school nor at work. The Education Aid Society found in 1862 in widely separate districts of Manchester that in 2,896 families investigated, out of every 15 children aged three to twelve, one was at work, 6 were at school, but 8 were neither at school nor at work.[66] (There were in these families a further 2,882 children over the age of twelve: while 81.3 per cent of these were at work, and 1.5 per cent at school, 17.2 per cent were neither at school nor at work.) Compulsory education was a necessity by the 1870's not because children were at work, but because increasingly they were not.

The Age of Marriage

Between the 1780's and the 1860's young people, particularly the working class young, were able to approximate to adult status because of their importance to the economy. Superfluous apprenticeship was an artifice which kept a diminishing proportion in unmerited subordination, particularly in the regions of most rapid social change:[67] in 1863, before the National Association for the Promotion of Social Science, its remaining vestiges were roundly attacked as "a species of slavery," "incompatible with the free institutions of this country," which, "unsuited to the present advanced state of society," "should be discontinued as a worn-out vestige of the past . . ." These were not strictures on "parish apprenticeship," but on normal apprenticeship for which high premiums might be charged, which might require seven years' training for "what might be acquired by a sharp lad in three or four."[68] The early nineteenth century offered youth a dominant and not a subordinate economic role. The young, in their 'teens, could attain an independence which gave them virtually adult status, a situation reflected in, and further confirmed by, the tendency to early marriage.

The independence and early marriage of young industrial workers were severely disapproved of by (middle class) social commentators and legislators.

[66] See E. Brotherton: "The State of Popular Education," *Transactions of the National Association for the Promotion of Social Science*, 1865: Also J. Hole: *Homes of the Working Classes*, 1866.
[67] See *Report of the Schools Inquiry Commission*, 1868, Vol. 9. "In the West Riding, there is so great a demand for juvenile labour, that the custom of paying premiums to masters with apprentices is almost obsolete. Indeed, indentures of apprenticeship are far less common than they were. Boys are seldom bound to masters; they begin to receive wages almost immediately after they enter a shop." (pp. 222-3)
[68] George Hurst: "On the System of Apprenticeship," *Transactions of the National Association for the Promotion of Social Science*, 1863. See W. Lucas: *A Quaker Journal*, 1934, Vol. 1, p. 44, for an account of a pointlessly long, expensive and futile tutelage in the early nineteenth century even for the profession of chemist.

The resentment of the high status of the young (and of employed women) echoed through the parliamentary debates on the regulation of factory employment. Social workers were surprised that people who worked long hours under conditions which the middle classes would have found distasteful did not feel sorry for themselves. Fanny Herz found young women factory workers "exceeding tenacious of their independence and jealous to a surprising degree of even the appearance of condescension or patronage in the conduct of those who would approach them with the kindest intentions . . ."[69] Lord Ashley, in the course of the debates on the Ten Hours Bill, wished to regulate the conditions whereby women were "gradually acquiring all those privileges which are held to be the proper portion of the male sex" and which promoted a "perversion as it were of nature which has the inevitable effect of introducing into families disorder, insubordination and conflict."[70]

Early marriage, the reflection and confirmation of the high status of young industrial workers, was generally deplored. Factory work was condemned for the young not because wages were low, but because they were high. "From the same cause, namely high wages, very many early and improvident marriages take place."[71] "The Census returns of 1861," runs a typical lament of the period, "show that among the population of Bolton, 45 husbands and 172 wives were coupled at the immature age of '15 or under'; in Burnley there were 51 husbands and 147 wives; in Stockport 59 husbands and 179 wives in the same category."[72]

This tendency to early marriage dated from the later eighteenth century and has been attributed to the breakdown of traditional apprenticeship with its requirement of celibacy, to changes in the organization of farming, particularly to the decline of the custom of labourers "living in," to the higher earnings of the young, and, more doubtfully, to the system of poor law allowances.[73] Because of the few hindrances to early marriage and the high birth rate of the period, the later eighteenth century and the early nineteenth have been described as "an almost, if not quite, unique epoch in the history of the human race."[74]

These circumstances prevailed in Ireland equally with England; and the social history of Ireland illustrates even more vividly than the history of England the close connection between the status of the young and the amount of marriage among them. The contrast between the Ireland of the later eighteenth century which Arthur Young described in his *Tour of Ireland* (1780) and the Ireland which American anthropologists described in the 1930's[75] is between a

[69] Fanny Herz: "Mechanics Institutes for Working Women," *Transactions of the National Association for the Promotion of Social Science*, 1859.

[70] *Parliamentary Papers*, 3rd Series, Vol. 73, col. 1096.

[71] R. Smith Baker: "The Social Results of the Employment of Girls and Women in Factories and Workshops," *Transactions of the National Association for the Promotion of Social Science*, 1868. Cf. Fanny Herz: *loc. cit.* "Owing to the liberal wages they earn, many of our young factory women become their own mistresses at a very early age . . ."

[72] R. A. Arnold: "The Cottone Famine," *Transactions* N.A.P.S.Sc., 1864.

[73] G. Talbot Griffith: *op. cit.*, pp. 112–22.

[74] See A. M. Carr-Saunders: *Population*, 1925, pp. 38–41.

[75] Conrad M. Arensberg and Solon T. Kimball: *Family and Community in Ireland*, 1940.

country with independent youth and early marriage and a country with subordinate youth and remarkably belated marriage.

Arthur Young was impressed by the independence of young people and the early age at which they married. The reclamation of waste land and the subdivision of land were important economic circumstances behind these developments. "There is no doubt at all that in the late eighteenth and early nineteenth centuries the Irish married while unusually young."[76] But whereas in 1841 only 43 per cent of males aged twenty-five to thirty-five were unmarried, in 1926 the percentage was 72. In the meantime the economic circumstances that had made early marriage possible had dramatically changed; in particular the shift from tillage to livestock production after the Famine, and the virtual cessation of the subdivision of land after 1852. By the 1920's, while 45 per cent of English males aged twenty-five to thirty were unmarried, 39 per cent of American, and 49 per cent of the Danish, 80 per cent of Irish males of this age were still single.[77]

Wherever social and economic institutions restrict the freedom of young people past puberty to marry, their social standing is depressed. The institutions may be as varied as protracted compulsory schooling, apprenticeship, exclusion from employment, the dowry, the bride-price, the monopoly of wives by elderly polygynists,[78] or exchange-marriage. A bride-price or dowry which is paid by parents enables the latter to regulate and impede the progress of youth towards adult status; exchange-marriage, whereby a man could marry only when his father supplied him with one of his daughters to give in exchange for a bride, was practiced by the Tiv of Nigeria until 1927 and effectively diminished the status of youth.[79] Arensberg and Kimball have described how in County Clare in the 1930's farmers arranged their children's marriages with a keen eye to economic advantage. Marriage conferred status, and until marriage, whatever his chronological age, a man remained a "boy." "Even at forty-five or fifty, if the old couple have not yet made over the farm, the countryman remains a 'boy' in respect to farm work and in the rural vocabulary." "It goes without saying that the father exercises his control over the whole activity of the 'boy.' It is by no means confined to their work together."[80] Groups of "young" (i.e. unmarried) men, unlike the "cuaird" of older men, discuss no serious adult concerns; their main activity together is gambling. They have been effectively reduced to a condition of social subordination and irresponsibility.

---

[76] K. H. Connell: *loc. cit.*

[77] C. M. Arensberg and S. T. Kimball: *op. cit.*, pp. 103–4.

[78] Cf. E. E. Evans-Pritchard: *Witchcraft and Oracles among the Azande*, 1937: "The older men had a monopoly of wives, and in the past it was difficult for young men to marry. The need of food and the hope of acquiring a sufficient number of spears with which to marry anchored a youth to his family and kin. The father of a family exercised great control over his sons who treated him with deep respect." (p. 16). Also K. L. Little: *The Mende of Sierra Leone*, 1951. "Married persons constitute a definite and more senior category to those who are unmarried irrespective of the actual age of the latter." "In the old days, few men had the opportunity of obtaining a wife before they were thirty, or even thirty-five years of age, and had proved their hardihood and diligence. Nowadays . . . a man has more opportunities to secure the amount of bride-wealth through his own efforts and so achieve a wife while still in his early twenties." (p. 140)

[79] M. Mead (ed.): *Cultural Patterns and Technical Change*, 1953, pp. 114–43.

[80] C. M. Arensberg and S. T. Kimball: *op. cit.*, p. 56.

The Position Since 1870

The depressed status of youth between 1870 and 1914, already foreshad-owed in the sixties in their increasing exclusion from the central concerns of the economy and signalized in the imposition of compulsory schooling in 1870, is further reflected in the rising average age of marriage. The proportion of married males and females between the ages of fifteen and twenty-four rose from 13.1 per cent in 1851 to 16.6 per cent in 1861, reaching a peak of 17.4 per cent in 1871; thereafter the proportion declined to 16.0 per cent in 1881, 10.5 per cent in 1891, 11.0 per cent in 1901, and the nadir of 9.7 per cent in 1911.[81] Recovery thereafter was faltering in the twenties and thirties, marked from the period immediately preceding the Second World War: 12.7 per cent in 1921, to 10.4 in 1931, 20.1 in 1947.

The diminished proportion of young people married after 1870 was par-ticularly marked in the middle classes—a reduction of status particularly keen for middle class girls who had as yet no compensation in widespread access to superior occupational statuses. As Hetty Widgett observed to Ann Veronica: "They used to marry us off at seventeen. They don't marry us off now until high up in the twenties. And the age gets higher. We have to hang about in the interval. There's a great gulf opened, and nobody's got any plans what to do with us. So the world is choked with waste and waiting daughters."[82] The average age of those professional men and gentlemen generally who married between 1840 and 1870 was 29.9 years, four-and-a-half years above the average for all classes of workmen.[83]

The recovery of youthful marriage in the forty years after 1911 was greater than the decline in forty years before. The proportion of males ever-married aged twenty to twenty-four declined by 38.6 per cent between 1871 and 1911, from 23.3 to 14.3 per cent; between 1911 and 1951 it rose by 66.4 per cent, from 14.3 to 23.8 per cent.[84] The recovery among young women has been more striking: the rate of marriage among young women aged twenty to twenty-four fell by 30 per cent between 1871 and 1911, from 34.8 to 24.3 per cent of the age group; it rose by 100 per cent (from 24.3 to 48.2 per cent) between 1911 and 1951. (The increase in the rate among girls aged fifteen to nineteen—266 per cent—is still more remarkable.)

Titmuss, drawing heavily on the work of Hajnal, has claimed that "These increases in the amount or quantity of marriage—in the apparent popularity of the institution of marriage—are . . . quite remarkable. They are also quite unprecedented in the history of vital statistics over the last hundred years."[85] This is misleading: to claim that "the amount of marriage" began to increase after 1911 and that the institution of marriage was never so popular as in the

---

[81] Calculated from *Papers of the Royal Commission on Population*, 1950, Vol. 2, *Reports and Selected Papers of the Statistics Committee*, pp. 195–7.

[82] H. G. Wells: *Ann Veronica*, 1909, ch. 2.

[83] C. Ansell: *op. cit.*, p. 45.

[84] These calculations are based on data in J. Hajnal: "Aspects of Recent Trends in Marriage in England and Wales," *Population Studies*, 1947, Vol. 1, and the returns of the 1951 Census.

[85] R. Titmuss: "The Family as a Social Institution," *The Family: Report of the British National Conference on Social Work*, 1953.

last fifteen years would require that the proportion ever-married in the population at risk—all those over the age of fifteen—had risen. In fact, there has been remarkable little variation over the past century: 59.3 per cent in 1851, 64.3 per cent in 1871, 59.7 per cent in 1911, and 63.8 per cent in 1931. The proportion of spinsters in the age group forty-five to fifty-four was 12.2 per cent in 1851, 12.1 per cent in 1871, 15.8 per cent in 1911, 16.4 per cent in 1931, and in 1951, at 15.1 per cent, almost as high as in 1911, and higher than at any time in late-Victorian and Edwardian England. What has recurred in the mid-twentieth century is the popularity of *youthful* marriage. It is a sensitive index of the changing status of the young.

The young have attained a new significance in the nation's economy since the thirties. It is true that they remain ever longer at school—although the really significant fact of educational history since 1944 is not the (belated) raising of the school leaving age to fifteen, but the refusal to raise it to sixteen. It is possible that in the 1960's, as in the 1870's, the young will pay the price of their importance and comparative abundance in the previous twenty years.[86] As the bulge moves on to the labour market, the school leaving age will in all likelihood be raised, as foreshadowed in the "Crowther" Report, *15 to 18* (1959), and the grammar school Sixth Forms, the universities and other institutions of higher education still further expand.

Since the twenties, and more particularly since the mid-thirties, the young have had the advantage of being born into an economy in which technological change has brought about widespread upgrading of occupations, the diminution of the proportion of labouring jobs, and an increase in the amount of skilled employment. Georges Friedman has argued that this is not the case: from his broad survey of trends in Western society, he scorns the notion of an imminent "technicians Utopia"[87] and claims that, while in the industrially advanced nations the proportion of unskilled labourers has declined, the proportion of semi-skilled, fragmentary, repetitive and mechanized jobs has greatly increased. The French[88] and American[89] statistics which he produces appear to support this contention that since 1910 the proportion of routine, semi-skilled workers in industry has greatly increased, while the proportion of skilled has shown relatively little change. The English statistics supplied by the Census Returns do not fit this picture: with skilled workers two-and-a-half times more numerous than semi-skilled (1951),[90] Friedman is driven to deny the validity of the Registrar General's data: "These surprising figures, which may even be regarded as mistaken when compared with the corresponding ones in France or the United States, can only be explained by fundamental differences in the definition and titles given to different occupational categories, partly perhaps also by the traditional policy of British unions, which attempt

[86] Sixteen-year-olds may increase by 31 per cent 1957–63, the age group 15–20 inclusive by 19 per cent. See *The Youth Service in England and Wales* (the "Albermarle" Report), 1960, Appendix 6, p. 129.
[87] Cf. P. F. Drucker: *The Practice of Management*, 1955, for the argument that mass production and automation mean more highly skilled and trained employees.
[88] Georges Friedman: *The Anatomy of Work*, London, 1961, p. 169.
[89] *Ibid.*, pp. 182–3.
[90] *Ibid.*, p. 172.

to maintain the status, and as far as possible the wages, of skilled trades for occupations that have been down-graded by mechanization." He has less difficulty with American statistics in showing that "from 1940 on, the proportion of semi-skilled workers is greater than that of either the skilled or the unskilled. Semi-skilled workers now constitute the largest group among the manual workers of American industry."[91]

There can be little doubt that Friedman's thesis, at least with regard to England, is wrong. Although Erich Fromm[92] and Paul Goodman[93] appear to lend some support to his picture of American employment, their concern is more with the psychological satisfaction of work today, rather than with the level of skill it involves. This, of course, is a quite different question: "alienated work," socially pointless and trivial work, may require high and rising levels of skill; it may nevertheless fall below the expectations of people who have lived through an age which has seen a revolution of expectation. But when Goodman argues that the status of youth is depressed, and their growing up to adulthood made difficult, because "there get to be fewer jobs that are necessary or unquestionably useful; that require energy and draw on some of one's best capacities; and that can be done keeping one's honour and dignity,"[94] he is, at least in the middle of this portmanteau proposition, stating an argument which is open to statistical verification. (He is forced by his initial assumption to the interesting conclusion that early (middle class) marriage is today a substitute for satisfactory employment.)

There can be little doubt that the entirely contrary view put forward by Talcott Parsons is nearer the truth: "We feel confident that a careful analysis would reveal that in contemporary organizations not only larger absolute numbers, but larger proportions of those involved are carrying more complex decision-making responsibilities than was true fifty years ago." "Now, not only have most of the older unskilled 'pick-and-shovel' type jobs been eliminated, but an increasing proportion of the 'semi-skilled' machine-tending and assembly-line types of jobs have followed them."[95] In England the Registrar General's classification of occupations shows a diminution in the proportion of employed males in unskilled and semi-skilled categories (classes V and IV) between 1931 and 1951: with jobs at both dates categorized on the 1931 classification, the proportion in class V declined from 17.7 to 14.3 per cent, in class IV from 18.2 to 16.0 per cent; on the other hand, the proportion of skilled men (class III) rose from 48.8 to 52.6 per cent.

The expansion and qualitative upgrading of skilled work has meant for

[91] *Ibid.*, p. 176.
[92] E. Fromm: *The Sane Society*, London, 1956. "There is one factor however which could mitigate the alienation of work, and that is the skill required in its performance. But here, too, development moves in the direction of decreasing skill requirements . . ." (p. 294) "To sum up, the vast majority of the population work as employees with little skill required, and with almost no chance to develop any particular talents . . ." (p. 295)
[93] Paul Goodman: *Growing Up Absurd*, London 1961.
[94] *Ibid.*, p. 17.
[95] Talcott Parsons and Winston White: "The Link between Character and Society," S. M. Lipset and Leo Lowenthal (eds.): *Culture and Social Character*, 1961, pp. 110–11.

the young that during the past quarter of a century they have grown up into a world in which the chances of obtaining skilled employment were steadily increasing. Mark Abrams has estimated that since 1938 the real earnings of "teenagers" (defined as young people aged fifteen to twenty-four) have increased far more rapidly than adult earnings, by some 50 per cent; and that discretionary spending has increased by 100 per cent.[96] Although only five per cent of total consumer expenditure is in the hands of this age group which constitutes 13 per cent of the population over fourteen years of age,[97] adolescent poverty may be said to have ended.

Young people have been obliged to enter "dead-end" jobs far less frequently than thirty years ago: in 1951 they constituted a far smaller proportion of workers in the less skilled occupations than in 1931. The proportion of the employed population under the age of twenty-five has, of course, declined, from 25 to 18 per cent; but the decline in the proportion employed, for instance, as messengers, roundsmen, bus and tram conductors and lorry drivers' mates has declined much more steeply: from 91 to 35 per cent, 44 to 22 per cent, 27 to 14 per cent, and 85 to 67 per cent respectively. Their decline among unskilled workers in miscellaneous trades was from 25 to 16 per cent.[98] The less skilled occupations have become topheavy with older people.

In consequence, as Abrams has claimed, young people "Nowadays . . . are increasingly spending their working hours in jobs that require adult, industrial and literary skills, and the capacity to work with adults more or less as equals . . . Thus, in their jobs too, quite apart from their earnings, they have, economically, come much closer to being adults and much further from the subservient rôles of the child."[99] These gains are by no means secure; they have given youth an importance and undoubtedly created an economic climate which favoured their greater reproduction; these very circumstances threaten their position in the future.

[96] Mark Abrams: *The Teenage Consumer*, 1959, p. 5.
[97] Mark Abrams: *Teenage Consumer Spending in 1959*, 1961, p. 4.
[98] *General Report, Census 1951*, Table 63, pp. 136–7.
[99] *The Teenage Consumer*, 1959, p. 13.

CHAPTER 2

Youth in Educational Settings

With the possible exception of organizing itself for overall functioning, none of society's tasks is taken more seriously than educating its young. The problem of socializing the young is practical in the sense of assuring social survival and utopian in the sense that hopes and goals for the future are invested in the molding process. Indeed, the young are the future of the society.

In industrial societies, of which America is the super-example, parents in many critical ways are obsolescent in their ability to prepare their children for economic roles in adulthood. While we would not dispute parental significance in playing behind-the-scenes roles as motivators and supporters, we note that in highly specialized societies parents have had to relegate education to an institutional arrangement outside of the family and, to a pronounced degree, independent of it. Today's bureaucratic educational organizations controlled by professional educators are a far cry from the colonial American community hiring its own barely-literate teacher. Large high schools are comparable to other large-scale organizations such as business corporations, hospitals, and government agencies with their formal and informal structures. The power of parents to control the educational process is very limited, and they are intimidated by the knowledge explosion and the growth of specialization which has reached even into the elementary school. The formal training of the young is largely out of their hands.

The majority of Americans live in urban places and of those who live in rural places, most are not farmers. Therefore, in an urban, industrialized society most fathers will not be able to pass on their specialized occupation to their sons and daughters. There is evidence from Coleman's study of the adolescent society[1] that most sons would not elect to pursue their fathers' occupations anyway. The rate of social change is so rapid that parents cannot afford to shape their children in time-bound images and

[1] James S. Coleman, *The Adolescent Society*, New York: The Free Press of Glencoe, 1961, pp. 7–8.

youth are not well acquainted with the specifics of their fathers' jobs. Adolescents are effectively prohibited from entering the labor market by compulsory school attendance laws, protective legislation, and formal employment practices.

Consequently, in advanced industrial societies youth is found in age-segregated circumstances for prolonged periods of time in schools, preparing for relatively non-specific economic futures. In the U.S. the proportion of the high school–age population found in school has increased from about 11 percent in 1900 to more than 90 percent today. In a system characterized by contest mobility where elite status is the price in an open contest[2] the elders have convinced the young that social mobility will be awarded to those who achieve degrees. According to Goodman,[3] more adolescents stay in school "terrified to jeopardize the only pattern of life he knows." The isolation of the adolescent from an age-integrated setting into a formal educational place as well as process has resulted in an unexpected circumstance. Youth come to constitute a small social system of peers that is separated from adult society. (Whether or not there is a separate adolescent subculture will be considered in selections in this book under the heading "Youth Peer Groups and Subculture.")

Our aim in making a point here about the genesis of the adolescent society is that youth seem to be looking increasingly to others of their own generation for approval, admiration, control, and respect—in a word, *status*, in school and out. The assumption that children are motivated and influenced by elders—parents and teachers—must be altered to include the effect of peers. Appreciation of the significance of peer behavior will increase understanding of what is happening (and what isn't happening) in education today—specifically, the blunting of scholarly and intellectual achievement values which the educational institutions espouse and student social systems depress.

What are the values in the adolescent culture with respect to school-rooted social systems? In the Coleman study of representative midwestern schools, high-school students were asked how they wanted to be remembered in schools, to which boys responded "an athletic star," and girls chose "activities leader" and "most popular."[4] For both sexes the "brilliant student" designation suffered. Scholastic success was only minimally helpful toward membership in the leading crowds, the social elite, after the attributes of personality, a good reputation, good looks, clothes, athleticism, and the like.[5] The effects of such a social system suppress scholastic

[2] Ralph H. Turner, "Sponsored and Contest Mobility and the School System," *American Sociological Review*, Vol. 25 (December 1960), pp. 855–867.
[3] Paul Goodman, "The Universal Trap," in Daniel Schreiber (ed.), *Profile of the School Dropout*, New York: Vintage Books, 1968, p. 32.
[4] Coleman, p. 30.
[5] Coleman, p. 39.

self-images in bright boys, and particularly discourage bright girls from accepting the self-image learned by them through their high achievements. Obviously the teacher has a problem in motivating not individuals *per se*, but an entire social system which does not reward serious scholarship to the degree to which the schools value it. Having measured the relative unimportance of academic achievement, Coleman suggests in the first selection that educational theory and practice seeem unaware of subsystem value priorities, for they focus on individuals and disregard competing value systems. It has been observed that interscholastic athletics play a dominating role in the high school because of the stress on intergroup competition rather than interpersonal competition. Athletic games function to bind the school and community together in a way that no other school-related activity does. Is it possible to restructure scholastic activities along the lines of intergroup competition and thereby direct the energies of the adolescent subculture toward learning?

In the second selection Irving Krauss looks for the sources of educational aspirations of working-class youth in family structural variables as well as in students' peer associations and participation in school activities. It is well established that the educational aspirations of working-class high school students are much lower than those of middle-class students. Krauss finds that the college-oriented working-class students have come to have middle-class values, that is, they are strikingly like their middle-class peers in a number of attitudes and behaviors. Status discrepancies betweeen parents, familial contact with middle-class people and the students' associations with college-oriented middle-class students may have produced anticipatory socialization toward upward mobility.

Socially sophisticated adolescents in the late sixties have been labeled "activist," meaning they have challenged traditional authority patterns which have held them in subordinated passive roles in schools. They are not content to sit quietly and be taught. Who would have predicted, given the relatively quiet campuses of the fifties, that the youth who followed the Silent Generation would embrace the first Civil Rights Movement, then the Berkeley campus free speech protest in 1964, and subsequently social protest patterns which filtered into the high schools in the late sixties? Protest was a media-managed theme of the sixties from which adolescents were not sheltered. The efforts of groups to effect changes in the *status quo* were also modeled for adolescents by the new militancy of the public school teachers, the pressure strategies of the black power advocates, the legal successes of the school desegregationists, and even the neo-feminism of the Women's Liberationists.

Perhaps the most significant legal precedent toward support of the expression of individual rights in the public high schools came on February 24, 1969, from the Supreme Court decision that First and Fourteenth Amendment rights were violated in Des Moines, Iowa, when black armbands in protest against American involvement in the Vietnam War were banned in the public secondary schools. We have included the full text of opinions written on that case: the opinion of the majority written by Mr. Justice Fortas as well as the dissenting opinions. The majority opinion establishes that neither students nor teachers shed their constitutional rights to freedom of speech and expression "at the schoolhouse door." It also affirms that school officials do not possess absolute authority over their students. Surely this already famous case will be invoked in the attempts students are making to challenge the legitimacy of the authoritarian hold of the educational organization on their in-school hours. "Ceremonies of humiliation in school," to use Friedenberg's meaningful phrase,[6] which refers to detailed rules governing personal grooming, length of hair on boys, and dress, have beeen subjected to criticism by the young and their adult advocates.

It is this basic question of legitimacy of regulation and restriction of student life which Jencks and Riesman explore in the final selection. Emphasis is on the undergraduate years of college but some attention is paid to the high school antecedents and the graduate program consequences. The roles and ambitions of students and faculty which are productive of intergenerational tensions are contrasted. The young may succeed in diminishing adult control in academic institutions, but they can ill afford to delay peacemaking, for adults ultimately control their future status in society.

[6] Edgar Z. Friedenberg, "Ceremonies of Humiliation in School," *Education Digest*, Vol. 32 (November 1966), p. 35–37.

ADOLESCENT SUBCULTURE
AND ACADEMIC ACHIEVEMENT[*,1]

JAMES S. COLEMAN

Industrial society has spawned a peculiar phenomenon, most evident in America but emerging also in other Western societies: adolescent subcultures, with values and activities quite distinct from those of the adult society—subcultures whose members have most of their important associations within and few with adult society. Industrialization, and the rapidity of change itself, has taken out of the hands of the parent the task of training his child, made the parent's skills obsolescent, and put him out of touch with the times—unable to understand, much less inculcate, the standards of a social order which has changed since he was young.

By extending the period of training necessary for a child and by encompassing nearly the whole population, industrial society has made of high school a social system of adolescents. It includes, in the United States, almost all adolescents and more and more of the activities of the adolescent himself. A typical example is provided by an excerpt from a high school newspaper in an upper-middle-class suburban school:

> Sophomores, this is your chance to learn how to dance! The first day of sophomore dancing is Nov. 14 and it will begin at 8:30 A.M. in the Boys' Gym. . . .
> No one is required to take dancing but it is highly recommended for both boys and girls. . . .
> If you don't attend at this time except in case of absence from school, you may not attend at any other time. Absence excuses should be shown to Miss ——— or Mr. ———.

In effect, then, what our society has done is to set apart, in an institution of their own, adolescents for whom home is little more than a dormitory and whose world is made up of activities peculiar to their fellows. They have been given as well many of the instruments which can make them a functioning community: cars, freedom in dating, continual contact with the opposite

* Reprinted from James S. Coleman, "The Adolescent Subculture and Academic Achievement," in *American Journal of Sociology*, Vol. LXV (January 1960), pp. 337–347, by permission of the author and University of Chicago Press. Copyright 1960 by the University of Chicago.
[1] The research discussed in this paper was carried out under a grant from the United States Office of Education; a full report is contained in "Social Climates and Social Structures in High Schools," a report to the Office of Education. The paper was presented at the Fourth World Congress of Sociology, Milan, Italy, September, 1959.

40

sex, money, and entertainment, like popular music and movies, designed especially for them. The international spread of "rock-and-roll" and of so-called American patterns of adolescent behavior is a consequence, I would suggest, of these economic changes which have set adolescents off in a world of their own.

Yet the fact that such a subsystem has sprung up in society has not been systematically recognized in the organization of secondary education. The theory and practice of education remains focused on *individuals;* teachers exhort individuals to concentrate their energies in scholarly directions, while the community of adolescent diverts these energies into other channels. The premise of the present research is that, if educational goals are to be realized in modern society, a fundamentally different approach to secondary education is necessary. Adults are in control of the institutions they have established for secondary education; traditionally, these institutions have been used to mold children as individuals toward ends which adults dictate. The fundamental change which must occur is to shift the focus: to mold social communities as communities, so that the norms of the communities themselves reinforce educational goals rather than inhibit them, as is at present the case.

The research being reported is an attempt to examine the status systems of the adolescent communities in ten high schools and to see the effects of these status systems upon the individuals within them. The ten high schools are all in the Midwest. They include five schools in small towns (labeled 0–4 in the figures which follow), one in a working-class suburb (6), one in a well-to-do suburb (9), and three schools in cities of varying sizes (5, 7, and 8). All but No. 5, a Catholic boys' school, are coeducational, and all but it are public schools.

The intention was to study schools which had quite different status systems, but the similarities were far more striking than the differences. In a questionnaire all boys were asked: "How would you most like to be remembered in school: as an athletic star: a brilliant student, or most popular?" The results of the responses for each school are shown in Figure 1,[2] where the left corner of the triangle represents 100 per cent saying "star athlete"; the top corner represents 100 per cent saying "brilliant student"; and the right corner represents 100 per cent saying "most popular." Each school is representedly a point whose location relative to the three corners shows the proportion giving each response.

The schools are remarkably grouped somewhat off-center, showing a greater tendency to say "star athlete" than either of the other choices. From each school's point is a broken arrow connecting the school as a whole with its members who were named by their fellows as being "members of the leading crowd." In almost every case, the leading crowd tends in the direction of the athlete—in all cases *away* from the ideal of the brilliant student. Again, for the leading crowds as well as for the students as a whole, the uniformity is remarkably great; not so great in the absolute positions of the leading crowds but in the direction they deviate from the student bodies.

[2] I am grateful to James A. Davis and Jacob Feldman, of the University of Chicago, for suggesting such graphs for presenting responses to trichotomous items in a population.

This trend toward the ideal of the athletic star on the part of the leading crowds is due in part to the fact that the leading crowds include a great number of athletes. Boys were asked in a questionnaire to name the best athlete in their grade, the best student, and the boy most popular with girls. In every school, without exception, the boys named as best athletes were named more often—on the average over twice as often—as members of the leading crowd than were those named as best students. Similarly, the boy most popular with girls was named as belonging to the leading crowd more often than the best student, though in all schools but the well-to-do suburb and the smallest rural town (schools 9 and 0 on Fig. 1) less often than the best athlete.

These and other data indicate the importance of athletic achievement as an avenue for gaining status in the schools. Indeed, in the predominantly middle-class schools, it is by far the most effective achievement for gaining a working-class boy entrée into the leading crowd.

Similarly, each girl was asked how she would like to be remembered: as a brilliant student, a leader in extracurricular activities, or most popular. The various schools are located on Figure 2, together with arrows connecting them to their leading crowd. The girls tend slightly less, on the average, than the

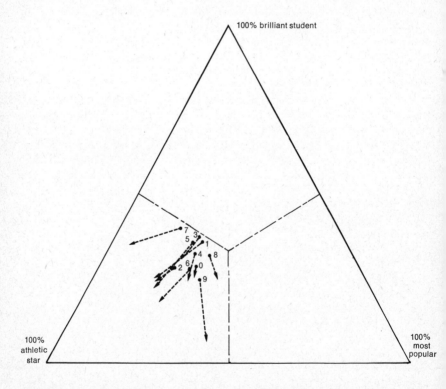

FIGURE 1.   Positions of Schools and Leading Crowds in Boys' Relative Choice of Brilliant Student, Athletic Star, and Most Popular.

boys to want to be remembered as brilliant students. Although the alternatives are different, and thus cannot be directly compared, a great deal of other evidence indicates that the girls—although better students in every school—do not want to be considered "brilliant students." They have good reason not to, for the girl in each grade in each of the schools who was most often named as best student has fewer friends and is less often in the leading crowd than is the boy most often named as best student.

There is, however, diversity among the schools in the attractiveness of the images of "activities leader" and "popular girl" (Fig. 2). In five (9, 0, 3, 8, and 1), the leader in activities is more often chosen as an ideal than is the popular girl; in four (7, 6, 2, and 4) the most popular girl is the more attractive of the two. These differences correspond somewhat to class background differences among the schools: 2, 4, 6, and 7, where the activities leader is least attractive, have the highest proportion of students with working-class backgrounds. School 9 is by far the most upper-middle-class one and by far the most activities-oriented.

The differences among the schools correspond as well to differences among the leading crowds: in schools 2, 4, and 6, where the girls as a whole are most oriented to being popular, the leading crowds are even more so; in the school

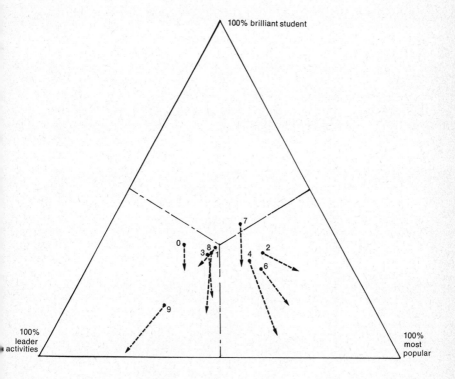

FIGURE 2. Position of Schools and Leading Crowds in Girls' Relative Choice of Brilliant Student, Activities Leader, and Most Popular.

where the girls are most oriented to the ideal of the activities leading, No. 9, the leading crowd goes even further in that direction.[3] In other words, it is as if a pull is exerted by the leading crowd, bringing the rest of the students toward one or the other of the polar extremes. In all cases, the leading crowd pulls away from the brilliant-student ideal.

Although these schools vary far less than one might wish when examining the effects of status systems, there are differences. All students were asked in a questionnaire: "What does it take to get into the leading crowd?" On the basis of the answers, the relative importance of various activities can be determined. Consider only a single activity, academic achievement. Its importance for status among the adolescents in each school can be measured simply by the proportion of responses which specify "good grades," or "brains" as adolescents often put it, as a means of entrée into the leading crowd. In all the schools, academic achievement was of less importance than other matters, such as being an athletic star among the boys, being a cheerleader or being good-looking among the girls, or other attributes. Other measures which were obtained of the importance of academic achievement in the adolescent status system correlate highly with this one.[4]

If, then, it is true that the status system of adolescents *does* affect educational goals, those schools which differ in the importance of academic achievement in the adolescent status system should differ in numerous other ways which are directly related to educational goals. Only one of those, which illustrates well the differing pressures upon students in the various schools, will be reported here.

In every social context certain activities are highly rewarded, while others are not. Those activities which are rewarded are the activities for which there is strong competition—activities in which everyone with some ability will compete.—In such activities the persons who achieve most should be those with most potential ability. In contrast, in unrewarded activities, those who have most ability may not be motivated to compete; consequently, the persons who achieve most will be persons of lesser ability. Thus in a high school where basketball is important, nearly every boy who might be a good basketball player will go out for the sport, and, as a result, basketball stars are likely to be the boys with the most ability. If in the same school volleyball does not bring the same status, few boys will go out for it, and those who end up as members of the team will not be the boys with most potential ability.

Similarly, with academic achievement: a school where such achievement brings few social rewards, those who "go out" for scholarly achievement will be few. The high performers, those who receive good grades, will not be the

[3] This result could logically be a statistical artifact because the leaders were included among students as a whole and thus would boost the result in the direction they tend. However, it is not a statistical artifact, for the leading crowds are a small part of the total student body. When they are taken out for computing the position of the rest of the girls in each school, schools 2, 4, 6, and 7 are still the most popularity-oriented and school 9 the most activities-oriented.

[4] Parenthetically, it might be noted that these measures correlate imperfectly with the proportion of boys or girls who want to be remembered as brilliant students. These responses depend on the relative attractiveness of other ideals, which varies from school to school, and upon other factors unrelated to the status system.

boys whose ability is greatest but a more mediocre few. Thus the "intellectuals" of such a society, those defined by themselves and others as the best
students, will not in fact be those with most intellectual ability. The latter,
knowing where the social rewards lie, will be off cultivating other fields which
bring social rewards.

To examine the effect of varying social pressures in the schools, academic
achievement, as measured by grades in school, was related to I.Q. Since the
I.Q. tests differ from school to school, and since each school had its own
mean I.Q. and its own variation around it, the ability of high performers
(boys who made A or A— average)[5] was measured by the number of standard
deviations of their average I.Q.'s above the mean. In this way, it is possible to
see where the high performers' ability lay, relative to the distribution of abilities in their school.[6]

The variations were great: in a small-town school, No. 1, the boys who
made an A or A— average had I.Q.'s 1.53 standard deviations above the
school average; in another small-town school, No. 0, their I.Q.'s were only
about a third this distance above the mean, .59. Given this variation, the
question can be asked: Do these variations in ability of the high performers
correspond to variations in the social rewards for, or constraints against, being
a good student?

Figure 3 shows the relation for the boys between the social rewards for
academic excellence (i.e., the frequency with which "good grades" was mentioned as a means for getting into the leading crowd) and the ability of the
high performers, measured by the number of standard deviations their average
I.Q.'s exceed that of the rest of the boys in the school. The relation is
extremely strong. Only one school, a parochial boys' school in the city's slums,
deviates. This is a school in which many boys had their most important associations outside the school rather than in it, so that its student body constituted
far less of a social system, less able to dispense social rewards and punishments, than was true of the other schools.

Similarly, Figure 4 shows for the girls the I.Q.'s of the high performers.[7]

---

[5] In each school but 3 and 8, those making A and A— constituted from 6 to 8 per cent
of the student body. In order to provide a correct test of the hypothesis, it is necessary
to have the same fraction of the student body in each case (since I.Q.'s of this group
are being measured in terms of number of standard deviations above the student
body). To adjust these groups, enough 6's were added (each being assigned the average
I.Q. of the total group of 6's) to bring the proportion up to 6 per cent (from 3 per
cent in school 3, from 4 per cent in school 8).
[6] The I.Q. tests used in the different schools were: (0) California Mental Maturity
(taken seventh, eighth, or ninth grade); (1) California Mental Maturity (taken eighth
grade); (2) SRA Primary Mental Abilities (taken tenth grade); (3) California Mental
Maturity (taken ninth grade; seniors took SRA PMA, which was tabulated as a per-
centile, and they have been omitted from analysis reported above); (4) Otis (ninth
and tenth grades; taken eighth grade); Kuhlman Finch (eleventh and twelfth grades,
taken eighth grade); (5) Otis (taken ninth grade); (6) California Mental Maturity
(taken eighth grade); (7) California Mental Maturity (taken eighth grade); (8) Otis
(taken ninth or tenth grade); and (9) Otis (taken eighth grade).
[7] For the girls, only girls with a straight-A average were included. Since girls get better
grades than boys, this device is necessary in order to make the sizes of the "high-
performer" group roughly comparable for boys and for girls. Schools differed somewhat

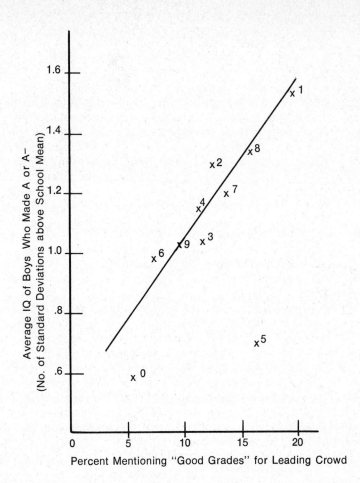

FIGURE 3. I.Q.'s of High Achieving Boys by Importance of Good Grades among Other Boys.

Unfortunately, most of the schools are closely bunched in the degree to which good grades are important among the girls, so that there is too little variation among them to examine this effect as fully as would be desirable. School 2 is the one school whose girls deviate from the general relationship.

The effect of these values systems on the freedom for academic ability to express itself in high achievement is evident among the girls as it is among

---

in the proportion of A's, constituting about 6 per cent of the students in the small schools, only about 3 per cent in schools 6 and 7, 1 per cent in 8, and 2 per cent in 9. In 8 and 9, enough girls were added and assigned the average grade of the 7 (A—) group to bring the proportion to 3 per cent, comparable with the other large schools. The difference, however, between the large and small schools was left.

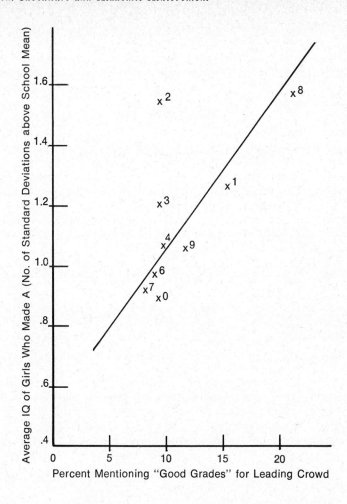

FIGURE 4. I.Q.'s of High Achieving Girls by Importance of Good Grades among Other Girls.

the boys. This is not merely due to the school facilities, social composition of the school, or other variables: the two schools highest in the importance of scholastic achievement for both boys and girls are *1* and *8*, the first a small-town school of 350 students and the second a city school of 2,000 students. In both there are fewer students with white-collar backgrounds than in schools *9* or *3*, which are somewhere in the middle as to value placed on academic achievement, but are more white-collar than in schools *7* or *4*, which are also somewhere in the middle. The highest expenditure per student was $695 per year in school *9*, and the lowest was little more than half that, in school *4*. These schools are close together on the graphs of Figures 3 and 4.

It should be mentioned in passing that an extensive unpublished study throughout Connecticut, using standard tests of achievement and ability, yielded consistent results. The study found no correlation between per pupil expenditure in a school and the achievement of its students relative to their ability. The effects shown in Figures 3 and 4 suggest why: that students with ability are led to achieve only when there are social rewards, primarily from their peers, for doing so—and these social rewards seem little correlated with per pupil expenditure.

So much for the effects as shown by the variation among schools. As mentioned earlier, the variation among schools was not nearly so striking in this research as the fact that, in all of them, academic achievement did not count for as much as other activities. In every school the boy named as best athlete and the boy named as most popular with girls was far more often mentioned as a member of the leading crowd, and as someone to "be like," than was the boy named as the best student. And the girl named as best dressed, and the one named as most popular with boys, as in every school far more often mentioned as being in the leading crowd and as someone "to be like," than was the girl named as the best student.

The relative unimportance of academic achievement, together with the effect shown earlier, suggests that these adolescent subcultures are generally deterrents to academic achievement. In other words, in these societies of adolescents those who come to be seen as the "intellectuals" and who come to think so of themselves are not really those of highest intelligence but are only the ones who are willing to work hard at a relatively unrewarded activity.

The implications for American society as a whole are clear. Because high schools allow the adolescent subcultures to divert energies into athletics, social activities, and the like, they recruit into adult intellectual activities people with a rather mediocre level of ability. In fact, the high school seems to do more than allow these subcultures to discourage academic achievement; it aids them in doing so. To indicate how it does and to indicate how it might do differently is another story, to be examined below.

Figures 1 and 2, which show the way boys and girls would like to be remembered in their high school, demonstrate a curious difference between the boys and the girls. Despite great variation in social background, in size of school (from 180 to 2,000), in size of town (from less than a thousand to over a million), and in style of life of their parents, the proportion of boys choosing each of the three images by which he wants to be remembered is very nearly the same in all schools. And in every school the leading crowd "pulls" in similar directions: at least partly toward the ideal of the star athlete. Yet the ideals of the girls in these schools are far more dispersed, and the leading crowds "pull" in varying directions, far less uniformly than among the boys. Why such a diversity in the same schools?

The question can best be answered by indirection. In two schools apart from those in the research, the questionnaire was administered primarily to answer a puzzling question: Why was academic achievement of so little importance among the adolescents in school 9? Their parents were professionals and business executives, about 80 per cent were going to college (over twice as high a proportion as in any of the other schools), and yet academic excellence counted for little among them. In the two additional schools parental background was largely held constant, for they were private, coeducational day schools whose students had upper-middle-class backgrounds quite similar to those of school 9. One (No. *10*) was in the city; the other (No. *11*), in a suburban setting almost identical to that of No. 9. Although the two schools were added to the study to answer the question about school 9, they will be used to help answer the puzzle set earlier: that of the clustering of schools for the boys and their greater spread for the girls. When we look at the responses of adolescents in these two schools to the question as to how they would like to be remembered, the picture becomes even more puzzling (Figs. 5 and 6). For the boys, they are extremely far from the cluster of other schools; for the girls, they are intermingled with the other schools. Thus, though it was for the boys that the other schools clustered so closely, these two deviate sharply from the cluster; and for the girls, where the schools already varied, these two are not distinguishable. Furthermore, the leading crowds of boys in these schools do not pull the ideal toward the star-athlete ideal as do those in almost all the other schools. To be sure, they pull away from the ideal of the brilliant student, but the pull is primarily toward a social image, the most popular. Among the girls, the leading crowds pull in different directions and are nearly indistinguishable from the other schools.

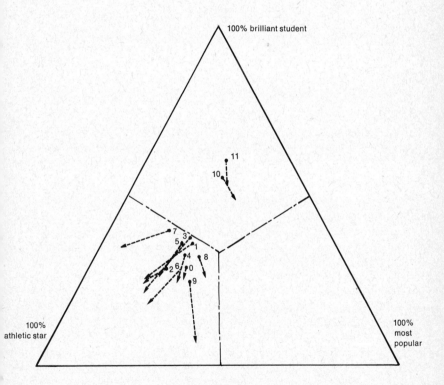

Figure 5. Positions of Schools and Leading Crowds in Boys' Relative Choice of Brilliant Student, Athletic Star, and Most Popular (Two Private Schools [*10, 11*] Included).

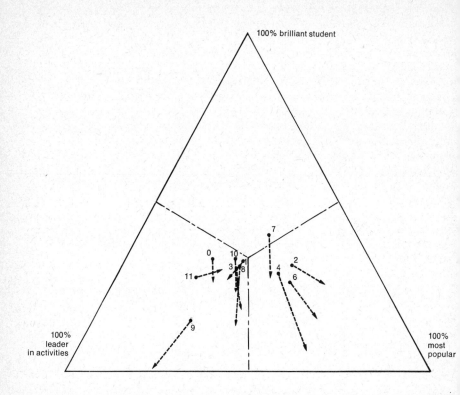

FIGURE 6. Positions of Schools and Leading Crowds in Girls' Relative Choice of Brilliant Student, Activities Leader, and Most Popular (Two Private Schools [10, 11] Included).

The answer to both puzzles, that is, first, the great cluster of the boys and now, in these two additional schools, the greater deviation, seems to lie in one fact: the boys' interscholastic athletics. The nine public schools are all engaged in interscholastic leagues which themselves are knit together in state tournaments. The other school of the first ten, the Catholic school, is in a parochial league, where games are just as hotly contested as in the public leagues and is also knit together with them in tournaments.

Schools *10* and *11* are athletically in a world apart from this. Although boys in both schools may go in for sports, and both schools have interscholastic games, the opponents are scattered private schools, constituting a league in name only. They take no part in state or city tournaments and have almost no publicity.

There is nothing for the girls comparable to the boys' interscholastic athletics. There are school activities of one sort or another, in which most girls take part, but no interscholastic games involving them. Their absence and the lack of leagues which knit all schools together in systematic competition means that the status system can "wander" freely, depending on local conditions in the school. In athletics, however, a school, and the community surrounding it, cannot hold its head up if it continues to lose games. It *must* devote roughly the same attention to athletics as do the schools surrounding it, for athletic games are the only games in which it engages other schools and, by representation, other communities.

These games are almost the only means a school has of generating internal cohesion and identification, for they constitute the only activity in which the school participates *as* a school. (This is well indicated by the fact that a number of students in school 10, the private school which engages in no interscholastic games, has been concerned by a "lack of school spirit.") It is as a consequence of this that the athlete gains so much status: he is doing something for the school and the community, not only for himself, in leading his team to victory, for it is a school victory.

The outstanding student, in contrast, has little or no way to bring glory to his school. His victories are always purely personal, often at the expense of his classmates, who are forced to work harder to keep up with him. It is no wonder that his accomplishments gain little reward and are often met by ridiculing remarks, such as "curve-raiser" or "grind," terms of disapprobation which have no analogues in athletics.

These results are particularly intriguing, for they suggest ways in which rather straightforward social theory could be used in organizing the activities of high schools in such a way that their adolescent subcultures would encourage, rather than discourage, the channeling of energies into directions of learning. One might speculate on the possible effects of city-wide or state-wide "scholastic fairs" composed of academic games and tournaments between schools and school exhibits to be judged. It could be that the mere institution of such games would, just as do the state basketball tournaments in the midwestern United States, have a profound effect upon the educational climate in the participating schools. In fact, by an extension of this analysis, one would predict that an international fair of this sort, a "Scholastic Olympics," would generate interscholastic games and tournaments within the participating countries.

SOURCES OF EDUCATIONAL ASPIRATIONS AMONG WORKING CLASS YOUTH[*,1]

IRVING KRAUSS

Characteristic of industrial society is growth in the proportion of better paid and more prestigeful occupations, increased educational requirements for the more desirable jobs, and greater availability of education. These conditions encourage individuals to develop mobility aspirations, and increasingly education is a primary channel for upward movement.[2] Yet, as is well known, only a limited proportion of working-class youths take advantage of this source of mobility.[3]

Many of the numerous studies of determinants of mobility have focused on lower-status youths.[4] In this paper I shall further probe the sources of educational aspirations among working-class youngsters, concentrating on five areas: 1) discrepant situations in the family of orientation; 2) the experience of family members and friends; 3) the relative status of the working-class family; 4) the influence of peers and participation in the school culture, and 5) working-class students' attitudes and middle-class values.

* Reprinted from Irving Krauss, "Sources of Educational Aspirations Among Working Class Youth," in *American Sociological Review*, Vol. 29 (1964), pp. 867–879, by permission of the author and publisher.

1 The data in this paper are from a thesis submitted in partial fulfillment of the requirements for the Ph.D. in the Department of Sociology, University of California, Berkeley. A grant of funds from the Committee on Research at the University of California helped defray research expenses. I wish to thank Seymour M. Lipset for several helpful suggestions, which were incorporated into this paper.

2 These phenomena are examined by Seymour M. Lipset and Reinhard Bendix in *Social Mobility in Industrial Society*, Berkeley and Los Angeles: University of California Press, 1959. See also Pitirim A. Sorokin, *Social and Cultural Mobility*, New York: The Free Press, 1959.

3 See William H. Sewell, Archie O. Haller and Murray A. Strauss, "Social Status and Educational and Occupational Aspiration," *American Sociological Review*, 22 (February, 1957), pp. 67–73 and Robert J. Havighurst and Robert P. Rodgers, "The Role of Motivation in Attendance at Post-High School Education Institutions," in Byron S. Hollinshead (ed.), *Who Should Go To College*, New York: Columbia University Press, 1953, pp. 135–165.

4 The literature is summarized by Lipset and Bendix, *op. cit.*, pp. 227–259. Recent studies include Richard L. Simpson, "Parental Influence, Anticipatory Socialization, and Social Mobility," *American Sociological Review*, 27 (August, 1962), pp. 517–522 nad Robert A. Ellis and W. Clayton Lane, "Structural Supports for Upward Mobility," *American Sociological Review*, 28 (October, 1963), pp. 743–756.

The Data

A precoded questionnaire was administered to 706 high school seniors in four San Francisco Bay Area high schools, approximately three weeks prior to their graduation in June, 1959.[5] The students were categorized according to their potential mobility, as expressed in their plans for *college, technical school,* or *no further education.* The most mobile students plan to enter a regular four-year college, or to attend junior college for two years and then transfer to a four-year institution. The students whose potential mobility is more limited plan to learn a trade or receive other training in a technical school, or in the vocational program of a junior college, where they will be one- or two-year terminal students. Those who are likely to be the least mobile have no definite plans for education after they leave high school. Some stated that they might seek additional schooling in the future, and the rest indicated that they definitely do not plan to obtain further education.

Table 1, which contrasts the post-high school plans of working- and middle-class students, shows that the educational aspirations of the working-class students are much lower than those of the middle-class students. While

[5] All the students in several classes in each school completed questionnaires, and of the 706 returned, 52 were not used: father's occupation was unclear for 38 respondents, 8 fathers were farmers, and six questionnaires were defaced or unanswered. Of the remaining 654 respondents, 387 whose fathers are in blue-collar work were defined as working-class, and 267 whose fathers are in white-collar occupations were defined as middle-class. The distinction was based on the U. S. Census classification of blue-collar and white-collar occupations. Evidence that this distinction is a meaningful one is summarized by Lipset and Bendix, *op. cit.,* pp. 14–17, 156–157 and 165–171. Cf. Peter M. Blau, "Occupational Bias and Mobility," *American Sociological Review,* 22 (August, 1957), pp. 392–399 and Robert S. Lynd and Helen M. Lynd, *Middletown,* New York: Harcourt, Brace, 1929, pp. 22–23.

Father's occupation was determined by responses to the following questions: "What is your father's occupation? Be as specific as possible. (If he is deceased, say what his occupation was.) *Tell exactly what he does* (for example, 'sells clothes,' 'operates a lathe,' etc.)," "In what kind of place does he work (for example, 'a department store,' 'a factory,' etc.)?" and, "Is he self-employed or does he work for someone else?" No distinction was made between employed and unemployed fathers, although my impression is that practically all were working at the time. The fathers of 20 working- and 13 middle-class students were deceased or out of contact, and these questionnaires are included.

Schools with a substantial number of working-class students were sought. A list of approximately 50 schools was compiled, excluding those whose students came almost entirely from upper middle-class neighborhoods. Because our resources were limited, we selected four schools on the basis of willingness to participate. The percentages of working-class fathers were 68, 62, 56, and 45. Students in all programs of study—college preparatory, commercial and vocational—were surveyed. Questionnaires were administered in mixed and in all-male classes, such as personal hygiene, where it was felt that the bases for segregation would not introduce bias. Thus 59 per cent of all respondents are working-class; 69 per cent of the working-class, and 67 per cent of the middle-class students are boys. Working-class students' post-high school plans, for boys and girls respectively, were: *college,* 43 and 37 per cent; *technical school,* 31 and 29 per cent, and *no further education,* 25 and 34 per cent. For middle-class students these percentages were: *college,* 66 and 61; *technical school,* 20 and 20, and *no further education,* 14 and 19. Since these sex differences were not large, male and female students were analyzed together to permit more detailed cross tabulations.

TABLE 1.   POST-HIGH SCHOOL PLANS OF WORKING-CLASS AND MIDDLE-CLASS
STUDENTS
(IN PERCENTAGES)

Student's Post-High School Plans	(N)	Working-Class Students (387)	Middle-Class Students (267)
College		41	64
Technical school		30	20
No further education		28	16
Total		99	100

64 per cent of those from middle-class homes plan to attend college, only 41 per cent of the working-class youths have similar plans.

This is a considerable, though not unexpected, proportion of the working-class students: what are the sources of their educational aspirations? That is, to what extent do the same conditions influence both working-class and middle-class youths to seek higher education? To what extent are the conditions most important for working-class students of limited significance for those from middle-class homes?

Sources of Educational Aspirations

DISCREPANT SITUATIONS

Among the possible sources of mobility aspirations are conditions or experiences that lead to dissatisfaction with a present status and interest in a new one.[6] Modern social conditions favor such dissatisfaction, while certain types of family structure may strongly encourage active interest in mobility. Previous research suggests that status discrepancies between husband and wife may be one of the structural factors responsible for mobility aspirations.[7]

Nearly one-fourth of the working-class mothers are employed in non-manual occupations. Fifty-three per cent of the children from these families plan to attend college, compared with only 29 per cent from families in which mother's occupation is manual. In fact, working-class students whose mothers are in manual occupations are less likely to have college plans than youngsters

[6] The process of breaking away from one group and entering a new one, of which this dissatisfaction is probably a part, has been examined in the framework of reference group behavior by Robert K. Merton, *Social Theory and Social Structure* (rev. ed.), New York: The Free Press, 1961, pp. 225–386. Other researchers who have studied this phenomenon with special reference to social mobility include Seymour M. Lipset, "Social Mobility and Urbanization," *Rural Sociology*, 20 (September-December, 1955), pp. 220–228; Lipset and Bendix, *op. cit.*, pp. 256–259 and Ralph H. Turner, "Reference Groups of Future-Oriented Men," *Social Forces*, 34 (December, 1955), pp. 130–136.

[7] Jean E. Floud, F. M. Martin and A. H. Halsey, "Educational Opportunity and Social Selection in England," *Transactions of the Second World Congress of Sociology*, 2 (1954), pp. 203–204.

TABLE 2.   STUDENTS' POST-HIGH SCHOOL PLANS BY MOTHER'S CURRENT OCCUPATIONAL STATUS
(IN PERCENTAGES)

	Working-Class Students			Middle-Class Students		
	Mother Currently Employed			Mother Currently Employed		
Student's Post-High School Plans (N)	In Non-Manual Work (91)	In Manual Work (55)	Mother Does Not Work (235)	In Non-Manual Work (100)	In Manual Work (10)	Mother Does Not Work (149)
College	53	29	39	67	(4)[a]	63
Technical school	23	44	30	16	(5)	20
No further education	24	27	30	17	(1)	16
Total[b]	100	100	99	100	(10)	99

[a] Numbers rather than percentages are given whenever the total number of cases is 15 or less.
[b] In this and in succeeding tables, unless otherwise noted, variations from the totals in Table 1 are due to omission of cases for which data were unavailable.

from homes in which the mother is not employed. Only ten middle-class students have mothers in manual occupations; of these, four have college aspirations, in contrast to 67 per cent from middle-class families where the mother's employment is non-manual, and 63 per cent where the mother does not work. (See Table 2.)

The working-class mother whose occupational status is higher than her husband's is likely to come in contact with middle-class persons and to acquire middle-class values. If her husband's status seems unlikely to improve, she may attempt to realize her aspirations through her children by encouraging them to develop middle-class interests and objectives.

Working-class students whose mothers were employed *prior* to marriage were more likely to express college aspirations, though mother's occupational level was not significant, if she did work. Perhaps employment prior to marriage indicates achievement motivation, which these working-class mothers may have passed on to their children. In middle-class families, whether the mother worked prior to marriage is not important; if she *was* employed, however, then her occupational level is strongly associated with her child's college aspirations. Among those whose mothers were in manual occupations, only 50 per cent have college aspirations, in contrast to 72 per cent among those whose mothers were in non-manual work.[8] (See Table 3.)

Another indicator of the wife's status relative to her husband's is the educational level of each at the time of marriage. Premarital educational

[8] Interpretation of these data must be tentative because of the number of mothers whose premarital occupational level is not clear.

TABLE 3.   STUDENTS' POST-HIGH SCHOOL PLANS BY MOTHER'S OCCUPATIONAL
STATUS PRIOR TO MARRIAGE
(IN PERCENTAGES)

| | | | Working-Class Families | | |
| | | | | Mother Worked in: | |
Student's Post-High School Plans (N)	*Mother Worked* (191)	*Mother Did Not Work* (196)	*Non-Manual Occupation* (71)	*Manual Occupation* (71)	*Occupational Level Not Clear* (49)
College	48	35	48	51	43
Technical school	28	33	28	28	29
No further education	24	32	24	21	29
Total	100	100	100	100	101

| | | | Middle-Class Families | | |
| | | | | Mother Worked in: | |
Student's Post-High School Plans (N)	*Mother Worked* (179)	*Mother Did Not Work* (88)	*Non-Manual Occupation* (116)	*Manual Occupation* (32)	*Occupational Level Not Clear* (31)
College	64	65	72	50	48
Technical school	19	22	16	25	26
No further education	17	14	12	25	26
Total	100	101	100	100	100

differences were significant in working-class families, but only under certain circumstances. When the working-class father has not completed high school the mother's educational achievement does not influence the youngster's post-high school plans. But when the father is a high school graduate, mother's education strongly affects the child's interest in college. For where the mother has married "down," as indicated by her having had more education than her husband, 76 per cent of the offspring plan to attend college—a larger percentage than among students whose fathers went to college. Where mother and father are both high school graduates, 44 per cent of the children plan on college. But where the mother married "up," that is, has had less education than her husband, only 29 per cent of the children have college aspirations. (See Table 4.)

In middle-class families, students whose fathers have had college training but whose mothers have not, are less likely to have college plans than those whose mother and father have both gone to college (70 compared with 82

TABLE 4. STUDENTS' POST-HIGH SCHOOL PLANS BY PARENTS' EDUCATION
(IN PERCENTAGES)

Working-Class

Student's Post-High School Plans	Father Has Not Completed High School			Father is a High School Graduate			Father Has Some College Training		
Mother's Education is:	More	Equal	Less	More	Equal	Less	More	Equal	Less
(N)	(98)	(69)	(13)	(26)	(63)	(21)	(6)	(13)	(33)
College	35	38	(3)	76	44	29	(3)	(10)	54
Technical school	32	35	(7)	12	30	38	(1)	(2)	21
No further education	32	27	(3)	12	26	33	(2)	(1)	24
Total	98	100	(13)	100	100	100	(6)	(13)	99

Middle-class

Student's Post-High School Plans	Father Has Not Completed High School			Father is a High School Graduate			Father Has Some College Training		
Mother's Education is:	More	Equal	Less	More	Equal	Less	More	Equal	Less
(N)	(25)	(15)	(1)	(11)	(49)	(5)	(11)	(45)	(73)
College	40	(8)	(0)	(7)	65	(3)	(7)	82	70
Technical school	28	(4)	(1)	(2)	18	(1)	(3)	11	22
No further education	32	(3)	(0)	(2)	16	(1)	(1)	6	7
Total	100	(15)	(1)	(11)	99	(5)	(11)	99	99

per cent). These students from status discrepant families, however, are more likely to plan to go to college than those whose parents are both high school graduates. Mothers who married "down" are numerous only among students whose father did not complete high school; these students are only a little more likely than their working-class counterparts to plan to attend college.

The significance of a working-class mother's educational achievement may be in the more important role she plays in child-rearing.[9] A college-trained mother may share her values and her aspirations for her child with middle-class college-educated people, even if she went to college for only a short time. Consciously or unconsciously, she may encourage her child to develop college aspirations rather than more limited working-class values. In working-class families in which the father has not completed high school, however, such factors as low occupational and income level may limit the effect of mother's greater education.

Another possible source of college aspirations may be the status of the preceding generation. Information on grandfather's occupational level was available for 71 per cent of the middle-class and for 65 per cent of the working-class students. Seventy per cent of the middle-class adolescents with at least one grandfather in a non-manual occupation planned to attend college, compared with only 54 per cent of those whose grandfathers were both manual workers. In middle-class families, college expectations for the children may be reinforced by white-collar occupational experience in the preceding generation.

In working-class families, having had at least one grandparent in a non-manual occupation also favors college aspirations. Fifty-six per cent of such students plan to attend college, compared with 41 per cent whose grandfathers were both manual workers. (See Table 5.) This may be a result of different factors, however, for these working class families have been downwardly

[9] See Ellis and Lane, *op. cit.*, p. 747.

TABLE 5.   STUDENTS' POST-HIGH SCHOOL PLANS BY GRANDFATHERS' OCCUPATIONAL LEVEL
(IN PERCENTAGES)

Student's Post-High School Plans		Middle-Class Students		Working-Class Students	
		Either Grandfather in Non-Manual Occupation	Both Grandfathers in Manual Occupation	Either Grandfather in Non-Manual Occupation	Both Grandfathers in Manual Occupation
	(N)	(135)	(54)	(126)	(126)
College		70	54	56	41
Technical school		16	26	22	33
No further education		14	20	21	26
	Total	100	100	99	100

mobile. Lipset and Bendix suggest the parents in such a family may be expected to compensate by encouraging their children to rise, and they cite Elizabeth Cohen's research[10]. My data support this thesis to some extent, although they are limited by the substantial number of students for whom information on grandparents' occupation was not available.[11]

COLLEGE EXPERIENCE OF FAMILY MEMBERS AND FRIENDS

Working-class students whose relatives or family friends have attended college may be encouraged to develop middle-class aspirations, including the desire for higher education. In this context, the college experience of parents, siblings and friends of the family is relevant.

Working-class parents who have attended college have not only been exposed to middle-class values that influence their children to seek further schooling, but in addition their having gone to college, even if for a limited time, may suggest to their offspring that such aspirations are not unreasonable. In addition, these parents know the requirements and procedures for entering college. Thus, in working-class families in which the father has college training, 61 per cent of the children plan to obtain higher education; in contrast, only 35 per cent of the youngsters whose fathers did not complete high school plan to attend college. (See Table 6.)

Middle-class students whose fathers did not complete high school are only a little more likely than their working-class counterparts to plan to attend

[10] Lipset and Bendix, *op. cit.*, p. 238. Also see Elizabeth G. Cohen, "Parental Factors in Educational Mobility," unpublished Ph.D. dissertation, Harvard University, 1958. Wilensky and Edwards show that the fathers in such families identify with the middle class, hold middle-class aspirations for themselves and have middle-class expectations for their children. See Harold L. Wilensky and Hugh Edwards, "The Skidder: Ideological Adjustments of Downward Mobile Workers," *American Sociological Review*, 24 (April, 1959), pp. 215–231, especially Table 1, pp. 221–225.
[11] Another source of mobility aspirations may be a working-class father's previous middle-class status. I have no data to probe this, but Wilensky and Edwards (*op. cit.*) found that these fathers are strongly middle-class oriented and expect their children to achieve middle-class status.

TABLE 6. STUDENTS' POST-HIGH SCHOOL PLANS BY FATHER'S EDUCATION
(IN PERCENTAGES)

Student's Post-High School Plans	*Working-Class Father's Education*			*Middle-Class Father's Education*		
	Less Than H.S.	*Completed H.S.*	*Some College or More*	*Less Than H.S.*	*Completed H.S.*	*Some College or More*
(N)	(183)	(113)	(54)	(46)	(67)	(138)
College	35	48	61	39	66	74
Technical school	34	27	19	30	15	18
No further education	30	25	20	30	19	7
Total	99	100	100	99	100	99

college. On the other hand, 74 per cent of those whose fathers experienced higher education, and 66 per cent of those whose fathers completed high school, have college aspirations.

The effects of mother's education are almost identical with those of father's education. As noted earlier, mother's education affects college aspirations most strongly when it differs from father's.

Students whose older siblings have attended college are, in working-class families, more likely to plan on college themselves. Where no older sibling has any higher education, only 26 per cent of the youngsters studied planned to attend college, while among those with one or more siblings who have gone to college, 53 per cent expected to go themselves. (See Table 7.)

A working-class child whose brothers or sisters have gone to college can benefit from their experience in coping with entrance requirements and the mechanics of enrolling. His siblings have demonstrated that college is attainable for a working-class child, they may provide a model for him, and their college experiences may allow him to participate vicariously in some aspects of middle-class life.

Older siblings who have gone to college have a less striking effect on the aspirations of a middle-class student. Seventy-six per cent of the middle-class students who have at least one older brother or sister with college training plan to obtain higher education themselves; but 61 per cent of those without a college-trained older sibling also have college aspirations.

The working-class student *and* his siblings may develop an interest in college for other reasons, of course, but an older sibling's college experience is clearly more relevant for the working-class than for the middle-class child, and probably reinforces other conditions favorable for college aspirations.

Of the working-class students who report that most of their parents' close friends are college graduates, 53 per cent plan to attend college, in contrast to 41 per cent in families where none of the close friends are college graduates. In middle-class families, all but one of the 20 students who report that all of their parents' close friends are college graduates have college plans,

TABLE 7.   STUDENTS' POST-HIGH SCHOOL PLANS BY NUMBER OF OLDER SIBLINGS WHO HAVE GONE TO COLLEGE[a]
(IN PERCENTAGES)

Student's Post-High School Plans		Number of Older Siblings Who Have Gone to College			
		Working-Class Families		Middle-Class Families	
		None	One or More	None	One or More
	(N)	(53)	(38)	(18)	(17)
College		26	53	61	76
Technical school		34	18	22	6
No further education		40	29	17	18
Total		100	100	100	100

[a] Includes only students with older siblings.

in contrast to 56 per cent where none of the close friends are college graduates.[12] (See Table 8.)

FATHER'S OCCUPATIONAL STATUS

Of the 387 working-class students, 49 per cent have fathers who are craftsmen or foremen, and 36 per cent have fathers who are semi-skilled workers. The remainder include protective service workers (5 per cent), other service workers (6 per cent) and laborers (3 per cent). Forty-seven per cent of the students whose fathers are craftsmen or foremen plan to attend college, in contrast to 36 per cent whose fathers are in semi-skilled service, or laboring work.[13]

Regardless of father's educational achievement, the children of foremen and craftsmen are more likely than the children of other manual workers to have college plans. (See Table 9.) This relationship, however, is strongest when the father is a high school graduate.[14] Where the father has some college education, the percentage planning to attend college among children of lower-level manual workers is relatively high. And where the father has less than a high school education, the difference between the children of craftsmen and foremen and the children of other manual workers is not very great; the

[12] Having uncles and aunts who are college graduates did not affect working-class students' post-high school plans. Having friends who are college graduates may indicate parents' interest in mobility either for themselves or for their children. Thus they have sought such friends, or if other considerations were the basis for friendship, acquaintance with college graduates may have resulted in the development of interests encouraging the children to seek college training. Status differences involving relatives may be a greater barrier to association than those involving friends, so that the latter may have more influence on the children's post-high school plans.

Middle-class students who reported that at least some of their uncles and aunts are college graduates were more likely to have college plans themselves, compared with those who reported that none of their uncles or aunts are college graduates.

[13] Cohen, *op. cit.*, also found that the status level of father's work affected college aspirations among working-class sons.

[14] Cf. Alan B. Wilson, "Residential Segregation of Social Classes and Aspirations of High School Boys," *American Sociological Review*, 24 (December, 1959), p. 841.

TABLE 8. STUDENTS' POST-HIGH SCHOOL PLANS BY NUMBER OF PARENTS' CLOSE FRIENDS WHO ARE COLLEGE GRADUATES

(IN PERCENTAGES)

Student's Post-High School Plans (N)	Number of Parents' Close Friends Who Are College Graduates							
	Working-Class Students				Middle-Class Students			
	None (51)	Some (154)	Most (32)	All (2)	None (16)	Some (94)	Most (68)	All (20)
College	41	52	53	(2)	56	57	71	95
Technical school	30	26	25	(0)	19	27	21	5
No further education	30	23	21	(0)	25	17	9	0
Total	101	101	99	(2)	100	101	101	100

TABLE 9.   STUDENTS' POST-HIGH SCHOOL PLANS BY FATHER'S EDUCATION AND OCCUPATIONAL LEVEL

(IN PERCENTAGES)

| | Working-Class Father's Education | | | | | |
| Student's Post-High School Plans (N) | Less than H.S. | | Completed H.S. | | Some College or More | |
	Fore-man, Crafts-man (82)	Other Manual (87)	Fore-man, Crafts-man (52)	Other Manual (51)	Fore-man, Crafts-man (33)	Other Manual (19)
College	40	36	60	37	58	48
Technical school	32	40	25	26	18	9
No further education	28	24	15	37	24	43
Total	100	100	100	100	100	100

| | Middle-Class Father's Education | | | | | |
| Student's Post-High School Plans (N) | Less than H.S. | | Completed H.S. | | Some College or More | |
	Profes-sional, Semi-profes-sional (4)	Other Non-Manual (42)	Profes-sional, Semi-profes-sional (4)	Other Non-Manual (63)	Profes-sional, Semi-profes-sional (66)	Other Non-Manual (72)
College	(2)	38	(3)	65	74	75
Technical school	(1)	31	(1)	14	17	19
No further education	(1)	31	(0)	21	9	6
Total	(4)	100	(4)	100	100	100

father's limited education mitigates against the family's developing values that might encourage the child to seek a college education.

As the elite of the working class, craftsmen and foremen have greater prestige and higher incomes than other manual workers.[15] In consumption patterns and aspirations for their children, the high status blue-collar family may to some extent approximate the middle-class ideal and therefore develop

[15] See Albert J. Reiss, Jr., *Occupations and Social Structure*, New York: The Free Press, 1961, pp. 95–97 and Appendix B. The median income of craftsmen and foremen is higher than that of many white-collar workers and small businessmen. Figures for 1960, for year-round, full-time male workers are: craftsmen, foremen and kindred workers, $5,905; self-employed managers, officials and proprietors (excluding farm), $5,396; clerical and kindred workers, $5,328. U. S. Bureau of the Census, *Statistical Abstract of the United States: 1962*, Washington, D. C.: U. S. Government Printing Office, 1962, p. 336.

middle-class aspirations, provided it is not handicapped by very little education.

For middle-class students, father's occupational level does not affect college aspirations, even in the college-educated group, the only one in which a substantial number of fathers have professional-level occupations.

THE PEER GROUP, AND PARTICIPATION IN EXTRA-CURRICULAR ACTIVITIES

College-oriented students may be expected to gravitate toward others with similar interests, and such associations are likely to reinforce college aspirations. While our data do not indicate how friends are selected, they show that working-class students whose acquaintances plan to go to college are more likely to plan to go themselves.[16] Among those who report that all their acquaintances are going to college, 81 per cent have similar plans, while only 6 per cent do not expect to obtain additional education. On the other hand, among those who report that none of their acquaintances plan to go to college, only 10 per cent expect to go themselves, while 45 per cent do not plan to obtain additional education. A similar relationship holds for middle-class students. (See Table 10.)

Previous research has shown that participation in the school culture is closely related to class position, and that participants are disproportionately from high-status families.[17] Working-class students who participate in extra-curricular activities have an opportunity to associate with middle-class students, most of whom plan to enter college, and as a result may be encouraged to develop interests leading them to seek higher education. Or, the association may reinforce pre-existing tendencies.

Both working-class and middle-class students who are extremely active in extra-curricular activities tend to have college aspirations: 74 and 80 per cent,

[16] Undoubtedly some choose friends who plan to go to college because they have similar aspirations, while others may develop an interest in college *after* associating with college-oriented students.

[17] See August B. Hollingshead, *Elmtown's Youth*, New York: John Wiley, 1959, esp. pp. 201–203, and Floud *et al.*, *op. cit.*, p. 204.

TABLE 10.   COLLEGE PLANS OF ACQUAINTANCES, AND STUDENTS' POST-HIGH SCHOOL PLANS

(IN PERCENTAGES)

	How Many of Student's Acquaintances Plan To Go to College							
	Working-Class Students				Middle-Class Students			
Student's Post-High School Plans (N)	None of Them (43)	Some of Them (177)	Most of Them (129)	All of Them (36)	None of Them (16)	Some of Them (91)	Most of Them (112)	All of Them (47)
College	10	29	60	81	(3)	47	77	83
Technical school	45	35	23	14	(5)	27	12	17
No further education	45	36	18	6	(8)	25	10	0
Total	100	100	101	101	(16)	99	99	100

respectively, plan to attend college. Only 28 per cent of the non-active working-class youngsters have college aspirations, however, compared with 55 per cent of the non-active middle-class students.[18] (See Table 11.) These data suggest that although active participation in extra-curricular activities encourages or reinforces all students' interest in college, such participation is more important for working-class youths.

The working-class student's peer group, and the extent to which he participates in extra-curricular activities, appear to be related to the development of college aspirations, but the context in which such behavior takes place is also important. That is, the atmosphere of the school and the general student body background are likely to affect working-class students' college aspirations. Alan Wilson suggests that students from working-class homes who attend a predominantly middle-class school are prone to identify with the middle-class.[19] He found that 59 per cent of these students plan to go to college, in contrast to 33 per cent of the working-class students in predominantly working-class schools. These findings are quite similar to those reported here. (See Table 12.)[20] The importance of school milieu for the development of college aspirations is also indicated by its effect on middle-class students in both

[18] In "The Pattern of Postponability and its Relation to Social Class Mobility," *Journal of Social Psychology*, 44 (August, 1956), pp. 33–48, Harry Beilin reports that of the lower-class high school boys in his study who planned to attend college, 84 per cent participated in extra-curricular activities, in contrast to 38 per cent of those who did not expect to go to college. See also Richard L. Simpson, *op. cit.*, pp. 519–520.
[19] Wilson, *op. cit.*, pp. 836–845.
[20] Wilson's eight schools cover a wider range than ours, for we sought mainly working-class schools. The data in Table 12 represent the "most" middle-class and the "most" working-class among the four schools in the present study, using basically the criteria Wilson used. See *ibid.*, pp. 837–838, and notes in Table 12 below.)

TABLE 11. EXTRA-CURRICULAR PARTICIPATION AND STUDENTS' POST-HIGH SCHOOL PLANS[a]

(IN PERCENTAGES)

	How Active Student Has Beeen in Extra-Curricular Activities					
	Working-Class Students			*Middle-Class Students*		
Student's Post-High School Plans	*Not Very Active*	*Fairly Active*	*Extremely Active*	*Not Very Active*	*Fairly Active*	*Extremely Active*
(N)	(199)	(138)	(50)	(101)	(120)	(46)
College	28	50	74	55	66	80
Technical school	36	29	14	22	21	13
No further education	37	22	12	24	13	7
Total	101	101	100	101	100	100

[a] The students were asked, "In general, how active have you been in extra-curricular activities in high school?" and were given the choices of "extremely active," "fairly active" or "not very active."

TABLE 12. COLLEGE ASPIRATIONS OF WORKING-CLASS STUDENTS IN MIDDLE-
AND WORKING-CLASS HIGH SCHOOL IN TWO STUDIES

Nature of the Schools[a]	(N)	*Per Cent of Working-Class Students Who Have College Aspirations*	
		In Wilson's Study[b] (260)	In Present Study (153)
Predominantly middle-class		59 (39)	53 (38)
Predominantly working-class		33 (221)	40 (115)

[a] The nature of the school was determined by father's occupation, social and economic characteristics of the neighborhood the students are drawn from and by an impression of the school's "atmosphere," through personal observation of the students in the classrooms, halls and playgrounds.
[b] Figures adapted from Wilson, *op. cit.*, Table 3, p. 839. Only working-class students from the "most" middle-class schools in Wilson's study (i.e. school Type A in Table 3, *ibid.*) and those from the "most" working-class schools (i.e. school Type C in Table 3, *ibid.*) are included.

surveys: those who attended a predominantly middle-class school were much more likely to have college aspirations than those who were in a predominantly working-class school.[21]

Characteristics of the College-Oriented Students

The sources of educational aspirations among working-class youth suggested by these data are largely structural in nature. That is, they refer mainly to the family's life conditions and only to a limited extent to the students' own attitudes and behavior. Yet several researchers have reported, and perceptive high school teachers have observed, that in many ways college-oriented working-class students resemble middle-class much more than other working-class youngsters. In Table 13 the college-oriented and non-college-oriented working-class students are compared with their middle-class counterparts on a number of selected characteristics. The similarities between the college-oriented work-

[21] Wilson found that among boys from professional homes who attended a predominantly middle-class school, 93 per cent planned to attend college, whereas this was true of only 64 per cent of those in a predominantly working-class school. Among boys from white-collar homes, the percentages with college aspirations are 79 per cent of those attending a middle-class school and 46 per cent of those in a working-class school. And among boys whose fathers were self-employed, 79 per cent of those in a middle-class school have college plans, in contrast to 35 per cent of those in a working-class school (see *ibid.*, p. 839). In the present sample, 80 per cent of the middle-class children attending a predominantly middle-class school plan to attend college, whereas 59 per cent of those in a predominantly working-class school have college aspirations.

TABLE 13. SELECTED CHARACTERISTICS OF MIDDLE-CLASS AND WORKING-CLASS STUDENTS ACCORDING TO THEIR INTEREST IN COLLEGE (IN PERCENTAGES)

	College Oriented		Non College Oriented	
A. *Student's Attitude toward Selected Occupations*	Middle-Class	Working-Class	Middle-Class	Working-Class
Student would be pleased to be . . .				
a doctor	56	57	40	39
a scientist	60	59	40	30
the owner of a small hardware store	22	29	26	39
an electrician	28	40	42	46
a machine operator in a factory	13	14	24	35
Total[a]	(172)	(160)	(95)	(227)
B. *Income Student Expects after Working for Ten Years*				
$10,000 or more a year	23	20	16	10
$7,000–$10,000 a year	43	45	35	39
Less than $7,000 a year	34	35	48	51
Total	100(154)	100(147)	99(85)	100(202)
C. *Belief in the Existence of Opportunity*[b]				
Strongly agrees	30	35	43	43
Agrees to some extent	59	58	47	54
Neither agrees nor disagrees; disagrees to some extent; strongly disagrees	11	7	9	4
Total	100(170)	100(158)	99(95)	101(114)
D. *How Often Student Goes to Church*				
Once a week or more	39	45	42	35
1–3 times a month	23	23	20	21
Less than once a month	29	25	32	30
Never	10	8	7	15
Total	101(168)	101(154)	101(92)	101(216)
E. *Interest in National and International Affairs*				
Very interested	26	29	17	14
Somewhat interested	59	59	58	56
Interested very little or not interested at all	14	11	25	29
Total	99(170)	99(158)	100(95)	99(217)

TABLE 13—*Continued*

	College Oriented		Non College Oriented	
	Middle-Class	Working-Class	Middle-Class	Working-Class
F. *Interest in Classical or Serious Music*				
Very much interested	33	32	24	20
Moderately interested	48	46	47	48
Not much interested	19	22	28	31
Total	100(170)	100(158)	99(95)	99(215)
G. *Number of Books Recently Read*				
7 or more	6	6	1	3
4–6	9	9	9	8
1–3	64	62	43	44
None	20	22	48	45
Total	99(172)	99(158)	101(94)	100(223)
H. *Political Preference*				
Republican Party	48	27	38	21
Sometimes one, sometimes the other	22	33	29	25
Democratic Party	30	40	33	54
Total	100(121)	100(123)	100(73)	100(169)
I. *Student's Views Regarding How Much Power and Influence Labor Should Have*[c]				
Labor's power is sufficient	55	42	38	35
Labor should have more power	45	58	62	65
Total	100(166)	100(150)	100(87)	100(205)
J. *Student's Attitude toward the Role of Government*[c]				
The government should be certain that there is opporunity	63	55	45	44
The government should guarantee jobs and a high standard of living	37	45	55	56
Total	100(164)	100(155)	100(86)	100(200)

[a] Only the percentage who responded that they would be pleased are reported. The other responses were "displeased," and "I don't know."

[b] The students were asked whether they strongly agreed, agreed to some extent, neither agreed nor disagreed, disagreed to some extent or strongly disagreed with the following statement: "Anyone who wants to can rise to the top. It just takes determination and hard work."

[c] The question from which these data were obtained was taken from Richard Centers, *The Psychology of Social Classes*, Princeton University Press, 1949, Appendix IV, p. 232.

ing-class and the college-oriented middle-class students are striking in regard to occupational preference, income expectations, belief in the existence of opportunity, interest in national and international affairs, interest in classical or serious music, and the number of books recently read. In political preference and attitude toward labor, the college-oriented working-class students are more "conservative" than other working-class youths, but less so than college-oriented middle-class youths. In their attitude toward the role of government, college-oriented working-class students were somewhat closer to the college-oriented middle-class youngsters than to other working-class students.

How do these college-oriented working-class students come to have middle-class values? To what extent are these values responsible for interest in college—or, to what extent does interest in college encourage the development of these values? Status discrepancies between parents, familial contact with middle-class groups and the youngsters' association with other middle-class children may have encouraged them to take the college-oriented middle-class students as their reference group. And the middle-class interests and values shared by the working-class students who plan to attend college as well as such behavior as participation in extra-curricular activities, may reflect anticipatory socialization. As Merton and others have pointed out,[22] taking on the values and forms of behavior of another group facilitates entry into that group.

Summary and Conclusions

My analysis has revealed two major sources of educational aspirations among the 387 working-class youths in this sample: primarily certain conditions in the family, and secondarily, the nature of the student's peer associations and his participation in school activities.

Significant influences in the family include the following: (a) *Status discrepancies*, especially where the working-class mother is currently holding a non-manual job, and also where the mother has had some college training while her husband has completed high school only. A history of downward mobility in the family, as indicated by a grandfather whose occupation was non-manual, also favored working-class youngsters' college aspirations. (b) *Family members, or friends of the family who have gone to college*: If parents, older siblings, or friends of the family have had college experience, the working-class student is more likely to have college aspirations. Such a person can furnish practical information about higher education, or, possibly, he may serve as a model for the child. (c) *Father's occupational status*: High occupational status within the working-class is associated with college aspirations in the offspring, and this relationship is strongest when the father has completed high school. If he has less than a high school education, high occupational status has little effect on children's college plans, whereas if he has gone to college, that experience appears to be more influential than high occupational status.

---

[22] See especially Merton, *op. cit.*, pp. 265, 290–291 and 384–385, and Lipset and Bendix, *op. cit.*, pp. 257–259.

As for the student's peer associations and participation in extra-curricular activities, these influences were significant: (a) College-oriented working-class students were very likely to have acquaintances who also have college aspirations. (b) They tended to be extremely active in extra-curricular activities. (c) They were more likely to be attending a predominantly middle-class than a predominantly working-class school.

In certain interests, values and activities, the college-oriented working-class youths were very similar to the college-oriented middle-class students. Reference group behavior may be involved, particularly anticipatory socialization.

Viewed from the perspective of familial responses to thwarted upward mobility, or attempts to arrest downward mobility, several of these findings may take on added meaning. For example, a wife's employment in a non-manual occupation, or a husband's employment in a high-status manual occupation, may reflect upward striving in the working-class family. In both cases upward mobility is limited by the husband's manual occupation, and the wife may attempt to realize her aspirations through her child. Hence educational attainment is encouraged. Similarly, families where the wife has more education than her husband, or where a grandfather was in a non-manual occupation, may have experienced downward movement and attempt to realize mobility aspirations through the children.[23]

[23] Not to be overlooked is the possibility of the husband rising or returning to a non-manual status. The data of Wilensky and Edwards, *op. cit.*, and Seymour M. Lipset and Reinhard Bendix, "Social Mobility and Occupational Career Patterns," *American Journal of Sociology*, 57 (January and March, 1952), pp. 366–374, 394–504 and Reinhard Bendix, Seymour M. Lipset and F. Theodore Malm, "Social Origins and Occupational Career Patterns," *Industrial and Labor Relations Review*, 7 (January, 1954), pp. 246–261 show that a considerable number of working-class men make such moves at some time in their careers. Thus a family's response to thwarted upward mobility or attempts to arrest downward mobility may involve the husband as well as the children.

ON STUDENT RIGHTS:
TINKER VERSUS DES MOINES*

John F. Tinker and Mary Beth
Tinker, Minors, etc., et al.,
Petitioners,

v.

Des Moines Independent Community School District et al.

On Writ of Certiorari to
the United States
Court of Appeals for
the Eighth Circuit.

[February 24, 1969.]

MR. JUSTICE FORTAS delivered the opinion of the Court.

Petitioner John F. Tinker, 15 years old, and petitioner Christopher Eckhardt, 16 years old, attended high schools in Des Moines. Petitioner Mary
Beth Tinker, John's sister, was a 13-year-old student in junior high school.

In December 1965, a group of adults and students in Des Moines, Iowa,
held a meeting at the Eckhardt home. The group determined to publicize
their objections to the hostilities in Vietnam and their support for a truce by
wearing black armbands during the holiday season and by fasting on December 16 and New Year's Eve. Petitioners and their parents had previously
engaged in similar activities, and they decided to participate in the program.

The principals of the Des Moines schools became aware of the plan to
wear armbands. On December 14, 1965, they met and adopted a policy that
any student wearing an armband to school would be asked to remove it, and if
he refused he would be suspended until he returned without the armband.
Petitioners were aware of the regulation that the school authorities adopted.

On December 16, Mary Beth and Christopher wore black armbands to
their schools. John Tinker wore his armband the next day. They were all sent
home and suspended from school until they would come back without their
armbands. They did not return to school until after the planned period for
wearing armbands had expired—that is, until after New Year's Day.

This complaint was filed in the United States District Court by petitioners, through their fathers, under § 1983 of Title 42 of the United States Code.
It prayed for an injunction restraining the defendant school officials and the
defendant members of the board of directors of the school district from
disciplining the petitioners, and it sought nominal damages. After an evi-
dentiary hearing the District Court dismissed the complaint. It upheld the
constitutionality of the school authorities' action on the ground that it was

* Excerpted by permission from The United States Law Week, Vol. 37 (1969),
pp. 4121–4128, published by The Bureau of National Affairs, Inc., Washington, D. C.
20037.

70

reasonable in order to prevent disturbance of school discipline. 258 F. Supp. 971 (1966). The court referred to but expressly declined to follow the Fifth Circuit's holding in a similar case that prohibition of the wearing of symbols like the armbands cannot be sustained unless it "materially and substantially interfere[s] with the requirements of appropriate discipline in the operation of the school." *Burnside* v. *Byars*, 363 F. 2d 744, 749 (1966).[1]

On appeal, the Court of Appeals for the Eighth Circuit considered the case *en banc*. The court was equally divided, and the District Court's decision was accordingly affirmed, without opinion. 383 F. 2d 988 (1967). We granted certiorari. 390 U.S. 942 (1968).

The District Court recognized that the wearing of an armband for the purpose of expressing certain views is the type of symbolic act that is within the Free Speech Clause of the First Amendment. See *West Virginia* v. *Barnette*, 319 U. S. 624 (1943); *Stromberg* v. *California*, 283 U. S. 359 (1931). Cf. *Thornhill* v. *Alabama*, 310 U. S. 88 (1940); *Edwards* v. *South Carolina*, 372 U. S. 229 (1963); *Brown* v. *Louisiana*, 383 U. S. 131 (1966). As we shall discuss, the wearing of armbands in the circumstances of this case was entirely divorced from actually or potentially disruptive conduct by those participating in it. It was closely akin to "pure speech" which, we have repeatedly held, is entitled to comprehensive protection under the First Amendment. Compare *Cox* v. *Louisiana*, 379 U. S. 536, 555 (1965); *Adderley* v. *Florida*, 385 U. S. 39 (1966).

First Amendment rights, applied in light of the special characteristics of the school environment, are available to teachers and students. It can hardly be argued that either students or teachers shed their constitutional rights to freedom of speech or expression at the schoolhouse gate. This has been the unmistakable holding of this Court for almost 50 years. In *Meyer* v. *Nebraska*, 262 U. S. 390 (1923), and *Bartels* v. *Iowa*, 262 U. S. 404 (1923), this Court, in opinions by Mr. Justice McReynolds, held that the Due Process Clause of the Fourteenth Amendment prevents States from forbidding the teaching of a foreign language to young students. Statutes to this effect, the Court held, unconstitutionally interfere with the liberty of teacher, student, and parent.[2]

---

[1] In *Burnside*, the Fifth Circuit ordered that high school authorities be enjoined from enforcing a regulation forbidding students to wear "freedom buttons." It is instructive that in *Blackwell* v. *Issaquena County Board of Education*, 363 F. 2d 749 (1966), the same panel on the same day reached the opposite result on different facts. It declined to enjoin enforcement of such a regulation in another high school where the students wearing freedom buttons harassed students who did not wear them and created much disturbance.

[2] *Hamilton* v. *Regents of Univ. of Cal.*, 293 U. S. 245 (1934) is sometimes cited for the broad proposition that the State may attach conditions to attendance at a state university that require individuals to violate their religious convictions. The case involved dismissal of members of a religious denomination from a land grant college for refusal to participate in military training. Narrowly viewed, the case turns upon the Court's conclusion that merely requiring a student to participate in school training in military "science" could not conflict with his constitutionally protected freedom of conscience. The decision cannot be taken as establishing that the State may impose and enforce any conditions that it chooses upon attendance at public institutions of learning, however violative they may be of fundamental constitutional guaranties. See, *e. g.*, *West Virginia* v. *Barnette*, 319 U. S. 624 (1943); *Dixon* v. *Alabama State Bd. of Educ.*,

See also *Pierce* v. *Society of Sisters*, 268 U. S. 510 (1925); *West Virginia* v. *Barnette*, 319 U. S. 624 (1943); *McCollum* v. *Board of Education*, 333 U. S. 203 (1948); *Wieman* v. *Updegraff*, 344 U. S. 183, 195 (1952) (concurring opinion); *Sweezy* v. *New Hampshire*, 354 U. S. 234 (1957); *Shelton* v. *Tucker*, 364 U. S. 479, 487 (1960); *Engel* v. *Vitale*, 370 U. S. 421 (1962); *Keyishian* v. *Board of Regents*, 385 U. S. 589, 603 (1967); *Epperson* v. *Arkansas*, 393 U. S. 97 (1968).

In *West Virginia* v. *Barnette, supra*, this Court held that under the First Amendment, the student in public school may not be compelled to salute the flag. Speaking through Mr. Justice Jackson, the Court said:

> The Fourteenth Amendment, as now applied to the States, protects the citizens against the State itself and all of its creatures—Boards of Education not excepted. These have, of course, important, delicate, and highly discretionary functions, but none that they may not perform within the limits of the Bill of Rights. That they are educating the young for citizenship is reason for scrupulous protection of Constitutional freedoms of the individual, if we are not to strangle the free mind at its source and teach youth to discount important principles of our government as mere platitudes. 319 U. S., at 637.

On the other hand, the Court has repeatedly emphasized the need for affirming the comprehensive authority of the States and of school authorities, consistent with fundamental constitutional safeguards, to prescribe and control conduct in the schools. See *Epperson* v. *Arkansas, supra*, at 104; *Meyer* v. *Nebraska, supra*, at 402. Our problem lies in the area where students in the exercise of First Amendment rights collide with the rules of the school authorities.

The problem presented by the present case does not relate to regulation of the length of skirts or the type of clothing, to hair style or deportment. Compare *Ferrell* v. *Dallas Independent School District*, 392 F. 2d 697 (1968); *Pugsley* v. *Sellmeyer*, 158 Ark. 247, 250 S. W. 538 (1923). It does not concern aggressive, disruptive action or even group demonstrations. Our problem involves direct, primary First Amendment rights akin to "pure speech."

The school officials banned and sought to punish petitioners for a silent, passive, expression of opinion, unaccompanied by any disorder or disturbance on the part of petitioners. There is here no evidence whatever of petitioners' interference, actual or nascent, with the school's work or of collision with the rights of other students to be secure and to be let alone. Accordingly, this case does not concern speech or action that intrudes upon the work of the school or the rights of other students.

Only a few of the 18,000 students in the school system wore the black armbands. Only five students were suspended for wearing them. There is no indication that the work of the school or any class was disrupted. Outside the

---

294 F. 2d 150 (C. A. 5th Cir. 1961); *Knight* v. *State Bd. of Educ.*, 200 F. Supp. 174 (D. C. M. D. Tenn. 1961); *Dickey* v. *Alabama St. Bd. of Educ.*, 273 F. Supp. 613 (C. A. M. D. Ala. 1967). See also Note, 73 Harv. L. Rev. 1595 (1960); Note, 81 Harv. L. Rev. 1045 (1968).

classrooms, a few students made hostile remarks to the children wearing armbands, but there were no threats or acts of violence on school premises.

The District Court concluded that the action of the school authorities
was reasonable because it was based upon their fear of a disturbance from the
wearing of the armbands. But, in our system, undifferentiated fear or appre-
hension of disturbance is not enough to overcome the right to freedom of
expression. Any departure from absolute regimentation may cause trouble. Any
variation from the majority's opinion may inspire fear. Any word spoken, in
class, in the lunchroom or on the campus, that deviates from the views of
another person, may start an argument or cause a disturbance. But our Constitution says we must take this risk, *Terminiello* v. *Chicago,* 337 U. S. 1.
(1959); and our history says that it is this sort of hazardous freedom—this
kind of openness—that is the basis of our national strength and of the independence and vigor of Americans who grow up and live in this relatively
permissive, often disputatious society.

In order for the State in the person of school officials to justify prohibition
of a particular expression of opinion, it must be able to show that its action
was caused by something more than a mere desire to avoid the discomfort
and unpleasantness that always accompany an unpopular viewpoint. Certainly
where there is no finding and no showing that the exercise of the forbidden
right would "materially and substantially interfere with the requirements of
appropriate discipline in the operation of the school," the prohibition cannot
be sustained. *Burnside* v. *Byars, supra,* at 749.

In the present case, the District Court made no such finding, and our
independent examination of the record fails to yield evidence that the school
authorities had reason to anticipate that the wearing of the armbands would
substantially interfere with the work of the school or impinge upon the rights
of other students. Even an official memorandum prepared after the suspension
that listed the reasons for the ban on wearing the armbands made no reference to the anticipation of such disruption.[3]

On the contrary, the action of the school authorities appears to have been
based upon an urgent wish to avoid the controversy which might result from
the expression, even by the silent symbol of armbands, of opposition to this
Nation's part in the conflagration in Vietnam.[4] It is revealing, in this respect,

[3] The only suggestions of fear of disorder in the report are these:

"A former student of one of our high schools was killed in Viet Nam. Some of
his friends are still in school and it was felt that if any kind of a demonstration existed,
it might evolve into something which would be difficult to control.

"Students at one of the high schools were heard to say they would wear arm
bands of other colors if the black bands prevailed."

Moreover, the testimony of school authorities at trial indicates that it was not
fear of disruption that motivated the regulation prohibiting the armbands; the regulation was directed against "the principle of the demonstration" itself. School authorities simply felt that "the schools are no place for demonstrations," and if the students
"didn't like the way our elected officials were handling things, it should be handled
with the ballot box and not in the halls of our public schools."

[4] The District Court found that the school authorities, in prohibiting black armbands,
were influenced by the fact that "[t]he Viet Nam war and the involvement of the
United States therein has been the subject of a major controversy for some time. When
the armband regulation involved herein was promulgated, debate over the Viet Nam

that the meeting at which the school principals decided to issue the contested regulation was called in response to a student's statement to the journalism teacher in one of the schools that he wanted to write an article on Vietnam and have it published in the school paper. (The student was dissuaded.)[5]

It is also relevant that the school authorities did not purport to prohibit the wearing of all symbols of political or controversial significance. The record shows that students in some of the schools wore buttons relating to national political campaigns, and some even wore the Iron Cross, traditionally a symbol of nazism. The order prohibiting the wearing of armbands did not extend to these. Instead, a particular symbol—black armbands worn to exhibit opposition to this Nation's involvement in Vietnam—was singled out for prohibition. Clearly, the prohibition of expression of one particular opinion, at least without evidence that it is necessary to avoid material and substantial interference with school work or discipline, is not constitutionally permissible.

In our system, state-operated schools may not be enclaves of totalitarianism. School officials do not possess absolute authority over their students. Students in school as well as out of school are "persons" under our Constitution. They are possessed of fundamental rights which the State must respect, just as they themselves must respect their obligations to the State. In our system, students may not be regarded as closed-circuit recipients of only that which the State chooses to communicate. They may not be confined to the expression of those sentiments that are officially approved. In the absence of a specific showing of constitutionally valid reasons to regulate their speech, students are entitled to freedom of expression of their views. As Judge Gewin, speaking for the Fifth Circuit said, school officials cannot suppress "expressions of feelings with which they do not wish to contend." *Burnside* v. *Byars, supra*, at 749.

In *Meyer* v. *Nebraska, supra*, at 402, Justice McReynolds expressed this Nation's repudiation of the principle that a State might so conduct its schools as to "foster a homogeneous people." He said:

> In order to submerge the individual and develop ideal citizens, Sparta assembled the males at seven into barracks and intrusted their subsequent education and training to official guardians. Although such measures have been deliberately approved by men of great genius, their ideas touching the relation between individual and State were wholly different from those upon which our institutions rest; and it hardly will be affirmed that any legislature could impose such restrictions upon the people of a State without doing violence to both letter and spirit of the Constitution.

---

war had become vehement in many localities. A protest march against the war had been recently held in Washington, D. C. A wave of draft-card-burning incidents protesting the war had swept the country. At that time two publicized draft burnings were pending in this Court. Both individuals supporting the war and those opposing it were quite vocal in expressing their views." 258 F. Supp., at 972–973.

[5] After the principals' meeting, the director of secondary education and the principal of the high school informed the student that the principals were opposed to publication of his article. They reported that "we felt that it was a very friendly conversation, although we did not feel that we had convinced the student that our decision was a just one."

This principle has been repeated by this Court on numerous occasions during the intervening years. In *Keyishian* v. *Board of Regents,* 385 U. S. 589, 603, MR. JUSTICE BRENNAN, speaking for the Court, said:

'The vigilant protection of constitutional freedom is nowhere more vital than in the community of American schools.' *Shelton* v. *Tucker,* 234 U. S. 479, 487. The classroom is peculiarly the 'market-place of ideas.' The Nation's future depends upon leaders trained through wide exposure to the robust exchange of ideas which discovers truth 'out of a multitude of tongues, [rather] than through any kind of authoritative selection'. . . .

The principle of these cases is not confined to the supervised and ordained discussion which takes place in the classroom. The principal use to which the schools are dedicated is to accommodate students during prescribed hours for the purpose of certain types of activities. Among those activities is personal intercommunication among the students.[6] This is not only an inevitable part of the process of attending school. It is also an important part of the educational process. A student's rights therefore, do not embrace merely the classroom hours. When he is in the cafeteria, or on the playing field, or on the campus during the authorized hours, he may express his opinions, even on controversial subjects like the conflict in Vietnam, if he does so "without materially and substantially interfering with appropriate discipline in the operation of the school" and without colliding with the rights of others. *Burnside* v. *Byars, supra,* at 749. But conduct by the student, in class or out of it, which for any reason—whether it stems from time, place, or type of behavior— materially disrupts classwork or involves substantial disorder or invasion of the rights of others is, of course, not immunized by the constitutional guaranty of freedom of speech. Cf. *Blackwell* v. *Issaquena City Bd. of Educ.,* 363 F. 2d 749 (C. A. 5th Cir., 1966).

Under our Constitution, free speech is not a right that is given only to be so circumscribed that it exists in principle but not in fact. Freedom of expression would not truly exist if the right could be exercised only in an area that a benevolent government has provided as a safe haven for crackpots. The Constitution says that Congress (and the States) may not abridge the right to free speech. This provision means what it says. We properly read it to permit reasonable regulation of speech-connected activities in carefully restricted circumstances. But we do not confine the permissible exercise of First Amendment rights to a telephone booth or the four corners of a pamphlet, or to supervised and ordained discussion in a school classroom.

If a regulation were adopted by school officials forbidding discussion of the Vietnam conflict, or the expression by any student of opposition to it

---

[6] In *Hammond* v. *South Carolina State College,* 272 F. Supp. 947 (D. C. D. S. C. 1967), District Judge Hemphill had before him a case involving a meeting on campus of 300 students to express their views on school practices. He pointed out that a school is not like a hospital or a jail enclosure. Cf. *Cox* v. *Louisiana,* 379 U. S. 536 (1965); *Adderley* v. *Florida,* 385 U. S. 39 (1966). It is a public place, and its dedication to specific uses does not imply that the constitutional rights of persons entitled to be there are to be gauged as if the premises were purely private property. Cf. *Edwards* v. *South Carolina,* 372 U. S. 229 (1963); *Brown* v. *Louisiana,* 383 U. S. 131 (1966).

anywhere on school property except as part of a prescribed classroom exercise, it would be obvious that the regulation would violate the constitutional rights of students, at least if it could not be justified by a showing that the students' activities would materially and substantially disrupt the work and discipline of the school. Cf. *Hammond* v. *South Carolina State College*, 272 F. Supp. 947 (D. C. D. S. C. 1967) (orderly protest meeting on state college campus); *Dickey* v. *Alabama State Board*, 273 F. Supp. 613 (D. C. M. D. Ala. 1967) (expulsion of student editor of college newspaper). In the circumstances of the present case, the prohibition of the silent, passive "witness of the armbands," as one of the children called it, is no less offensive to the Constitution's guaranties.

As we have discussed, the record does not demonstrate any facts which might reasonably have led school authorities to forecast substantial disruption of or material interference with school activities, and no disturbances or disorders on the school premises in fact occurred. These petitioners merely went about their ordained rounds in school. Their deviation consisted only in wearing on their sleeve a band of black cloth, not more than two inches wide. They wore it to exhibit their disapproval of the Vietnam hostilities and their advocacy of a truce, to make their views known, and by their example, to influence others to adopt them. They neither interrupted school activities nor sought to intrude in the school affairs or the lives of others. They caused discussion outside of the classrooms, but no interference with work and no disorder. In the circumstances, our Constitution does not permit officials of the State to deny their form of expression.

We express no opinion as to the form of relief which should be granted, this being a matter for the lower courts to determine. We reverse and remand for further proceedings consistent with this opinion.

Reversed and remanded.

MR. JUSTICE WHITE, concurring.

While I join the Court's opinion, I deem it appropriate to note, first, that the Court continues to recognize a distinction between communicating by words and communicating by acts or conduct which sufficiently impinge on some valid state interest; and, second, that I do not subscribe to everything the Court of Appeals said about free speech in its opinion in *Burnside* v. *Byars*, 363 F. 2d 744, 748 (C. A. 5th Cir. 1966), a case relied upon by the Court in the matter now before us.

MR. JUSTICE STEWART, concurring.

Although I agree with much of what is said in the Court's opinion, and with its judgment in this case, I cannot share the Court's uncritical assumption that, school discipline aside, the First Amendment rights of children are co-extensive with those of adults. Indeed, I had thought the Court decided otherwise just last Term in *Ginsberg* v. *New York*, 390 U. S. 629. I continue to hold the view I expressed in that case: "[A] State may permissibly determine that, at least in some precisely delineated areas, a child—like someone in a captive audience—is not possessed of that full capacity for

individual choice which is the presupposition of First Amendment guarantees."
Id., at 649–650 (concurring opinion). Cf. *Prince* v. *Massachusetts*, 321 U. S.
158.

MR. JUSTICE HARLAN, dissenting.

I certainly agree that state public school authorities in the discharge of
their responsibilities are not wholly exempt from the requirements of the
Fourteenth Amendment respecting the freedoms of expression and association.
At the same time I am reluctant to believe that there is any disagreement
between the majority and myself on the proposition that school officials should
be accorded the widest authority in maintaining discipline and good order in
their institutions. To translate that proposition into a workable constitutional
rule, I would, in cases like this, cast upon those complaining the burden of
showing that a particular school measure was motivated by other than legitimate school concerns—for example, a desire to prohibit the expression of an
unpopular point of view, while permitting expression of the dominant opinion.

Finding nothing in this record which impugns the good faith of respondents in promulgating the arm band regulation, I would affirm the judgment
below.

MR. JUSTICE BLACK, dissenting.

The Court's holding in this case ushers in what I deem to be an entirely
new era in which the power to control pupils by the elected "officials of state
supported public schools . . ." in the United States is in ultimate effect transferred to the Supreme Court.[1] The Court brought this particular case here on
a petition for certiorari urging that the First and Fourteenth Amendments
protect the right of schools pupils to express their political views all the way
"from kindergarten through high school." Here the constitutional right to
"political expression" asserted was a right to wear black armbands during
school hours and at classes in order to demonstrate to the other students that
the petitioners were mourning because of the death of United States' soldiers
in Vietnam and to protest that war which they were against. Ordered to
refrain from wearing the armbands in school by the elected school officials
and the teachers vested with state authority to do so, apparently only seven
out of the school system's 18,000 pupils deliberately refused to obey the
order. One defying pupil was Paul Tinker, 8 years old, who was in the second
grade; another, Hope Tinker was 11 years old in the fifth grade; a third member of the Tinker family was 13, in the eighth grade; and a fourth member of
the same family was John Tinker, 15 years old, an 11th grade high school
pupil. Their father, a Methodist minister without a church, is paid a salary by
the American Friends Service Committee. Another student who defied the
school order and insisted on wearing an armband in school was Chris Eckhardt, an 11th grade pupil and a petitioner in this case. His mother is an
official in the Women's International League for Peace and Freedom.

[1] The petition for certiorari here presented this single question:
"Whether the First and Fourteenth Amendments permit officials of state-supported public schools to prohibit students from wearing symbols of political views
within school premises where the symbols are not disruptive of school discipline or
decorum."

As I read the Court's opinion it relies upon the following grounds for holding unconstitutional the judgment of the Des Moines school officials and the two Courts below. First, the Court concludes that the wearing of arm-bands is "symbolic speech" which is "akin to pure speech" and therefore protected by the First and Fourteenth Amendments. Secondly, the Court decides that the public schools are an appropriate place to exercise "symbolic speech" as long as normal school functions are not "unreasonably" disrupted. Finally, the Court arrogates to itself, rather than to the State's elected officials charged with running the schools, the decision as to which school disciplinary regulations are "reasonable."

Assuming that the Court is correct in holding that the conduct of wearing armbands for the purpose of conveying political ideas is protected by the First Amendment compare, *e.g.*, *Giboney* v. *Empire Storage & Ice Co.*, 336 U. S. 490 (1949), the crucial remaining questions are whether students and teachers may use the schools at their whim as a platform for the exercise of free speech—"symbolic" or "pure"—and whether the Courts will allocate to themselves the function of deciding how the pupils' school day will be spent. While I have always believed that under the First and Fourteenth Amend-ments neither the State nor Federal Government has any authority to regulate or censor the content of speech, I have never believed that any person has a right to give speeches or engage in demonstrations where he pleases and when he pleases. This Court has already rejected such a notion. In *Cox* v. *Louisiana*, 379 U. S. 536 (1964), for example, the Court clearly stated that the rights of free speech and assembly "do not mean that anyone with opinions or beliefs to express may address a group at any public place and at any time." 379 U. S. 536, 554 (1964).

While the record does not show that any of these armband students shouted, used profane language or were violent in any manner, a detailed report by some of them shows their armbands caused comments, warnings by other students, the poking of fun at them, and a warning by an older football player that other, non-protesting students had better let them alone. There is also evidence that the professor of mathematics had his lesson period prac-tically "wrecked" chiefly by disputes with Beth Tinker, who wore her armband for her "demonstration." Even a casual reading of the record shows that this armband did divert students' minds from their regular lessons, and that talk, comments, etc., made John Tinker "self-conscious" in attending school with his armband. While the absence of obscene or boisterous and loud disorder perhaps justifies the Court's statement that the few armband students did not actually "disrupt" the classwork, I think the record overwhelmingly shows that the armbands did exactly what the elected school officials and principals foresaw it would, that is, took the students' minds off their classwork and diverted them to thoughts about the highly emotional subject of the Vietnam war. And I repeat that if the time has come when pupils of state-supported schools, kindergarten, grammar school or high school, can defy and flaunt orders of school officials to keep their minds on their own school work, it is the beginning of a new revolutionary era of permissiveness in this country fostered by the judiciary. The next logical step, it appears to me, would be to hold unconstitutional laws that bar pupils under 21 or 18 from voting, or from being elected members of the Boards of Education.[2]

The United States District Court refused to hold that the State school orders violated the First and Fourteenth Amendments. 258 F. Supp. 971. Holding that the protest was akin to speech, which is protected by the First and Fourteenth Amendments, that court held that the school orders were "reasonable" and hence constitutional. There was at one time a line of cases holding "reasonableness" as the court saw it to be the test of a "due process" violation. Two cases upon which the Court today heavily relies for striking down these school orders used this test of reasonableness, *Meyers* v. *Nebraska*, 262 U. S. 390 (1923) and *Bartells* v. *Iowa*, 262 U. S. 404 (1923). The opinions in both cases were written by Mr. Justice McReynolds; Mr. Justice Holmes, who opposed this reasonableness test, dissented from the holdings as did Mr. Justice Sutherland. This constitutional test of reasonableness prevailed in this Court for a season. It was this test that brought on President Franklin Roosevelt's well-known Court fight. His proposed legislation did not pass, but the fight left the "reasonable" constitutional test dead on the battlefield, so much so that this Court in *Ferguson* v. *Skrupa*, 372 U. S. 726, 729, 730, after a thorough review of the old cases, was able to conclude in 1962:

> There was a time when the Due Process Clause was used by this Court to strike down laws which were thought unreasonable, that is, unwise or incompatible with some economic or social philosophy. . . . The doctrine that prevailed in *Lochner, Coppage, Adkins, Burns,* and like cases—that due process authorizes courts to hold laws unconstitutional when they believe the legislature has acted unwisely—has long since been discarded.

The *Ferguson* case totally repudiated the old reasonableness due process test, the doctrine that judges have the power to hold laws unconstitutional upon the belief of judges that they are "unreasonable," "arbitrary," "shock the conscience," "irrational," "contrary to fundamental 'decency,' " or some other such flexible term without precise boundaries. I have many times expressed my opposition to that concept on the ground that it gives judges power to strike down any law they do not like. If the majority of the Court today, by agreeing to the opinion of my Brother FORTAS, is resurrecting that old reasonableness due process test, I think the constitutional change should be plainly, unequivocally, and forthrightly stated for the benefit of the bench and bar. It will be a sad day for the country, I believe, when the present day Court returns to the

[2] The following Associated Press article appeared in the Washington *Evening Star,* January 11, 1969, p. A–2, col. 1.

"BELLINGHAM, Mass. (AP)—Todd R. Hennessy, 16, has filed nominating papers to run for town park commissioner in the March election.

" 'I can see nothing illegal in the youth's seeking the elective office, said Lee Ambler, the town counsel. 'But I can't overlook the the possibility that if he is elected any legal contract entered into by the park commissioner would be void because he is a juvenile.'

"Todd is a junior in Mount St. Charles Academy, where he has a top scholastic record."

McReynolds' due process concept. Other cases cited by the Court do not, as implied, follow the McReynolds' reasonableness doctrine. *West Virginia* v. *Barnette*, 319 U. S. 625, clearly rejecting the "reasonableness" test, held that the Fourteenth Amendment made the First applicable to the States, and held that the two forbade a State to *compel* little school children to salute the United States flag when they had religious scruples against it.[3] Neither *Thornhill* v. *Alabama*, 310 U. S. 88; *Stromberg* v. *California*, 283 U. S. 359; *Edwards* v. *South Carolina*, 372 U. S. 329, nor *Brown* v. *Louisiana*, 382 U. S. 131, related to school children at all, and none of these cases embraced Mr. Justice McReynolds' reasonableness test; and *Thornhill*, *Edwards*, and *Brown* relied on the vagueness of state statutes under scrutiny to hold it unconstitutional. *Cox* v. *Louisiana*, 379 U. S. 536, 555, and *Adderley* v. *Florida*, 385 U. S. 39, cited by the Court as a "compare," indicating, I suppose, that these two cases are no longer the law, were not rested to the slightest extent on the *Meyers* and *Bartell* "reasonableness-due process-McReynolds' " constitutional test.

I deny, therefore, that it has been the "unmistakable holding of this Court for almost 50 years" that "students" and "teachers" take with them into the "schoolhouse gate" constitutional rights to "freedom of speech or expression." Even *Meyer* did not hold that. It makes no reference to "symbolic speech" at all; what it did was to strike down as "unreasonable" and therefore unconstitutional a Nebraska law barring the teaching of the German language before the children reached their eighth grade. One can well agree with Justice Holmes and Mr. Justice Sutherland, as I do, that such a law was no more unreasonable than it would be to bar the teaching of Latin and Greek to pupils who have not reached the eighth grade. In fact, I think the majority's reason for invalidating the Nebraska law was that they did not like it or in legal jargon that it "shocked the Court's conscience," "offended its sense of justice," was "contrary to fundamental concepts of the English-speaking world," as the Court has sometimes said. See, *e. g., Rochin* v. *California*, 342 U. S. 165, and *Irvine* v. *California*, 347 U. S. 128. The truth is that a teacher of kindergarten, grammar school, or high school pupils no more carries into a school with him a complete right to freedom of speech and expression than an anti-Catholic or anti-Semitic carries with him a complete freedom of speech and religion into a Catholic church or Jewish synagogue. Nor does a person carry with him into the United States Senate or House, or to the Supreme Court, or

---

[3] In *Cantwell* v. *Connecticut*, 310 U. S. 296, 303–304 (1939), this Court said: "The First Amendment declares that Congress shall make no law respecting an establishment of religion or prohibiting the free exercise thereof. The Fourteenth Amendment has rendered the legislatures of the states as incompetent as Congress to enact such laws. The constitutional inhibition of legislation on the subject of religion has a double aspect. On the one hand, it forestalls compulsion by law of the acceptance of any creed or the practice of any form of worship. Freedom of conscience and freedom to adhere to such religious organization or form of worship as the individual may choose cannot be restricted by law. On the other hand, it safeguards the free exercise of the chosen form of religion. Thus the Amendment embraces two concepts—freedom to believe and freedom to act. The first is absolute but, in the nature of things, the second cannot be. Conduct remains subject to regulation for the protection of society."

any other court, a complete constitutional right to go into those places contrary to their rules and speak his mind on any subject he pleases. It is a myth to say that any person has a constitutional right to say what he pleases, where he pleases, and when he pleases. Our Court has decided precisely the opposite. See, *e. g., Cox v. Louisiana,* 379 U. S. 536, 555; *Adderley v. Florida,* 385 U. S. 39.

In my view, teachers in state-controlled public schools are hired to teach there. Although Mr. Justice McReynolds may have intimated to the contrary in *Meyers* v. *Nebraska, supra,* certainly a teacher is not paid to go into school and teach subjects the State does not hire him to teach as a part of its selected curriculum. Nor are public school students sent to the schools at public expense to broadcast political or any other views to educate and inform the public. The original idea of schools, which I do not believe is yet abandoned as worthless or out of date, was that children had not yet reached the point of experience and wisdom which enabled them to teach all of their elders. It may be that the Nation has outworn the old-fashioned slogan that "children are to be seen not heard," but one may, I hope, be permitted to harbor the thought that taxpayers send children to school on the premise that at their age they need to learn, not teach.

The true principles on this whole subject were in my judgment spoken by Mr. Justice McKenna for the Court in *Waugh* v. *Mississippi University* in 237 U. S. 589, 596–597. The State had there passed a law barring students from peaceably assembling in Greek letter fraternities and providing that students who joined them could be expelled from school. This law would appear on the surface to run afoul of the First Amendment's freedom of assembly clause. The law was attacked as violative of due process and as a deprivation of property, of liberty, and of the privileges and immunities clause of the Fourteenth Amendment. It was argued that the fraternity made its members more moral, taught discipline, and inspired its members to study harder and to obey better the rules of discipline and order. This Court rejected all the "fervid" pleas of the fraternities' advocates and decided unanimously against these Fourteenth Amendment arguments. The Court in its closing paragraph made this statement which has complete relevance for us today:

> It is said that the fraternity to which complainant belongs is a moral and of itself a disciplinary force. This need not be denied. But whether such membership makes against discipline was for the State of Mississippi to determine. It is to be remembered that the University was established by the State and is under the control of the State and the enactment of the statute may have been induced by the opinion that *membership in the prohibited societies divided the attention of the students and distracted from that singleness of purpose which the State desired to exist in its public educational institutions.* It is not for us to entertain conjectures in opposition to the views of the State and annul its regulations upon disputable considerations of their wisdom or necessity. (Emphasis supplied.)

It was on the foregoing argument that this Court sustained the power of Mississippi to curtail the First Amendment's right of peaceable assembly. And the same reasons are equally applicable to curtailing in the States' public schools the right to complete freedom of expression. Iowa's public schools, like Mississippi's university, are operated to give students an opportunity to learn, not to talk politics by actual speech, or by "symbolic" speech. And as I have pointed out before, the record amply shows that public protest in the school classes against the Vietnam war "distracted from that singleness of purpose which the State (here Iowa) desired to exist in its public educational institutions." Here the Court should accord Iowa educational institutions the same right to determine for itself what free expression and no more should be allowed in its schools that it accorded Mississippi with reference to freedom of assembly. But even if the record were silent as to protests against the Vietnam war distracting students from their assigned class work, members of this Court, like all other citizens, know, without being told, that the disputes over the wisdom of the Vietnam war have disrupted and divided this country as few other issues ever have. Of course students, like other people, cannot concentrate on lesser issues when black armbands are being ostentatiously displayed in their presence to call attention to the wounded and dead of the war, some of the wounded and the dead being their friends and neighbors. It was, of course, to distract the attention of other students that some students insisted up to the very point of their own suspension from school that they were determined to sit in school with their symbolic armbands.

Change has been said to be truly the law of life but sometimes the old and the tried and true are worth holding. The schools of this Nation have undoubtedly contributed to giving us tranquility and to making us a more law-abiding people. Uncontrolled and uncontrollable liberty is an enemy to domestic peace. We cannot close our eyes to the fact that some of the country's greatest problems are crimes committed by the youth, too many of school age. School discipline, like parental discipline, is an integral and important part of training our children to be good citizens—to be better citizens. Here a very small number of students have crisply and summarily refused to obey a school order designed to give pupils who want to learn the opportunity to do so. One does not need to be a prophet or the son of a prophet to know that after the Court's holding today that some students in Iowa schools and indeed in all schools will be ready, able, and willing to defy their teachers on practically all orders. This is the more unfortunate for the schools since groups of students all over the land are already running loose, conducting break-ins, sit-ins, lie-ins, and smash-ins. Many of these student groups, as is all too familiar to all who read the newspapers and watch the television news programs, have already engaged in rioting, property seizures and destruction. They have picketed schools to force students not to cross their picket lines and have too often violently attacked earnest but frightened students who wanted an education that the picketers did not want them to get. Students engaged in such activities are apparently confident that they know far more about how to operate public school systems than do their parents, teachers, and elected school officials. It is no answer to say that the particular students here have not yet reached such high points in their demands to attend classes in order to exercise their political pressures. Turned loose with law suits for damages and injunctions against their teachers like they are here, it is nothing but wishful thinking to imagine that young, immature students will not soon believe it is their right to control the schools rather than the right of the States that collect the taxes to hire the teachers for the benefit of the pupils. This case, therefore, wholly without constitutional reasons in my judgment, subjects all the public schools in the country to the whims and caprices of their loudest-mouthed, but maybe not their brightest, students. I, for one, am not fully persuaded that school pupils are wise enough, even with this Court's expert help from Washington, to run the 23,390 public school systems[4] in our 50 States. I wish, therefore wholly to disclaim any purpose on my part, to hold that the Federal Constitution compels the teachers, parents, and elected school officials to surrender control of the American public school system to public school students. I dissent.

[4] Statistical Abstract of the United States (1968), Table No. 578, p. 406.

THE WAR BETWEEN THE GENERATIONS*

CHRISTOPHER JENCKS
DAVID RIESMAN

The Role of Student Sub-Cultures

Among the many myths which afflict contemporary thinking about American colleges, none is more persistent than the one which maintains that in the good old days, when colleges were small, faculty and students had intimate personal contacts on a day-to-day basis. This myth has several sources. One is the assumption that because the faculty were not busy with research or consultations, they had time and energy for their students. A second reason for this myth is the general American tendency, perhaps the human tendency, to assume that if things are presently bad, they were once better, rather than realizing that they are likely to be *considered* bad precisely because they are getting better.

Whatever its origins, the myth does not square with the facts. Even a cursory reading of academic history makes clear that eighteenth and nineteenth century colleges, while small enough, were neither harmonious nor intimate. The students were continually struggling with the faculty, whom they almost all regarded as the enemy. The faculty reciprocated in kind, devoting itself mainly to the enforcement of academic and social rules, often of the most trivial kind. There was always a somewhat autonomous and rebellious student culture, just as there was a somewhat autonomous juvenile culture in many of the large families chronicled in Victorian novels.

The conflicts which inhibited faculty-student communication about non-disciplinary issues should not surprise us. Colleges have always been institutions through which the old attempt to impose their values and attitudes on the young. They have therefore taken over from parents the tension-filled and affect-laden tasks of socialization. This was particularly difficult in a frontier society where many parents were fearful lest their children lapse into the seeming barbarism of the ever-visible Indians. They therefore clung tightly to small as well as large manifestations of their inherited tradition. These parents and their clerical spokesman saw colleges as a device for protecting them against the danger of losing their precarious ties to an Eastern or even European past. It was therefore natural for the colleges to resist all compromise with the interests and predilections of the young. There could not but be con-

* Reprinted from Christopher Jencks and David Riesman, "The War between the Generations," *The Record*, Vol. 69 (1967), pp. 1–21, by permission of the authors and the publisher.

flict in such institutions, just as there could not but be conflict (however well repressed) in such families.

This conflict was intensified by the fact that most colleges also took over from the adult intelligentsia the task of transmitting some version of High Culture—in the narrow literary as well as the broad anthropological sense—to the semi-civilized young. It is true that adult versions of High Culture have never had the same authority in America as in countries like France and Japan, and perhaps this is true of adult culture in the broad sense as well. Nonetheless, nineteenth century American educators believed in the value of what they had to teach, and sought to impose it on the young, whether the young enjoyed it or not. They seldom succeeded very well but the mere attempt was often enough to keep the young on the warpath and produce continuing guerrilla resistance.

STUDENT AUTONOMY

One of the attractions of a college, even in nineteenth century America, was that it enabled its students to find at least a small measure of freedom from adult control. The students were very closely regulated on paper, but they gained strength from numbers and were often quite successful in resisting the intent (and often even the substance) of college rules. The young man who would otherwise have had to stay on the family farm or go to work under the watchful eye of an office supervisor therefore found a kind of freedom in college. He had co-conspirators in breaking the rules, and while he could be punished by expulsion, this was a common and far from serious fate in an age where records seldom followed a man from one place to the next.

So while colleges were designed to familiarize the young with the best that had been thought and said by their elders, to give them a sense of continuity between their own problems and those of previous generations, and thus hopefully to spare them learning everything again by trial and error, they sometimes had precisely the opposite effect. Even when the college was in no sense a university, and its faculty was fully committed to transmitting the conventional wisdom rather than questioning or expanding it, the autonomy of the student culture could make the college a *de facto* instrument of cultural change. Whether it wished to or not, a college could become the crucible in which the younger generation shaped its distinctive values and acquired a sense of separate identity, rather than one in which the young were shaped by those who had gone before and acquired their predecessors' sense of history and purpose. The extent to which a college separated the young from their elders depended in part on the degree of cultural homogeneity among students, faculty, and administrators. Colleges whose personnel came from similar backgrounds were usually less subversive than those which for one reason or another mixed dissimilar students and faculty. Yet even relatively homogenous colleges could be the locus of generational conflict and evolution within a given sub-culture.

CHALLENGING ADULT LEGITIMACY

The lack of intimacy and harmony between young and old is, then, hardly a twentieth century novelty. Nor are youthful efforts to meet adult pressure by sabotage and selective inattention a uniquely modern phenomenon. Nonetheless, we are convinced that nineteenth century conflicts between the generations differed from today's in some important respects. Nineteenth century young people seldom challenged the legitimacy of their elders' authority. They merely claimed that it had been abused in a particular case, or even more commonly, they defied it without creating any ideology to bolster them. Even the riots which marked the nineteenth century college life were more like peasant revolts against tyranny than like revolutionary movements. In the twentieth century, on the other hand, the increasing separatism of teen-age culture and the massing together in high schools and colleges of very large numbers of young people of identical age and social condition have gradually led to a new atmosphere in which the basic legitimacy of adult authority has been increasingly called into question.

By the 1960's this challenge reached quasi-revolutionary proportions and led to the establishment of the free universities. The distinctive features of these ephemeral institutions have been a deep distrust of those over thirty and a rejection of the kinds of academic learning adults normally insist on. They have been initiated and in good part staffed by the young, unlicensed, and relatively inexperienced. Thus far these efforts to create education "of the young, by the young, for the young" are important both as symptoms of present malaise and perhaps as portents of things to come. Nonetheless, they do not have a wide following, and we have not the space to discuss them here. Nor will we take up the earlier and opposite species of generationally defined special-interest colleges for adults of the kind sometimes sponsored by the YMCA. Instead, we will concern ourselves with the way generational tensions affected the overall pattern of higher education. Indeed, in the discussion which follows we will not even be able to take up all aspects of the growing conflict between the generations, but will focus on two specific changes in the character of higher education which help give the collegiate manifestations of this conflict their present character. The first of these changes is the professionalization of the teaching staff. The second is the changing position of the undergraduate years in the over-all maturational cycle.

FROM PSEUDO-PARENT TO SCHOLAR

There was a time, as we have already said, when most college instructors saw themselves, however reluctantly, as policemen whose job was to keep recalcitrant and benighted undergraduates in line, exacting a certain amount of work and imposing a measure of discipline. These men were more often clergymen than scholars, even though a few were both. They found it natural to justify their work in terms of improving the social and moral character of the young rather than in terms of their intellectual attainment. This cast them in a quasi-parental role.

Today's college faculty seldom sees itself this way. In the better universities and university colleges, professors are usually scholars or at least pseudo-scholars and have much less emotional investment in their students' social and moral development than did professors a century ago. Today's scholars are still willing to monitor the academic lives of the young, at least by proxy, insisting that students take certain courses, pass certain examinations, and so forth. But few have any interest in dominating the non-academic lives of the young—in shaping what is no longer even called the students' moral character. In part this is because they think the role of moral tutor (or worse, policeman) would interfere with their ability to work with students on academic matters. In part it is because while they often disapprove of hedonism and athleticism and shower sarcasm on young people who indulge in such heresies, they do not care enough to invent or supervise alternatives.

AMBIVALENCE ON PRINCIPLE

Many professors and administrators are also less certain than they once were what students *ought* to be or become, and are reluctant to go to the mat with the young over principles in which they themselves only half believe. Then, too, even those professors and administrators who are individually sure of their ground and opposed to permissiveness in their personal dealings with the young sometimes find that it is politically expedient to avoid collective regulation of student behavior. If the adult community is divided on those matters, as it often is, any effort to impose adult standards on the young inevitably deepens and intensifies divisions within faculty and administration. Thus it often turns out that the wisest course is to avoid the issue. The easiest way to do this is to deny the need for any rules in a controversial area, leaving it to the students' discretion.

The result of all this is that many faculty and some administrators develop a Veblenian deal. They want undergraduates to act like graduate apprentices, both socially and intellectually, and when a particular undergraduate deviates from this norm they tend to say that he "doesn't belong at a university." Since only a minority of undergraduates have either the talent or the motivation to act like apprentice scholars, many professors disclaim responsibility for the majority, urge more selective admission, and hope for the best. They view the faculty and its apprentices as the "heart of the university," and the still uncommitted undergraduates as an expendable penumbra. The easiest way to ensure that the penumbra does not interfere with the main business of the university is to let its members go their own way relatively undisturbed, hoping that they will educate one another or pick up something in the library or from lectures.

There are, of course, exceptions. Some faculty, perhaps especially in the humanities, are more eager to have their students adopt a particular cultural style than to become imitative and not very capable scholars, while some, especially in the social sciences, look to students to carry out political mandates, either in alliance with them or in compensation for their defections.[1] Some who have become professors in recent years see themselves as ever young, hedonistic, and hep, and revel in the more anti-intellectual manifestations of student rebelliousness even when it is directed at themselves. Even in a scholarly faculty some are ambivalent about their own scholarship and nurture other and contrasting qualities in the young. Transference obviously

Cf. Joseph Gusfield and David Riesman, "Academic Standards and 'The Two Cultures' in the Context of a New State College," *The School Review*, vol. 74, no. 1, Spring 1966.

enters all these cross-generational transactions. There are occasionally deviant academicians who are willing to participate at the adolescent level in both the make-believe and the reality of student life. Such men are sometimes frivolous but often dedicated. On the most academic campuses they sometimes protect the young from becoming too adult too soon. The danger is that they will also reenforce the incompetent amateurism and the self-indulgent or self-pitying protective cults by which young people so often counteract adult expectations.

THE RISE OF THE T.A.

Nonetheless, the character of most faculties *has* changed, not only over the past hundred years but even over the past thirty. Until World War II even senior scholars at leading universities did a good deal of what they defined as scut work, teaching small groups of lower-level students, reading papers and examinations, and so forth. Their labors were supplemented by ageing but unscholarly instructors and assistant professors, who were not given tenure, status, or high salaries, but were kept around precisely because there were lots of routine teaching jobs to be done and they were willing to do them. Today, however, few well-known scholars teach more than six hours a week, and in leading universities many bargain for less. Even fewer read undergraduate examinations and papers. At the same time the AAUP and other faculty groups have pushed through "up or out" rules on faculty promotion, so that the permanent assistant professor is now practically unknown at leading universities. The routine problems of mass higher education have therefore fallen by default to graduate students. These students have assumed the role of shop stewards, mediating between the highly professionalized faculty who run the curriculum and the still amateur undergraduates who pursue it. Graduate teaching assistants handle quiz sections, read examinations, listen to complaints, and generally protect the professors from over-exposure to the ignorant.[2]

CHANGING STUDENT OUTLOOKS

The changing needs and expectations of the adults on college and university campuses are one side of the equation which define faculty-student relations; the other side is the changing needs and expectations of the entering students. Today's students are quite different from those who entered college

[2] The impact on all this of increasingly generous fellowships and research assistantship varies from field to field. In the natural sciences most graduate students have no economic need to teach. This means that routine teaching chores of the traditional sort may simply not be performed. Exams, for example, may be multiple choice and machine scored; papers may be eliminated; and laboratory work may be supervised by advanced undergraduates. Even outside the natural sciences, moreover, the competition for graduate students' services is so stiff in the more esoteric fields that many cannot be dragooned into teaching assistantships. A good ABD (All But Dissertation) student in some fields can earn as much as $10,000 a year as an assistant professor in a small college near his university, often with a lighter load than he would have had as a T.A. at the institution where he is taking his Ph.D. If, as is often the case, his appurtenances include a wife, two or three children, pets, a summer place, and so forth, the salary advantage of teaching in such a college will more than offset the frequent drabness of the students.

a generation or two ago. They have lived in a very different sort of adolescent sub-culture before matriculating, and college occupies a different place in their overall life cycle. There was a time in the not so distant past when a middle-class high school boy could goof off in class or get in trouble on his block with almost complete confidence that his misadventures would not be held against him. If he decided to go straight he could do so simply by applying to a reputable college. If his parents could pay the tuition his other failings would usually be forgotten. No more. Today's high school student is told that his future position in life depends on getting good professional training, that this depends on his getting into a good college, and that this in turn depends on his performing well in high school. A misstep in high school may, in other words, count against him forever. (Or so the myth says. In reality America still offers a great many second chances, explicitly as at Parsons College, covertly else-where.) This does not, of course, mean that high school boys always *act* as if they will be held permanently answerable for the mistakes they made in high school or as if they will get permanent credit for their triumphs, though girls often do act this way. But even the boys are more inclined than in the past to feel that this is the case, at least with regard to their work. This is especially true in the East, where gradations of college prestige are finer and fear of not making the right college is correspondingly enhanced.[3]

The effect of such assumptions is difficult to chart, but they appear to hasten a kind of maturity. High school students seem to feel that they are more on their own, and that their fate depends more on what they do and less on what their parents do for them. Success seems to depend on what they have in their heads, not what kinds of property their parents have in the bank. Partly as a result, many children feel relatively little obligation to maintain strong ties with their parents or to conform to their parents' standards. Some begin relating almost exclusively to their peers by the time they are twelve or thirteen. They also become involved with the opposite sex earlier than their parents did, partly because physical maturity comes sooner and partly because post-Freudian parents are ambivalent in their opposition to adolescent sexual-ty, perhaps partly because the greater flexibility of sexual identities has heightened anxiety about the possibility of being homosexual and has thus made it more important to prove one's heterosexuality.

SELF-DETERMINATION IN HIGH SCHOOL

Breaking out of the family circle has always left the young uncertain where their loyalties lie and what limits still restrict their behavior. They become involved in all sorts of quasi-familial groups which arouse at least temporary faith in something larger than themselves. The residential college, with its fraternities, football games, and general emphasis on school spirit, was once such a group. Today the suburban high school plays this role, at least among the middle classes, just as the junior high school is now the scene for

For a discussion of the complex pressures discussed here and their differential effects on boys and girls in the sixth grade of a suburban school, see Michael Maccoby, *The Game Attitude,* unpublished doctoral dissertation, Harvard University Department of Social Relations, 1960.

many early adolescent dramas once associated with high school. By the time today's young people reach college they have therefore already partly broken away from their families and are ready for a more mature role. Whether one looks at the books they have read, their attitudes towards the opposite sex, their allergy to mickey mouse extracurricular (or curricular) makework, or their general coolness, today's entering freshmen seem older than those of the 1920's and 1930's. Class, ethnic, rural-urban, and other differences exist here, but have been little charted. We believe that the mass media—especially television —have a large role in the earlier maturation of the young, making them sophisticated cynics about advertising (although also diligent consumers) almost before they can read, and exposing them to adult fare that would once have been kept out of reach or only read under the covers late at night.[4]

At the same time certain kinds of responsibility come later and later. While young people still hold various kinds of temporary jobs during adolescence, they find it hard to embark on a career in the traditional sense before they reach 22. The most interesting work usually requires professional training beyond the BA and often is not begun in earnest until 25 or older. This means not only that the young usually are denied the kinds of responsibility which go with many jobs, but that they often depend on their families for money until at least 21 and often even later.

Thus, while adolescence begins earlier, it also continues longer. Students must begin making good records sooner, yet these records bring tangible results later and later. This combination of precocity and enforced dependence encourages students to create a make-believe world in which it is as if they were grown up. To achieve this they must organize their own lives, define their own limits, set their own ideals, and deny the authority and legitimacy of the adult world which they cannot join.

DISSIDENT MINORITIES

As in all class struggles, the actors in the war between the generations often take positions contrary to what an outside analyst would regard as their class interest. Just as the civil rights movement had to fight Negro apathy as well as white supremacy for many years, and depended in many ways on white liberals for both money and legitimacy, so too students who oppose adult discrimination and segregation have found that they are a minority among their agemates and that both their political success and their internal morale depend on finding adult supporters. (Their political successes seem to depend mainly on the tacit support of the faculty; their morale depends more on over support from graduate students and from non-students of that age.)

Broadly speaking, undergraduates assert themselves in one of two ways. Some temporarily repress the fact that they will eventually become adult themselves, and act like "permanent students." Others construct visions of the

---

[4] One set of studies in California suggests that adolescents who do not attend college (after applying) go through some of the same changes as their agemates who are attending college. See the discussion in John C. McCullers and Walter T. Plant, "Personality and Social Development: Cultural Influences" in *Motivational Research*, 1964 Vol. 34, pp. 604–606. The studies directed by Dr. Plant cover only a fraction of the problem but suggest its magnitude.

adult world which are in some sense harmonious with the student culture in which they are currently immersed. Many, of course, do both things, either simultaneously or sequentially.

The attitudes of the scholarly faculty, and the ways in which these encourage unscholarly students to create a counter-reality, have already been touched on. Feeling guilty about their neglect of unscholarly undergraduates, some professors talk about the importance of students' taking responsibility for their own education and about the impossibility of anyone else's doing the job for them. The faculty justify their neglect of the students by pointing to the students' neglect of them. Some precocious and sophisticated students welcome such talk, arguing that students are indeed mature and responsible, and that the university should recognize this and treat them accordingly. The net result is often that both sides conspire to encapsulate the undergraduates in their own world.

ENCOUNTERS WITH FACULTY

It is important to recognize the mutuality of this relationship. Students, for example, often complain about "lack of faculty-student contact" and tell horror stories about professors who have office hours once a month in an ill-publicized place. But the professors rightly counter by noting that few students come to whatever hours they keep, and that those who do come usually argue about grades. Similarly, students complain that they have no unofficial, personal contact with their nominal mentors. Professors respond by pointing out that when they ask students to their homes many make excuses and the rest seem uncomfortable and eager to go. While we think this latter observation underestimates the significance of such encounters to some students, it is certainly true that they seldom provoke significant communication, much less rapport. What the students really need is a sense that an adult takes them seriously, and indeed that they have some kind of power over adults which at least partially offsets the power adults obviously have over them. In order to be taken seriously and exercise power they must, despite their youth, contribute in some way to the world which they are about to join. They seldom get this sense directly from their professors, for the academic enterprise in which professors are engaged seldom excites them. Even if the academic world does excite them, they seldom find any way to contribute to it, even at the margins. It is true that imaginative faculty members, especially in the less fully organized fields, have found ways to bring eager undergraduates into research, so that some have published papers, with or without their mentors, in leading specialized journals. In microbiology it has been possible until recently for an undergraduate to come to the frontier by the time of his junior year; this has also been possible in sociology and in some areas of psychology. It is evidently more difficult in most branches of economics or physics. Whether it is attempted seems to depend in part on whether faculty members feel they stand to gain from success. In highly selective colleges such as Reed, Swarthmore, or Amherst, scholarly professors have long made do with undergraduate research assistants and have organized seminars for advanced undergraduates; but where graduate students and post-doctoral fellows are available as subordinates and colleagues, the greater effort needed to bring undergraduates along is generally less common. Nonetheless, it seems clear that the possibility exists, at least for a minority of students. When we look, for example, at the work published by undergraduates at the University of Kansas in the annual volume sponsored by that institution, or at the work published by Harvard undergraduates in the volumes of papers done for the second author's undergraduate course, it seems to us that undergraduates should be taken seriously as colleagues by even distinguished scholars. So, too, if one looks at undergraduate journals such as Reed College's *Journal of the Social Sciences*, the *Bard Papers*, or the journals published by several of the Harvard undergraduate Houses, the academic quality of the work is impressive. Yet most faculty members accustomed to the colleagueship and discipleship of a large research university seem to feel that they do not get much feedback along the central lines of their research from even the brightest undergraduates.

The central problem here is probably not so much one of age as of the relationship between professionals and amateurs. The academic profession like almost all others has been very reluctant to admit even the possibility that amateurs could make significant contributions. Such an admission would imply, for one thing, that all its training and certification machinery were superfluous and that those who had fought their way through had wasted their time. Euphoric but untalented amateurs can, moreover, often do considerable damage—though this is far less of a danger in academic life than in, say, medicine or engineering. Whatever the merits of the case, however, the academic profession is at least as elitist and exclusive as the American professional norm. This makes it in some ways very unsuited to the socialization of young people who are by definition outside the charmed circle. While some students nonetheless identify with their professors, the majority cannot afford to take the professorial model too seriously, for they have no reason to think they could approximate it if they tried.

SYMPTOMS OF ANTI-ORGANIZATION

Feeling excluded from the world of work in which their professors participate, many students retreat to a more hedonistic world of football and fraternity parties, or sex and drugs. Since today's students are increasingly anti-organizational in outlook, the latter have gradually displaced the former as a focus of interest. The appeal of sex and drugs is compounded by the bitterness of adult opposition, for anything which evokes such hostility from adults becomes almost by definition "grown up." The decline of the double standard has also made sex more important to undergraduates, for male undergraduates no longer have to depend on lower-class partners and therefore find it easier to blend sex with sociability and even study. The availability of coeds has not only driven the old campus prostitutes out of business but encourages proto-marital relationships which consume far more time and emotional energy than was once common. These relationships occupy such a central place in many undergraduates' lives that they are no longer willing to endure the inconveniences and humiliations adults have traditionally imposed on pre-marital sex. There are few campuses on which the rules surrounding relations between the sexes are not under attack, both as irritations and hypocrisies.

When one turns from the external forces which drive students to seek a self-contained sub-culture to the internal forces which give this sub-culture strength to resist adult pressure, the role of the graduate student assumes considerable importance. There was a time when undergraduates were almost as remote from graduate students as from professors. Undergraduates were often from more affluent families than graduate students on the same campus, and they were almost always less committed to intellectual values. The graduate students, in turn, felt that undergraduates were a frivolous lot, and had little or nothing to do with them. Today, however, undergraduates are more mature and more thoughtful, and the gap seems narrow at some points. It is true that graduate students in professional schools like law and medicine still keep pretty much to themselves. They have no institutional contact with undergraduates, and they already identify to some extent with their future professions.[5]

GRADUATE DOUBLE AGENTS

Graduate students in the arts and sciences, on the other hand, often seem somewhat less professionalized. While many of them make strenuous efforts to emulate their professors rather than undergraduates, others become double agents, maintaining ties with their past as well as their future. These dissident graduate students often become the leaders and legitimizers of undergraduate discontent—a phenomenon well documented at Berkeley in recent years but increasingly common elsewhere too. (At Stanford, for example, a bearded graduate student was head of the student government in 1965–6, and similar developments are taking place on other campuses.)

The mere existence of this sort of graduate student has an effect on the self-conception of many undergraduates. Graduate students are not yet quite adults, but they have many of the adult prerogatives to which undergraduates aspire: somewhat responsible jobs, reasonably satisfactory incomes which do not depend on parents, the right to live where and how they please, sexual liberty, and fairly long academic tethers. They are, moreover, committed to this way of life for a more or less indefinite period, which they are often in no hurry to end. A graduate student may therefore look to his juniors—and sometimes to himself—like a perpetual student in the Latin American tradition. For the undergraduate who finds himself unable to identify with any of the career alternatives he knows about, this life may seem a lesser evil—avoiding a difficult choice, preserving a measure of youthful noncommitment, and yet not exacting the full price usually demanded of those who remain dependent on their elders. Such identification is even possible at those university colleges where no graduate students are actually enrolled but where large numbers of undergraduates nonetheless assume they will eventually do graduate work.

Graduate students of this kind, along with the undergraduates who identify in whole or in part with them, form a semi-stable occupational group. Unlike those undergraduates and professional students who expect to be on campus for a fixed period and then depart for something better, these students

The frequent and partly proto-professional involvement of law students in Young Republican, Young Democratic, and other political groups is an exception.

see no immediate prospect of changing their status.[6] They are therefore far more interested than other students in trying to improve their present circumstances. Most students have what might be called a white-collar mentality, which assumes that if they conform to their superiors' demands they will be rewarded and rise to a new role in the world. The dissident minority on the other hand, has what might be called a blue-collar mentality. This outlook excludes promotion as remote or unlikely, and focuses on improving the conditions associated with its present work. While this dissident group is small, it includes many of the most competent and articulate students.

SUB-CULTURES IN PERSPECTIVE

Looking at undergraduate sub-cultures in historical perspective we are inclined to predict that the dissident minority will continue to grow. It represents a natural response to the extension of adolescence, both back into what was once childhood and forward into what was once adulthood, and extension in both directions is likely to continue. Psychologically if not chronologically, college therefore comes later in the overall life cycle, and its role *in loco parentis* is increasingly subject to challenge. If stern administrators formed a united front and refused to yield, they might perhaps hold the line against this challenge. But unity is hardly likely. Given the appealing Continental example, the growing logistical difficulties of enforcing rules made *in loco parentis*, and the increasing moral and emotional doubts of the administrators and faculty who must make most of these rules, it seems likely that undergraduates who demand an end to the doctrine will slowly get their way on most campuses. A generation hence most undergraduates will probably be treated like today's graduate students, both socially and academically.

There are colleges, public and private, where undergraduates' impatience for such changes threatens the very survival of the institution, by arousing the ire of powerful adults who regard student pranks as funny but cannot laugh off student solemnity. We have talked to students on such campuses who say that if the college authorities would frankly admit that the rules exist to protect the college from community reprisal, they would cooperate; what they say they cannot abide is being told that the rules are for their own good. Whether most would in fact cooperate we are not sure. Some among the current student generation are in revolt against all authority, obsessively testing all limits. Clothes are a constraint; razors are a constraint; courses and examinations are constraints; intervisitation hours are a constraint; refined language is a constraint. This revolt is supported by developments in the arts and also in the bohemias of the world—developments which are readily visible to undergraduates. It is a revolt which has also won a measure of long overdue support in the courts. On many campuses the rebels can also count on the tolerance of their fellow students, who fear to be thought square or chaste or fearful or finks. In this situation there may be some students who will inhibit themselves in order to save the institution, but there are likely to be others

[6] The draft has, of course, been a major factor for some in prolonging student status, especially since the Vietnam war became a political issue. The elimination of graduate student deferments should change the pattern somewhat, but probably not dramatically.

who relish the prospect of the institution's succumbing to community disapproval, thus revealing the community's rottenness for all to see.

Nonetheless, despite some students' refusal to present a cleancut fact to the public, virtually all the colleges which now feel threatened will survive and even prosper. The real question is therefore how the increasing autonomy of many undergraduate sub-cultures will affect the individual participants' long-term growth and development—and thus how it will affect the larger society. We find it hard to imagine, for example, that students who spend four (sometimes ten) years in the more alienated Berkeley hippie scene will slip easily into the established adult institutions within which the middle classes now earn their living. Even four years in Cambridge can develop a set of assumptions and habits rather poorly suited to the occupations for which Harvard has traditionally prepared its alumni.[7] Some of these alumni may be permanently out of tune with the world of work.

HIPPIES AND ACTIVISTS

In examining this question one must distinguish between students whose estrangement from adult life is so complete that they withdraw into passivity and privatism (often nourished by drugs) and students who, while alienated from the adult society they observe around them, still have enough hope for the future to make an active effort at political change. The activists may seem almost wholly committed to anti-organizational ideologies and behavior but they can often change their views quite suddenly, especially if institutions they had defined as hopelessly rigid and square take them seriously, adopt their rhetoric, and toy with their program. The relations between some radicals and the federal poverty program illustrate this. But even the hippies who have no political program may find a place in the corporate state if they have technical competence. Thus one finds industries employing computer programmers whose dress and demeanor remain aggressively bohemian and who often continue to live in colonies of like-minded souls on the fringe of some ethnic or academic ghetto. Technical writing and the academic profession itself absorb others of the same species. The continuing shortage of men with technical skills is likely to force traditionally less adaptable and progressive industries to emulate the data processors.

It could be argued, however, that as students acquire more freedom their world may become more like that of adults—as, for example, the world of graduate students in some ways already is. One of the distinguishing features of student life is that its participants are allowed to make mistakes without paying too heavy a price. They can, in other words, be somewhat irresponsible. If students do not do their work they may get a bad grade, and if they get enough bad grades they may be fired, but the amount of absenteeism, indolence, and sheer incompetence permitted students is far greater than that permitted almost any other sort of worker.[8] Similarly, if a student gets arrested

[7] See Kenneth Keniston, "The Sources of Student Dissent," *Journal of Social Issues*, Spring 1967 for a more detailed discussion of some of these themes; also Keniston's *The Uncommitted*, N.Y., Harcourt Brace, 1965.
[8] By setting the passing grade at 60 or 70 percent instead of the 95 percent or more required on most real jobs, colleges can offer students more interesting and difficult

for smoking marijuana his parents will usually go to bat for him, find lawyers, pay bail, and the like. Not only that, but the civil authorities are likely to be relatively lenient, chalking up his failings to youthful excess rather than moral turpitude. Radicals and idealists often deplore all this, saying that students should have no greater privileges than other members of society. Yet if this were really to happen students would probably become far more cautious in their outlook, taking fewer risks and supporting fewer radical causes, both moral and political. Look, for example, at those students who plan professional careers. These are the students whose work is "real" in the sense that their failures count heavily against them. And these are by and large soberly professional as undergraduates even in their dress.

Observing such students, we are inclined to believe that other students' sympathy for deviant ideas and life styles is in good part a transitional phenomenon—a by-product of their currently ambiguous status as neither quite children nor quite adults. If so, a clear commitment to treating students as adults in all off-the-job respects might reduce the levels of discontent. It might, on the other hand, exacerbate discontent by dramatizing the tension between off-the-job freedom and on-the-job subordination, as has happened in some cases with graduate students. It might be argued that this contrast causes relatively little trouble in other enterprises, where workers do what they are told on the job but enjoy full citizenship after hours. This is, however, only partly true. First, workers *don't* do what they are told in many cases, and it might be small consolation to educators to think that if they abandoned all efforts in *loco parentis*, they would still have as much trouble with students as employers have with unions. Educators' sights are, perhaps foolishly, set higher. Second, workers' limited willingness to do what they are told depends on being paid. Students, on the other hand, are presumed to be working for their own good. Under such circumstances, insubordination seems inevitable once the general principle of adult authority is abandoned.

The Adult Backlash and the "Safe" Colleges

The customs and concerns of student sub-cultures vary enormously, but all are in one way or another at odds with the adult sub-cultures from which they spring. The growing autonomy of such sub-cultures has therefore been greeted with less than universal enthusiasm by responsible adults. Fearful parents believe that if they let their children immerse themselves in one of these sub-cultures, the children may never outgrow it. This fear flourishes especially among parents who have not themselves been to college. Not having

challenges than most employers dare offer. Real jobs are therefore almost certain to bore most workers, for they must be over-qualified and unchallenged in order to ensure that they won't make too many mistakes. (There are exceptions here, especially in organizations with no competition or no choice of employees. The Army, which has competition only in wartime and never enough money to pick and choose among applicants, seems to set "passing" at a level even lower than most colleges; some of the service trades are not much better off.)

been undergraduates themselves, these parents have not had the experience of passing through this particular phase and slipping into the post-collegiate adult world. This may make them exaggerate the difficulty of the transition and underestimate the probability that it will eventually take place. But even college educated parents worry about whether their children will prove as resilient as they themselves did. They worry doubly when they see that the distance between many student sub-cultures and adult society is wider than it was a generation ago. And even we ourselves, while less anxious about these matters than most parents and professors, are not sure that such fears are wholly unfounded.

Parental worries are compounded by ambiguities. Parents and other adults usually conform to the achievement ethic of the highly organized society in which they work, but many are also attracted by more spontaneous, hedonistic, impractical, and pre-industrial possibilities. As David Matza has pointed out, this means that there is a kind of secret sharing between many adults and those adolescent sub-cultures which defy adult ambition, taste, and sobriety.[9] Adults may patronize teenagers whose immaturity finds symbolic expression in panty-raids, but only the most puritanical are alarmed by them. When frivolity turns to defiance, however, the adults' response changes correspondingly. Even those who view themselves as liberals are frequently upset by long hair, marijuana and LSD, miscegenation, and seemingly unpatriotic anti-militarism. There is, in other words, some point at which almost every parent wants to draw the line, even though not every parent dares to try. Not only that, but some parents seem to succeed at least in part.

ATTRACTING THE CONVENTIONAL

All over America there are children who want to eschew the youth sub-culture and move with maximum safety and minimal delay into some kind of adult world. A number of otherwise undistinguished colleges have been able to attract substantial numbers of students by catering to these hopes and fears. These safe colleges fall into two general categories: the closely regulated residential colleges, most of which are church-controlled, and the commuter colleges, most of which are publicly controlled.

The church colleges are a study in themselves. Here it need only be noted that church colleges are in most cases colleges first and church related second. This has several consequences. First, they feel obliged to meet at least some of the standards of academic excellence established in secular colleges. One consequence of this is that many church colleges have recently raised their charges faster than devout families have raised their incomes. This has changed their potential clientele. At the same time, the church colleges' quest for financial viability and academic quality has forced them to

[9] See David Matza, *Delinquency and Drift*, N.Y., The Free Press, 1963. See also the writing of Bennett Berger concerning youth cultures. Talcott Parsons and S. N. Eisenstadt see these matters in somewhat different perspective, arguing that the young are licensed to deviate from adult norms for a few years in order to tie them to non-fraternal achievement norms more securely later on. See, e.g., Eisenstadt's *From Generation to Generation: Age Grades and the Social Structure*, Glencoe, The Free Press, 1956.

grow in order to support more specialized faculty, better libraries, and the like. As a college grows, its dissident minorities also grow, until they reach the critical mass at which a partially self-contained sub-culture is possible. Once established this sub-culture can proselytize and can at least sporadically evoke minority impulses in a wide range of apparently contented students. The existence of such a sub-culture is in turn likely to frighten away the more repressed high school students and their parents, who fear corruption by all too tempting friends. Thus while church colleges are still much closer than leading secular universities to their Victorian ancestors, they are usually considerably more emancipated from the past then their clientele, and are often eager to widen their lead. Furthermore, even where the college authorities remain very conservative, their capacity to control the student culture is extremely limited in a residential setting. Undergraduates are too numerous to be constantly monitored, and in any case relatively few faculty even at church colleges have a taste for this. And so youth culture tends to take hold and go its own way, even though it is seldom as unbridled as at a scholarly residential university. Many parents of limited means and views have therefore felt obliged to look elsewhere for a safer (and a cheaper) route to the B.A. Many seem to have found it in public commuter colleges, especially public junior colleges.

MARRIED AND UNMARRIED COMMUTERS

The apparent safeness of the commuter college derives from the fact that students spend almost all their campus time in class. This gives adult faculty an almost completely effective veto over what students do while on the campus. As soon as the students leave the controlled classroom environment they normally leave the campus too, unless they are so unfortunate as to have a schedule with a dead hour or two between classes. Once they leave the campus they usually head for home or for a job. In either case they are likely to be interacting mainly with people substantially older or younger than themselves or their classmates. A distinctive student culture is therefore unlikely to develop.

There are however, exceptions to this rule. Not all students at commuter colleges live with their parents. Some get married.[10] Married students almost all set up their own households, often in apartments near the commuter college which one or both of them attends. Even those who do not marry are likely to find both reasons and resources to move out of their parents' home as they grow older.[11] Regardless of whether the owners are single or married,

[10] U.S. Bureau of the Census, 1960, *Census of Population, Final Report PC (2)-5A, (School Enrollment)*, Washington, U.S. Government Printing Office, 1964, Table 9 shows that less than two percent of all college men under 19 are married, compared to nine percent of those aged 20 and 21, thirty percent of the juniors and seniors aged 22–24, and thirty-five percent of graduate students aged 22–24. The proportions are somewhat lower for women, presumably because women are more likely to drop out of college when they marry.
[11] The Census, *ibid.*, shows that among unmarried men not living in college dormitories 79 per cent of those 19 or under, 64 per cent of those aged 20 or 21, and 54 per cent of those aged 22–24 were living with parents or relatives.

apartments of this kind tend to become the nucleus of an unsupervised and independent student culture which embraces single as well as married commuters.[12] Commuters of this sort often create a semi-residential, entirely unofficial student community around their university. Such a community will center near the campus if cheap housing is available nearby, as it is for example at NYU and Wayne State. Since at a place like UCLA or San Francisco State, however, there is little suitable housing nearby, the commuter who does not live with his parents tends to merge with whatever incipient bohemia his city sustains. The result may be a Left Bank pattern of student life more in the European than in the Anglo-American tradition. Under these circumstances the very absence of dormitories may paradoxically encourage the creation of a student sub-culture more independent, more embracing, and more at odds with adult attitudes and values than a dormitory-based sub-culture could possibly be. While such bohemianism almost never appeals to more than a small minority of the students enrolled at non-residential institutions, it can exercise a certain subtle but pervasive influence on a larger fraction. By frightening adults, moreover, it can polarize conflict with the college authorities and thus win more converts to the anti-adult cause—as the activist non-dormitory students have periodically done at Berkeley.

TWO YEAR COLLEGE SOBRIETY

Almost any institution with graduate students is likely to spin off such a sub-culture as one of its by-products, and in large cities even the four year commuter colleges often acquire some such penumbra. Two year colleges, on the other hand, tend to be relatively immune. While the public ones often have a fair number of older students who are not living with their parents, these are seldom promising candidates for student leadership or taste-making. Many are working full-time. Many others have children and the sobriety that usually comes with them. While some are friends with other students of their own age at a more advanced level, others spend their time mainly with high school chums who never went to college at all, have worked for some years, and now see themselves as part of the adult world. As a result, the public two-year college usually conforms quite closely to the archetypal commuter pattern discussed earlier, in which students see one another mainly in classrooms and hence mainly under adult supervision. When one combines this with a faculty which is seldom drawn from leading graduate schools and includes relatively few intellectual or social eccentrics, it is easy to see why two-year colleges have attracted a growing proportion of those who want the advantages of advanced certification and (perhaps) training without exposure to the dangers or distractions of the youth culture.[13]

[12] An illuminating variant is provided at Oakland University outside Detroit, which began as a commuter branch of Michigan State University and has recently begun building dormitories. These attract students with more sophistication and probably more money than the commuters. The dormitory students then sometimes form alliances with commuters to use the commuters' parents' homes for weekend parties, escaping a "dry" campus with few amenities.

[13] There are, of course, many other reasons for these colleges' appeal, including minimal admissions requirements, the famous open door, non-academic programs, easy commuting and low cost.

Some community college advocates look forward to the day when virtually all high school seniors will go to a junior college, regardless of aptitude, income, or career plans. These prophets expect that today's undergraduate colleges will gradually cut back or abandon their freshman and sophomore years, recruiting students from junior college just as they now do from high school. Under these circumstances senior colleges would probably deemphasize the B.A. and enroll most students in three or four year Masters' degree programs.[14] The net result would be to alter the present 6-6-4-Plus (or 8-4-4-Plus) sequence of American education, making it 6-6-2-Plus (or 8-4-2-Plus).

NEW SEQUENCES

Such a development would resolve the present ambiguous status of undergraduate education, making the 13th and 14th grades more clearly an upward extension of high school general education and for 15th and 16th grades more clearly a downward extension of graduate professional training. The 13th and 14th grades would be taught by men and women recruited from much the same pool as high school teachers. They would not be expected to have Ph.D's or to do scholarly research. Some would be graduate students at universities. Others would be alumni of the burgeoning MA programs at former teachers colleges. By freeing the Ph.D's who now devote some of their time to teaching freshmen and sophomores, this kind of reorganization would ensure a more adequate supply of Ph.D's to teach juniors and seniors.[15] These men would mostly be scholars first and teachers second, and would make no pretense of offering their students non-professional education. Their colleges would also presumably abandon the last pretense of acting *in loco parentis*, while the junior colleges would continue in this role, or at least in active collaboration with parents who retained this role.

Enrolling all high school graduates in comprehensive junior colleges would postpone the college admission trauma two additional years. Instead of making the first irrevocable choice of their lives at seventeen, most middle-class youngsters would make it at nineteen. And instead of beginning to ready themselves for this choice at fourteen, most young people might well procrastinate until eighteen. If all students could enter the local junior college regardless of how badly they did in high school, and if none could enter a more prestigious college regardless of how well they did in high school, academic competition in high school would presumably lose much of its present

[14] See, e.g., Alvin Eurich, "A Twenty-First Century Look at Higher Education," *1966 Current Issues in High Education,* Proceedings of the 10th Annual National Conference on Higher Education, Washington Association for Higher Education (NEA), 1962.
[15] Allan M. Cartter (The Supply and Demand for College Teachers, *Journal of Human Resources,* Vol. 1, Summer 1966, p. 29) estimates that between 40 and 50 per cent of all college teachers now have Ph.D.'s *1960 Census, op. cit.,* Volume I, Part I, Table 160, shows that about 47 per cent of all college and university students are juniors, seniors, or graduate students. These latter get something like 70 per cent of all faculty time. (Estimated from data on California in *A Master Plan for High Education in California,* 1960–1975, Sacramento, California, State Department of Education, 1960, pp. 156 ff.) The elimination of freshmen and sophomores would, then, reduce college teaching requirements by 30 per cent and mean that about 65 per cent of all teaching of juniors and seniors could be done by Ph.D.'s.

intensity and significance. The junior colleges would supplant the high schools as first-round sorting and screening institutions in the occupational rat race. Only when students reached junior college would they begin to feel that they were playing for keeps, that their successes would really help them in later life, and that their failures would really count against them. Only then would they be forced to expose themselves to impersonal adult judgments from whose consequences neither their peers nor their parents could protect them. (This is not to deny that some high school students would continue to take their teachers' demands very seriously, just as some junior high students do today. There will always be Calvinists eager to prove themselves elected for future glory, even when nobody with power over their fate is watching.)

PRECOCITY VERSUS DEPENDENCY

Those who find the current precocity of the young alarming might greet such delays with enthusiasm. There would, however, be serious problems. They would probably have increasing difficulty recruiting competent male teachers, since many of the men who now teach high school would be drawn into the junior colleges. The male students' tendency to equate learning and effeminacy would thus continue even longer than it now does. In addition, the high schools would be deprived of their main claim to seriousness, namely their role in preparing students for their first quasi-adult choices, both among colleges and among jobs.

The main problem would, however, be the prolongation of youthful dependency. Many young people live at home too long even today. The universalization of junior college would make this even more common. Instead of striking out on their own at eighteen, both geographically and intellectually, most students would have to wait until twenty. The gradual extension of adolescence has already produced a variety of problems which America cannot handle satisfactorily; universal junior college would make the situation appreciably worse.

For better or worse, however, junior colleges are unlikely to become universal. While highly rationalized state planning agencies may create a few new colleges like Florida Atlantic, which begins in the junior year and caters to junior college alumni, existing colleges and universities are unlikely to drop their freshman and sophomore years so long as they keep attracting competent applicants. For one thing, universities often make a financial profit on freshmen and sophomores. This is used to subsidize upper-classmen and graduate students. Even if they do not provide a short run profit, the freshmen and sophomores often justify themselves over the long haul, for it is the four undergraduate years rather than the graduate years which seem to evoke the loyalty and generosity of alumni. Then, too, colleges are in stiff competition with one another for able students, and a college which admits freshmen and sophomores has an enormous competitive advantage over one which tells prospective applicants to wait two years. We doubt that many colleges will relinquish this advantage voluntarily.[16] And so long as universities and uni-

---

[16] The only way we can imagine this happening would be for a cartel of elite private colleges to abolish the freshmen and sophomore years. This might give the new pattern enough status to make it attractive to able students.

versity colleges keep admitting high school graduates, we expect high school graduates will keep applying. We see no prospect of junior colleges competing successfully for students who have the money, ability, and drive to make it at a selective brand-name institution.

JUNIOR COLLEGE AND THE MAJORITY

There is, however, more reason to expect the junior colleges to become the major vehicle for educating the less affluent, the less adept, and the less ambitious students, who are the great majority. This has happened in California, and it could easily happen elsewhere. This development seems especially likely in states where the adult backlash against student emancipation is strongest. In California, for example, adult reaction against youthful rebellion at Berkeley may lead to some redirection of resources to other, safer enterprises. The decision of the Regents to equalize certain kinds of expenditure between Berkeley and UCLA preceded recent unruliness on the cosmopolitan Berkeley campus, as did the decision to develop a new university in the pastoral setting of Santa Cruz. However, these and other campuses may look more appealing as Berkeley looks less so. Furthermore, Governor Reagan's tuition proposals would have the effect of establishing higher tuition at the University than at the state colleges, and none at the junior colleges. Whether this was the aim or not, the consequence might be to push more students into relatively trouble-free local commuter colleges.

Despite these political pressures, however, we do not see how adults can indefinitely contain the generational revolt. In the long run undergraduates are almost certain to win increasing autonomy, and the doctrine of *in loco parentis* is likely to be abandoned in post-secondary institutions. The minority which is officially charged with such work, usually concentrated in the dean's office, has little more chance of success than a colonial administration confronted with a determined guerrilla movement. The dissident students are only a small minority on most campuses, as the administration constantly emphasizes. But the young troublemakers swim in a sea of relatively tolerant fellow travelers, many of whom will protect student rights against the adult administration even if they themselves feel little impulse to exercise such rights. While there are also many conservative students sympathetic to adult values, they tend to be apathetic and cannot be counted on to play an active role in defending the status quo against youthful defiance. Likewise, while there are many adult faculty nominally allied with the administration, who are put off by student insolence, dissidence, and resistance, they have mixed feelings about the time-consuming tasks of enforcing *in loco parentis*, and in a crisis the administration cannot count on them.

Indeed, the whole idea of self-government in communities whose student members all expect to be gone in a few years, and many of whose faculty members hope to go to a better place, may well be unworkable. Those who lack a deep stake in the future of the community as a whole may have a disproportionate interest in protecting their civil liberties as against meeting their civic responsibilities. (Even the phrase "responsibility" usually elicits a look of disgust from student activists, who have heard it invoked so often for reasons of institutional public relations.) Self-government can only work if a substantial fraction of the community in question is willing to give up time, convenience, and a measure of personal freedom to promote the general welfare. Undergraduates are willing and able to do this under the right circumstances. (Antioch seems to have managed this, though perhaps with increasing difficulty; Goddard, Marlboro, Franconia tremble on the edge of it.) But it is far from clear that a college can create these circumstances so long as most students take an instrumental view of higher education, see their college mainly as a place which they can induce to give them a degree, and are already looking forward to moving on.

All metaphors can, of course, be pushed too far. We do not expect the generational revolt to achieve victory in the same sense that the Algerian revolt did. Neither legislators nor trustees are ready to haul down the banner of adult responsibility and turn over the regulation of student affairs either to the students themselves or to the police who regulate other citizens. College administrators eager to be loved, or at least not abused by the young, may in some cases want to abandon the struggle to impose their will on undergraduates, retrenching to the "neo-colonialist" position they now take vis-à-vis graduate students. But they will seldom feel free to go this far, even if they want to. Adults will therefore continue to regulate and restrict undergraduate life in a variety of ways for many years to come, making periodic attacks on the students' sense of maturity and dignity. But as in guerrilla warfare, the occupying powers may win all the battles while gradually losing the war. The problem is at bottom one of legitimacy, and the claims of adults on undergraduates seem to achieve this less and less.

Nonetheless, the metaphor of guerrilla warfare and colonial liberation suggests another side to our prophecy. It is one thing for undergraduates to win the same actual rights as other adults; it is quite another thing to win the freedom which they *imagine* goes with adult status. The waning of formal adult control over the social aspects of undergraduate life is unlikely to be accompanied by comparable waning of control over undergraduate work. Today's graduate students are after all nominally free, but they are actually very much constrained by the fact that adults control their future status in society. This will probably be the case with tomorrow's undergraduates. Generational revolt, in other words, will probably bring the appearance of victory, but it will also lead to neo-colonialism, for the young can no more afford to go their own way independent of adults than Ghana or Cuba can get on without making peace with at least some of the Great Powers.

CHAPTER 3

Family Roles
and Youth

Adolescence is an intermediate stage in the series of dramas which constitute ever-changing family life.[1] Some observations on the structure and functions of the modern American family in which the adolescent is caught may be helpful toward appreciating dilemmas which arise. The structure of the family is described as being "isolated nuclear," that is, the spouses and their still-dependent children live separately and sometimes at considerable distance from kinsmen. But the nuclear family is not independent of society; it is, according to Parsons,[2] a small and highly differentiated subsystem of the society. The parents function as humanizers for their children. As socializing agents, the parents occupy not merely their familial roles but more diffuse roles representing other hats they wear in society. Socialization of the child is not strictly into the family but into structures which extend beyond the family and cut through it: the school, the peer group, the family of procreation this child will create, and adult occupational roles. Primary socialization is therefore a critical function which families perform for other social systems. It is important to emphasize the significance of this function of the nuclear family since it is fashionable to note with lament that many functions of families are being lost or usurped by other institutions in modern society. While it is true that modern families do not have major economic, political, religious, or educational duties (nuclear families may never have had these duties), certain functions, such as primary socialization, are almost exclusively the province of the modern family.[3]

As the child becomes an adolescent and grows out of the primary

[1] Clifford Kirkpatrick applies the life cycle approach in his classic sociological text *The Family*, 2d ed., New York: The Ronald Press, 1963.
[2] Talcott Parsons and Robert Bales, *Family, Socialization and Interaction Process*, Glencoe, Ill.: The Free Press, 1955, p. 35.
[3] Norman W. Bell and Ezra F. Vogel, "Toward a Framework for Functional Analysis of Family Behavior," in Norman W. Bell and Ezra F. Vogel (eds.), *A Modern Introduction to the Family*, rev. ed., New York: The Free Press, 1968, p. 7.

socializing unit, parents become less able to socialize their children for adult roles. Considerable conflict is manifested between parents and youth. Kingsley Davis, in a paper which has become classic, attempted to distinguish the universals or constants that appear to underlie all such instances of friction from the specific conditions or variables distinctive to modern American society which interact with the universals to produce conflict in families and perhaps the generational gap in society at large.[4] The universals are the birth cycle and decelerating socialization of the parent, the physiological differences which are greater than the chronological age differences between parents and children and the conservative realism of adults versus the Utopian idealism of youth. These universal factors are activated toward the production of conflict; by our rapid rate of social change which gives the parent a different historical content from his offspring; by the extent of complexity in the social structure; by the lack of agreement on methods of childrearing, routes to adulthood, and rites of passage into adulthood and power; and by a social mobility system which demands an early choice toward preparation for an occupation which is not likely to be the same for fathers and sons.

What are the characteristics of the family which is successful with respect to the primary socialization of its children? One man's view, admittedly a controversial one, is provided by British educational sociologist Frank Musgrove. His "good home" is definitely not the ladies magazines' romantic confection of togetherness, happiness, acceptance, and rock-like stability. Instead, he finds through empirical analysis, a family in which there are few children whose intellectual accomplishments may be traced to their close associations with adults. He finds that the child's progress in school is related to "favourable parental attitude" but this attitude is not found to be an attractive one of kindly understanding and encouragement. It is, rather, equated with ambitious and demanding behavior which is conjoined with the ample opportunity to do well, to achieve. The love-oriented disciplinary technique in which love is given on contractual terms appears to be an effective way of producing conscientious students with well developed capacities for guilt and anxiety. In less direct ways than formerly in the Western cultures, parents as mediators of the social class membership continue to influence the life chances of their children.

The role of the mother in the "good home" of the adolescent may be in need of an updated definition. Musgrove notes that if the mother works, this may be more indicative of striving than neglect, and for this reason the child's achievement is enhanced rather than depressed. Since maternal employment is more and more a cross-class characteristic of

---

[4] Kingsley Davis, "The Sociology of Parent-Youth Conflict," *American Sociological Review*, V (August 1940), pp. 523–536.

American families, we would wish to know more of the relationship between adolescent development and the mother's working before passing judgment on this trend.

On the basis of a national sample of intact families in which the father was employed, Douvan was able to analyze her formulations relative to the full-time and part-time maternal employment variables and their effects on adolescent girls and adolescent boys. We are given the impression that, for adolescent girls, part-time employment of the mother is more frequently associated with positive effects than is full-time employment or no outside employment. These effects are the encouragement of autonomy, activity, and responsibility in the daughter, without the precocious separation of the daughter from the mother's influence and control.

And what of sons of employed mothers? The findings are less clear; however, maternal employment appears to be a less important factor in the life of the adolescent boy. His model for ego development and male-appropriate role behaviors is his father, not his mother. When the mother's employment is based on factors of personal choice, rather than on perceived inadequacies of the father, there seems to be no established effect on the son's development.

Generational differences rather than generational relationships is the concern of the paper written by Krystall and his colleagues. The possibility of a generational gap in civil rights orientations between Negro high school seniors and their mothers is suggested through data analyses of responses to questions constructed around the themes of integration and black consciousness. The adolescents, maturing in an era of black power movements and successful attempts toward the enhancement of racial pride, are notably more aware of the special case of being black than are their mothers. Moreover, the young people are more pro-integration in their sympathies. The term cultural pluralist is applied to these students who are resolving the traditional bind between favoring integration, on the one hand, and cultivating black awareness, on the other.

As mentioned earlier, the involvement of youth in the social institution of the family has two main aspects: youth in the child status in the family of orientation, and youth in the transitional status toward spouse-parental roles in the family of procreation. Since married adolescents represent only a small, though conspicuous segment of the adolescent population, we will concentrate on the heterosexual, premarital activity of the majority of adolescents.

Sociologists of the family have advanced many theoretical statements concerning the American courtship system as practiced in the adolescent subculture. One of the earliest conceptualizations of the dating system as a rating system was set forth by Willard Waller before World War II.[5] His notion was that dating was not actual courtship but was a dalliance relationship, strongly materialistic and superficial, an end in itself. More recent writers have taken the sanguine view that the dating experience functions as an educational experience which aids individuals in developing and assessing mature criteria for future mate selection.

In the earlier part of the century, the random dating pattern with rapid changing of partners was the characteristic one. This pattern has been supplanted somewhat in the past twenty years by the "going steady" complex, a temporary monogamous relationship in depth. The going steady practice has been associated with changes in the sexual codes of teenagers by Ira Riess.[6] He argues that the association of sexual behavior with mutual affection is more easily achieved in the going steady situation than in casual dating.

Because of inconsistencies in the literature on dating behavior relative to function, process, and motivation, McDaniel sought to systematically discover the relationship between the female roles in dating and her reasons for dating in each stage of courtship. His paper provides us with a tentative theory of the socialization process operating in dating and courtship and concomitant role behavior changes from assertive to receptive. It is clear that if the girl wishes to marry, she must eventually take a receptive role, or risk rejection by males who strongly dislike assertiveness in girls in later stages of courtship.

[5] Willard Waller, "The Rating and Dating Complex," *American Sociological Review*, II (October 1937), pp. 727–734.
[6] Ira L. Reiss, "Sexual Codes in Teen-Age Culture," *The Annals*, CCCXXXVIII (November 1961), pp. 53–62.

THE "GOOD HOME"*

FRANK MUSGROVE

The "good home" is an aid to success in our school system. It is small; the parents are ambitious for their children; the father is at least a skilled manual worker; and if it is a working-class home, the mother has preferably "married down." The father is somewhat ineffectual, perhaps rather feckless; but one or both parents are demanding, even ruthless in their expectations of achievement. Relationships in the home are emotionally bleak. The family is unstable and has moved often; the mother goes to work. The children grow up to be rather withdrawn and solitary, conscientious and given to self-blame. They are "good grammar-school material."

Birth-Order and Family Size

The feature of the "good home" which is least in doubt is its size. In general the small family produces the most intelligent children as measured by intelligence tests, presumably because "intelligence" is to a considerable extent inherited, and intelligent parents show their intelligence by limiting the size of their families.

It is also possible that in the small family the child is in closer touch with its parents and habitually uses more grown-up language and ideas than he would if he were lost in a cloud of siblings. He may therefore appear to have a higher level intelligence than he "really" has, particularly on tests which are wholly or mainly verbal. The trend to smaller families may thus, conceivably, mask a real decline in innate intelligence by giving a boost to the environmental component.

The negative correlation of approximately point three between intelligence and family size has been established in numerous surveys, such as the Scottish Mental Survey of 1947. A correlation of this magnitude means, roughly, that in a random sample of a hundred families, sixty would demonstrate this relationship; but in twenty there would be high average intelligence in large families, and in the remaining twenty low average intelligence in small families.

If intelligent parents are not directed by their intelligence to limit their

* Reprinted from Frank Musgrove, *The Family, Education and Society* (London: Routledge & Kegan Paul, Ltd.; New York: Humanities Press, Inc.) 1966, pp. 72–93, by permission of the publishers.

families, then their families may be large and their children of high intelligence. There does not appear to be the same connection between family size and intelligence among Catholic as among Protestant families (and presumably in the past, before the advent of modern birth-control methods, there was no connection in the population at large). In one fairly recent survey in Middlesbrough only 6 per cent of children from families of four or more children gained grammar school places, but 18 per cent of Catholic children from families of this size did so. Catholic children from small families showed no such superiority.[1]

It seems that even children of good intelligence will not use their intelligence as effectively as they might if they are members of large families, particularly when their fathers are manual workers. In her inquiries in boys' grammar schools in 1951 Himmelweit found that working-class boys from small families (one or two children) had a better chance of gaining a grammar school place than working-class boys from large families. "Since no such differences were found in the non-manual groups they require an explanation over and above that of the known negative correlation between I.Q. and family size."[2]

More recently, in his research on a national sample of primary school children, Douglas found that middle-class boys (but not girls) were also less likely to succeed in the eleven plus selection tests if they came from large families. However, in the middle class it was only families of four or more children that had a depressing effect; among working-class children the prospects became progressively worse as the family increased in size above one or two.[3]

In working-class families of three children, 14.1 per cent were expected to gain grammar school places judging by their measured abilities, but only 13.2 per cent did so; in middle-class families of the same size 33.9 per cent were expected to gain places, and a still higher percentage (38.6) in fact did so. The explanation appears to lie very largely in the attitudes, expectations and assumptions of parents with large families. If the school is very good, and if the parents' attitudes are favourable, the handicap for working-class children from large families can almost, though not entirely, be eliminated.

The significance of birth-order is also reasonably well established, although the interpretation of the facts is neither easy nor certain. In his nineteenth-century studies of eminent scientists Galton found that it was an advantage to be an eldest or an only son. Subsequent research in the general population both here and in America has amply confirmed this judgement.

Social-class differences have been found in this connection too. It matters much more to be an eldest son or daughter in a working-class than a middle-class family, at least as far as eleven plus selection is concerned. One investigation demonstrated that "a working-class boy, whatever the size of his family, is

[1] J. E. Floud, A. H. Halsey and F. M. Martin, *Social Class and Educational Opportunity* (1956), p. 137.
[2] H. T. Himmelweit, "Social Status and Secondary Education since the 1944 Act: Some Data for London" in D. V. Glass (ed.), *Social Mobility in Britain* (1954).
[3] J. W. B. Douglas, *The Home and the School* (1964), p. 170.

more likely to attend a grammar school if he is an eldest child, and . . . this again does not apply in the case of a middle-class boy. . . ."[4]

Douglas's findings were similar. The eldest child tended, in the eleven plus examinations, to exceed the expectations based on his measured ability. This was found to be the case among both middle-class and working-class children, but to a more marked extent among the latter.

Douglas did not find that only children did any better than "expected," and attributed this principally to lack of sibling rivalry. Other investigators have found both onlys and eldests more scholastically able than intermediates and youngests. There is no evidence that they are more intelligent; they are more disposed to use their intelligence with effect in the school setting.

Lees and Stewart established in two Midland cities in 1955 that both eldests and onlys were found in grammar schools significantly more often than in modern schools. Thus onlys were 18.3 per cent of the grammar school population in one city, but only 11.7 per cent of the modern school population. The advantage of being an eldest girl diminished in families of four or more.[5]

The interpretation of these findings is not easy. In earlier research into the background of a group of adult students Lees, like Douglas, attributed the superiority of eldests principally to sibling rivalry, particularly when younger brothers and sisters were getting on well and so seriously threatening the eldest's status.[6] Clearly this cannot account for the success of onlys; and in their later work Lees and Stewart advance an explanation which might apply to any first-born child—his rather lonely position of eminence and perhaps responsibility in the family which provides him with an early training for handling "situations demanding individual intiative, and, incidentally, of coping with such situations as those presented by intelligence tests and examinations at eleven plus years."

This explanation is diametrically opposed to that offered by Stanley Schachter to account for the superiority in some situations of first-born Americans. Lees and Stewart say the first-born is successful because he has a capacity for loneliness; Schachter says he is successful because he has not.

First-born children, argues Schachter, are less rather than more able to cope on their own with their problems and anxieties. Far from being highly "individualistic," they will seek solutions to their problems in groups. First-borns undergoing group therapy have been observed to continue their treatment longer than necessary; later-borns drop out before they should. There is a greater tendency for later-borns to become alcoholics, handling their anxieties in non-social ways. The first-born, as an infant, has enjoyed a concerned and attentive mother, fussing over her first child: she has come to his side whenever he faced discomfort or fear. Later-born children have a mother who is probably more blasé; they will more often be left to deal with their problems

[4] A. H. Halsey and L. Gardner, "Selection for Secondary Education and Achievement in Four Grammar Schools," *British Journal of Sociology* (1953), 4.

[5] J. P. Lees and A. H. Stewart, "Family or Sibship Position and Scholastic Ability," *Sociological Review* (1957), 5.

[6] J. P. Lees, "The Social Mobility of a Group of Eldest-born and Intermediate Adult Males," *British Journal of Psychology* (1952), 43.

alone and will grow up accustomed to handling their anxieties in solitude.[7]

The significance of birth order has attracted a great deal of attention. Much has been written about it and psychologists have conducted a variety of experiments to check their theories. Recent experiments by Sampson in America indicate that first-born males, at least, are inclined to greater social conformity: they fall into line more readily when rewards are offered and are more susceptible to social pressures. (They also have a stronger need for achievement than later-borns.) First-born girls, on the other hand, showed a greater independence than later-borns.[8] It is not easy to reconcile these findings, particularly with regard to sex differences, with other research, although in a general sense they are in line with Schachter. But it seems reasonable to suggest that first-born boys at any rate may be successful in our school system not because they are individualistic, but because they are not: because they need the approval of adults and conform closely to the expectations of teachers.

"Favourable Parental Attitudes"

The importance of parental attitudes to a child's progress at school seems to be firmly established. Yet the concept of "favourable parental attitude" is perhaps one of the most ambiguous and misleading in the contemporary discussion of educational achievement. The measurement of this attitude has been crude in the extreme; and precisely what has been measured is open to very serious doubt. It would be very dangerous indeed to equate parental interest and concern with kindly, beneficent and understanding encouragement. The usual measures of parental interest might equally signify ruthless, unreasoning, inexorable and even quite unrealistic demands.

The most common and apparently objective measure of parental interest is the frequency of visits to school. Middle-class parents score high here, and working-class mothers higher than working-class fathers. But while the frequency of school visits undoubtedly provides some indication of the level of parental interest, it also measures the level of parents' social competence and assurance.

Other factors which have usually been taken into account are the age at which parents wish their children's education to end; and the type of school or institution of further education they wish them to attend. (One inquiry, for example, obtained favourable-unfavourable attitude scores according to (1) the frequency of parents' school visits, (2) their preference for selective secondary education, (3) the intention to keep the child at school until at least 16, and (4) their preference for further education after school.[9]) The longer the period of education envisaged and the more selective and academic

---

[7] *The Psychology of Affiliation* (1959).

[8] E. E. Sampson, "Birth Order, Need Achievement, and Conformity," *Journal of Abnormal and Social Psychology* (1962), 64.

[9] J. E. Floud *et al.*, op. cit., p. 93.

the type of institution preferred, the more favourable is parental attitude judged to be.

Attempts have been made to take into account more intangible aspects of parents' attitudes, but these are often difficult to incorporate into attitude scales. Teachers' judgements of parental interest have also been taken into account (by Douglas), and cultural interests have been estimated in the light of the Sunday newspapers they take, their membership of public libraries and cultural organizations. The emotional atmosphere of the home has been estimated, the degree of harmony prevailing, and the emotional security afforded the child. The level of material wellbeing in the home is easier to establish; and it has been shown (in Middlesbrough) that below a certain level, low material standards may nullify the advantages of favourable parental attitudes as conventionally judged by visits to the school and ambitions for the child.

There is no doubt that parents who visit the school often and wish their children to enjoy a selective and protracted education in general give a boost to their children's educational progress. At all social levels, and in socially contrasted areas, children tend to be more successful in the eleven plus examinations if they have parents who have discussed their future with the primary school teacher and would prefer them to stay at school till 18.[10] There are clear signs in recent research that parental interest (measured by similar crude means) is more important with children of borderline ability, and from working-class rather than middle-class homes.

This is the conclusion of Douglas's report on his national sample of primary school children. Children of borderline ability obtained 23 per cent more places in grammar schools than had been expected in the light of their measured ability, if their parents were educationally ambitious for them; but they gained 69 per cent fewer places if their parents were unambitious. Children with ambitious parents tended to be "over-achievers." When the school's academic standard, the material standards of the home, and parental ambitions were analysed for their relative importance, parental encouragement was shown to have the greatest effect.

"Parental encouragement" is not necessarily the same thing as humane consideration and kindly, understanding interest. It may be a ruthless and inflexible demand for achievement. When "family dynamics" have been investigated by clinical psychologists for their bearing on achievement, unambitious parents have obviously been of little help to their children; but neither have "normal" parents, setting reasonable and realistic goals. The most effective parents are, it is true, ambitious for their children; but it is not a particularly attractive characteristic, ruthless and demanding.

This is the picture that emerges from the research of Kent and Davis in Cambridgeshire, and is amply supported by inquiries in America. Kent and Davis investigated the relationship between "discipline in the home" and intellectual development among a sample of primary school children (as well as a group of juvenile offenders and children referred to a psychiatric outpatients' clinic). The homes of the children were investigated and classified as "normal", "unconcerned", "over-anxious" and "demanding."

[10] Ibid., p. 102.

"Normal" parents were tolerant, patient, but firm, making reasonable demands on the child, realistically related to his abilities, interests and needs. The unconcerned were indifferent to the child's progress, without ambition for his success, content if he kept out of trouble and made few demands upon them. But the effective home was the "demanding" home: the parents set high standards from an early age; they were ambitious for their child; they "reward infrequently and without generosity"; approval and affection are conditional upon achievement. But within the general framework of high demands and expectations the child is free to learn and good opportunities are afforded for him to do so. In the light of other research on achievement which is reviewed in the next section, it is perhaps the conjunction of demands and opportunity which is important.

Such homes were not confined to middle-class social levels. Whatever their social position, they tended more than other types of home to produce children of high ability. "One may argue therefore that the cause of the high development of verbal and academic abilities lies in their demanding discipline, and that the poor development of these abilities in the children of the unconcerned class is due to the lack of encouragement given them by their parents."[11]

There seem to be few rewards in our educational system (and perhaps in our society generally) for "normality" or even for humanity. The driving, demanding home, with exacting standards and expectations and remorseless pressure on the children, appears to be the "good home." The kindly, reasonable, understanding, tolerant and helpful home pays less handsome dividends. This may be why frequent moves, working mothers, and wives who have married beneath themselves are valuable ingredients in the good home: they are symptoms or causes of the striving and straining which seems so invaluable.

Research in America into the family background of able schoolchildren and university students lends support to the view that family relationships which are demanding and lacking in warmth are associated with high intellectual capacity. In their studies of adolescents who were of high intelligence but comparatively low in "creativity" on the one hand, and of others who were of rather lower intelligence but high in creativity on the other, Getzels and Jackson found that the former more often had mothers who were "vigilant", "critical" and "less accepting." Mothers of the children of high I.Q. both observed more about their children and observed a greater number of objectionable qualities. The mothers of the children who did best in tests of creativity apparently subjected their children to a less intensive and censorious scrutiny; and they were more at ease with themselves and with the world.[12] (We are given no information about fathers.)

American studies of university students are in general congruent with these findings. Very thorough investigations have been made of the academic performance, personality development, family background and subsequent careers of the women graduates of Vassar College. The early family life of

---

[11] N. Kent and D. R. Davis, "Discipline in the Home and Intellectual Development," *British Journal of Medical Psychology* (1957), 30.
[12] J. W. Getzels and P. W. Jackson, *Creativity and Intelligence* (1962).

"under-achievers" at college had been happy and secure. "Fathers are seen as having been competent, loving, lots of fun. . . . Mothers were warm, sociable, happy and accepting." Over-achievers, on the other hand, tended to have mothers with high social aspirations and fathers who were self-made men. "On the whole there is close conformity with strict parental demands."

Those graduates who achieved distinction in their subsequent careers (typically by middle life they had not married or had few children if they had) did well in their studies at Vassar. They had been lonely at college and "In their early life and adolescence they have experienced conflict arising from domineering and talented mothers, against whom there is considerable repressed hostility associated with strong guilt. As a group their early lives tended not to be free from upsetting events such as deaths, moves, economic crises and the like, nor were their childhoods outstandingly happy."[13]

A more impressionistic picture is given by Jackson and Marsden, in their study of "Marburton," of the home circumstances of successful grammar school pupils. Sixth-formers in "Marburton" came mainly from driving and ambitious homes with frustrated parents who belonged to the "sunken middle class" and fathers who were foremen without hope of rising to managerial rank. Some of the children, successful at the grammar school, in the end failed their degrees. For one girl this failure brought a great sense of release: "I decided then and there that I'd go and do what I wanted. I'd been doing what other people wanted for so long and now it was time that I did what I wanted. I went to the employment exchange and they offered me all kinds of academic things—but I decided definitely that I was going nursing."[14]

Kent and Davis found frequent moves of home closely related to the highly productive demanding discipline. "An especially large proportion of the children of the 'demanding' class had experienced three or more moves' compared with the normal class. Douglas found a similar situation: "When the average test performance of children of families which have never moved is compared with the performance of those in families that have moved, it is found that the former make lower average scores in the tests than the latter. . . ." But there were slight indications that the disadvantages of a stable home-background were less marked for pre-school children.

Investigations in an American university have isolated early geographical mobility as a common factor in the background of students of high ability who, when subjected to a battery of personality and attitude tests, undervalued themselves, felt insecure and lonely, and were strongly inclined towards guilt feelings and self-punishment. These able students had one significant early experience in common: geographical instability. "In all of their histories are accounts of moving from one town to another. One of the girls probably expressed the feelings of the group when she wrote in her autobiography, Several times I was dead sure that my whole life was being torn completely asunder. . . ." '[15]

[13] D. R. Brown, "Personality, College Environment and Academic Productivity" in Nevitt Sanford (ed.), *The American College* (1962), pp. 536–62.
[14] *Education and the Working Class* (1962), pp. 151–2.
[15] E. Paul Torrance, "Personality Dynamics of Under-self-evaluation among Intellectually Gifted Freshmen" in E. P. Torrance (ed.), *Talent and Education* (1960).

Of course such a history of family instability is not a necessary condition of academic excellence. And it would be a mistake to ascribe the intellectual development associated with it to the stimulus of changing environments. The migrant home is often the striving home, and it is the attitudes of migrant parents rather than the migration itself which probably accounts for these findings. The value to working-class children of a mother who has "married down"[16] perhaps has a similar explanation: she strives to make up for her social decline through the achievements of her children.

The fact that mothers go to work is also more commonly a symptom of parental striving and ambition than of selfishness and negligence, and for this reason assists rather than impedes the child's educational progress. During research in Aberdeen, Frazer found no evidence that children were handicapped at the secondary stage by having a mother at work: "if there is any difference at all, it appears to be very slightly in favour of the children whose mothers go out to work, especially in the middle ranges of intelligence."[17]

In America there is more positive evidence that working mothers may foster educational ambitions and promote higher attainment. The greater tendency for urban as opposed to rural wives to take up paid employment outside the home has been held to account for the backwardness of rural children. "A mother who works at least part time in a small town or larger city is likely to be exposed to the fact that a college education is required for most high status jobs, whereas the mother who is submerged in the home-making problems of a farm family is unlikely to be impressed with this reality."[18]

Permission and Punishment

One of the most interesting but as yet rather inconclusive ways of examining the influence of family background has been to compare social groups which differ significantly in their general level of occupational and educational achievement. Urban children are generally superior to rural children; middle-class children to working-class children; the children of Jewish immigrants to the United States to Italian immigrants. Can broad differences in attainment between these groups (of course there is a great deal of overlap too) find an explanation in differences in child-care practices and family dynamics?

The general tendency for middle-class children to do better in the school system in both England and America has been attributed not only to differences in parental encouragement but to social-class differences in early child-rearing practices. The training of middle-class infants, it is argued, makes them particularly able to succeed later on in scholastic pursuits and perhaps in the activities involved in professional work. Working-class children of good intelligence may be defective in other attributes which ensure academic success. Whatever the long term consequences of social-class differences in infant

[16] J. E. Floud *et al.*, op. cit., p. 88.
[17] E. Frazer, *Home Environment and the School* (1959), p. 66.
[18] G. H. Elder, "Achievement Orientations of Rural Youth," *Sociology of Education* (1963), 37.

care, there can be no doubt that these differences are still with us. As the Newsons observe after their recent exhaustive investigations in Nottingham: "The classless society in Britain is still a long way off. Men may be born equal; but, within its first month in the world, the baby will be adapting to a climate of experience that varies according to its family's social class."[19]

Scholastically able people are not only intelligent, they also tend to be conscientious, capable of long-term effort and planning, able to forgo many immediate satisfactions for more distant gains. Often, too, they are orderly, careful, meticulous, and punctual. Some or all of these attributes have been ascribed to the stricter methods of infant care which are perhaps characteristically middle-class: early and severe toilet training; early punishment of aggression; feeding by rigid schedule, and early weaning; early independence training; and control through "love-oriented" techniques of discipline. It has also been claimed that middle-class upbringing induces "adaptive, socialized anxiety" which deters the child from incurring the disapproval of his parents and teachers.[20] Working-class upbringing, though not unproductive of anxieties too, was supposed to be more permissive and indulgent, less likely to produce far-sighted, controlled and conscientious personalities.

These views are currently under heavy fire. The relevance of early toilet training to a controlled and orderly adult personality has been seriously questioned.[21] Hallworth has shown that the academically successful are not generally more anxious, at least at the secondary school stage, than the less academically gifted.[22] But most startling of all has been the apparent demonstration both in England and America that the middle classes are more permissive and less punitive in their child-care practices than the working classes. These claims need very careful scrutiny for the limits of their validity.

Recent research with mothers in Devonshire seemed to show that, with reference to 5-year-old children, "In England, as in the U.S.A., middle-class mothers are less punitive than working-class mothers," and that "English middle-class mothers are also like American middle-class mothers in being more permissive of aggressive behaviour."[23] And indeed there seems little doubt that with regard to "immodesty" and aggression the middle-class mother of today is more permissive than twenty or thirty years ago. She has been lectured by the psychologists, and she has taken heed. This was clear too in the Newsons' study of mothers of one-year-old babies in Nottingham. Middle-class mothers breast-fed their babies more often than working-class mothers, and were no less inclined than the latter to "demand feeding." They checked the child's inclination to play with its genitals less often than working-class mothers, and less often smacked the child for "naughtiness."

[19] J. and E. Newson, op. cit., p. 217.
[20] Allison Davis, *Social Influence upon Learning* (1948).
[21] I. L. Child, "Socialization" in Gardner Lindzey (ed.), *Handbook of Social Psychology* (1954), vol. 2.
[22] H. J. Hallworth, "Anxiety in Secondary Modern and Grammar School Children," *British Journal of Educational Psychology* (1961), 31.
[23] R. Lynn and I. E. Gordon, "Maternal Attitudes to Child Socialization: Some Social and National Differences," *British Journal of Social and Clinical Psychology* (1962), I.

But all this does not add up to a revolution in middle-class child-care methods to an unprecedented general permissiveness. Over many areas of behaviour, and in essence, middle-class child training remains ruthless. The Newsons found that in some respects middle-class mothers had high and inflexible expectations of their children: toilet training began earlier and was less casual; they were less inclined to soothe the baby to sleep ("There seems to be a strong middle-class feeling that babies should learn early to go to sleep at a 'reasonable' hour without help and without making a fuss"); and while they are now much given to breast feeding, the dummy ("secondary oral gratification") finds little approval.

The working class seems to be less permissive principally in the sense that it is more inclined to resort to physical punishment. Middle-class discipline is more subtle, unflinching and effective; working-class discipline is simply more desperate.

The most authoritative review of recent research in this field concluded that "the most consistent finding . . . is the more frequent use of physical punishment by working-class parents. The middle class, in contrast, resort to reasoning, isolation, and . . . "love-oriented" discipline techniques." "Yet . . . it would be a mistake to conclude that the middle-class parent is exerting less pressure on his children." "Though more tolerant of expressed impulses and desires, the middle-class parent . . . has higher expectations for the child. The middle-class youngster is expected to take care of himself earlier, to accept responsibilities about the home, and—above all—to progress further at school."[24]

The "love-oriented" technique of discipline would be repugnant to many working-class parents; for in essence it is a tacit bargain between child and parents, love and affection given in return for good behaviour, withdrawn for misdeeds. Love is offered on strictly limited, contract terms. This appears from the cross-cultural surveys of anthropologists to be the most effective way of producing conscientious people prone to high guilt feelings and self-blame[25]—the very stuff of high academic promise.

Within the fringe of middle-class permissiveness exists a hard core of inflexible demand. Over many areas of behaviour there is simply no question that things should be otherwise than parents decree or just quietly, tacitly assume. This applies not least to the age of school leaving and the type of school attended. When the author investigated the attitudes to education of parents in Leicester in 1960, working-class parents were inclined to say with regard to the choice of secondary school: "Wherever he'll be happy." Middle-class parents were quite clear on this issue, there was really no choice—the grammar school (or in some cases a public school) was the obvious place. "Happiness" was an irrelevance.[26]

[24] U. Bronfenbrenner, "Socialization and Social Class through Time and Space" in E. E. Maccoby, T. M. Newcomb and L. Hartley (eds.), *Readings in Social Psychology* (1958).
[25] J. W. M. Whiting and I. L. Child, *Child Training and Personality* (1953).
[26] F. Musgrove, "Parents' Expectations of the Junior School," *Sociological Review* (1961), 9.

Need-Achievement

The will to achieve—indeed the need to achieve—has its roots in family circumstances. Of particular importance are the child's relationships with its parents. If these are close, warm, and affectionate, he is likely to be handicapped for life.

Moralists in the past, Freudian psychologists today, and our own common sense, suggest that the young boy needs an adequate example and model in his father. The latter should be an effective human being with whom the boy can "identify." The evidence seems to be—in spite of Betty Spinley's *Deprived and the Privileged* and Madeline Kerr's *People of Ship Street*—that the moralists, Freudian psychologists, and common sense are wrong. The boy's long term interests are best served by an inadequate and feckless (if "demanding") father.

Family relationships ("interaction patterns") have only quite recently been subjected to direct study and analysis for their bearing on children's development and achievement. There has long been a great deal of clinical evidence on family life, but this is of an indirect nature, drawn from patients' recollections of the often quite distant past. Of particular interest have been attempts to measure the strength of an individual's need for achievement (nAch) and to relate it to his family background. These attempts have not yet given a consistent and reliable picture and a great deal more work remains to be done. There is the further complication that high "need-achievement" may not necessarily, for a wide variety of reasons, lead to actual achievement, at least in any specific field of endeavour.

Need-achievement has been measured by projective tests. Subjects write stories about pictures which are shown to them, and the stories are scored for their achievement imagery. The subjects, who have been aroused and put on their mettle by impressing on them the significance of the tests as indicators of their organizational abilities, will put their own hopes for success and fears of failure into their stories. But of course people hope for different kinds of success; and perhaps success for women is more typically in terms of getting on well with people, while for men it is getting on well in a career. Some individuals with high need-achievement scores may be indifferent to scholastic success, but hope for it in the sphere of athletics or the conquest of women. As one American investigator has pointed out: "Motives have both force and direction. Present measures of need-achievement consider only the former while neglecting the latter."[27] It is perhaps for this reason that general need-achievement scores have not been shown to relate very closely to success or failure at school.

Families of Jewish and Italian immigrants in America have been closely studied in an attempt to discover why children of the former tend to succeed at school and in their subsequent careers while children of the latter in general make poor progress.[28] It has been supposed that the subordination of the

[27] M. C. Shaw, "Need Achievement Scales as Predictors of Academic Success," *Journal of Educational Psychology* (1961).
[28] F. L. Strodtbeck, "Family Interaction, Values and Achievements" in D. C. McClelland *et al., Talent and Society* (1958).

Italian child to the interests of the family might induce a sense of resignation and undermine the will to achieve. But Italian and Jewish fathers of similar occupational standing did not differ in the extent to which they expected children to be tied to their families. The investigators suggested—although the evidence is not really very firm—that very capable fathers produce a sense of helplessness in their sons, who feel they can never be masters of their own fate.

When family interaction processes were analysed, Italian fathers were found to give more support to their sons than Jewish fathers to theirs. The helpfulness of fathers seemed at best a mixed blessing: the fact that help is necessary tends to underline or suggest the son's incompetence. In line with this is the quite firm finding among American university students that people with high need-achievement scores perceive their parents as unfriendly and unhelpful. (Much may depend on the age of the person who is offered help. American high school pupils who are high in need-achievement do *not* see their parents as unhelpful.) [29]

The friendliness or unfriendliness of parents to their children of whatever age, their authoritarian or non-authoritarian attitudes, are perhaps an irrelevance. What matters is the independence they accord. The unhelpful parents, the non-authoritarian parent, the negligent parent, the ineffectual parent—all tend to be alike in this respect, that for no doubt quite different reasons they leave their children alone. But it is perhaps a help if, while leaving them alone, they also expect them in a general sense to do well.

Farmers in America make considerable demands on their children. Their expectations are detailed and specific; their control and guidance close. Perhaps for this reason farm families produce comparatively few successful children for non-farming careers. Farm boys have heavy demands made upon them for various kinds of achievement at a very early age; but the tasks are quite specific. In caring for livestock, milking and the like, they may have close guidance, help and instruction; but they have no freedom to explore, to shape their lives in their own way, to experiment with some degree of freedom in their growth towards independence.[30] Theirs is the opposite of the "negative education" which Rousseau recommended before puberty. They need a good dose of neglect. As they then discovered for themselves a mastery of problematic situations, the confidence and will for achievement might be born.

To be left alone is perhaps one of the most urgent needs of children in a child- and home-centred society. (Studies of the careers of successful American scientists and scholars indicate that at some stage of their education their teachers have had enough sense to leave them alone. They have often suffered prolonged "neglect," but in a general context of high expectation.) It is not only the kindly and tolerant parent who might, as a conscious decision, grant a child such freedom. "The contrast should not be thought of too simply in terms of the autocratic-democratic dimensions, currently so popular in psychological literature."[31] The important thing is that, for whatever reason, there is scope for "the independent development of the individual."

[29] D. C. McClelland *et al.*, *The Achievement Motive* (1953), p. 283.
[30] G. H. Elder, "Achievement Orientations and Career Patterns of Rural Youth," loc. cit.
[31] D. C. McClelland *et al.*, op. cit., p. 329.

This may account for the high achievement, both scholastically and in professional careers, of men whose family relationships in youth were anything but warm and supportive. The men who have risen through education and their own efforts to the top of American business life perceive their early relationships with their fathers as at best detached, reserved, cool.[32] Fathers were often weak, inadequate and unreliable (although mothers were often strong and competent).

Perhaps such a childhood was a good preparation for the somewhat impersonal relationships of modern large-scale bureaucracy. The essential characteristic of these men in adult life was their independence. Similar rather detached and vague relationships with their parents seem to characterize the childhood of men who succeed in the physical sciences. Often in childhood they have had the experience of bereavement. Eminent social scientists have usually had a more stormy involvement with their parents, though scarcely more satisfactory from the point of view of psychology, humanity or common sense.[33] Neither humanity nor common sense seems to pay the highest dividends in the educational system and social order which we have devised.

A Question of Class

It is possible that our notion of the "good home" needs to be redefined, or at least less naïvely defined. But there can be no doubt about the continuing influence of home background on educational and vocational advancement. In our contemporary democracy the influence of birth remains great and shows signs of increasing. Modern sociology and psychology are invoked to justify and promote enhanced parental power. Social science is used to support a position which social philosophy has discredited.

In less crude and direct ways than formerly, but no less effectively, parents have a powerful influence on the life-chances of their children. Their influence is particularly great in the intermediate ranges of ability, among border-line cases for selection and promotion. The outstandingly able will often make their own way whatever their family circumstances; and the outstandingly dull will have difficulty whatever backing they receive. But the great majority are neither outstandingly able nor dull; for them parents are often decisive.

The relationship between educational opportunity and attainment and "social class" has been demonstrated often enough during the past decade. When middle-class children make use of the state system, they tend to get more grammar school places in proportion to their numbers than working-class children, to stay longer when they get to the grammar school, to be more involved in its extra-curricular activities, to have better examination results,

---

[32] W. L. Warner and J. C. Abegglen, *Big Business Leaders in America* (1955), pp. 59 ff.
[33] Anne Roe, "A Psychological Study of Eminent Psychologists and Anthropologists, and a Comparison with Biological and Physical Scientists," *Psychological Monographs* (1953), 67.

to pass more often into the sixth form, and still more often to the university. Indeed, the further through the system we look, the more are children from white-collar and professional homes "over-represented" in our grammar schools and institutions of higher learning.

There is no doubt that the children of skilled manual workers have benefited greatly from the "scholarship system," particularly since 1944; but in the Ministry of Education's inquiry into early leaving in the nineteen-fifties they were somewhat under-represented in the grammar school intake at twelve, and more markedly under-represented in the sixth-form entry. (The children of skilled workers were 51 per cent of all children, 43.7 per cent of the grammar school entry at twelve, 37 per cent of the sixth-form entry. In contrast children of professional and managerial families were 15 per cent of all children, 25 per cent of the grammar school intake, 43.7 per cent of those entering the sixth form. Children of unskilled labourers were strikingly under-represented in the sixth form: they were only 1.5 per cent of the entry, but constituted 12 per cent of the age group.)

Although the general tendency is for children from the homes of manual labourers to deteriorate even when they enter the grammar schools, some do very well and exceed their initial promise. The Ministry's inquiry found that 12 per cent of these children who began in bottom streams had risen to top streams over five years. Although these children are, in general, a bad risk, it is a risk that must be taken: there is no way of telling which individuals will in fact do better than expected, and which will do worse.

The influence of family background operates today in more subtle ways than in the past—there is undoubtedly far less flagrant nepotism and patronage; but it is still very pervasive. The open competitive examination is the great social invention of the past century which has done most to eliminate it; and those who would abolish such examinations must face the certainty that the advantages of birth and family circumstances would be greatly enhanced.

With all its limitations and unfortunate side-effects, the open competitive examination for entrance into schools, universities and the public services is the main safeguard of the interests of people of humble origins, and our main guarantee of a measure of social justice. Only the lottery would remove altogether the advantages and disadvantages of birth. The open competitive examination remains the most effective instrument we have yet devised for the elimination of parents.

But they remain astonishingly potent. This is reflected in the high degree of self-recruitment still to be found in the major professions—and, indeed, in humbler employment, such as dockwork, where there may be special encouragement and opportunity for sons to follow in their fathers' footsteps. The sons of lawyers, doctors, parsons and teachers themselves become lawyers, doctors, parsons and teachers to a quite remarkable degree. In some professions this tendency to follow in father's footsteps has actually increased in a quite dramatic manner over the past century.

Only 6 per cent of Cambridge graduates who become teachers in the second half of the nineteenth century were the sons of teachers; in 1937–8, 14 per cent were teachers' sons. At both dates about a third of those who became doctors or parsons were the sons of doctors or parsons. Fifteen per cent of those entering law at the earlier date had lawyer fathers; in 1937–8, 26 per cent had lawyer fathers.[34] If we take a longer time span, over some two hundred years, the most remarkable change among Cambridge graduates is the extent to which the Church has become self-recruiting. In the eighteenth century the extent to which the sons of parsons became parsons barely exceeded what might happen by chance; by the nineteen-thirties they became parsons five times the chance expectation.[35]

Even in the academic world of twentieth-century Cambridge, where examinations and other objective tests of merit might be expected to have eliminated family influence, it is still a marked advantage in securing senior, or even junior, appointments to be a Macaulay, a Butler, a Trevelyan, a Huxley, or a member of the Wedgwood-Darwin connection, for example. The Provost of King's College, Cambridge, has analysed these intricate family alliances and has shown how once again, even at this level, the importance of having chosen the right father comes out at the borderline of ability (a very high borderline, of course, in this particular case).

> Clearly certain families produce a disproportionately large number of eminent men and women. But equally clearly the study shows that men of natural but not outstanding ability can reach the front ranks of science and scholarship and the foremost positions in the cultural hierarchy of the country if they have been bred to a tradition of intellectual achievement and have been taught to turn their environment to account. Schools and universities can so train young men, but such a training has a far stronger command over the personality when it is transmitted through a family tradition.[36]

It is the task of schools in the second half of the twentieth century to achieve a similar command over the personalities entrusted to them even when the family has not done more than half their job for them.

[34] R. K. Kelsall, "Self-recruitment in Four Professions" in D. V. Glass, op. cit.
[35] C. A. Anderson and M. Schnaper, *School and Society in England* (1952), Tables 2 and 6.
[36] Noel Annan, "The Intellectual Aristocracy" in J. H. Plumb (ed.), *Studies in Social History* (1955).

MATERNAL EMPLOYMENT
AND THE ADOLESCENT*

ELIZABETH DOUVAN

For forty years or more the working mother has walked in our world like a lady in a fun house of mirrors, watching one or another of her features now exaggerated, now diminished, nearly always distorted. Even now, when it is clear that maternal employment is a permanent feature of our world, popular discourse about the issue carries the heady tone of a good fight. On a popular level, this kind of involvement is not to be decried. But passion serves poorly as the muse of science, and unfortunately in the past research has on occasion been all too close to the heat of debate.

More recently, as our editors indicate, social scientists have returned to the problem in a more dispassionate mood, raising more sophisticated, more disinterested questions about the impact of maternal employment on family life or child development in various settings, under various conditions. We seem at last on the way to a clarification of the issue.

We are not yet very far on the way, however. And it is this fact that justifies including the present chapter in a book on the issue. The data on which the chapter is based were not originally gathered for a systematic analysis of maternal employment. They suffer the usual limitation of such data: the crucial measure is unrefined because the variable it seeks to measure was not a central concept in the design of the study. Nonetheless, where knowledge is scarce, even fragments may be useful.

The Data

Our data are seriously limited in that we gathered no information (from adolescent subjects) about the length of time the mothers worked. We asked only whether the mother was currently employed and whether she worked full- or part-time. This obviously is a crucial problem, one which bars us from critical tests of many aspects of the theory of maternal employment. Nonetheless, we can report some interesting findings about the relationship between the mother's employment and adolescent development, and can suggest a theoretical scheme to account for the findings, one which knits them into a coherent pattern.

Our data come from two large national sample interview studies of

* Reprinted from Elizabeth Douvan, "Employment and the Adolescent," in F. Ivan Nye and Lois W. Hoffman (eds.), The Employed Mother in America (Chicago: Rand McNally), 1963, pp. 142–164 by permission of the publisher.

adolescent boys and girls. The studies, conducted at the Survey Research Center of the University of Michigan, were sponsored by the Boy Scouts of America and the Girl Scouts of the U.S.A.

Respondents were selected in a multi-stage probability sampling (1) and represent school children of eleven through eighteen years for the girl sample and of fourteen through sixteen for boys. Each subject was interviewed at his school by a member of the Center's field staff; interviews followed a fixed schedule and lasted from one to four hours. For details about the studies and copies of the complete questionnaire readers may refer to the basic reports (3, 4).

Preliminary Findings

The analysis we report is limited to youngsters from intact families in which the father is employed. Two preliminary findings about the distribution of working mothers in major population groups should be stated at the outset since they affect the validity of all of our interpretations. We do not, to begin with, find any consistent or striking relationship between the social class position of the family (gauged by father's occupation) and the likelihood that the mother works outside the home. Except in farm families, where only about 15 per cent of all the mothers work, the proportion ranges between 32 and 45 per cent for all status groups in both of our samples.[1]

The second finding concerns the relationship between mother's employment and the age of the child, and it also is a negative finding: That is, there is no relationship between the age of the child and the likelihood that his mother works outside the home. We know that there is a significant association between these variables in studies of younger children, but apparently within the adolescent range it breaks down.[2]

[1] In the girls' sample, the range is 33 to 41 per cent, and the direction of difference is not the same as we move down the ladder of skills represented by the father's occupation. So the figures are: 33 per cent for the wives of professionals and business executives; 41 per cent among wives of white-collar, sales, and clerical workers; 38 per cent for the skilled and semi-skilled blue-collar class; and 41 per cent in the families whose heads are unskilled workers. In the boys' sample, we find the highest proportion of working mothers in the professional class (45 per cent), and the lowest proportion outside the farm group in the skilled and semi-skilled blue-collar group (32 per cent). All other status groups are practically identical in the proportions of working and non-working mothers (38 per cent of wives of business executives, 40 per cent in the white-collar group, and 38 per cent in the unskilled blue-collar group). The largest difference in the analysis—between the professional and skilled worker groups in the boys' sample—is in the direction opposite from that one would predict on the basis of economic necessity.

[2] Since the entry of mothers into the labor market has been shown to have multiple sources—economic necessity and the woman's desire to absorb increasing leisure are among the more critical factors—one might expect the child's age to have a greater effect in higher social classes where, presumably, the mother has a choice between working and not working and where simple economic pressure is not so decisive a force. When we analyze maternal employment in relation to the child's age in the higher social strata, however, we again find no relationship.

Most women probably make the commitment to return to work when the child enters school. By the time the child is eleven the mother is no longer delaying her return because of the child's age. A woman may delay the decision beyond this point for other reasons—including the fact that she has other younger children—but these delays will not bear any significant relationship to the age of our subjects.

These two findings reduce the need to exercise special controls in the analysis of the mother's employment. Yet we were interested in making separate analyses for the two major social classes on the grounds that the meaning of maternal employment must be quite different when the general economic position of the family is good or poor. We shall discuss the results of this controlled analysis after a description of our basic findings. We shall describe the results from the study of girls first, since girls seem most crucially affected by the mother's employment.

Findings: Adolescent Activities and Employment

On the basis of previous research and our own analysis of adolescent activity patterns, we developed certain conceptions about the meaning of full-time and part-time maternal employment—its impact on family life, the motivational factors that underlie the mother's work, and the significance of these factors for performance of the maternal role, particularly in relation to adolescent children. We looked at data on adolescent development and family life for tests of some of these derivations.

The analysis of adolescent activities that led to our formulations about full-time and part-time maternal employment can be summarized briefly.[3] Both groups of working-mother daughters are active in some sense—daughters of non-working mothers are never the most active on any index in our study —but the spheres of their activity are quite different. The single area they share—and in which they contrast with girls whose mothers do not work—is household responsibility: the proportion of girls who carry major responsibilities at home is larger where the mother works either full-time (22 per cent) or part-time (17 per cent) than in homes where the mother is not employed (5 per cent). Girls whose mothers do not work most often report that they do token jobs or none at all (59 per cent, compared to 43 per cent of girls whose mothers work part-time and 42 per cent of girls whose mothers work full-time).

Daughters of women who are employed full-time most often work hard at home, carry some kind of paying job, and date actively; in particular, they go steady more often than other girls at each age level. On the other hand, they report very few of the kinds of engagements we conventionally think of as "healthful leisure activities." They do not as commonly belong to clubs or other organized social groups, nor do they have as many group attachments as girls whose mothers work part-time or not at all. They have tried significantly fewer of the leisure activities suggested in a fixed list (compared to

[3] The findings from this analysis are summarized in Table 1.

TABLE 1. MATERNAL EMPLOYMENT RELATED TO ACTIVITIES OF ADOLESCENT GIRLS

Adolescent Activity	Maternal Employment		
	Full-time (n = 235)	Part-time (n = 158)	None (n = 769)
		Per Cent	
Household Responsibility			
Major	22	17	5
Moderate	30	36	30
Light or none	42	43	59
Work			
Holds a part-time job	81	74	70
Dating			
At age 13 or under			
Goes steady	5	1	—
Dates	17	22	14
Doesn't date	78	77	86
At age 14 to 16			
Goes steady	18	10	12
Dates	54	64	55
Doesn't date	26	26	32
At age 17 or 18			
Goes steady	45	38	27
Dates	50	61	65
Doesn't date	5	—	8
Group Membership			
None	30	16	25
Belongs to 1 or 2 groups	48	55	52
Belongs to 3 or more groups	21	29	23
Leisure Activities			
Low	27	14	14
Medium	48	37	47
High	35	49	39
Suggest Other Activities			
Yes	27	42	34
No	72	57	66
Leisure Reading			
None	16	4	10
Spend Leisure			
Alone	12	2	6
With friend(s)	46	41	42
With family	38	52	47

Note: Data in this and subsequent tables apply only to non-farm subjects. However, a separate analysis of farm subjects produced similar results where numbers were large enough to permit any reliable analysis.
— Less than half of 1 per cent.

girls in the other two groups), and they have less interest in trying new sports, games, or hobbies. Fewer of these girls report any leisure reading. One gains the impression that the daughters of women who hold full-time jobs are active girls, but that their activity has a serious character. They work hard and their social life consists primarily of dating. They begin dating earlier than girls whose mothers are at home part- or full-time, and they go steady earlier and more commonly than other girls. Even in leisure they seem bent on early assumption of adult-like patterns.

Daughters of women who work part-time are outstandingly active girls, no matter what measure we employ. They are almost as responsible for home tasks as the girls whose mothers work full-time, and they often have jobs outside the home—not, again, as frequently as the full-time group, but more than girls whose mothers do not work. Practically all girls in this group have some formal group affiliation, and they belong to a larger number of clubs and organizations than girls in the other two categories. They date early and actively; they date as much as girls whose mothers work full-time, but they do *not* as often go steady. At each age level girls in the part-time group are less likely to go steady than are girls in the full-time category. Only after sixteen do they approach the full-time group in this regard.

The part-time group also has the largest number of specific leisure activities. They are enthusiastic about sports, games, and hobbies already experienced (compared to girls in either of the other categories), and they suggest a greater number of other activities they would like to try. In short, the daughters of women who work part-time are active in every sphere. They are different from the girls whose mothers work full-time in that they have a broader range of social and leisure activities.

One other difference among our groups in the area of leisure commitment: girls whose mothers work full-time spend relatively little leisure time with the family. They, more often than other girls, spend time "alone," and they share leisure activities with a friend more often than with family members. Girls from families in which the mother works part-time most often report that they spend their leisure with their families—more, even, than do the girls whose mothers do not work. Girls in the non-working-mother group fall between the other two groups on the distribution of time spent with family and with friends.

From their daughters' activities, we can infer something about the mothers who work full-time: they do not apparently spend much time with their daughters or take a highly active role in promoting and supervising a varied program of leisure activities for their children. The out-of-school activities which their girls most often report—part-time jobs and dating—do not make as many demands on parents as some other activities. They require no special parent involvement—as a child's group memberships often do—and they require no special facilities or equipment as many leisure sports and hobbies do. Both part-time working and dating can be carried on outside the parents' sphere. We may have in the daughters of full-time working women a precocious separation of the child from the family. Their early and frequent steady dating and the fact that they spend little time with the family suggest that they have shifted some major portion of their emotional involvement away from the home. One might suggest further that they form these extra-family involvements in order to supply emotional needs which have not been met at home, perhaps because their mothers are over-extended in their own commitments outside the home. In short, we thought that a pattern of neglect might mark the families of women who carry full-time jobs.

PART-TIME GROUP

The activities of girls whose mothers work part-time suggest quite a different family pattern. Specifically we get the impression of active parents who participate energetically in the child's life. They spend a good deal of time with their children—according to girls' reports—and their children's pattern of leisure engagement is one which implies parent involvement.

The fact that a mother works part-time in itself implies certain things about her psychological make-up—more, it seems, than can be inferred from a full-time job commitment. Economic factors do not, we suspect, contribute as simply or forcefully to the decision to work in the case of part-time work. Very likely all women who look for employment are motivated by economic desires of some order—either they must supplement the husband's income to make ends meet at all, or they choose to work in order to increase the family's level of living and enlarge the number of luxuries the family can enjoy. We suspect that women who work part-time are less often directed by economic interests of a bare subsistence kind. Since full-time jobs are generally easier to find than part-time, we assign relatively greater weight to personal motivation as a determinant of this choice, and assume that the women themselves limit their work commitment. We suggest that these are women who, while they want to contribute to the family's economic well-being, are at the same time bound by a sense of responsibility to reserve their major emotional investment for direct care of the family.

This group may also include a relatively large proportion of women who seek in work some measure of personal fulfillment. Again, assuming that they are less economically pressed, and considering that it takes a degree of initiative to find part-time jobs, we might expect these women to be active and energetic, the kind of women who need some individual fulfillment beyond that provided in the roles of wife-homemaker and mother.

If these speculations are correct—and the high energy level of mothers in this group gains some support from the data on girls' activities—we might expect the part-time working mother to feel split loyalties and to have a rather complex personal integration based on a high level of energy and on a personal goal system in which one seeks challenges in the environment and takes pleasure in mastering them.

Women of this type would be similar to the "guilt motivated" working mothers that Lois Hoffman has described in her study of younger children; these are women who enjoy their outside jobs and feel some measure of guilt because they choose to spend part of their time away from the family in a personally gratifying activity. To reduce the guilt over what they conceive to be a self-indulgence, women of this type show a pattern of overprotective concern for their children, tend to demand less from them and to provide few opportunities for the child to learn through doing or meeting challenges unaided; they tend, in other words, to supply the child's needs too readily and completely through their own activity. Their children show the effects of maternal overprotection in dependency and an impaired capacity for individual problem-solving.

Our adolescent girls whose mothers work part-time do not look over-protected. They are highly active youngsters. Their activities are too many and too varied to permit any conclusion except that they have a great deal of initiative and responsibility. Yet for several reasons we cling to the view that the part-time working mother is like Hoffman's guilt-motivated mother at least in her high activity level, her strong sense of responsibility, and in the fact that she works primarily because she wants to work and enjoys the work role. We could explain the difference in effects on the child—between our subjects and Hoffman's—largely on the basis of the age difference in the two groups. Many of our working mothers may have returned to work only when their children approached adolescence. Even women who work while their children are young may feel less guilt as the children gain maturity and self-sufficiency, so that by the time their children reach adolescence, most working mothers may be more realistic and less selfless in their expectations *vis à vis* the child. The active woman who overprotects a younger child may become a model of activity for the older one.

The girls in our sample whose mothers work part-time certainly seem to be using some high energy model. From the fact that they spend a good deal of time with their families, and from the parent-involving activities they engage in, we ventured the not very radical speculation that the mother is the model they use. If this is the case, and if modeling is the process involved, we would expect these girls to be independent and responsible as well as energetic.

Our data generally support these speculations about the girls whose mothers work part-time. They are unusually developed in the area of autonomy. They show an independence of thought and values generally rare among girls, and their autonomy is apparently permitted and encouraged by the parents. Altogether this group can be said to show a pattern of development more common to boys than to girls in our culture (Table 2).

Their independence shows itself in many forms. For one, they have more open disagreements with their parents than girls in either of the other groups; they name more disagreements in answer to the general question, and in each of the specific areas probed—clothes, dating, hours, driving, friends, ideas—this group is consistently lowest in the proportion who say that the particular issue is not a source of disagreement between them and their parents. They are particularly likely—compared to the girls whose mothers work full-time or not at all—to say they disagree with their parents about ideas. In a series of picture-story questions, girls in this group think the heroine would question a parental restriction more than other girls do. In all, we get a picture of considerable verbal discussion and argument in the home. And this pattern is apparently accepted and stimulated by the parents: according to girls' reports, parents of this group frequently expect their daughters to be self-reliant and independent at the same time that they stress good manners and ladylike deportment. They allow their daughters a share in rule-making more often than other parents, at the same time that they maintain a clear and

TABLE 2.   MATERNAL EMPLOYMENT RELATED TO FEATURES OF ADOLESCENT
          DEVELOPMENT AND FAMILY LIFE

	Maternal Employment		
Item	*Full-time* (N = 235)	*Part-time* (N = 158)	*None* (N = 769)
		Per Cent	
Disagreement with Parents			
Reports no disagreement	27	11	21
Disagreement with Parents			
on Issues			
Dating	26	35	30
Lipstick	16	21	20
Clothing	46	52	44
Cars, driving	30	37	35
Friends	40	44	35
Ideas	22	41	29
Index of Disagreement			
High (3 or more issues)	24	39	28
Response to Parents'			
Restriction (Projective)			
Questions restriction	2	13	8
Parents' Expectations of R			
Self-reliance	12	17	3
Good manners	48	59	50
Obedience, respect for authority	25	23	33
Part in Rule-Making			
R shares in rule-making	61	68	53
Parents' Strictness			
(Projective)			
Strict	16	15	15
Strict but reasonable	16	27	20
Lenient	58	46	52
Very lenient	8	9	11
Adult Ideal			
Mother	42	43	31
Father	1	6	—
All in-family choices	67	53	55
Intimacy of Friendship			
Can be as close as family tie	34	51	44
Cannot be as close as family tie	41	33	37
Response to Lonely Mother			
Return home	49	36	38
Choice of Confidante			
Mother	51	49	37
Friend	22	31	33
No one	12	3	5
Friendship Development Index			
High	10	27	18
Low	23	5	12

TABLE 2. (Cont.)   MATERNAL EMPLOYMENT RELATED TO FEATURES OF ADO-
LESCENT DEVELOPMENT AND FAMILY LIFE

	Maternal Employment		
Item	Full-time (N = 235)	Part-time (N = 158)	None (N = 769)
		Per Cent	
Expectations about Friendship			
Stress mutuality, relationship	22	38	33
Index of Traditional Femininity			
High	19	15	27
Low	23	26	18
Job Aspirations			
Choice of traditional masculine job	4	12	7
Mobility Aspirations			
Upward mobile	20	28	16
Index of Internalization			
High	21	34	23
Low	24	15	28
Response to Peer Pressure to Break Promise to Parents			
Resists pressure, sense of trust	16	28	13
Tell Parents of Misdeed			
Yes	45	58	40
Characteristics of Future Husband			
Ego skills	37	40	31
Family attitudes	24	37	27
Nature of Punishment			
Physical	13	9	12
Deprivational	69	69	65
Psychological	17	20	21
Attitude toward Authority			
Relies heavily on adults	30	33	40
Relies moderately on adults	59	47	49
Tends to reject adult authority	6	16	5

strong personal authority. The girls in this group picture parents as "strict and reasonable" in their exercise of authority more than girls in the other groups. They less often see their parents as lenient.

Another fact also leads to the conclusion that their self-assertion is encouraged: although these girls argue and assert themselves with the parents, they apparently have close and happy relationships with them. They spend a good deal of time with their families, we recall, and they show both love and respect for the parents. Girls in this group very often choose their own mothers as an adult ideal. Both groups of girls who have working mothers choose the mother more often than do daughters of non-working women, but in the part-time group this looks less like a dependency sign than in the full-time group. These girls do *not* choose other relatives very often—their choices are not narrowly restricted to the family group. And they show other signs of independence from the family: they think a friend can be as close as a relative more than girls in either of the other groups, and they are least likely of any group to say (in response to a projective question) that a girl should leave a good job to return home to her lonely mother. They try most often to work out some alternative solution to this problem. In light of their general auton-omy—in these instances and in the apparent ease with which they disagree with their parents—we take the choice of the mother as a model to indicate uncomplicated respect and affection.

Two other series of findings fill out our picture of girls with part-time working mothers. They are, in the first place, highly developed and mature in their ideas about friendship. For all their warm and apparently satisfying relationship within the family, they are not retarded in friendship develop-ment.

The other set of findings relates to something we mentioned earlier—that the girls in the part-time working mother group may be developing an integra-tion which does not adhere closely to traditional concepts of femininity. They score relatively low on an Index of Traditional Femininity—as do all of the girls whose mothers work. But this group shows certain other signs of a non-feminine orientation: they choose traditionally masculine occupational goals more than other girls do. In line with this last finding—although not the same finding, since it is based on the jobs they want their future husbands to hold—girls in this group aspire to upward social mobility more often than other girls. They choose their fathers as adult models somewhat more often (although still infrequently), and they show some signs of moral development that are more characteristic of our boy sample than of the general population of girls.

They are slightly higher on an index of internalization, and markedly different on responses to two individual questions in the index: the daughters of part-time working women more often say that the girl in the projective picture-stories would obey her parents because she had promised, because of a sense of trust, and they are much more likely than other girls to feel that if the girl *did* break her promise to her parents, she would tell them of her mis-deed later. They show, in our view, a sense of commitment to the promise they have made—more than do girls in other categories.

These findings can be interpreted in light of our earlier speculations about the part-time working mother and her relationship to her adolescent children. We suggested on the basis of the adolescents' activity patterns that family relationships in these cases were strong and actively cultivated by energetic mothers. We find the daughters of these women to be, on one hand, warmly related to their families and apparently strongly identified with active mother-models. On the other hand, they show a degree of autonomy in rela-tion to the family which is rare indeed among girls in our sample. The model-ing concept forms the theoretical bridge between these two findings: the girls have warm and close ties to families which provide them a feminine model of unusual energy, independence, and responsibility. In modeling themselves after their mothers, they develop an autonomy which seems at first glance to contradict their close family ties. But this autonomy grows out of an identification with an independent mother and is encouraged by the parents. It implies not a rejection of the parents, but rather an internalization of their values.

The part-time working mothers apparently offer a model of integration that is not primarily based on traditional concepts of femininity and the feminine role. Daughters of women in this group express somewhat masculine predispositions in their occupational aspirations, their independence, their desire for social mobility. Girls in this group not only aspire to social mobility more than other girls, but they more often fit the pattern we designated a masculine mobility model: that is, they expect to acquire high status at least in part through their own efforts to achieve high prestige positions. They apparently conceive future achievement as a family enterprise which they will share with ambitious husbands.[4]

FULL-TIME GROUP

We can turn at this point to the other working mother group—i.e., to those girls whose mothers hold full-time jobs outside the home. We speculated, on the basis of the activity pattern that characterizes this group, that the girls whose mothers work full-time receive somewhat inadequate attention and companionship from their families and that they turn to friends and boyfriends for the warmth and closeness they fail to find at home. Our findings in this case are not, however, consistent or strongly supportive of the initial hypotheses. We find no indication that parents in the full-time working mother group neglect their children or deny them emotional support. We have suggested that they do not enter very actively into their children's leisure lives, but, apart from this, they apparently fulfill their obligations very much as other parents do.

We expected, for example, that signs of parental neglect might show up on measures of discipline and strictness, or in the attitudes adolescents express toward their parents. But we find no evidence of peculiar harshness or of rejection, no signs of excessive family conflict among girls whose mothers work full-time. In fact, they tend to disagree with their parents somewhat less than other girls do. They show no special resentment toward their parents, nor do they express an unusually strong desire for a closer relationship with their parents (on a projective question about a girl who would like her parents to be different). Girls in this group admire and respect their mothers more than the daughters of non-working women: they choose their mothers as models more frequently than do the girls whose mothers are not employed and about as often as girls in the part-time group. They think of their mothers in the role of confidante more than other girls do, and they are more tied to the mother emotionally if we can judge from their answers to the situation in which a girl is asked by her lonely mother to return home. They more often say the girl should go home than do girls in either of the other patterns.

[4] Another finding fits this general interpretation: when asked what kind of man they hope to marry, girls in the group whose mothers work part-time tend to stress ego skills *and* family values. They would like the man they marry to have talent and drive and also strong family values: to like children, enjoy family life, spend time with the family.

The daughters of full-time working women show a mixed pattern of developed autonomy and unresolved dependency. The only interpretation which seems to lend any coherence to the findings is this: these girls are developed in ego skills which equip them for managing practical aspects of reality well and with ease, but emotionally their major commitment is still to the family. In this latter regard (i.e., emotional dependency) they appear to be less autonomous than other girls in this age group.

We have seen evidence of their autonomy in practical affairs in the unusual work load they manage. They share in rule-making at home more than girls whose mothers do not work, and about as often as those whose mothers work part-time. Their parents expect them to be independent and self-reliant, and they are least likely of all three groups to rely heavily on adult authority.

With respect to emotional dependence on the family, girls in the full-time working mother group distinguish themselves on a number of items. In addition to their responses to the question about the lonely mother who asks her daughter to return home, daughters of full-time working women choose their adult models exclusively from within the family more than girls in either of the other groups. They have fewer conflicts with their parents than the part-time group, and are similar in this regard to the non-working group. They also are less likely than the daughters of part-time working women to think that friendship can be as close as a family relationship. When we ask them to think of the person to whom a girl might confide a misdeed, these girls most often think of the mother.

Impact of Employment by Social Class

This peculiar combination of ego autonomy and affective dependence—and it is peculiar in that ordinarily we find adolescents moving toward independence at about the same pace in the two areas—leads into our second analysis, of the differential impact of maternal employment in the two major social classes. It seemed highly probable to us that the meaning of maternal employment would be different in the two classes, and, in the case of the full-time working mother, this is borne out in the analysis. A part-time work commitment has a relatively stable meaning and implication in both the middle and working classes, but full-time maternal employment apparently depends upon different motivational sources in the two groups, and has distinct meanings for family interaction. The findings we have reported for this group represent a combination of two quite different patterns.

MIDDLE CLASS

In the middle class the girls of full-time working women look more like those whose mothers work part-time: they are relatively active, autonomous girls who admire their mothers but are not unusually closely tied to the family. They have a high rate of participation in leisure activities and in organized groups—higher than either working-class girls whose mothers work full-time or middle-class girls whose mothers do not work. They do not have as active leisure lives as girls in the middle-class part-time group, but the differences between the two patterns are not large on our measures of leisure activity.

The serious and adult-like activities decrease in this group when we factor out class: middle-class girls in the full-time pattern do not have as much responsibility at home, and they do not hold part-time jobs as often as girls in the working class whose mothers work full-time. They date just as actively, but again look more like other girls of their class level whose mothers work part-time: they do not go steady as often as their counterparts in the working class. They spend more time with their families than the daughters of full-time working women in the lower class, and their relationships within the family look like those we have described for the part-time working mother pattern. Their parents expect them to be self-reliant, give them a share in rule-making, and apparently permit discussion and open disagreement. In all these respects, girls in the middle-class full-time group are more like those in the part-time patterns and different from girls in the working class whose mothers work full-time. They choose their mothers as ideals more than daughters of non-working women—this holds for all the working mother groups at both class levels—but they do *not* choose in-family models as exclusively as do their working-class counterparts. They think of the mother as confidante, but they also think that a friend can be as close to one as a family member. They do not characteristically think that a girl should yield personal work interests to return home to a lonely mother.

WORKING CLASS

The dependency which distinguished the total group of girls whose mothers hold full-time jobs is primarily a feature of working-class girls in the pattern. Here we find both a strong positive affection for the mother and a strong dependency component. The working-class girls in families where the mother works full-time show the primary characteristics of premature seriousness, deprivation in social and leisure activities, and emotional dependency. Compared to other working-class girls or to middle-class daughters of full-time working women, they have fewer group memberships and leisure activities, and they are more often responsible for major housekeeping tasks and part-time jobs. They are not striving toward emotional independence, nor are they encouraged by their parents to be self-reliant. In this regard they look most like girls whose mothers do not work and differ from all of the other working mother groups. (Table 3).

Compared to any other group in this analysis, the working-class girls whose mothers work full-time have strong emotional ties to the family: they admire and feel close to their mothers, and seem psychologically highly dependent on the family. In choosing an adult ideal, girls in this group name their mothers as often as girls in other working mother categories, and when we consider all in-family choices, they are far and away the group most family-oriented (76 per cent of this group name an ideal from the family group, compared to 60 per cent of the working-class non-working mother group, the second highest of all categories in this regard). They have fewer disagreements with their parents than any other group of girls, and they more often reject the notion that friendship can be as close as kinship. On the question about

TABLE 3.   FULL-TIME MATERNAL EMPLOYMENT IN RELATION TO GIRLS'
ACTIVITIES AND ATTITUDES IN THE MIDDLE- AND WORKING-CLASS
GROUPS[1]

Item: Adolescent Girls' Behavior, Attitudes	Full-time Maternal Employment	
	Middle Class (N = 104)	Working Class (N = 131)
	Per Cent	
Leisure Activities		
Low	18	34
Medium	42	51
High	40	15
Group Membership		
None	21	34
Belongs to 1 or 2 groups	54	49
Belongs to 3 or more groups	25	17
Household Responsibilities		
Major	15	27
Moderate	32	28
Light or none	47	39
Work		
Holds job	74	86
Dating[2]		
Goes steady	5	16
Dates	49	33
Doesn't Date	45	51
Spends Leisure Time		
Alone	5	17
With friend(s)	43	48
With family	47	32
Parents' Expectations		
Self-reliance	19	5
Good manners	54	43
Obedience	21	28
Part in Rule-Making		
R shares in rule-making	71	57
Disagreement with Parents		
Reports no disagreement	15	36
Index of Disagreement (specific issues)		
Disagrees with parents on 3 issues or more	43	28
Adult Ideal		
Mother	40	43
Father	1	1
All in-family choices	55	76
Intimacy of Friendship		
Can be as close as family tie	46	25

TABLE 3. (Cont.) FULL-TIME MATERNAL EMPLOYMENT IN RELATION TO GIRLS' ACTIVITIES AND ATTITUDES IN THE MIDDLE- AND WORKING-CLASS GROUPS[1]

Item: Adolescent Girls' Behavior, Attitudes	Full-time Maternal Employment	
	Middle Class (N = 104)	Working Class (N = 131)
	Per Cent	
Choice of Confidante		
Mother	60	44
Friend	28	18
No one	7	16
Response to Lonely Mother		
Return home	37	56

[1] Middle-class status was assigned whenever the father's job was a professional, managerial, or white-collar one. The working class category includes all girls whose fathers hold manual jobs.

[2] Analysis of dating patterns with age and class both controlled reduced numbers severely. In the interest of reliability, we have run the analysis for all age groups. The class groups did not differ significantly in age, in any case.

the lonely mother who wants her daughter to come to live with her, girls in this group give the traditional response of loyalty to the mother more than girls from any other constellation. The contrast is again a striking one—56 per cent of this group think the girl should return, compared to 42 per cent of the next highest group.

On the other hand, these girls do not spend a great deal of time with their families; they are more likely than other girls to say they spend most of their free time alone or with a friend. In many cases, this friend may be a steady boyfriend, since a large proportion of these girls go steady. If we take steady dating to indicate a transfer of emotionality from the family, then we are faced with the paradoxical fact that girls in this pattern are both very tied to their families and at the same time more likely to have shifted the focus of their emotional lives. One other indication that at least in some spheres they do not in fact rely on their mothers as much as one might think from their attitudes toward family relationships: they do not think of the mother as confidante as often as girls in the other working mother groups.

PATTERNS OF EFFECTS

The analysis of maternal employment within social classes has distinguished two patterns of effects that may accompany a mother's full-time work commitment. The patterns break on class lines in the following manner: in the middle class the effect of the mother's working full-time appears to be similar to the effects of a partial work commitment in either class group—family interaction is high and is geared to training children toward autonomy and self-reliance. Girls in such families are active in both organized and non-organized leisure activity, spend a good deal of time with their families, and are relatively autonomous in issues of judgment and authority. They admire their mothers, but do not seem particularly dependent on them.

The lower-class girl whose mother works full-time is not like other daughters of working women. The girls in this pattern come closest to our original conception of the girl who is neglected and suffers a serious loss in family life because her mother is overextended in her commitments, harassed, perhaps resentful. Here we find girls who carry very heavy responsibilities, lack normal leisure commitments, and apparently find in extra-family relationships (i.e., the steady dating relationship) the secure and stable companionship which they do not find at home. Though in fact they share very little time with their families, the girls in this group have a strong and sentimental conception of the importance of family ties, and continue to be emotionally dependent on the family at an age when other girls have begun to break their ties of dependency. This last set of findings does not, we think, contradict our original notion that full-time maternal employment might imply neglect: one reason girls from such families might be sentimental about the family and more dependent on it is that their needs for family-based security have never been adequately met. At the same time that girls with such backgrounds take unusual responsibility for daily realities, they may continue to yearn for the closeness and security of more normal family interaction.

EXPLANATION

Why should full-time maternal employment have such different effects in the two status groups? The simplest hypothesis relies on economic factors: the middle-class mother who works either part- or full-time very likely has some degree of choice in the matter. In the working class the two commitments may reflect quite different degrees of personal choice and financial press —the lower-class woman who works full-time may be responding to a much simpler and more imposing condition of economic need. Two minor findings from our study support this suggestion. When we asked girls to think of ways in which a girl might like her parents to be different, the girls in our working-class full-time group differed clearly from the other three working mother groups in one respect: while the other three groups all stand out for their reference to the parents' life style ("she'd like them to have a nicer home, go out, entertain more"), the working-class full-time group rarely gives such answers. On the other hand, the working-class full-time group gives economic *problems* as a source of worry for girls much more than any of the other working mother groups.

If in fact this is the case—that the working-class full-time pattern is the only one of our four working mother groups that represents serious economic deprivation—then we can make some ordered interpretations of our findings. The mother who works because of serious economic need is not necessarily one whose psychological make-up prepares her for the dual roles of homemaker and worker. She may feel herself taxed by the demands of a life complication which she did not choose and does not feel up to. Sheer economic deprivation adds a further burden of concern, and in many cases we might expect to find such women both harried and resentful or passively resigned to an unsatisfying and burdensome life situation. The pattern is similar to the one Lois Hoffman has characterized as guilt-free (4). Pressed themselves, such women feel no special obligation to their families. They expect to get their children to take a good deal of responsibility at home; they spend very little time and energy in managing or sharing their children's leisure affairs; and they engender in their children a strong sympathy and sentimental loyalty.

One is reminded of the mothers who so regularly appear in the short stories of Frank O'Connor and other Irish authors: the strong and stable support in a family whose father deals primarily in alcoholic charm and irresponsibility. The key for such a woman is to convert the children to her side, as emotional suppliers and supporters in the real problems of life. She inspires her children with both the strength to cope with reality and also the dependency that assures her some emotional gratification in an otherwise bleak life. To be sure this fictional Irish mother is an exaggerated form, but we suspect that some such pattern is the paradigm for understanding the emotional nexus that dominates many lower-status families in which the mother's employment is a condition for family survival.

We have already described the motivational pattern that we think underpins part-time maternal employment. The distinctive features here are that the woman herself chooses to work and that she maintains a vivid sense of obligation and responsibility toward her family. She chooses a complex rather than a simple life pattern, but the conditions of the pattern are set by her primary commitment to her family role. We see this as a pattern requiring unusual energy and one which results in a high degree of family interaction. Derivative effects of the pattern we note in the degree of parent participation in the leisure lives of their adolescent children and in the energy, autonomy, and responsibility that characterize girls from this family setting. These psychological features of the girls develop, we suggest, from a modeling process in which the girls identify with and draw their ideals from their own active and autonomous mothers.

The only pattern remaining to be accounted for is the middle-class mother who works full-time. We found this group of girls to be indistinguishable in most critical respects from the daughters of women who work part-time. We must now ask how a full-time work commitment might for a middle-class woman be the same—have the same meaning—as part-time employment. One suspects that economic need alone does not distinguish the two kinds of employment for middle-class women, and the woman of higher social status who works full-time does so, at least in part, because of personal choice.

Maternal Employment and Adolescent Boys

One would expect—from the findings in the girls' study—that maternal employment might be a less important factor in the life of the adolescent boy. If we are right in our view that much of the influence of maternal employment comes about through a modeling process in which the girl fashions her ego-ideals and activities in keeping with the pattern set by her mother, then we can expect that this pattern will be less effective in predicting the boy's devel-

TABLE 4. WORKING-CLASS BOYS WITH FULL-TIME WORKING MOTHERS COMPARED TO OTHER BOYS ON SELECTED MEASURES OF ACTIVITY, EGO DEVELOPMENT

Item: Boys' Attitudes, Behavior	Maternal Employment	
	Full-time Working Class (N = 71)	All Other Patterns (N = 631)
	Per Cent	
Adult Ideals		
Father	12	27
No ideal	15	6
In-family models (including father)	45	41
Time Perspective		
Extended	32	45
Restricted	12	5
Dating		
Date	68	53
Doesn't date	32	47
Group Membership		
None	43	26
Belongs to 1 or 2 groups	48	53
Belongs to 3 or more groups	9	21
Leisure Activities		
Low	33	18
Medium	38	45
High	29	37
Work		
Holds a job	51	47
Intimacy of Friendship		
Can be as close as family relationship	46	41
Cannot be as close	52	56
Reliance on Parents: Advice on Issues		
Relies heavily on parents	40	44
Relies somewhat on parents	47	45
Does not rely on parents	13	10

oping integration. For the boy, the model provided by his father will be the key to ego development, and the mother's activity or employment should be a comparatively minor factor (Table 4).

Our interpretations of the meaning of work to mothers in the part-time and full-time patterns gain some general support from our data on boys. Here again we find that the lower-class family in which the mother works full-time has more pressing financial troubles—or, at least, that financial problems come through to the children more clearly. Boys in this group think of financial problems as a source of worry and also as something they would like to change about their own lives more often than do boys in any of the other working mother patterns, and often more than those whose mothers do not work at all. The other three types of working mother (i.e., higher-status women who work full-time and women of either high or low status who hold part-time jobs) again seem to be women who are unusually conscientious, active mothers. Their sons, like their daughters, report sharing leisure activities with their parents more than other boys do, and they have a larger number of leisure activities of the kind that imply parental involvement (i.e., membership in organized groups and active sports and hobbies).

Beyond these few findings, the working mother variable shows relatively little power to predict the boy's activities and psychological characteristics. When the mother's work stems from personal choice—or so we infer, at least —the boy has a relatively high leisure activity index, but he differs in no other area from boys whose mothers do not work. He is no more likely to work or date; he shows no signs of unusual achievement striving,[5] of special forms of ego development, or of precocious loosening of dependency ties.

The boys from families in which the mother's work is the product of economic necessity (i.e., lower-status women who work full-time) do differ from other boys in some respects, and this seems to us interesting in light of the fact that this is the one case in which maternal employment implies something about the father as a model. The fact that a mother "must" work— irrespective of her personal wishes—does not speak well for the father's capacity as a provider. Considering the importance of economic prowess in the American definition and evaluation of the male, a father who cannot or does not support his family adequately can hardly serve as an effective ideal for his son. And it is in the area of modeling that the boys differ most clearly from their age mates. They choose their own fathers significantly less often than other boys do, and they more frequently say that they have no adult ideals. Beyond this we find that boys in this group are somewhat rebellious in response to adult authority, and that they show signs of a poor ego integration. They have a relatively short time perspective and a low level of general activity. Only in dating are they especially active. They do not have part-time jobs as often as other boys; they have very few organizational ties and active leisure engagements. Our information on their family attitudes is limited: we did not ask boys as many questions in this area as we did girls. But boys in the lower-class full-time group do not seem to be emotionally dependent on the family in any way that compares with our findings for girls from similar family backgrounds. They do not think that family ties are always closer than friendships, and they do not rely heavily on parental advice or on in-family models more than other boys do. We would very much like to have information on the boy's relationship to his mother distinguished from his attitude toward his father, but in this our data on boys are specifically lacking.

We can say, by way of a general conclusion, that the effect of maternal

---

[5] When we consider only urban boys from lower-middle and upper-middle working-class homes, we do find a relationship between the boys' mobility aspirations and maternal employment. Boys who aspire to upward mobility more often report that their mothers work part-time than do boys whose orientation is non-mobile or downwardly mobile. While maternal employment is generally a less imposing force in the life of the boy, this finding suggests that in certain cultural settings, the fact that a boy has an ambitious mother may crucially affect the direction of his development. Kahl's work (5) supports this suggestion.

employment in the boy's development is significant only when it serves to inform us about general features of family integration and, specifically, about the relationship between the boy and his father. When the mother's work rests to any significant degree on factors of personal choice—when, that is, it reflects qualities and motives of the mother but does not yield specific information about the father—it fails to predict a unique pattern of adjustment in the boy, although it appears to be an important force in the girl's integration. This difference in the findings for boys and girls supports our earlier view that the kind of woman who assumes an occupational role through a desire for some self-realization exerts an influence on her daughter's development through a modeling process in which the girl identifies with and incorporates many of her mother's ego characteristics.

REFERENCES

1. Bergsten, Jane W. "A Nationwide Sample of Girls from School Lists," *Journal of Experimental Education*, XXVI (March 1958), 197–208.
2. Douvan, Elizabeth, and Adelson, Joseph. *Themes in American Adolesence*. Unpublished manuscript.
3. Douvan, Elizabeth, and Kaye, Carol. *Adolescent Girls*. Ann Arbor, Mich.: Survey Research Center, University of Michigan, 1956.
4. Douvan, Eliabeth, and Withey, S. B. *A Study of Adolescent Boys*. Ann Arbor, Mich.: Survey Research Center, University of Michigan, 1955.
5. Kahl, J. A. "Educational and Occupational Aspirations of 'Common Man' Boys," *Harvard Education Review*, XXIII (Spring 1953), 186–203.

ATTITUDES TOWARD INTEGRATION AND BLACK CONSCIOUSNESS: SOUTHERN NEGRO HIGH SCHOOL SENIORS AND THEIR MOTHERS*

ERIC R. KRYSTALL
NEIL FRIEDMAN
GLENN HOWZE
EDGAR G. EPPS

A recent issue of *Ebony* pictures Izell Blair, one of the four original Greensboro sit-in students, garbed in African dress at the Newark Black Power Conference.[1] This picture symbolizes two tendencies, two strains in the civil and human rights movements. The thesis is integration—the insistence by Negroes on full legal and social equality in a color-blind society. The antithesis is black consciousness—the reaffirmation of Negritude, of the African heritage, of the specialness of being black. Everyone awaits the new synthesis.

This dialogue, this integration vs. black consciousness debate, so prevalent today, has in fact been with us since before the Mayflower. Some early Negro voluntary associations called themselves "Colored";[2] others labeled themselves "African."[3] Frederick Douglass, militant abolitionist, thanked God each day for making him a man; Martin Delaney, champion of colonization, thanked God each day for making him a black man.[4] Du Bois worked with the National Association for the Advancement of Colored People; Garvey chartered The Black Star Line. Martin Luther King led sit-ins, pray-ins, swim-ins, and walk-ins; Elijah Muhammed exhorted so-called Negroes to get

---

* Reprinted from Eric R. Krystall, Neil Friedman, Glenn Howze, and Edgar G. Epps, "Attitudes toward Integration and Black Consciousness: Southern Negro High School Seniors and Their Mothers," in *Phylon*, Vol. 31 (Summer 1970), pp. 104–113. Revised version of a paper delivered at the Thirty-First annual meeting of the Southern Sociological Society, April 1, 1968, held in Atlanta, Georgia.

[1] David Llorens, "Natural Hair: New Symbol of Race Pride," *Ebony*, XXIII, No. 2 (December 1967), 143.
[2] For example, Society for the Promotion of Education Among Colored Citizens (1857); Convention of Colored Citizens of America (1830).
[3] For example, The Free African Society (1787); The Bethel African Methodist Episcopal Church (1794); The African Union Society (1780). For more on the topic see Harold Isaacs, *The New World of Negro Americans* (New York, 1964), pp. 62–72.
[4] Philip Foner, *Biography of Frederick Douglass* (New York, 1955), p. 461.

out. And since the assassination of Malcolm X, while the NAACP and the Southern Christian Leadership Conference have continued battering at the walls of segregation, the Student Non-Violent Coordinating Committee and the Congress of Racial Equality have been building new fences of separation.

How strong are these two impulses relative to each other in the Negro community? Which members of the community—the young or the old—does each force attract? Who is more likely to favor integration—high school seniors or their mothers? Who is more likely to develop black consciousness?

It was to questions such as these that attention has been directed.

The data collected were part of the 1967 Tuskegee Area Study, which is an annual social survey carried on by junior and senior social science majors at Tuskegee Institute.

The 1967 study site was Montgomery, Alabama.[5] The city has four Negro high schools—two public and two private. A sample was taken of the seniors in these high schools. The entire senior classes of the two private schools were interviewed in order to increase the number of respondents from middle- and upper-class backgrounds. A random sample was taken from a complete list of the seniors at one public high; a sample was take from a partial list of the seniors at the other public high school. Interviews were completed with over 90 percent of the students in the sample and with 240 of the mothers or female guardians of the 266 students interviewed (see Table 1).

Attitudes toward integration were assessed through questions concerning feelings about integration in housing and schools, intermarriage, and civil rights participation (see Table 2). The table shows that both students and their mothers express overwhelmingly favorable attitudes toward living in the same neighborhood as whites, going to the same school as whites and intermarriage. In the two comparisons where there are significant differences

[5] The 1968 study sites were Birmingham, Alabama, and the Tuskegee Institute campus. The comparative data on black consciousness and pro-integration sympathy among high school and college students in those two locales are currently being analyzed.

TABLE 1. SAMPLE CHARACTERISTICS AND RESPONSE RATE

	Sample Size	Completed Interviews	Percentage Completed
Public School 1	141	131	92.9
Public School 2	74	63	85.1
Private School 1	53	51	96.2
Private School 2	26	21	80.8
Total	294	266	90.5

NOTE: Unless otherwise indicated, Parent N = 240; Student N = 266. All figures reported are percentages. In the calculation of Chi Squares "other" categories have been omitted.

between the groups, the children are more prointegrationist than are their parents, and they are more likely to have taken part in civil rights activity.[6]

Black consciousness was assessed through questions concerning feelings toward black power, Stokely Carmichael, Africa, violence, group labels (Negro, Afro-American, black), and the Afro (natural) hair style. Tables 3 and 4 show that black consciousness is not as prevalent in the sample as is pro-integration sympathy. The tables also show that seniors have more black consciousness than do their mothers.

Table 3 shows that the seniors are more likely than their mothers to have heard of Stokely Carmichael, to rate him as a good or very good leader, and are more likely to say that they disagree with none of his ideas.

The table also shows that the seniors are more likely to have heard of

[6] This tendency is more striking in Tables 8 and 9. Students are significantly more likely to say they would approve close friends marrying whites than are parents to say they would approve their children marrying whites. Table 9 indicates that when parents do approve intermarriage, they do so most often out of tolerance for other peoples' "business"; when children approve they are more likely to take the positive view that love can conquer racial barriers.

TABLE 8. SUPPOSE YOUR (SON) (DAUGHTER) (CLOSE FRIEND) WANTED TO MARRY A WHITE, WOULD YOU APPROVE OR DISAPPROVE?

Response	*Parents*	*Students*
Approve	42	84
Disapprove	53	12
Other	5	4
Total	100	100

$x^2 = 100.80$; $P < .001$

TABLE 9. WHY WOULD YOU APPROVE (OF INTERMARRIAGE)?

Response	*Parents*	*Students*
If they love each other	20	33
They know what they are doing	11	24
Not my business; would not interfere with their happiness	63	36
Other	6	7
Total	100	100
N =	107	209

$x^2 = 22.62$; $P < .001$

Of course, it should be pointed out that the referents in the two questions differ in psychological distance from the respondent—in the one case, a member of the immediate family; in the other case a friend. If parents had been asked the same question with a "close friend" as referent, their attitudes may not have differed from those of students.

TABLE 2. ITEMS RELATING TO INTEGRATION

Item	Parents	Students
Percentage which would send a younger child or sibling to an integrated school $x^2 = 5.74$; P $<$ .02	73	82
Percentage which feels that a Negro and a white can have a successful marriage $x^2 = .64$; N.S.	65	74
Percentage which thinks Negroes and whites should live in the same neighborhood $x^2 = 1.48$; N.S.	90	89
Percentage which has taken part in civil rights activity $x^2 = 74.72$; P $<$ .001	37	74

black power and to think it means black supremacy. They are a bit more willing than their mothers to join a black power movement and much more willing to give it active rather than financial support. Forty percent of the high school seniors say they are willing to join the black power movement; they are more likely than their mothers to think demonstrations will cease to be nonviolent.

The data also show that the seniors are significantly more likely to think of their forefathers as having come from Africa, significantly more likely to want to visit Africa, and significantly more likely to know the names of African leaders.[7]

And finally, Table 3 shows that the seniors are very significantly more likely to approve of the Afro hair style than are their mothers.

Table 4 shows that very few seniors or mothers prefer being called Afro-Americans or blacks. As of January, 1967, in the Montgomery sample, *Negro* was still the favored term.[8] But the seniors are less likely to mind being called blacks or Afro-Americans than are their mothers.

First, is it certain that these data reveal a generational difference? May it not be that there is a sex difference, with the male students differing from the female students and mothers? Analysis of the student data broken down by sex reveals only two significant sex differences: male students are more likely to join a black power movement than are female students; female students are more likely to have agreed in the past when Negro leaders asked their followers to be nonviolent. Male and female seniors do not differ significantly in their evaluation of Stokely Carmichael, Afro hair styles, group names, or integration. The data, then, show mostly a generational difference, with high school seniors in Montgomery slightly more pro-integration and much more black conscious than their mothers.

[7] Knowledge of African leaders was practically nonexistent for the parents, and miniscule for the children. Considering their school curricula, with the purposeful ignoring of African and Afro-American culture and history, this lack of knowledge is not altogether surprising. However, it does indicate that for this sample emotional feeling of ties to Africa far surpasses concrete knowledge of Africa.

[8] Data from Birmingham high school students in 1968 show little or no trend toward preference for either "black" or "Afro-American" as group labels.

TABLE 3. ITEMS RELATING TO BLACK CONSCIOUSNESS

Item	Parents	Students
Percentage which has heard of Stokely Carmichael $x^2 = 2.72; P < .10$	58	66
Percentage which thinks of Stokely Carmichael as a good or very good leader $x^2 = 7.55; P < .01$	54	73
Percentage which disagrees with any of Stokely Carmichael's ideas and actions $x^2 = 9.25; P < .01$	51	45
Percentage which has heard of the expression "Black Power" $x^2 = 29.07; P < .001$	77	95
Percentage which thinks "Black Power" is: Negro dominance or superiority Militance or violence $x^2 = 19.11; P < .001$	25 6	35 4
Percentage which would join or take part in the "Black Power" movement $x^2 = .95;$ N.S.	33	40
Percentage of those who would take part in the "Black Power" movement who would be active $x^2 = 16.38; P < .001$	15	45
Percentage which think demonstrations will continue to be nonviolent $x^2 = 3.53; P < .10$	36	34
Percentage which considers their forefathers having come from Africa $x^2 = 31.52; P < .001$	27	57
Percentage which knows the names of any African leaders $x^2 = 2.82; P < .10$	8	13
Percentage which approves of Afro hair styles and cuts $x^2 = 6.14; P < .02$	27	49

Do the results present something of a paradox? The students are both more integrationist and more favorable to black consciousness than are their mothers. They seem to be capable of maintaining apparently opposing ideologies without the bind of obvious psychological conflict one would expect in such a situation.[9]

To explain this apparent paradox it is necessary to make clear that integration and black consciousness are not psychological opposites. Focus can be

---

[9] It should be mentioned that in the heat of the present crisis people tend to gloss over logical differences in favor of superficial stereotypes. It is felt that the latest stereotype by whites is that every black person with an Afro haircut and an African robe plans to become a mau-mau (or already is). The typology has endeavored to show that black people with the same hair and dress styles can be either integrationist or separatist in their orientation.

TABLE 4. WHICH OF THESE NAMES DO YOU PREFER TO BE CALLED BY,
WHICH DO YOU NOT MIND, AND TO WHICH DO YOU OBJECT?

Response	Parents	Students
Negro		
Prefer	36	58
Do Not Mind	61	39
Object to	3	3
$x^2 = 24.65; P < .001$	100	100
Afro-American		
Prefer	4	3
Do Not Mind	42	47
Object to	34	38
Other	20	12
$x^2 = .80;$ N.S.	100	100
Black		
Prefer	2	2
Do Not Mind	28	33
Object to	68	64
Other	2	1
$x^2 = 1.34;$ N.S.	100	100

sharpened on this by constructing a typology based upon the assumption of
theoretical independence of orientations toward integration and black consciousness. The typology utilizes the four categories of racial orientation which
it is felt are prevalent today. These four orientations are labeled as follows:
(1) assimilationist; (2) cultural pluralist; (3) traditional separatist;[10] and (4)
nationalistic separatist. These categories have been listed in descending order
of the willingness of their occupants to interact with whites in day-to-day
patterns of living. A description of each type follows:

| Black | *Favorableness to Integration* | |
Consciousness	HIGH	LOW
LOW	Assimilationist (1)	Traditional Separatist (3)
HIGH	Cultural Pluralist (2)	Nationalistic Separatist (4)

FIGURE 1. Typology Based on Black Consciousness and Favorableness to Integration.

[10] The most difficulty was experienced with this item. Malcolm X pointed out an
important difference between segregation and separation: "segregation is when your
life and liberty are controlled, regulated by someone else. To segregate means to control.
Segregation is that which is forced upon [the people they call] inferiors by [people
who call themselves] superiors. But separation is that which is done voluntarily by
two equals. . . ." (*The Autobiography of Malcolm X*, New York: Grove Press, 1964,
p. 246.) In this usage, then, "traditional separatists" are those who live segregated
(not separated) lives.

The assimilationist accepts the American Creed without question. The melting-pot ideal is, for him, an attainable goal. The assimilationist resembles the figure on the cover of *Stride Toward Freedom*,[11] walking briskly through the opening doors which promise a society without racial barriers, a society through which Negroes will be randomly distributed and lose their group identity. Killian calls this type of person "whitewardly mobile."[12]

The cultural pluralist relishes his African heritage and cultivates his Afro-American identity, but he also pushes for all his freedom here and now. He may be willing to live, work, and study with whites, but he prefers to maintain traditionally Negro cultural patterns and life styles in areas such as diet, music, extended family relationships, etc. On the level of social organization, he may prefer building up the power of Negro institutions so as to achieve an ultimate integration of groups of equal position. Especially among collegians, African dress and hair styles are often an outward expression of this inner feeling.[13]

The traditional separatist (often called "Uncle Tom") accepts the American Creed but stays within a "protected" market. His stated goals are those of the white American middle class. But he lives in the ghetto, holds jobs traditionally held by Negroes, attends segregated schools, and generally makes no overt move in the direction of integration. He does not fight the system; he believes in integration, often, but will not fight for it. He is a black Anglo-Saxon who does not interact much with white Anglo-Saxons.[14] He sticks with Negro organizations and institutions primarily[15] because he subsconsciously accepts the label of inferiority placed on him by white society. He maintains a whitewashed mind in a black environment.

The nationalistic separatist wants to link his pride in being black with a land he can call his own. His black nation may be more a desire than a reality, but it provides him with a mythical "homeland" and a rallying cry for his call to arms. To compare him with another minority group, he could be called a black Zionist. The emphasis on black superiority and black supremacy is often accompanied by an emphasis on violence and urban guerrilla warfare. The nationalist wants to live in his own world without whites or their culture.

[11] Martin Luther King, Jr., *Stride Toward Freedom* (New York, 1958). It is well to recognize that in his later works, King played up black consciousness more than he did in his early efforts.

[12] Lewis Killian, *The Impossible Revolution* (New York, 1968). There is considerable confusion about the relation between assimilation and integration. Some black militants insist that integration is assimilation. For example, Malcolm X wrote: " 'Integration' is called 'assimilation' if white ethnic groups alone are involved: it's fought against tooth and nail by those who want their heritage preserved," Malcolm X, *op. cit.*, 277. It is felt that one important value of the typology might be to rescue integration from its conceptually inaccurate identification with assimilation. It is possible to physically integrate without giving up one's heritage. It is also felt that it is important for the integration leadership—black and white—to start stressing this point if it wishes to keep integration from becoming a dirty word among black militants.

[13] Llorens, *op. cit.* For a profound discussion of the cultural pluralist and his need for social institutions through which to express his blackness, see Harold Cruse, *The Crisis of the Negro Intellectual* (New York, 1968).

[14] See Nathan Hare, *Black Anglo-Saxons* (New York, 1965).

[15] The acceptance is not necessarily total. It is also possible that he fears to find out whether he is in fact capable of competing with whites.

How do the findings look when viewed within this framework? The typology suggests that the students, who are relatively high on both integration and black consciousness, should tend to be "cultural pluralists," while the parents, who are high on integration and low on black consciousness, should be predominantly "assimilationist" in orientation. Few students should be "traditional separatists"; few parents should be "nationalistic separatists."

In order to test the utility of the typology, two scales were constructed. These were called "Favorableness to Integration" and "Black Consciousness" scales.[16] Cross-classification of students and parents on these scales resulted in the distribution shown in Table 5. The expectation that students would tend to be cultural pluralists is strongly supported. The expectation that parents would be predominantly assimilationist is also supported. More parents than students are traditional separatists. Unexpectedly, students are slightly less likely than parents to be nationalistic separatists.

What does this mean in terms of the civil and human rights movements? It suggests movement from traditional separatism toward assimilation and cultural pluralism on the part of parents and movement toward cultural pluralism on the part of students. These attitudes are probably influenced by socioeconomic status. It would be hypothesized that higher-status parents and students are more likely to move toward pluralism, while lower-status parents and students are more likely to move toward some form of separatism. Preliminary analysis bears out this hypothesis (see Tables 6 and 7).

Table 6 indicates that for the parents there is a strong association between low income and nationalistic separatism. Table 7 is concerned with voter registration. It shows that while the assimilationists back their belief in the

---

16 The Likert type of scaling technique was employed in the construction of the "Orientation to Integration" and the "Black Consciousness" scales. Scale scores were not constructed for persons with missing data on any item. The Orientation to Integration Scale was constructed from four items: (1) Suppose that you had a younger (child) (brother) would you send (him) (her) to a white school? (2) Do you feel that a Negro and a white can have a successful marriage? (3) Do you think Negroes and whites should live in the same neighborhood, and (4) Have you ever taken part in civil rights activity? A positive response was 1 and a negative response was scored 0. The scale scores ranged from 0 to 4. For purposes of this paper, the scale was dichotomized between scale scores 2 and 3. Persons with scale scores 0–2 were categorized as being Low on Orientation to Integration and those with scale scores of 3–4 were classified as being High on Orientation to Integration.

The Black Consciousness Scale was constructed from four items: (1) Which country do you consider your forefathers having come from? (2) Would you join a Black Power movement? (3) Do you prefer, do not mind, or object to being called Afro-American or Black?, and (4) Do you approve of the Afro hair styles and cuts? Persons indicating that their forefathers were from Africa (or the West Indies) were given a score of 1 and those indicating that their forefathers were from elsewhere were assigned a score of 0. Persons reporting that they would join a Black Power movement were scored 1 and those who said they would not were given a score of 0. Those who preferred or did not mind being called Afro-American or Black were given a score of 1 and those who objected to both labels were assigned a score of 0. Those who approved of Afro hair styles were given a score of 1 and those who did not approve of them were given a score of 0. The scale scores ranged from 0–4. For purposes of this paper, the scale was dichotomized between scale scores 1 and 2. Persons with scale scores 0 and 1 were categorized as being Low on Black Consciousness and those with scale scores of 2–4 were classified as being High on Black Consciousness.

TABLE 5. COMPARISONS OF PARENTS AND STUDENTS ON ORIENTATION TO INTEGRATION AND BLACK CONSCIOUSNESS

Typology	Parent		Student		Total	
	(N)	Percent	(N)	Percent	(N)	Percent
1. Assimilationist	58	40	62	28	120	33
2. Cultural pluralist	42	29	124	57	166	46
3. Traditional separatist	29	20	18	8	47	13
4. Nationalistic separatist	15	10	15	7	30	8
Total	144	100	219	100	363	100

$x^2 = 29.02$; $P < .001$

TABLE 6. TYPOLOGY BY FAMILY INCOME

Income	Assimilationist	Cultural Pluralist	Traditional Separatist	Nationalist Separatist
Over $3,000	72	74	79	27
Under $3,000	28	26	21	73
Total	100	100	100	100
N =	54	38	24	11

$x^2 = 10.91$; $P < .02$

TABLE 7. TYPOLOGY BY VOTER REGISTRATION

Registered To Vote	Assimilationist	Cultural Pluralist	Traditional Separatist	Nationalist Separatist
Yes	97	90	79	67
No	9	10	21	33
Total	100	100	100	100
N =	58	42	29	15

$x^2 = 12.98$; $P < .01$

system by registering as voters, the separatists are much less likely to register. Thus there is reason to believe that the nationalist separatist group represents a lower-class element of the population which is alienated from the system.

The hypothesis is that both cultural pluralists and nationalistic separatists are often self-assertive and may be hostile toward whites. In one case the combination of assertion and hostility leads to aggressive movement toward increased integration; in the other it leads to withdrawal from whites, or violence. At the time and place of this survey, the latter tendency was decidedly less pronounced. There is every reason to believe it will gain adherents in the future if resistance of whites continues to increase and the traditional civil rights organizations continue to have diminishing success.

Data have been presented which show that high school seniors are: (1) more favorable toward integration than their parents; (2) more strongly identified with "blackness" or black consciousness than their parents; and (3) more willing to join or participate in a black power movement than their parents. The parents are pro-integrationist, but not pro-black consciousness.

The fact that the students are both pro-integration and pro-black consciousness led to the construction of a typology based on the assumption that these two concepts are not psychological opposites. A person who favors integration and has black consciousness is called a cultural pluralist. A person who favors integration and does not have black consciousness is called an assimilationist. These two categories typify the majority of the respondents. It is expected that the distribution of the types will change with shifts in the course of the civil and human rights movements.

DATING ROLES AND REASON
FOR DATING*,[1]

CLYDE O. McDANIEL, JR.[2]

There is a large inconsistency within the literature on female dating behavior. On the one hand, the female is characterized as assertive and unmindful of the marriage-oriented reasons for dating.[3] Bowman declares that

> The woman plays a role and has a vital part in making choices and in developing the [dating] relationship. . . . There are indications that women are losing their traditional reserve and are more direct and aggressive in their approach to men.[4]

Herman's 1955 study shows that dating represents, for many girls, merely doing as others do and a means for lessening competition.[5] He labels this type of dating "dalliance."

On the other hand, the female is characterized as receptive and very much aware of the marriage-oriented reasons for dating.[6] Tyler declares that

> [While dating] women assume the role of the pursued. Women respond favorably to pursuit by men. . . . It is worth keeping in mind that there is a feminine as well as a masculine role in dating. We have not yet reached the stage where both sexes widely accept the principle of "dutch dating." An open display of aggression or initiative on the part of a woman makes men avoid her.[7]

* Reprinted from Clyde O. McDaniel, Jr., Ph.D., "Dating Roles and Reasons for Dating," in *Journal of Marriage and the Family*, Vol. 31, No. 1 (February 1969), pp. 97–107, by permission of the author and publisher, The National Council on Family Relations.
[1] This paper is based on the author's doctoral dissertation, "Relationships between Female Dating Roles and Reasons for Dating" (unpublished Ph.D. dissertation, University of Pittsburgh, 1967). The author is grateful for the advice of Robert W. Avery, Jiri Nehnevajsa, Morris Berkowitz, Ray Elling, Howard Rowland, and Jacquelyn A. Alford in preparing the dissertation. Data for the study were gathered from December, 1966, through February, 1967.
[2] *Clyde O. McDaniel, Jr., Ph.D., is Director of Research and Evaluation, Urban Laboratory in Education, Atlanta, Georgia.*
[3] An assertive girl is one who takes the initiative or acts as aggressor in most dating activities.
[4] Henry A. Bowman, *Marriage for Moderns* (New York: McGraw-Hill Book Company, Inc., 1960), pp. 9 and 128.
[5] Robert D. Herman, "The Going Steady Complex: A Re-Examination," *Marriage and Family Living*, 17 (1955), pp. 92–98.
[6] A receptive girl is one who is responsive in most dating activities to male initiative.
[7] Leona E. Tyler, *The Psychology of Human Differences* (2nd ed.; New York: Appleton-Century-Crofts, Inc., 1956), p. 310.

153

Cameron and Kenkel's 1960 study shows that 70 percent of the students in their sample were thinking of marriage,[8] and Hewitt's 1958 study shows that most of the traits his sample desired in a date were also desired in a marriage partner.[9]

One of the reasons for such inconsistence is the failure, on the part of current dating theorists, to specify which stage of courtship is being used as a reference point. While studies have been done to assert that courtship is a progressive phenomenon and that girls do assume different roles for different reasons, no one has related stages and reasons for dating, or stages and dating role. This study was aimed at answering a set of questions which inquire about some of the relationships between the female's role in dating and her reasons for dating (in each stage of courtship). Since these questions also inquire about the conditions under which the relationships obtain, their answers aid in placing dating-courtship firmly within the boundaries of socialization.

This study was designed essentially to discover what impact stages of courtship have on the relationship between female dating role and reasons for dating by answering the following specific questions:

1. In what sequence do stages of courtship occur?[10]
2. What is the relationship between stages of courtship and dating roles?[11]
3. What other factors influence dating roles?[12]
4. What is the relationship between stages of courtship and reasons for dating?[13]
5. What is the relationship between dating roles and reasons for dating?
6. Is a penalty paid by girls if their dating roles do not change as they move through the stages of courtship?
7. What impact do the perceptions of males have on facilitating change in female dating behavior?

Methodology

Survey methodology was employed to execute the study. Of the 600 questionnaires which were distributed to undergraduate students at the University of Pittsburgh, 396 were returned from single females while 181 were returned from single males.

[8] William J. Cameron and William F. Kenkel, "High School Dating: A Study in Variation," *Marriage and Family Living*, 22 (1960), pp. 74–76.
[9] Lester Hewitt, "Student Perceptions of Traits Desired," *Marriage and Family Living*, 20 (1958), pp. 344–349.
[10] Only three stages of courtship were used in this study: random dating, going steady, and pinned/engaged.
[11] Three types of dating roles were used in this study: assertive, assertive-receptive, and receptive. The assertive-receptive role type is manifest when the girl alternates about evenly between assertiveness and receptivity.
[12] Other factors used in this study were three types of reference sources (original family, peer group, and personal-boyfriend), degree of dissatisfaction with dating role, commitment to boyfriend, and complementarity of girl's and boyfriend's personality traits.
[13] Three reasons for dating were used in this study: recreation, mate selection, and anticipatory socialization (training to become good marriage mates).

Determining adequate sample sizes and selecting respondents were not done arbitrarily. In order to determine the sample size for single females, the author used the following criterion as a guideline: select a sample size which is practical and manageable and yet which is large enough to allow for subgroup analyses. This criterion was buffered by the awareness that the aim of the study was not to generalize to any particular population, but to test relationships. The author consequently decided on a sample size of 400. Since the major intent of the study was to discover the impact of stages of courtship (a trichotomized variable) on the relationships between two sets of dichotomized variables—role behavior (assertiveness and receptivity) and reasons for dating (recreation, mate selection, and anticipatory socialization)—a sample size of 400 allowed the possibility of simultaneously analyzing these relationships. Such a cross-tabulation scheme would result in forty-eight subgroups with a chance possibility of eight to nine cases in each.

In order to place female "subjects" on a sample list, simple random sampling was employed: random sampling, not for the purpose of facilitating accurate generalization to the parent population, but for the purpose of making sure all categories in the antecedent and independent variables would be substantially represented. Since there were about 5,000 single dormitory females in the population from which the sample of 400 was to be drawn, from a list of all the single females in the population, every eighth one was designated as a respondent for the study.

A sample size of 200 for single males was arrived at in much the same way. Since there were 9,000 single male students at the University from which a sample of 200 was to be drawn, from a list of all the single male students, every forty-fifth one was designated as a respondent. The reason for using the smaller sample was to make simple comparative analyses of females who were actually dating (and had not completed progress through the courtship system) with males' perceptions of how females should act while dating. The smaller sample facilitated the testing of implicit hypotheses such as the following: "dating males, at certain stages of courtship, expect their girl friends to be assertive (or receptive)."

Summarily, the entire sample can be described in a few statements. It was composed predominantly of young single female students. Further, being undergraduates, they were principally freshmen and sophomores. They were overwhelmingly democratic, upper middle-class, and white. Most of them began dating at or around junior-high-school age. The girls, in a typical middle-class fashion, were somewhat sensitive about revealing their ages or anything connected with age. Most of them had had the experience of the first two stages of courtship—random dating and going steady—but few had been pinned or engaged. Finally, most of the sample presently were either random dating or going steady.

It was impractical to observe directly the behavior which constituted the data for this study. However, indirect observation was practical. Among the many methods available which would facilitate indirect observation, the self-administered questionnaire seemed most appropriate. The foregoing was especially true because the self-administered questionnaire lent itself to simultaneously questioning members of the respondent group with a minimum of interaction among them. The method, which did not require an interviewer because each respondent read the questions herself (himself) and filled in her (his) own answers, took the following form: After each of the potential respondents had been identified and placed on a sample list, each of them was contacted via campus mail. Upon such contact, they were notified that they had been selected and were asked to be available on a specified date in order to fill in the questionnaires. Then, with the aid of the Dean of Men, the Dean of Women, and relevant dormitory heads, the questionnaires were distributed and promptly returned via campus mail.

The contents of the questionnaire were based on a list of items which are characteristic of dating behavior. These were categorized and judiciously assigned to each variable (see the next section for conceptual and operational definitions of each variable). Where feasible, the items were incorporated in the critical-incident technique form.[14] Furthermore, most of the questions incorporating the items were either phrased normatively or hypothetically in order to allow the respondents to answer the questions freely and nonthreateningly.[15] The items came from published results of research and from observations of the author and referred to both attitudinal sets and to behavior, such as engaging in sex. In assigning items to variables, the author employed the Guttman Scalogram model. Adherence to this measurement model made it possible to construe each variable along a unidimensional scale and to make no measurement assumptions which exceeded ordinality.

The questionnaire was pretested with small samples of graduate and undergraduate students at the New Kensington branch of the University of Pennsylvania, at Carnegie Institute of Technology, and at Chatham College. In analyzing the data, all zero-order relationships were assessed through the use of Spearman's Rho along with a conservative level of significance (.05). All higher-than-zero-order relationships were assessed through the use of elaboration and percentaging with no level of significance being chosen. That is, where it was necessary to tease out subgroup relationships, percents were employed with modal differences being indications of the patterns of relationships. One essential feature of elaboration is that it allows no single hypothesis to be viewed independently of others. Instead, there is a series of hypotheses which must be looked at in combination. Consequently, the tactic here was to capitalize on *patterns* of percentage differences.

Data Analysis and Discussion

1. STAGES OF COURTSHIP

Since it was postulated that significant changes take place among females within certain stages of courtship, it was necessary to hypothesize the sequence

---

[14] John C. Flanagan, *The Critical Incident Technique* (Pittsburgh: The American Institutes for Research, July, 1954).
[15] There is clear evidence that expressed value positions do provide insight into behavior. See, for example, Winston Ehrmann. *Premarital Dating Behavior* (New York: Henry Holt and Co., 1959), pp. 213–276. In this section of his book, Ehrmann provides convincing evidence that girls' most intimate courtship behavior correlates quite well with their expressed personal codes about intimate courtship behavior.

in which the changes were expected to occur. Dating is known to manifest itself in at least three stages: random dating, going steady, and pinned/engaged. Random dating occurs when the female is dating but not with any special person; going steady occurs when she is dating a special person but has not made any commitment to marry; and being pinned/engaged occurs when she is dating a special person and has made a commitment to marry.

Hypothesis I: *It was expected that these three stages were progressive, i.e., that girls randomly date before they go steady, and randomly date and go steady before they become pinned/engaged.*

The rationale for the progression is based on the assumption that girls must scout around a bit before they learn that society expects them to choose special persons who are suitable for marriage mates. When they find such persons, they must test their compatibility by dating them steadily. If compatibility cannot be attained, the girls revert back to random dating, and the process starts again. If and when compatibility is attained, the girls commit themselves to marriage and become engaged.

In order to discover whether or not occupancy in one stage of courtship presupposes occupancy in other stages, the three stages were incorporated as items in the questionnaire. Table 1 shows that, among single females, all the items scaled and yielded a very high Coefficient of Reproducibility (.972) and Minimal Marginal Reproducibility (.820). In the order of their decreasing attractiveness, the stages arranged themselves in the following manner: (1) random dating, (2) going steady, and (3) pinned/engaged. One can be sure, with such a high Coefficient of Reproducibility, that if a girl is going steady, she has random dated; and if she is pinned/engaged, she has random dated and gone steady; and any variable which correlates fairly well with stages of courtship participated in can, to that extent, be used in the same manner in which the latter can be used. While it must be remembered that stage of courtship participated in is not synonymous with present stage of courtship, it appears that Hypothesis I was not disconfirmed.

TABLE 1.   STAGES OF COURTSHIP PARTICIPATED IN

Scale Scores		Single Females	
		F	%
Random Dating, Going Steady, Engaged	1	103	26
Random Dating, Going Steady	2	186	47
Random Dating	3	107	27
Total		396	100

Coefficient of Reproducibility = .972; Minimal Marginal Reproducibility = .820; no non-scalable questions.

2. ROLE BEHAVIOR

Robert Winch, *et al.*, while empirically elaborating the Winch theory of the complementarity of needs in mate selection, suggested an excellent analytical role scheme which was used in assessing role behavior in this study.[16] The scheme was suggested when, through cluster analysis, Winch and his associates arrived at the general hypothesis that "an important dimension of dating for both sexes is the assertive-receptive dimension."[17] They found, on the one hand, that the *assertive* dater was achievement-oriented, autonomous, dominant, hostile, a status aspirant, and a status striver; they found, on the other hand, that the *receptive* dater was abasive, deferential, succorous, prone to vicariousness, an approacher, and anxious.[18] The behavioral indicants of these were used in this study as assertive and receptive roles respectively.[19] The assertive-receptive role was a combination.

Although eighteen items were included in the questionnaire to measure assertiveness, only nine scaled such that an acceptable Coefficient of Reproducibility (.90) and Minimal Marginal Reproducibility (.76) were produced. The items which scaled acceptably—in the order of their decreasing attractiveness—were the ones dealing with a girl's (1) always being in control on dates, (2) wishing to marry only a potential success, (3) not being dependent on her date, (4) reprimanding her date for misbehavior, (5) being cautious on dates, (6) staying at least one step ahead of her date, (7) wishing to stay at least one step ahead of her date, (8) subtly manipulating her date, and (9) making all the decisions on dates.

As was the case in measuring assertiveness, eighteen items were used to measure receptivity. Again, in order to achieve an acceptable Coefficient of Reproducibility (.90) and an acceptable Minimal Marginal Reproducibility (.819), nine of the items had to be discarded. The items which conformed to an acceptable scale—in the order of their decreasing attractiveness—were those

---

[16] Robert F. Winch, Thomas Ktsanes, and Virginia Ktsanes, "Empirical Elaboration of the Theory of Complementary Needs in Mate Selection," *Journal of Abnormal and Social Psychology*, 51 (1955), pp. 508–518.

[17] *Ibid.*, p. 513.

[18] *Ibid.*, pp. 509–513. Winch and his associates defined each need (n) and each trait (t) behaviorally as follows: a. *achievement* (n)—to work diligently to create something and/or to emulate others; b. *autonomy* (n)—to get rid of constraint of other persons or to be unattached and independent; c. *dominance* (n)—to influence and control the behavior of others; d. *hostility* (n)—to fight, injure, or kill others; e. *status aspiration* (n)—to desire a socioeconomic status considerably higher than one has; f. *status striving* (n)—to work diligently to alter one's socioeconomic status; g. *abasement* (n)—to accept or invite blame, criticism, or punishment or to blame or harm the self; h. *deference* (n)—to admire and praise another; i. *succorance* (n)—to help sympathetically; to nurse, to love, to protect, to indulge; j. *vicariousness* (t)—the gratification of a need derived from the perception that another person is deriving gratification; k. *approach* (n)—to draw near and enjoy interaction with another person or persons; and l. *anxiety* (n)—fear, conscious or unconscious, of harm or misfortune arising from the hostility of others and/or social reactions to one's behavior.

[19] From a strict role standpoint, these two concepts may appear to be polar extremes of a single continuum and thus analytically inseparable. From a behavioral and empirical standpoint, however, the two concepts comprise two separate continua, because a given act can only be either assertive or receptive. Since a role is manifest by acts, by modal definition it may be either of the three role types.

dealing with a girl's (1) rejoicing when her date rejoices, (2) enjoying being near her date, (3) admiring her date, (4) wanting to be tenderly cared for by her date, (5) dressing to suit her date, (6) being disturbed if her date is disturbed with her, (7) allowing her date to make the decisions on dates, (8) accepting her date's criticisms, and (9) never going stag to a party.

Hypothesis II: *It was expected that the girls in this study would be assertive in the first stage of courtship, assertive-receptive in the second stage, and receptive in the last stage.*

                  The rationale for such a progression is as follows: Girls, in the early stage of courtship, are inexperienced and unsophisticated with regard to appropriate role behavior. They are assertive initially because they view their right to act as aggressors in social interaction as identical with boys' right to act as aggressors. In heterosexual interaction on dates, however, they are made aware of their inappropriate role behavior through negative reinforcement from boys. In this way, they learn that receptivity is more frequently approved than assertiveness. At the same time, they are beginning to place a premium on attaining a mate. Both of these are seen as significant features in the definition of their adult status. They resort to receptivity, then, because it enables them to obtain a mate, and because it is consistent with their adult status definition.

To test Hypothesis II, present stage of courtship was related to assertiveness and to receptivity. The first stage, of course, is random dating and was assigned a lower weight than the later stages—going steady and pinned/engaged.

The first column in Table 2 shows that (1) *there is a tendency for girls in the early stage of courtship to be assertive,* and (2) *there is a tendency for girls in the later stage of the courtship to be receptive.* Although the correlations are small, they are significant, indicating that a fairly high degree of confidence can be placed in them. Since stages of courtship scale, there is reason to believe that girls in the early stage of courtship approach heterosexual relationships with the belief that they have just as much right, power, and authority as boys. Their immediate goal is to initiate cross-sexual relationships, and the data indicate that they do so with straightforwardness. However, something happens between early dating and later dating, because female role behavior tends to shift toward receptivity. Whatever the influence is, it is difficult to say, but an attempt is made in the succeeding sections to tease out much of it.

It is interesting to note that the two correlations in the first column of Table 2 differ not only in direction (or sign) but also in magnitude. This seems to imply that there is a stronger tendency for girls to be assertive in the first stage than there is for them to be receptive in the last stage, or that fewer girls have changed to receptivity in the later stages. The differences in the sizes of the correlations are probably due to the fact that those girls who

TABLE 2. THE RELATIONSHIPS AMONG OTHER FACTORS AND ASSERTIVENESS, RECEPTIVITY AMONG SINGLE FEMALES

			Other Factors				
Role Behavior	Stages of Courtship	Original Family Orientation	Peer-Group Orientation	Personal Orientation	Degree of Dissatis-faction	Commit-ment to Date	Traits Desired in a Date	Actual Traits of Date
Assertive	−.35	.13	.18	−.12	—	.20	−.16	.14
Receptive	.24	.26	.12	.12	.23	.29	−.13	.17

N = 396, P ≤ .05

have not changed cluster in the second, or transitional, stage of courtship—going steady—wherein they are becoming receptive while not actually relinquishing assertiveness. If this is true, it can be said that the girls in the second stage of courtship are assertive-receptive. Furthermore, it means that a certain amount of credence is accorded to Hypothesis II.

3. THE INFLUENCE OF REFERENCE SYSTEMS, DEGREE OF DISSATISFACTIONS, COMMITMENT, AND COMPLEMENTARITY ON ROLE BEHAVIOR[20]

Many other factors can be hypothesized to account for the girls' being assertive in the first stage of courtship and receptive in the last stage. The author thought that if some of these other factors related significantly with role behavior, then confidence could be placed in the assumption that they influence assertiveness initially and receptivity later. The last seven columns in Table 2 show the relationships among some of the other factors and role behavior.

[20] *Original-family orientation*—From among the ten items used to measure the extent of orientation to the original family, only one proved non-scalable. The ten items were hypothetical activities wherein the respondents were asked to indicate how they would be affected if their parents (or parent substitutes) disapproved of their participation in the activities. The nine remaining items yielded a Coefficient of Reproducibility of .911 and a Minimal Marginal Reproducibility of .669. The nine items—arranged in the order of their decreasing attractiveness—were the ones concerning the respondents' (1) becoming engaged, (2) dating a particular person, (3) dating, (4) petting on dates, (5) going to the movies with a date, (6) attending a football or basketball game with a date, (7) talking to strange boys, (8) studying alone with a boy, and (9) having lunch with a boy.

Peer Orientation—The extent of peer-group orientation was measured by asking respondents to indicate how they would be affected if their age-association sex group (peer group) disapproved of their participation in the same ten hypothetical activities used in measuring the extent of original-family orientation. Again, only one item proved non-scalable. In this case, the Coefficient of Reproducibility was .925 and the Minimal Marginal Reproducibility was .753. The nine scalable items—in the order of their decreasing impact on the respondents assuming their peer groups' disapproval—were the ones concerning their (1) becoming engaged, (2) dating a particular person, (3) dating, (4) petting on dates, (5) talking to strange boys, (6) going to the movies with a date, (7) attending a football or basketball game with a date, (8) having lunch with a boy, and (9) studying alone with a boy.

Personal Orientation—Ten items were used to measure the extent to which the respondents evaluate and determine their own dating behavior. All of the items scaled except two. With a Coefficient of Reproducibility of .915 and a Minimal Marginal Reproducibility of .832, the eight scalable items—in the order of their decreasing attractiveness—were concerned with whether the respondents (1) would prefer to be the sole determiner of whether or not to pet on dates, (2) would enjoy having interesting experiences on dates in spite of whether or not they could be related to friends, (3) would prefer not to discuss with friends the fact of their having sexual intercourse on dates, (4) would disregard her friends' opinions if she wished to hold hands on dates, (5) would prefer to be the sole determiner of whether her dating conduct was rewarding to her, (6) would prefer not to have her friends around when she is with her date, (7) would rather go to the movies alone with her date, and (8) would prefer going to games alone with her date.

The Extent of Satisfaction with Dating Role—Ten items were used to measure the extent of satisfaction-dissatisfaction with the dating situation. Only five of them did not scale. Those which did scale yielded a Coefficient of Reproducibility of .900 and a minimal Marginal Reproducibility of .666. The five items included in the scale—

A number of facts became apparent when these columns are perused. It seems that as the girls make the shift from assertiveness to receptivity, they simultaneously become: (1) more original-family oriented, (2) less peer-group oriented, (3) much more personally oriented, (4) much more dissatisfied with their dating role, (5) more committed to their dates, and (6) relatively unchanged in terms of complementarity (both assertive and receptive girls desire fewer traits in their dates than they actually get).

In view of the foregoing, it is believed that a series of events occur in the process of girls' changing from assertiveness in the first stage of courtship to receptivity in the last stage. Some of the events cause assertiveness, some of them result from assertiveness and cause receptivity, and some of them result from receptivity.

It is believed that achievement as prescribed by the peer group and the original family dominates the first stage of courtship. The girls are much more aware of peer-group norms than they are of original-family norms, but they are unaware of their own ability to prescribe the content of their dating behavior. First, the peer group demands that they initiate cross-sexual relationships; and later the original family demands that they select particular dates and exclude others. Concurrently, the girls in the first stage have not learned that they have less power than the males in initiating cross-sexual relationships, since

---

in the order of their decreasing attractiveness—concerned whether the respondent would be disturbed if she found it necessary to (1) ask her date to talk to her when he is obviously preoccupied in conversation with someone else, (2) ask her date for another date, (3) "pay the tab" for her and her date's dinner, (4) tell her date where the two of them are to go on a date, and (5) straighten her date's tie, hat, hair, etc.

Commitment to Dating Partner—Twenty-one items were used to measure the extent of commitment to dating partner. Ten of these did not scale. With a Coefficient of Reproducibility of .918 and a Minimal Marginal Reproducibility of .774, the eleven items which did scale—in the order of their decreasing attractiveness—were those concerned with whether the respondent would comply if her dating partner wished her to (1) run an errand for him, (2) correct her general, apparently disorderly conduct, (3) raise her scholastic average, (4) travel a long distance to visit his parents, (5) help him pass a test, (6) "pay the tab" for their dinners, (7) give him expensive presents, (8) defy her parents, (9) change her religious preference, (10) change her political preference, and (11) ostracize a long-time friend.

Complementarity of Traits—Complementarity of traits was measured by combining a scale of traits desired in a date with a scale of perceived traits of respondent's date. *Traits Desired in a Date*—Ten items were used to measure traits desired in a date. These were incorporated in the questionnaire as a list of traits, and respondents were asked to indicate whether or not they desired each one in an ideal date. Five of them did not scale. Yielding a Coefficient of Reproducibility of .900 and a Minimal Marginal Reproducibility of .690, the five traits which did scale—in the order of their decreasing attractiveness—were: (1) emotional maturity, (2) stability and dependability, (3) affection, (4) industriousness, and (5) family-mindedness. *Perceived Traits of Respondent's Date*—The same ten traits used in measuring traits desired in a date were used to measure perceived traits of date. The only difference is that this time the respondents were asked to indicate whether or not they thought their dates actually possessed the traits. None of the traits proved non-scalable, and at the outset a Coefficient of Reproducibility of .900 and a Minimal Marginal Reproducibility of .730 were obtained. In the order of their decreasing attractiveness, the traits were as follows: (1) neat appearance and good manners, (2) pleasantness of disposition, (3) physical attractiveness, (4) considerateness, (5) affection, (6) industriousness, (7) poise and confidence, (8) stability and dependability, (9) emotional maturity, and (10) family-mindedness.

they were socialized, in the past, on the same generational plane as the males.[21] As a result, they feel that they have just as much right and power to act as aggressors in attaining their goals—heterosexual though they may be—as the males. This causes them to be assertive in their dating behavior and to be fairly satisfied with their dating role, since it conforms with the expectations of their most important reference groups (at that time) and is consistent with their past socialization.[22]

Continuing, the early daters are not nearly as much "in love" with their dates as are their "sisters" in the later stages of courtship. But it appears that many of them are sometimes inclined to indicate that they are committed to their dates. They have a fairly high evaluation of their dates (even though they do not necessarily desire many traits in their dates). It is quite likely that some of the early daters are "falling in love" with their dates. If this is true, it means that their reference source is shifting to themselves and their boyfriends. When these two phenomena occur, the girls move into the later stages of courtship wherein their boyfriends more seriously reject assertiveness among girls. With emotional investment in boyfriends, the girls are forced to become receptive, because now it conforms to the expectations of their new reference source.

Receptivity, however, is not consistent with past socialization,[23] and one of the interesting findings in this study is that the receptive girls are dissatisfied with having to play their receptive role. The girls in the later stages play the receptive role, but this does not mean that they have accepted the role. This, indeed, seems to provide a built-in conflict for newlyweds, especially since it is known from a separate finding that married females are more avant-garde than single females and that they advocate assertiveness in some of the more crucial areas of dating behavior much more strongly than single females.[24]

As a summary, it may be well to speculate on the order in which the dating roles are probably subscribed to by the girls in this study. It appears that the girls are assertive first; that is, they enter the courtship process feeling themselves equal to boys in rights, power, and authority, and they express themselves accordingly while random dating. At a second stage—going steady—the girls are assertive-receptive; that is, receptivity is gradually being learned and is gradually supplanting assertiveness. And finally, at the third stage—pinned/engaged—when the girls are ready to be married, they are receptive.

4. REASONS FOR DATING

The findings from a study done by Lowrie in 1951 were applicable here.[25] Lowrie's study was designed to discover why students date. Four reasons were identified: (1) mate selection, (2) recreation, (3) anticipatory socialization,

---

[21] See Talcott Parsons and Robert F. Bales, *The Family, Socialization, and the Interaction Process* (Glencoe, Illinois: The Free Press, 1955).

[22] *Ibid.*

[23] *Ibid.*

[24] Clyde O. McDaniel, Jr., "Relationships among Female Dating Roles and Reasons for Dating" (unpublished Ph.D. dissertation, University of Pittsburgh, 1967), p. 135.

[25] Robert H. Lowrie, "Dating Theories and Student Responses," *American Sociological Review*, 16 (1951), pp. 334–340.

and (4) adult role clarification. Because of ambiguity of definition, adult role clarification was not used in this study. Mate selection is the conscious searching for compatible dating and/or marriage partners. Recreation is dating solely for the purpose of enjoying heterosexual interaction. Anticipatory socialization is learning, through dating, the knowledges and skills which are prerequisite to assuming specific marital roles.

In the present study, ten items were incorporated in the questionnaire to measure the extent to which mate selection was used as a reason for dating. All ten items scaled and yielded a Coefficient of Reproducibility of .911 and a Minimal Marginal Reproducibility of .818. In the order of their decreasing attractiveness, the ten items were concerned with a girl's (1) making herself as attractive as possible to attract the boy of her choice, (2) *incidentally* dating to choose the right husband, (3) dating, prior to engagement, enough boys to make a choice from a wide range of potential husbands, (4) being provided, through dating, with opportunities to refine her standards for good husbands, (5) not thinking of incompatible dates as good husbands, (6) comparing, in the dating situation, her ideal mate choice with reality, (7) *not just incidentally* considering mate selection while dating, (8) considering "romantic love" as secondary to her other standards for a good husband, (9) dating only those boys whom she considers potentially good husbands, and (10) *primarily* dating to choose the right husband.

Again, ten items were used to measure the extent to which recreation was used as a reason for dating. Only one of these proved non-scalable. With a Coefficient of Reproducibility of .916 and a Minimal Marginal Reproducibility of .820, the remaining nine scalable items—in the order of their decreasing attractiveness—were those concerning a girl's (1) *incidentally* dating to have lots of fun, (2) considering dating as a pleasant opportunity for companionship with the opposite sex without the responsibility of marriage, (3) having fun while dating in order not to miss a large portion of the beauty of youth, (4) considering enjoying herself as a major issue when contemplating going out on a date, (5) dating only those boys with whom she feels most comfortable, (6) obtaining sexual enjoyment while dating, (7) not worrying about marriage while on dates, (8) *primarily* dating to have lots of fun, and (9) not worrying about pleasing her date, just herself.

From among the ten items used to measure anticipatory socialization, only one proved non-scalable. The Coefficient of Reproducibility and the Minimal Marginal Reproducibility were quite satisfactory, being .917 and .800, respectively. In the order of their decreasing attractiveness, the remaining nine scalable items are those concerning a girl's (1) not being marriageable to a particular boy until he has seen her assuming a variety of different roles, (2) learning, through dating, the general attitudes and behaviors of boys in order to facilitate initial marital adjustment, (3) *incidentally* dating in order to learn what behavior is necessary for being a good wife, (4) learning how to please a date in order to learn how to please a husband, (5) testing sexual compatibility with a potential mate while dating, (6) allowing engagement to serve as a trial marriage, (7) not seeing anything "wrong" with trial marriages, (8) *primarily* dating in order to learn what behavior is necessary for being a good wife, and (9) dating only those boys who can teach her something about marital roles.

Hypothesis III: It was expected that the girls in this study date for the purpose of recreation in the early stage of courtship, mate selection in the second stage, and anticipatory socialization in the
last stage.

The rationale for the progression is based on the assumption that girls are either not aware of or not interested in the
maritally oriented functions of dating in the early stage. They
learn soon that, women, to be socially acceptable, must be
married. As a result, a conscious mate selection process en-
sues; this is done in a sequence of tests while going steady.
Once a mate has been selected and tested, girls' emphases
shift to the more immediate future wherein they begin actively to anticipate some of their perceptions of their roles
as wives.

While these three reasons for dating are isomorphic with the implicit
deductions of each of three theoretical schools of thought (see next section),
Lowrie failed to cash in on a major theoretical contribution by not relating
them with certain types of dating roles, stages of courtship, or with any of the
variables involved in courtship. However, Lowrie's study does indicate that
young people do not date solely for the purpose of having fun. Many are
seriously concerned with other functions, particularly the marital and socialization functions.

The first three cells in the first three columns of Table 3 show the relationships among present stage of courtship and the three reasons for dating
among single females. The data indicate that anticipatory socialization is

TABLE 3. SOME OF THE RELATIONSHIPS AMONG STAGES OF COURTSHIP,
FEMALE REASONS FOR DATING, FEMALE ROLE BEHAVIOR, AND
MALE ATTITUDES TOWARD FEMALE ASSERTIVENESS AND RECEP-
TIVITY

Female Reasons for Dating	Present Stage of Courtship			Female Role Behavior	
	Random Dating	Going Steady	Engage-ment	Assert-iveness	Receptivity
Anticipatory Socialization	—.28**	—.15**	.30**	—**	.16**
Recreation	.24**	—.17**	—.30**	.23**	—**
Mate Selection	.15**	.32**	.12**	.29**	.32**
Male Attitudes Toward Female Assertiveness	.10*	—.12*	—.24*		
Toward Female Receptivity	.16*	.20*	.30*		

* N = 181 (Number of Males).
** N = 396 (Number of Females).
P ≤ .05.

positively correlated with the engagement stage of courtship; recreation is positively correlated with the random dating stage of courtship; and mate selection is positively correlated with all three stages of courtship, but the highest correlation obtains with the going-steady stage of courtship. This makes it highly probable that the following relational pattern obtains: (1) in the early stage of courtship, there is a tendency for the girls to justify their dating on the basis of mate selection and recreation (however, recreation dominates); (2) in the interim stage of courtship, there is a tendency for them to justify their dating on the basis of mate selection; and (3) in the last stage of courtship, there is a tendency for the girls to justify their dating on the basis of mate selection and anticipatory socialization (however, anticipatory socialization dominates). If such a pattern obtains, a certain amount of credibility is accorded to Hypothesis III and to the assumptions underlying it.

5. RELATIONSHIPS AMONG ROLE BEHAVIOR AND REASONS FOR DATING
From the foregoing it follows that role behavior and reasons for dating among single females are related to each other in the following manner:

Hypothesis IV: *The females who date primarily for the purpose of recreation are very likely to be assertive.*
Hypothesis V: *The females who date primarily for the purpose of mate selection are very likely to be assertive-receptive.*
Hypothesis VI: *The females who date primarily for the purpose of anticipatory socialization are very likely to be receptive.*

The main focus of Hypotheses IV, V, and VI is: "Exactly what do assertive and/or receptive girls get out of courtship?" As seen in the last two columns of Table 3, this question was answered by relating types of role behavior to reasons for dating. The data indicate that (1) *the assertive girls date for the purposes of mate selection and recreation;* (2) *the receptive girls date for the purposes of mate selection and anticipatory socialization;* and, since both assertive and receptive girls justify their dating on the basis of mate selection, (3) *the assertive-receptive girls date for the purpose of mate selection.*
It seems that if girls were continually assertive throughout courtship, two of the functions uncovered by Lowrie would go lacking, but if they were continually receptive, they would get no fun out of dating. If they were sometimes assertive and sometimes receptive, they would be continually searching for mates. Assertiveness does not undermine the functions of courtship; it merely contributes to specialized aspects of them. Since it is known that the girls shift from assertiveness to receptivity as they move through courtship and that their dating emphases also shift, the findings in the last two columns of Table 3 were expected. However, the findings indicate that Hypotheses IV, V, and VI are not disconfirmed.
The data show that at least three schools of thought can be used to summarize the role behavior of modern-day females.[26] Waller and Gorer's school (an Assertive school) seems to present a neat characterization of early

[26] These three schools can be abstracted from a careful reading of the following sources: Willard Waller, *The Family: A Dynamic Interpretation* (New York: Holt, Rinehart

female daters as assertive and motivated by hedonistic consideration.[27] Burgess and Locke's school (an Assertive-Receptive school) seems to give a fairly accurate presentation of females who are in transit from the early stage (random dating) to the last stage (pinned/engaged).[28] Their girls are pictured as sometimes assertive and sometimes receptive and motivated by desires to select mates. The stage of courtship which best describes this school is going steady. Lowrie's school (a Receptive school) more properly portrays later daters, wherein the girls are receptive and motivated by desires to attain anticipatory socialization benefits.[29] The stage of courtship which best describes this school is pinned/engaged.

Each of the schools is valuable as far as it goes. Each characterizes a part of the dating process. When the three schools are combined, however, a much clearer picture of dating roles and functions is presented, wherein one can see that dating roles and functions change as the girls move through courtship. The question immediately arises as to what would happen if the roles and functions do not change. Apparently, some penalty is paid by the girls if they do not change their role behavior from one stage to another. The next section presents insight into the nature of this penalty.

6. ASSERTIVENESS, RECEPTIVITY, AND SOCIALIZATION

If the girls do not change from assertiveness to receptivity while moving through courtship, one wonders what happens. The data, in this study, show that two things happen: (1) society imposes negative sanctions, and (2) the girls do not progress to later stages of courtship, or if they do progress, they soon regress to earlier stages. The first finding is presented in the last two cells of the first three columns of Table 3. These six cells show that "society" (in the form of the male) does not, in fact, like females who are assertive. And more significantly, they dislike them most in the last stages of courtship.[30] The more advanced the men are in the stages of courtship, the more they de-emphasize female assertiveness and the more they emphasize female receptivity. It can be assumed, then, that with such an attitude toward the female role in dating, the males impose serious negative sanctions on the expression of female assertiveness during the later stages of courtship. Credibility is added to this statement when one remembers (from Table 2) that girls become, during the later stages, more personally and boyfriend oriented.

---

and Winston, 1938); Geoffrey Gorer, *The American People* (New York: W. W. Norton and Company, 1948); Ernest Burgess and Harvey Locke, *The Family: From Institution to Companionship* (New York: American Book Company, 1945); and Samuel H. Lowrie, "Dating Theories and Student Responses," *American Sociological Review*, 16 (1951), pp. 334–340.

[27] Waller, *The Family*; and Gorer, *The American People*.

[28] Burgess and Locke, *The Family*.

[29] Lowrie, "Dating Theories and Student Responses."

[30] The attitudes of males toward female assertiveness and female receptivity were assessed by asking the 181 single males in the study to respond to the same items which were used to measure assertiveness and receptivity among females. For both attitudes toward female assertiveness and attitude toward female receptivity, about half of the items had to be discarded in order to obtain Coefficients of Reproducibility of .90. The items which were retained were identical with those included in the scales of assertive and receptive dating behavior among females.

Table 4. The Relationship Between Present Stage of Courtship and Stage of Courtship Participated In

Present Stage of Courtship		Stage of Courtship Participated in	
	%		%
Random Dating	55	Random Dated	26
Going Steady	30	Random Dated, Gone Steady	47
Pinned/Engaged	15	Random Dated, Gone Steady, Pinned/Engaged	27
Total	100(396)		100(396)

$r_s = -.60$, $P \leq .05$.

This means that they are, indeed, aware of the types of sanctions imposed by their boyfriends and that they are more concerned with learning the proper role behavior for an adult woman and wife.

The second finding is presented in Table 4 which shows that a significant number of girls do, in fact, regress or fail to progress to further stages of courtship. This is evidenced by the fact that the correlation between present stage of courtship and stage of courtship participated in is −.60, indicating that (1) most of the girls who presently reside in later stages of courtship are quite likely to have participated in earlier stages, and (2) *many of those who have participated in later stages are quite likely to be presently residing in earlier stages.* The negative exchange which is implied by the second statement seems to take place between random dating and going steady, pinned/ engaged. More girls are presently random dating than have *only* random dated in the past. And fewer girls are presently going steady or are pinned/engaged than have gone steady or have been pinned/engaged in the past. The residue of present random daters is accounted for in the two succeeding categories under "Stages of Courtship Participated In" ("Random Dated, Gone Steady" and "Random Dated, Gone Steady, Pinned/Engaged"). This means that some of the girls who are presently random dating were once going steady and were once pinned/engaged.

Since it is known that the early daters (random daters) are assertive and the later daters (pinned/engaged) are receptive, one would guess that one of the main reasons for the negative exchange is the failure, on the part of some later daters, to shift from assertiveness to receptivity. One can visualize a learning cycle wherein girls learn through trial and error to become receptive. If they do not become receptive, they never get married. Admittedly, the foregoing is a very strong statement, but the evidence in Table 2 shows that most of the later daters are not assertive, and most of the early daters are not receptive in spite of the fact that many of them were once residents of later stages of courtship. Presumably, the later daters who are still assertive will repeat the cycle until they become receptive.

Summary

In order to provide a picture of the foregoing findings, elaborate cross-tabulation procedures (contingency analyses) were performed, the results of which are reported in Figure 1. The cross-tabulation involved: (1) dichot-omizing each of the variables in the paradigm (except stages of courtship and commitment which were trichotomized); (2) cross-tabulating role behav-ior with reasons for dating among single females (modal categories were pulled out and placed in column 2); and (3) sequentially cross-tabulating the results in column 2 with present stage of courtship, reference groups, complementar-ity, commitment, and degree of dissatisfaction. The modal categories were pulled out and placed in column 1, 3, 4, 5, and 6.

Such a picture makes it quite clear that the six hypotheses raised at the outset are credible. Now it is possible to summarize the major findings of this study. The findings are as follows:

1. There is a tendency for the girls in this study to random date first, to go steady second, and to become pinned/engaged third or last.
2. There is a tendency for girls in this study to be assertive in the first stage (random dating) and receptive in the last stage (pinned/engaged). They are assertive-receptive in the second stage (going steady).
3. There is a tendency for girls in this study who are assertive to be original-family and peer-group oriented, complementary plus, low-medium in com-mitment, and mostly satisfied-dissatisfied with their dating roles.
4. There is a tendency for girls in this study who are receptive to be original-family and personally and boyfriend oriented, complementary plus, medium-high in commitment, and mostly dissatisfied with their dating roles.

It is believed that some of the intervening variables cause assertiveness, some result from assertiveness and cause receptivity, and some result from receptiv-ity. However, further research is needed to assess the exact causal status of the intervening variable set.

5. There is a tendency for girls in this study who are in the first, second, and third stages of courtship to give recreation, mate selection, and anticipatory socialization, respectively, as their primary reasons for dating.
6. There is a tendency for the girls in this study who give recreation as their primary reason for dating to be assertive. They are probably participating in the first stage of the courtship socialization sequence (random dating). This is consistent with Waller and Gorer's Assertive school with regard to reason for dating and role behavior.
7. There is a tendency for the girls in this study who give mate selection as their primary reason for dating to be assertive-receptive. They are probably participating in the second stage of the courtship socialization sequence (going steady). This is consistent with Burgess and Locke's Assertive-Receptive school with regard to reason for dating and role behavior.
8. There is a tendency for the girls in this study who give anticipatory socialization as their primary reasons for dating to be receptive. They are probably participating in the third stage of the courtship socialization sequence (pinned/engaged). This is consistent with Lowrie's Receptive school with regard to reason for dating and role behavior.

Assertive dating behavior does not undermine the functions of courtship, but contributes to specialized aspects of them, i.e., recreation and mate selection.

Specialization Sequence: Stages of Courtship	Relationship between Role Behavior—Reasons for Dating	Reference Group Orientation	Degree of Complementarity	Degree of Commitment	Degree of Satisfaction with Dating Role
1. Random Dating	Assertive—Recreation	Original Family, Peer Group	Complementary Plus	Low/Medium	Satisfied
2. Going Steady	Assertive Receptive—Mate Selection	Original Family, Peer Group	Complementary Plus	Medium	Satisfied/Dissatisfied
3. Pinned/Engaged	Receptive—Anticipatory Socialization	Self and Boyfriend	Complementary Plus	Medium/High	Dissatisfied

FIGURE 1. Summary

9. Tentatively, evidence is offered to the effect that girls in this study do learn to be receptive. If they are not receptive in the early stages, they probably have a lot of fun while dating. If they are not receptive in the later stages, they either regress to earlier stages, or at least they fail to progress to more advanced stages. Such a phenomenon is enhanced by the males' strong dislike for girls who are assertive in the later stages.

A single testing of a theory is never definitive. Each hypothesis included in a theory is always threatened by the possibility of its rejection. Such a possibility is allowable only through an appeal to more research. A single testing only heightens the awareness that further research, to be useful, should be conducted with different and more sophisticated methods. In the present study, a college population, the use of the questionnaire technique, the use of percentages, and the use of ordinal statistics may have presented impediments to the validity of the findings. Further testing of the theory in this study must attempt to avoid these limitations.

CHAPTER 4

Youth Peer Groups
and Subcultures

For almost three decades, the description of adolescence in the sociological literature has included propositions concerning a subculture of youth. It is probably safe to claim that social scientists are disposed to accept the adolescent culture as a subculture if by subculture we mean loosely that adolescents are observably different in behavior or in value orientation than some other age group. In a sense, a subculture is a special case, a subsidiary of a culture; the subcultural scheme is a behavioral blueprint for the people whose needs for status and acceptance are not entirely met by the overall cultural scheme. Thus, there arise many subcultures or subgroups distinguishable from other groups on the basis of their associational patterns, values, norms, and symbols: delinquent gangs, narcotic addicts, jazz musicians, air traffic controllers, astronauts, mental hospital ward residents, Green Berets, public school teachers, and adolescents.

Youth subculture, peer culture, adolescent society, and combinations thereof are terms used broadly and somewhat interchangeably to refer to the age group which emerges in societies in which participation in the family becomes insufficient for developing full identity and social maturity. The assumption that guides this discussion of a separate adolescent culture does not go unchallenged, however. While many sociologists and anthropologists (Margaret Mead, Willard Waller, Talcott Parsons, James S. Coleman, Albert K. Cohen, Kingsley Davis, Robin M. Williams, Jr., Ralph H. Turner, and David Gottlieb, to name a few) have commented on the nature of the subculture, Turner has suggested that it is sometimes problematic to find the empirical referent of the adolescent subculture.[1] We are not entirely clear as to where and how the adolescent subculture departs from the total or universal culture. Does the subcultural hypothesis stand or fall on the degree of difference observed between

[1] Ralph Turner, *The Social Context of Ambition*, San Francisco: Chandler Publishing, 1964, pp. 138–146.

adolescents and other age-grade groups? What do we mean by differences anyway?

In an article in the mid-fifties, Frederick Elkin and William Westley took a dissenting view on the subject of adolescent subculture.[2] Analysis of their data obtained from a small sample of suburban Montreal teenagers did not furnish support toward the subcultural view. Instead of finding discontinuities in socialization from adolescence to adulthood, they found a picture of conformity, i.e., young people well integrated into adult society and accepting of their parents' dicta. The "storm and stress" of adolescent development was decidedly lacking.

The question of whether an adolescent subculture does or does not exist should not depend on the types and degrees of differences found between adolescents and adults. Differences may indeed be found, but they are not necessary for the establishment of this phenomenon. The more productive questions seem to be related to how and why adolescents enter into certain types of peer associations and how membership, involvement, and allegiance to the group influences the beliefs and behavior of the person. On answering these questions we would be better able to understand and evaluate the meaning of adolescent subcultures. Selections in this chapter conceptualize youth cultures with respect to their core structural and functional features.

If we follow Eisenstadt's theoretical reasoning that age groups (read youth groups) emerge to ease the transition from one stage of life to another,[3] we might infer that the adolescent association is a collective response to young peoples' uncertain status in the adult world and functions to ease the transition into full adult family and occupational status. James S. Coleman has charted the conditions antecedent to the adolescent subculture in modern industrial America.[4] (We discussed his formulation earlier in the chapter on the adolescent in the school.) An industrialized society characterized by open opportunity and mobility beliefs recognizes that parents cannot provide the requisite training for preparing their children for specialized jobs bound to be different from their own. Therefore, the educative function becomes established outside the family and is largely governed by professionals. Youth becomes age-segregated for a prolonged period of time. "They have taken not only job training out of the parents' hands, but have quite effectively taken away the whole adolescent himself. The adolescent is dumped into a society of his peers. . . ."[5] While we might interpret Coleman's conclusions in the

[2] Frederick Elkin and William Westley, "The Myth of the Adolescent Culture," *American Sociological Review*, XX (December 1955), pp. 680–684.
[3] S. N. Eisenstadt, "Age Groups and Social Structure," *From Generation to Generation*, Glencoe, Ill.: The Free Press, 1956.
[4] James S. Coleman, *The Adolescent Society*, Glencoe, Ill.: The Free Press, 1961.
[5] Coleman, p. 4.

negative, findings that the attributes for nomination into the leading crowds focused on popularity, athleticism, and material advantage, we must note that most adolescents do make their way to the station of full adulthood without visible scars.

In the next selection, Bennett Berger examines the characteristics of youth cultures which are relevant to other groups in society. He is critical of the transitional-stage conceptualization that has been the dominant framework for discussions of adolescence because it minimizes the orientation of adolescents to their peers. If we conceptualize adolescence as a way of life, then we take seriously the effects of this later socialization process on adult values and behavior. His point is that youthfulness is not an exclusive property of youth (and some youth seem not at all youthful but precociously mature) and that youthfulness may thread its way into certain adulthood careers and life styles.

Continuing with elaboration of distinguishable properties of adolescent peer groups, Gary Schwartz and Don Merten have used the language of adolescents as a means of understanding the evaluative standards, world views and life styles of the youth culture. En route to the main contributions of their papers, Bennett and Schwartz and Merten give their own views on the problems of models of youth cultures which are worth the reader's consideration in view of the professional controversy as to the existence and characteristic features of separate youth cultures.

A highly descriptive and somewhat less formal view of the youth culture phenomenon is written by James Q. Wilson, after returning to his own high school in California some twenty years after graduation. He concentrates on the evidence of social structuring organized around differences in behavior in a highly homogeneous student body, on the adolescent values of friendliness and sincerity, on the decline of participation in formal activities and school spirit. In an era of youthful protest, these students do not seem to be "aroused" by events in the outside world to the extent one might expect; rather, they tend to resolve controversial issues via the reaffirmation of traditional values.

Separated by a short distance geographically, but by an enormous distance culturally from the relatively affluent and blandly homogeneous adolescents in Wilson's neighborhood, are Mexican youth populating a low-income area of East Los Angeles. Robert Derbyshire's paper provides a richly descriptive statement of the adaptation traumas experienced by an ethnically divergent group having limited access to the mainstream of American culture. Recent migrants are compared with established Mexican American "chicanos" on attitudes, values orientations, and sex-role conceptualizations. Clues on the conditions of the emergence of youthful gangs are uncovered. Membership is found in association with extreme feelings of uncertainty toward Mexican culture held by the established adolescents. With some poignancy, we learn that adaptation to the new environment is facilitated by maintaining traditional Mexican cultural values (in the face of American cultural denials) while simultaneously learning the United States culture. All this, and coping with adolescence too!

There are some qualifications which come to mind when discussing a general model of youth subculture, which should be mentioned. First, there is a tendency to discuss youth subculture as if there were one monolithic universal American adolescent subculture. There are, however, in reality many forms of subculture differentiated by social, racial, religious, residential, and other characteristics, including socially deviant behaviors. Second, youth subculture is usually a partial rather than a total or comprehensive way of life. In some other subcultures (that of black Americans serves as a prime example) an individual's whole social life may be lived rather exclusively with others who share the common subculture. But we know that adolescents live in the fire of "parent-peer cross pressures;"[6] these are at least two reference groups to which he seeks an accommodation. Third, the unique aspect of individuals may strain the solidarity and the conformity required by the subcultural membership. Uniqueness is managed variably: The student who excels in scholarship may be required to make a more impressive loyalty display than is expected of a youth who excels in a popular team sport or in rock music. The athletically or musically talented student does not threaten the autonomy of the subculture to the degree of the scholastically performing student who seems to bow to the values and desires of teachers and parents. Fourth, there is a potentially disintegrative element of competitiveness within the subculture which is more pronounced among girls than boys. Girls compete against each other earlier than boys for recognition, approval, and affiliation with the opposite sex. This tends to break up their monosexual cliques whereas the interests of boys in sports, cars, and other activities function to extend the solidarity of their cliques.

[6] Clay V. Brittain, "Adolescent Choices and Parent-Peer Cross Pressures," *American Sociological Review*, XXII (June 1963), pp. 385–391.

ON THE YOUTHFULNESS
OF YOUTH CULTURES*

BENNETT M. BERGER[1]

For more than twenty years now, sociologists have increasingly concerned themselves with the study of "youth culture." Talcott Parsons' very influential article, published in 1942,[2] with its much quoted characterization of youth culture as "more or less specifically irresponsible" has become a point of departure for an enormous amount of research and discussion on youth. Parsons' characterization of youth culture, however, inadvertently suggests that whatever it is that constitutes the "youthfulness" of youth culture may have less to do with chronology than with culture. To characterize youth culture as "irresponsible" or to describe its "dominant note" as "having a good time" or to say that it has "a strong tendency to develop in directions which are on the borderline of parental approval or beyond the pale . . ." (note 1) clearly excludes those large numbers of adolescents who have had no important experience in anything remotely resembling such a milieu. Many, and probably most young persons, while they experience the classic problems of adolescent psychology described in the textbooks, seem to make their way through to full adult status without grave cultural damage, without getting into serious trouble, without a dominating hedonism, and without generalized attitudes of rebellion toward parents and the world.

These introductory remarks are not intended as a preface to a "defense" of adolescents against the bad press they have been getting in recent years. I intend, rather, to suggest that 1) "youth culture" should refer to the normative systems of *youthful* persons, not necessarily of young ones; and 2) since whatever it is that is normatively distinctive about youth culture is probably not characteristic of all or even most adolescents, it is not attributable solely or even primarily to chronological age; and hence 3) that the definitive characteristics of youth culture are relevant to groups other than the age-grade we call adolescence.

While Frederick Elkin and William A. Westley believe they have exploded "The Myth of Adolescent Culture"[3] with survey data showing that a sample of middle-class adolescents comply with the norms of deferred gratification, get

---

* Reprinted from Bennett M. Berger, "On the Youthfulness of Youth Cultures," in *Social Research*, Vol. 30 (1963), pp. 319–342, by permission of the author and publisher.
[1] Author's Note—A revised version of a talk given at the annual banquet of Alpha Kappa Delta, Purdue University, May 19, 1961.
[2] "Age and Sex in the Social Structure of the United States," *American Sociological Review* (October 1942).
[3] *American Sociological Review* (December 1955).

along well with their parents, without hostility or resentful feelings that "they don't understand us," what they have actually done is present evidence that certain adolescents do not share the norms of youth culture. By thus implicitly distinguishing the facts of chronological age from the phenomena of culture, they invite us to consider the hypothesis that what we are in the habit of calling "youth culture" is the creature of some young and some not so young persons. If hedonism or irresponsibility or rebelliousness are essential features of youth culture, then it may be unwise as well as unnecessary to restrict the consideration of youth culture to adolescent groups—since these qualities are dominant in several adult groups as well; and the fact that this is so is probably not fortuitous. I am suggesting, in short, that youthfulness, like fertility, is unequally distributed in society, and not satisfactorily explained by reference to chronological age. This essay is an attempt to explore theoretically some of the conceptual problems that an investigation of the structure and dynamics of youth culture will encounter.

Youth Cultures of the Young

TWO IMAGES OF THE YOUNG: "TEENAGERS" AND "AMERICAN YOUTH"[4]

To begin, let us note a recurrent ambiguity in the images with which American adolescents are usually conceived. The "teen-agers" are those who, in Dwight McDonald's apt ethnography,[5] spend an hour a day on the phone and two hours a day listening to disc jockeys; they are the most assiduous movie-goers in the nation, preferring especially films about monsters, rock and roll music, and teenagers like themselves. More than half of them "go steady" and practice the sexual or proto-sexual intimacies implied by that phrase. The boys are very car-conscious, and spend a good deal of their leisure reading about, talking about, and working on hot rods. They read *Mad*, and its imitators *Frenzy* and *Thimk*; they don't read the Bible, don't go to church regularly, are bored by politics, ignorant of the Bill of Rights, and so on.

If one shifts one's perspective for a moment, and begins to think of the adolescents who populate Boy Scouts, Youth for Christ, 4H clubs, Future Farmers of America, and other groups of this sort, McDonald's characterization (based in part upon the results of Remmers' work[6] and Eugene Gilbert's youth polls) has a rather jarring effect. These doers of good deeds and raisers of prize pigs and winners of essay contests on Americanism are clearly not the adolescents who have seemingly become a permanent "problem" on the American scene.

"Teenagers" and "American youth" are, of course, images, and as such, they may be little more than stereotypes; we may, and likely will, find rock and rollers belonging to the FFA. But it is also likely that these distinctive images express differences in social and demographic variables like class,

---

[4] I am indebted to Barbara Williams for the terms of this distinction.
[5] See his two-part "profile" of Eugene Gilbert in *The New Yorker* (November 22 and 29, 1958).
[6] H. H. Remmers and D. H. Radler, *The American Teenager* (Indianapolis, Ind.: The Bobbs-Merrill Co., 1957).

region, ethnicity, and religion. In any case, the initial distinction between "teenagers" (the adolescents publicly worried about) and "American youth" (the adolescents publicly praised) does suggest the useful banality that some adolescents engage in ways of life essentially at odds with or indifferent to the official desires and expectations of "responsible" adults, whereas other adolescents comply with or actively pursue the aims and expectations set down for youth by adult authorities.

TRANSITIONAL STAGE AND SUBCULTURE

One way of extending this distinction between types of adolescents is to contrast two ideas that are frequently used in psychological and sociological discussions of youth. Most standard works on the social psychology of adolescence speak of it as a "transitional stage" between childhood and adulthood, a period of years ridden with conflicts and tensions stemming partly from an acceleration in the individual's physical and cultural growth but also from the age-grading norms of our society that withhold from adolescents most of the opportunities, rights, and responsibilities of adults. When sexual desires are more powerful than they will ever again be, sexual opportunities are fewest; obedience and submission are asked of adolescents at precisely the time when their strength, energy, and desire for autonomy are ascendant; responsible participation in the major institutions is denied them at the moment when their interest in the world has been poignantly awakened.[7] Such tensions, generated by our age-grading system and exacerbated by a decline in parental control and a world in a state of permanent crisis, are frequently cited as the major source of adolescent difficulty. Conceived as a "transitional stage," adolescence is a very difficult period; it is described—and caricatured—as a time of awkwardness and embarrassment and trouble and pain—something to be got out of as soon as possible by orienting oneself primarily toward eventual membership in the adult community.

For many years, apparently, this conception of adolescence as a difficult transitional stage was the dominant framework in which adolescent problems were discussed. As recently as 1944, Caroline Tryon could write, "we have a tendency to disregard or to minimize the educational significance of the child's experience in his peer group."[8] Today, this statement strikes the eye as incredible; certainly it is no longer true. Very few contemporary discussions of youth fail to mention the significance of the involvement of young persons in their own age-graded peer groups. The emphasis in these discussions, however, is quite different from that contained in discussions of adolescence as a transitional stage; the stress is on the orientation of adolescents to their peers. From this perspective emerged the idea of an adolescent subculture[9] as

---

[7] These are a few of the "discontinuities" made famous by Ruth Benedict in her celebrated article "Continuities and Discontinuities in Cultural Conditioning," *Psychiatry* (May 1938). See also Kingsley Davis' related discussions: "Adolescence and the Social Structure," *The Annals* (November 1944) and "The Sociology of Parent-Youth Conflict," *American Sociological Review* (August 1940).

[8] Caroline Tryon, "The Adolescent Peer Culture," *43rd Yearbook of the National Society for the Study of Education* (Chicago, Ill.: University of Chicago Press, 1944).

[9] This is not the place to go into the problems of applying the concept of "subculture," developed on ethnic models, to age groups. See, however, J. Milton Yinger,

a "way of life" relatively autonomous, and controlled internally by a system of norms and sanctions largely antithetical or indifferent to that offered by parents, teachers, and clergymen—the official representatives of the adult world.

By itself, the subcultural view of adolescence suggests nothing *inherently* transitional, except in the sense that all experience is transitional, representing, as it does, the passage from what one was to what one is about to become. But oddly enough, it is precisely this element that is missing from the conventional usage of the concept of "transitional stage." To suggest that adolescence is "a stage they go through"—something that adolescents "grow out of," is to violate much of what we know about the permanent effects of socialized experience. It is as if adolescence, frequently designated "the formative years," formed nothing, but was simply a rather uncomfortable period of biding one's time until the advent of one's twenty-first birthday or that one's graduation from school induces the adult world to extend a symbolic invitation to join it. But if the transitional view of adolescence minimizes the permanent influences of adolescent experience, the subcultural view exaggerates the degree to which adolescents create an insulated, autonomous milieu in which they may with impunity practice their anti-adult rites. No large scale study of high school youth, for example, has successfully demonstrated the existence of a really deviant system of norms which governs adolescent life.[10]

The point I wish to stress here, however, is that our understanding of the varieties of adolescent experience depends heavily upon whether adolescent group life is primarily conceived in the vocabulary of developmental psychology as a transitional stage, or in the sociological vocabulary of subcultures. Conceived as a transitional stage, adolescence is typically described in ways which make its termination devoutly to be wished.[11] When adolescence is discussed in subcultural terms, no such implication is carried with it. The literature on youth culture most consistently describes it in terms of hedonistic, irresponsible, and "expressive" behavior. Although most adults may believe that this behavior and the norms that constrain it *ought* to be terminated at the threshold of adulthood, it is by no means self-evident that a group which can "get away with" a life of hedonism (read: fun, kicks), irresponsibility (read: freedom, license), and expressiveness (read: immediate gratification, ego enhancement) may be expected to terminate it easily in exchange for the mixed blessing of recognition as adults, and the sometimes baleful responsibilities that this entails. Objectively—and at the very least, adolescence is a portion of a life lived—*formative* attitudes and orientations, talents and commitments, capacities, *and incapacities* develop that affect adolescents' various modes of adaptation into adult worlds, which more or less facilitate or obstruct their

---

"Contraculture and Subculture," *American Sociological Review* (October 1960) and my own comments in "Adolescence and Beyond," *Social Problems* (Spring 1963).
[10] The most ambitious attempt to demonstrate this is James Coleman, *The Adolescent Society* (Glencoe, Ill.: The Free Press of Glencoe, 1961).
[11] The characterization of adolescence as "the awkward age" full of pimples and embarrassment has validity only for the very early teen years. It may merely be a survival from a period when adolescents were completely dependent and completely subordinate. Today, high school students, free and relatively affluent, frequently feel that they are currently living what they expect will be the best years of their lives.

eventual recruitment into a specific adult milieu. If the child is father of the man, an understanding of the varieties of experience adolescents undergo, the varieties of milieu they touch, should contribute to the understanding of the kind of adults they are likely to become—and *not* to become.

CHRONOLOGICAL AGE AND YOUTHFULNESS

Before attempting to describe the groups that might fit the categories of "teenagers" and "American youth," and the groups that might be usefully analyzed with the concepts of "transitional stage" and "subculture," I wish to make explicit one more distinction alluded to earlier, and conceptually parallel to the two sets of distinctions I have already made. To say that youthfulness is far from perfectly correlated with chronological age is to imply that some adolescents are more youthful than others. Once the distinction is made, we can speak categorically of youthful young men, unyouthful young men, youthful old men and unyouthful old men. This fourfold classification suggests, perhaps over-sharply, that chronological age and the culture-personality variables associated with it may be analytically separated. To render the distinction fruitful, however, it is necessary to specify what is meant by youthfulness. Rather than approach this problem directly, it may be wiser to do it indirectly, by contrasting with it the relative lack of youthfulness in "American youth."

In this connection, let me draw attention to a recent book called *The Vanishing Adolescent* in which Edgar Friedenberg argues that adolescence as a stormy decade of identity-seeking and as a distinctive stage of human development is disappearing in the United States largely as a result of premature socialization primarily in the high schools.[12] Without digressing into a discussion of Friedenberg's thesis, we *can* say that we have all known adolescents of the kind about which he is concerned. They do well enough in school, are "well-adjusted," popular with their peers, have few great conflicts with their parents or other authorities, and in general have few if any serious quarrels with the value system into which they are being socialized or with the institutions representing these values. Grant this image some validity; then let us ask: in what sense are these young persons youthful? Certainly they are young and probably inexperienced in the affairs of the world. But adolescents who respond docilely to the expectations of school authorities, who accept as legitimate the limits imposed on them by their parents,[13] who engage in the activities that are deemed appropriate by adult authorities, are more aptly described as going through the final phase of their pre-adult socialization, as junior grown-ups, rather than as incarnations of youthfulness. For when, in common usage, we describe persons as "youthful," we mean not primarily that they are obviously young, and hence relatively naive and inexperienced; we mean that they tend to manifest certain qualities in their behavior, and that although these qualities do seem to be empirically

---

[12] (Boston, Mass.: The Beacon Press, 1959).
[13] There actually are many adolescents who respond to questionnaires with the opinion that teenagers are not really old enough to smoke or drink or in general to know what is good for them.

*associate*d with tender years, they are not *exclusively* age-graded. Regardless of chronological age, youthful persons tend to be impulsive, spontaneous, energetic, exploratory, venturesome, and vivacious; they tend to be candid, colorful, blunt in speech (having not acquired the skill and habit of dissimulation); they are often irreverent, frequently disrespectful; extreme, immoderate, they know no golden mean; they are "action seekers"[14] rather than seekers of stable routine. They joke a lot; the play motif dominates much of their activity—which they tend to transform into games, even in the most apparently unpropitious of circumstances. Lacking caution and judiciousness, they tend to throw themselves with full passion and sexually alert intensity into those activities that promise thrills and excitement, which they tend to pursue with little regard for consequences.

Notice that these are primarily the qualities of persons, not roles, and certainly not rationalized, bureaucratic roles—although they may become quasi-institutionalized as "deviant" roles. Notice too that they are all very active——one might say erotic. When abstracted from behavior and become conscious, qualities such as these assert themselves on *ideological* grounds. When, that is, they take on the character of moral imperatives, we can properly speak of a system of subcultural norms.[15] Such norms underlie the content of youth culture. Clearly, they are dangerous: from the perspective of the major institutions of social order, youthfulness is excess; it is implicit or incipient disorder; for society, it is a "problem" that requires handling, control, co-optation, or channeling in socially approved directions.

Society has at its disposal a great armory of means to control this implicit threat of disorder. I mean not the police and the courts or the more informal sanctions wielded by parents and other authorities; I mean the community youth center, the chaperoned dance, organized sports, school-sponsored extracurricular clubs, and the junior auxiliaries of business, religious, fraternal and veterans' associations—for adults have learned that adolescents will frequently accept from their peers the same norms they may reject from adults. But the effectiveness of these organizational weapons in coping with youth varies with the location of particular youths in the social structure. Where, for example, adult leadership is poor and community facilities limited, as in urban slums and certain new suburbs; or where sudden discontinuities in style of life create inter-generation tensions and anxieties, and disqualify parents as models worthy of emulation and respect, as frequently occurs in immigrant or highly mobile families; or where failure or anticipated failure in academic competition leaves the failer with the perception of a bleak future and with no approved alternative sources of self-respect, as frequently occurs among ethnic and working class boys in schools dominated by middle class norms—where these and other early experiences of incipient

---

[14] The term "action seeker" is taken from Herbert Gans' characterization of some working-class Bostonians. See his *The Urban Villagers* (New York: The Free Press of Glencoe, 1962).
[15] For modern formulations of this ideology, see Norman Brown, *Life Against Death* (New York: Random House, 1960); Herbert Marcuse, *Eros and Civilization* (Boston, Mass.: The Beacon Press, 1959) and Paul Goodman, *Growing Up Absurd*, (New York: Random House, 1960).

social disaffection can mobilize ideological supports and some degree of structural insulation from the major institutions, there we are likely to find fertile ground in which the seeds of youthful excess and disorder can grow, and, eventually, bear the exotic flower called "youth culture."

VARIETIES OF YOUTH CULTURE

The flower has many blooms; the varieties of youth culture are as wide as the variety of cultural contexts and opportunity systems offered by a pluralistic society. At its broadest and most innocuous, the youth cultures of the young touch the fringes of what is called "teenage culture": popular songs, rock and roll, disc jockeys, juke boxes, portable phonographs, movie stars, dating, and romantic love; hot rods, motorcycles, drag racing, and sports cars, panty raids and water fights, drive-in hamburgers and clandestine drinking, football games, basketball games, dances and parties, and clubs and cliques, and lovers' lanes. At its delinquent extreme, youth culture is black leather jackets, gang rumbles and switch blades, malicious mischief, and joy riding in stolen cars. Politically, it is expressed in sit-ins, freedom rides, peace marches, and folk songs; it is jazz at Newport, vacations at Fort Lauderdale—and their attendant riots. And it is also bohemians and beatniks and beards and hipsters, and coffee shop desperadoes plotting everything from literary magazines to assaults on the House Committee on Un-American Activities.[16]

I intend by this apparently formless catalogue of symbols to suggest how wide a variety of group styles and expressions the youth cultures of the young include. Intimations[17] of youth culture will be found more frequently among "teenagers" than among "American youth," more frequently among "conflict" and "retreatist" delinquent gangs than among the "rational" criminal delinquents,[18] more among "bohemian" and "collegiate" undergraduates than among academically or vocationally oriented college students,[19] and more among politically militant and extreme student groups than among the student adherents of "moderate" sentiment within the two major political parties. The wide social spectrum represented by these groups should reassure the skeptical that I have no ideological axes to grind; few of those prone to moral judgments of youth could unambiguously approve or disapprove of *all* of these groups at the same time. But what delinquents and bohemians and campus radicals and even some high school hot rodders and college fraternity boys have in common is, I am suggesting, their youthfulness, that is, their tendency to behave in patterned ways normatively hedonistic, irresponsible, and expressive.

In spite of the wide variety of dissimilar forms in which it is expressed,

[16] For a very similar formulation, see David Matza, "Subterranean Traditions of Youth," *The Annals* (November 1961) in which Matza argues that radicalism, bohemianism, and delinquency are the three basic forms which subterranean traditions (that is, subcultures) of youth take.

[17] I say "intimations" because "teenage culture" is what David Matza calls a "conventional version" of what I would call a genuine youth culture.

[18] See Richard Cloward and Lloyd Ohlin, *Delinquency and Opportunity*, (Glencoe, Ill.: The Free Press, 1960) for a discussion of these types of gangs.

[19] See the typology of college student orientations in Martin A. Trow and Burton Clark, "Determinants of College Student Subcultures," in *College Peer Groups*, T. M. Newcomb and E. K. Wilson, eds. (Chicago: Aldine, 1966).

it seems reasonable and useful—and also more objective—initially to designate this normative behavior as "youthful" (rather than, say, "deviant" or "delinquent" or "alienated"—although it may *become* these) because it is in large part the autonomous creature of sub-societies of the recalcitrant young. Although, as I have suggested above and will argue at some length below, it is also selected from, supported by, and modeled after a long cultural tradition, nourished by several contemporary subcultures of adults, and is hence in principle viable into adulthood and beyond. The youth cultures of the young are an adaptive response by *some* adolescents to problems presented to them by their parent society and culture (for example, contradictions or imbalances in norms, blockage of opportunity, inadequately defined roles, ambiguities of age-grading, the prospect of meaningless work), and the forms they take in specific groups reflect a choice from traditions available to them. To see the matter this way takes account of both the autonomous character of the subculture and its linkage to important traditions which antedate it. The significance of the adjective in the term "youth culture," however, rests not in the fact that many of its participants are young, but in the fact that their selective interaction with one another, under the difficult conditions generated by our age-grading norms and in contexts that limit the exercise of adult supervision and control, may sustain a set of more or less counter-norms which encourage and support, however ambivalently, a pattern of behavior at odds with the official norms of the culture in which it is located, but *adaptive* in the sense that it can provide—not just temporarily—a more or less viable way of life.

Adult Youth Cultures

THE PRESERVATION OF YOUTH CULTURE: ITS LINKS WITH THE ADULT WORLD

Earlier, I criticized the usage of the concept of "transitional stage" because it did not sufficiently specify the differential impact of adolescent experience upon subsequent careers. We already know that adolescents eventually become adults; but we do not know much about the ways in which variations in adolescent experience affect subsequent adult adaptations. The concept of "transitional stage" is often employed largely as a palliative for society's functional problems of recruiting and integrating youth into adult worlds: if it's merely "a stage they're going through," then adults need not frankly confront the problems their behavior raises because, after all, "they'll grow out of it."

Most of them, it is true, do grow out of it, and the fact that they do is testimony not only to the power of adult agencies of socialization but to the vulnerability to co-optation of "teen-age culture"—to its lack of resources to sustain it in crisis and insulate it from attack.[20] But some do not or cannot grow out of it. What becomes of those young persons whose "youthful rebelliousness" turns out to be not "a stage they're going through," but a series of

---

[20] It is this lack which distinguishes "teen-age culture" from more genuine subcultures such as ethnic communities, delinquent gangs in urban slums, and bohemias. Ethnic communities frequently have a full blown institutional structure to shield

subculturally rewarding experiences that subjectively validate their initial opposition to or irritation with the official demands of adults? And what becomes of those whose participation in political, delinquent, and bohemian forms of youth culture leaves permanent stigmata that render them permanently visible to a henceforth skeptical and suspicious world? Delinquency statistics, the "beatnik" craze, student militance and riots suggest that for substantial numbers (how many, no one knows) adolescence is not simply an awkward but benign transitional stage, and it is these facts to which we refer when we speak of youth and their growing up as a "social problem." To the extent that we can conceive of growing up as a *career* (and in this psycho-analytical age it is not difficult to do so), "*not* growing up" (that is, the preservation of the essential features of youth culture in later life) can also be considered as a career. Although there is a certain joylessness in the idea of "maturity" (identified, as it is, with sober responsibilities and solemn commitments), there are relatively few niches in the adult social structure where "youthfulness" does not receive severe negative sanctions, and those adolescents whose peer group experience has developed in them trained incapacities for growing up or perhaps even conscientious objections to it may be expected to gravitate toward them.

Those adolescents among whom youthful attributes are weakest—for example, those studied by Elkin and Westley, the prematurely socialized type described by Friedenberg, and the bulk of adolescents only superficially involved in teenage culture—will probably have the least difficulty in making the transition to the typical adult careers offered in a highly industrialized, bureaucratized society. On the other hand, those in whom youthful attributes are strong will have the greatest difficulty in making those sacrifices of youthfulness that most executive and professional and other prestigious adult careers require.

What kinds of adult occupations and milieu are likely to reward or at least to tolerate youthfulness, and thus normatively support an attempt not to grow up or an inability to grow up? If it is true that some adolescents are more youthful than others, it is also true that some adults are more youthful than others, and it is likely that some of the important forces that sustain youthfulness in those who are no longer young may be found in the norms of the occupations they choose (or which choose them) and in the milieu that those norms help create.[21] What are some of these types of occupations?

YOUTHFUL CAREERS

I submit the following short list for illustrative purposes. My best hope is that it will be taken as suggestive of one way of theoretically linking the

its members from the society's encroachment; delinquent gangs emphasize the inviolability of "turf" for good sociological reason; bohemias are usually ecological communities as well as subcultures, and even political radicals have, at the very least, a strong ideology to sustain them. Teenagers have very little.

[21] Statuses other than occupational ones, of course, may also help sustain youthfulness: bachelor, divorcé(e), student, for example. Periodicals such as *Esquire* and *Playboy* are apparently directed at youthful adult audiences, and an analysis of their readers might provide evidence of youthful adult statuses.

content of adolescent youth cultures with important subterranean or deviant traditions in the adult world, and hence of linking certain kinds of youthful experience in the adolescent milieu with the subsequent taking up of adult careers.

Bohemian Business. By bohemian businessmen, I mean the proprietors or managers of small enterprises that cater to the needs, tastes, and desires of bohemians. These enterprises range all the way from those that are central to bohemian subcultures (*espresso* coffee houses, small art galleries, sandal and leather shops, pottery shops, jewelery shops, and so on) to other marginal businesses serving other markets as well ("art" theaters, paperback book-stores, small night clubs specializing in modern jazz, accessory and specialty shops for women, and so on). Wherever a "deviant" community exists (in this case a bohemian community), a business community is likely to exist to supply the wants that symbolize and define its deviance—in a sense analogous to that in which organized crime is symbiotically interrelated with government, law enforcement agencies, and parts of the legitimate business community. Bohemian business enterprise is one of the relatively few types of careers available to persons who, having had their basic orientations to the world shaped by experience in an adolescent subculture, have developed trained incapacities for pursuing more conventional kinds of business or professional or "bourgeois" careers—although the ironic and economically "reactionary" character of bohemian enterprise is that it gives its entrepreneurs the status of shopkeeper.

But their status as shopkeepers is less important and less revealing than the fact that they are likely to be bohemians. Bohemian businessmen, that is, are more like their customers than like other small businessmen. Even in their strictly economic capacities, bohemian businessmen are likely to reflect the habits of their customers. They may, for example, be expected to keep irregular hours, to open their shops late in the day, and remain open late in the evening. Located primarily in the "Latin quarter" of large cities or near university campuses, they frequently take long summer vacations or move their shops to summer resorts of the "art colony" type. They are not likely to keep rigorous books and their prices are frequently not standardized—sometimes because their wares are not. Often, they do not have a primarily commercial or instrumental orientation to what they sell, but rather an expressive one.[22] Dealing mainly in beauty—in esthetic objects or experience—they are not likely to think of themselves primarily as businessmen, but either as craftsmen or as esthetic functionaries performing services for the community of avant-garde good taste. However they think of themselves, bohemian businessmen (recruited largely from the student bohemian world of craftsmen, failed or insufficiently talented artists, and hangers-on and camp followers of the cultural avant-garde) live in a milieu that tolerates and rewards a youthful

[22] As an example a customer walks into an "art mart" to purchase a teapot that goes with a set of china that the customer knows the shop stocks. With some hauteur, the proprietress informs the customer that she does not sell the teapot (although she sells all the other pieces in the set) because it is "poorly designed."

adaptation to the world. Bohemian business offers a moderately viable niche in the adult world for those unable or unwilling to grow out of youth culture.

Perhaps an *image* of a viable niche in the world would be a more accurate statement. For it is, of course, true that the actual opportunities for a successful career in bohemian business are probably not very good. Although it is a theoretically open milieu, the rate of business failure seems high, and the population of bohemia is probably not large enough to support the commercial enterprises of very many of those young persons who are more or less successfully resisting or evading middle-class socialization. Nevertheless, the image of an adult bohemian life is culturally fertile and ambiguously seductive to many. Bohemia is always newsworthy; its consistent coverage in the mass media, its consistent status as a "tourist attraction" means that it is of great interest to the vicarious lives of large numbers of people. For every core bohemian there are probably five fringe bohemians; for every fringe bohemian there are probably five "weekend bohemians"; and for every weekend bohemian there are probably scores of Walter Mittys each of whom might be secretly flattered to have one of his perhaps idiosyncratic habits labeled "bohemian" by a suspicious and surly neighbor. My point is simply that although full-time bohemianism as a career may not be viable very long for very many, its part-time or fantasy appeal is apparently much stronger than the actual opportunities it offers. But it is the existence of this appeal and the ambiguous possibilities represented by it that enable it to serve for the youthful as a *milieu of orientation* tolerant of their behavior and to which they may look for permanent sustenance.

Show Business. Many actors, singers, dancers, musicians, comedians, and other entertainers inhabit a world suffused by the myth of youth——a world in which grandmothers and grandfathers are noted for their sex appeal. The professional milieu of jazz musicians interpenetrates with the hipster and bohemian varieties of youth culture, bonded by a common antipathy to "squares." Much like the jazz milieu, the world of the off-Broadway theater is heavily populated with aspiring actors and actresses, committed to their expressive art, who live on the fringe of bohemia. The celebrity world of Hollywood stars is, for public consumption at least, "La Dolce Vita," with its dominating motifs of sex, speed, alcohol, drugs, and perversion set in a context of luxury. Most of the "new" American comedians have come up from the dark basement clubs catering to bohemian-intellectual audiences into the bright glare of the legitimate stage and the TV studio to continue, somewhat diluted, their savage satires of the routine, the usual, the ordinary (that is, the "adult")—but now to the masochistic audience upon whose lives and opinions their material is based. Finally, teenage pop singers, despite their ritual affirmation of God, Home, and Mother, and their pious promises to "continue their education" (directed, one supposes, at the parents of their admirers), create a professional image compounded of thinly disguised erotica and forlorn adolescent alienation and, with the help of publicity, transform their slum or otherwise poverty stricken backgrounds into a romantic determination to "be somebody." ("I want to become a really good actor instead of just a teenage singer.")

That show business careers and similar occupations are in fact subject to much the same economic circumstances and bureaucratic controls as are other occupations, and that many show folk in fact live model middle-class lives are less important than the carefully nurtured Dionysian images of show business life, the persistent myth that careers are made "overnight," that its durable stars are ageless, and that "expressive" opportunities are offered by the public spotlight. Like other "creative" occupations, show business tends to be tolerant of irregular, spontaneous, unpredictable, exhibitionistic behavior— indeed, these are sometimes built into the very conditions of employment; more, show business expects this kind of behavior, and sometimes rewards it (in publicity, if nothing else—and publicity is seldom nothing else), at least among its stars. The hedonism and public irresponsibility of show business celebrities is disingenuously mythologized as "artistic temperament," suggesting that in those industries in which "creativity" is a basic commodity, perversities of other sorts must also be accepted: great beauty, great talent, great acclaim imply great vices. Thus Ava Gardner (a living Lady Brett) leaves a trail of discarded lovers across the bull rings of Spain; thus Maria Callas sails the Mediterranean in her Greek billionaire's yacht, telling the press at Riviera ports that they are "just friends"; thus Ingrid Bergman illegitimately conceives a child on a volcanic Aegean island to the merely temporary dismay of her fans; thus Lana Turner rears a daughter who becomes the killer of her mother's gangster-lover; thus Eddie leaves Debbie for Liz and Liz leaves Eddie for Richard to a breathless watching world of column readers. Billie Holiday, the greatest jazz singer of the era, wasted from years of addiction to heroin, dies under guard in a hospital; idols of teenage girls get picked up for homosexuality; Dean Martin nurtures a lucrative public image built on a reputation for alcoholism, and the Frank Sinatra clique spread across the night life of the country their money, their liquor, their arrogance, and their talent to delight the press.

With this newsreel, I intend neither a documentation of the lurid nor a righteous cry of decadence but only a vivid suggestion that, manufactured or not, the image of show business careers exists in a milieu in which Dionysian excess has a long tradition and an honored place—a cautious and implicit honor (given its dependence on the whims of public opinion), but a milieu in which one neither loses face nor gets fired for scandalous behavior, a milieu in which the only bad publicity is no publicity at all. The extremes to which the public behavior of show business celebrities is constrained are, like that of gang delinquents, justified by the "rep" it engenders; the Dionysian comings and goings of middle-aged Frank Sinatra and his middle-aged friends are apparently regarded by the public with the same chuckling benignity reserved for the pranks of teenagers. There is a normative kinship between the Dionysian motifs of the celebrity world of show biz and the hedonistic, expressive values of youth culture. A substantial part of the material content of youth culture is provided and sustained by the industries of mass entertainment and a large part of the entertainment business depends upon youth for its markets. Notice also that show business careers (and satellite show business careers such as disc jockeying and modeling) are virtually the *only* occupations or occupational images offered to adolescents in the pages of the "teenage magazines." Like bohemian business, show business offers the image of a career to talented young people with trained incapacities for business or the bureaucratized professions. People with "artistic talent" have, according to legend, no "business sense," and show business careers are often said to require the kind of single-minded dedication that is unable even to imagine another kind of future. Like bohemian business, show business tolerates or rewards a youthful orientation to the world and offers the inducement of "romantic" or "glamorous" careers to those unable or unwilling to "grow up."[23]

Like bohemian business too, show business has an important component of vicarious appeal; there is a sense in which show business is everyman's vicarious business; there are probably thousands of Americans who sit in front of their TV sets quietly confident that they can sing as well, dance as well, tell jokes as well, ride a horse and sling a gun as well as those merely lucky ones on the screen. Show business not only involves the audience in the imaginary worlds it creates, it involves them vicariously in show business itself. This may be one of the reasons for the proverbial interest of Americans in the private lives of celebrities, and why professional, in-group banter and jokes about show business is virtually the only kind of esoteric humor of interest to out-groups. So that in addition to the promise of an actual career, show business, again like bohemia, offers an abundance of vicarious careers to the imperfectly socialized, and is thus, in an oddly perverse sense, functional to the extent that, by mollifying largely unfulfilled yearnings for a freer, more spontaneous that is, more youthful life, it softens the tensions and frustrations engendered by socialization without internalization. Like the Horatio Alger myth, which told us that we too could succeed, the myths of the adult milieu which combine the exciting with the unsavory tell us that our lives need not be routine and colorless. The Alger myth succored an age of economic growth preoccupied with objective success; the youthfulness myth succors an age of psychology preoccupied with subjective "fulfillment."

Working-Class Occupations.   Many of the adolescents whom I have called "youthful"—the high school rebels, the flouters of adult authority, the claimers of autonomy for adolescents—are likely to be of working-class background, especially ethnics, culturally "deprived," without much talent, who drop out of high school or do poorly in it, and are probably headed not for the glamorous careers I have mentioned but for the lower reaches of the manual labor force. Nevertheless, there are good reasons for believing that many working-class occupations and the subcultural norms associated with some of them are more supportive of youthful orientations than most middle-class occupations.

Several otherwise disparate intellectual traditions converge in their charac-

---

[23] Moss Hart, who should know, writes, "I would hazard a guess . . . that the temperament, the tantrums, and the utter childishness of theater people in general, is neither accidental nor a necessary weapon of their profession. It has nothing to do with so-called 'artistic temperament.' The explanation, I think, is a far simpler one. For the most part they are impaled in childhood like a fly in amber." Moss Hart, *Act One* (New York: Random House, 1959).

terizations of working-class life in terms akin to my conception of youthfulness. The Marxist tradition, for example, confers upon labor the innocent dignity of useful work, the tragedy of exploitation and alienation, and the heroic mission of carrying within it the seeds of a bright and revolutionary future. Having nothing to lose but their chains, the proletariat can take dramatic and passionate steps in its own interest. Sabotage, walkouts, general strikes, the Marxist myth of a militant working class—bold, defiant, resentful of its oppressors, impatient to bring down the system of authority which victimizes it—strikingly partakes of much the same spirit and imagery as rebellious adolescents *vis-à-vis* the world of adults. Both groups claim for themselves, in the strident tones characteristic of those without a parliamentary voice, autonomy, freedom from their illegitimate subordination to an authority they never chose, that consigns them to a future they do not want.

There is also a literary tradition more than 150 years old that bestows upon laborers—especially rural laborers—greater energy, vitality, and sexuality than the pale, thin, beardless, repressed pencil pushers who inhabit the offices of the world. In this literary tradition, workers are impulsive, strong, intuitive, passionate—capable of great anger and great tenderness; above all, they are, like adolescents, *personal*, largely alienated from and disgusted with the rationales and rationalizing of the impersonal bureaucratic world.

Paralleling these two romanticisms of working-class life is a third intellectual tradition that emphasizes the common values and long history of both the highest and the lowest classes of traditional Europe, which the despised, calculating minds of the *arriviste* middle class could never share: aristocrats and peasants share a tendency to violence, to alcoholic excesses, and to blood sports. This kinship between the highest and the lowest may be rather forced, but the peculiar combination of aristocratic and vulgar motifs, or élite and egalitarian themes which crystallize around a disdain for middle class life has persisted for nearly two hundred years.[24] The intellectual core of this tradition is the belief that the powers, privileges, and immunities of aristocratic life, and the passion, desperation, and anarchy of life in the depths are both preferable to the calculated moderation and mediocrity inherent in bourgeois definitions of maturity and responsibility. Each extreme is, in its different way, transcendent; the middle class is forever earthbound. Translating this tradition into my own terms, the lower classes and the upper classes are more youthful than the middle class.

Finally, recent empirical descriptions of working class culture by sociologists lend considerable support to these romanticized versions of working-class life. These studies show a highly remarkable but generally unremarked upon similarity to standard descriptions of youth culture. Thus workers tend to be hedonistic, unable to plan ahead or defer gratification; they are highly expressive rather than instrumental in their basic orientations, given to violent and

[24] Especially strongly in the bohemian literary tradition from, say, Diderot to Norman Mailer. One is reminded that "teddy boys" affect the garments of Edwardian gentlemen and the manners of hoodlums. Leslie Fiedler has argued at some length that "highbrow" and "lowbrow" culture have more in common than either has with "middlebrow" culture. See his, "Both Ends Against the Middle," reprinted in Rosenberg and White (eds.) *Mass Culture* (Glencoe, Ill.: The Free Press, 1957).

extreme views, irrational, anti-intellectual, "person-centered" (rather than "role-centered"), and generally neglectful of their civic responsibilities.[25] Certain working class occupations, then, especially *lower* ones, are likely to require much less in the way of sacrifice of youthfulness than most other occupations, and it should come as no surprise that recalcitrant youth without academic ability or usable deviant talents should gravitate toward these jobs.

Conclusion

What I have offered here is in a sense a conceptual model for the analysis of adolescent behavior and the youthful adult milieu to which, under certain conditions, it may lead. There are youthful occupations and milieu other than those I have described. I have not, for example, mentioned free lance art or the military or professional sports, nor have I mentioned several niches in the academic and intellectual worlds that support youthful orientations. But I think that by now my major point should be clear: I have tried to suggest that the successful socialization of children into the dominant value system is always problematic especially in pluralistic societies, that recalcitrance can be spotted early, and that what I have called youth culture begins when adolescent rebellion against dominant adult norms take on ideological supports from existing deviant traditions. For many adolescents, of course, this is only "a stage they go through," and most of them eventually internalize or at least comply with the norms constrained on them by the major agencies of socialization. At the same time, it is important to recognize that many adolescents do not, that the experience of many in adolescent subcultures shapes their futures by incapacitating them for bureaucratic roles. Most of these, it is true, wind up at the lower end of the occupational hierarchy, especially those who are unable to survive high school. But those who do survive and who are fortunate enough to discover the other face of their trained incapacities—in college or elsewhere—are uniquely enabled to take advantage of the few sheltered places a pluralistic society offers in its occupational structure which will permit them, as adults, to sustain that normative variation without which pluralism is emptied of its cultural meaning. This leaves a society highly differentiated on the level of social structure but homogeneous on the level of culture.

With this analysis, I am not offering only a more differentiated view of socialization—substituting a frame of reference emphasizing conformity to milieu rather than to general cultural norms. I mean also to emphasize that groups differ in the extent to which they tolerate or encourage normative

[25] See, for example, William F. Whyte, *Street Corner Society*, (Chicago, Ill.: University of Chicago Press, 1943); S. M. Miller and Frank Riessman, "The Working Class Subculture," *Social Problems* (Summer 1961); Richard Hoggart, *The Uses of Literacy*, (London: Chatto and Windus, 1957); A. K. Cohen and H. M. Hodges, "Characteristics of the Lower-Blue-Collar Class," *Social Problems* (Spring 1963); Herbert J. Gans, (Note 13), and Seymour Martin Lipset, "Working Class Authoritarianism," in *Social Controversy*, W. Petersen and D. Matza, eds. (Belmont, Calif.: Wadsworth Publishing Co., 1963).

dissension, and the extent to which this is true is directly relevant to the *roles* that inveterate dissenters can find in the social structure. In groups which require a high degree of uniformity, dissenters are constrained to yield or to withdraw from active participation; but in groups that place a high value on innovation—and many youthful groups are prominent among these—dissenters are much more likely to be able to retain the privileges of active association.[26]

This analysis also bears upon the problem of adaptation to failure, and casts a little light on the ingenious way in which society provides for the comfort of its failures while using its own failure to socialize some of its members as a way of easing the tensions engendered by its excessive success with others: those who are relegated to the bottom of the occupational heap. for example, are heir to a ready-made ideology, a myth that invidiously contrasts their own vigor, vitality, and authentic humanity with the repressions, the desk-boundness, and the futile status-seeking of the successful. Society uses the luckier ones too—those who are able to find loftier, more glamorous, youthful adult niches. These feed the vicarious appetites of the nation, and are living testimony to the bored, the alienated from work, and the otherwise vaguely dissatisfied that exciting careers *do* exist. And the definition of these careers as newsworthy by the mass media peculiarly fits them for the strategic role they play in the vicarious lives of others.

[26] For empirical data on this point, see Yrjo Littunen, "Deviance and Passivity in Radio Listener Groups," *Acta Sociologia* (Vol. 4).

THE LANGUAGE OF ADOLESCENTS*

GARY SCHWARTZ
DON MERTEN[1]

For insiders language becomes a chief key to the taste socialization and mood currents that are prevalent in this group at any moment. For outsiders, including adult observers, language becomes a mysterious opacity, constantly carrying peer-group messages which are full of precisions that remain untranslatable—DAVID RIESMAN, *The Lonely Crowd.*

The Problem

The question of whether there is a relatively self-contained adolescent subculture in this society stimulates recurrent, inconclusive sociological controversy. Contrary to the model of the youth culture as a contraculture, we hold that its reality as a subculture does not rest upon its power to repudiate or undermine basic adult values. We shall argue that peer-group interaction is guided by expectations which do not govern the behavior of other members of the community. And we claim that the understandings which transform what might otherwise be transitory encounters into stable peer-group relationships are not fully comprehensible to the rest of the community. More simply, adolescent social relationships are predicated upon premises not completely accessible or intelligible to adults.[2]

* Reprinted from Gary Schwartz and Don Merten, "The Language of Adolescents: An Anthropological Approach to the Youth Culture," in *American Journal of Sociology*, Vol. LXXII (March 1967), pp. 453–468, by permission of the authors and University of Chicago Press. Copyright 1967 by the University of Chicago.
[1] This paper reports on the first part of an on-going anthropological study of the youth culture in an urban community which is supported by the National Institute of Mental Health grant MH 12172–01. Our data are derived from field observation of peer groups operating in their natural habitats and from intensive, free-flowing interviews with selected informants. Initial contacts were made with this youth population through an established youth-serving agency, and subsequent relationships were established by following out friendship networks, i.e., meeting and talking with friends of our initial contacts. We found that these networks seldom bridged the several strata of the status system; thus, it was necessary to establish new contacts and follow out friendship networks in each of the strata. Thus far most of our informants have come from the higher reaches of the adolescent status system (24), rather than its lower levels (10). There are more girls (23) than boys (11) at present in our formal interview sample. Much of our data on the boys came from less structured contexts, such as conversations in cars, etc. Although the number of interviews with each informant varies, we find that some of our more articulate informants have remained with the

From our point of view, the specifically subcultural aspects of adolescent social life reside in those symbolic elements (values, beliefs, and standards) which integrate various concrete norms[3] into a coherent system of action. Later in this paper we will examine some of the symbolic resolutions of adolescent role dilemmas and ambiguities, for example, adolescent beliefs about their own social world which reduce logical and moral inconsistencies between incongruous orientations to various social situations.

As Riesman suggests, the significance of much of adolescent social life is partially hidden from adults by linguistic devices. Consequently, the data which can best reveal the character of the youth culture are linguistic, and the relevant aspect of adolescent language is obviously semantic.

Language and Action

In this paper, we will show that adolescent perceptions and assessments of their own social universe are embodied in a distinctive argot, their status terminology. These status terms refer to moral attributes (those qualities which make some persons admirable, others reprehensible, etc.) and moral dispositions (the kinds of things these people are likely to do and say). The members of a status category are thought to possess common social virtues and defects. Status terms, then, are not affectively neutral labels for structural positions in the youthful social system. They bestow either negative or positive esteem on those who manifest or exemplify these personal characteristics. Consequently, an individual's rank in the local prestige hierarchy is partly a function of the meanings inherent in those terms his peers use to describe his character and his group affiliations.

Following the logic but not the exact method of componential analysis,[4] the lexical set we call the adolescent status terminology constitutes a

---

study for a year on the basis of two or three hour-and-a-half tape-recorded interviews per month. The interviews were usually with individual informants, although occasionally small groups of 2–4 students were interviewed. A considerable portion of our data was gathered in talks with students at dances, parties, hangouts, card games, etc.

We would like to thank Solomon Kobrin and David M. Schneider both for their comments on this paper and their generous advice on the design of this study. We also would like to thank Cal Cottrell, Daniel Scheinfeld, and Henry McKay for their comments on this paper. We alone are responsible for its deficiencies.

[2] In a comparatively recent view of the "adolescent society," Bennett Berger, "Adolescence and Beyond," *Social Problems*, Vol. X (1963), asserts that "there is absolutely no good body of data on adolescents, Coleman's included, which indicates the existence of a really deviant system of norms which govern adolescent life" (p. 395).

[3] By concrete norms we mean specific prescriptions and proscriptions which refer to particular types of social contexts (e.g., dating) and which govern or which actors feel ought to govern behavior (e.g., sexual) in these kinds of social settings.

[4] Componential analysis is a technique for the investigation of semantic domains modeled after descriptive linguistics. It should enable an observer both to describe and predict the ways in which the members of a culture will classify phenomenological reality. Anthony Wallace, "The Psychic Unity of Human Groups," *Studying Personality Cross-culturally*, ed. Bert Kaplan (Evanston, Ill.: Row, Peterson, 1961), succinctly describes this method: "The fundamental and intuitive idea on which the

semantic domain:[5] a culturally defined and verbally expressed area of social experience bounded by the existence or occurrence of certain types of objects, events, or behaviors. Although the exact boundaries of this semantic domain are sometimes vague, it comprises an internally consistent system of meanings. At one level of meaning, these terms refer to the kind and the amount of respect the occupants of a status category can claim in the adolescent social system. From the perspective of formal linguistic analysis,[6] the problem concerns the conceptual (i.e., cultural) criteria which assign particular status terms to larger status classes or categories. However, we are not interested in arranging these terms so that their value is specified along these conceptual dimensions and so that the intersection of these values predicts the occurrence of each term in this classificatory scheme. Rather, we want to know how the cognitive and evaluative meanings of this semantic domain are related to social contexts.[7]

---

semantic calculus is based is a simple one: that the signification of a 'term' (which may be an extrinsic linguistic symbol, such as a word, or any other overt behavior) is given by a particular pattern of predicates which evoke or are evoked by, that term. A predicate is a symbol for the common property of the members of a class. In the technique of componential analysis, the various criteria (predicates) relevant to the definition of the terms in a lexicon are conceived of as values on dimensions, such that each cell in the space represents a unique combination of values, one from each dimension. Each term can then be mapped onto the space by stating to which combination or combinations of criteria it corresponds. When all the terms have been so mapped, their logico-semantic relationships can be explicitly stated" (p. 143).

[5] There has been a good deal of discussion about replicable, empirical discovery procedures for establishing the boundaries of semantic domains, such as the use of standard control questions which specify the exact level of linguistic contrast. But we rely upon more impressionist techniques for delimiting this semantic domain because we are concerned with the expressive (i.e., the connotational) as well as the referential (i.e., the definitional) meanings of this terminology. This is a more elusive universe of discourse than the usual subjects of componential analysis, e.g., kinship, color, plant, and disease terminologies. Even when componential analysis is applied to purely cognitive domains it experiences some difficulty when these terminologies have an oblique or tangential relationship to observable events or physical objects. Thus, Charles Frake, "The Diagnosis of Disease among the Subanum of Mindanao," *Language in Culture and Society*, ed. Dell Hymes (New York: Harper & Row, 1964), says that "it is difficult, then, to define Subanum diagnostic categories in terms of analytic or perceptual attributes of the denotata" (p. 201). And Robbins Burling, "How To Choose a Burmese Numeral Classifier," *Context and Meaning in Cultural Anthropology*, ed. Melford Spiro (New York: Free Press, 1965), has found for a clear-cut semantic domain that "the attempt to find pervasive semantic dimensions which unambiguously apportion the entire set of classifiers into clear subsets has hardly been successful" (p. 263). In light of these considerations, our inability to determine the exact boundaries of this semantic domain does not constitute an insuperable obstacle to discovering the meaning of the cognitive distinctions and moral oppositions inherent in this terminology.

[6] Paul Kay in a comment on R. N. Colby's "Ethnographic Semantics: A Preliminary Survey," *Current Anthropology*, Vol. VII (February 1966), says that "componential analysis is best conceived as an *analytic process* in which the investigator searches for (a) the *dimensions* of meaning underlying the domain and (b) the mapping of the values on these dimensions *(the features of meaning)* onto the set of lexemes. The process of looking for these mappings is not to be confused with particular types of such mappings such as paradigm, taxonomy, and tree" (pp. 20–21, italics in original).

[7] As we have seen, status terms refer to certain kinds of social predicates. In order to elicit these predicates, we rely upon a basic methodological postulate of componential analysis: the contextualization of meaning. Hymes, "A Perspective for Linguistic

The linguistically conditioned ways in which the members of a group perceive and evaluate their social environment have determinant consequences for their behavior. Here we follow Clyde Kluckhohn, who says that "the *vocabularies* of different languages both reflect and perpetuate habitual and distinctive ways of categorizing experience or modes of thought."[8] He goes on to say that "how people behave toward one another is, in part, a function of what they call each other and of *how* they conceive objects, themselves, other people and types of events which enter into their relations."[9] Elucidation of the meanings implicit in the adolescent status terminology will illuminate the complex relationships between the norms of this subculture and the behavior of its members in various social settings.

Stated in functional terms, cultural categories contained in language do not usually determine the particulars (i.e., the who, how much, and when) of any behavioral sequence but, rather, provide the cognitive and evaluative parameters of social interaction in any social setting.[10] These categories identify the appropriate motives, values, roles, and rules which transform the actor's external physical world into what Hallowell calls the behavioral environment of the self. "A *second* function of all cultures is the orientation of the self to a diversified world of objects in its behavioral environment, discriminated, classified, and conceptualized with respect to attributes which are culturally constituted and symbolically mediated through language. The role of language in object-orientation is as vital as in self-orientation."[11] As we shall see in the case of the meaning of the term "cool," these categories tie both the actor's moral orientations and cognitive definitions of social situations to the critical motivational dimensions of the self, that is, his judgments about his own worth—"Any kind of self-depreciation, loss of self-esteem, or

---

Anthropology," *Horizons of Anthropology*, ed. Sol Tax (Chicago: Aldine Publishing, 1964), says that "as is widely recognized, a term's meaning depends upon the interaction between its own semantic properties and those recognized in the context in which it occurs. A term can indicate a wide range of meanings, and a context can support a range of meanings. In a given case the term does not so much positively name, as does the intersection of the term and context eliminates most, or all but one, of the possible meanings" (p. 97). This stress on the intersection of linguistic meanings and social context is particularly applicable to the study of the evaluative aspects of the youth culture. Here there is a complex relationship among the actor's motives, the norms which govern behavior in a social situation, and the ends or goals this subculture defines as worthwhile, i.e., what its members should strive to achieve or become. We hold that the meaning of a particular status term can only be understood after the observer knows the contexts in which it is used and the norms which govern behavior in this situation. Then, for example, he can ask his informants whether "cool" and "mellow" mean the same or different things. Hymes, *ibid.*, claims that the "fact of contrast, and the dimensions, can be determined only by knowing the context of the situation, and discovering what expressions have functional unity through being mutually substitutable for a given end within it" (p. 98).

[8] "Culture and Behavior," *Handbook of Social Psychology*, Vol. XX, ed. Gardner Lindsey (Reading, Mass.: Addison-Wesley Publishing, 1954), p. 938, italics in original.
[9] *Ibid.*
[10] For a persuasive statement of a somewhat different point of view, see Frake, "A Structural Description of Subanum 'Religious Behavior,'" *Explorations in Cultural Anthropology*, ed. Ward Goodenough (New York: McGraw-Hill Book Co., 1964).
[11] A. I. Hallowell, "The Self and Its Behavioral Environment," *Culture and Experience* (Philadelphia: University of Pennsylvania Press, 1955), p. 91, italics in original.

threat to the self impairs the complex motivational systems that focus upon the self and its needs. At the same time, self-evaluation through culturally recognized norms is inescapable."[12]

The Structural Origins of the Youth Culture

Considered as a phenomenon indigenous to modern societies, the youth culture can be traced to the problem of socialization in industrial societies.[13] Certainly adolescent norms refer to these structural problems at various levels of meaning. But this does not exhaust the cultural connotations and the behavioral implications of distinctively adolescent modes of communication. For there is great latitude in the selection of the cultural forms which provide adequate solutions to these structural exigencies and concomitant developmental crises—witness the differences in the content of the peer-group norms in various communities and classes.[14] Therefore, it is not possible to account for the substance and imagery of the youth culture solely in terms of the difficult passage from childhood to adulthood in a highly differentiated society.

The Youth Culture Defined

Part of our society's ideology about the nature of human growth asserts that youth must not prematurely assume adult roles. Thus, it is often said that adolescents need an exemption from the pressures of adult responsibilities in order to discover their individual talents. These ideological sanctions encourage adolescents to transform developmental necessities into aesthetically satisfying as well as socially adaptive modes of behavior. In other words, the efflorescence of adolescent styles results from this license to experiment with the possibilities inherent in adult roles. In turn, the youth culture symbolically affirms and celebrates its freedom from conventional restraints on social behavior which has little or no immediate practical significance. For example, many of our informants lavishly praise what they call "idiot"[15] behavior:

---

[12] *Ibid.*, p. 106.

[13] S. N. Eisenstadt's classic study, *From Generation to Generation* (Glencoe, Ill.: Free Press, 1956), points out that there is a radical social-psychological transition between childhood and adulthood in industrial societies. Thus, every child in our society must eventually leave his family circle where he is appreciated for *who* rather than *what* he is. According to this theory, the youth culture serves as a "halfway house" between a young person's particularistic and universalistic associations. While youth groups are based upon ascriptive ties, the youth culture enables adolescents to try out roles and form relationships which involve more universalistic considerations: An adolescent must *earn* his status in the peer group. The youth culture, then, allows the adolescent to experiment with objective, universalistic standards without sacrificing the psychological security of highly solidary primary groups.

[14] For a very detailed account of the attitudes and activities of various types of adolescent peer groups, see Muzafer and Carolyn Sherif, *Reference Groups: Exploration into Conformity and Deviation of Adolescents* (New York: Harper & Row, 1964).

[15] Words enclosed by quotation marks (e.g., "cool") are terms used with considerable frequency by our informants. This is not to say, however, that the notions contained in these words are not also expressed by circumlocution. These terms are ordinarily used in reference and rarely in address.

actions and attitudes which are childish or foolish from an adult point of view and which sometimes treat situations from seemingly incompatible perspectives, for example, dealing with a love relationship in a manner that is at once flippant and romantic. According to some of our most articulate informants, the ability to engage in any sort of silly collective action requires a certain amount of inner freedom and *joie de vivre*. In general, these informants tend to associate these sorts of peer-group activities with independence from adult supervision and with actions which demonstrate this autonomy.[16]

Stated more formally, the youth culture consists of those adolescent norms, standards, and values which are discussed in a language particularly intelligible to members of this age-grade. At this point, we should note that members of the youth culture do not deal with or even "talk" about all the concerns which vitally interest or agitate adolescents, and they may even ignore or overlook those concerns which are of enduring significance to the members of this society.[17] Yet the youth culture contains a distinctive vision of social reality. It is embodied in a normative order predicated upon conceptions of those personal qualities which its members believe make a male admirable and a female desirable.

The Youth Culture as a Contraculture

The sociological conception of the youth culture as a contraculture assumes that the cultural and structural aspects of the youth culture are inextricably linked. Thus, evidence which reveals serious structural discontinuities between the generations is also supposed to show a set of youth norms which are opposed to adult values.[18] According to the contraculture model, if adolescents substantially accept core adult roles and values, then the youth culture is essentially epiphenomenal.[19] But if they doubt the legitimacy

---

[16] According to some of our informants, "idiot" should not be equated with childish behavior. We have been told that those persons who are able to act this way are often the same people who appear most sophisticated (i.e., adult-like) in other social contexts. Perhaps, this connection between silly and sophisticated personal styles is a symbolic means of demonstrating what Erving Goffman (*Encounters* [Indianapolis: Bobbs-Merrill, 1961]), calls role distance. They seem to say that we now have mastered the developmental tasks of childhood, and hence these sorts of performances (playing games which have no extrinsic social significance) can now be slightly ridiculed because it no longer constitutes a vital part of our social identities.

[17] This idea was stimulated by James F. Short's remarks on delinquent gangs in "Social Structure and Group Processes in Gang Delinquency," *Problems of Youth: Transition to Adulthood in a Changing World*, ed. Sherif and Sherif (Chicago: Aldine Publishing, 1965), esp. p. 173.

[18] Cf. James Coleman, *The Adolescent Society* (New York: Free Press, 1961), and F. Elkin and W. Westley, "The Myth of Adolescent Culture," *American Sociological Review*, Vol. XX (1955), who have tried to determine whether the norms of the youth culture impede or inhibit the socialization of adolescents into adult occupational roles.

[19] As subordinate and quite powerless members of our society, youth are said to experience social and psychological deprivation because of the conflicting demands which are placed upon them. Viewed as a contraculture, the youth culture evolves

of societal values, then the youth culture is the appropriate label for this truly rebellious posture. In contrast, our approach to the youth culture holds that the symbolic components of adolescent social life form a relatively coherent subculture *irrespective* of whether its norms eventually subvert, reinforce, or have no lasting effect upon adult values. Our position rests upon a basic theoretical assumption: that the cultural categories which shape adolescent orientations to their own social milieu are largely autonomous inasmuch as they are embodied in systems of meanings whose implications are not immediately apparent to adults.[20]

The structure of advanced societies generates a certain amount of adolescent rebelliousness against adult authority.[21] But this does not mean that opposition to the goals of the older generation is the only, or even the most important, disjunction between adolescent and adult views of social reality. Nor is it true that the norms of the youth culture derive their subcultural attributes from intergenerational conflict.

In fact, the traditional cycle of intense intergenerational conflict followed by reconciliation when the younger generation takes its place in society seems less common today than in the past. Instead of direct confrontations over the moral validity, the relevance, and the appropriateness of the other generations' goals and aspirations,[22] both the older and younger members of this society subscribe to a laissez faire ideology. This encourages generational segregation, rather than opposition. Keniston notes that "another salient fact about young people today is a relative lack of *rebelliousness* against their parents or their parent's generation. . . . The result is frequently an unstated 'gentleman's agreement' between the generations that neither will interfere with the other."[23] According to one of our informants, a senior girl:

Q. Do you know what adults in this community think about various issues?
A. I'd say there is a very small amount of contact between the teen-agers and the adults because we're self-centered, I think, and the adults are too. We think 'I'll leave them alone,' and they do too.

---

out of a normative "reaction-formation" to these pressures. According to Milton Yinger, "Contra-Culture and Subculture," *American Sociological Review*, Vol. XXV (1960), it involves "the creation of a series of inverse or counter values (opposed to those of the surrounding society) in face of serious frustration or conflict" (p. 627).

[20] For example, most adults in this community are aware of, and many approve of, the fraternity and sorority system which operates despite an official school ban on such activity. However, if our adolescent informants are correct, very few adults know why one person is "rushed" and another is not. Though many parents seem to want their children to succeed in this social world, most adults are ignorant of the specific social criteria fraternity and sorority youth use to select certain kinds of persons for their exclusive social circles.

[21] See K. Davis, "The Sociology of Parent-Youth Conflict," *Social Perspectives on Behavior*, ed. H. D. Stein and R. A. Cloward (Glencoe, Ill.: Free Press, 1958).

[22] See Walter Laquer, *Young Germany* (New York: Basic Books, 1962), for a description of youth movements which opposed the prevailing ethos of their society in their early stages of development.

[23] K. Keniston, "Social Change and Youth in America," *Daedalus*, XCI (1962), 151–56, italics in original.

Our informants almost instinctively measured their own worth against the standards of the youth culture. And the cardinal concerns of the youth culture are in those domains over which they exercise direct control: friendships, relations with the opposite sex, and various types of expressive activities. This sort of partial cultural isolation is reinforced by the paucity of enduring intergenerational contacts outside of formal socializing agencies, such as the school and family.[24] Thus most of the adolescents we have observed accept a socially imposed hiatus in their life cycle, regardless of whether they are eager, reluctant, or uninterested in becoming an adult; and most of them assume that only their peers can truly understand those kinds of interpersonal accomplishments and failures which make their lives in the adolescent world either gratifying or mortifying.

Open intergenerational conflict in this community revolves around the question of how much control adults rightfully can exercise over adolescents.[25] Both sides in these disputes agree that intrusion into private generational matters is generally unwarranted, for example, adults usually allow adolescents to arrange their own social affairs. The issue, then, concerns the definition of those aspects of adolescent behavior which are legitimately public and hence subject to adult control.

The Relationship between Adult Values and Youth Norms

In our study of this upper-middle-class urban community,[26] we found that these adolescents successfully internalized adult occupational goals. None of our informants questioned the notion that a high school diploma was a

[24] See F. Musgrove, *Youth and the Social Order* (Bloomington: University of Indiana Press, 1965), for an interesting historical perspective on the present separation of the generations.
[25] According to the data collected by Henry McKay for the Institute for Juvenile Research, this area, in the 35-year period from 1927 to 1962, had the lowest-mean delinquency rate in the city (these rates are based upon official Juvenile Court cases). However, this low rate of delinquency should not be interpreted as evidence of a complete lack of intergenerational conflict. We have observed that behavior which slightly violates adult norms, such as surreptitiously playing poker for high stakes or putting a fraternity picture in the school annual (fraternities and sororities are forbidden), is often sufficient to demonstrate one's autonomy vis-à-vis adult controls. Since the tolerance of deviant youth behavior in the community is small, one can establish one's autonomy through relatively minor acts of defiance of adult authority.
[26] The community we studied is located in a large midwestern city and has a population of approximately 25,000. It has most of the socioeconomic characteristics commonly associated with upper-middle-class residential areas. Since it may be useful to compare this community to the city as a whole, the figures for the latter will be given in parenthesis; and the figures for both will be given in approximate percentages. According to data from the 1960 Census, the median family income in this community was $11,000 ($6,700). Only 5 per cent (14 per cent) of the families earned less than $3,000 a year, and 58 per cent (21 per cent) had an income of $10,000 a year or more. Eighty-six per cent (24 per cent) of the families lived in single-dwelling units, and of these 82 per cent (33 per cent) were owned by the occupants. For this population the median number of years of education was almost 13 (10), and 21 per cent (6 per cent) had four years of college or more. Seventy-two per cent (37 per cent) of this population held white-collar jobs.

minimal requirement for even a half-decent job, and comparatively few students in the local high school dropped out before graduation. Most of these adolescents intended to go to college, and many of them worked reasonably hard to get good grades. They wanted a college degree because they felt it would help them get the professional job or husband which insures a middle-class way of life. However, very few of these adolescents, even the best students, had marked intellectual or scholarly interests. In short, we discovered that adolescent conceptions of the validity of adult roles and values are, at least, largely independent of the standards they use to estimate the relative excellence of their peers.[27]

The youth culture in this area is not completely oblivious to an individual's potential capacity to assume his adult roles. But, as far as his peers are concerned, his success or failure in the academic system of the high school (i.e., his grades) is a relatively minor component of his social identity, although very negative connotations are associated with the status of a "brain" —a person who devotes all his energies to getting high marks. Our informants usually call such a person "twinky," which implies that his demeanor manifests an underlying effeminacy. The choice of a term which connotes less-than-manly behavior follows a peculiarly subcultural logic. The standards of the youth culture are focused on those sorts of behaviors which its members think reflect one's sex-role identity. Their judgments of personal worth are closely linked to general conceptions of those attributes and performances which are thought to reveal a person's masculinity or femininity. For boys, the crucial external signs of inner manhood are physical strength, athletic talent, courage in the face of aggression, a willingness to defend one's honor at all costs, and sexual and drinking prowess. According to girls, the most admirable feminine traits are physical attractiveness, personal vivacity, and the ability to delicately manipulate various sorts of interpersonal relationships.

As a cultural system, the youth culture in this area consists of those norms, life styles, and ideals which are intimately associated with a *variant*, age-graded system of cultural meanings. Of course, the youth culture does not emerge out of a cultural vacuum. Adolescent social patterns obviously are based upon adult conceptions of the desirable types of social relationships and upon adult images of personal virtue. Adolescents, however, do not slavishly copy these general cultural norms. The youth culture experiments with and elaborates on some of the partially unrealized or alternative possibilities in the adult moral order. This is particularly true in the interpersonal realm: Adolescents distinguish various kinds and degrees of trust among friends. Our informants habitually discriminate among "good," "best," and "casual"

---

[27] In "Values and Gang Delinquency: A Study of Street-Corner Groups," *American Journal of Sociology*, Vol. LXIX (1963), R. A. Gordon, J. F. Short, D. S. Cartwright, and F. L. Strodtbeck report that even the most socially disadvantaged, delinquent youth not only evaluate a middle-class way of life very highly but that they also see the conventional path to this end—saving, working at a steady job, and education— as a legitimate, although not always realistic, way to attain a respectable adult status. Yet, as Short, *op. cit.*, points out, these adolescents do not use these values to regulate peer-group life. Similarly, it is wrong to infer that, just because middle-class adolescents are even less ambivalent about adult values, these standards determine the norms of their peer groups.

friends. One informant distinguished among these types of friends in the following terms:

Q. What are some of the things you expect of a friend?
A. When you leave [a group], when you walk out, they don't all of a sudden start stabbing knives in your back. It all depends upon the degree of friendship you want [in response to the question].
Q. What are the various degrees of friendship?
A. With some girls you just have a casual friendship, and she's got her friends and I've got mine, but we'll sit down and talk. Then like the girls in my club, we are pretty good friends. We know who we are going out with. With the casual friend you don't sit and talk about your boyfriend to them. I have one best friend.
Q. Are there certain things you share with a best friend that you don't share with a fellow club member [i.e., "pretty good friend"]?
A. You talk about your boyfriends if you had an argument, but you wouldn't tell them personal things [i.e., to a "pretty good friend"]. I could tell my best friend anything, and she wouldn't think badly of you. You don't have to worry that, will she tell anybody else? While the members of my club, I expect them not to stab knives in my back when I leave, *but my best friend, if someone else does, I expect her to stand up for me. My club members, I wouldn't expect them to stand up for me.*

From a comparative point of view, then, the differences among the cultural categories which shape adult and adolescent orientations to some social situations are admittedly slight. Nevertheless, and this is the important point, the differences between adult standards of personal worth and the meaning of adolescent status terms are great enough to sustain an independent adolescent status system. The multitude of discrete norms which regulate a person's relations with his peers are integrated into a meaningful system of action by distinctively adolescent conceptions of personal worth. The cultural core of the adolescent social system is formed by the meanings of adolescent status terms and prestige categories. An adolescent's estimation of his own interpersonal competence depends, to a great extent, upon whether the particular terms his peers use to describe his status have laudatory or pejorative connotations. These terms indicate whether he is able convincingly to present a "cool" self-image in highly competitive social contexts.

The Meaning of Key Status Terms

The adolescents in this community do not see their status system as a perfectly linear, clearly defined series of hierarchically arranged status positions. Rather, they perceive it as a set of ranked, slightly ambiguous prestige categories which are internally differentiated. This status system is structured along two dimensions. First, there are horizontal social strata defined by differentially evaluated life styles, that is, modes of dress, speech, and interpersonal demeanor. In general, our informants perceive two salient life styles which they refer to as "hoody" and "socie." However, we see another way of life which lacks an explicit folk designation, though most of our informants distinguish it from "socie" and "hoody" styles. For the lack of a better term, we call this the conventional way of life. It is an essentially residual category which includes all those patterns which are neither clearly "socie" nor "hoody."

The dominant values institutionalized in the status system of the local high school are those held by the majority of the upper-middle-class segment of this youthful population (the high school draws students from a stable working- and lower-middle-class community as well as from our upper-middle-class area).[28] Consequently, most adolescents in this area perceive the "socies" as the top stratum of this prestige system. Since "hoody" and "socie" youth do not agree about who has the most valuable way of life (e.g., our "hoody" informants tell us that "socies" are hypocrites, etc.), an individual's estimation of his own status depends, in part, upon his particular adolescent reference group. From an observer's point of view, the "hoody" adolescents have evolved a truly independent style of life. Nevertheless, our "hoody" informants see their own life style as at least a partly antagonistic response to "socie" values and material advantages. "Hoody" adolescents, by and large, refuse to and often cannot financially afford to compete with "socies" on the latter's terms, and they feel that their mode of life is not accorded general esteem in this system. Those who adopt what we have called a conventional way of life gain some social recognition only to the extent to which they can imitate "socie" patterns.

The vertical component of this status system locates an individual's rank within one of these horizontal strata. As far as we can ascertain, a person's rank is a function of how well he is known by the other members of his stratum, and this, in turn, seems closely related to his ability to conspicuously live up to its standards of excellence. This vertical dimension, then, is quantitative rather than qualitative and refers to what our informants mean when they say someone is more or less "popular." Since public renown is a basic value in the "socie" world, those who achieve fame are called "elites." This, however, says nothing about their commitment to one of the various substyles available to the members of this stratum. Although all our informants subscribe to a highly egalitarian social ideology (no one is inherently better than anyone else), "hoody" adolescents take it very seriously. Though many of our "hoody" informants admitted that certain persons in their social circle are more "popular" than others, they have no term which designates high position.

An adolescent's socioeconomic status certainly affects his ability to assimilate "socie" styles. Nevertheless, the decisive factor is his ability to act in terms of these standards whatever his family background. In other words,

---

[28] In numerical terms, this upper-middle-class group does not constitute a majority of this school population. Yet, through the fraternity and sorority system which it dominates and through less overtly stratified, adult-sponsored youth groups which it co-opts as a recruiting ground, these adolescents control both the formal (e.g., the cheerleaders at this high school are not only restricted to sorority girls but to the members of one sorority) and informal activity systems which emerge out of school associations but which are definitely not confined to this location.

an adolescent's status identity is created by his overt commitment to an adolescent life style.[29] Some of our lower-middle- and stable working-class informants are among the most influential "socies," while a few of our informants from upper-middle-class homes are labeled "hoods" by their peers. "Socies" tend to associate "hoody" life styles with very stereotyped conceptions of the attitudes and aspirations which distinguish the lower and middle classes. For instance, even those "socie" informants from stable working- and lower-middle-class families, repeatedly tell us that "hoods" are the sort of people who do not care about their grades, about school activities, about their personal appearance, about morals, etc. In essence, they believe that the "hoods" incorporate what they think is the critical lower-class social-psychological attribute—a complete lack of interest in "bettering oneself."

At this point, we should note that there are alternate terms for these status categories; for example, the words "socie" and "socialite" are used interchangeably. Also, certain status terms change over time. For instance, many of our informants feel that it is more "in" to use the term "mellow" in those contexts where they formerly used the term "cool," but they also agree that these terms have the same meanings. Status terms also take on special meanings according to the structural position of the speaker. Thus, a "socie" speaker will use the term "hoods" interchangeably with "greasers," "scraggs," etc; all of these terms have very derogatory implications. Similarly, "hoods" use the terms "snob" and "stuck-up" as synonyms for "socie."

"Hoods" and "socies" very rarely use these terms to describe themselves but almost obsessively use them to describe each other. It is difficult for adults to appreciate the discrepancy between the adolescent meaning of a term like "hoody" and its conventional referents, that is, to delinquents. For example, one of our most articulate informants belongs to the "hoody" stratum, and she accepts this designation insofar as she defines her own personal style as one which consistently opposes "socie" styles. Yet adults would not ordinarily call her "hoody" because she takes a college mathematics course in her spare time and participates in a tutoring project for culturally deprived children.

These status terms do not refer directly to bounded social units which have a clearly demarcated membership. Yet membership in certain cliques, clubs, fraternities, and sororities makes it very likely that a person will be considered a "socie" by his peers. The precise meaning of these terms, however, cannot be understood apart from the nature of the youth culture in an upper-middle-class community. Here adolescents have a dual orientation to the standards of the youth culture and to the values of the adult world.[30]

---

[29] Most of the adolescents who fall into the conventional category seem more oriented to "socie" than "hoody" dress styles, and some have attempted and failed to join "socie" groups. In contrast to "socies" and "hoods," conventionals have a life style which does not appear to involve a code of honor vis-à-vis other groups. Conventionals, however, tend to define the local social system in terms of what all its members perceive as polar, antagonistic social categories, i.e., "socie" and "hoody." Hence conventionals are difficult to place unambiguously in the status system and lack the definite social identities ascribed to "socies" and "hoods."

[30] N. Riley, J. Riley, and M. More, "Adolescent Values and the Riesman Typology: An Empirical Analysis," *Culture and Social Character*, ed. Seymour M. Lipset and

The adult world is represented by the achievement orientation of the high school. Our "socie" informants claim that this stratum is divided into the "clean-cut" or "all-around" and the "hoody-socie" segments. The "clean-cut socies" stress role performances which are explicitly linked to the school's activity system. They usually do well in team sports, get fairly good but not necessarily high grades, and most importantly, know how to get along with their teachers and classmates—they are very "sociable."[31] In fact, it seems that part of a non-"socie" social identity involves the belief that one does not have enough social skill and organizational ability to give a "swinging" or "cool" affair, and non-"socie" social gatherings generally reinforce this self-fulfilling prophecy.

"Clean-cut socies" must also realize the "cool" patterns of adolescent social life. They must succeed in the intense competition for dates with high-status persons; the social circle from which a person selects his dating partners partially establishes his or her standing in the larger social system. After the second year of high school, "socie" boys must be "conditioned" drinkers, which means not getting prematurely or obnoxiously inebriated in social situations. Sexually, "socie" boys must "make out" and thereby provide some concrete evidence for their frequent and exaggerated boasts about their sexual prowess.

For these boys, drinking and dating are the definitive areas in which one's manhood is tested and proven. They talk a great deal about and admire toughness but studiously avoid situations where they might have to fight. Buying liquor or beer in a store is viewed as a potential threat to their image as autonomous "men," and, conversely, it is seen as a challenge which, if handled properly, can add greatly to one's stature in the group. As our informants perceive it, buying beer in a bar or package store is a battleground reserved only for the courageous: the risks to one's self-esteem are great. If a boy reveals that he is afraid to show a false identification card or otherwise bluff his way through demands that he prove his age, then he loses considerable face within his peer group. But if he stands his ground when accused of

---

Leo Lowenthal (Glencoe, Ill.: Free Press, 1962), found this same dual orientation to parental and peer-group standards. Also see C. V. Brittian, "Adolescent Choices and Peer Cross Pressures," *American Sociological Review* Vol. XXIII (June 1963).

[31] Being "sociable" often means that a person is able to articulate previously unconnected persons or cliques into larger and sometimes bounded social networks. This trait, in turn, is closely related to a person's standing in the "socie" world. For example, one of our informants who actively aspired to this stratum told us that part of her lack of success was due to her inability to bring her various, disparate friendship groups together. She sat in the middle of the lunch table between these two groups but could not promote social intercourse between them and felt marginal to both. However, another informant, who lacked the usual physical attributes of a "socie" girl, was an "elite" largely because she could not only integrate separate dyads into larger friendship networks, but could then combine these networks into a named group whose membership was drawn from both the sorority world and from those girls who were by and large sorority "material" but who were excluded by the "blackball" system—one vote against a prospective member was enough to reject her. This girl provided the rationale, the occasions (e.g., "hen parties"), and most importantly, the contacts which enabled some girls to validate their status in the larger social system through membership in this group.

being under age and does not give in to his desire to flee the situation, then he proves that he has "guts" regardless of whether the store ultimately sells him the beer. Our informants tell us that it is crucial not to "lose your cool" in these situations, and anyone who fails to rise to the occasion has his claims to "coolness" ruthlessly deflated by his peers.

Girls prove their worth in a more contracted arena. They must attract many high-status boys as dates, and to do so they must occasionally engage in rather intense petting without endangering their "reputations." While their prestige depends partly on the status their presence bestows upon their dating partners, it can be compromised if they give sexual favors to all who request them.

The "socies" (our informants usually employ the term "socie" and qualify it when they want to refer to those who adhere to the "clean-cut" or "hoody" variant) fully realize the adolescent dimensions of this social system. Though a member of the "clean-cut socies" adopts many "cool" patterns, he never relinquishes his commitment to adult standards of accomplishment. On the other hand, the "hoody-socies" devote themselves wholeheartedly to adolescent conceptions of excellence. They are the most enthusiastic fraternity and sorority members and are not usually very interested in academic pursuits. Instead they spend a good deal of time and energy systematically refining their dating and drinking techniques. And they are the avant-garde leaders in musical tastes, dress styles, etc.

The "hoods" and the "hoody-socies" should not be confused. The latter represent the furthest an adolescent in the "socie" stratum can move away from adult values without openly rejecting them, that is, they rarely openly defy adult authority in acts of serious delinquency, and, unlike some of the "hoods," they rarely drop out of high school before graduation.

"Socies" have developed a special set of status terms which distinguish various social segments among those who occupy the lower orders of the status system. These terms have depreciatory connotations because they imply that these social types are represented by persons with morally defective or socially underdeveloped personalities. From the "socie" perspective, the "hoods" belong to the more encompassing social category of "out-of-its." One informant described the "out-of-its" as follows: "They're misfits; they're insecure, they don't think they're cute enough, or they're awkward, or they have a lisp or something." This is a heterogeneous category; here one finds the rebels, the retarded or slow learners, the intellectuals, and anyone else who is deviant from the point of view of the prestige criteria which define this status system.

"Socies" also perceive another category of persons who are not attached to or even loosely associated with "socie" cliques and yet who do not fit into the "out-of-its." Some of our "socie" informants call them the "others," and they are just ordinary students who are not distinguished by some success or blatant failure in the adolescent social system. One student described the "others" in this way: "Some of them may not come out of their shell until they get to college, and they may find a group whether it's intellectual or social. These kids will usually gravitate toward getting the higher grades—some don't concentrate on anything at all. They just go along and get by in school and don't join activities, but just sit home and watch television all the time."

The derogatory implications associated with the term "others" do not simply derive from exclusion from "socie" social circles: It means that a person has no definite social identity in this social system. As far as "socies" are concerned, these people are faceless because they are not demonstrably attached to a discernible adolescent style. As one of our informants put it, "others" are people you do not notice or know anything about unless you happened to go to elementary school with them.

As we have seen, the process of status attribution is quite complex and does not result simply from objective talents and characteristics, for example, a boy's athletic ability, a girl's physical attractiveness, etc. Thus, an individual must take the esteem he has gained in a variety of contexts and transform this diffuse prestige into a subculturally validated image of the successful adolescent. He must present himself as "cool," and our informants tell us that if a person truly believes he is "cool" he generally acts "cool." In other words, concrete achievement buttresses the crucial mode of presentation of self in the adolescent subculture, and *it is this self-image and not the concrete role performance which ultimately interests adolescents. Confidence about one's essential masculinity or femininity and the ability to manifest this in smooth performances in many spheres is the essence of high status in this social system.*

One might expect a normative shift toward adult success standards over time in a youthful population largely oriented to college. But as an adolescent progresses through high school he discovers that the tension between adult and adolescent patterns increases rather than decreases. By the final year of high school the social category of the "clean-cut socies" has very few members. Those who cling to "clean-cut" patterns and hence are not trying to be "cool" no longer dominate the status system. In fact, those "clean-cut socies" who do not perceive this shift toward "cool" patterns are called "milk and cookies boys" and rapidly descend in the status system. One informant described what happened to a fraternity which did not make the shift to the "socie" patterns: The Lambdas aren't well liked now because the Lambdas don't drink, and the other kids are all getting to drink, and they [the Lambdas] are not that well liked anymore because they look down upon it [drinking]. So now if you want social prestige with the kids, you wouldn't dare mention the Lambdas." The former members of the "clean-cut socies" who retain their social supremacy do so by appearing to adhere to responsible adult standards while, at the same time, actively participating in covert adolescent patterns.

Cultural Sources of Integration in the Youth Culture

Every cultural system has internal normative inconsistencies. In this section, we will show how certain cultural categories partially resolve some of the paradoxical or contradictory behavioral implications of the norms which govern dating. "Cute" and "cool" are prestigeful terms in this system, and an "elite" girl should be both. Girls see these as consistent personal attributes when they refer to the norms which regulate the ways in which a person achieves pre-eminence in the prestige system. But when girls talk about the ideal norms which should control relationships between members of the opposite sex, these two terms assume partly antagonistic meanings.

Both our male and female informants define a "cute" girl as a person who exudes a certain kind of sexual attractiveness but who does not demonstrate her sexual superiority in intercourse. In fact, if it is widely known that a high-status girl has had sexual intercourse, she very likely will be dropped from the "elite" circles even if she did not get pregnant. Yet, if she is "cool," a girl must be quite adept in the dating system. This means that she must "make out" with a comparatively large number of boys without, on the other hand, being "made." She must allow herself to reach a relatively high level of sexual excitement and intimacy without giving into what are described as persistent demands for greater sexual favors. Consequently, if a girl is considered both "cool" and "cute" by her age mates, she must not only by physically attractive but also confidently manage the sexual self-aggrandizement which marks these temporary unions.

So far, "cuteness" and "coolness" are somewhat different but essentially complementary social categories. But girls have their own moral standards which form part of the meaning of these terms. When the social context is restricted to feminine interests and when the norms of proper behavior vis-à-vis males are at issue, "cool" and "cute" become partly contradictory categories.

Adolescent girls in this community discuss the motives and the norms which should govern dating in terms of "good clean fun." A good dating partner should be companionable, have similar interests, and should be a sympathetic and lively person. In this context, the "cute" girl is viewed as the friendly, "all-American girl" whom everyone likes and admires. She is vivacious, attractive, and, above all, not overly interested in the leverage one can obtain over boys through the judicious allocation of her affections. In short, she is a very wholesome girl. However, this category of the "all-American girl" quickly drops out of the picture when the girls talk about the realities of the power struggle which almost invariably accompanies dating. Incidentally, "going steady" is an institutionalized way of emphasizing the solidarity rather than the individualism of dating oriented to the status system. But among "elites" the dominant concern of who is going to control the relationship—all of our informants were convinced that long-term dating was an intrinsically asymmetrical relationship and were afraid that their peers would see them as the subordinate partner[32]—almost inevitably leads to its dissolution in a relatively short time. One girl viewed dating as follows:

Q. You see this [dating] as pretty much of a game of strategy?
A. Definitely! It's one of the most fun games around too. Because you never know what's going to happen. . . . It's up to you. There are no rules really. There might be a couple of rules that you take for granted, but basically. . . .
Q. Like what [rules]?
A. Well, not to do anything really nasty. Like go out with his best friend—

[32] Many of our male informants expressed what seemed to us an almost pathological fear of being "pussy whipped," but we shall let psychoanalysts reveal the psychological implications of this term.

break a date with him and go out with his best friend or something like that. Nothing really drastic, but aside from that there aren't too many rules, and you've just always got to make sure that you're on top, that you're winning because otherwise if you're not winning you're losing and there's no tie. So you always make sure you're winning.

According to ideal feminine norms, real sex, as distinguished from the "good-night kiss," is out of place, undesirable, and, in some sense, morally wrong on a good date. The feminine vision of a romantic relationship holds that a date should come from mutual concern with the other partner's true or inner qualities. As even a cursory glance at love comics and true romance magazines will attest female ideology maintains that it is possible to appreciate the true worth of another person only if one is willing to rise above the ordinary trivial absorption in the competitive aspects of cross-sex relations, that is, with the other person's physical appearance, with his or her superficial manners (usually with their sophistication or lack of it), with the other person's prestige value (whether one's peers think he or she is "cool"), etc.

In light of these norms, "coolness," which is manifest in an attachment to "making out," is apparently incompatible with purely feminine conceptions of "cuteness." Thus, when girls talk solely in terms of their own moral standards, the "cute" girl is defined less by reference to her physical attractiveness than by her attractive "personality." Nevertheless, if a "cute" girl is to retain or achieve a position among the "elite" of the adolescent social system, she must attract high-status boys. How, then, does she retain her image of "cuteness" and the esteem that goes with it in the eyes of her girlfriends if she must also engage in a wide range of petting activities with many boys? Or, to phrase this in motivational terms, how does she keep her "cool" orientation toward sex within the moral boundaries of the feminine universe? That is, how can she participate in a rather promiscuous pattern of sexual intimacy with many boys and, at the same time, exercise considerable control over her sexual encounters?

This somewhat contradictory pattern of normatively encouraged sexual promiscuity and restraint is resolved by a higher-order cultural category. This category defines the sexual nature of boys in both cognitive and evaluative terms. Our girl informants tell us that boys "naturally" try to "get all they can" sexually because boys are born with uncontrollable sexual urges.[33] One girl discussed the issue in the following terms:

Q. Whose responsibility is it [regarding how far things go sexually on a date]?
A. The girl's. I mean because guys can't help it. I mean they are born that way, but then girls get carried away because guys can't help themselves and girls can. To a point, but once past that point there's no hope.
Q. Are all guys like this or just particular guys?
A. Some guys would get as far as they could get, just for kicks, but there are other boys who are just as nice as they can be, but any boy who likes a girl

---

[33] The Ngulu, by way of contrast, are convinced that women are born sexually insatiable (see T. Beidelman, "Pig (Gulwe): An Essay on Ngulu Sexual Symbolism and Ceremony," *Southwestern Journal of Anthropology*, Vol. XX (1964).

enough . . . I don't think he would do it intentionally to hurt her, but just can't help to get as far as he can get. I don't think even the nicest guy can help being that way.

In terms of dating norms, girls say that it is their responsibility both to satisfy part of this inborn male desire for continual sexual satisfaction and to keep the situation from getting out of hand. Though girls admit that they also have strong sexual feelings, they agree that they and not the boys are capable of rational control, of setting limits.[34] Thus, girls claim that nature has burdened them with the responsibility of keeping petting relationships within the prescribed moral limits. In a basic sense, girls see boys as morally defective—or, if not as morally defective, at least as morally immature. Boys are said to be simply incapable of realistically assessing the negative consequences of giving free rein to sexual impulses in a dating situation. And, from what we have been able to observe, boys often fulfil these cultural expectations which have been phrased in such biological terms.

Although success in dating seems superficially completely tied to ascriptive criteria, there are important performance aspects to dating. Female competence is culturally defined as the ability to manipulate the sexual component of dating relationships to one's own advantage. Some girls have told us about a technique of "dumping" which they use to entice boys and yet keep them in a dependent position, never certain of whether they will be abandoned for a more attractive partner. One girl described her dating relationship in the following way:

> Like when Jim and I first started dating we got along just fine. Then I started to dump on him, being a little snotty once in a while and stuff like this. Then I decided to be nice because it would be nice to be nice for a while, just as a change. Then I figured if he was so nice to me when I was dumping on him, just think if I was nice to him, he would really be nice to me. Well then he decided that wasn't such a hot idea [and] that he would start dumping on me which I didn't think was such a good idea either. So when he started dumping on me, I just decided to give him the shaft.

One of the latent and unintended consequences of this dating system is the widespread fear among "popular" girls that they are being exploited by the boys. A "popular" girl often feels that if she becomes too attached to a boy he may, in reality, be dating her only for the prestige which comes from being in the company of a "cool" and "cute" girl or, what is worse, he may play upon her romantic proclivities to seduce her.

Incidentally, we have found that many of the girls who "fall in love with" a popular entertainer, such as one of the Beatles (an English singing group), are often marginal in a very special way. They may have all the prerequisites

---

[34] For a long time we were puzzled about the reasons why one of our informants was systematically excluded from the girls' group mentioned above. Our other informants in this group told us, at first, that her clinical attitudes toward sex repulsed them, but upon reflection they admitted that they too collectively discussed sex in a similar manner. Upon further investigation, we found that this girl revealed her desire for sex, she "needed it," and hence she violated these norms.

for success in the dating system; they are often physically attractive and personable. But these girls reject the hostility and exploitation inherent in the dating system and prefer an imaginary but romantically perfect relationship with these remote figures.

Conclusion

In conclusion, we do not hold that the youth subculture is a closed normative system. The normative integrity, coherence, and identity of a sub-culture is not always based upon estrangement from the larger culture nor does it always reside in social organizations which resist integration into the larger society. On the other hand, in a discussion of the reality of the youth culture, Berger declares that subcultures must not only have "relatively dis-tinctive styles of life, but styles of life which are to a great extent self-generated, autonomous, having institutional and territorial resources capable of sustaining it in crisis and insulating it from pressures from without."[35] In our opinion, this limits the concept of a subculture to very special, and possibly almost non-existent, cases of cultural differentiation in this society. The high degree of interdependence of functionally differentiated subsystems in this society makes it unlikely that many subcultures will fulfil all of Berger's stringent prerequisites.

In contrast to Berger's strictures, we propose a more catholic and perhaps more fruitful view of a subculture. Rather, we suggest that the core of the youth culture resides in its distinctive evaluative standards. They endow the adolescent status terminology (and thus the social categories through which the members of this age-grade orient themselves to their peers) with qualities and attributes which do not dominate adult status judgments. Here we follow Anselm Strauss's view of the connection between social categories linked to a person's position in age and other societal structures and the ways in which people perceive social reality:

> These changes in conceptual level involve, of course, changes in be-havior, since behavior is not separate from classifying. Shifts in concept connote shifts in perceiving, remembering and valuing—in short, radical changes in action and person. . . . Terminological shifts necessitate, but also signalize new evaluations: of self and others, of events, acts and objects; and the transformation of perception is irreversible; once having changed, there is no going back. One can look back, but he can evaluate only from his new status.[36]

From our point of view, then, the members of a subculture can be inte-grated into basic societal institutions even though their definitions of ordinary social situations are predicated upon a special set of cultural meanings. Conse-quently, the crucial criterion for the identification of a youth subculture is whether its norms provide its members with a distinctive world view, a style

---

[35] Berger, *op. cit.*, p. 396.
[36] Strauss, *Mirrors and Masks: The Search for Identity* (Glencoe, Ill.: Free Press, 1959), p. 92.

of life, and the standards against which they can measure their own worth. Here again it is worthwhile to quote Strauss on age-graded perceptions of the world: "But the world is different for persons of different age and generation even if they share in common sex, class, and nationality, and occupation."[37]

Finally, our approach emphasizes the element of free cultural play in the genesis of the youth culture. Of course, we do not deny that the typical psychological and role problems of this age-grade provide the raw materials out of which youth culture is built. But we do point to the ways in which the meanings inherent in this adolescent normative order transcend the requirements of simple adjustment to these exigencies. In other words, these adolescent cultural inventions and innovations impose a discernible order upon the crises and dilemmas of adolescence.

[37] *Ibid.*, p. 138.

YOUTH CULTURE IN A HIGH SCHOOL*

JAMES Q. WILSON

North Long Beach, where I grew up, is one of the many communities in the
Los Angeles basin that, blending imperceptibly into one another, seem to be
neither city nor suburb. It is also a community that has reached maturity and
begun to show its age. The period of rapid growth of the Thirties and Forties
is at an end, and has been for some time. Even in the Fifties, the population
increased only by about 7,000 to a 1960 total of 48,000. An area of single-
family houses, it has for many years seen little new construction of this sort;
instead, the few remaining vacant lots, as well as the backyards of existing
homes, are being filled in with small apartment buildings, two or three stories
high, having little open space and catering to older persons, young couples
without children, or "singles." Long Beach was never the center of whatever
youth culture Southern California may have—if any age-group in the city
received special attention and concern, it was the old folks to be found near
the public shuffleboard courts—and now with the population changes young
people are even less at the center of gravity. North Long Beach has begun to
change from being an outlying area in which child-rearing was the focus of
life to a place out of which young couples move in search of larger or newer
homes.

Today, as twenty years ago, the area is neither affluent nor squalid—it
combines in a way unfamiliar to Easterners a suburban life-style (single-
family homes, neat gardens) with a working-class and lower-middle-class
population. Driving north on Atlantic Avenue from downtown Long Beach,
one passes through Bixby Knolls, now, as in the past, a prosperous neighborhood bordering on the Virginia Country Club and with an attractive, off-the-
street shopping center. North Long Beach begins abruptly as one passes under
the Union Pacific railroad tracks and encounters, on each side of the street,
small, semidetached stucco storefronts, painted various pastel shades and
cluttered with a patchwork of neon signs. The street is broad, wider than
many big-city thoroughfares, but the shops are almost all one-story and
together they convey no clear sense of line, mass, or color. Things seem
strangely out of scale and slightly out of focus—the stores are too low for the
width of the road, and the muted green, beige, and pink colors offer no sharp
contrast with the hazy, often smog-filled sky. Even the low-income public

* Reprinted from James Q. Wilson, "The Young People of North Long Beach," in
Harper's Magazine (December 1969), pp. 83–90, by permission of the author and
publisher. Copyright © 1969, by Harper's Magazine, Inc.

housing project on county land near the railroad tracks is distinctively Southern Californian. Though built over twenty years ago, it is set back off the main street and consists of one- and two-story buildings surrounded with grass and vegetation and painted the same yellow, green, and coral shades as private housing. It is into this area that most of the few Negro families in North Long Beach have moved, though many of the tenants are still white.

David Starr Jordan Senior High School, which I attended, first appears along Atlantic Avenue like an oasis. Towering palm trees border the wellkept part adjacent to the school, and the campus itself has tall eucalyptus trees that impart a sweetly pungent smell to the walks. In my student days, it was filled with children born in the Depression. For many, the bungalows of North Long Beach were their first non-farm homes, or at least their first taste of a city of any size. Though the war had just ended and many parents had saved a good deal of money from wages earned at the Douglas aircraft plant or in the Long Beach shipyards, there was not yet much to spend it on (the new postwar cars were eagerly awaited) and little inclination to hand it over to the kids. Many people spent what they had to pay off as much as they could on their house. Accordingly, there was little exotic clothing and few expensive hobbies—surfboards, for example, cost more than anybody I knew could afford. The young people were mostly Protestant and Midwestern, and all white.

Twenty years later, the young people look very much the same, only more prosperous. They are still Protestant, but now they are Californians, not Okies, Arkies, and Missourians. By 1968 eighteen black students had entered the high school, but a majority lived outside North Long Beach. Many, indeed, were transferred to Jordan High from other schools for disciplinary reasons, a system that may not augur well for the development of friendly interracial contacts among the students.

The young people, especially the girls, are better-dressed (and I think better-looking, though I can't trust my judgment on that) than in 1948, when I graduated. But their general style is very much the same—"really" or "real" is for them, as probably for all adolescents, still the standard, all-purpose adverb ("Gee, that's real great!") and "ya know" still serves as a kind of oral punctuation ("I think, ya know, he's all right, ya know?"). Big or difficult words are still avoided, even by bright students, because they convey ostentatious intellectuality; as one girl told me, "In class, I've gotta talk in words of one syllable, or the guys will think I'm a kiss-up" (*i.e.* teacher's pet).

Names have changed, at least for the girls. It is almost as if their parents, symbolizing the greater security and prosperity they felt as compared with *their* parents, wished to bestow first names that conveyed fashion and what they took to be urbanity. In the class of 1948, my yearbook tells me, girls' names were simple, straightforward—Patricia, Jo-Ann, Barbara, Shirley, Mary. Though there was one Darlene and a few other "stylish" names, they were the exception. Many boys had rural names—LaVerne, Dwayne, Dwight, Verlyn, Delbert, Berl, Virgil, Floyd. In the class of 1968, the girls had blossomed out with unusual names and unusual spellings of familiar names——no fewer than eight Sharons, six Cheryls, two Marlenes, two Sherrys, two Charlenes, and one each of Melodee, Jorjana, Candy, Joy, Cherry, Nanci, Carrolyn, Cyndi, and Darlene. Mary may be a grand old name, but it is no longer a very common one.

In a school where ethnic and class distinctions are either nonexistent or invisible, the social structure is organized around differences in behavior. There are distinct social groupings, complete with names, at Jordan High, though there is no agreement that they are hierarchically arranged, and little agreement as to the membership of each group. Most students, of course, belong to no particular group at all. Three that have names are the "soshes," the "surfers," and the "cruisers." "Sosh" is a word with a double meaning—perjorative for someone who is snobbish, aloof, or preoccupied with matters of dress and appearance, and descriptive for the well-dressed, personable young people who get elected to most of the student offices, are active in the clubs, and "support the school." They are great favorites of the teachers and the administrators, though they are also fearful of being thought "kiss-ups." Because the term has two meanings, no one with these attributes likes to apply it to himself, but for better or worse the obvious non-soshes use the label frequently and with respect to a clearly visible group.

"Surfers" may or may not be people who actually surf—indeed, most don't, though they all like the beach. The term applies not so much to what they do as to what they look like. Unlike the soshes', their hair is long (at the extreme, and there are a few cases at Jordan, the surfers fade into the hippies) and blond as a result of inheritance, sun, or chemicals. Compared to the soshes, they are more casual in dress and less deferential to teachers (though hardly rude). "Cruisers" (sometimes called "Northtowners") are the "rough" group oriented to automobiles and with little interest in studies. The boys wear their hair neither short (as do the soshes) nor long (as do the surfers) but in modest pompadours or otherwise waved. Their pants are tight, their shirts untidy (and, whenever they can get away with it, out of their pants), and their shoes run toward suede, sharp-toed, elevator-heel boots. Their girlfriends are called "hair girls" because they wear wigs or have their own hair arranged in fantastic creations rising precariously almost a foot above their heads and held in place with a hair spray that must have the adhesive power of epoxy cement. During compulsory physical education classes, all girls turn out for softball or other games dressed in regulation blue gym suits designed, no doubt intentionally, so as to make a Sophia Loren look like something out of Louisa May Alcott. The hair girls will be out, too, their towering creations waving unsteadily as they run about. A softball hit into one of those hairdos would have to be called a ground-rule double since it could not possibly be extracted in less than half an hour.

Cruisers cruise. The accepted routes are Atlantic Avenue and Bellflower Boulevard; the accepted cars are the ones that have been lowered, equipped with mag wheels (sometimes fake), and their windows decorated with a tasseled fringe and a hand-painted slogan ("Midnight Hour"); the accepted driving style is slowly, with the driver slumped down in his seat until only the top of his head shows and his hand draped casually out the window. Pinstriping, metallic paint, and other car fashions described by Tom Wolfe are no longer much in evidence around high schools (partly, no doubt, because customizing has become very expensive). And, sadly, the classic hot rods of the 1940s, with exposed, reworked engines, straight pipes, and minimal driver comfort are rare. Perhaps they have been taken over by adults whose nitro-methane fueled super-eliminators make a conventional hot rod look now like what it once emphatically was not—kid stuff. Or perhaps no one in North Long Beach knows how to make them anymore, or perhaps the parts are unavailable, or perhaps no one cares.

(For the benefit of middle-aged suburbanites anxious to close the generation gap, I should report seeing a customized Volkswagen driven by a young cruiser. It had a lowered front end, wide-oval racing tires on the rear, glistening paint, an extractor exhaust, and the word "Hessians" written in elegant script on the rear window. The beetle has been gilded.)

Casual observation of the campus conveys chiefly an impression of sameness—middle-class Wasp students preoccupied with social life, school activities, and class work. But the students themselves see differences where adults see similarities, and though the differences might be narrow indeed on a scale that included all teen-agers in the country, they are nonetheless important. I suspect the differences may be even more important today than twenty years ago, and that there are now fewer uniformities in behavior and manner. For example, in 1948 styles of dress were more or less standard (simple skirts, sweaters or blouses, and white Joyce shoes for girls; jeans or cords, and T-shirts and lettermen's sweaters for most boys); today, though scarcely radical by the standards of contemporary fashion, clothing is more varied, reflecting in part the freer choice that comes from prosperity and in part the emergence of more distinctive sub-groups with which students consciously identify.

Dress regulations have always been a major issue in the high school and a not infrequent cause of disciplinary action. The rules are set by a city-wide committee of students and teachers, subject to administrative approval, and revised annually. The effort to define what constitutes an acceptable mini-skirt has been abandoned as dress lengths have steadily risen, an inch or two ahead of the regulations every year. In resignation, the rule-makers have retreated into comfortable ambiguity, saying only that "skirts must be of reasonable length and appropriate for school wear." My close study of the situation suggests that the meaning of "reasonable" is not self-evident—some skirts come almost to the knee, some remain defiantly (and gloriously) at mid-thigh. For the boys, clothing must "avoid extremes," hair may come down to the collar but not below it, and sideburns and moustaches (but not beards) are all right. A few young men display long hair (thereby becoming surfers even if they don't know how to swim) but going beyond modest deviance is risky. As one football player and student officer told me, "The guys don't like hippies much. One of the guys walked up to a fella with hair down to his shoulders and just hauled off and hit him. A lot of guys will say something to the hippies, sort of challenge them, and if they answer back, then it can get rough."

One might suppose, to judge from the breathless accounts given by a mass media fascinated by "youth culture," that teen-agers today thrive on individuality, independence, and fancifulness—each person "doing his own thing." Though this state of nature may prevail in some places, it is not found in North Long Beach, nor, I suspect, in most communities. Young people of course are always struggling to rebel against adult authority, but precisely because of that they tend to place even greater stock in the opinion of their peers. Teen-agers draw together, discovering themselves in the generalized opinion they form of each other—seeing themselves reflected, as it were, in the eyes of their friends. What is surprising is not that their life tends to a certain uniformity in manners and dress, but that there is any heterogeneity at all.

The chief social values of the young people to whom I spoke (and whom I remember from two decades ago) are friendliness and, above all, "sincerity." Anything smacking of a pose, a "front," or "phoniness" is hotly rejected. The emphasis in Media Youth Culture on love, honesty, communication, and intense self-expression are not reactions *against* traditional youth values, but only extreme expressions *of* these values. Affluence, freedom, and rapid social change produce more exaggerated statements of the enduring concerns of young people (or, for that matter, most people) than a repudiation of those concerns. Of course, to a true hippie or young political radical, the Jordan High School student is at best a square—the embodiment of tradition, philistinism, and middle-class preoccupation with property, dating, and booster-ism. Though in behavior and ideology the hippie and the square could not be more different, the animating impulse in both cases is similar—a deep concern with honesty in personal relations. For the "square," honesty is simply not as complex a value as for others.

Among surfer and sosh alike, as well as among the mass of unaffiliated students, the strongest criticism voiced about the behavior or attitude of others is that it seemed "snobbish" or "phony" or that the individual was part of a "clique." The most popular students are not those one might imagine if one remembers the Hollywood musical comedies about campus life; they are not the socially aggressive "big men on campus." They are instead rather quiet persons who are socially at ease but who also embody in greatest degree the quality of being "sincere." The student-body president said little in meetings I attended of student leaders, but when he spoke, he was listened to respectfully—perhaps precisely because he did not chatter or try to be a wise guy and because he seemed to think carefully about what he wanted to say, and when he spoke he was neither flustered nor bombastic.

Still, I detect sharper cleavages among the social groupings of the students, sharper, that is, than I would have expected knowing merely that young people seek to find a place where they can belong and a circle they can join. I think that one new factor, almost unknown to my generation of students, helps explain these wider distinctions—drugs. There is no doubt whatever that at Jordan, as (according to the police) at all Long Beach high schools, illegal drugs (marijuana, barbiturates, amphetamines) are widely used. During the fall semester preceding my arrival on campus, twenty-six drug cases came to the attention of the school authorities. Every student I spoke to knew of persons who used drugs, several implied (without quite admitting) that they had used them, two or three told me they could make a purchase for me "within the hour" if I wanted. (I did not.)

Students were concerned about this and aware that certain social groupings were heavily populated with "dopies." (The term connotes more than it should. No one believes there are any addicts, or users of physiologically addicting drugs, among the students; drugs—"reds" and "whites"—are used much like alcohol, on weekends and at parties and occasionally at school.) Many kids are worried about drugs because of fears over health or acquiring a police record, and leery of groups or parties where the dopies gather. For the city as a whole, police arrests of juveniles in cases involving marijuana increased between 1962 and 1968 from 18 to 186; cases involving pills rose from 12 to over 650. For a student, being a user—or worse, being caught as a user—intensifies normal social cleavages.

For some boys, athletics is seen not only as fun but as an absorbing activity that increases one's chances of staying away from a social life involving dopies. One player told me that "if it hadn't been for football" he probably "would have wound up where the guys I used to hang around with are"—in trouble with the school and the police. On the other hand, the same young people reject as "phony" many of the materials they see in class designed to warn them of the dangers of drug use. One complained that "The stuff they show you in those movies about dirty old men hanging around school trying to push dope—that's all pretty stupid, that's not the way it is at all. Anybody who wants to buy drugs can get them easy."

Perhaps because social groupings are more sharply defined, perhaps for other reasons, most students complained that there was not enough "school spirit" and that many of the formal student organizations were "meaningless" or ineffective. "Nobody cares about the school," one girl said. "There are no cheers at the pep assemblies." Many students think student government is a "waste of time" (only a third of the students voted in the last election), and most of those in student government worry about the same thing—organizations seem weak, "spirit" is flagging.

If the football team could have a winning season, this all might change, but it has not for some time, mainly, it appears, because it is playing over its head in a league composed of several larger schools with more and bigger talent to draw on. But nobody is convinced that a losing record in football is the whole reason. One girl (labeled by others a surfer though she herself, as everybody else, refused to accept any label) said that students want to be "more individual" not "try to act just like the soshes," but then complained of the absence of school spirit. I asked her whether more intense individualism was incompatible with school spirit; she puzzled over it a moment and then said she guessed that was right.

The formal student organizations cut across the informal social groupings, and that may be one reason for their weakness. More than thirty clubs exist in a student body of 2,200, chiefly to serve social, vocational, or hobby interests. The Shutterbugs enjoy camera, the Rooks play chess, the Thespians participate in drama, the Girls' Rifle Team does whatever girls do with rifles. There are chapters of Future Teachers of America and Future Medical Leaders of America. Music produces the most organizations, partly because many grow directly out of elective classes—the Concert Band, the Orchestra, the

Marching Band, the Military Band, the String Quartet, A Capella, the Girls' Choir, the Mixed Chorus, the Choraliers, the Straw Hatters. An important way in which the community reaches into the school is through the sponsorship of student organizations by business and civic associations—the Kiwanis sponsors the Key Club, Rotary sponsors Interact.

Because the formal organizations crosscut, rather than coincide with, informal groupings, their vitality is compromised (except those which pursue a clear activity, such as the music organizations). Social organizations are not, and under school rules cannot be, exclusive as to membership, and thus a number of unofficial, "secret" organizations flourish. These are mainly fraternities and sororities that have no (and want no) approved adult sponsor, and thus are illegal. The administration struggles against them, but with little success. Students differ as to the importance of the secret organizations; some members feel they have declined in recent years but all members compare them favorably to the official clubs with open memberships, no hazing, adult sponsors and, thus, no fun.

One official organization that has both a large number of followers and considerable respect is Campus Life, a quasi-religious group begun by members of the Youth for Christ movement. It holds a number of dances during the year and in addition has education programs featuring, for example, films about LSD or other controversial subjects. The popularity of Campus Life is one current indication of an enduring feature of community and school—the extraordinary importance of churches. The area from the first had many storefront Protestant sects and the more successful of these have become large, active organizations. The local Brethren church, for example, has a huge physical plant, including a school, and runs a number of well-attended youth activities. Mormons for decades have accounted for a sizable fraction of the student population, and Baptists, Methodists, and Presbyterians are also numerous. It is difficult to assess the religious significance of the strong and clear church affiliations, but their social and institutional importance are unmistakable.

The most striking aspect of organizational life, however, is the complete absence of any group devoted to questions of public policy, world affairs, or community issues. Only one club, Cosmopolitan, touches matters external to the school (it organizes and raises money for an exchange-student program that brings one foreign student to campus each year and sends one Jordanite abroad). Twenty or twenty-five years ago, in the years of slowly fading optimism following the second world war, the World Friendship Club was an active organization, sponsoring an annual World Friendship Day and meeting regularly to study international events with heavy emphasis, as I recall, on the Chinese government of Chiang Kai-shek and especially on the views of Madame Chiang. Neither the club nor the day remains, and no new policy area has generated any substitutes.

I asked various groups of students what questions other than personal or campus matters concerned them, but other than one boy who mentioned the draft, I got no clear answers. To be sure, if I had asked them whether they were interested in, say, civil rights or the Vietnam war, many would have said they were. And most issues of this sort are discussed, often heatedly, in their classes. But what is impressive is that no general question, couched in broad terms, elicited any strong feelings or active, spontaneous concern. The issues which they did volunteer were wholly campus-oriented—the students had argued with the principal over the date of the senior prom, there was some indignation about a fence that had been erected between the school and the adjacent park (not, it seems to keep the kids in but to keep "undesirables" out), and some complaints about the tight control the administration was believed to exercise over the contents of the student newspaper. Some students noted wistfully that another high school in the city had an underground newspaper but almost in the same breath said they did not like the recent efforts of a group of older men, perhaps college students, to distribute such a paper on the Jordan campus.

In an era of "aroused" youth preoccupied with "relevance," why should the young people of North Long Beach be neither aroused nor relevant? It is easy, too easy, to think of explanations, some plausible but none convincing. The students are "middle-class," they are Wasps, they live in a "sheltered community," there are few Jewish students on campus, North Long Beach is not a "central city," they are all part of Southern California and probably "just another crop of young backlashers." And of course their parents were not radical; no Jordan student could be a "red diaper baby." Some explanations, especially the last one, have partial significance but none satisfies me. What is perhaps equally important, none would even be intelligible to the persons described. To them, almost everybody is middle-class; extremes of wealth or poverty are outside their experience. Some may know what "Wasp" means, but the term is still an Eastern invention, largely marketed in the East. Long Beach is, to them, neither sheltered nor "non-central"—to them, it is highly "central." ("We've got everything around us here," one said. "The beach, the mountains, LA, Hollywood, Disneyland. It's really great.") As for the idea that families have a tradition of liberalism or radicalism, they can scarcely imagine it. And they would be embarrassed to hear anyone speak of the influence of Jewish culture on social change—it's "not nice" to speak of a person's religion, you "shouldn't generalize" about other people, and besides the Jews are supposed to be just like everyone else.

The most important fact about these students is not their class, ethnicity, religion, or location; the most important thing about them is their age. They are sixteen years old, give or take a year or two. They are coming to grips with problems of identity, sex, career, and adult authority. Their responses to these central concerns produce the social groupings we see—the soshes, with their ready acceptance of adult values, especially the virtues of work, service, neatness, neighborliness; the cruisers, with their rejection of those values, their open pursuit of girls as objects of conquest, their contempt for studies that signifies either rebellion or despair; the surfers, who are reevaluating standards, suspending judgments, and above all resisting a premature commitment to the adult world or any abandonment of values of individuality, which they greatly prize. When one is sixteen, the larger world does not touch one, except in crisis or because one's parents make involvement in that world a central adult value. In a profound sense, community or world issues are irrelevant to the focal concerns of the students, and not vice versa.

Now, as when I was in that world, young people have great natural idealism, but the objects of that idealism are principally personal relations (friendship, the team, the "crush") or else distant and lofty goals (religiosity, human brotherhood in some ultimate sense, world peace). There is rarely any middle ground (again, except when circumstances provide it) of public policy toward which one acts or about which one thinks with much intensity. When an issue from the middle range intrudes, an effort is made to translate it into simpler human values. One student leader spoke critically of the demonstrations on college campuses because they showed a "lack of respect for other people"; another (in a classroom discussion) was critical of de Gaulle's policies toward the United States because he had displayed neither gratitude nor fairness; a third, in a class report on pornography, concluded that censorship wouldn't work but that we must be careful, as parents, to inculcate "the right moral values" in our children.

There is less aversion to classroom discussion of controversial issues than when I attended Jordan but the same tendency to evaluate or resolve those issues by reaffirming traditional values. It would have been most unlikely that, twenty years ago, a girl would have given an illustrated report on pornography, much less gather material for that report by attending (with her brother) a skin flick and patronizing a downtown dirty book store. Had the discussion occurred, the boys in the back of the room would have nervously snickered over the (rather mild) illustrations and concluded that the girl must not be "nice" and thus fair game. There were no snickers, nervous or otherwise, the discussion was matter-of-fact (and rather quickly branched off to include student use of marijuana and drugs), and the girl was obviously "nice." The teacher played almost no role in the uninhibited discussion that followed but despite this, a general agreement on the importance of morality and family training was quickly reached. At this point, several girls spoke disapprovingly of the looseness of the "younger generation," by which they meant their ten-year-old kid brothers. "They are learning too much, too soon," one said. "You'd be amazed at the words and things they know *already!* It wasn't like that for *me*."

The one major issue that has touched their lives, and that they speak about frequently though still in guarded tones, is race. No Negroes attended Jordan when I was a student there and scarcely any lived in the area. Though Compton, which is two-thirds black, is just across the city line and Watts not far away, almost no Negro families have yet moved into North Long Beach—apparently, because no one has been willing to sell to them. In time, that line will break (there is a great deal of housing in the area within the buying power of the blacks) and Jordan High School will face what for it will be a crisis, unless the district lines are redrawn. (Such a strategy is conceivable, since a new freeway now under construction runs east and west across North Long Beach just south of the Compton line, thereby providing a "natural" barrier to immigration.)

The young whites with whom I spoke are obviously torn between two standards which they think ought to be consistent but which, when applied to what they see as the "Negro problem," produce incompatible judgments. One is that people ought to be judged as individuals, fairly, and without regard to skin color; the other is that people ought to have a common standard of behavior, and in the adolescent world this includes not being ostentatiously cliquish and not occupying a place of special favor in the adult-managed authority system (not, as they put it, being able to "get away with something" by reason of privilege rather than cunning). The two standards are familiar enough—liberty and equality—and the tension between them gives rise to the same problems for young people as for older ones.

The Jordan High whites spoke approvingly of a few Negroes whose behavior did not produce any dilemmas—who could be judged as individuals *because* they were "like everybody else." Liberty tended toward equality in these cases, and the Negroes involved were singled out for special praise: "he is real boss," "one of the guys," he "goes around with a bunch of white guys." They spoke critically of others who were a "clique" and "got away with murder" because "the teachers are afraid to do anything about it." One white claimed she had seen a Negro girl "crowd in line in the cafeteria and a teacher who saw it just stood there." A boy said he thought some of the Negroes had stolen ballots in the student-body election, again without penalty. "If you say anything to them, they say you're picking on them because they're black."

Them. When the standard of equality is violated (in white eyes), the violators are set apart as outside the school's social system and given a collective label. Soshes, surfers, and cruisers all resist and resent the labels given them and struggle to show that they do not really fit, each person insisting that he is "an individual" (valuing liberty but unwilling to accept its price, which is inequality—at least in the mind of the beholder). But the blacks, being black, cannot escape or argue about the collective label and with growing race pride they now understandably flaunt it.

It would be easy to stigmatize the racial views of these white youngsters by putting in their mouths a phrase I never heard them use, perhaps because they are aware that it has become a symbol of complacent bigotry—"some of my best friends are Negroes." Whatever they may become as adults, few are now complacent bigots by any means—their sense of fair play is much too strong for that precisely, I would argue, because they are adolescents. When a Negro did act like "one of the guys," there was no visible resistance or resentment. At a Friday night dance at the Canteen, a popular youth center run by the city Recreation Department and located in the park next to the school, I saw two Negro high-school boys dancing with white girls. Nobody paid any attention. I asked one of the more conservative students (he had told me earlier of his outrage at the "disrespectful" attitude of college students who "rioted and demonstrated" at their campuses) if anybody cared about the interracial dancing and he said, in some surprise, "No, they're good guys." He then said that the previous year a Negro boy had married a white girl after graduation and there had been "no fuss." A Canteen official said there hadn't been any racial problems with the young people but that she imagined some of their parents (whom she thought "less honest" than their children) might be upset.

With the growth in numbers of black students at the school, it will be increasingly difficult either for many blacks to be "one of the guys" in white society or for the whites to continue to apply individual tests of worth in the face of increasing collective differences. One white girl who liked a Negro boy and was seen with him frequently on campus reported growing undercurrents of criticism from both blacks and whites.

When I asked some white student leaders if there was anything they thought should be done about the Negro students, they strongly reasserted the value of equal treatment. "Everybody should be treated the same," "no special favors," "the rules ought to apply to everybody equally" were the common views. Teachers and administrators were criticized sharply for not (in the students' opiniom) acting this way. They were "afraid" to enforce the rules on the blacks, students said. If Negroes stayed together, it was because of "self-segregation." (Some students dissented, however. One came up to me afterwards and said he thought Negroes needed extra help and "some breaks" but he clearly didn't feel he could push this view too hard in a public discussion.) The administrators, of course, had a more complicated view of the situation, concerned as they were about avoiding friction and forestalling an incident, but what to school officials may have been prudence was to the students inequity.

Such racial tension as exists, however, is at a very low level. Most of the black students live out of the school attendance area, and thus there is little after school contact. Nor are there many community problems that would provide fuel for racial conflict—there are no teen-age gangs, delinquency is (in police eyes) no more than what might be expected in a middle-class area, and church and civic groups are influential. It is an area of almost numbing wholesomeness.

The social life of Jordan students remains much as it was twenty years ago. The most important events are the Friday night dances at the Canteen at which four or five hundred boys and girls regularly turn out to enjoy bands picked by the student officers of the Canteen; as always, far more girls than boys are interested in actually dancing. On Saturday night, there are movies, perhaps a church dance, "cruising," working at the Kentucky Colonel Fried Chicken shop, or hanging around the A&W Root Beer stand. A big date means a trip to Melodyland or Disneyland or occasionally to the Shrine for a rock show. The "secret" fraternities and sororities will have an annual dance at the Elks Club or a nearby veterans' hall. Parties at homes are less common than formerly, apparently, as one girl said, because the "boys get too wild and wreck the place or steal things." During Easter Week, those with access to cars (and a little money) will drive to Palm Springs or Balboa; during the Christmas vacation, many go to Big Bear in the mountains.

The sexual revolution like "youth culture" has not had the radical effect its middle-aged chroniclers (and admirers) sometimes suggest. Teachers and counselors with many years' experience at Jordan find no evidence of a dramatic increase in premarital sex but a good deal more candor about what actually does occur. An unmarried girl who got pregnant used to be whisked off, in shame, to some distant relative to have the baby; now, she is likely to stay in town and be given a shower by her friends. The chief restraints on libertinism remain what they have always been—the conflict between a boy's desire for action and a girl's quest for commitment, together with each other's fears of rejection and embarrassment.

The opportunities that money and automobiles are supposed to have provided adolescents generally have long since been available in Southern California. The perimeter of youthful social life—Hollywood to the north, Big Bear and Palm Springs to the east, Balboa to the south—is far-flung, but it has always been so, and there is therefore little sense of newfound freedom or heavy "experiences." Perhaps like children in European families who grow up familiar with wine, Southern California teen-agers take their environmental stimulants pretty much for granted.

Within that perimeter, they are highly mobile, but the world beyond is still known primarily by hearsay. Other than those young people who make a summer pilgrimage back to their grandparents' home in Kansas, Missouri, or Iowa, very few Jordan students know anything at all of the East and rather little of the urban Midwest. Students frequently asked me "what's it like" at Harvard, or in New England. I asked them what they thought it was like, and they said that New England was "really cold" and Harvard has a lot of "rich snobs who are big brains." I tried to assure them that Boston temperatures do not preclude all forms of life, that Harvard students are on the whole not very rich, and those who are rarely are very smart, but I could see in the eyes of my questioners that nothing I could say would dispel the mystery of the East.

Nobody I spoke to knew anyone who had gone away to college in the East and no one intended to go himself. A survey of Jordan's class of 1968 showed that 52 per cent had gone on to college full or part time, but the vast majority of these (over 80 per cent) attended the two-year Long Beach City College and a large but unknown proportion dropped out in their first year. The record college enrollments around the country, and especially in California, conceal the fact that for most students their formal education ends with high school or within a year or two after graduation. Very few (only about 7 per cent at Jordan) go directly on to a four-year college or university; most go to tax supported institutions located in the immediate area.

Even though California State College at Long Beach, a four-year school, is located just a few miles from the Jordan campus, very few seniors (perhaps 16 out of over 700) go even that far away. One reason is transportation—even a few miles in Southern California, given the state of public transportation, is a big distance if one doesn't have a car (Cal State has very few dormitories). But the more important reasons are probably social and cultural—Cal State is a big place (over 25,000 students), it is "overcrowded" with large classes, and there are a lot of "weird" people there (during my visit, it was convulsed by a conflict over a black-studies program). City College, by contrast, is nearby, familiar, and attended by all one's friends. As one girl said, "It's like a high school with ashtrays."

Cost is also a factor. Jordan students are keenly aware that their parents can't afford everything and probably can't afford even the cost of UCLA, much less a private school. Jordan has its share of bright students (one represented Southern California at a youth science conference in Chicago) and some of these will get scholarships, but most will think wistfully that while it might be nice to go to UCLA or Santa Barbara it is easier to enroll in LBCC. Even among the "academically talented" members of the class of '68 included in the survey, the furthest east one had gone was to the University of Redlands—seventy miles away.

Jordan High School, like North Long Beach, has not changed in any fundamental way. New buildings of green and pink stucco have replaced the wooden bungalows in which I attended class, but the social structure and the values of the people are essentially the same, modified, perhaps, by the influence of higher incomes and the settled sense of being a "Californian" rather than a migrant. So striking is the continuity one finds in North Long Beach that one is tempted to describe it under a pseudonym, and then let the reader guess where it is actually located. Many will suppose, even as I might have supposed, that it is an isolated backwater of the nation—a small town in Iowa, perhaps, or a suburb of Omaha. But it is not: it is near the center of one of the most populous, affluent, mobile, media-conscious areas in the United States, part of a state where Robert F. Kennedy and Eugene McCarthy met head-on in a bitter, closely watched primary election, and very near the place where, in August of 1965, the "black revolt" is thought to have begun. At one nearby university, two Black Panthers were recently shot and killed; at two others, a fraction of the student body has been in open revolt.

The Jordan students are aware of the turmoil but not seized by it. How it has affected them will probably not be apparent for years. Already, of course, the older teachers lament that the "work ethic" has been eroded: "They just don't seem to work as hard in class as they used to," one told me. "There's no real discipline problem, but it seems as if they want to be entertained more, they want to know what they'll get out of it if they do an assignment." Another veteran teacher agreed, but thought the reason was not in broad social changes or in student values, but in the school itself: "Increasingly, the emphasis here is on college preparation, but when you get right down to how many actually go to a four-year college, the answer is, damned few. For the rest, we're not preparing them for much of anything. Some shouldn't even be here—they ought to be out learning a trade, but the law says we have to keep them here until they're sixteen."

It is hard to evaluate such comments. Men in their fifties are bound to see young people somewhat differently than the same men in their thirties. At the end of one's career, students may not seem as bright, or as hard-working, or as exciting as they did when one first started teaching. But there is another possibility: the great increase in the proportion of students going on to college, even if only to City College, as a result of both parental pressure and their own assessment of career needs, has undoubtedly placed great strains on the normal social processes of the high school. The new definition of success—college and a "good" job, rather than immediate marriage and "any" job—represents simultaneously a school norm, an adult expectation, and an adolescent hope. The normal (and normally minor) symptoms of youthful rebellion against those adult expectations that seem excessive, unreal, or unrelated to their own needs and opportunities may have been intensified by these newer and more demanding expectations which have made high school seem less "fun," less responsive to adolescent interests, and more a system to be beaten by doing what is necessary but doing it without zeal. Even the elusive school spirit that students find so lacking may be in part the victim of a process that has made the high school less an end in itself and more a means to a larger and more equivocal end—career success.

Underlying the continuity of manner and style, there may thus be deeper changes at work. But it is unlikely they arise from what, in our intense preoccupation with the immediate crises of race and peace, we imagine —not from the issues and fashions of the moment, but from a fundamental restructuring of the ways in which one enters society and the labor force, and thus of ways in which one grows up.

ADAPTATION OF ADOLESCENT MEXICAN AMERICANS TO UNITED STATES SOCIETY*

ROBERT L. DERBYSHIRE

Culturally divergent ethnic categories and adolescents have much in common in the United States' society. Both are minorities excluded from the mainstream of American adult culture and each lacks adequate access to economic, political and social power. Each is struggling toward acceptance yet each has difficulty locating adequate and functional acculturative frames of reference for culturally integrated participation. Functional relations between simultaneous membership in culturally excluded minority worlds for different migratory generations and relationship of these forces to adolescent attitudes is the subject of this paper. Adolescent attitudes are based upon data gathered from Mexican American adolescents residing within the most economically depressed area of East Los Angeles. Identity crisis, as described by these attitudes, with its subsequent strain, resulting from role conflict, stimulated by the adolescent's desire to identify with family, peer and greater adult worlds, concomitantly influenced by the dominant culture's lack of acceptance of Mexican American cultural diversity and the role conflict it engenders, suggests that adolescence for Mexican American migrants in an urban setting is vulnerable to deviant behavior (Derbyshire, 1968).

Migration is a complex phenomena. The term does not imply a discrete, mutually exclusive category. However, as they do many other categories describing social phenomena, researchers and laymen frequently view the concept as implying that all persons fitting into the category maintain similar social, cultural, and psychological characteristics.

The psychosocial dynamics of those who migrate are myriad. Therefore, one's socially visible pattern of moving from one nation to another, one social configuration to another, or one culture complex to another is viewed as the apparent unifying criterion of commonality. Behavioral similarities are often expected after placing into the same category all persons who have migrated. For example, even when an external force such as a revolution appears influential in a migratory pattern, there is every reason to believe that persons who migrate are not necessarily basically motivated to migrate because of the revolution, but the revolution provides them with a stimulus for responding to already unmet migratory needs. In other words, migration of a large number of Cubans, during and after the Cuban Revolution, may appear on the surface as a large segment of people being pushed out to "seek freedom"

* Reprinted from Robert L. Derbyshire, "Adaptation of Adolescent Mexican Americans to United States Society," in American Behavioral Scientist, Vol. 13 (September 1969), pp. 88–103, by permission of the author and publisher.

when more accurately the revolution may be the mechanism or the stimulus for acting upon and carrying out migratory wishes encouraged by the drawing forces of United States culture.

A major problem for such migrants is their willingness or resistance to fitting into a prescribed social role (i.e., "seeker of freedom from Communism") which may or may not fit into their identity needs. Therefore, if Americans with whom the migrant comes into contact treat him and expect him to play the "freedom seeker game," then the migrant must either fit into the pattern and adapt, which may be uncomfortable, or reject the pattern and receive behaviors which may enforce social distance and alienation.

Too frequently, as social scientists and laymen, we pay little attention to the reciprocal relationship between actors. The importance of examining and understanding this reciprocity is essential when examining minority-majority relations. What is perceived by the stationary population as acceptable role behaviors for migrants and what migrants perceive as acceptable behaviors for self in relation to migrants and others is frequently divergent. When one moves from a culture in which he was born and reared, where he has maintained a comfortable, adaptive set of behavior patterns at cognitive, affective, and cultural levels, old ways of feeling, thinking, and acting remain the only criteria upon which the migrant can validate new experiences. When trying to validate new experiences with self as a social barometer, comfortable, old ways of behaving do not provide the same fulfillment as they did in the old world, culture, or social group, because feeling states, interaction patterns, and cultural mechanisms are less successful at tension reduction in this new environment.

By virtue of moving and seeking to establish territorial rights, one sets up within the organism's psychology, a need to feel and display, among other things, dominance and security over some aspects of one's life. Overdetermined fears of rejection, alienation, and just plain discomfort increase the possibilities for carrying out a self-fulfilling prophecy (Thomas and Znaniecki, 1927). Migrant-nonmigrant interaction, by virtue of manifest differences as well as the more subtle behavioral and feeling nuances, often decreases communication validation. Therefore, with social interaction there is a potential for the migrant to receive and communicate a fear of role nonacceptance which, in itself, when it is recognized at a conscious or subliminal level in the other participant creates a distrust which forces the maintenance of social distance to provide safeguards against uncomfortable feelings of strangeness between the two participants.

These psychodynamics become intensified and of greater importance when one examines the social dynamics for migration. Some expressed reasons for migration are: (a) social factors over which the individual feels he has little or no control (i.e., revolution, economic depression, acts of God, e.g., floods, hurricanes, fires and other disasters); (b) external social forces over which he feels he may have some control yet he is unable to cope with these in his present environment (i.e., loss of job, extrusion of close family member from society to prison, hospital, etc., death of a loved one, unexpectedly poor return on self-employed endeavors, e.g., farming, light manufacturing, etc.); (c) social forces which perpetuate the appearance that the new land of the immigrant has greater opportunities than where he presently lives. These and other migratory forces are not mutually exclusive and become weighted determinants in family and individual decision-making processes. Therefore, it seems reasonable to conclude that any understanding of differences between migrants and nonmigrants must be examined in terms of both psychodynamic and social reasons for the migratory patterns. For example, one can hypothesize that the length of time a migrant family maintains the old cultural identity will be inversely related to social-psychological traumas (i.e., unanticipated culturally shocking experiences created by moving and the quality and quantity of subsequent experiences) which force sanctuary in one's cultural identity. Also it can be hypothesized that those persons who perceive their migration as forced or maladaptive, yet have a desire to return to the donor culture, will participate in less effective social-psychological interplay between migrant and nonmigrant (Scotch, 1963).

The following interview brought to my attention the many feeling problems engendered during migration. A seventeen-year-old Mexican-American youth had arrived in East Los Angeles at the age of thirteen with his father, mother, three brothers and two sisters. He stated:

> The ride from Mexico to Los Angeles was long, hot and troublesome. With each stop for gas and truck repairs people acted funny. When they smiled I did not know why. When they frowned I was puzzled and hurt. Even though I understood English, the tongue was strange and not easy to follow. People's faces made me feel strange and unwanted. We ate very little and I was hungry all the way. I did not know what people wanted or how to act. I was scared. I did not trust anyone. It was this way everywhere. People, land and smells, all were strange. I remember feeling lost, helpless and unhappy yet my father said he was happy to be going to a new job in Los Angeles.

This paper compares the attitudes and behaviors of lower class Mexican American migrants and nonmigrants. It is assumed that recent migrants will have attitudes affected by Mexico and their more recent nomadic type experiences while second- and third-generation migrants will have adapted to a ghettoized more or less supported life of the host culture. Although the data presented here do not adequately validate the aforementioned hypotheses and assumptions, some insights are provided.

Mexican American

Terminology difficulties are inherent within minority populations who are citizens of the United States of America (Heller, 1966: Chap. 1). All members of minorities, either born or naturalized in the United States, are legally considered, tend to be, but frequently are not responded to as American citizens first. Aside from American citizenship, however, there are certain ethnic characteristics which promote or inhibit human interaction and relationships within the United States culture (Marden, 1952). These differences are based upon physiognomy, i.e., hair structure and color, nasal index, height and weight, eye color and eye fold and skin color. There is no conclusive evidence that physiognomic characteristics of ethnic categories determines their behavior. However, determinants of behavior are related to gross cultural differences, linguistic nuances of persons from varying backgrounds and societal reactions to physiognomic differences. When these differences interact with the dominant white, Protestant, "capitalistic," Anglo-Saxon "democratic" culture of the United States, prejudicial and discriminatory behavior often occur. In other words, differences in behavior among ethnic groups is the result of at least two major phenomena: (a) the "right" and "wrong" of behavior due to socialization supporting the dominant values within one's culture (Williams, 1960), and (b) these behaviors in interaction with the United States culture which views minority persons and their behavior as "alien."

Mexican American, without the hyphen, is used to identify the minority population with whom this project is related. Although we recognize numerous identity conflicts exist within the community of East Los Angeles, it is not the intention of this research to alienate, determine consensus, or ameliorate feelings of group identification. Although other Spanish-speaking populations, i.e., Cubans, Puerto Ricans, and other South and Central American nationalities, reside in East Los Angeles, statistical analysis of the community indicates that the bulk of the population originally migrated from Mexico. Overtones of group identity problems are not dismissed. Self-reference labels of Latin Americans, Americans of Spanish descent, Americans of Mexican descent, Mexican Americans, or Spanish-speaking Americans and others are frequently heard in East Los Angeles (Weaver, 1968). Although the lack of consensus over semantic identification problems is recognized, I use the abbreviated form without the hyphen for identifying Mexican Americans. The persons described in this research are Americans who by virtue of their Mexican ethnicity have received differential and inferior treatment. However, one teenager, searching for an equal or superior identity, stated, "Mexican American means bicultural and bilingual a little more than other Americans."

The East Los Angeles Mexican American

A brief subjective view of the area where data were gathered may help to interpret the findings (Derbyshire, 1968: 75–80).

East Los Angeles, the unincorporated area, in which this study was carried out, lies east of Boyle Heights, south of City Terrace and Alhambra, west of Monterey Park and north of Commerce and Montebello. Those census tracts in East Los Angeles which supply the greatest amounts (in Los Angeles County) of family disorganization, juvenile delinquency, crime, drug addiction, dilapidated housing, poverty, and other indicators of community pathology, are surrounded by four huge concrete and steel freeways. Apparently these freeways tend to limit ecologic mobility. The Long Beach Freeway on the east, Santa Ana Freeway on the south, San Bernardino Freeway on the north, and Golden State Freeway on the west are the "Anglo" curtains segregating the most economically deprived Mexican Americans.

On a clear day, when smog neither settles in this basin nor nestles against the San Bernardino Mountains, snow-capped Mount Baldy is seen as it over-looks Los Angeles County. On humid days yellowish, eyeburning, mucous-generating smog devastatingly increases the health hazards of this community. Although a California state college and junior college are located in or near this area, few residents join its student body. Fewer East Los Angeles residents are members of the faculties. Statistics on junior high and high school dropouts are the highest in the County.

The "Serape Belt" as East Los Angeles has been designated, was at one time a predominately Jewish neighborhood. Today, however, on main thoroughfares, Brooklyn Avenue, Third Street, and Whittier Boulevard one notes advertisements in Spanish, cantinas, corner fruit stands, motion picture theaters with Spanish-speaking movies and Anglo merchants who display signs reading "hablo Espanol." Many merchants' and some physicians' offices have television tuned to Spanish language programs during the day. Tortillas and tacos are sold at small sidewalk carry-out shops. Signs designating the office of a "curendero" (a folk curer or medicine man) and "abogado" (a false lawyer) are visible.

From second-hand furniture and clothing stores filter the sounds of Spanish language radio programs. On the streets Spanish can be heard more frequently than English. Dark complexioned faces of older males reveal the rugged outdoor manual labors of a lifetime. While women are frequenting the shops and stores, groups of young men are visible on several corners. Clothing is worn, tattered, yet neat; hands, face and eyes appear fatigued; a massive pride is characterized by the erectness of body posture and lightness of gait.

Houses in East Los Angeles are small, colorfully painted, with dilapidated fences and small flower gardens. Much of the housing is rented, not owner occupied. In many neighborhoods the interdependent atmosphere of the barrio (small community) exists. Females, particularly mothers and wives, are often busy with local church and neighborhood affairs. Children frequent the streets for companionship and peer activities. Local settlement houses as well as more recent poverty programs provide some recreational and social facilities.

The sheriff and his deputies, and the state police are avoided when possible. Church and its responsibilities are taken most seriously by females, while males pay lip service. Immigration officers are well known and avoided. Unknown Anglos asking questions in the neighborhood are viewed suspiciously. Middle- and upper-class "chicanos" (slang for Mexican Americans) are also viewed with trepidation for fear they are investigators from Anglo institutions.

Although families in this ghetto appeared to be patriarchal and matri-centric, there was excellent evidence that male strength and dominance exists only because females feel it is best to play the subordinate role. Females frequently verbalized dissatisfaction with their husbands' and fathers' positions in the family but give and promote family respect out of deference to his loss of status in Anglo culture. Among families interviewed, there was a apparent role deception by females to provide a foundation for the emascu-lated if not lost "machismo" of their Mexican heritage. This was most frequently revealed through the wifes' lack of condemnation for their husbands' extramarital sexual exploits. Praise was often given for the male's lack of fear and his physical combativeness outside of the house. Although sexual and aggressive behavior was seldom condemned, most mothers and wives were able to verbalize to the interviewer that these actions were dysfunctional for getting ahead in Anglo land. "The poor man fights so many problems every day that the least I can do is support him in the ways of his father."

Child-rearing practices are punitive and severe. Girls are protected while boys are encouraged to be aggressive. Gang life is most usual for boys. "Pachuco" gangs have their distinct dress and speech patterns (Meeker, 1964). Gangs frequently attack isolates, dyads or triads of their rivals. Large gang warfare is seldom encountered although it does exist. These gang disagreements most frequently involve territory or females. Most youngsters in these gangs are not delinquent.

Although East Los Angeles, no doubt, produces a variety of family belief systems, most older persons give lip service to the Mexican family prototypes. This has been described by Oscar Lewis (1949).

> According to the ideal pattern for husband-wife relations in Tepoztlan, the husband is viewed as an authoritarian patriarchal figure who is head and master of the household and who enjoys the highest status in the family. His prerogatives are to receive the obedience and respect of his wife and children as well as their services. It is the husband who is expected to make all important decisions and plans for the entire family. He is responsible for the support of the family and for the behavior of each member. The wife is expected to be submissive, faithful, devoted, and respectful toward her husband. She should seek his advice and obtain his permission before undertaking any but the most minor activities. A wife should be industrious, frugal and should manage to save money no matter how low her husband's income. A good wife should not be critical, curious, or jealous of her husband's activities outside the home.

Adolescents, in this study, of both a recent and not so recent migratory background have interacted within this milieu and each has been uniquely affected by these transactions.

Adolescent Migration Research

The problem of growing up as a first-generation Mexican migrant in the United States was discussed as early as 1931 (see Gamio, 1931; Humphrey, 1946; Leonard and Loomis, 1941; McWilliams, 1949; Sanches, 1943; Taylor, 1932). Children born to the migrant Mexican and reared in East Los Angeles, present unique United States adaptation patterns. Conflicts due to diversity of cultures create adaptive problems within American institutional life in areas of values, education, religion and occupation.

During the initial data gathering phase of this experiment I was fortunate to receive aid and support from an East Los Angeles teen center and its leader. One Friday evening while approximately thirty teenagers were completing the questionnaire, a rival gang harassed members of the teen center. Not only was the experiment interrupted during this encounter but many of the forms were destroyed. This incident extended the data gathering period several months because these adolescents were then brought in two at a time to complete the 34 page questionnaire.

PURPOSE

The purpose of this research is to compare the attitudes of Mexican American adolescents who were born and reared or whose parents were born and reared in the United States with those adolescents who migrated or whose parents migrated from Mexico to the United States.

In an earlier work Seward (1958) suggested ". . . the paradoxically sounding assumption that the more firmly an individual is embedded in his primary ingroup the better integration he may be expected to make with the dominant culture." Peak (1958) writes, "The great differences in philosophy of acceptance and resignation, passivity, dependency, etc. between Mexicans and Anglos have been the cause of much misunderstanding of Mexicans by the Anglo population who misinterpret Mexican philosophy and see these people as indifferent, lazy or unambitious." These differences appear to be exaggerated early in the migratory process. Since Mexican values are the antithesis of values cherished by American adults, then unless Mexican American adolescents can find congruence in, and lack ambivalence toward, their subcultural values, transition into adulthood may be filled with conflict over the necessity of giving up one's sacred beliefs in order to be accepted by a hostile environment, which results in role strain and social deviance.

The dominant pattern in Mexican families is to develop in the growing child, obedience, humility and respect for elders (Guerrero, 1955). Adolescent crisis is turbulent with problems of authority and self-determination. An intensification of ambivalence toward obedience, humility and respect is encountered at this time for most Mexican American adolescents. It is hypothesized that role strain is particularly evident for youngsters of Mexican parentage who, having been born and reared in the United States, have not adequately internalized the dominant Mexican values.

Associated with these difficulties is the humility of the older generation. A lower-class Mexican lady indicated, "when my teenage children do wrong I blame nobody but myself for not being more strict." In response to being asked how she felt when the children lived up to her expectations she stated. "I thank God for making them that way." The Mexican American adult, with his extreme humility associated with success and self-punishment associated with failure, establishes a psycho-social situation within which the developing child, when in contact with the Anglo world, finds difficulty integrating the concepts of responsibility, aggressiveness, authority and independence. To manifest a world view that "man can do only bad" and "God can do only good" is functional only with strong (Mexican) cultural support and a lack of interference from outside (United States) cultures. Culture shock for Mexicans is apparent when the Anglo world suggests that man is responsible for his "good" and his "bad" deeds. This, no doubt, establishes for the growing child a conflicting situation, creating uncertainty toward the Mexican value system, while concomitantly supporting acceptance of the Anglo culture which is more functional for upward mobility, yet has only limited usefulness for self-preservation (Derbyshire, 1966; Brody, 1966; Derbyshire, 1964).

Since adolescence is a time for breaking away from authority, both parental and religious, the Mexican American youngster who has uncertain feelings toward his culture may strike out at his parents through deviant acts, without offending God. Mexican American informants in East Los Angeles indicate that youthful gangs are most frequently those boys with extreme feelings of uncertainty toward Mexican culture.

According to Erikson's assumption (1950), the mastering of future life experiences (for adolescent Mexican Americans) depends upon the success with which their own culture is mastered (and later the culture of the Anglo world). It may be hypothesized that if one successfully gains "wholehearted" cultural support for his Mexican identity, then later success at coping with incongruent Anglo modes of behavior may be functional for political and socioeconomic success, yet not necessarily dysfunctional for ego identity. If, as it has been suggested by other investigators (Spiegel and Kluckhohn, 1954), the Mexican American family has been, during the last generation, moving away from overt father dependence to the American pattern of individualism, then the strong dominant father and passive, submissive mother of the Mexican cultural pattern is no longer functional as a "successful variant of group identity" (Erikson, 1950). As stated by Seward (1964), "This change has had a disorganizing influence on family structure and adversely affected the personalities of family members, often resulting in antagonism between eldest and younger sons, and becoming manifest in delinquent behavior."

Information gathered in this study describes differences in attitudes between two groups of Mexican American adolescents. It is the hypothesis of this research that the values, attitudes, and behavioral patterns of teenagers who were born in Mexico, or who are children of parents who were born in Mexico, are significantly different from those teenagers in the same socioeconomic situations who were born to parents who have resided in the United States for two or more generations.

METHODOLOGY AND SOCIAL CHARACTERISTICS OF SAMPLE POPULATION

The sample consists of eighty-nine adolescents of Mexican American background who lived in a low-income area of East Los Angeles. These young persons, forty-two males and forty-seven females, were between the ages of thirteen and nineteen. Each youngster anonymously completed a thirty-four-page questionnaire. This included ten pages of information covering a personal and family history as well as subjective feelings and attitudes toward persons and values significant in the life of adolescents.

Together with these data was a series of twenty-four concepts followed by nineteen Osgood semantic differential scales. These scales were selected to reveal concept differences for male-female roles and American and Mexican value orientations, (e.g., proud-humble, dark-light, etc.). Each concept concerns itself with attitudes related to persons who may, for these adolescents, present problems of ego integration during adolescence (e.g., Mexican, Father, Mother, bullfighter, etc.).

The eighty-nine adolescents who contributed data to this study were divided into two categories: (a) Mexican American migrants who had moved to East Los Angeles within their lifetime or whose mother or father moved from Mexico to East Los Angeles; (b) Mexican Americans whose father and mother as well as themselves were born and reared in the United States. Forty-one adolescents were defined in the migrant category, twenty-six male and fifteen female. The nonmigrant or what is also labelled as the "established" category consisted of forty-eight adolescents, twenty-one male and twenty-seven female. When comparing the median age (fifteen years) of the migrants with the established category (sixteen years) there is only a one year difference. However, the mean age of the established category is two years older than the migrants. Only fifteen migrants were born in Mexico while twenty-six of those adolescents had one or both parents who were born in Mexico. An overwhelming majority of both categories professed Catholicism as their religious preference. However, church attendance was significantly more frequent among migrants.

When comparing migrants with nonmigrants, the fathers of nonmigrants were significantly more highly educated (formally by three years) while there is no difference between mother's education for the two groupings. The majority of mothers in both categories were unemployed and remained at home, (according to these youths) because their mothers "desire to be with family."

Twelve adolescent nonmigrants had forty-six arrests while seven migrants were involved in twenty arrests. There was no difference in school failures between these two categories. Nonmigrants were further ahead in their formal education, but this was, no doubt, due to the fact that they were somewhat older. School dropouts, however, were most frequent for the established grouping.

Only one nonmigrant is an only child. Established families average two children more than the migrant families. Although migrants speak Spanish significantly more than nonmigrants, there is no difference in the reading of Spanish newspapers. Reading appears to be more influenced by social class than ethnicity since there is also very little reading of English newspapers by both categories of adolescents.

Findings and Discussion

Although significant differences between categories do not appear on attitudes concerning family, father, mother and Mexican cultural patterns (e.g., "control over environment," "sickness as punishment," and "present-time orientation") large differences exist in attitudes toward premarital sex. While migrant adolescents, somewhat more strongly, feel premarital sexual relations are appropriate for boys, nonmigrants are significantly more willing to suggest premarital sexual behavior for girls. The lower class established adolescents do not have a dual standard for premarital sexual relations while the immigrant category maintains a dual standard.

Nonmigrants view formal education as a means for upward mobility while migrant adolescents less frequently see education in this manner. "Getting even" for perceived injustices and "turning to authority" when difficulties arise is significantly more important to migrants than established adolescents. Established adolescents also see employment as a means to success. Significantly fewer migrants see work in terms of future orientation but work is viewed by these adolescents as a present-oriented phenomena.

There is also a surprising sophistication within both categories concerning mental illness. Most of these youngsters view mental illness as a "misfortune," an illness which "can be cured," and something for which "one should not be punished."

Significantly more migrants than nonmigrants desire to live in Mexico. Somewhat fewer migrants than nonmigrants want to continue to live in Los Angeles. The gang as a mechanism of identity is significantly more important to established adolescents than to migrants.

When there is a "problem" both migrant and nonmigrant adolescents see their parents seeking assistance in the following order: (a) family; (b) God; (c) priest, policeman and doctor; (d) friends and social worker; (e) curendero. However, when seeking help with mental illness migrants feel their parents would turn to: (a) God; (b) physician; (c) priest; (d) family and psychiatrist; (e) friend; (f) social worker; (g) policeman. Nonmigrants, on the other hand, see their parents using: (a) physician; (b) God; (c) family; (d) psychiatrist; (e) priest; (f) social worker; (g) friend; (h) policeman. These data indicate that migrants are less likely to use traditional American mental health resources than nonmigrants. Apparently Mexican cultural heritage plays a more important role than social class when dealing with disordered behaviors designated as mental illness.

Table 1 compares migrants and nonmigrants as each category evaluates self with reference to other meaningful Mexican and American roles. Each plus and minus indicates the direction of the significant difference between self and other. Squares which are blank indicate no statistically significant difference. Migrants more frequently (twenty-four) than nonmigrants (seventeen) differentiate themselves from other role categories on potency scales. These data indicate the self-determination concerns of migrants. Evidently nonmigrants are less concerned, deny or have dealt with their feelings of control over their lives.

Nonmigrants are more concerned than migrants with evaluative responses. Viewing the world in terms of good and bad is important to both categories; however, nonmigrants are more likely to differentiate between self and others in evaluative terms.

Activity scales do not differentiate migrant adolescents from the established category.

While migrants see little difference between their fathers as they are and as they wish them to be, they view their mother as extremely different from what they wish her to be. The established category, on the other hand, reverses this perception by indicating high congruence between what mother is and how they wish her to be while fathers lack this congruence to a high degree.

These data raise an interesting question as to sex role differentiation and

TABLE 1. SIGNIFICANT DIFFERENCES (T > 2.0) ON NINETEEN ADJECTIVE SCALES WHICH COMPARE THE MANNER IN WHICH MIGRANTS AND NONMIGRANTS "SEE MYSELF" AND THE MANNER IN WHICH THEY VISUALIZE A SERIES OF MEXICAN AND AMERICAN ROLES

P = Potency
E = Evaluation
A = Activity
(+) or (−)

		Nonmigrants (N = 41) / Females (N = 15) / Males (N = 26)													Nonmigrants (N = 48) / Females (N = 27) / Males (N = 21)												
		Mexican	Anglo	Negro	Bullfighter	Police	Priest	Crazy Person	God	Babies	Father	Father as I like him to be	Mother	Mother as I like her to be	Mexican	Anglo	Negro	Bullfighter	Police	Priest	Crazy Person	God	Babies	Father	Father as I like him to be	Mother	Mother as I like her to be
P	Brave or Cowardly	+	−		+	+	+	−	+		+	+	+	+	+	+	−		−	−	−	−	−		+	+	+
E	Unfriendly or Friendly		+				−	+	−	+				+	+	+	+		+	−	+		+			+	+
E	Sober or Drunk	+		+		+	+	−	+	+			+	+	+	+	−	−	+	+	+	−	+			+	+
E	Sinful or Virtuous						−	+	−	−				+	+	−		−	+	+			−			+	−
E	Dark or Light	+	+	+				−	+	−	−				+	+	+					−	−	−			
A	Rash or Cautious			+		+		+	−						−		+				+		+				
E	Proud or Humble							−	−				+			−	+				−		−	−			
A	Excitable or Calm	+			+		+	+	−	+	+				+	+	+		+	+	+	+	+				
P	Weak or Strong	+				+	+	+	+	+	+		+		+	+	+	−	+	+	+		+				+
A	Following or Leading	−	−		−	−	−	+	−			−		−					+				+				
A	Competitive or Cooperative	+	+		+	+	−	+	+	−	+	+		+					+		+	+	+	−	−		−
E	Inferior or Superior	+	+			+	−	+	+	+	+									−		+	−			+	
E	Beautiful or Ugly	+			+		−	+	+	+	+			+								+	−	−	+	+	
P	Unintelligent or Intelligent	−					−	−	+	−				−		−							+	+			−
E	Sensitive or Insensitive							+	−		+											+					
A	Active or Passive	−		+	+		+	−		+	+		+	+			−					−	−		+		+
E	Wise or Foolish	−	+		+	+	+	+	+	−	+	+	+	+	−	+	+		−		+	+	−		+	+	+
P	Hard or Soft	−	−		+		+	+	−	−				+			−						−	+			
E	Kind or Cruel	+	−		+		−	−	+	+	+	+		+			−		−	−		−	+		+	+	+
	Responses	9	7	1	5	4	10	16	16	6	6	7	3	11	4	6	9	1	9	6	12	6	15	3	10	6	7

confusion for migrants and nonmigrants. Migrant adolescents who see their fathers as they desire them to be but do not view their mothers in a similar fashion may be responding to the Mexican mother's "lack of fit" in terms of behavioral prototypes in American culture. Fathers meet the required behavior of these adolescents. Apparently, fathers of migrants are able to carry out role expectations of their children while mothers are not.

Migrant adolescents view themselves as most highly different from "crazy person," "God," "priests," and "Mexican." Adolescents of the established category see themselves as highly different from "babies," "crazy person," "father as I would like him to be," "police," and "Negro."

Differentiation of self from others for nonmigrants appears to be based on an age-masculinity complex, strangeness, father's desired behaviors and lower-class American culture stereotypes. However, migrants differentiate themselves on the basis of strangeness, religion, Mexican culture.

While nonmigrant adolescents highly identify themselves as being least different from bullfighter, father and Mexican, the migrant category see themselves as most similar to Negro, mother, and police. Nonmigrants see little difference between self and those whose role includes highly aggressive, masculine and proud behaviors while migrants identify more closely with less potent, supportive yet aggressive categories.

During this process of acculturation, migrant Mexican American adolescents in search of self and adaptively meaningful behavior, utilize father, religion and Mexican culture as positive value orientations. Migrants not only place high value on these items but they also view representatives of these values as being different from self in a culturally positive direction. As the acculturation process extends through two or more generations, a major shift in value orientation takes place. Nonmigrants in their search for a positive identity utilize inadequacy and strangeness as self-differentiating factors. In other words, babies, crazy persons, father as I would like him to be, police, and Negro are all viewed by the established adolescent as people not like himself. Adolescent migrants utilize culturally positive value orientation representatives in differentiation of self, while nonmigrant adolescents adhere to culturally negative value orientation representatives as a comparative reference group. This major switch from a positive value orientation reference group to a negative value orientation reference group probably has significant behavioral adaptive functions. Seeing oneself as different from, yet working toward, behavior which has positive meaning in the culture increases interest in behavior and behavioral alternatives which support sociocultural expectations. On the other hand, viewing oneself as different from, yet focusing upon, representatives of negative value orientation, does not provide role models which support acculturative behavior with sociocultural expectations.

Although intrapsychic mechanisms assisting successful adaptation are not delineated, this research indicates that most recent migrant Mexican American adolescents tenaciously hold Mexican ideals and values by viewing them as desirable goals. However, the established category see themselves as extremely similar to the role categories displaying Mexican American values. The impact of United States society either reduces the importance of Mexican values as a personal goal or more established adolescents view themselves as a part of these goals for adaptive reasons. In other words, after one or two generations in the United States it may be adaptively necessary for Mexican American adolescents to overly view themselves as highly Mexican in order to defend against the "cultural stripping" process of American society.

To maintain the values and seek the goals of Mexican culture while learning the culture of the United States may be the most adequate mechanism for adapting. However, as American culture consistently denies the importance of Mexican values, established adolescents are forced to over-identify and to some degree identify with the most visible or masculine aspects of the culture (bullfighter, father and Mexican). This overidentification has in the past been a deterrent to upward mobility, acculturation and assimilation. According to others (Meeker, 1964) moving up for Mexican Americans has meant leaving the ethnic community, changing names and assimilating into the Anglo-white community. Apparently, the overidentification with Mexican values is functional to identity maintenance for established Mexican American adolescents, but not necessary for new immigrants. However, it appears as though this overidentification has been dysfunctional to upward mobility and acculturation.

For these Mexican American adolescents, adaptive behavior learned at the onset of migration becomes maladaptive during succeeding steps in the migratory process. If adolescents, their families, or society's institutions cannot provide adaptive techniques for rapid change during the several generations of the migratory process, then the ghettoes of East Los Angeles with their social disorganization will be perpetuated.

REFERENCES

Brody, E. B. (1966) "Cultural exclusion, character and illness." *American J. of Psychiatry* 122: 852–858.

Derbyshire, R. L. (1968) "Adolescent identity crises in urban Mexican Americans in East Los Angeles." Pp. 73–110 in E. B. Brody (ed.) *Minority Group Adolescents in the United States*. Baltimore: Williams & Wilkins.

―――― (1966) "Cultural exclusion: implications for training adult illiterates." *Adult Education* (October): 3–11.

―――― and E. B. Brody (1964) "Marginality, identity and behavior in the American Negro: a functional analysis." *Sociology and Social Research* 48 (April): 301–314.

Erikson, E. (1950) *Childhood and Society*. New York: W. W. Norton.

Gamio, M. (1931) *The Mexican Immigrant: His Life Story*. Chicago: Univ. of Chicago Press.

Guerrero, R. D. (1955) "Neurosis and the Mexican family structure." *American J. of Psychiatry* 112: 411–417.

Heller, C. S. (1966) *Mexican American Youth: Forgotten Youth at the Crossroads*. New York: Random House.

Humphrey, N. D. (1946) "The housing and household practices of Detroit Mexicans." *Social Forces* 21 (no. 4): 433–437.

Leonard, O. and C. P. Loomis (1941) "Culture of a contemporary rural community, El Cerrito, Mexico." *Rural Life Series*, No. 1. Washington, D.C.: U.S. Department of Agriculture, Bureau of Agricultural Economics.

Lewis, O. (1949) "Marriage and the family: husbands and wives in a Mexican village: a study of role conflict." *American Anthropology* 51: 602–610.

Marden, C. F. (1952) *Minorities in American Society.* New York: American Book.

McWilliams, C. (1949) *North From Mexico.* (People of America Series) Philadelphia: J. B. Lippincott.

Meeker, M. (1964) *Background for Planning.* Los Angeles: Welfare Planning Council.

Peak, H. M. (1958) "Search for identity by a young Mexican American." In G. Seward (ed.) *Clinical Studies in Culture Conflict.* New York: Ronald Press.

Sanches, G. I. (1943) "Pachucos in the making." *Common Ground* 4 (Autumn): 13–20.

Scotch, N. A. (1963) "Social change and personality: the effects of migration and social mobility on personality." Pp. 323–330 in N. J. Smelser and W. T. Smelser (eds.) *Personality and Social Systems.* New York: John Wiley.

Seward, G. (1964) "Sex identity and the social order." *J. of Nervous and Mental Disease* 139: 126–136.

——— [ed.] (1958) *Clinical Studies in Culture Conflict.* New York: Ronald Press.

Spiegel, I. P. and F. R. Kluckhohn (1954) "Integration and conflict in family behavior." *Group for Advancement in Psychiatry,* monograph 27.

Taylor, P. S. (1932) *An American-Mexican Frontier.* Chapel Hill: Univ. of North Carolina Press.

Thomas, W. I. and F. Znaniecki (1927) *The Polish Peasant in Europe and America.* (2nd. ed.) New York: Alfred A. Knopf.

Weaver, T. "Sampling and generalization in anthropological research on Spanish speaking groups." Paper presented at the American Ethnological Society, Detroit, May 3, 1968.

Williams, R. (1960) *American Society.* New York: Alfred A. Knopf.

CHAPTER 5

Youth Prepares
for Work

Work is the hallmark of adulthood, yet "It's hard to grow up when there isn't enough man's work."[1] There is little simple, noble subsistence work left for men in American society. Urban American men and women surrender their freedom in working for others in jobs which have become increasingly specialized and professionalized. "Increasingly a young person's success in his career is determined by the quality and quantity of his preparation."[2] Provision of equal educational opportunities with the ability to persevere to the completion of the degree "job ticket" have come to play an important role in determining occupational and social mobility.

In urban industrialized society, the family is no longer a production unit, rather it is a consumption unit. Father—and with increasing frequency, mother—works out of the purview of the children. Adult work is characterized by "invisibility";[3] a young man may grow up never having observed his father at his employment. Parents carry home random snatches of their total work experience making it very difficult for a youth to conceptualize a whole picture of what his father or mother does as a worker. Given the fictional nature of jobs as youth reconstruct them, it is understandable that it takes great effort to sustain the motivation to complete long years of formal education in preparation for occupational objectives.

Although the proportion of young people graduating from high school is expected to continue to rise substantially, the Bureau of the Census estimates that the increase in the youth population will inflate the total number of school dropouts.[4] The object of much official concern in the

[1] Paul Goodman, "Jobs," *Growing Up Absurd*, New York: Vintage Books, 1960. pp. 17–35.
[2] Eli Ginzberg (ed.), *The Optimistic Tradition and American Youth*, New York: Columbia University Press, 1962, p. 53.
[3] Hans Sebald, *Adolescence: A Sociological Analysis*, New York: Appleton-Century-Crofts, 1968, p. 37.
[4] U. S. Department of Labor, *Manpower Report of the President and a Report on Manpower Requirements, Resources, Utilization, and Training*, March 1966, p. 95.

240

sixties (Presidents Kennedy and Johnson brought the phenomenon to the attention of the Congress and the nation), the school dropout is defined as a social and economic problem. Alternative paths to growing into adulthood have disappeared. It is no longer as possible as it once was to quit school, find a job, and become a participating adult. The school way is the only way to job entry and acceptable personal status. The high school diploma has become a screening device used by employers to simplify the recruitment-hiring process, even when the job does not specifically require an incumbent with a diploma.[5]

Best estimates of the proportions of youth leaving high school before graduation run to one-third and beyond. The dropouts are not evenly distributed among the social classes of course; they are concentrated in the lower socioeconomic classes. Daniel Schrieber, who is an educational expert on work-experience programs for the socially disadvantaged, has provided this profile of the average dropout:[6]

> The dropout is a child just past his sixteenth birthday who has average or slightly below average intelligence, and is more likely to be a boy than a girl. He is not achieving according to his potential; he is not reading at grade level; and academically he is in the lowest quarter of his class. He is slightly overage for his grade placement, having been held back once in the elementary or junior high school grades. He has not been in trouble with the law although he does take up an inordinate amount of the school administrators' time because of discipline problems. He seldom participates in extra-curricular activities, feels rejected by the school and his fellow classmates, and in turn rejects them as well as himself. He is insecure in his school status, hostile toward others, and is less respected by his teachers because of his academic inadequacies. His parents were school dropouts as were his older brothers and sisters. His friends are persons outside the school, usually older dropouts. He says he is quitting school because of lack of interest. . . . He strongly resents being called a dropout. . . . To a great extent he is a fugitive from failure, fleeing Kafka-like into more failure.

That these youth tend to lack a realistic orientation to the job market and/or are held back by a low self-concept and fatalistic attitude toward their environment is explained in the selection by Leshner and Snyderman. It was immediately obvious to the authors that the job-seeking and job-holding patterns of the youth could not be ameliorated entirely through verbal means via the provision of occupational information and counseling. Rather it was imperative to design a process of changing work attitudes and improving skills based on performing real work in a simulated environmental context which could be manipulated

[5] For a recent critical analysis of the consequences of this phenomenon, see George Pettitt, *Prisoners of Culture*, New York: Charles Scribner's Sons, 1970.
[6] Daniel Schreiber (ed.), *Profile of the School Dropout*, New York: Random House Vintage Books Edition, 1968, pp. 5–6.

by the planners. In the guided development experience the individual youth was able to integrate his emotional resources. He learned to cope with work complexities and associated social stresses, thereby improving his self-work conception. Attention was also given to the problem of reaching and sustaining the disadvantaged youth who quit or were terminated from vocational programs.

Since adolescence may be considered as a state of becoming, attention should focus on the aspirations or orientations of youth toward life plans, generally taken to mean occupational choice. The educational and occupational aspirations of young Americans have been among the most studied sociological dimensions. Many factors have emerged in association with aspirational levels of adolescents: the position of the family in the class system, parental thrust, level of I.Q., racial/ethnic background, peer influences, social class composition of secondary schools, and need for achievement, to name some of the well-researched factors reported in the sociological journals.

There is wide support for the American Dream that boys have equal opportunity to become almost anything if they work hard. (We have never thought about the systematic application of the Dream ideology to girls!) The consensus regarding equality of opportunity and open upward mobility has been challenged, however, by blacks and their white supporters who question the degree to which the ideology operationally extends to non-middle-class whites. But, by and large, we are a people distinguished by an ethos of social hope and occupational ambition. Eli Ginzberg examines three decisions which largely determine the success of a young man's efforts to give shape and meaning to his values and goals in life: occupational choice, compulsory military service, and early marriage. He argues the interrelationship of these three factors, for the problem of choosing a career becomes even more complicated when the youth must coordinate his military commitments with his career plans. While it is possible to identify positive effects of a period of military service, and these are enumerated, it must also be noted that anticipatory socialization toward the eventual period of service is usually not part of the positive life planning of young men. The extensively publicized resistance to the draft by young men during an unpopular Vietnam War makes the perception of the compulsory military service all the more negative. Early marriage and compulsory military service are linked via an escape hypothesis. Early marriage and career are not necessarily antithetical any longer although the author expresses some reservations relative to their compatibility.

One of the major factors influencing occupational aspiration and achievement is that of residential differences based on the rural-urban dichotomy. Recent emphasis in the literature on the occupational problems of the urban socially disadvantaged youth have somewhat masked the admittedly less critical plight of rural youths who will not be able to utilize their talents on farms. The technological success of American farming methods has produced the displacement of most contemporary farm youth. The displacement, coupled with the considerable evidence that boys reared on farms or in rural areas have less success in the urban labor market than boys reared in urban areas,[7] strengthens the concern that educational achievement and advancement are apt to become a more integral part of orientation to the occupational success in the urban setting. Success in the drastically updated business of farming, as well, promises to become increasingly associated with advanced educational training.

From a detailed review of the literature to which he has contributed research, Glen Elder hypothesizes three sets of variables which account for the relatively depressed achievement orientations of rural youth as compared with urban youth: access to achievement opportunities, exposure to achievement goals and values, and motivation toward achievement. Of these, motivation is thought to be the basic variable influencing college attendance and achievement in life. Much more needs to be known about child-rearing philosophies and methods in farm families before helpful advice can be offered to parents who would wish to prepare their children well for independence.

While the first three selections included in this chapter have focused primarily on the occupational planning and preparation of the adolescents of secondary-school age, the last will attend to the interplay of the work and the wish to serve motivations of college and post-college youth. There are many reasons why the Peace Corps idea, the Vista program, the Civil Rights Movement, and radical causes have appealed to the motivation in young American people to work and serve simultaneously. One general reason has to do with a major value orientation in American culture which has been labeled by a well-known sociologist as "worldly, instrumental activism."[8] It is an aggressive attitude of actively mastering a situation, quite the antithesis of passive fateful acceptance of one's lot. Instrumental activism applies especially to work, to one's occupation and also to other voluntary activities in which one is encouraged to participate. Another reason for work-service program favor has been well-developed by Kenneth Keniston in his final chapter of *Young Radicals.*[9] As he sees it, there are growing numbers of young men and women moving into an emergent

[7] Lee G. Burchinal, "Career Choices of Rural Youth in a Changing Society," North Central Regional Publication No. 142, Agricultural Experiment Station, University of Minnesota, 1962, p. 10.
[8] Talcott Parsons, *The Social System*, Glencoe, Ill.: The Free Press, 1959, pp. 180–200. Also see: Robin Williams, Jr., *American Society*, New York: Alfred A. Knopf, 1960, pp. 421–424.
[9] Kenneth Keniston, *Young Radicals*, New York: Harcourt Brace Jovanovich, Inc., 1968.

stage suspended between adolescence and adulthood. This stage made possible by the affluent, post-modern world is called youth. It is a period of life wherein psychological criteria of adulthood have been met: inner identity is resolved, the capacities to work, to make a love relationship, to play have been developed. However, the prime sociological characteristics of adulthood are lacking: youth have not fully integrated themselves into the institutional structures of marriage, family, and occupation in society. While the great majority of America's young people move directly from adolescence into adulthood, some of the most talented, most affluent, most reluctant young continue to experiment with life's possibilities and their own potentialities and defer entry into sociological adulthood for a time. There are only a small number of institutions which shelter the young who seek a temporary moratorium before joining the Establishment: the Peace Corps, VISTA, the New Left, the hippie movement, the graduate and professional schools, ombudsman type or quasi-administrative roles in colleges, and so forth. In such roles, youth realize the values of openness, flexibility, and movement. Identification is made with a generation rather than with a tradition. These generations succeed each other quickly as anyone over thirty has learned through rebuffs when seeking affiliation with youthful causes.

But, we would not suggest that the need to stop, integrate, and stabilize before launching into traditional adult roles is the only need underlying the enthusiastic response of some of the young to programs of national service. Joseph Colmen, who was associated with the Peace Corps in its early years, makes it clear in his paper that the motivation to volunteer is a healthy combination of "giving and getting." Certainly the Peace Corps has become one of the more durable and imaginative of the New Frontier creations, although its heyday has obviously passed. The idealism of youth is stirred by the positive American values of humanitarian concern, problem solving, aid to the common man, and faith in the ability to master one's environment. In future years it is likely that domestic programs which offer avenues for service will be chosen by youth, and their idealism will find its application at home.

PREPARING DISADVANTAGED YOUTH FOR WORK*

SAUL S. LESHNER
GEORGE S. SNYDERMAN

Jobseeking Patterns of Disadvantaged Youth

This article describes the findings of a project designed to evaluate and pre-pare a group of school dropouts for training or jobs. The project was under the supervision of the Philadelphia Council for Community Advancement, with services performed by the Jewish Employment and Vocational Service (JEVS) and the local offices of the Pennsylvania State Employment Service (PSES).

Four hundred and fifty youths selected for study lived in the section of North Philadelphia that has sometimes been referred to by popular writers as the "jungle." High proportions of unemployment, school dropouts, poverty, dependency, crime, delinquency, illegitimacy, illiteracy, and inferior housing reflect the depressed condition of the area. All had in common a lack of direction and commitment to finding and holding a steady job.

All of the youths were interviewed by PSES counselors prior to their selection for the project. The first series of questions posed to each youth was aimed at revealing his insight into his problem. They were not asked in any particular order, and the youth was permitted to ventilate all his feelings without interruption. The following points were explored: What does he think is keeping him from finding suitable work? How does he view his occupational future? What does he think he ought to do about it?

As might be expected, some of the reasons given overlapped or were implicit in others. Forty-three said they "lacked training," 63 said they "lacked a high school diploma," 56 coupled training with experience, and 24 coupled lack of training and experience. Another 24 said they were "not qualified for anything." It is evident that many of these school dropouts believed that their failure to find jobs was somewhat related to their failure to complete school or, at least, to acquire a salable skill while in school. Others were so passive as to seem unresponsive or impervious to any stimula-tion aimed at helping them. Twelve girls said they were unemployed because they were pregnant, and 6 girls had to stay home to care for their children, 19 youth said their "delinquency record" was held against them by employers. Three youth said they had looked for the wrong job, 138 youth admitted that

* Excerpted from Saul S. Leshner and George S. Snyderman, U.S. Department of Labor, *Employment Service Review* (November 1965) pp. 1–3, (December 1965) pp. 4–6, (January 1966) pp. 7–10, (April 1966) pp. 14–16.

they did not seriously look for work, and 9 said they did not know why they were unemployed.

Regardless of length of unemployment, only 84 (19 percent) of the 450 youth had made one or more contacts with an employer per week; 39 percent never made a single contact; and only 4 percent made more than five contacts per week. It appeared, however, that the longer the period of unemployment, the less the youth engaged in jobseeking activities. Evidently, the youth's motivation and ability to direct his energies toward seeking a job lessen as the length of unemployment increases.

KINDS OF JOBS SOUGHT

Nearly half (46 percent) of the youth were unable to express any kind of job preference. When responses indicating a preference were grouped and examined according to such variables as skill content, opportunity to acquire training, possibilities for upgrading, and work environment, the choices were, in fact, realistic. Only one boy said he had been seeking what might appear to be an unrealistic job opportunity: e.g., acting.

The youth who could state their preferences most frequently were seeking low level jobs. In the main, these were the types of jobs which nonwhites with meager educational attainment could actually get. Traditionally, these were the jobs in which relatives and friends were employed. They required little skill, were of poor to fair working conditions, offered little chance for advancement. Even the so-called "semiskilled" jobs to which the youth aspired were repetitive in nature or required persons able to "serve others." This seems to contradict some statements in the literature which point out that "lower class" youth set high values on occupations related to athletics and entertainment.

Significant also is the fact that 45 percent of the youth could state only one kind of a job that they were seeking as a first choice; 60 percent could not state a second choice; and 70 percent could not state a third choice. When these are added to the numbers who were seeking "any kind of work," there is additional evidence of the deep uncertainty and almost blind groping of these youth in attempting to deal with their job problems.

In line with the commonly held view of disadvantaged youth, our findings indicate that most of these youth could not make a vocational choice. Where they could, the choice was usually concrete and realistic.

WHERE THEY APPLIED

Possibilities for job-finding and upgrading were also limited because of the types of establishment to which the youth applied for work. Twenty-two percent made their first application at a factory. They seemed to have vague notions about what they wanted to or could do. Some seem to have been seeking jobs which exist in limited numbers in factories, e.g., janitors, stock and shipping, etc. From the youth's point of view, working in a factory meant better pay rates and working conditions.

Forty-three youth applied at hospitals or nursing homes; nearly all were girls who felt that these establishments were less likely to insist that applicants be high school graduates or have specific training. More than half of these youth had been "steered" to the prospective employers by friends or relatives. Several said that the free meals given to workers more than offset the lower wages.

Forty youngsters said they first applied to "stores," usually small retail or variety shops situated in the neighborhood in which they lived. Twenty-five other youth applied at food and grocery stores, but in their immediate neighborhoods; only two applied at the large chain stores. Twenty-one more youth applied at department stores, but 18 told the PSES counselor they did not expect to be hired.

Thirty of the youth who appeared to be interested in securing work in the retail trade were further interviewed at some length by JEVS counselors. These boys and girls said they had not applied at department stores or large chain stores because they did not have a high school diploma, or they did not have proper clothing, or they did not think they could pass the tests.

Perhaps more revealing is the fact that of those youth who did apply for jobs in retail trade, very few tried for sales or cashiering jobs. Most looked for jobs with duties like "filling shelves," "unpacking crates," "delivery," "sweeping up," etc. They said they were "playing it safe" and looking for work which they could do and for which nonwhites are acceptable. Few of the youth were seeking "white-collar" or clerical openings; only four applied for jobs in offices.

HOW JOB SOURCES WERE SELECTED

Although all of these youth needed considerable assistance in finding a job, only 15 went first to an employment office, public or private. All 15, at the time of their initial application, were seeking service jobs in hospitals, hotels, restaurants, or private households.

Few read want-ad columns in newspapers, even though jobs were listed that they could do and might conceivably get. Only 10 of the 15 youth were referred to prospective employers by the employment agencies, but only 2 of the 10 secured jobs through these agencies, and the jobs were temporary. Those who registered with private agencies said that they were "brushed off" if they "did not have the fee to pay in advance." Only 4 of the 15 had registered with PSES.

Only a small number seemed to have valid reasons for applying at a particular establishment, and were able to verbalize their reasons. Specifically, 7 said they had some experience and could describe the experience; 13 said they were interested in a specific job and could say why; 30 said they had seen or thought about the work as performed in the particular establishment and thought they could do it or learn to do it.

WHY THEY STOPPED JOBSEEKING

On this point the youth tend to generalize or rationalize. For example, 31 were discouraged (22 of the 31 appear to have been seeking work for more than 6 months; these averaged two contacts per week but had not produced even a day's work). Fifty said they "did not know where else to look" (36 of these had averaged less than 1 contact per month; 19 had made less than 5 contacts during their entire time of unemployment). Five became ill and were hospitalized but did not attempt to secure work when their health problem was resolved. Twenty-one had no carfare (all were being supported by the Department of Public Assistance); 52 of the girls became pregnant or had to stay home to care for one or more of their children. Five doubted their ability to work because of a physical handicap, and 32 were "away for a while" in a correctional institution.

Added to the above were "vague" reasons which, taken with the foregoing, have resulted in such youth being labeled as "aimless" and "unmotivated" and unable to assume responsibility. Thus, 26 said they "did not know why" they stopped looking; 89 "just stopped"; 77 "never really looked for work"; 8 filed applications with employers and decided to "wait" for the employer to call them; 3 thought they were "too young" to work (none of these contacted the Employment Service or Board of Education to check this point); 8 were satisfied with occasional odd jobs and appeared to have been unable or unwilling to seek permanent work; 12 registered with an employment agency but did not apply elsewhere; 2 slept "too late to look for a job"; one was considering enlisting in the army, and one was considering returning to school, but neither boy took action.

CONCLUSIONS

Some of the major findings of other students of employment of disadvantaged youth were confirmed. The youth tended to have little understanding of concepts of success and achievement. They tended to view the existing occupational structure as irrelevant and without personal reference, and to view middle class goals as vague or impossible of attainment. They set up personalized goals which can be achieved, and they regard these goals as "good enough." They lack or do not view occupational goals seriously. Their negative attitudes toward work in general, and steady work in particular, result from their failure to accept an occupational role.

Occupational titles of jobs meant little to these youth. The number of occupations of which these youth had knowledge was very small. The youth's exposure to persons with real work experience was almost exclusively limited to those in unskilled, semiskilled, service and domestic occupations. Lack of knowledge about jobs and the job market, in part at least, explains why so many youth restricted their search to a few occupations and industries. It also underscores why so many could not state a vocational choice or goal.

Most youth preferred to stay as close to home as possible. Some youth felt that the chances of securing a job were better since the prospective employer "might know" them and would be more apt to hire them. Several boys said they were afraid to travel through territories of other gangs. Several others "did not know their way around the city" and said they thought they might get lost.

In summary, a large proportion of the youth had vague and random job-seeking patterns. These appeared to stem from a lack of orientation to the job market. For those who were motivated to seek employment, aspirations tended to be realistic in terms of their own competencies and personal and social limitations. Aspirations, however, reflected a devalued self-concept and a lack of any belief that they could escape the bonds of their environment.

Despite a general awareness that they needed training, comparatively few of the youth had confidence that an investment in preparation through schooling or training would pay off. This appears to be due, in part at least, to feelings of self-devaluation, discrimination in hiring, and to their inability to engage in long term effort for future rewards. The youth tended to live in the present and were unable to project expectations into the future, and defer immediate gratifications for later well-being.

IMPLICATIONS FOR SERVICE

It seems probable that the deep-rooted problem of finding and holding a job for a disadvantaged youth cannot be resolved through verbal means. In spite of initial counseling at the Employment Service, half the youth rejected the offer to enter the adjustment and training programs. The depth of the youths' problems was related to the fact that their development occurred without social guidelines and standards. Many lacked personal identity and a concept of anything other than relations and behaviors affecting their immediate survival. Absence of purpose or goal, in a sense, resulted in a bewilderment with, or a psychological withdrawal from any involvement with matters not tied to their immediate experiences. Their attitude was one of little hope or expectation of having a more fruitful life.

It is, therefore, an oversimplification of the problem to suggest that counseling and occupational information for these youth are enough. Rehabilitation would imply first a wide and intensive variety of health, welfare, and educational measures for them and their parents.

The depth of the problem is reflected in the alien character of the subculture, the constricted developmental and life experiences of the individual youth, and the lack of relatedness of middle-class norms to their survival needs. The first steps in the youths' vocational development must involve a broadening of fundamental experiences through social learnings, which will enable them to deal with matters which offer a high sense of well-being.

The attitudes and conformance patterns to be cultivated must consolidate those healthy forces which can be made available within the home, neighborhood, school, and employing community.

The rewards of self-improvement should be geared to prescribed efforts and related to achievement. Recommendations for sound jobseeking and vocational development cannot be intelligible or intelligent for this population until the youth are prepared through elementary experiences for dealing with them.

Counseling and Work Adjustment

In the counseling situation the youth served were generally unmotivated and unresponsive. Because of limited verbal abilities they were unable to cope with the GATB; e.g., the average reading levels were at the 4th grade; arithmetic achievement was lower; more than half were classified as functionally retarded. The population was drawn from the slums of North Philadelphia. Cultural impoverishment, together with a paucity of economic advantages, resulted in a lack of motivation for work or school. Even though delinquency records could not be routinely checked, at least 36 percent of the boys and 33 percent of the girls had been so adjudicated by the courts. In addition, at least 30 percent of the remaining boys and 25 percent of the girls were known to the police. Eighty-three boys admitted membership in fighting gangs.

These youth presented special and difficult problems to counselors. They represented a population which is culturally alienated from the mainstream of middle-class aspirations and vocational values. They viewed work as a punitive and not as a rewarding activity. For them, work was arduous and menial and offered neither wages above minimal subsistence needs (which were already met by public assistance sources), nor the opportunity to move up the occupational ladder.

Most of the youth had dropped out of school in the 10th or 11th grade after a history of chronic truancy. Academic materials were unrealistic in terms of their life experiences. They seem to have existed in a relatively primitive society in which the survival demands of today obviated their ability to consider long-range values. They lived primarily in the present, lacked planfulness, and were impulsive and unable to defer immediate needs for larger rewards that result from self-preparation and improvement.

Their limited and negative attitudes towards education and employment were reinforced by the home and neighborhood. Whatever brief exposures they had had with middle-class values were offset by the pervasive realities of their family and neighborhood life. Middle-class values, perceived only vaguely, produced reactions of withdrawal, frustration, or aggression. Many of the youth were unable to understand these alien standards and, finding no meaning in them, lacked any desire to meet them.

In addition to this "psychological blindness" to most of our middle-class mores the youth were generally unaccustomed to dealing with their own inner feelings. Communication with each other commonly touched on only the superficial and the obvious. Their need to stifle profound anxieties and hostile impulses resulted in their building a protective shield around intimate personal issues.

DEVELOPMENT IS GUIDED

The primary approach in the JEVS work adjustment process consists of providing a guided developmental experience through which the individual may integrate his emotional resources. He begins in a setting in which the demands imposed are within his grasp. Work tasks are simple, peer relationships are casual, and supervisory attitudes are benign and understanding. As the youth is helped to relate to these simple conditions, increased difficulties, and more complex work and relationships are introduced progressively. The youth is helped to develop increased tolerance for work and social stresses and to acquire the behavior patterns which enable him to accommodate to discipline and to cope with the demands of competitive employment. Eventually, the youth begins to feel more positively about himself and work.

The function of counseling in the work adjustment process was a supporting and reinforcing one. As the youth developed suitable attitudes and coping behaviors, counseling enabled him to bring to awareness the changes that were occurring within him. Periodic counseling interviews crystallized his feelings and provided a mental image of his new worker identity. He was helped to verbalize the positive and negative feelings he experienced, to express in words the values and purposes of working that he felt were satisfying. Thus, counseling helped him to develop a worker self-concept which clearly reflected personal status and vocational goals and the ways to achieve those goals.

Counseling occurs when the counselor can communicate verbally with the youth in terms which are meaningful because they relate to the youth's background and experience. Initially, discussions deal with matters and problems that are immediate and part of the present. There is no point in talking about feelings with a youth who is accustomed to ignoring his feelings. It is meaningless to discuss vocational plans with a youth who cannot project his ideas beyond the present. It is logical, however, as a first step to put into words what the youth is doing, how and with whom he is doing it, why he does it, and what more he will be asked to do. To this base of contemporary experience, a broader range of experiences accrues. As it builds and is brought to consciousness, the individual is enabled to grow and use himself more meaningfully. Further, as feelings of identity and self-worth emerge and are put into words, the youth's personality is organized and he is enabled to deal better with both abstractions and futures. In this way, the rationality with which the youth meets internal problems and environmental demands improves.

Most contemporary students agree that growth stems from a positive relationship between the counselee and the counselor. The relationship is made up of mutual respect and trust. It should be expected, therefore, that in a population with life experiences of rejection, mistrust, misunderstanding, and none of the benefits of middle-class society, the counselor will meet many difficulties and resistances to establishing a sound relationship. The counselor is apt to be viewed with suspicion, simply because the youth will not have understood him. The youth will alternately oppose, withdraw from, or try to manipulate, as he tests out the counselor's reliability, sincerity, and willingness to help.

In the environment of work, the initial relationship of the youth is with himself as he engages in the work tasks. It is the task of the counselor to unite and transfer the non-threatening relations with the object world to the interpersonal relationships in which highly threatening factors of self-esteem and social value are involved. As a confident relationship begins to prevail, it becomes possible to particularize and discuss the youth's strengths and weaknesses. The counselor can now proceed to point up where development is needed and why the youth can benefit from taking specific actions. In effect, the youth becomes able to appreciate the fact that his present experiences are "paying off" in gratification and self-worth. Consequently, other ideas of personal development will also be acceptable as he continues. Such are the roots of motivation and counseling direction.

As the youth progressed through the Work Adjustment Center his occupational orientation was sharpened. His functioning as he "produced" was carefully observed and nurtured. Industrial foremen, not psychologists, helped him deal with problems involving his work tempo, persistence, coordination, dexterity, quality, and quantity of task performance.

Throughout the adjustment process, individual and group counseling was provided to help the youth mobilize his energies, learn to cope with inter-personal relations, and make vocational choices. Counseling always related to the work situation. If, for example, a youth failed to meet the foremen's expectations in a particular respect, the youth was invited to discuss the matter privately with the psychologist. The problem was discussed in concrete voca-tional terms, e.g., "Would an employer permit this or might he fire you?" If this kind of discussion failed, the psychologist referred the youth to the super-vising psychologist who used a more personal, subjective approach to help him develop insights.

WEEKLY COUNSELING

Individual counseling interviews and small group counseling sessions were held at least once a week for each youth. At first, topics and content covered personal matters relating to the immediate work experience. Eventually, these were extended to home, peer group, and social matters which, in turn, related to vocational development issues. As the vocational aspect became predomi-nant, the realities of job-finding became the focus of discussion. Presentability, handling the interview, employer expectation were discussed. The youth was helped to recognize and understand that he might be rejected by many employ-ers before he was finally accepted. It was indicated that these rejections might not be failures on his part but were generally implicit in the normal job-finding process.

Counseling therefore was an accompanying and significant component of the evaluation and work adjustment process. It capitalized on the youth's present status and his new experiences. It progressed from impersonal to personal considerations and finally to matters wherein external employment conditions were separated from personal anxieties. Thus, near the close of the program, counseling was mainly vocational and designed to help the youth about to "graduate" to face and grapple with problems of choosing, entering upon, and succeeding in training or a job. To this end, both individual and group sessions were considered essential.

When these were completed, the youth was referred to the PSES local office counselor, with an understanding that until he was placed in either a job or an MDTA course, he should continue in the Work Adjustment Center several days a week, where a climate of continuing acceptance and the means of earning pocket money were provided.

The vocational program described here is an extended one by the stand-ards set for most public welfare programs. It requires, in addition to the pro-cedures described above, built-in methods to continue to support the disad-vantaged youth's struggle to rehabilitate himself. Followup by mail generally fails. It requires that someone, preferably a knowledgeable counselor, visit the youth in his home. This is costly, because these youth are highly mobile and revisits are often necessary. Valuable help can be given on the spot. Incidentally, data can often be gathered to clarify problems and the value of services ren-dered. For example, JEVS learned that 40 percent of the youth followed up wished to continue in counseling even after they had found jobs. They were encouraged to do so, and even though the program officially ended January 31, 1965, each week several called to talk in person or by phone with their psychologists at the Center.

Not all disadvantaged youth are amenable to immediate vocational help. As indicated above, years of poverty, deprivation, and discrimination have created not only a "hard core" socioeconomic problem but also psychological and health difficulties which must be treated before the youth can be helped. Actually, 21 percent of the youth entering the program needed some other service before they could begin to think about and relate to the world of work. Counseling was used to help these boys and girls accept a referral to a suitable community agency for medical, psychiatric, or family case work services. Seventy-one percent of these did accept a referral and were receiving the services at the close of the program.

There is no "sure-fire, quick and easy" method to help all disadvantaged youth. Many will be able to accept and use counseling and other services available in the Youth Opportunity Centers of the Employment Service. But a sizable number will have severe emotional or personality problems and will require services such as those offered by JEVS *before* they can accommodate to and use the YOC services. The experience of PSES in Philadelphia clearly demonstrates that these youth can be placed in competitive industry.

Work Adjustment Training

The Work Adjustment Center was established in 1957 to experiment with procedures aimed at improving employability through the cultivation of suitable work patterns and attitudes. Inadequacies of routine selection, evaluation, training, and placement for the special problems and needs of "hard core" youth indicated a need for new methods to assess and improve trainability and employability.

This program for out-of-school, unemployed youth lacking sufficient verbal skills and educational background to enter available training is based upon job sample evaluation in a workshop situation. JEVS maintains two well-lighted, well-ventilated workshops, one 15,000 square feet in a factory loft building, the other 10,000 square feet. Both contain work benches, fixtures, tools, time clocks, and a belt line used in both the evaluation and adjustment phases. Work areas were planned by an industrial engineer so that both individual and team work are possible. Space has been allocated for offices, storage, shipping, and receiving, as well as for remediation and for individual and group counseling.

Work, obtained by contract from private industry at competitive prices and in accordance with Federal wage and hour standards, was typically simple or repetitive. While it consisted mainly of hand operations, some contracts required the use of such equipment as staplers, heat sealers, scales, or punch presses. Jobs were broken down into basic components in order to fulfill the qualitative and quantitative demands of the contract. The young people were exposed to a variety of job tasks and situations. The pressures of the contracts were used to teach what to expect, accept, and deal with in industry. At the same time, they permitted the staff to observe the youths' adjustment to meeting actual industrial standards.

The purpose of the program was to show that with personal redevelopment, work adjustment training, and increased motivation, "hard core" youth could become employable and be placed in open competitive employment in Philadelphia.

INTAKE PROCEDURES

Standard operating procedure of the Employment Service required all school dropouts with little or no work history or with vocational adjustment problems to be referred to local office employment counselors.

The PSES Project Counselor conducted an intake interview with a two-fold purpose: (1) to determine whether the youth was actually in need of the program and could benefit from it; and (2) to instill in him a desire to take long-term actions that would result in his becoming occupationally competent. Where the youth appeared to be adequately adjusted, reasonably motivated, and possessed of specific occupational potential, he would be offered referral to an MDTA training course already in operation. However, where the youth's test scores were negative and/or his attitudes and values were such as to preclude the likelihood of successful employment, an effort was made to interest him in referral to a Work Adjustment Center.

Acceptance into the program was based on the judgment of the Work Adjustment Center's intake psychologist regarding the youth's readiness for evaluation and willingness and ability to travel to the centers unaided each day. The psychologist interviewed each youth, took him on a tour of the Center to which he would be assigned, explained the program, and encouraged him to ask questions about the process and his place in it. If the youth indicated interest in entering the program, he was given a starting date, usually within 24 hours. Arrangements were made to interview one or both of his parents or guardians, and the PSES counselor was notified of his acceptance.

PREVOCATIONAL EVALUATION

Evaluation was incorporated into every phase of the project and changed in purpose and emphasis as the youth progressed through the program. Initial evaluation, encompassing 4 or more weeks of observing the yough and encouraging him to test himself on work samples, was concerned mainly with determining readiness for vocational help and the kinds of activities that will be of value to him. It was originally estimated that a decision regarding trainability and/or employability of the youth could be made in about 4 weeks. However, 76 percent had to be retained in the program for 8 to 13 weeks before a clear evaluation could be made. (Many of the group who stayed 7 weeks or less either dropped out or were dropped from the program.)

The psychologist decided the level and task category at which the youth would begin an established sequence of the tasks to be administered from elected industrial groupings. Whether the youth began in one occupational area or another was determined by personal or aspirational considerations, or on a trial and error basis to ascertain preferential work areas.

Before the youth began each task, the evaluation assistant explained its nature and significance and gave detailed instructions on how to proceed. He observed the youth as he worked on each task, lent encouragement, expressed those attitudes and demands agreed upon with the psychologist, and recorded times used to complete the task and behavior. If the youth seemed able to function on higher levels than those assigned initially, this was discussed with the psychologist. The newly identified strengths, if persisting, were incorporated as a series of new assignments, and the client transferred to a higher level of tasks. Similarly, adjustments were made if the level of tasks was too high. The youth earned no money in this phase of evaluation.

Grading of work samples extended over five levels, each of which represented a different degree of psychological activity involving intellectual and motor performance. The increased complexity of work tasks ranged from those requiring simple specific directions to tasks involving more complex directions, abstract reasoning, and problem-solving. Likewise, tasks progressed from those which can be performed almost automatically to those which required multicoordinated sensory motor activities. Work sample tasks were distributed within broad occupational categories, such as small parts assembly, packaging, sewing, building maintenance, clerical, electronic, and auto parts repairing. Each level in a category may comprise several tasks of equal complexity.

For each task within each occupational area and at each level of difficulty, the trainee was rated for performance and accuracy and was observed for punctuality, attendance, appearance, frustration tolerance, learning speed, and psychomotor activity.

Some youth progress through work samples very rapidly and then tend to become bored if left on a fixed schedule. Others perform well on work samples but experience difficulty adjusting to real work. To improve the accuracy of the final evaluation and enable the professional staff to examine and verify the results achieved on work samples, the youth was placed on simple production tasks. He was again required to be careful in task performance, observe rules, be punctual, accept criticism and increased pressures, participate and communicate with other workers, and generally to meet progressively higher performance standards.

Minimal wages and automatic increments served as incentives for forming appropriate behavior patterns. Together with observing the client's reactions to pressures and more stringent regulations, they enabled the psychologist to evaluate the youth's ability to improve in such areas as personal and social attitudes, neatness, precision of work tasks, persistence, learning and adaptability. For some, wages were a stimulus to mobilize personal resources and function more effectively. Other youth failed to change their behavior patterns despite the payment of wages.

The weekly automatic wage increases during the first half of the work adjustment program tended to support and stimulate most youth and their productivity kept pace with their pay increases. However, others increased their productivity faster than their pay and a few tended to pace themselves and produced less.

During the latter part of the production program, the youth were paid the shop rate or the piece rate, whichever was higher. During this phase, the youth tended to earn status among his peers on the basis of his wage level. By the same token, the foreman and the floor psychologist used the earnings of the youth as an important basis for determining his employability. As the sole indicator of employability, wages were sometimes misleading, however. For example, one youth was earning $1.25 per hour by the time he was in the tenth week of the program. At the same time, he was involved in several fights because he had been trying to "shake-down" other youth. He was frequently late for work. Despite his high productivity, he tended to cheat on his counts of work done.

Regardless of problems they may present, incentive rates are necessary because they represent the reality of many industrial jobs. Many youth were obviously motivated by them, although the exact degree and kind of motivation could not be measured. Incentive rates for many youth were more meaningful than the guaranteed shop rate.

Each youth evaluated generally spent approximately 2 weeks on work samples and 2 weeks on real production work. The actual time necessary to secure information which predicts ability to learn to work well and use vocational help varies from youth to youth. Some spend a few days on work samples and even this time may need to be extended for a definite evaluation.

When the results of both types of evaluation were taken as a unit, the psychologist had a rounded picture of the youth and judged if he could proceed with the work adjustment program or whether he was ready for skill training or placement. Evaluation provided a reliable estimate of general and specific competencies and a prediction of particular kind and level of vocational adjustability and was therefore continued in Personal and Work Adjustment Training.

PERSONAL AND WORK ADJUSTMENT

The process initially offered a benign and permissive climate which gradually progressed to the disciplined, structured environment commonly found in competitive industry. The beginning objective was promotion of personal adjustment to the general work setting and helping the individual youth accommodate to the personal and social factors which, aside from production, are traits required of good workers. A generalized kind of personality integration was promoted. Variables most emphasized at this point related to the client's ability to observe rules and regulations, personal grooming, communication and behavior acceptable to others, and respect for authority.

The first level in the process was the industrial foreman's attempt to help by stressing work of good quality; teaching the youth to pace himself properly; emphasizing persistence; and stressing productivity, attendance and punctuality, personal responsibility, group goals, and reality factors specific to being an efficient worker. If a youth evidenced difficulty in any one of these areas, the foreman attempted to help him work out his problem. If the foreman failed, he referred the youth to his rehabilitation counselor, who tried to help him understand and accept the problem so that he could deal more effectively with it.

Occupational orientation was gradually sharpened and made more concrete as the client's personal adjustment improved. His functioning was more selectively production-oriented in terms of how he performed assigned tasks, as contrasted with how well he related to the general situation emphasized in the diagnostic phases of the program. Variables treated in adjustment training are work tempo, task persistence, coordination and dexterity, self and peer competition in output, quality and quantity in performance.

This phase of the project was administered by a supervising psychologist and controlled by counseling psychologists (rehabilitation counselors) and industrial work foremen, intermittently supplemented by vocational counselors. It was a flexible process for those youth considered potentially trainable or employable after prevocational evaluation. To help the youth develop a self-image of a good worker, organize his effects and energies, and acquire suitable work patterns and attitudes, the process became progressively less permissive. Gradually, more insistent and structured standards of quality and quantity were imposed. Industrial foremen, at the instruction of a floor psychologist, introduced the kinds of pressures to be expected in competitive work. The foremen used prescribed techniques and devices to help the client learn to function more adequately. Individual and group counseling helped on problems inhibiting progressive adjustment.

PILOT COMMUNICATIONS IMPROVEMENT PROJECT

As part of the work adjustment training program, a pilot project was set up to determine its effectiveness in improving listening, speaking, reading, writing, and arithmetic skills. The dropouts' severe lack of these skills makes them difficult to train for many types of vocations and may completely preclude training for some. Few had the reading and writing ability needed to complete a job application; some were nonreaders.

An 8-week course of three 1-hour sessions a week was established for two groups of seven trainees—those who placed highest and those who placed lowest on the screening tests and other measuring methods. Participation was voluntary and the group members were paid at their regular hourly rate.

There were indications, especially in the lower group, that negative attitudes toward learning could be changed. There seemed to be increased interest of members in both groups in additional training. Members in the higher group expressed desire to attend prep schools and complete their high school work. In final individual conferences, each trainee expressed a willingness to continue in the Center's program on a nonpay basis, if given the opportunity. However, the program did not affect the trainees sufficiently to enable them to transfer their gains to their overall adjustment. They appeared quite able to work in a socially acceptable job while at the Center, and to continue in antisocial, unproductive behavior elsewhere.

Experience in this program indicates that daily 1-hour sessions would be preferable, especially in view of the brief duration of the program. It would also seem wise to investigate the possibility of extending this type of program to on-the-job training or as an evening program after trainees leave the Center and are placed in vocational opportunities appropriate to their training and experience.

Most effective were those activities which related most closely to (a) the experience and cultural background of the trainees, (b) vocational training tasks currently being executed in the Center, and (c) enhancing the trainees' understanding of such things as withholding of pay for social security, income taxes, etc.

OBSERVATIONS AND CONCLUSIONS

The following are some of the observations and conclusions drawn from the project:

1. Traditional techniques of evaluation and preparation for work which are useful with the average unemployed or displaced workers fail with disad-

vantaged youth. New methods—youth- and problem-centered—must be used with these youth.

2. Evaluation procedures involving the use of work samples and productive work were effective with disadvantaged youth in designating areas and levels of training and employment. It was possible to evaluate a majority of the youth who could not be evaluated by normal Employment Service methods. Youth who were rejected in routine examinations could use and profit from extended and individualized evaluation. Adaptability to training and work is least revealed in standard psychological testing.

3. Evaluation, work adjustment training, and other remedial procedures must be tailored to the particular needs of disadvantaged youth. Tasks and procedures must be culturally oriented and acceptable to the youths' value system.

4. Work provided in an Adjustment Center should be real and equivalent to work in private industry and where possible should be contracted from private industry and involve competitive standards.

5. Wages should be realistic and based on production. Unrealistically high minimum rates tend to reward inadequate work behavior and stifle rather than promote vocational development.

6. Individual and group counseling must be integrated with personal and work adjustment processes to help the youth work through emotional difficulties which hinder his entrance to and success in training or work; followup counseling is needed to reinforce gains made by the youth in the adjustment process.

7. A substantial number of youth regarded as slow learners and borderline mentally retarded respond to and reveal average competencies in a work setting. Youth who lack competencies in basic skills (i.e., reading and arithmetic) can be motivated to acquire these skills through individualized techniques in a work setting.

Much that has been written about the lack of motivation of disadvantaged youth is only partially correct. Dreary implications that they are hopeless and therefore predestined to failure are without substance. "Traditionally unmotivated," "hard to reach," "disadvantaged," or "hard core" youth can learn and will respond if there are persons who wish to help them. When these youth learn and understand, they become more accepting of and amenable to vocational treatment. They learn to handle time limits. Clocks are no longer "for squares." They report regularly and punctually for service.

The Failure Cases in a Vocational Development Program

Rehabilitating "hard-core" jobless youth presents a number of difficulties to agencies engaged in counseling and placement. Recruiting and motivating these youth to accept and use vocational help is a long, arduous, and costly process. Many accept the programs and then drop out, while others are not immediately amenable to vocational service. Obviously, the loss of even a portion of these youth is expensive to the agency offering the services, and it is a traumatic experience to the young person who leaves the program feeling he has not been helped. These are the failures which counselors should not merely "learn to live with," but rather should find some way to minimize. But before we can design and implement a method for attacking the problem of holding these youth until they can maintain themselves in, and benefit from, training or work, we need to know far more about their reactions to vocational services as they now exist.

/This is a report of a study of youth who were referred to the Work Adjustment Center of the Philadelphia Employment and Vocational Service by counselors of the Pennsylvania State Employment Service, but failed to use the vocational help offered.

Of the 331 youth who were accepted into the program, 135 failed to complete it, 66 (20 percent) dropped out, and 69 (21 percent) were terminated. Although some of the terminated group needed services which were not available in the Work Adjustment Center, it may be observed that none of the "failure" cases actually could profit from a vocational service, even though it was individualized and custom-tailored to meet the needs of each person.

We use the term "failure" here to mean a youth who did not successfully complete the entire program. He is considered a "success" case only if he finished his program at the JEVS Work Adjustment Center and returned to his PSES counselor for placement. If for any reason he quit or was dropped from the program by JEVS or PSES, he was considered a failure.

Virtually all disadvantaged youth in the sample, whether successes or failures, shared common characteristics and had histories laden with psychosocial problems. Even when these were readily apparent, JEVS psychologists could rarely state with assurance that a particular youth would or would not respond. All they could do was to apply a repertory of techniques such as individual and group counseling, work adjustment procedures, and remedial reading—and expect that a sizeable percentage of the youth would find a success experience on which they could capitalize. Even then, there were 25 youths who successfully completed this comprehensive rehabilitation program but then did not return to the PSES for placement service. Since few of these were able to find jobs, they are considered to be failures.

We attempted initially to predict success by studying data procured at intake. However, nothing in a youth's socioeconomic or personal history yielded clues by which to predict success or failure in a vocational program except a general attitude that failure was inevitable. In approximately 8 percent of the 331 cases, this attitude could be detected at intake, and attention was given to helping the youth cope with feelings of inadequacy. Generally, however, this failure expectancy was masked and could not be ascertained until relatively late in the program.

Excluding those youth who had to be dropped for medical reasons and who entered a medical program, JEVS psychologists classified the failure cases into four categories:

1. Youth who typically could not relate to anyone or sustain an organized mode of behavior. Some of these acted out their problems and disrupted service for others in the program; others exhibited superficial conforming

behavior as a means of testing or manipulating authority. All of the youth tended to respond impulsively and to seek immediate need gratification. They were oriented to the survival demands of the moment and were unwilling or unable to pursue long-range larger goals. These youth may be classified broadly as individuals with a character problem.

2. Youth who were highly immature, suggestible, and responsive to any diverting stimulus. They also lacked ability to make plans and could neither organize systematic behavior patterns nor direct their activities. They tended to "drift off" and had no "staying power." They may be considered emotionally and socially immature as a result of constricting and shallow developmental backgrounds.

3. Youth who were unable to tolerate any structured activity or restraint. Since by definition work implies a channeling of energies, these youth rebelled against supervision, worked sporadically, attended when the occasion suited them, and resisted any attempts to regulate and rehabilitate them. They had inadequate defense mechanisms with which to deal with their psychological conflicts, and were therefore classified as emotionally unstable.

4. Youth who could perceive no meaning in a work situation because it was not relevant to any of their life experiences. These boys and girls reacted inappropriately to work situations and demands, or they withdrew from involvement with them, or they reacted with frustration, fear or aggressive behavior. Like group 2, they were unable to cope with social or vocational demands.

The above grouping oversimplifies the dynamic aspects of their responses, but it offers an etiological framework for determining why so many failed. Their needs and problems were not always clear; reasons for failures were highly individualized, and differentiating factors were a matter of degree. The data which are presented and discussed do not purport to be specifically defined. However, we may draw some broad conclusions which may help us to deal better with the failures.

As mentioned before, of the total of 135 youth, 69 were terminated and 66 dropped out or quit. All but 4 of those terminated and 19 dropouts were interviewed at least once by PSES counselors. JEVS psychologists had interviewed all of these 23 failures prior to their termination from the Center, and the data from these interviews are used in this report. JEVS staff also interviewed 29 additional failures and 19 other dropouts. The results of these interviews were utilized to supplement the data obtained by PSES counselors.

For purposes of discussion, the joint findings of PSES and JEVS are grouped under the following categories: Male Dropouts (QM); Female Dropouts (QF); Terminated Males (TM); Terminated Females (TF).

THE QM GROUP

Thirty-five boys, or 19 percent of those entering the program, quit (QM). Twenty-four of the 35 said they had to or wanted to go to work, but few really were so motivated or actually did look for jobs. None seemed to have been able to adjust to a job even when they found one, and not one of the program failures placed by PSES was able to hold the job. Consequently, we may infer that the failure of these youth in a vocational program is dynamically similar to their failure to adhere to a constructive jobseeking pattern.

Several youth who dropped out to go to work said that they were not being paid enough at the Work Adjustment Center. Individual and group counseling was ineffectual in helping them understand and accept the program's developmental or training aspects. Their insistence that they were employed at the Center reflected an inability to differentiate between work as a preparatory or developmental process and work as a means of earning a living. At one point in the program, JEVS staff considered the advisability of supplementing base earnings, but it was believed that allowances paid would not deter these youth from dropping out. Since their basic behavior patterns would not be modified, they would soon find other ways to evade program demands. Also, it was felt that if income is not correlated directly with effort, the incentive value of earning money would be diluted. This may be a controversial point, for there seems to be some indication that these youth are not generally oriented to amounts of income, except perhaps for large differentials which have symbolic value.

Eleven boys quit the program for the following reasons: Five were picked up by the police and detained for extended periods of time; four had chronic or prolonged illness; and two had family difficulties with excuses such as "had to help at home," "have to help my girl friend who is pregnant."

Generally, we were not able to check the validity of any of these reasons. Some of the boys who had been arrested and detained by the police returned to the Center to brag about their escapades, to create a series of difficult situations, and then quit when called to account. Most boys, including those who obviously were ill, refused to accept a referral for medical or psychiatric help. Of the seven who did, only three kept their first appointment.

THE QF GROUP

Thirty-one, or 20 percent of the girls entering the program, quit (QF). Their reasons included personal responsibilities which could not be avoided. When a girl said she was dropping out to take care of her child because her own mother no longer could, it is likely that such was the case. It was reasonable, also, to expect that girls would have to help around the house, an activity usually not required of the boys. Nevertheless, personality factors such as those described for the boys accounted for 13 of the QF group. The other dropouts are as follows: Health reasons, nine; family problems, seven; economic reasons, one; and detained by police, one. Pregnancy was included under health reasons.

THE TM GROUP

As indicated previously, 69 youth, or 21 percent of those who entered the program, were terminated because they were unable to profit from the vocational assistance. Forty-six of these terminations were boys (TM), some of whom exhibited the same modes of behavior as the dropouts.

Thirty-two of the boys terminated from the program said that they "could not behave," "could not get along with superiors," and the like; 3 said that they "could not do the work"; and 11 were ill and could not attend regularly. It may be assumed that the failure of a majority of the TM boys was psychologically based, since all were physically able to perform the assigned tasks. None indicated an urgent need for more money, although all talked freely about their own personal failure or their inability to use available help. This apparent willingness to verbalize the basis for their problem is perhaps the most significant difference between the boys who dropped out (QM) and those who were terminated (TM).

THE TF GROUP

Twenty-three of the youth terminated were girls (TF). Their readiness to talk about their inability to profit from vocational help differentiates them from the girls who dropped out (QF). None dropped out for economic reasons; none was picked up by the police; but 12 had a health problem (including pregnancy); 5 "could not do the work"; 4 "disliked working"; and 2 had family problems. JEVS psychologists observed that generally these girls attempted to maintain communication with the Center. This desire to continue contact also differentiates the TF from the QF cases, and is a factor which may have significance in planning future programs.

CONCLUSIONS

For many of the 135 youth who failed, this project was the first time any vocational help had been offered. Despite its failures, the program apparently did reach and provide some help to them. All 135 interviewed by PSES counselors were asked what benefits they had received from the program. As there were no perceptible differences between the Q and T groups or the sexes, the data are consolidated. The responses were as follows:

	No.	Percent
Total	135	100
Learned more about work	42	31
Learned to work with others	23	17
Enjoyed a real work experience	19	14
"Something, but I don't know what it is"	17	13
Learned to take orders	4	3
Don't know	3	2
No benefit	27	20

Thus, it appears that at least 105, or 78 percent, of the youth whom we consider as failure cases stated that they did derive some benefit from the program. It is anticipated that some portion of this group may be reached at a later date, as they gradually become more aware of their real needs.

PSES counselors also attempted to learn whether some other service might be acceptable to these boys and girls by asking them to state what they wished most to achieve. Only 106 of the 135 could answer this question; the others said they "did not know" or "had never thought about the matter." The primary wishes of those who responded were as follows:

	No.	Percent
Total	106	100
Stay out of trouble	38	36
Get and hold a job	29	27
Acquire a skill	15	14
Become self-supporting	13	12
Get a high school diploma	7	7
Support my child	3	3
Learn to read or write	1	1

More than a third expressed an avoidance goal, i.e., to stay out of trouble, etc.; 60 percent stated conventional achievement goals of a job, a skill, self-support, or a diploma; and only 4 percent a practical objective of supporting a dependent or acquiring literacy. These expressions of aspirations also reflect deep-rooted anxieties and suggest a need for continuing intensive help, perhaps preceded by a thorough counseling effort. They also suggest that counselors must formulate new concepts and devise new techniques for penetrating resistances if they are to reach and hold these youth in vocational programs.

DYNAMICS OF REACHING AND HELPING FAILURES

Whatever the source of their difficulties, it is evident that the disadvantaged youth who are vocational failures have many common behavior problems. Vocational treatments initially must be broadly therapeutic and cultivate a sense of mutuality and confidence between the counselor and the youth. The counselor must use methods which are organized and benignly controlling. The process requires patience and time for the youth to test out both the counselor and his new experiences.

Vocational treatments *per se* for these youth are not likely to be effective unless accompanied by work with the youth's family and neighborhood, to improve home relationships and secure the support of peers. Unless family members and peers understand and accept the youth's struggle to rehabilitate himself, and reinforce his motivation during regressive lapses, lasting benefits are not likely.

The psychological problems which the counselor must face as he attempts to rehabilitate the youth who quit or are terminated from vocational programs appear to fall into the following categories: Those who need a sustained, controlled, but protective program; those who need to learn through benign relationships; those who need therapy; and those who need to learn through new experience.

Youth in the first group may be viewed as "character problems" and represent the largest number who dropped out of the program. They are the most resistant to constructive help. The profound egocentricity of their responses and their intolerance for anxiety indicate a rigid defense system against threats to their self-esteem. Since they tend to act out their hostility, the counselor must be prepared to be the target of their latent and overt aggressions. Only by maintaining a firm, unchanging but protective relationship can the counselor help these youth expose their anxieties, acquire a tolerance for dealing with their fears, and develop a balance of emotional expression which can be used to further personal and vocational growth.

The emotionally and mentally immature youth make the most radical improvement when counseling and other vocational services are intensive and continuing. Superficially, their behavior is similar to those designated as "character problems," but intrinsically they need a systematic and controlled emotional and intellectual development experience. They are willing and able to accept help if it incorporates small increments of easily assimilated new experiences. Because these youth are easily distracted by more enticing activities elsewhere and tend to drift away in an irresponsible manner, they must be followed up and periodically brought back into the program. The followup and continued responsibility for these youth may be vested best in a single counselor who represents parent, teacher, and friend during the progressive stages of cultivating readiness for training and employment.

THEY LEARN TO FACE PROBLEMS

Emotionally unstable youth require a long-term therapeutic environment and relationship. They are accustomed to using devious means to acquire satisfactions and commonly evade coming to grips with clearcut goals. Intensive group and individual counseling often enables them to acquire healthy defenses against the stresses of work, and helps them develop healthier attitudes in dealing directly with their vocational problems.

Youth in the fourth problem group, the nonperceivers, resemble the character-disordered youth in that they require a learning experience in which new activities become extensions and enlargements of their own way of life before they can achieve understanding and purpose. They learn best when activities are initially organized around materials similar to their current life patterns. New perceptions are introduced best through small increments which the youth find within their grasp, and which offer them meaning and satisfaction.

On the basis of data collected at intake, it would appear that the disadvantaged youth who quit or were terminated could not be differentiated from the youth who successfully completed the program. Generally, those who quit were more elusive than those who were terminated because the latter tended to maintain communication with the professional staff even after they left the Center. Since there are no clear criteria for detecting failure by interviews, it would appear that sustained observation and evaluation of the individual's behavior in a work situation and his response to supervision, counseling, and remedial help are the avenues through which more accurate predictions can be made. It is noted that there was staff skepticism at intake concerning successful outcomes for many youth who, in fact, completed their programs and were placed in competitive industry. This further suggests that counselors need to handle disadvantaged youth with patience, understanding, and optimism for success.

FIT PROGRAMS TO SPECIAL NEEDS

It is safe to assume that more disadvantaged youth who quit or are terminated from vocational programs want this help than are receiving it, and that many more can profit from it than currently are doing so. The problem of getting them to accept counseling and other vocational treatment could be resolved, in part at least, if the Youth Opportunity Centers would formulate programs specially designed for these youth. Such programs should relate to the various underlying problems manifested in modes of behavior characterized by hostility, passivity, personal irresponsibility, inability to invert the self, elusiveness, impulsiveness, distractibility, and the like. There is need for the YOC's to apply special techniques for prolonged and deep evaluations and for reaching these youth through peer groups, neighborhood organizations, churches, and schools, so as to provide more individualized and continuing vocational adjustment services.

PLANNING OF WORK CAREERS*

ELI GINZBERG

The foregoing chapters (Ginzberg, 1962) have shown how ideology and reality in the United States have reinforced each other to create a favorable environment for the improvement of youth. Parents assume that it will be possible for their children to live a better life than they did, and their offspring in turn grow up assuming that they will be able to improve the circumstances which characterized the lives of their parents. Beyond the immediate family, the community as a whole is committed by belief and deed to establishing and strengthening those institutions that will contribute to this end.

What is sometimes overlooked, however, is the fact that the outcome—whether children will in fact lead a life noticeably better than that of their parents—depends to a large extent on the values and goals of youth and that these values and goals will determine how effectively young people will make use of their capabilities.

Folklore holds that all Americans would like to get to the top, that every boy would like to be President. Yet the proof of this is lacking. To most of its native-born citizens, and more particularly to most of the immigrants who came to its shores, the United States offered an opportunity to get ahead simply by standing still. The very thrust of westward expansion and the resulting economic prosperity have produced a more or less steady rise in living standards since the colonial period. At the same time there have been striking gains in religious and political freedom. Binding the two together and in part the result of them has been the remarkable fluidity of social classes, which has meant that no person has had to resign himself to permanent membership in a lower class. The uniqueness of this American situation was suggested by one of our earlier monographs, *European Impressions of the American Worker*, and it is documented more extensively in *The American Worker in the Twentieth Century*.

In short, every American could, with only a moderate effort, get on the escalator of rising material benefits. If he decided that he wished to ascend more rapidly, as many in each generation did, he could simply run up the moving stairs. If he did not slip, he could make a very speedy ascent.

For every young man three decisions largely determine the success of his efforts to give shape and meaning to his life. The first is his choice of a career, including the antecedent decisions with respect to education. The second is his

* Reprinted from Eli Ginzberg, *The Optimistic Tradition and American Youth* (New York: Columbia University Press), 1962, pp. 72–92, by permission of the publisher.

choice of a program to fulfill his military commitment. The third is his choice of a marital partner. This is not to ignore the fact that a young person's margins of freedom may be limited and, in many instances, may be quite narrow. Yet they are relatively greater in American society than in any other.

A person's values, the mainspring of his actions, are much more than simply the product of his own struggle for identity and independence. They are also the outgrowth of his cumulative experience since infancy. With puberty and adolescence, a youth gains more freedom for self-expression and self-determination, but he is still forced to remain within the grooves cut earlier. In the shaping of a young person's values, the influence of parents and peers is likely to be greater than the searchings of the individual himself. And yet the scope for individual choice is substantial.

The young person's emerging values and goals provide important anchors that enable him slowly to give up his fantasies of adulthood and seek to orient his efforts in a more realistic direction. In the event that he has rather modest goals for himself, a reflection of lack of stimulation and help from his parents and from others in his immediate environment, or else of unresolved emotional conflict, the consequence may be lack of motivation. This will result in an underdevelopment of his potentialities and capacities, involving among other things a failure to utilize effectively the opportunities which exist in the larger environment.

For a person to be successful later in life, he requires while still young a strong spiritual foundation—that is, the nourishment of certain fundamental values and a setting of challenging goals. Yet if his parents cannot provide him with the proper stimulation or if he himself cannot resolve his emotional conflicts, a young person may fail to utilize his full potential. Or it may happen that the parents make themselves appear so successful to the youngster that he fears he can never match their accomplishments and so sets himself a less than fully challenging goal. Hence the expression arises, "Three generations from riches to rags."

Of the three types of decision which a young man must make—occupational, military, and marital—the first provides him with the most direct opportunity to realize his values and goals. For the work that a man does usurps such a large part of his time and energies that it inevitably shapes his life off the job too. Here deliberate choice—the objective assessment of the advantages and disadvantages of various alternatives—is possible to a much larger extent than in the other two areas. In regard to military service, the margins for individual maneuver are relatively narrow, and in the event of a national emergency may all but disappear. And in the case of marital choice, emotional and instinctual pressures may radically reduce the area of rational discretion.

Occupational Choice

In 1951, we published the results of an exploratory study, *Occupational Choices: An Approach to a General Theory*. The following draws heavily from this research.

A person's occupational choice is not a one-time decision but the cumulative result of many decisions over time. These decisions reinforce each other until the occupational path open to an individual has been narrowly delineated. The facts that one is young only once, that one goes to school only once, and that one can prepare for only one profession at a time effectively limits the alternatives open to an individual at various stages of his life. But certain alternatives exist nonetheless. It is well, therefore, to point out the framework in which these alternatives are weighed.

Even very young children will tell you what they want to be when they grow up. Usually it is some exciting, dramatic occupation, such as aviator, soldier, or nurse. Without having to worry about how practical such dreams are, young children can easily give their fantasy full reign. But even fantasy can be the first step in the long, tortuous process crystallizing one's thinking about the kind of work one would like eventually to do. A four-year-old girl, if asked whether she would like one day to be a physician, may reply that this is not possible. Only men, not women, are doctors, she may tell you. Faulty as this judgment is, it shows that the four-year-old is already making important distinctions about the world of work and the jobs appropriate to each sex.

Around the age of eleven, when young people begin to recognize for the first time that sooner or later they will have to choose the type of work they would like to do later in life, the process of occupational choice enters a new stage. First the young person chooses a field of study that interests him; then, as he nears the end of high school, he tries to match an occupation with his academic interests. This is the transition from tentative to realistic choice, from exploration to crystallization.

The very nature of the educational system constantly forces a young person to choose among various alternatives—which high school to enter, what course to pursue, whether or not to apply to college, what major to select, whether or not to enter professional or graduate school. And each decision reduces the alternatives open to him.

This is the complex process of choosing an occupation, which begins in early childhood and continues for almost twenty years. During the last ten years, the young person himself is directly involved in making choices, even if these consist of no more than following the line of least resistance.

It is a rare youngster indeed who experiences little or no difficulty in resolving the problem of occupational choice. No matter how narrow the areas of discretion may be, the number of options available to him is considerable, whether he be a diligent student or a sluggish one, whether he come from an affluent home or a low-income family. That he will reach the age of partial discretion—puberty or adolescence—so deeply committed to one career goal that he has no doubts about it is unlikely. Some may be strongly drawn to certain fields, but even they are likely to consider various alternatives. More typically, however, young people do not feel a powerful pull in any direction. Instead, they find it difficult to translate their academic interests into meaningful careers. Contrary to what many parents and counselors think, a student who does well in science will not necessarily be happy as a doctor, nor will one who does well in history necessarily be happy as a teacher.

At the same time, the failure of parents and counselors to understand the process of occupational choice often makes the decisions of youngsters more difficult. Many parents push their children to decide on a career long before they are intellectually and emotionally capable of doing so. If this pressure is great enough, the result may well be an over-anxious, confused, or prematurely committed child. But the opposite danger also exists. Some children are not pushed enough. At key stages in their life, when they should make important career decisions, they may simply ignore the problem so that, when they are finally ready to leave school, they are without definite career plans. While they will sooner or later find jobs, they may not be the ones that will satisfy them, and they may spend several years or longer looking for the type of work that will prove suitable to them. Their failure to think seriously about the future probably prevented them from getting very much out of school, and this in turn probably made a satisfactory occupational adjustment later on more difficult.

There is another danger. Young people may commit themselves to a particular career goal before they have had an adequate opportunity to test the depth of their interest or the strength of their capability. By the time they discover what their true interests or strengths are, however, it may well be too late for them to change their career plans and they may wind up dissatisfied with their work. Such a premature commitment is likeliest to occur in fields which require long years of study and preparation.

The problem of choosing a career, difficult as it may be, can become even more complicated when a young person must also decide how he will fit his military commitments into his career plans. To this second major area of decision making, we now turn.

Compulsory Military Service

Since 1940, approximately 25 million men have served in the armed forces. Throughout most of these two decades, except for one brief period in 1947–48, the great bulk of these men have entered the military service because of the draft. But the significance of this for the lives of young people has not been fully appreciated. Apparently our antimilitaristic tradition has led the American public to view the armed forces as something apart from the rest of its life, except in war or in time of national emergency. Men enlist or are drafted, they serve for two, three, or four years, and then, except for a small number who decide to make armed services a career, they return to civilian life and quickly turn their backs on their military experience.

In recent years a new factor has been added. Young men coming of draft age are no longer certain that they will have to serve. While the numbers deferred or exempted for various reasons have always been larger in the United States than among our allies, until recently about seven out of every ten young men eventually served in some capacity. But currently the ratio is dropping, and, unless the international situation should worsen perceptibly or the entire system of military manpower procurement be altered, the proportion of young men called to duty may decline to one out of two in the eligible age group and, later in the decade to only one out of three. The numbers of young men coming of draft age are very much larger than those required to fill the needs of the armed services, particularly in light of the services' strenuous efforts to build up a career force.

Military service, instead of being an obligation which all young men recognize, has become more and more of a gamble in which certain players hold marked cards. For instance those who go on with their studies, the more intelligent and the more well-to-do, are deferred until their studies have been completed. While they are technically subject to call until they are thirty-five, most of them will probably not see service because, among other reasons, the armed services prefer younger men. There are also many young men who marry early. They, too, while technically subject to call, are not generally being inducted. And finally, there are the ever-increasing proportions of each age group who are being turned down because, in the opinion of the armed services, they do not possess the intellectual ability, the physical strength, the emotional stability, or the moral integrity to make good servicemen. Able to pick from a more-than-adequate pool, the armed services have steadily raised their standards of acceptability.

While young men are subject to service under an act entitled Universal Military Training and Service, each year sees the concept of universality further violated. Admittedly, the country faces a difficult problem in working out a sound solution. The armed forces must be able to secure the number of men that Congress has authorized, either by enlistment or through Selective Service. Since enlistments are insufficient to supply the armed services with all the manpower they need, recourse to the draft is unavoidable. But the supply of eligible young men is increasing far in excess of the numbers required, with the result that more and more young men will not be called upon to serve.

Until the Berlin crisis in the fall of 1961, only an occasional congressman or student of public affairs had expressed concern about the implication of a system of military manpower procurement that deviates increasingly from the criterion of universality. The armed forces were getting the men they needed; the Selective Service system continued in business, and most individuals chose the time they would serve, whether in the army, air force, navy, or marine corps. Sometimes they even chose the type of duty they would perform. Under such circumstances, it was not surprising that the critics were few and that their criticism failed to evoke a large-scale and favorable response. Even today the public accepts the fact that the country requires sizable military forces to halt the expansion of international communism and it is apparently willing to accept the deviation from universality in favor of a practical resolution to an admittedly difficult predicament, in which the armed forces need some but not all of the men eligible to serve.

But it may well be that the public does not fully realize the implications of acquiescing to the present arrangements, which stem largely from the Department of Defense and interested congressional committees.

The last time the Universal Military Training and Service Act was extended, in 1959, Congress was unwilling to authorize, as one congressman suggested, a detailed evaluation of the complex problem of military manpower needs and requirements. Rather than open Pandora's box, the lawmakers extended the old act as quickly and unobtrusively as possible.

The fact that military manpower policy has been left to the interested few and has not caught the attention of the larger public goes far to explain why so little thought has been given to the consequences of a system that encourages young people to "play the odds." Currently, the young man who "gets caught" and who serves for two or more years on active duty is likely to consider himself a "sucker," for that is how his friends who escape military service regard him. The uncertainty that surrounds a man's obligation to serve makes it more difficult for him to plan intelligently when to serve and in what capacity. And it makes it much more difficult for those who eventually do serve to consider their assignments and responsibilities constructively—to do their best and to try to profit as much as possible from their experience. They are much more likely to consider themselves as unfortunate "victims of the system," who are "serving time." Military service, they are convinced, has little if anything to contribute to their development. As a result, their major objective is to find a good asignment, which means an easy assignment, preferably one where passes are frequent.

In point of fact, the armed services have made and are continuing to make a major contribution to the development of a great many young men on a great many different fronts—in terms of education, occupation, health, social skills, and general personal development. Indicative of the American public's attitude toward military service is the fact that this wide impact of the armed services on youth has largely gone unnoticed.

We cannot here do justice to the full range of this impact, but it may be helpful to suggest within the general theme of this book (Ginzberg, 1962) on the improvement of youth some of the principal lines of influence which the armed forces exert.

There is little question but that the occupational horizons of many young men are considerably expanded as a result of their military service. Through travel, they have an opportunity to learn about many types of work which are unknown in their home communities. They also can learn about job opportunities from their barrackmates and officers. Moreover, they are encouraged to pursue their education on off-duty hours, and this opens areas of potential employment for which they may not have been qualified previously. And most importantly, they are able to secure training in such skilled occupations as electronics, medicine, communications, and mechanics, many of which have direct counterparts in civilian life. Many who acquired the elements of a skill while on active duty are later able to develop a satisfactory civilian career on this foundation.

Those who became entitled to veteran's benefits through their service— and that covers most of the men who have served since 1940—have had new and expanded opportunities for education and training. They were frequently able to reconsider their occupational choices. With tuition and maintenance assured for two, three, or even four years, they could even look forward to entering a scientific, professional, or skilled occupation which previously would have been beyond their reach, though not necessarily beyond their ambition or capacity.

The armed services have also done much to improve the physical health and emotional stability of American youth by introducing millions of them to proper regimens of diet and personal hygiene, acquainting them with the potentialities of modern medicine and dentistry, and providing them with a heterogeneous social environment where they were challenged and encouraged to get along with individuals from diverse backgrounds.

In this connection it is well to emphasize that outstanding progress on the racial front has occurred as a result of the final desegregation of the armed services during the early 1950s. In this important sector of our national life, Negroes have a pilot model of an environment in which every form of legal discrimination has been eliminated. And equally, if not more important, millions of young white men have learned to live with Negroes in every relationship—as superiors, equals, subordinates. There has been no more forceful lesson in race relations than when white boys from the deep South learned through personal experience that Negroes were capable of command, that they were often skilled and talented, and that their response to danger, challenge, or opportunity was not greatly different from their own.

While it has been relatively easy to identify many positive contributions the armed services have made to the improvement of American youth, the fact that the country must still make use of Selective Service to fill its armed ranks is incontestable. Most young Americans look upon active military duty with distaste. Such an attitude derives first, from the national ethos that in times of peace any forced restriction of individual freedom is bad; next, from the belief that the years that a man spends in uniform are wasted and will set him back in his career; lastly, from the widespread feeling that large-scale forces are unnecessary in an age of atomic weapons.

Whatever the rationale, the simple fact remains that young men are growing up without any sense of obligation to serve in the armed forces. As they approach the end of high school, many confront the situation for the first time. But many others who are on their way to college and graduate school can push the issue far into the future. Although much foolishness has been written about the American prisoners of war in Korea who went over to the enemy, it cannot be gainsaid that in Korea, as in World War II, a disturbingly high percentage of the men on active duty had little perception of the relationship between the sacrifices they were asked to make and the predicament of their country. They had grown up without being conditioned to the necessity of military service—in fact many had been negatively conditioned by the widespread pacifist agitation prior to World War II. There is a disturbing parallel in the current situation where once again the anticipation of eventual military service is not part of the positive life planning of most young men. They know that they may have to serve but they hope not to.

The fact that in Korea a few prisoners went over to the enemy and many more collapsed to a point where they would not struggle to stay alive does not bespeak, as some military psychiatrists have argued, a collapse in the moral fiber of American youth. Instead it bespeaks serious shortcomings in the education which these men received, both in civilian life and in the military; more particularly, it bespeaks the failure of the military command structure after the men were taken prisoner. In view of the half-hearted support which the fighting men received from the home front it can even be argued that the small number who defected is testimony to the character of American youth.

Shifting the focus from past to future, it is not possible to be sanguine. Despite the appalling seriousness of the power struggle in which this country is currently engaged, most young men grow up without any understanding of military obligation, with the consequence that if and when they are called to duty, they view it as an imposition, an annoyance, or a stroke of bad luck that they were caught while so many others escaped.

To make matters worse, Congress provided an option in 1955 for a considerable number of young men, enabling them to discharge their military obligation by serving for six months on active military and then five and a half years in the active reserve. These men are usually set apart and trained separately in the army; and all too many of them are assigned to reserve units characterized by inadequate leadership, equipment, and training. As a result, they become even more disillusioned with the military. They talk loosely about the waste they see in their training and service and thereby reenforce the negative attitudes of others.

There are many inherent difficulties in operating a large-scale reserve system effectively—difficulties stemming from lack of funds, equipment, leadership, and time. Many reserve units have succeeded in surmounting these very real difficulties, but many more have not.

There are many other ramifications of compulsory military service that could be explored, but the preceding summary discussion should highlight the crucial issue: the necessity to reevaluate the system and to refashion it in such a manner that it contributes as much as possible to the security of the nation and the welfare of the individual. Nothing is more dangerous, especially for a democracy, than to permit basic military manpower policy to escape continuing and penetrating public discussion. Only if the public understands why demands are being made on it can it be motivated to respond effectively. For a democracy to permit and encourage its young men to grow up viewing military service as a burden to be avoided is an invitation to national disaster.

The call-up of reservists incident to the Berlin crisis of 1961 revealed still another order of difficulty with the system. Despite the widespread criticism of the inequities that occurred during the Korean hostilities when men who had never served were permitted to remain in their civilian pursuits while veterans who had not been actively participating in a reserve program were called back to active duty to serve a second time, and despite the effort of the 1955 Reserve Act to prevent a repetition of such inequities, the recent call-up caught a considerable number of individuals with prior service—some few with two previous stints—while many others in the active reserve without prior extended duty but in pay status were not ordered to active duty. The complaints have reached such a high pitch that some corrective action is likely.

Early Marriage

While at first it may be difficult to see any logical connection between compulsory military service and the age at which young people marry, a moment's reflection should make clear that there are many. Most obviously, an unknown but probably sizable number of young men are encouraged to marry, to escape military service by becoming fathers. Moreover, whether a young man goes into service or not will determine whether he will be around during the next two to four years, and this in turn may encourage him to reach a quicker decision about a young woman whom he has started to court. In turn, his impending removal from the scene may lead the young woman to press the matter to a successful conclusion before he gets away.

The fact that military pay represents for many young men their first steady, if modest, income encourages many of them to marry, for they also take into account that their wives will receive a special allowance.

Nor can one overlook the fear of loneliness in the hearts of many who are wrenched away from their familiar surroundings for the first time in their lives. A considerable number of young men who enter the army single marry during the course of their military service, often in a desperate effort to find some substitute for what they had to leave behind.

These are but a few of the connections between military service and early marriage. While it would be possible to identify factors that tend to delay rather than hasten marriage, on the balance it seems that military service is one of the forces in American society today making for early nuptials.

At present, about one quarter of all young women are married before the age of eighteen and more than half are married before they are twenty-one. This represents the lowest average age of marriage in the nation's history, and one of the lowest, if not the lowest, of any modern industrial society.

Historically, the very wealthy and improvident poor married early—and for largely the same reason. Money was no barrier, for the rich because they had all they needed; for the poor because they lived only for the moment without regard to the future. In recent decades, the high level of employment has made it possible for young people, even for those without advanced education or special skill, to find jobs where they could earn from the start as much as $60 a week, and before long, even more. This means that a young couple can look forward to a combined income of over $6,000 a year—more than enough to set up and run a home. Able to support themselves, many young couples see no reason even to ask their parents' consent. If their parents object to such an early marriage the young couple can take care of themselves.

Early marriages today occur among a large number of college students as well as among a small number of high school students. Among the college group there are many who require and receive continuing support from their parents. When the parents are unable or unwilling to help, or where the young people prefer not to ask them, the wife frequently drops out of school and goes to work while the young man continues his studies. Among graduate students, it is understood that a wife can underwrite a man's studies just as effectively— and perhaps even more so—than a graduate scholarship or fellowship.

There is no single or simple explanation for the trend toward early marriage. It has resulted from the confluence of a great many forces, including the puritanical view of most Americans towards sexual relations outside of matrimony, the acceleration in sexual maturation through improved dietary and living conditions, the increasingly heterosexual nature of our educational and recreational facilities which throw boys and girls together from puberty on, the uncertainties of military service which make many young people fear the consequences of prolonged separation, and the relaxed attitudes of young people about what the future holds in store for them. They are sure that they will find jobs and discharge their responsibilities, including the support of a family, the size of which will be under their control.

There is a close relationship between the changing attitudes of Americans, already sketched, towards work and the increased frequency of early marriage. One of the major reasons that men postponed marriage in earlier decades was their desire to be well-set in their careers before assuming responsibility for a wife and children. Much has changed. As argued in the last chapter (Ginzberg, 1962), the nonwork areas of life have grown in importance over the work areas. In *The Nation's Children*, Moses Abramovitz pointed out that in recent years professionally trained persons no longer have to accumulate considerable capital to get started in their careers. What they need is supplied them by the organizations, profit or nonprofit, for which they work. Nor must one overlook the fact that one of the concomitants of a growing affluence is the even larger number of young people who have some money of their own—which they have been given or which they have been able to save.

For these and other reasons, the young man no longer faces a sharp choice—wife or career. He is often in a position to have both, as shown by the large number of young physicians who marry while still in medical school and the much larger number who marry before completing their internship and residency training.

Until now, the emphasis has been on the male because young women have always been interested in marrying early, but have usually had to wait until their young men were in a position to do so. For most young women see their fulfilment in marriage and children.

This last point helps to explain not only why young people marry early but also why many of them have children shortly afterward. In fact, many marriages take place because a child is on the way. But the more typical pattern is for a young couple to start their family shortly after they are married. This is, at first glance, not easy to understand in a society where knowledge of contraception is widespread. The explanation must be sought in the social pressures which produce not only early marriage but also early family formation.

Young people are sensitive to the behavior of their peers. They hesitate to deviate. When they find many of their friends marrying early, they are strongly impelled to do likewise. When a college junior finds that her three best friends have dropped out of school during the summer because they married, this may be enough to tip the scales in favor of her accepting a proposal which, up to that point, she has been uncertain about. She does not want to return to school alone and face the task of developing a whole new set of friends. And young men also become restive when they notice that the most attractive girls are being taken out of circulation.

The same competitive pressures operate with respect to children. When their friends have a child every year and a half or every two years, most young couples will indeed feel pressure to do likewise. Moreover, they are likely to be impressed with the conventional wisdom that young parents make the best parents.

Many thoughtful people, professionals and laymen, have questioned the soundness of early marriage. One expert, concerned about the high rate of divorce among young couples, has remarked that today the first marriage is really a trial marriage. Despite these strictures there is every reason to expect the present trend to continue, and if the level of employment remains high it is likely that the average age of marriage may drop even lower.

There is one important consequence of the present pattern that has not been fully appreciated—its influence on the career choices and occupational behavior of young men of high ability. Even in those instances where the young wife is willing to see her husband through graduate school she is not likely to want to support her husband after he has completed his degree. As soon as he has his course work behind him, she is likely to press him to start their family, for this is the pattern of the day. And the young man at the beginning of his career may then make his job decisions in light of his growing family responsibilities. He will be much more interested in current income than in future prospects, in fringe benefits than in opportunities to broaden and deepen his skills. Moreover, his mobility will be limited. He will have to weigh job offers not only in terms of what they might contribute to his future but also their desirability from the viewpoint of locating his family.

The overriding fact is that at the very outset of his career the young husband and particularly the young father must pay more attention to the immediate needs of his family than to his future career. He must be concerned with exploiting what he already knows rather than with accumulating additional knowledge so that he can perform in the future on a higher level of competence.

While it is reasonable to question whether young people whose life experience has been limited to attending school have acquired the requisite maturity to make a good marital choice, or whether on balance it is desirable for a couple to marry even though they must be supported for several years by their parents, there is little likelihood that the present pattern will change. And as far as the majority of young people are concerned, the advantages and disadvantages of this new pattern may balance.

The disadvantages may be more social than individual. While early marriage may yield many satisfactions to those personally involved, a society cannot ignore the fact that it may interrupt the higher education of many able young women and may interfere with the occupational development of many able young men. These untoward results, however, stem more from young couples' having children early than from their marrying early.

Whether the link between the two——early marriage and early family formation—will continue as in the recent past, will depend on a great many factors, including the extent to which young men and women in the future question the wisdom of tying themselves down early in their married life. But as long as the family and children continue to furnish young people their major gratification, it will be only the exceptional individual who stands against the trend and concentrates during his twenties on advancing his education and getting a good start in his career.

ACHIEVEMENT ORIENTATIONS AND
CAREER PATTERNS OF RURAL YOUTH*

GLEN H. ELDER, JR.

Major technological developments in American agriculture, the industry and ingenuity of the independent American farmer, and favorable environmental conditions have resulted in one of the most remarkable production systems in the contemporary world. The enormous accumulation of agricultural surpluses, encouraged by government price supports and the failure of regulatory efforts, bears testimony to the capability of this system. These and other changes in agriculture have implications for the educational training and occupational preparation of rural youth who desire to farm: 1) although only 5% of all employed workers are farm owners and managers, this percentage is likely to decrease if it changes at all, thus reducing occupational opportunities for youth who have little chance of inheriting a farm;[1] 2) capital needed to begin farming is likely to increase, thereby strengthening farm inheritance as the essential precondition for entrance into this occupation; and 3) high level skills are apt to become more important as requisites for the successful operation of a farm.

These trends clearly indicate that scholastic achievement and a college education are apt to become a more integral part of the preparation of youth,

* Reprinted from Glen H. Elder, Jr., "Achievement Orientations and Career Patterns of Rural Youth," in *Sociology of Education*, Vol. 37 (1963), pp. 30–58, by permission of the publisher.
[1] Donald J. Bogue, *The Population of the United States*, New York: The Free Press of Glencoe, 1959, Chapter 17, "Occupational Composition and Occupational Trends."

The employment and educational implications for rural youth of the changing occupational structure in the United States as vividly illustrated by the per cent change in employment of civilian workers by major occupation groups between 1950 and 1960. For all 51 states:

Professional, technical and kindred workers	47.0%
Managers, officials and proprietors except farm	7.4
Clerical and kindred workers	33.8
Sales workers	18.7
Craftsmen, foremen, and kindred workers	11.8
Operators and kindred workers	6.4
Laborers except farm and mine	−9.6
Service workers, except private household	26.7
Private household	22.3
Farmers and farm managers	−41.9
Farm laborers and farm foremen	−40.2

Data are obtained from Stella Manor "Geographic Changes in U. S. Employment from 1950 to 1960," *Monthly Labor Review* (Jan. 1963). Table 2, p. 5.

in addition to existing informal apprenticeship procedures, for those who intend to succeed in the drastically changing enterprise of farming. Since most non-farm occupations with high status require a college education, education beyond high school provides more attractive occupational alternatives to youth who eventually find they dislike farming, who lack farming opportunities, or who decide against farming immediately after high school. In short, achievement in farming, as well as in urban occupations, promises to become increasingly contingent on advanced educational training in the near future.[2]

Educational attainment is crucial in determining the mobility chances of the large proportion of rural youth who migrate to urban areas. From an analysis of the community origins of a sample of principal wage earners in Oakland, Lipset found that men from farms were located in disproportionate numbers in manual and entrepreneurial occupations.[3] Rural farm migrants were even less likely than men with lower class urban origins to be upwardly mobile. The major explanation of this difference which Lipset advances involves education; he suggests that rural-farm men are apt to have less and perhaps poorer educational training. They were pictured as less likely to live near a college, to have highly skilled teachers, to be exposed to a wide selection of occupational opportunities, and to have high aspirational levels. A comparison of the ranked median years of education of major occupational groups clearly indicates that farm managers, owners and laborers are very close to the bottom of the hierarchy with an average of less than nine years.[4] Another analysis of the characteristics of farm-reared persons who reside in nonfarm areas indicates that the ranking of this population group is similar on other measures of status as well; they tend to be over-represented in low status categories as indexed by occupation, family income, and subjective

[2] See for instance Otis D. Duncan and Robert W. Hodge, "Education and Occupational Mobility: A regression Analysis," *American Journal of Sociology*, 68 (May 1963), pp. 629–644.

[3] Seymour M. Lipset, "Social Mobility and Urbanization," *Rural Sociology*, 20 (Sept.-Dec. 1955) pp. 220–228; see also Gunnar Boalt, "Social Mobility in Stockholm" in *Transactions of the Second World Congress of Sociology*, Volume II (London: International Sociological Association, 1954). In a cross-national analysis of data on social mobility, Miller found that the mobile independent farmer's son was most likely to move into the working class, next most likely to enter the farm worker category, and was least likely to move into the non-manual class. Whether the movement into the working classes was upward or not was impossible to determine with the available data. Social mobility was even more characteristic of the sons of farm workers, although it followed a pattern similar to that of the sons of independent farmers. S. M. Miller, "Comparative Social Mobility," *Current Sociology*, 9 (1960), No. 1, pp. 51–53. The complex problems of adaptation experienced by rural emigres in urban-industrial environments are comprehensively assessed by H. Krier in a report for the Organization for European Economic Cooperation. See *Rural Manpower and Industrial Development: Adaptation and Training*, August, 1961.

[4] Bogue, *op. cit.*, The low educational attainment of farm managers, owners and laborers appears to be continuing in the high dropout rate among youth with fathers in these occupations. Of the 350,000 young people over age 16 who left elementary or high school before graduation between January and October of 1961, a larger proportion were from rural than from urban areas. However, proportionally more of the rural than urban dropouts were able to find employment. See Jacob Schiffman, "Employment of High School Gaduates and Dropouts in 1961," *Monthly Labor Review* (May 1962), 502–509.

social class status.[5] The low mobility of the farm-reared in urban areas cannot be entirely accounted for by an education deficit, however. In a Chicago area study, Duncan and Hodge found that males with farm origins and relatively poor education achieved considerably less than non-farm males with similar education.[6] Thus, it appears that rural youth with relatively little education may be doubly disadvantaged with respect to their chances for upward mobility.

In a significant research operation, the Bureau of the Census and the Economic Research Service of the Department of Agriculture have engaged jointly in two surveys of the college plans and attendance of a large sample of American youth.[7] In the October, 1959 Current Population Survey of the Bureau, data were obtained on the college plans of high school seniors and their personal and family characteristics. These data were combined with information obtained from a follow-up questionnaire to high school principals in the fall of 1960 on the reported college enrollment of the students and on their school records. Slightly over half of the respondents indicated in 1959 that they planned to go to college (53%); however, only 42% actually did attend college in 1960. Some of those who did not follow through on their plans will undoubtedly do so in later years. As we shall see in a later part of this paper, a disproportionate number of these late entrants come from rural areas. The proportion of rural farm youth who were enrolled in college was considerably smaller than the attendance rates of rural nonfarm and urban youth. Of the male graduates, 53.9% of the urban, 37.3% of the rural non-farm, and 32.2% of the rural farm youths enrolled in college. Rates of college attendance by residence differed among girls only for those living in urban and rural non-farm areas, 41.7% and 31.2%. Thus, variations in college attendance by residence are sharper among boys; urban youth are over one and one-half times as likely to attend college as rural farm boys. An analysis of the relation between occupation of household head and college attendance produced an even sharper rural-urban difference; 62.7% of the sons and daughters of white-collar workers entered college in contrast to only 27% of the youth from "farm worker" homes.

In addition to the effects of occupation and residence on college attendance, the effects of eleven other variables were assessed in a multiple regression analysis; in order of predictive value, they are college plans, obtained usually from the mother, type of high school curriculum, I.Q., scholastic standing, family income, occupation, number of siblings, private or public high school, urban-rural residence, sex, region of residence, size of high school class, and color. All thirteen independent variables accounted for 48% of the variance in

[5] Ronald Freedman and Deborah Freedman, "Farm-Reared Elements in the Non-Farm Population," *Rural Sociology*, 21 (March 1956), pp. 50–61.
[6] Duncan and Hodge, *op. cit.*, p. 642.
[7] James D. Cowhig and Charles B. Nam, "Educational Status, College Plans and Occupational Status of Farm and Non-Farm Youths: October, 1959," Series Census-ERS (P-27), No. 30, 1961; Charles B. Nam and James D. Cowhig, "Factors Related to College Attendance of Farm and Non-Farm High School Graduates: 1960," Series Census-ERS (P-27), No. 32, 1962. See also Roy C. Buck and Bond L. Bible, *Educational Attainment Among Pennsylvania Rural Youth*, Agriculture Experiment Station, Pennsylvania State University Bulletin 686, Nov., 1961.

college attendance and the first six variables accounted for three-fourths of the explained variance. This regression analysis suggests that the residence or socioeconomic status of a youth is not the crucial factor. However, other data which were presented indicate that these two background factors are significantly related to two factors which explained a large portion of the variance in college attendance, namely college plans and placement in a college preparatory curriculum. From these results we may derive the following major causal sequence: residence and father's occupation→college plans and placement in a college preparatory curriculum→enrollment in college. We shall examine this sequence in more detail at various points in this paper.

A majority of youth do not enroll in college, and this remainder includes two groups; those who have graduated from high school and school drop-outs. In an earlier survey, Cowhig and Nam found that the occupational placement of youth in these two streams differed substantially.[8] Approximately 40% of rural-farm males in the labor force aged 16 to 24, who had dropped out of school, were farm laborers; urban youths of similar characteristics were most commonly employed as operatives. Only 26% of the rural males who graduated from high school were farm laborers and 16% were in higher status positions, such as farm operators or managers. Although large numbers of rural youth in this age group were in non-agricultural jobs, those who remained on the farm were generally less likely to be unemployed than urban youth of similar status.[9] In contrast to the low occupational placement of youth who have not gone beyond high school in their formal education, over four-fifths of the male college graduates in the labor force were employed in white-collar jobs.[10] Similar results were obtained for rural and urban women aged 16 to 20 who were not enrolled in school. The importance of a college education for high occupational placement among rural and urban youth is plainly evident in these statistics.[11]

---

[8] Cowhig and Nam, *op. cit.*

[9] James D. Cowhig, "Early Occupational Status as Related to Education and Residence," *Rural Sociology*, 27 (March 1962), pp. 18–27. The relatively low unemployment rate of rural youth with less than a high school education is due in large measure to the unique ability of farm units to absorb additional, albeit low wage, workers. McDonald describes this capacity as the "institutional ability of agriculture to absorb additional workers in hard times." In prosperous times, high wages in urban areas draw off many of these surplus workers and thereby reduce unnecessary labor costs. See Stephen L. McDonald, "Farm Out-migration as an Integrative Adjustment to Economic Growth," *Social Forces*, 34 (December 1955), pp. 119–128.

[10] Small business careers seem to represent a major avenue of advancement into the white-collar ranks for poorly educated rural youth. A recent study of the origins of small businessmen in Lexington, Kentucky disclosed that 37% came from business owner or executive families, and 35% from farm families. The former group was the best educated whereas the businessmen from farm families were the most poorly educated of all subgroups in the sample. It should be noted that the casualty rate among small businessmen is generally high and thus this type of entrepreneurial career carries many of the hazards associated with farming. Gordon F. Lewis, "A Comparison of Some Aspects of the Backgrounds and Careers of Small Businessmen and American Business Leaders," *American Journal of Sociology*, 65 (January 1960), pp. 348–355. See also C. T. Pihlblad and C. L. Gregory, "Occupational Mobility in Small Communities in Missouri," *Rural Sociology*, 22 (March 1957), pp. 40–49.

[11] As more and more American youth enter college, it is possible that the relation between occupational attainment and education will decrease. Among the college edu-

If we grant that the role of a college education and diploma is crucial in determining success in the labor market and couple this fact with the relatively low rate of college attendance among rural youth, it becomes apparent that a large portion of future workers in low status jobs in urban areas is likely to continue to be drawn from a population of rural youth with quantitatively and perhaps qualitatively inferior education. Since the demands of industry for unskilled labor are decreasing and are certain to decline further in the face of technological advancement and automation, there is little need for rural surpluses of unskilled and semiskilled workers. In his analysis of employment rates among high school graduates and drop-outs, Schiffman cogently suggests that more research interest should be shown in the farm school drop-out. "His lack of experience in non-farm work, combined with deficient education, ill prepares him for job competition in industrialized areas and makes doubly difficult any job training or retraining."[12]

Data on selective net rural-urban migration in the United States and the South between 1940 and 1950 indicated that the migration stream of young people between the ages of 15 and 30 is characterized by a relatively high proportion of youth with a high school or college education and of those with very little education.[13] From the rural population over 30 years of age, migration to urban areas draws most heavily from lower grade educational categories. The net effect of this rural-to-urban movement is that urban and rural non-farm areas are receiving a disproportionate number of newcomers at low educational levels.

What are the factors which account for the relatively low educational attainment of the rural population?[14] This is a question of considerable

---

cated the level of post-graduate training represents an important status determinant. See C. Arnold Anderson, "A Skeptical Note on the Relation of Vertical Mobility to Education," *American Journal of Sociology*, 66 (May 1961), p. 560.

[12] Schiffman, *op. cit.*, p. 509.

[13] C. Horace Hamilton, "Educational Selectivity of Net Migration from the South," *Social Forces*, 38 (October 1959), pp. 33–42. See also Gladys K. Bowles, "Migration Patterns of the Rural-Farm Population, Thirteen Economic Regions of the United States, 1940–1950," *Rural Sociology*, 22 (March 1957), pp. 1–11. Several other studies have shown that migration from farms is selective of the best educated youth. C. Horace Hamilton, "Educational Selectivity of Rural-Urban Migration: Preliminary Results of a North Carolina Study" from *Selected Studies of Migration Since World War II*, (New York: Milbank Memorial Fund, 1958): C. T. Pihlblad and C. L. Gregory, "Selective Aspects of Migration Among Missouri High School Graduates," *American Sociological Review*, 19 (June 1954), p. 314–324. This educational selectivity of migration among rural youth coupled with the greater diversity of occupations in urban areas are undoubtedly major determinants of the relatively higher occupational achievement which has been noted among youth who migrate out of rural areas and small towns. See Richard Scudder and C. Arnold Anderson, "Migration and Vertical Occupation Mobility," *American Sociological Review*, 19 (June 1954), pp. 329–334.

[14] Several recent studies have found that boys who desire to farm are generally not inclined to have college plans. In samples of Wisconsin and Michigan high school boys, Haller has found that boys who plan to farm are highly unlikely to have college plans, whereas boys with non-farm occupational ambitions are much more likely to have such goals. Haller suggests among other explanations that boys with non-farm plans have greater primary group support for college and high status occupations than do farm-oriented boys. We shall examine these results in greater detail in the following pages. A. O. Haller, "The Influence of Planning to Enter Farming on Plans to Attend

importance since the farm-reared population is a major source of the urban labor supply. In the remainder of the paper, through a review of the literature, we shall investigate several factors which seem likely to account for a large proportion of the rural-urban difference in educational achievement. The concluding section focuses upon the achievement and career development of rural and urban youth who enter and are graduated from colleges and universities.

Some Determinants of an Achievement Orientation

We suggest that three sets of variables account in large part for the relatively low educational achievement of rural youth. Compared to urban youth, we hypothesize that rural adolescents are less likely 1) to have access to *achievement opportunities*; 2) to have close, social contact with persons who espouse *achievement values and goals*; and 3) to experience child rearing practices and learning opportunities which develop the *potential for achievement* as evidenced in the desire to achieve, personal autonomy, and intellectual ability.[15] The effects of each of these sets of independent variables on the educational and occupational achievement of rural and urban youth will be examined in the above order.

ACHIEVEMENT OPPORTUNITIES

The position of rural youth within the family and in the broader social structure determines whether they will have the financial resources for a college education, and will have access to occupational and educational information presenting mobility opportunities. A farm family's position in the class structure indicates the availability of financial support for the college education of children in the family and the extent to which the "labor foregone" during the college years jeopardizes the farming operation. The size of the family determines the theoretical maximum of support for each child, while the

College," *Rural Sociology*, 22 (June 1957), pp. 137–141; "Planning to Farm: A Social Psychological Interpretation," *Social Forces*, 37 (March 1959), pp. 263–368; "Research Problems on the Occupational Achievement Levels of Farm-Reared People," *Rural Sociology*, 23 (Dec. 1958), pp. 355–362; "The Occupational Achievement Process of Farm-Reared Youth in Urban-Industrial Society," *Rural Sociology*, 25 (Sept. 1960), pp. 321–333; similar differences in educational orientations of farm-oriented and non-farm orienteed youths were obtained by Burchinal in a small sample of high school boys in Iowa. Lee G. Burchinal, "Differences in Educational and Occupational Aspirations of Farm, Small-Town, and City Boys," *Rural Sociology*, 26 (June 1961), pp. 107–121.

[15] In a recent study of the scholastic achievement and mobility aspirations of a large sample of urban and rural non-farm white youths from unbroken families in Central Ohio and North Carolina, strongly achievement-oriented youth experienced the most favorable set of achievement opportunities, were most exposed to achievement values and high mobility goals in their social environments, and experienced more frequently than other youths parental training practices in the home which tend to develop intellectual ability, interpersonal competence, and the desire to achieve. See Glen H. Elder, Jr., *Adolescent Achievement and Mobility Aspirations*, Chapel Hill: Institute for Research in Social Science, 1962.

youth's birth order rank indicates if he reaches college age first and hence qualifies first for economic support. The economic resources of families sending children to a school place some limit on the wealth of the school as evident in the availability of educational facilities and the salaries paid to teachers. Do these indexes of the structure of opportunities disadvantage adolescent girls and boys in rural areas?

The average income level of rural farm families is well below that of urban families in every geographic region of the country.[16] Although there is considerable variation in the income of families residing in rural farm areas, the rural-urban discrepancy is large and consistent throughout. For the country as a whole, urban families draw almost twice the median income of rural farm families. Thus, rural adolescents are much less likely than urban youth to have the financial resources to enter college.

Youth from low-income farms are likely to be drawn into the farm labor force often to such an extent that scholastic progress in school, and chances for a college education, are severely undermined. In three low income farming areas of Kentucky, Youmans found that high school drop-outs reported more often than in-school youth that they had stayed home during their last year in school to do unpaid work.[17] Although the causal sequence is not clear in this finding, it does seem reasonable that a heavy work load may result in gradual alienation from educational endeavors. Involvement in the farming operation may lead inadvertently to commitments and induce premature closure in vocational opportunities which further reduce the chances of completing school or of breaking away for a two or four year post-high school education. In addition, the opportunity to take over or work on a farm is likely to initiate countervailing pressures to a college education, particularly when decision pressure is great and the youth's time perspective is restricted.[18]

Besides the relatively low average income of farm families, rural youths are additionally disadvantaged by the fact that they are likely to have more siblings in the family than their urban counterparts. Since the number of children in a family is inversely related to median family income, and average family size is larger among the rural than urban population regardless of

---

[16] Bogue, *op. cit.*, Chapter 20.
[17] See E. Grant Youmans, *The Educational Attainment and Future Plans of Kentucky Rural Youths*, Lexington, Kentucky: Kentucky Agriculture Experiment Station Bulletin, January, 1959: Youmans, "Factors in Educational Attainment," *Rural Sociology*, 24 (March 1959), pp. 21–28; and Alvin L. Bertrand and Marion B. Smith, *Environmental Factors and School Attendance*, Baton Rouge, Louisiana: Louisiana Agriculture Experiment Station, Bulletin 533, May, 1960.
[18] The urgent need for meaningful work for lower class youth is convincingly presented by Miller. See S. M. Miller, "Youth and the Changing Society," in "Youth and Work" issue of the *Journal of Social Issues*. The beneficial aspects of work roles is shown by Murray Straus in "Work Roles and Financial Responsibility in the Socialization of Farm, Fringe and Town Boys," *Rural Sociology*, 27 (September 1962), pp. 257–274. Apparently very few adolescents have not at some time or other held a part-time or full-time job. In a probability sample of high school seniors in the state of Washington, Slocum discovered that 93% reported either one or both types of work experience. W. L. Slocum, *Occupational and Educational Plans of High School Seniors from Farm and Non-Farm Homes*, Washington Agricultural Experiment Stations Bulletin, 564 (1956), Pullman, Washington.

income, the average income per member of a large rural family is relatively small. In 1956, the income per person in a family of seven persons or more was less than $713, whereas in a two-person family, it was $2,618.[19] A large number of studies have found that college attendance and college aspirations are negatively related to the size of family.[20] In a national survey, David and associates found that youth from low income families who were expected to go to college were more likely to be expected to live at home, and to share in meeting the expenses of college.[21] The low income parents interviewed in this study were more apt to believe that their children could go to college if they lived close to low-tuition community colleges. A system of community colleges may be the answer to the financial predicament of farm youth rather than an increase in scholarship funds and educational subsidies.[22] In addition to the inadequacy of financial resources, the large family makes it less possible for parents to foster and direct learning experiences for each child and to provide each child with individual attention. Parents tend to be more controlling and less communicative in large families.[23]

While youth with a large number of siblings appear to be disadvantaged in academic achievement and in chances for a college education, the first-born in the family seems to enjoy the greatest probability of going to college.[24] This advantage is almost non-existent in the low-income family; all possible economic resources are marshalled in the low-income family and the first-born represents the first child to reach the potential status of wage earner.[25] In fact, the eldest child in a low-income farm family may be encumbered with

[19] Bogue, *op. cit.*, p. 667.
[20] Elder, *op. cit.*, Chapters 1 and 2; A. H. Halsey and Jean Floud, *Social Class and Educational Opportunity*, London: Heineman and Co., 1956; Nam and Cowhig, *op. cit.*; Glen Stice, William G. Mollenkopf and Warner S. Torguson, *Background Factors and College—Going Plans Among High Aptitude Public High School Seniors*, Princeton, New Jersey: Educational Testing Service, August, 1956; Martin David, Harvey Brazer, James Morgan and Wilbur Cohen, *Educational Achievement—Its Causes and Effects*, Ann Arbor, Michigan; Survey Research Center, 1961, p. 42; Paul B. Wilson and Roy C. Buck, "The Educational Ladder," *Rural Sociology* 25 (December 1960), pp. 408–409.
[21] David *et al.*, *ibid.*; Chapter 5. Before 1959, the distance from school to home seemed to be a major determinant of the French youth's life chances. Ferrez notes that many parents were reluctant to send their children great distances to school. The concurrence of distance (and low density) and low social class in rural areas severely limited the rural youth's likelihood of getting to the university. The chances for a university education for the children of professional and civil servants were about fifty times better than those of farmer or farm workers' sons. The 1959 reform in the French school system was designed to correct these inequalities. Jean Ferrez, "Regional Inequalities in Educational Opportunity," in A. H. Halsey (ed.) *Ability and Educational Opportunity*, Organization for Economic Cooperation and Development, 1961.
[22] For a description of the "democratization" of higher education through community and junior colleges, see Burton R. Clark, *The Open Door College*, New York: McGraw-Hill, 1960.
[23] Glen H. Elder, Jr. and Charles E. Bowerman, "Child Rearing in Large and Small Families," unpublished manuscript.
[24] Elder, *op. cit.*, Chapters 2 and 3; James V. Pierce, *The Educational Motivation of Superior Students Who Do and Do Not Achieve in High School*, U.S. Office of Education, November, 1959; Wilson and Buck, *op. cit.*
[25] Elder, *ibid.*

such heavy economic responsibilities that he is possibly less apt than his siblings to go to college. Results from one study indicate that neither family size nor order of birth are related to the choice of farming as an occupation.[26] Since the farm families in this study in the state of Washington were relatively well-off financially, it is possible that inequality in the distribution of resources and socializing pressures within the family may be contingent upon the economic status of the farm. When disposable income is scarce, the position of first-born may be a handicap.

Turning to the broader social environment of rural youth, we find that they may be disadvantaged in achievement opportunities due to the relatively few education-requiring jobs in rural areas. Since occupational opportunities are related to community size, urban youth are more likely to be exposed to the desirability and availability of education-requiring occupations in business and the professions.[27] Grigg and Middleton found that the occupational aspirations of high school boys were positively related to size of community; the relationship decreased some, but did not disappear, with I.Q. and occupation of father controlled.[28]

Achievement opportunities in the family and in the rural community differ substantially between boys and girls. Boys are faced with the necessity of making a living and the chances of realizing success in this venture are often seen as enhanced by a college education, although college tends to be seen as less necessary by boys who plan to farm. Girls, on the other hand, are confronted by several vocational options: they may go on to college, go to work, or marry. In the rural community, marriage and having a family is perhaps the most rewarded vocation for a girl, but whether a girl from a farm family goes on to college or obtains employment, marriage is generally a foremost aspect of her vocation.[29] To the extent that a boy's major task is to earn a living and a girl's calling is to marry and bear children, a college education from a purely vocational viewpoint is less apt to be seen by farm parents as necessary for daughters than for sons.[30] In contrast to these differences in parental educational goals are forces which differentially attract girls

[26] Murray A. Straus, "Personal Characteristics and Functional Needs in the Choice of Farming as an Occupation," *Rural Sociology*, 21 (September-December 1956), pp. 257–266.

[27] Lipset, *op. cit.*

[28] Charles M. Grigg and Russell Middleton, "Community of Orientations of Ninth Grade Students," *Social Forces*, 38 (May 1960), pp. 303–308.

[29] Even on college campuses, marriage and a family is the major vocational preference of women. On the Cornell campus, Goldsen and associates discovered that almost all of the girls planned on marrying between the ages of 20 and 25. The general pattern they observed was for "the girls to plan for a career, to work at it before marriage, to continue working after marriage until the birth of the first child, to interrupt professional life while the children are young, and perhaps to resume occupational life after the children have reached a certain age." Rose K. Goldsen, Morris Rosenberg, Robin M. Williams, Jr., Edward G. Suchman, *What College Students Think*, New York: D. Van Nostrand, Inc., 1960, p. 46.

[30] College is quite often viewed as providing an ideal mating ground by high school girls. In a national sample of adolescent girls, Douvan found that only 13% of those planning to go to college were doing so for academic reasons. The rest had non-intellectual goals such as an exclusive concern with marriage and family and the

and boys in rural communities to their home territory. The small rural community and farm are potentially more attractive in a vocational sense to boys than to girls. This sex difference in the impact of "pull" forces may override the presence or lack of educational opportunities within the farm family. For instance, in Coleman's study of the value climates and associational networks in ten high schools in the midwest, the college-going of girls and boys was found to differ between large and small high schools.[31] With father's education held constant, boys were more likely and girls less likely to plan on college in large schools than in small schools in rural communities. In addition, the boys in the small towns were less likely to plan on college than were girls of similar family background in these communities. These differences seem best explained by the requirements of sex-linked vocations. The girls in the rural communities were much more likely to want to leave town, while the boys were more likely to express the intention of staying in the community. Coleman tentatively suggests that:

> It is likely that many boys can follow their father's occupation, business, or farm. In the city or suburb, following in parental footsteps is not so easy, since father works away from home, often outside the community. Thus, the city or suburb has little to offer a boy unless he has formal training, and can get a job by virtue of training through bureaucratic channels. In contrast, the girls' "career chances," that is, their chances of making a good marriage, are more augmented by college for the small-town girl than for the city girl. For a small-town girl, college expands the range of boys from whom she can find a mate more than it does for the large-school girl, who already has a larger selection in her school and community.[32]

Considering the relatively low median income of rural farm families, it is not surprising that the median income of communities is positively related to their size. Hence the financial resources of a community for support of schools are likely to decrease as community size decreases. Even with education and occupation controlled, the direct relationship between community size and median income remains.[33] To a certain degree, there is an association between both community and school size and wealth. Of the more than 20,000 high schools in the United States, the large schools are generally located in large urban areas, while the rural countryside is sprinkled with a majority of the small schools. Rural areas are generally less able to provide schools with adequate financial support for supporting a counselling staff, providing laboratory facilities and other educational materials and for paying teachers well. In addition, a school with no more than 25 or 50 seniors

---

search for a marital partner. Elizabeth M. Douvan, "Adolescent Girls: Their Attitudes Toward Education," in Opal D. Davis (ed.) *The Education of Women*, Washington, D.C.; American Council on Education, 1959, pp. 23–24.

[31] James S. Coleman, *The Adolescent Society*, New York: The Free Press of Glencoe, 1961, pp. 270–272.

[32] *Ibid.*, p. 272.

[33] Otis Duncan and Albert Reiss, *Social Characteristics of Urban and Rural Communities, 1950*, New York: John Wiley & Co., 1956, p. 103.

cannot offer a variety of scholastic programs without increasing the cost of education per student. Since many rural schools are not geared to preparing students for college as evidenced by their resources and by the fact that over 70% of rural-farm youths are enrolled in the vocational curriculum, it is probable that rural youth who are exposed to influences and opportunities to go to college are a small minority.[34]

Preliminary analyses of data collected in Project Talent, a large-scale longitudinal study of the abilities and aptitudes of 440,000 American youth, do reveal that the achievement level of students varies according to the economic characteristics of the schools they attend.[35] The average salary paid to teachers was found to be directly related to student achievement. In a study of Detroit schools, Sexton found similar relations among income level of students attending the school, social and physical characteristics of the school, and student achievement.[36] In lower-income schools, class size was larger, substitute teachers were more common, teacher and pupil turn-over rates were higher, teachers had less experience, buildings were older, and science and conservatory facilities were either substandard or absent. These attributes may similarly characterize many secondary schools in low-income rural areas. However, neither size of school nor rural-urban residence was found to be related to student achievement in the national sample of 1,353 high schools in Project Talent.[37] These preliminary results are much too scanty to enable us to draw conclusions with any confidence, although they do suggest that a large portion of the variations between the educational achievement of rural and urban youth may be explained by income differentials. It is also possible, and we

[34] Nam and Cowhig, *op. cit.*, p. 17. Inadequacies in school personnel and in facilities are most sharply evident in the one-teacher grade school. In 1917–18, there were 196,037 one-teacher schools; by 1958–59, this number had dropped to 23,695. *One-Teacher Schools Today*, Washington, D.C., NEA Journal, June, 1960.

[35] Since we shall refer to various findings from this most significant interdisciplinary study, the objectives and scope of this project should be mentioned. Project Talent was launched in 1960 as the first national census of the abilities and aptitudes of students in secondary school ever conducted in this country. The study is longitudinal in design and was conceived as a search for the most useful methods by which to identify, develop, and utilize human talents. Data were to be collected on available talent, relations among aptitudes, interests and other factors, factors related to vocational and educational goals, creativity and productivity, and the effectiveness of different types of educational experience. A total of 1,353 senior high schools were selected by stratified sampling procedures. The sample design called for the inclusion of all 15 year-olds, whether in or out of school. Those out of school were to be analyzed separately. In March, 1960, 440,000 students in the schools selected were administered a two-day battery of tests and other instruments. In addition, all of the school principals completed a questionnaire on school characteristics. A follow-up study has been made of these students one year after they graduated from high school. Similar follow-up studies are planned at intervals of five, ten, and twenty years after graduation from high school. See John C. Flanagan, "Project Talent Preliminary Findings," paper presented at the annual meetings of the American Educational Research Association and the American Association of School Administrators, Atlantic City, New Jersey, February 1962. See also John C. Flanagan, John T. Dailey, Marion F. Shaycoft, William A. Gorham, David B. Orr and Isadore Goldberg, *Design for a Study of American Youth*, Boston: Houghton-Mifflin Co., 1962, Chapter 3.

[36] Patricia C. Sexton, *Education and Income*, New York: Viking Press, 1961.

[37] John C. Flanagan, "Project Talent: Preliminary Findings," *op. cit.*

suggest it is likely, that the college plans of rural and urban youth will be found to differ in this study even though their achievement levels are similar.

We have examined a number of factors which restrict the educational opportunities of rural youth. A youth who comes from a large low-income farm family, who is needed for work on the farm, who has the opportunity to take over the farm, who attends a low-income school, who is enrolled in a vocational curriculum, who does not live near a public college, and who is not the eldest child in the family is likely to experience very few opportunities for going on to college. Although favorable mobility opportunities undoubtedly encourage youth to broaden their horizons and develop their talents, the values, goals and socializing pressures to which youth are exposed in home and school environments are likely to have an even greater effect on the life chances of adolescents since they foster or discourage the utilization of educational opportunities.

ACHIEVEMENT VALUES AND GOAL-ORIENTATIONS

The farm family and the school with its informal peer system are major agents in the socialization of rural youth. In relations with parents, teachers counselors, and peers, they are exposed to sets of beliefs, expectations, and personal ambitions. To the extent that these social relationships are valued by adolescents, they will shape and guide their perspectives toward the future. It should be added that, valued or not valued, authority figures such as counselors are likely to have a substantial effect on adolescent goals. A recent study of the determinants of educational aspirations in a large sample of adolescents in a Massachusetts public high school is most revealing in showing the relative influence of expectations from significant others.[38] From a multiple correlation analysis, the educational goals of father, mother, older sibling or relative, friend of same age, friend a few years older and senior high counselor were found to have independent effects on level of aspiration which were significant at the .001 level. The expectation perceived from a friend of the same age was most related to level of aspiration, with senior high counselor and parents next in order of relationship. Thus, we find that in terms of influencing educational plans, significant others include the family, and the school guidance counselor, and peers. In the following pages, we shall examine the role these significant others play in shaping the goal-orientations and educational plans of rural youth.

As with college attendance, rural males are less likely than urban boys to have college plans[39] and high occupational aspirations.[40] These results were obtained in samples from the Midwest and South and controls on I.Q. and

[38] Robert E. Herriott, "Some Social Determinants of Educational Aspirations," *Harvard Educational Review*, 33 (Spring 1963), pp. 157–177.

[39] A. O. Haller and W. H. Sewell, "Farm Residence and Levels of Educational and Occupational Aspiration," *American Journal of Sociology*, 62 (January 1957), pp. 407–411; Russell Middleton and Charles Grigg, "Rural-Urban Differences in Aspiration," *Rural Sociology*, 24 (Dec. 1959), pp. 347–354; and Lee G. Burchinal, "Differences in Educational and Occupational Aspirations of Farm, Small-Town, and City Boys," *Rural Sociology*, 26 (June 1961), pp. 107–121.

[40] Grant Youmans, "Occupational Expectations of Twelfth Grade Michigan Boys," *Journal of Experimental Education*, 24 (June 1956), pp. 259–271; Middleton and Grigg, *ibid*; and Burchinal, *ibid*.

occupation of father did not seem to depress the negative relationships. Rural and urban girls seem to differ relatively little in either type of goal. The relationship between educational plans and actual enrollment in college shows even sharper rural-urban differences. A re-analysis of data obtained by Nam and Cowhig in their national sample of 1959 high school seniors is presented in Table 1. Here we have the relation between college plans of the youth reported by mother or some other adult in the family, and whether or not the adolescent actually attended college, by residence and occupation of household head. A rural-urban comparison of the percentage of youths who had college plans and actually fulfilled them reveals almost twice as many urban adolescents to be characterized by this pattern. Rural adolescents were more apt to attend college without any predisclosed plan. This finding is of considerable interest since a number of farm youth report that they are undecided on their educational and occupational plans.[41] This lack of crystallization may be due in part to a lack of guidance counseling in school, a lack of information concerning possible vocational alternatives, and a lack of parental interest and help. The factors which encouraged the uncommitted to enter college are unknown and represent a problem worthy of investigation. The relation between college plan and attendance patterns and occupation of household

[41] See Burchinal, "Difference in Educational and Occupational Aspirations of Farm, Small-Town and City Boys," *op. cit.*

TABLE 1. THE EFFECTS OF RESIDENCE AND OCCUPATIONS OF HOUSEHOLD HEAD ON COLLEGE PLANS AND ATTENDANCE DURING FALL OF 1960[a]

		College Plans—College Attendance Type				
					Non-	
			Planners	Non-	Planners	Total
Family	Number of	Planners	Non-	Planners	Non-	Per-
Background	Respondents[b]	Attenders	Attenders	Attenders	Attenders	cent
Residence:						
Urban	1,032,429	42.1	15.5	5.7	36.7	100
Rural non-farm	511,761	30.0	21.2	4.1	44.7	100
Rural farm	257,780	24.0	12.0	8.7	55.3	100
Occupation of household head:						
White-collar worker	660,694	57.9	14.3	4.9	22.9	100
Manual or service worker	859,534	23.4	18.3	5.8	52.5	100
Farm worker	170,553	19.1	15.1	8.1	57.7	100
Unemployed or not in labor force	112,021	29.0	20.1	4.6	46.3	100

[a] Data are drawn from Table 7 in *Factors Related to College Attendance of Farm and Nonfarm High School Graduates: 1960*, Charles B. Nam and James D. Cowhig, Series Census—ERS (P—27), No. 32, p. 15.
[b] Estimated number in the population as projected from the sample.

head is similar, with youth from white-collar homes three times as likely as farm youth both to plan and to attend college.

One explanation for this large rural-urban difference is in the goals rural farm parents have for their adolescent offspring. In a national sample of approximately 3,000 heads of spending units, David and associates found that farmers had lower educational goals for their sons than men in any other occupational group.[42] The level of education desired for daughters was quite similar to the level expected for boys. Spending unit heads who were born and reared in rural areas tended to have lower educational expectations than those who were born on farms and currently lived in small towns or cities. In a study of the future plans of 80 farm girls, 117 small town girls and 134 high school girls living in Des Moines, Iowa, fathers of farm girls were less involved in their daughters' occupational plans and farm parents provided less encouragement regarding a college education.[43] Perhaps as a response to this parental orientation, farm girls were less likely to plan on college and were more apt to express interest in purely vocational training such as provided in a business school. In addition, an interest in marriage may be fostered more intensively in the farm family, and thus may represent more of a vocational alternative to farm girls.[44]

Another factor which is related to the low educational goals of farm parents is that some of these parents have expectations which preclude the possibility of going to college. Boys who plan to farm appear to be encouraged in this vocational pursuit by their parents and are frequently discouraged from obtaining a college education before taking over major responsibility on the farm.[45] The lack of educational goals beyond high school is strongly associated with plans to farm among farm boys. In a small sample of Iowa farm boys of high school age, Burchinal compared boys who planned to farm, to enter non-farm employment, and boys who expressed uncertainty. Boys who planned to farm were much more likely than other youths to have fathers who were owner-operators of the farm and eight out of ten believed that they would have a farm to run after completion of high school.[46] Since fathers

---

[42] David and associates, *op. cit.*, 72–75. See also Howard W. Beers, "Rural-Urban Differences: Some Evidence from Public Opinion Polls," *Rural Sociology*, 18 (March 1953), pp. 1–11. From opinion poll data collected between 1946 and 1950, it was discovered that farmers, compared to other occupational groups, were least likely to consider a college education important for sons and were next to wage earners in the value placed on a college education for daughters. From a secondary analysis of national survey data, Hyman obtained similar results. Herbert H. Hyman, "The Value Systems of Different Classes: A Social Psychological Contribution to the Analysis of Stratification," in *Class, Status and Power* (eds.), Reinhard Bendix and Seymour M. Lipset, Glencoe, Illinois: The Free Press, 1953, pp. 426–442.

[43] Lee G. Burchinal, "What About Your Daughter's Future," *Iowa Farm Science*, 14 (June 1960), pp. 9–10.

[44] See Lee G. Burchinal, "How Successful Are School-Age Marriages," *Iowa Farm Science*, 13 (March 1959), pp. 7–10.

[45] Burchinal, *op. cit.*, and "Who's Going To Farm?," *Iowa Farm Science*, Volume 14 (April 1960), pp. 12–15.

[46] In another study Straus found that boys who planned to farm more often came from high income families and were more likely to be sons of full-time farm owners. This study is based on 148 boys who were farmers' sons in the state of Washington.

who are owner-operators have vested interests in their business and might be forced to sell the farm if their sons went on to college and lost interest in farming, it is not surprising that farm-oriented boys considered their fathers as having the most important influence on their decision. Both mothers and fathers were least likely to provide encouragement regarding college for farm-oriented boys.[47] Nonfarm-oriented boys listed counselors and teachers first, with parents next. The farm-oriented boys showed considerable evidence of premature closure on vocational development. Over half indicated that they had not talked with a teacher or counselor about occupational plans during the past year; they were much less interested in obtaining information about other occupations; and they were less likely to have even considered vocational alternatives. The decision to farm does not appear to have been coerced by parents since very few boys even mentioned that their parents wanted them to farm.[48]

In various ways, farm-oriented boys acquire values consonant with the "farming life"; in Burchinal's study, three-fourths of these boys favored farming over non-farm work; none of the boys felt that urban life was superior to farm life; and they ranked "freedom on the job" as the most valued attribute of a job. In addition, farm-oriented boys, in contrast to boys who plan to leave the farm, are more likely to espouse traditional rural values and beliefs,[49] are more apt to view change as undesirable,[50] and are more likely to have positive attitudes toward work.[51] In his Washington state sample, Straus found that farm-oriented boys were more likely to consider "work with things" as the most important work value, while non-farm boys more frequently favored "work involving relationships with people," and "working with ideas."[52] The work values least favored by farm-oriented boys in Burchinal's study were "chance of advancement" and "intellectual challenge."[53] Since farm boys are

---

See Murray Straus, "Personal Characteristics and Functional Needs in the Choice of Farming as an Occupation," *op. cit.*

[47] Similar results were obtained by Haller in his Lenawee County study.

[48] Straus, "Work Roles and Financial Responsibility in the Socialization of Farm, Fringe and Town Boys," *op. cit.* Slocum and Empey found "actual work in the field" to be the most frequently mentioned important influence in the occupational decision making of high school seniors and college undergraduates in the state of Washington. Thus, early and continuous exposure to farming is likely to be registered in premature commitments to farming among boys who feel they have the opportunity to enter this occupation. W. L. Slocum and L. T. Empy, *Occupational Planning by Young Women*, Washington Agricultural Experiment Stations Bulletin, 568 (August 1956), Pullman, Washington.

[49] Rural residence does not seem to be an important correlate of social conservatism among youth in the highly urban state of Pennsylvania. Residence accounted for less than 1% of the total variance in social conservatism scores. See Fern K. Willits and Robert C. Bealer, "The Utility of Residence for Differentiating Social Conservatism in Rural Youth," *Rural Sociology*, 28 (March 1963), pp. 70–80.

[50] Haller, "The Occupational Achievement Process of Farm-Reared Youth in Urban-Industrial Society," *op. cit.*

[51] Straus, "Personal Characteristics and Functional Needs in the Choice of Farming as an Occupation," *op. cit.*

[52] *Ibid.*

[53] Burchinal, "Who's Going to Farm?," *op. cit.* The willingness to move if an excellent job opportunity came along is often considered to be one aspect of the orientation

given tasks at an earlier age than urban boys, this early and continuous indoctrination in farming as a desirable way of life coupled with parental support for this line of work may be the crucial factors in dissuading them from continuing their education. In fact, Schwarzweller discovered that rural youth who planned on college did not hold "hard work" and "security" as important values, but did favor "service to society" and "mental work."[54] Thus, in the socialization of farm boys toward farming or away from farming, substantially different culture content is transmitted.

Since values frequently have their origin within the work setting of father and mother, one way in which urban values might enter the family other than through associations of the father is through work experiences of the mother. Several studies have shown that the mother tends to be the more active parent in encouraging and promoting college orientations; thus her current and past work life may be an important determinant of the kinds of perspectives she fosters. A mother who works at least part time in a small town or larger city is likely to be exposed to the fact that a college education is required for most high status jobs, whereas the mother who is submerged in the homemaking problems of a farm family is unlikely to be impressed with this reality. There is some evidence which indicates that farm-oriented boys are less likely to have mothers who work outside the home.[55] In another study the employment status of the mother was found to have a different effect upon the achievement and college plans of rural and urban youth.[56] Rural adolescents were more likely to go to college if their mothers worked, while the reverse was true in the urban sample. The actual explanatory significance of maternal employment with respect to the socialization of farm boys remains to be determined; the effects of other factors such as income of family and type of farm operation should be removed in order to clarify the relationship.

Although boys who plan to farm generally do not intend to go on to college, there is a sizable number who do have such plans. In fact, 39%, or

---

of upwardly mobile persons. Available data seem to indicate that urban boys differ from their rural counterparts in this respect. Haller reports that urban boys tend to evaluate physical mobility more positively, while Payne found that youth who had a history of geographic mobility were more apt to have positive attitudes toward moving. Since rural farm families are less mobile than urban families, this positive attitude is more likely to be held by urban youth. See A. O. Haller and Carole Ellis Wolff, "Personality Orientations of Farm, Village and Urban Boys," *Rural Sociology*, 37 (September 1962), pp. 275–293; Raymond Payne, "Rural and Urban Adolescents' Attitudes Toward Moving," *Rural Sociology*, 22 (March 1957), pp. 59–61, and "Development of Occupational and Migration Expectations and Choices Among Urban, Small Town and Rural Adolescent Boys," *Rural Sociology*, 21 (June 1956), pp. 117–125.

[54] Schwarzweller makes the point that values are more apt to influence curriculum choice in college than the actual likelihood of attending college. Harry K. Schwarzweller, "Value Orientations in Educational and Occupational Choices," *Rural Sociology*, 24 (September 1959), pp. 246–256.

[55] Straus, "Personal Characteristics and Functional Needs in the Choice of Farming as an Occupation," *op. cit.*

[56] Prodipto Roy, "Maternal Employment and Adolescent Roles: Rural-Urban Differentials," *Marriage and Family Living*, 23 (November 1961), pp. 340–349.

approximately 12 of the farm-oriented boys in Burchinal's study were planning on education beyond high school.[57] In what ways do these two groups of farm-oriented boys differ? It would be of interest to know the characteristics of the family life and farming operation of the farm-oriented boys who intend to acquire additional education. Does this type of boy have more highly educated parents and is his father more progressive in his farming operations? These are some questions which seem to warrant further investigation since the highly mechanized progressive farm is one which is most likely to be a financial success in the years to come. In addition, it is this type of farming operation which most requires managers with highly developed skills.

In addition to the influence of farm parents in forming the achievement-orientations of their sons, the rural school and the youths' classmates are also likely to be influential. A large number of the high schools in rural areas are vocationally-oriented and seem to stress preparation for college much less than urban secondary schools. Many high schools in working class neighborhoods in metropolitan areas seem to manifest a similar goal-orientation. For instance, in Nam and Cowhig's national survey of the college plans and attendance of 1959 high school graduates, 63% of the youths from white-collar homes were enrolled in the college preparatory curriculum, while this was true of only 32% and 27% of those from blue-collar and farm families.[58] Since occupational groups tend to be segregated in urban areas as well as in rural areas, these data tend to support the above statements. However, college rates are not even similar among youth enrolled in the college preparatory track; 81.5% of the white-collar, 63.6% of the blue-collar, and 48.1% of the farm worker youths who were in this track in 1959 were enrolled in college in 1960. In schools characterized by a heavy vocational training emphasis, it seems plausible that guidance counselors may be inclined to recommend a job rather than a college education even to youths who have the ability to benefit from college.

Vocational agriculture is a vital part of the vocational program of a majority of rural high schools. Youth who take a large number of courses in this program are socialized into farming as an occupation, are likely to be exposed to more information which concerns farming as a vocation than which describes other vocations, and are likely to be classified, inadvertently or not, as "boys who plan to farm." In addition, a student who takes a number of vocational courses may in the same process exclude himself from consideration for college by not taking academic courses such as algebra which are crucial for entrance into many colleges and universities. Some of the adult-directed youth organizations in rural schools, such as the FFA, require enrollment in vocational agriculture as a precondition for membership.[59] Since the

[57] A total of 62 boys planned to farm in Haller's study of the educational and occupational plans of 12th grade boys in Lenawee County, Michigan. Slightly more than one-third (22) had plans to go to college. See A. O. Haller, "Research Problem on the Occupational Achievement Levels of Farm-Reared People," *op. cit., p.* 361.
[58] Nam and Cowhig, *op. cit.,* p. 17.
[59] Cf. Selz C. Mayo, "An Analysis of the Organizational Role of the Teacher of Vocational Agriculture," *Rural Sociology,* 25 (September 1960), pp. 334–345.

FFA may be quite popular among boys in a high school, it is likely to be instrumental in drawing students out of college preparatory tracks and into the vocational program.[60]

It is, of course, true that a large number of boys who plan to farm do plan to go on to college even though a vocational program is, by definition, not designed to give a student adequate preparation for academic studies in college. The lower entrance requirements of community colleges seem to represent the most feasible solution to the educational needs of capable rural students who have specific job plans and lack high school credits as well as funds necessary for entrance into more expensive four-year educational institutions. Since relatively little is known about rural schools, and since it is well recognized that high schools play an important role in allocating youth to positions in the occupational structure, considerable research effort should be focused on the kind of influence the rural school has in shaping adolescent and adult careers. When a school places a youth in a vocational program, for instance, it places him in a path which is unlikely to lead to the education required in high status occupations.

Another indicator of the values and goal-orientations to which rural youth are exposed and the impact of these on the adolescents' educational plans is the class characteristics of the student body as a whole. Since working-class youth typically have lower educational and occupational goals than white-collar adolescents, a school which is largely composed of working-class youth would have a relatively unfavorable climate for youth who have some interest in acquiring a college education. This type of low aspiring climate has been shown in several studies to have a somewhat depressive effect upon the goal-orientations of youth who, according to class background, might otherwise be expected to attend college.[61] Since the median income and median education of farmers are relatively low compared to other occupational groups, it is likely that a large number of rural high schools are characterized by an unfavorable academic climate. The significance of this type of educational milieu for the educational goals of youth is clearly evident in a recent study conducted by Alan Wilson.[62] The percentage of students planning on going to college was examined in three groups of schools in Oakland, California: upper white-collar, lower white-collar, and industrial. Among youth from "professional" homes, college plans were acknowledged by 93% of the students in upper white-collar schools, 77% in lower white-collar schools, and 64% in "industrial" schools. Even among straight "A" students, the prevalence of college plans differed substantially across these three types of schools.

In addition to simply providing a norm for achievement, a school characterized by an unfavorable milieu provides students with a population of low

---

[60] Haller notes that the boys in his Lenawee County Study who were planning on farming had taken relatively more course work in agriculture. "The Occupational Achievement Process of Farm-Reared Youth in Urban-Industrial Society," *op. cit.*
[61] See Alan B. Wilson, "Residential Segregation of Social Classes and Aspirations of High School Boys," *American Sociological Review*, 24 (December 1959), pp. 836–845, and John A. Michael, "High School Climates and Plans for Entering College," *The Public Opinion Quarterly*, 25 (Winter 1961), pp. 585–595.
[62] Wilson, *ibid.*

aspirers as potential friends. Herriott, in his study of adolescents in a Massachusetts high school, found the expectations of a close friend of the same age to be more strongly related to adolescent educational plans than any other expectation.[63] The college plans of best friends were most strongly related to the college plans of boys among youth in three rural counties of Utah.[64] The social class status of best friends likewise seems to have a substantial effect on the occupational plans of adolescent boys.[65] If a farm youth's friends are college-oriented and are planning on professional jobs, it is most likely that he will hold similar views. This is especially true if there is very little opposition from other salient reference groups. Thus, if a majority of students in a school have low aspirations, the probability of selecting such a friend is relatively great.

Simply in terms of the values and expectations of family members, the school, and classmates, farm youth (especially boys) are less likely than urban boys to have contact with models, climates and pressures that direct them toward college and a high status occupation. Given the opportunity to obtain a college education, they would be less likely to use it to full advantage. A farm boy who experiences little impetus in the direction of education beyond high school might be characterized in the following manner: He comes from a large family and lives on a farm which his father owns and operates in a low-income farming area. College is not encouraged by his father since he would like his son gradually to take over the farm; his mother is relatively indifferent to a college education. The school he attends is small, understaffed, and is largely focused on a vocational training program in which he is enrolled. Although the probability of such a boy entering college is relatively small, other factors may make a difference in his life chances. The motivation and ability to achieve, as well as social-psychological competence, are dimensions of a youth's achievement potential which may over-ride all obstacles in his path. A boy with an unusually high record of grades, for instance, may be lifted over all other barriers to a college education by a four-year scholarship.

ACHIEVEMENT POTENTIAL

Development of the desire and ability to achieve takes place in large part within the family; if parents are interested in developing the talents of their children, the child is confronted by standards of excellence, is given supervised liberty to explore and acquire confidence in self-control and in mastery of problematic situations. Are farm parents less likely to develop these capacities for achievement and success in later life than urban parents? Unfortunately, there is relatively little information on child rearing in the contemporary farm family; but the evidence we do have suggests that farm families are less likely

---

[63] Herriott, *op. cit.*
[64] John R. Christiansen, James D. Cowhig, John W. Payne, *Educational and Occupational Progress of Rural Youth in Utah: A Follow-up Study*, Social Science Bulletin No. 2, Brigham Young University, August, 1962, p. 6. See also the prior report on plans, *Educational and Occupational Aspirations of High School Seniors in Three Central Utah Counties*, Social Science Bulletin No. 1, Brigham Young University, June, 1962.
[65] Richard L. Simpson, "Parental Influence, Anticipatory Socialization, and Social Mobility," *American Sociological Review*, 27 (August 1962), pp. 517–522.

than those in urban areas to rear their children in ways which seem to develop achievement potential. We do not intend to convey the impression that parents necessarily engage in a deliberate effort to develop achievement capacities in their children. Obviously, parental motives for using such tactics may be completely unrelated to developing the desire to achieve in their children. Many of the rural-urban differences, as we shall see, are inferred from studies which do not bear directly on rural-urban differences and thus should be considered as merely suggestive. Much more research needs to be done in this area.[66]

McClelland suggests that four conditions discourage the development of high achievement motivation: paternal dominance, low standards of excellence, an indulgent attitude toward the son, and very early achievement demands.[67] Several studies indicate that rural boys are more likely than urban boys to experience both paternal dominance and very early achievement and task demands. In the study of Ohio and North Carolina youth, the percentage of adolescents who reported that their parents were highly controlling was compared across rural farm, rural non-farm and urban residence groups in each state.[68] Residence differences in parental control were large and consistent only among North Carolina adolescents, a result which is entirely consistent with known differences between the two states. Ohio is more urban and industrialized than North Carolina. Among boys of high school age, urban-rural farm comparisons show dominance to be more common among rural mothers (16.7 vs. 27.0%) and fathers (30.2 vs. 39.1%). Differences are greater among boys of junior high age, e.g., rural vs. urban dominance of mothers, 19.9 vs. 41.6%. Differences between parents residing in the two states were evident only among rural farm families; in all possible comparisons, North

---

[66] Although a large number of studies have compared samples of rural and urban children on personality adjustment and orientations, we know very little about the correlates of personality development in the rural farm family. Due to variations in method, research design, and concepts, the results of the following studies have not resulted in an accumulation of knowledge on the personality development of rural and urban children. On rural-urban analyses of personality differences, see L. G. Burchinal, G. R. Hawkes, and B. Gardner, "Adjustment Characteristics of Rural and Urban Children," *American Sociological Review*, 22 (1957), pp. 81–87; A. R. Mangus, "Personality Adjustment of Rural and Urban Children," *American Sociological Review*, 8 (October 1948), pp. 566–575; Paul H. Landis, "Personality Differences of Girls from Farm, Town and City," *Rural Sociology*, 14 (March 1949), pp. 10–20; Byron E. Munson, "Personality Differentials Among Urban, Suburban, Town, and Rural Children," *Rural Sociology*, 24 (September 1959), pp. 257–264; and Starke R. Hathaway, Elio P. Monachesi, and Lawrence A. Young, "Rural-Urban Adolescent Personality," *Rural Sociology*, 24 (December 1959), pp. 331–346. For a carefully designed study, see A. O. Haller and Carole E. Wolff, "Personality Orientations of Farm, Village and Urban Boys," *Rural Sociology*, 27 (September 1962), pp. 275–293. This study, like most of the above research, is not based on well developed theoretical formulations. As a result, a popular approach has been to use a "shotgun" technique in the search for rural-urban differences.
[67] David C. McClelland, *The Achieving Society*, New York: D. Van Nostrand Company, Inc., 1961. See also Bernard C. Rosen and Roy D'Andrade, "The Psychosocial Origins of Achievement Motivation," *Sociometry*, 22 (September 1959), pp. 185–218.
[68] See Glen H. Elder, Jr., "Structural Variations in the Child Rearing Relationship," *Sociometry*, 25 (September 1962), pp. 241–262.

Carolina parents were more likely to be highly authoritarian than were Ohio parents. An analysis of parental control in families of high school seniors in the state of Washington revealed no significant residence differences.[69] Thus, these observed variations among rural farm families and the relatively small differences obtained in parental control by residence suggest that rural-urban differences as well as class differences are relatively small.

A large number of rural farm families are in the low-income, low education bracket and some evidence suggests that these families may be relatively uninvolved in preparing their adolescents for eventual independence. These data were obtained from the above described study of Ohio and North Carolina adolescents who lived in urban and rural nonfarm areas. Thus, inferences about the rural family which are based on this study must be cautiously interpreted. In an analysis of the determinants of achievement among urban adolescents, a five-item index of preparation for independence was developed for mother and for father.[70] A parent high on preparation for independence was one who allowed freedom for learning the skills of self-government, but at the same time supervised this freedom, offered explanations of rules and discipline which were not understood, made adjustments in level of parental control as the child grew older, and used reasoning as the principal mode of discipline. The degree to which parents engaged in the preparation of their adolescent offspring for independence was directly related to their education and to the level of prestige of father's occupation. In addition, it was discovered that youths who indicate that their parents are highly dominant and do not prepare them for self-government were low achievers in school, had low educational aspirations and were least likely to have self-confidence and to feel self-reliant. These findings are supported by several studies of rural-urban differences in personality. Urban boys in the Lenawee County study were found to have the highest mental test scores, and were highest on independent self-sufficiency, and in the belief in the internal determination of events (social class was controlled).[71] Using the MMPI, Hathaway and his colleagues found that rural adolescents in Minnesota were less assertive and more socially self-conscious than urban youths.[72]

Compared to urban children, those who live on farms are likely to have their lives structured around tasks and responsibilities at an earlier age. On a farm, there is always work to be done and assignments to fulfill. According to a study of high school boys in a county adjacent to Milwaukee, farm boys were much more likely to have regular jobs at the age of six or under than were fringe and town boys; 40% of the farm, 24% of the fringe and 20% of the town boys held regular jobs by this very early age.[73] Although no

[69] Paul H. Landis and Carol L. Stone, *The Relationship of Parental Authority Patterns to Teenage Adjustments*, Washington Agriculture Experiment Station, Bulletin 538 (Pullman, Washington: Institute of Agricultural Sciences, September, 1952).

[70] Elder, *Adolescent Achievement and Mobility Aspirations, op. cit.*

[71] Haller and Wolff, *op. cit.*

[72] Hathaway et al., *op. cit.*

[73] Murray A. Strauss, "Work Roles and Financial Responsibility in the Socialization of Farm, Fringe and Town Boys," *op. cit.* The three residence groups—farm, fringe,

evidence is presented on the level of difficulty of the jobs and the number of hours worked at this young age, some data are shown on these aspects of work for the current work situation of the 18 year olds. Fringe and town boys were much more commonly employed in household jobs than were farm boys and they also worked more hours per week on this type of job. Farm youths, on the other hand, were largely employed on a non-paying basis in farm work and 61% worked 20 hours or more on this type of job. The mean age at which certain chores were started and worked on regularly was 8.9 for helping with the garden, 10.3 for helping with the milking, and 12.5 for doing the milking. The farm boys were more likely to report that they enjoyed working with their parents, that their work contributed something to the family's well-being, and that they seldom needed to be reminded to do their chores. Thus, the farm boy is more likely than his urban counterpart to assume regular jobs at a young age, to work, perhaps, on more physically taxing jobs, to work longer hours per week and to receive relatively little pay for his labors. The excessive burden of work on youth from farms is a dominant theme in a study of 712 eighth graders who lived on high and low income farms in California.[74] Smitters describes one fifteen-year-old boy from a farm family with over $6,000 per year net income who wanted to drop out of school and who had the following work schedule: he worked 56 hours per week in the summer at $100 per month and 36 hours per week during the school year. In his own words:

> I get up at four thirty or sometimes five o'clock. I go to the milk house and set up the milking machines. At seven thirty I am finished and I start washing the milking machines. At fifteen minutes to eight, I am through doing the barn chores. Then I eat breakfast and get ready for school. I put my coat on, I go and get the car, and I call for my step-father to take me to school.
>
> I get home at fifteen minutes to four, undress and put my milking clothes on. Then I drive the car over to the haystack and put some hay in the trailer and drive the car out on the field where the milk cows are. I start feeding them. At fifteen minutes to five I put the trailer where it was and the car in the garage and go into the milk house. I set the milking machines and I am through by five minutes to five.
>
> Then I put the cows in the barn and I start washing them with a water hose to get the mud out of their bags. I get the milking machines and put them on the cows. At seven thirty I am all through with the chores.[75]

The farm boy generally has early access to an economic system which can use his labor and consequently is likely to devote more of his energy and time to such an enterprise. It is not known whether apprenticeship procedures

---

and town—were roughly similar in median income, although significant differences were obtained in median education and size of family. Straus made an admirable attempt to control for extraneous variables in this research unlike a majority of studies of rural and urban life.
[74] Faith W. Smitter, "Experiences, Interest and Needs of Eighth Grade Farm Children in California," unpublished Ed.D. thesis, University of California, Berkeley, 1951.
[75] *Ibid.*, p. 126.

instituted early in a child's life and becoming more demanding as each year passes frustrate or encourage achievement motivation and the broadening of a youth's intellectual horizons, although it seems plausible that some youth who are socialized in this manner acquire interests and motivations which are specific to the farming operation. As a result, scholastic programs in school and other experiences which do not bear directly on this focus may be relatively unattractive.

We have examined three sets of factors which influence the development of achievement orientations among youth: achievement opportunities, achievement values and goals, and achievement potential. Since it is known that rural compared to urban youth are less likely to graduate from high school, enter college and achieve high status jobs, we have sought explanations for these rural-urban differences by surveying studies which compare rural and urban families on these independent variables and/or which show how these factors influence the achievement and career patterns of youth. The extent to which rural-urban differences in the conditions for achievement and mobility will remain when variables such as education, income, and family size are controlled, is as yet unknown, and should be investigated. Tentatively we suggest that development of the motivation to achieve represents the essential foundation for achievement in life, the acquisition of high educational and occupational goals provides direction for achievement motivation and ability,[76] and achievement opportunities facilitate the realization of these life goals. This order of factors according to their salience is implied by Havighurst and Rodgers who consider motivation to be the key determinant of college attendance, more so than income.[77]

Rural and Urban Students in College; Their Academic Progress and Social Affiliations

Do urban and rural youth who do enroll in colleges and universities each year differ at all on entrance tests, choice of field, occupational specialization, academic progress, and social affiliations? Answers to some of these questions are provided by a recently completed longitudinal study of students who enrolled at Iowa State University in the fall of 1955.[78] Data on the students was collected from university records in 1955 and in the fall of 1959. Approximately 40% of the students were from rural areas and only one-third

---

[76] Rosen found value orientations to be related to college aspirations, while achievement motivation was more related to grades in high school. Bernard C. Rosen, "The Achievement Syndrome; A Psychocultural Dimension of Social Stratification," *American Sociological Review*, 21 (April 1956), pp. 203–211.

[77] Robert J. Havighurst and Robert R. Rodgers, "The Role of Motivation in Attendance at Post-High School Educational Institutions," in Byron S. Hollinshead, *Who Should Go to College* (New York: Columbia University Press, 1952). See also Robert H. Beezer and Howard F. Hjelm, *Factors Related to College Attendance* (Office of Education: Cooperative Research Monograph, No. 8, 1961).

[78] William S. Folkman, *Progress of Rural and Urban Students Entering Iowa State University, Fall, 1955*, Agricultural Economic Report No. 12, U.S. Department of Agriculture, July, 1962.

were females. The average size of the high school graduating class of the urban students was 196; of the rural, 33. Although most of the entering students were between 16 and 20 years of age, 15% had delayed entering college after high school. Rural males represented the largest proportion of older students. This finding is particularly interesting in view of the fact that farm boys are highly vulnerable to pressures which tend to divert them from college immediately after high school.

Students from rural areas were more likely to have deficiencies in high school credits and achieved lower scores on the college entrance examination. In contrast to lower achievement on these measures, rural youths were slightly above their urban counterparts in high school grade-point average and on their scholastic rank in their graduating class. These results imply that teachers in rural schools have normalized their grading system on a lower level of performance than have urban teachers. In other words, academic standards in rural schools may be lower than those in urban schools. Judging by the size differential between rural and urban schools and by the greater credit deficiencies of rural students, this conclusion seems quite plausible.

Rural and urban students differ substantially in choice of a general field of study and in selection of fields of specialization. The vocational training orientation of this land-grant institution should be noted because it places a limit on possible fields of study. A freshman could enroll in any one of four colleges; Agriculture, Engineering, Home Economics, and Science (this division includes the social sciences as well as the physical and biological sciences). Iowa State does not have a degree program in the humanities. Rural males were more likely to enroll in Agriculture (34.9 vs. 18.0%) and were less likely to enroll in Engineering (50.6 vs. 59.9%) and Science (14.4 vs. 21.9%). Over 85% of the urban and rural females enrolled in Home Economics: the Science Division was the only other female choice and slightly more urban than rural girls entered this college. Thus, Agriculture and Engineering represented major alternatives for rural males. The choice between these two divisions was highly contingent on their college entrance scores; if they scored high, they were apt to choose Engineering over Agriculture, while the low scorers were more apt to enroll in Agriculture. Similarly, Science was more likely to be selected by high scoring girls than by girls who achieved low entrance scores. Rural males were slightly more likely than urban men to select a specialty within their chosen college at the beginning of their college careers. Since agriculture and engineering appeal to rural youth according to their intellectual talents (particularly in mathematics), it is of interest to note that students in these curricula tend to have similar occupational values.

In the Cornell Study of Values, Rosenberg found that "engineering" and "farming" students were neither strongly for nor against self-expression and were low on people-orientation.[79] Research at the center for the Study of Higher Education at Berkeley has revealed that engineering students are, in comparison to other students, less "imaginative," less "creative," less "theoreti-

---

[79] Morris Rosenberg, *Occupations and Values*, Glencoe, Illinois: The Free Press, 1957, Chapter 11.

cal" and more "authoritarian," characteristics which Trow suggests may reflect a strongly committed, goal-oriented student who has no patience with anything that does not directly bear on his goals.[80] Unfortunately, we do not know what kinds of farm families produce youth with vocational interests and a dedication to achievement in engineering or for that matter in farming.

Once having chosen a college, relatively few Iowa State students moved to another division. Engineering students were most likely to move, with 26% changing to either Agriculture or Science. However, in a panel study of Cornell students, Rosenberg discovered that engineering students were less likely than any other occupational group to change programs.[81] Residence seems to have considerable influence on the stability of farming as an occupational choice.[82] In the Cornell study, students who selected farming in 1950 were more likely to have this same occupational choice in 1952 if they came from small rather than large communities. In addition, over the two year period, "farming" gained recruits from among students who came from small communities; it lost students, however, from among men with homes in large communities. Undoubtedly, many of these career changes are moves in the direction of reality; men from large cities are likely to recognize the hard economic facts of entering farming without inheriting a farm. New recruits to this career may have perceived new opportunities in farming and perhaps may be pressured by parents and others engaged in farming to make this choice.

Rural and urban students at Iowa State did not differ in grade-point average, in dropping out of school and in graduating ahead or behind time. Boys, however, were more likely to drop out of school for scholastic reasons than were girls. Urban students were more likely to graduate with honors.

On social affiliations on the Iowa State campus, urban men and coeds were approximately twice as likely to join a fraternity or sorority as were rural students. Since other studies have shown that membership in a fraternity or sorority is related to the income of a student's family, this finding suggests

[80] Martin Trow, "Some Implications of the Social Origins of Engineers," in *Scientific Manpower*, New York: National Science Foundation, 1958. Vocationalism is relatively strong among college youth from rural and working class homes. From questionnaires mailed to 741 male under-graduates at Washington State College, Case found that farm boys were more apt to cite occupational preparation as their main reason for going to college. Herman M. Case, "College as a Factor in Occupational Choice: A study of Different Perception by Farm and Non-Farm Youth," *Journal of Educational Sociology*, 30 (December 1956), pp. 191–199. When asked what educational goals the ideal college should emphasize, lower and working class youths are more apt to reply, "provide vocational training, develop skills and techniques directly applicable to your career," while middle and upper class students are more inclined to answer that it "provides a basic general education and appreciation of ideas." Vocational courses in college are generally more popular among students from working class homes. See Martin Trow, "The Democratization of Higher Education in America," *European Journal of Sociology*, 3 (December 1962), pp. 231–262. Clark and Trow discern two types of college student vocationalism; an interest in college for what it can provide in terms of saleable skills and knowledge, and for the credentials it offers such as a saleable diploma. See Burton R. Clark and Martin Trow, "Determinants of College Student Subcultures," unpublished manuscript, 1962, p. 17.
[81] Rosenberg, *op. cit.*, p. 64.
[82] *Ibid.*, pp. 88–89.

that the rural students entering Iowa State in the fall of 1955 came from generally lower-income families than did the urban youths. Unfortunately, no data are presented on the median income, education and occupational status of the urban and rural students' families. In addition, no information was collected on student attitudes, job perspectives, and ideology. Controls on extraneous variables and the collection of data from the students themselves are procedures which would have added greatly to the value of this study. As it is, this writer knows of no other study which has even attempted to assess the progress of rural and urban students in college.

One of the goals of a liberal arts education is to broaden a youth's outlook and horizons and to deepen his understanding of the world about him. A strong vocational orientation and an early vocational choice, which we suggest chaacterize a large number of rural youth, are likely to lead them to institutions of higher education and associations on the campus which may further narrow rather than broaden their interests. Riesman and Jencks note that this constriction generally does not occur at San Francisco State College; students with strong vocational perspectives in their freshman year tend to evaluate the objective of their college education in other terms as well by their senior year.[83] However, from the research we have examined, a "constricted self" is a likely product of socialization on a farm and as such, poses an educational problem in the secondary school as well as in college for the minority who make it that far.[84] If intolerance and provincialism are fostered in the farm family as Stouffer's research suggests,[85] it seems important for us to determine ways in which the education of rural youth can enlarge their self-conceptions, free their minds for the consideration of many alternative occupations, and prepare them for their chosen vocation.

Summary

American agriculture has changed drastically during the 1950's, and these changes have many implications for youth reared in rural areas and, in particular, on farms. In the future, a higher level of skills will be required to farm successfully and fewer farming opportunities will be available. As a consequence, education beyond high school has assumed crucial significance as a determinant of the life chances of rural youth, whether they farm or seek non-farm occupations. Against this situation, we see the problem of a relatively high dropout rate from high school and a relatively low rate of college attendance among youth from rural areas. Three sets of factors were suggested as providing possible explanations for the rural-urban differential in

[83] David Riesman and Christopher Jencks, "The Viability of the American College" in *The American College* (ed.), Nevitt Sanford, New York: John Wiley & Sons, 1962, pp. 74–192.
[84] Lerner used the concept of "constricted self" in a highly insightful social and psychological analysis of modernization in the Near East. Daniel Lerner, *The Passing of Traditional Society* (Glencoe, Illinois: The Free Press, 1958).
[85] See Samuel A. Stouffer, *Communism, Conformity and Civil Liberties* (Garden City, New York: Doubleday and Company, 1955, Chapter 5).

college attendance. By surveying the research literature which was relevant to each of these sets of variables, we found that rural youth are more apt than urban adolescents (even on the same income level) to be disadvantaged in achievement opportunities, exposure to achievement values and high goals, and achievement motivation. An examination of the progress of rural and urban youth in a large land grant institution revealed rural youth to be less adequately prepared for college and to choose fields of specialization which differed from the choices of urban students.

DISCOVERY OF COMMITMENT*

JOSEPH G. COLMEN

So far, over 175,000 Americans have applied to become members of the Peace Corps. Some 17,000 have actually made it through the rigorous selection process. Of course, not all of those who apply are available within a reasonable time; some apply and then withdraw; others fail to meet basic eligibility criteria. Some do not make it through the training program. But what impels a sizable portion of the population to take the trouble to fill out a demanding, twelve-page questionnaire?

The answer to this question has intrigued almost everyone. One of the favorite pastimes of reporters, psychologists, parents, friends, educators, and others when the Peace Corps began was to ask: "Why did you join?" Asked so frequently, the applicant, trainee, and Volunteer found the question tiresome, particularly when for so many the question was asked with some degree of implicit ridicule. And the interesting sidelight of the question was that, tiresome or not, the respondent really was hard put to give a simple, succinct answer.

Arnold Zeitlin, a television reporter and an applicant for the Peace Corps in 1961, described it as follows:

> Pittsburgh's correspondent for *Variety*, the show business weekly, asked, "Why did you do it? Was it TV?" . . . I told him volunteering was a challenge and a chance to help a worthy cause. The *Post-Gazette* assigned a reporter to interview me. With a friendly wink he said, "Don't worry. I won't ask you why you did it." He put me in the same league with any aging ingénue worried that some newsman would embarrass her with a question about her birthday.[1]

Another applicant, who was offered an attractive job while waiting to hear from the Selection Division of the Peace Corps, wrote:

> I have chosen the possibility of a challenging and rewarding opportunity to serve my country in an unusual way over the certainty of interesting employment, and such a choice always involves risk. Nevertheless, I believe that life's greatest gains can often be made only at considerable risk—at this point I feel that I can afford that risk.

Marquis Childs is reported to have said:

* Reprinted by Joseph G. Colmen, "A Discovery of Commitment," in *The Annals*, Vol. 365 (1966), pp. 12–20, by permission of the author and the publisher.
[1] Arnold Zeitlin, *To the Peace Corps, With Love* (Garden City, N. Y.: Doubleday, 1965), p. 18. Zeitlin was among the first group of Volunteers to serve in Ghana.

Those who see themselves in the role of noble messiahs had better stay home. They will only be frustrated, while they alienate those they are seeking to help.

And way back in 1961, Albertson *et al.* wrote:

Motivation is one of the most important factors to be considered in the selection of Volunteers. Although it is recognized that the motivation of young adults in applying might appropriately be of several kinds, it is felt that a humanitarian desire to serve others and a pioneering spirit must be present.[2]

Before proceeding to a more systematic look at "what makes Johnny join," it may be helpful to know something about the nature of the population that has become Volunteers. To be eligible at all for Peace Corps service, one must be over eighteen years of age, be a citizen of the United States, and be single, or, if married, have no dependents under eighteen. As of September 1965, with 12,207 Volunteers and trainees counted, they were distributed as shown in Tables 1, 2, 3, 4, and 5.

The "typical" Volunteer, one can see from these tables, is between 21 and 25 years of age, single, and a college graduate, most often with a liberal arts degree. Among the states most often represented (over 200 Volunteers) are California, Connecticut, Illinois, Iowa, Massachusetts, Michigan, Minnesota, New Jersey, New York, Ohio, Pennsylvania, Texas, Washington, and

TABLE 1.   PEACE CORPS VOLUNTEERS AND TRAINEES, 1965: SEX

Sex	Number	Per Cent
Male	7,204	59
Female	5,003	41
	12,207	100

TABLE 2.   PEACE CORPS VOLUNTEERS AND TRAINEES, 1965: AGE

Age	Number	Per Cent
Under 20	228	1.9
21–25	10,021	82.1
26–30	1,349	11.0
31–40	320	2.6
41–50	92	.8
51–60	97	.8
61–70	87	.7
71–80	13	.1
	12,207	100.0

[2] Maurice L. Albertson, Andrew E. Rice, and Pauline E. Birkey, *New Frontiers for American Youth* (Washington, D.C.: Public Affairs Press, 1961), p. 66.

Wisconsin. Figures on racial or religious composition of the Peace Corps are not available since records by these variables are not kept. It may be of interest to note that Volunteers from Southern states are serving effectively in Africa as well as in other regions of the world, though the racial character of these Volunteers is not known.

Why People Join the Peace Corps

Motivation for joining the Peace Corps was of such serious interest to the nation, and had such important implications for the quality of the Peace Corps, that a systematic study was undertaken in 1962 to provide this kind of information.[3]

What we were interested in was the relationship of specific motivational statements to over-all quality of the applicant, as measured by a rating given by an assessor of an applicant's total file. The study was based on 2,612

TABLE 3.   PEACE CORPS VOLUNTEERS AND
TRAINEES, 1965: MARITAL STATUS

Status	Number	Per Cent
Single	10,471	85.8
ªMarried	1,736	14.2
	12,207	100.0

ª Either entered training as married couple, married while in training, or married while overseas.

TABLE 4.   PEACE CORPS VOLUNTEERS AND
TRAINEES, 1965: EDUCATION

Education	Number	Per Cent
High school	247	2.0
Other than college	119	1.0
1 or 2 years college	726	5.9
3 or more years; no degree	760	6.2
A.A. degree	193	1.6
A.B. degree	6,561	53.8
B.S. degree	2,775	22.8
M.A. or M.S. degree	730	5.9
Ph.D, LL.B., etc.	96	.8
	12,207	100.0

[3] Suzanne N. Gordon and Nancy K. Sizer, *Why People Join the Peace Corps* (Washington, D.C.: Institute for International Services, 1963; Contract PC-W-136). Out of print.

TABLE 5.   PEACE CORPS VOLUNTEERS AND TRAINEES,
1965: OVERSEAS EXPERIENCE

Nature	Number	Per Cent
Resided three months or more abroad	1,674	14
No overseas residence	10,533	86
	12,207	100

applicants' replies (22.5 per cent of total) to a question on the application
form: "What do you hope to accomplish by joining the Peace Corps?"
Gordon and Sizer summarize the findings as follows:

> Some write long essays, complete with quotations from Lederer, Bur-
> dick, Shakespeare or President Kennedy. Others scribble half a sentence.
> But most fill the entire question space with their ideas about the Peace
> Corps—what they want to contribute to it, advantages they believe it
> offers, and a variety of statements about their attitudes, values, opinions,
> and experiences.
>
> Almost all of them write about what they want to *do* for the Peace
> Corps. And what most of them want to do is to "help people." Those
> with well-developed skills want to apply their talents overseas. Teachers
> (and many others as well) want to teach. Others are willing to "work
> hard" at whatever task the Peace Corps gives them.
>
> Many applicants express a belief in the Peace Corps itself and
> simply want to help further its goals. To them, serving as a Volunteer
> is a way to work for peace, serve the United States, help to improve
> international relations, or participate in the progress of developing nations.
> As a TV newscaster put it, "I've reported helplessly the hot spots in
> South America. Now I'd like to be able to do something about it."
>
> Much of the Peace Corps' attraction lies in the fact that it does
> offer people an opportunity to "do something." It is a chance to help peo-
> ple of other countries attain the "better life" which so many Americans
> take for granted; it is a chance to apply the skills and knowledge which
> are the fruits of an affluent and highly mechanized society while gaining
> the experience of living and working abroad at the same time. These are
> some of the main reasons why people say they want to join the Peace
> Corps.
>
> There are many other reasons. More than half of the applicants men-
> tion potential advantages to themselves—experience, knowledge, a chance
> to develop as individuals and to further their careers or vocations. Many
> note the personal satisfaction which would result from helping others or
> from feeling that they were identified with a worthwhile cause. The ad-
> vantage mentioned most often, however, is the opportunity the Peace
> Corps provides for learning about other cultures, getting to know and
> work with people of other nations, and becoming familiar with different
> customs, philosophies, and ways of life.
>
> Expressions of patriotic feelings are likely to show a broad concern
> for strengthening the United States in its relations with other countries
> rather than a desire to "Americanize" others. Religious motives are more
> likely to emphasize humanitarian service than a desire to proselytize.

These findings, and the eagerness of many applicants to gain understanding of people in other countries, indicate that most prospective Volunteers do not want to cast others in the image of their own political or religious beliefs.

More than half of the applicants wrote about themselves and their previous experiences, or made statements concerning their personal beliefs and philosophies. General moral and ethical considerations provided the rationale for many applicants; duty to one's fellow man or one's country lay behind others. These substantiating statements covered many academic, political, and personal topics, including the applicant who was bored with his present job, the student of Latin American affairs who wanted to do his Ph.D. dissertation while helping to further the economic development of the area, and the grandmother who wanted to keep her grandchildren from fighting another war.

The narrative statements were classified by content-analysis techniques. More detailed statistical results appear in Table 6. Most notable of the findings is that 93 per cent of the applicants reported a desire to give as basic to applying, while only 65 per cent reported a desire to gain. The overlap between the two, that is, a "giving" and a "getting" statement combined, was 60 per cent. Only 6 per cent reported a "getting" statement without a "giving" one, but 33 per cent reported a "giving" statement without a "gaining" one. Only 2 per cent reported neither.

More specific motivational-statement content categories reported were as shown in Table 7.

Here we note the small proportion of applicants concerned with travel or adventure or fighting communism, while helping humanity, improving international relations, and gaining an intercultural experience represent the largest specific bases for applying. Mostly, it will be noted, applicants do not

TABLE 6.   CLASSIFICATION OF PEACE CORPS
APPLICANTS' STATEMENTS

Giving Statements (93%)	Per Cent
Ideal-oriented	35
International-oriented	36
People-oriented	57
Task-oriented	48

Getting Statements (65%)	Per Cent
Personal gain	32
Social gain	35
Practical gain	32

Substantiating Statements (65%)	Per Cent
Personal	31
Idealistic	41

respond in terms of their own psychological needs, but rather in terms of behavior or end results possible through joining.

Some of the specific statements for which these content categories were fashioned are:

> I wish to make the Peace Corps part of my conscientious effort on behalf of the 'Peace Race.'

> To make the 'Good Life' possible for the whole world community.

> In the past 48 years we have been in two World Wars and the Korean War. Isn't it about time we changed our technique? What has the money we've lent brought us? . . . If I could at least reach one person with knowledge and understanding.

> I would be helping a new nation to develop in the way it has chosen —would be helping to make its people *aware*, not to compare values. I would be doing a job that the African government, not the U.S., first decided was needed.

TABLE 7. CONTENT ANALYSIS OF PEACE CORPS APPLICANTS' STATEMENTS

Content Category	Per Cent of Sample
To work for peace or against war	23
To spread or promote freedom and democracy; to fight tyranny	7
To serve or strengthen U.S.; become a better U.S. (or world) citizen	24
Belief in the Peace Corps as an organization, or instrument of change	24
To build a better world, encourage international brotherhood	8
To help other countries	7
To improve international relations, represent the U.S., promote international understanding	31
To fight communism	6
To correct past "mistakes" in U.S. foreign policy, change U.S. image abroad	7
To help people, humanity	35
To work with people, help them help themselves	11
Person-to-person contact	9
To give of oneself, serve, work hard	19
To teach (general)	17
To apply specific skills or knowledge	16
To help a specific geographic area	13
General personal satisfaction	14
Develop or improve as an individual	13
Identification with something bigger than self	9
Get to know or understand people in general	
Gain intercultural experience	27
Learn or gain general or specific experience	19
Travel or adventure	7
Further career or vocation	12
Previous relevant experience	14
Sense of duty or guilt	9
General moral or ethical considerations	11

I have great faith that person to person contact and association will influence future political cooperation and tolerance as much as foreign military installations. I believe our strongest weapon in this current 'cold war' is the 'putting into practice' of our American ideals and beliefs abroad, while at the same time being cognizant of each individual's right to follow his own cultural way.

To become more aware of myself as a person.

Service with this group would also give me a chance to test some of my beliefs—that I am understanding, can live with less, not a cultural stereotype, and can face unique and challenging situations. I like to see little faces light up with the thrill of discovery, be they black, white, yellow, or red.

Applicants Who Decline Invitations

Motivation for serving in the Peace Corps can be tested in another way. After an applicant's qualifications are assessed favorably, he is invited to enter training for a specific project in a specific country. At this point, acceptance or rejection of the invitation may be viewed as a further test of motivation. A study was therefore conducted of a sample of 149 persons who declined and another sample of 151 who had accepted invitations to training.[4] The study involved personal, depth interviews at the respondents' places of residence and covered a variety of topics relating to influences on the decision to accept or decline.

A major finding revealed that parental influence was among the most imposing factors that predisposed an applicant toward or away from the invitation. Eighty per cent of the applicants discussed the invitation with their parents, and half said that their parents' feelings had considerable weight in

TABLE 8. CONCEPTS OF RESPONDENTS TO PEACE CORPS INVITATIONS

Concern	Per Cent Concerned	Per Cent Believing Important
Adapting to strange customs	6	80
Chance of accomplishment	9	78
Learning a language	30	66
Medical help	21	34
Isolation	20	21
Separation from family and friends	23	15
Weather	34	9

[4] Stanley E. Seashore and David C. Bowers, *Research Providing for an Investigation of the Attitudes, Motivations and Life Circumstances Associated with the Decision by Peace Corps Applicants to Reject Offered Peace Corps Assignments* (Ann Arbor: Survey Research Center, University of Michigan, 1964; Contract PC-W-219). Out of print.

their decision. Decliners more often had jobs or were more career-oriented than accepters; or they had more concern about the specific nature of the work they would be doing; or they had problems connected with disposal of property, debts, or the like.

When asked what their concerns with an assignment might be, the results were as shown in Table 8.

It is interesting to note that the psychological question of adjustment is the most important concern to invitees, though expressed by fewest of them.

The Peace Corps and the College Senior

The latest study of motivation was conducted in 1964 among college seniors, the Peace Corps' most important source of applicants.[5] The study addressed itself *in toto* to the perceptions, value systems, and interests of college seniors. The sample interviewed included 388 male and female students at twenty colleges dispersed geographically throughout the United States. It included 5 per cent who actually submitted an application; 2 per cent who plan to apply; 8 per cent still debating, but positively motivated; 17 per cent still debating, but negatively motivated; 33 per cent who decided against applying; and 35 per cent who never really considered it.

Students were shown eighteen statements which indicated various possible advantages and asked to indicate for each advantage their evaluation of its importance.

The eighteen statements which the students were shown centered on three different concepts—the National Interest, Self-Orientation, and Social Orientation. Each concept was expressed in several different ways, with each

TABLE 9. COLLEGE SENIORS' OPINIONS OF ADVANTAGES OF PEACE CORPS SERVICE

Statement	Concept	Mean Importance	Per Cent Indicating Statement Is Most Important
Increase knowledge of others	Social	2.75	16
Broaden scope of personal horizon	Self	2.68	11
Give a better picture of Americans	National	2.62	7
Improve the lot of the less fortunate	Social	2.61	20
Promote international co-operation	Social	2.54	8
Work for peace	Social	2.54	11
Improve U.S. image abroad	National	2.54	6
			79

[5] *The Peace Corps and the College Senior* (New York: Young & Rubicam, 1965; Contract PC-W-338).

expression having its own set of connotative implications. Each of the eighteen statements was rated on a three-point scale of "very important" (weighted 3), "somewhat important" (weighted 2), and "little or no importance" (weighted 1). For each statement and for each concept, average scores were derived.

Advantages that expressed the concepts of Social Orientation were, on the whole, considered more important than advantages expressing the concepts of National Interest and of Self-Orientation. The average importance ratings of statements within each of these three concepts were:

Social Orientation	2.48
National Interest	2.24
Self-Orientation	1.83

The specific statements thought to represent the most important advantages to Peace Corps service were as shown in Table 9.

Students were also asked to select the one statement they believed expressed the most important advantage of Peace Corps service. As is indicated in the last column of the table above, the seven advantages that were most highly rated accounted for 79 per cent of the student choices. The one advantage most frequently considered as the most important was improving the lot of the less fortunate, which was selected by 20 per cent of all students. The second most frequently mentioned advantage was increasing knowledge of others, cited by 16 per cent of the students.

The statements that students rated lowest in importance, and the ones which were most often cited as "least important" were:

Break off old ties	(Self)	1.12	(59%)
Take a breathing spell after college	(Self)	1.45	(13%)

Sixteen statements describing possible barriers to Peace Corps service were rated by students according to their own personal feelings. The scale used was the same for the "advantages" question—"very important" (weighted 3), "somewhat important" (weighted 2), and of "little or no importance" (weighted 1). Also, students were asked to select the one statement that was most important to him (or her), and the one least important statement.

The statements to which students were exposed centered on four different concepts—Personal Inadequacies, Prior Commitments, Peace Corps Negatives, and Doubt That the Peace Corps Needs Me. The average importance of each of these statement groupings as expressed by all students was as follows:

Prior Commitments	1.86
Personal Inadequacies	1.48
Doubt That Peace Corps Needs Me	1.40
Peace Corps Negatives	1.34

On the whole, barriers to Peace Corps service are rated as less important to the student than are the advantages to Peace Corps service. This difference may stem from a general reluctance to impute importance to a barrier to joining an organization that is admired, or at least felt to be admired or respected by others. This conclusion is partly substantiated by the observation that the type of statements that were rated lowest were those expressing negatives about the Peace Corps as an organization. The barriers rated as the more important ones to students were those of personal prior commitments.

In terms of the specific statements that were rated, the two that were seen as most important in preventing Peace Corps application were:

Desire to pursue career	2.29
Desire to get married	1.92

(Both of these statements are included in the Prior Commitments category.) Fifty per cent of all students felt that one or the other of these statements was the most important barrier to Peace Corps service.

Other statements that had importance to students in possibly preventing application to the Peace Corps were:

Desire to be financially independent	1.88
Lack of language skills	1.75
Desire to get ahead	1.70

Psychological Aspects of Volunteering

Colmen[6] has postulated six factors which may be behind the desire of thousands of young people to apply to the Peace Corps:

1. Self-testing. The variety of unknowns in Peace Corps service offer opportunities to test oneself emotionally, physically, intellectually, and vocationally.
2. Independence or emancipation from parental or parent-substitute influence.
3. Search for one's own values or dissatisfaction with the values represented in our society today.
4. Co-operative activity toward worth-while service goals.
5. A desire to be needed and recognized for what one is and what one can contribute.
6. Chance for a "political" experience, a challenge to develop in a microcosmic village the skills of group problem-identification and co-operative solution: in short, the skills of democratic involvement.

In 1960, before the Peace Corps was started, Maurice Albertson at Colorado State University investigated motivation for Peace Corps-type service. He found that

a desire to broaden personal background and experience ranked first, with concern for people in developing countries a close second; value to career and adventure ranked last.

[6] Joseph G. Colmen, "Volunteerism: a Constructive Outlet for Youthful Energy," *Journal of Marriage and the Family*, Vol. 27, No. 2 (May 1965), pp. 171–175.

The picture has changed largely in respect to the predominantly heavy weight being given to the service nature of Peace Corps, the "giving" dimension. It certainly has not been the pay or the glamour which has attracted the applicant. In fact, Peace Corps recruiting literature itself discourages those motivated along these lines.

Some believed that, in 1961, a high element of risk-taking, a pioneering spirit, was behind the applicant's interest. Later, someone invented a new term, the "bland" Volunteer, someone who was colorless, an organization man, reflecting the joiner who saw the Peace Corps as something nice to do, who was moderately productive, but not as creative, who saw the Peace Corps as a "good bet." The data do not support this view. Today's Volunteers are, perhaps, more varied but nonetheless capable; they are greater in numbers but just as well motivated.

It may be that we will never have a perfect fix on why people do something as complex as join the Peace Corps. Some reasons probably dip into the unconscious; others are only reluctantly discussed or admitted; still others are too multidimensional to sort out. We can say that those moved by flight from problems or by grossly self-seeking or grossly masochistic needs will not succeed in the Peace Corps environment abroad. Beyond that, there is room in the Peace Corps for many kinds of people, with many different combinations of motives; there is as yet no direct correlation between possession of any one set of motivations and success.

When Lyndon B. Johnson, as Vice President, was addressing Peace Corps Volunteers at Inter-American University in Puerto Rico in July 1962, he said:

> I flatly refuse to ask you, "Why did you join the Peace Corps?" I understand you expect that question now for the thousandth time. Let me suggest the next time someone asks you that question, simply turn it around—like Thoreau turned Emerson's question around.
>
> Emerson had paid a visit to his friend in the Concord jail. "My dear Thoreau," Emerson said, "Why are you here?"
>
> To which Thoreau replied, "My dear Emerson, why are you not here?"

CHAPTER 6

Political Action
and Youth

The political roles of youth were energized in the decade of the 1960s which has beeen labeled by social commentators as the "decade of protest." In spite of the fact that the vast majority of American college students are politically quiescent, reasonably content with the vocational-professional training they are undergoing, and looking forward to accepting the traditional adult responsibilities in our society, an important minority—variously described as protestors, activists, militants, the new student left, and radicals—has already made a tremendous impact on institutions of higher education and on the larger society. To a lesser degree there has been politicization of high school and junior high students relative to their individual rights and to an even lesser degree the non-school youthful populations such as young men in the military service.

Had we presented this anthology ten years ago, we might have passed over a section on the political involvement of youth with an exhortation to the effect that youth should concern themselves more with conscious political socialization, public affairs, the amelioration of social problems, and political action. The youth of the fifties were seen as passive, conformist, uninvolved, uninterested in social questions, and security and retirement-planning oriented. They were the mildly maligned Silent Generation.

Then, as the sixties began some black and white students joined the Civil Rights Movement and earned the sympathy of American liberals for their idealistic, democratic goals, their use of militant nonviolence, their willingness to suffer the punishments prescribed by law for civil disobedience. Howard Zinn has described with feeling the committed new abolitionists who participated in the early years of this social movement.[1] The flow of the student movement traveled from South to North, from slum to campus. As targets changed, so did tactics. In a recent issue of *Change* magazine, Kenneth Keniston wrote that there has been

[1] Howard Zinn, SNCC, *The New Abolitionists*, Boston: Beacon Press, 1965, pp. 1–15.

a change toward militancy, anger, and dogmatism in the white student movement.[2] In place of the willingness to accept punishments levied by the courts for violations of laws, there are non-negotiable demands for amnesty. Are more nihilistic than idealistic students recruited into "the movement" as it becomes more politically revolutionary? That is a question which social clinicians are considering.

Why has the university come to be the major vehicle of organized dissent? Why was there a revolt at Berkeley in 1964, at Columbia in 1968, at many other universities and colleges all over this country in the years since 1964, and in many other countries as well? While there is a place for the protest-prone personality hypothesis, it is not sufficient to account for the development of activism by groups within the institutional environment. Hence we turn to the more sociologically framed explanations. Some of the factors contributing to activism within the university which have been suggested are: the increased and increasing size of the student population which increases their national visibility; the high expectations students have of the quality of campus life based on the improved academic quality of their secondary school experiences; the propinquity of inquiring, intelligent, equalitarian students leading to protest-prone subcultural behavior; the presence of teaching assistants and graduate students whose marginal positions place them in temporary social suspension; the hugeness of the multiversities harboring administrators, faculty, and students in various relationships characterized by conflicts of interests; the concentration of the mass media on campus happenings encouraging acting-out behavior, etc., with other interpretations to which lengthy essays have beeen devoted.

Essential to an understanding of youthful activism is the nationally unpopular war in Vietnam, which brought thousands of young people (as well as people of all ages) to the Moratorium March in Washington in November of 1969. For many youth, the Civil Rights Movement and the Vietnam War are perceived as interrelated phenomena in which powerless people are trampled by an unjust Establishment. Draftable students, black citizens, and Southeast Asian peasants are seen as sharing the common fate of victims. On perhaps no other issue in our history have universities played such an important role as in making the Vietnam War involvement a subject of national debate. Are the major educational roles played by the university significantly endangered when it becomes the locus of political struggle and when many of its resources are mobilized to political ends?

Psychological studies of the styles of dissent have distinguished between alienated and activist types and among subtypes of each. The

---

[2] Kenneth Keniston, "Notes on Young Radicals," *Change Magazine* Vol. 1 (November-December 1969), pp. 25–33.

values of the alienated, apolitical hippie subculture preclude the belief that America is worth saving, while the activist dissenters usually manifest more hope for society and a more sustained willingness to act for change—within or without the existing social structure. Studies of activist students tend to conclude that protestors are academically and intellectually superior to non-activist students. Keniston and others go beyond this to present evidence toward the moral superiority of activists, i.e., more activists have reached the stage of moral reasoning in which right and wrong are not as indicated in the law necessarily but are identified with the future good of the community, the sacredness of all life, the Golden Rule literally applied.[3] These post-conventionally moral individuals are in the same camp, however, with egocentrically moral persons, hence the idealistic-nihilistic ambivalence.

Sociological studies have illuminated some surprising factors characteristic of the social backgrounds of politically active students. This is, in Richard Flacks' terms, "a revolt of the advantaged," for the white activists he studied were primarily of upper-middle-class origins from professional homes wherein intellectual and liberal values were espoused. Subsequent studies have supported the contention that white activist students are definitely not an underprivileged group but are among the most advantaged groups of students.

So, why do these relatively affluent students protest the political status quo? It is not, we believe, permissiveness in upbringing in the pejorative sense of parental permissiveness as productive of greedy, infantile, maladaptive responses in their offspring. Rather it may be permissiveness in the more positive sense of parental intervention within the context of socialization in a family which has a highly principled family culture wherein the methods of disciplining the child are more psychological than physical. However, existing research leaves unanswered the question of why these students protest. The established sociodemographic characteristics of activists have known social-psychological concomitants. But such answers take the form of hypotheses which must be tested in future studies.

Now, lest we forget that the intense left-leaning activism identified with the names of some campuses is not pervasive and that most students are as conforming as ever—or appear to be—we must consider another minority group of students whose political leanings are decidedly to the right of center. These are the students who are tagged "the obedient rebels" by Lawrence Schiff. Students for a Democratic Society (SDS) finds its opposite in Young Americans for Freedom (YAF). In fact, in recent years these groups have openly opposed each other on various issues such as the role of ROTC in university life. While we have main-

[3] *Ibid.*, pp. 27–28.

tained that most students are inclined toward conformity and hence toward political conservatism, they have not rushed to join specific conservative political groups. Schiff's paper probes the common elements of the conversion to conservatism pattern. It will be interesting for the reader to make gross comparisons of the family milieu of activists as described by Flacks with the family dynamics of conservative converts as presented by Schiff. What factors in the family contexts predispose toward the ideological choices of the "activist rebellion" or "obedient rebellion?"

An articulate young student, nineteen years old at the time of the publication of his book, writes a highly personalized account of the Columbia protests of 1968. Since analyses of events often seem detached and even unrelated to what happened in more concrete terms, James Kuen's testimony concerning the student occupation of President Kirk's office provides us with the subjective reality of involvement. This final selection is decidedly "human" as Kuen shares, with running asides, what he does, and his rationale for doing it.

THE LIBERATED GENERATION[*][1]

RICHARD FLACKS

As all of us are by now aware, there has emerged, during the past five years, an increasingly self-conscious student movement in the United States. This movement began primarily as a response to the efforts by southern Negro students to break the barriers of legal segregation in public accommodations— scores of northern white students engaged in sympathy demonstrations and related activities as early as 1960. But as we all know, the scope of the student concern expanded rapidly to include such issues as nuclear testing and the arms race, attacks on civil liberties, the problems of the poor in urban slum ghettoes, democracy and educational quality in universities, the war in Vietnam, conscription.

This movement represents a social phenomenon of considerable significance. In the first place, it is having an important direct and indirect impact on the larger society. But secondly it is significant because it is a phenomenon which was unexpected—unexpected, in particular, by those social scientists who are professionally responsible for locating and understanding such phenomena. Because it is an unanticipated event, the attempt to understand and explain the sources of the student movement may lead to fresh interpretations of some important trends in our society.

Radicalism and the Young Intelligentsia

In one sense, the existence of a radical student movement should not be unexpected. After all, the young intelligentsia seem almost always to be in

* Reprinted from Richard Flacks, "The Liberated Generation: An Exploration of the Roots of Student Protest," in *Journal of Social Issues*, Vol. 23 (1967), pp. 52–75, by permission of the publisher.
1 The research reported here stemmed from a coalescence of interests of the author and of Professor Bernice Neugarten of the Committee on Human Development of the University of Chicago. The author's interests were primarily in the student movement and the families and social backgrounds of student activists. Professor Neugarten's interests have been primarily in the relations between age-groups in American society. The plan to gather parallel data from students and their parents accordingly provided a welcome opportunity for collaboration. The research has been supported in part by grant #MH 08062, National Institute of Mental Health; in part by grants from the Carnegie Fund for the Advancement of Teaching and the Survey Research Center of The University of Michigan. I wish to thank Professor Neugarten, Charles Derber and Patricia Schedler for their help in preparing this manuscript; its flaws are entirely my own responsibility.

revolt. Yet if we examine the case a bit more closely I think we will find that movements of active disaffection among intellectuals and students tend to be concentrated at particular moments in history. Not every generation produces an organized oppositional movement.

In particular, students and young intellectuals seem to have become active agents of opposition and change under two sets of interrelated conditions:

When they have been marginal in the labor market because their numbers exceed the opportunities for employment commensurate with their abilities and training. This has most typically been the case in colonial or underdeveloped societies; it also seems to account, in part, for the radicalization of European Jewish intellectuals and American college-educated women at the turn of the century (Coser, 1965; Shils, 1960; Veblen, 1963).

When they found that the values with which they were closely connected by virtue of their upbringing no longer were appropriate to the developing social reality. This has been the case most typically at the point where traditional authority has broken down due to the impact of Westernization, industrialization, modernization. Under these conditions, the intellectuals, and particularly the youth, felt called upon to assert new values, new modes of legitimation, new styles of life. Although the case of breakdown of traditional authority is most typically the point at which youth movements have emerged, there seems, historically, to have been a second point in time—in Western Europe and the United States— when intellectuals were radicalized. This was, roughly, at the turn of the century, when values such as gentility, laissez faire, naive optimism, naive rationalism and naive nationalism seemed increasingly inappropriate due to the impact of large scale industrial organization, intensifying class conflict, economic crisis and the emergence of total war. Variants of radicalism waxed and waned in their influence among American intellectuals and students during the first four decades of the twentieth century (Aaron, 1965; Eisenstadt, 1956; Lasch, 1965).

If these conditions have historically been those which produced revolts among the young intelligentsia, then I think it is easy to understand why a relatively superficial observer would find the new wave of radicalism on the campus fairly mysterious.

In the first place, the current student generation can look forward, not to occupational insecurity or marginality, but to an unexampled opening up of opportunity for occupational advance in situations in which their skills will be maximally demanded and the prestige of their roles unprecedentedly high.

In the second place, there is no evident erosion of the legitimacy of established authority; we do not seem, at least on the surface, to be in a period of rapid disintegration of traditional values—at least no more so than a decade ago when sociologists were observing the *exhaustion* of opportunity for radical social movements in America (Bell, 1962; Lipset, 1960).

In fact, during the Fifties sociologists and social psychologists emphasized the decline in political commitment, particularly among the young, and the rise of a bland, security-oriented conformism throughout the population, but most particularly among college students. The variety of studies conducted then reported students as overwhelmingly unconcerned with value questions, highly complacent, status-oriented, privatized, uncommitted (Jacob, 1957; Goldsen, *et al,* (1960). Most of us interpreted this situation as one to be expected given the opportunities newly opened to educated youth, and given the emergence of liberal pluralism and affluence as the characteristic features of postwar America. Several observers predicted an intensification of the pattern of middle class conformism, declining individualism, and growing "other-directedness" based on the changing styles of childrearing prevalent in the middle class. The democratic and "permissive" family would produce young men who knew how to cooperate in bureaucratic settings, but who lacked a strongly rooted ego-ideal and inner control (Miller and Swanson, 1958; Bronfenbrenner, 1961; Erikson, 1963). Although some observers reported that some students were searching for "meaning" and "self-expression," and others reported the existence of "subcultures" of alienation and bohemianism on some campuses (Keniston, 1965a; Trow, 1962; Newcomb and Flacks, 1963), not a single observer of the campus scene as late as 1959 anticipated the emergence of the organized disaffection, protest and activism which was to take shape early in the Sixties.

In short, the very occurrence of a student movement in the present American context is surprising because it seems to contradict our prior understanding of the determinants of disaffection among the young intelligentsia.

A Revolt of the Advantaged

The student movement is, I think, surprising for another set of reasons. These have to do with its social composition and the kinds of ideological themes which characterize it.

The current group of student activists is predominantly upper middle class, and frequently these students are of elite origins. This fact is evident as soon as one begins to learn the personal histories of activist leaders. Consider the following scene at a convention of Students for a Democratic Society a few years ago. Toward the end of several days of deliberation, someone decided that a quick way of raising funds for the organization would be to appeal to the several hundred students assembled at the convention to dig down deep into their pockets on the spot. To this end, one of the leadership, skilled at mimicry, stood on a chair, and in the style of a Southern Baptist preacher, appealed to the students to come forward, confess their sins and be saved by contributing to SDS. The students did come forward, and in each case the sin confessed was the social class or occupation of their fathers. "My father is the editor of a Hearst newspaper, I give $25!" "My father is Assistant Director of the ———Bureau, I give $40." "My father is dean of a law school, here's $50!"

These impressions of the social composition of the student movement are supported and refined by more systematic sources of data. For example, when a random sample of students who participated in the anti-Selective Service sit-in at the University of Chicago Administration Building was compared with a sample composed of non-protesters and students hostile to the protest, the protesters disproportionately reported their social class to be "upper middle," their family incomes to be disproportionately high, their parents' education to be disproportionately advanced. In addition, the protesters' fathers' occupations were primarily upper professional (doctors, college faculty, lawyers) rather than business, white collar, or working class. These findings parallel those of other investigators (Braungart, 1966). Thus, the student movement represents the disaffection not of an underprivileged stratum of the student population but of *the most advantaged* sector of the students.

One hypothesis to explain disaffection among socially advantaged youth would suggest that, although such students come from advantaged backgrounds, their academic performance leads them to anticipate downward mobility or failure. Stinchcombe, for example, found high rates of quasi-delinquent rebelliousness among middle class high school youth with poor academic records (Stinchcombe, 1964). This hypothesis is not tenable with respect to college student protest, however. Our own data with respect to the anti-draft protest at Chicago indicate that the grade point average of the protesters averaged around B to B+ (with 75% of them reporting a B— or better average). This was slightly higher than the grade point average of our sample of nonprotesters. Other data from our own research indicate that student activists tend to be at the top of their high school class; in general, data from our own and other studies support the view that many activists are academically superior, and that very few activists are recruited from among low academic achievers. Thus, in terms of *both* the status of their families of origins *and* their own scholastic performance, student protest movements are predominantly composed of students who have been born to high social advantage and who are in a position to experience the career and status opportunities of the society without significant limitations.

Themes of the Protest

The positive correlation between disaffection and status among college students suggested by these observations is, I think, made even more paradoxical when one examines closely the main value themes which characterize the student movement. I want to describe these in an impressionistic way here; a more systematic depiction awaits further analysis of our data.

Romanticism. There is a strong stress among many Movement participants on a quest for self-expression, often articulated in terms of leading a "free" life—i.e., one not bound by conventional restraints on feeling, experience, communication, expression. This is often coupled with aesthetic interests and a strong rejection of scientific and other highly rational pursuits. Students often express the classic romantic aspiration of "knowing" or "experiencing" "everything."

Anti-authoritarianism. A strong antipathy toward arbitrary rule, centralized decision-making, "manipulation." The anti-authoritarian sentiment is fundamental to the widespread campus protests during the past few years; in most cases, the protests were precipitated by an administrative act which was interpreted as arbitrary, and received impetus when college administrators continued to act unilaterally, coercively or secretively. Anti-authoritarianism is manifested further by the styles and internal processes within activist organizations; for example, both SDS and SNCC have attempted to decentralize their operations quite radically and members are strongly critical of leadership within the organization when it is too assertive.

Egalitarianism, Populism. A belief that all men are capable of political participation, that political power should be widely dispersed, that the locus of value in society lies with the people and not elites. This is a stress on something more than equality of opportunity or equal legal treatment; the students stress instead the notion of "participatory democracy"—direct participation in the making of decisions by those affected by them. Two common slogans— "One man, one vote"; "Let the people decide."

Anti-dogmatism. A strong reaction against doctrinaire ideological interpretations of events. Many of the students are quite restless when presented with formulated models of the social order, and specific programs for social change. This underlies much of their antagonism to the varieties of "old left" politics, and is one meaning of the oftquoted (if not seriously used) phrase: "You can't trust anyone over thirty."

Moral Purity. A strong antipathy to self-interested behavior, particularly when overlaid by claims of disinterestedness. A major criticism of the society is that it is "hypocritical." Another meaning of the criticism of the older generation has to do with the perception that (a) the older generation "sold out" the values it espouses: (b) to assume conventional adult roles usually leads to increasing self-interestedness, hence selling-out, or "phoniness." A particularly important criticism students make of the university is that it fails to live up to its professed ideals; there is an expectation that the institution ought to be *moral*—that is, not compromise its official values for the sake of institutional survival or aggrandizement.

Community. A strong emphasis on a desire for "human" relationships, for a full expression of emotions, for the breaking down of interpersonal barriers and the refusal to accept conventional norms concerning interpersonal contact (e.g., norms respecting sex, status, race, age, etc.). A central positive theme in the campus revolts has been the expression of the desire for a campus "community," for the breaking down of aspects of impersonality on the campus, for more direct contact between students and faculty. There is a frequent counterposing of bureaucratic norms to communal norms; a testing of the former against the latter. Many of the students involved in slum projects have experimented with attempts to achieve a "kibbutz"-like community amongst themselves, entailing communal living and a strong stress on achieving intimacy and resolving tensions within the group.

Anti-institutionalism. A strong distrust of involvement with conventional institutional roles. This is most importantly expressed in the almost universal desire among the highly involved to avoid institutionalized careers. Our data suggest that few student activists look toward careers in the professions, the sciences, industry or politics. Many of the most committed expect to continue to work full-time in the "movement" or, alternatively, to become free-lance writers, artists, intellectuals. A high proportion are oriented toward academic careers—at least so far the academic career seems still to have a reputation among many student activists for permitting "freedom."

Several of these themes, it should be noted, are not unique to student activists. In particular, the value we have described as "romanticism"—a quest for self-expression—has been found by observers, for example Kenneth Keniston (1956b), to be a central feature of the ideology of "alienated" or "bohemian" students. Perhaps more important, the disaffection of student activists with conventional careers, their low valuation of careers as important in their personal aspirations, their quest for careers outside the institutionalized sphere —these attitudes toward careers seem to be characteristic of other groups of students as well. It is certainly typical of youth involved in "bohemian" and aesthetic subcultures; it also characterizes students who volunteer for participation in such programs as the Peace Corps, Vista and other full-time commitments oriented toward service. In fact, it is our view that the dissatisfaction of socially advantaged youth with conventional career opportunities is a significant social trend, the most important single indicator of restlessness among sectors of the youth population. One expression of this restlessness is the student movement, but it is not the only one. One reason why it seems important to investigate the student movement in detail, despite the fact that it represents a small minority of the student population, is that it is a symptom of social and psychological strains experienced by a larger segment of the youth—strains not well understood or anticipated heretofore by social science.

If some of the themes listed above are not unique to student activists, several of them may characterize only a portion of the activist group itself. In particular, some of the more explicitly political values are likely to be articulated mainly by activists who are involved in radical organizations, particularly Students for a Democratic Society, and the Student Non-violent Coordinating Committee. This would be true particularly for such notions as "participatory democracy" and deep commitments to populist-like orientations. These orientations have been formulated within SDS and SNCC as these organizations have sought to develop a coherent strategy and a framework for establishing priorities. It is an empirical question whether students not directly involved in such organizations articulate similar attitudes. The impressions we have from a preliminary examination of our data suggest that they frequently do not. It is more likely that the student movement is very heterogeneous politically at this point. Most participants share a set of broad orientations, but differ greatly in the degree to which they are oriented toward ideology in general or to particular political positions. The degree of politicization of student activists is probably very much a function of the kinds of peer group and organizational relationships they have had; the underlying disaffection and tendency toward activism, however, is perhaps best understood as being based on more enduring, pre-established values, attitudes and needs.

Social-Psychological Roots of Student Protest: Some Hypotheses

How, then, can we account for the emergence of an obviously dynamic and attractive radical movement among American students in this period? Why should this movement be particularly appealing to youth from upper-status, highly educated families? Why should such youth be particularly concerned with problems of authority, of vocation, of equality, of moral consistency? Why should students in the most advantaged sector of the youth population be disaffected with their own privilege?

It should be stressed that the privileged status of the student protesters and the themes they express in their protest are not *in themselves* unique or surprising. Student movements in developing nations—e.g., Russia, Japan and Latin America—typically recruit people of elite background; moreover, many of the themes of the "new left" are reminiscent of similar expressions in other student movements (Lipset, 1966). What is unexpected is that these should emerge in the American context at this time.

Earlier theoretical formulations about the social and psychological sources of strain for youth, for example the work of Parsons (1965), Eisenstadt (1956), and Erikson (1959), are important for understanding the emergence of self-conscious oppositional youth cultures and movements. At first glance, these theorists, who tend to see American youth as relatively well-integrated into the larger society, would seem to be unhelpful in providing a framework for explaining the emergence of a radical student movement at the present moment. Nevertheless, in developing our own hypotheses we have drawn freely on their work. What I want to do here is to sketch the notions which have guided our research; a more systematic and detailed exposition will be developed in future publications.

What we have done is to accept the main lines of the argument made by Parsons and Eisenstadt about the social functions of youth cultures and movements. The kernel of their argument is that self-conscious subcultures and movements among adolescents tend to develop when there is a sharp disjunction between the values and expectations embodied in the traditional families in a society and the values and expectations prevailing in the occupational sphere. The greater the disjunction, the more self-conscious and oppositional will be the youth culture (as for example in the situation of rapid transition from a traditional-ascriptive to a bureaucratic-achievement social system).

In modern industrial society, such a disjunction exists as a matter of course, since families are, by definition, particularistic, ascriptive, diffuse, and the occupational sphere is universalistic, impersonal, achievement-oriented, functionally specific. But Parsons, and many others, have suggested that over time the American middle class family has developed a structure and style which tends to articulate with the occupational sphere; thus, whatever youth culture does emerge in American society is likely to be fairly well-integrated with conventional values, not particularly self-conscious, not rebellious (Parsons, 1965).

The emergence of the student movement, and other expressions of estrangement among youth, leads us to ask whether, in fact, there may be families in the middle class which embody values and expectations which do *not* articulate with those prevailing in the occupational sphere, to look for previously unremarked incompatibilities between trends in the larger social system and trends in family life and early socialization.

The argument we have developed may be sketched as follows:

First, on the macro-structural level we assume that two related trends are of importance: one, the increasing rationalization of student life in high schools and universities, symbolized by the "multiversity," which entails a high degree of impersonality, competitiveness and an increasingly explicit and direct relationship between the university and corporate and governmental bureaucracies; two, the increasing unavailability of coherent careers independent of bureaucratic organizations.

Second, these trends converge, in time, with a particular trend in the development of the family; namely, the emergence of a pattern of familial relations, located most typically in upper middle class, professional homes, having the following elements:

a. a strong emphasis on democratic, egalitarian interpersonal relations
b. a high degree of permissiveness with respect to self-regulation
c. an emphasis on values *other than achievement*; in particular, a stress on the intrinsic worth of living up to intellectual, aesthetic, political, or religious ideals.

Third, young people raised in this kind of family setting, contrary to the expectations of some observers, find it difficult to accommodate to institutional expectations requiring submissiveness to adult authority, respect for established status distinctions, a high degree of competition, and firm regulation of sexual and expressive impulses. They are likely to be particularly sensitized to acts of arbitrary authority, to unexamined expressions of allegiance to conventional values, to instances of institutional practices which conflict with professed ideals. Further, the values embodied in their families are likely to be reinforced by other socializing experiences—for example, summer vacations at progressive children's camps, attendance at experimental private schools, growing up in a community with a high proportion of friends from similar backgrounds. Paralleling these experiences of positive reinforcement, there are likely to be experiences which reinforce a sense of estrangement from peers or conventional society. For instance, many of these young people experience a strong sense of being "different" or "isolated" in school; this sense of distance is often based on the relative uniqueness of their interests and values, their inability to accept conventional norms about appropriate sex-role behavior, and the like. An additional source of strain is generated when these young people perceive a fundamental discrepancy between the values espoused by their parents and the style of life actually practiced by them. This discrepancy is experienced as a feeling of "guilt" over "being middle class" and a perception of "hypocrisy" on the part of parents who express liberal or intellectual values while appearing to their children as acquisitive or self-interested.

Fourth, the incentives operative in the occupational sphere are of limited efficacy for these young people—achievement of status or material advantage is relatively ineffective for an individual who already has high status and affluence by virtue of his family origins. This means, on the one hand, that these students are less oriented toward occupational achievement; on the other hand, the operative sanctions within the school and the larger society are less effective in enforcing conformity.

It seems plausible that this is the first generation in which a substantial number of youth have both the impulse to free themselves from conventional status concerns *and can afford to do so.* In this sense they are a "liberated" generation; affluence has freed them, at least for a period of time, from some of the anxieties and preoccupations which have been the defining features of American middle class social character.

Fifth, the emergence of the student movement is to be understood in large part as a consequence of opportunities for prolonged interaction available in the university environment. The kinds of personality structures produced by the socializing experiences outlined above need not necessarily have generated a collective response. In fact, Kenneth Keniston's recently published work on alienated students at Harvard suggests that students with similar characteristics to those described here were identifiable on college campuses in the Fifties. But Keniston makes clear that his highly alienated subjects were rarely involved in extensive peer-relationships, and that few opportunities for collective expressions of alienation were then available. The result was that each of his subjects attempted to work out a value-system and a mode of operation on his own (Keniston, 1965b).

What seems to have happened was that during the Fifties, there began to emerge an "alienated" student culture, as students with alienated predispositions became visible to each other and began to interact. There was some tendency for these students to identify with the "Beat" style and related forms of bohemianism. Since this involved a high degree of disaffiliation, "cool" non-commitment and social withdrawal, observers tended to interpret this subculture as but a variant of the prevailing privatism of the Fifties. However, a series of precipitating events, most particularly the southern student sit-ins, the revolutionary successes of students in Cuba, Korea and Turkey, and the suppression of student demonstrations against the House Un-American Activities Committee in San Francisco, suggested to groups of students that direct action was a plausible means for expressing their grievances. These first stirrings out of apathy were soon enmeshed in a variety of organizations and publicized in several student-organized underground journals—thus enabling the movement to grow and become increasingly institutionalized. The story of the emergence and growth of the movement cannot be developed here; my main point now is that many of its characteristics cannot be understood solely as consequences of the structural and personality variables outlined earlier—in addition, a full understanding of the dynamics of the movement requires a "collective behavior" perspective.

Sixth, organized expressions of youth disaffection are likely to be an increasingly visible and established feature of our society. In important ways, the "new radicalism" is *not* new, but rather a more widespread version of certain subcultural phenomena with a considerable history. During the late 19th and early 20th century a considerable number of young people began to move out of their provincial environments as a consequence of university education; many of these people gathered in such locales as Greenwich Village and created the first visible bohemian subculture in the United States. The Village bohemians and associated young intellectuals shared a common concern with radical politics and, influenced by Freud, Dewey, etc., with the reform of the process of socialization in America—i.e., a restructuring of family and educational institutions (Lash, 1965; Coser, 1965). Although many of the reforms advocated by this group were only partially realized in a formal sense, it seems to be the case that the values and style of life which they advocated have become strongly rooted in American life. This has occurred in at least two ways: first, the subcultures created by the early intellectuals took root, have grown and been emulated in various parts of the country. Second, many of the *ideas* of the early twentieth century intellectuals, particularly their critique of the bourgeois family and Victorian sensibility, spread rapidly; it now seems that an important defining characteristic of the college-educated mother is her willingness to adopt child-centered techniques of rearing, and of the college educated couple that they create a family which is democratic and egalitarian in style. In this way, the values that an earlier generation espoused in an abstract way have become embodied as *personality traits* in the new generation. The rootedness of the bohemian and quasi-bohemian subcultures, and the spread of their ideas with the rapid increase in the number of college graduates, suggests that there will be a steadily increasing number of families raising their children with considerable ambivalence about dominant values, incentives and expectations in the society. In this sense, the students who engage in protest or who participate in "alienated" styles of life are often not "converts" to a "deviant" adaptation, but people who have been socialized into a developing cultural tradition. Rising levels of affluence and education are drying up the traditional sources of alienation and radical politics; what we are now becoming aware of, however, is that this same situation is creating new sources of alienation and idealism, and new constituencies for radicalism.

The Youth and Social Change Project

These hypotheses have been the basis for two studies we have undertaken. Study One, begun in the Summer of 1965, involved extensive interviews with samples of student activists and non-activists and their parents. Study Two, conducted in the Spring of 1966, involved interviews with samples of participants, nonparticipants and opponents of the tumultuous "anti-ranking" sit-in at the University of Chicago.

STUDY ONE—THE SOCIALIZATION OF STUDENT ACTIVISTS

For Study One, fifty students were selected from mailing lists of various peace, civil rights, and student movement organizations in the Chicago area. An additional fifty students, matched for sex, neighborhood of parents' residence, and type of college attended, were drawn from student directories of Chicago-area colleges. In each case, an attempt was made to interview both parents of the student respondent, as well as the student himself. We were able to interview both parents of 82 of the students; there were two cases in which no parents were available for the interview, in the remaining 16 cases, one parent was interviewed. The interviews with both students and parents averaged about three hours in length, were closely parallel in content, and covered such matters as: political attitudes and participation; attitudes toward the student movement and "youth"; "values," broadly defined; family life, child-rearing, family conflict and other aspects of socialization. Rating scales and "projective" questions were used to assess family members' perceptions of parent-child relationships.

It was clear to us that our sampling procedures were prone to a certain degree of error in the classification of students as "activists" and "nonactivists." Some students who appeared on mailing lists of activist organizations had no substantial involvement in the student movement, while some of our "control" students had a considerable history of such involvement. Thus the data to be reported here are based on an index of Activism constructed from interview responses to questions about participation in seven kinds of activity: attendance at rallies, picketing, canvassing, working on a project to help the disadvantaged, being jailed for civil disobedience, working full-time for a social action organization, serving as an officer in such organizations.

STUDY TWO—THE "ANTI-RANKING" SIT-IN

In May, 1966, about five hundred students sat-in at the Administration Building on the campus of the University of Chicago, barring the building to official use for two and a half days. The focal issue of the protest, emulated on a number of other campuses in the succeeding days, was the demand by the students that the University not cooperate with the Selective Service System in supplying class standings for the purpose of assigning student deferments. The students who sat-in formed an organization called "Students Against the Rank" (SAR). During the sit-in, another group of students, calling themselves "Students for a Free Choice" (SFC) circulated a petition opposing the sit-in and supporting the University Administration's view that each student had a right to submit (or withhold) his class standings—the University could not withhold the "rank" of students who requested it. This petition was signed by several hundred students.

Beginning about 10 days after the end of the sit-in, we undertook to interview three samples of students: a random sample of 65 supporters of SAR (the protesters); a random sample of 35 signers of the SFC petition (the anti-protesters); approximately 60 students who constituted the total population of two randomly selected floors in the student dormitories. Of about 160 students thus selected, 117 were finally either interviewed or returned mailed questionnaires. The interview schedule was based largely on items used in the original study; it also included some additional items relevant to the sit-in and the "ranking" controversy.

SOME PRELIMINARY FINDINGS

At this writing, our data analysis is at an early stage. In general, however, it is clear that the framework of hypotheses with which we began is substantially supported, and in interesting ways, refined, by the data. Our principal findings thus far include the following:[2]

[2] A more detailed report of the procedures and findings of these studies is available in Flacks (1966).

Activists Tend To Come from Upper Status Families. As indicated earlier, our study of the Chicago sit-in suggests that such actions attract students predominantly from upper-status backgrounds. When compared with students who did not sit-in, and with students who signed the anti-sit-in petition, the sit-in participants reported higher family incomes, higher levels of education for both fathers and mothers, and overwhelmingly perceived themselves to be "upper-middle class." One illustrative finding: in our dormitory sample, of 24 students reporting family incomes of above $15,000, half participated in the sit-in. Of 23 students reporting family incomes below $15,000, only two sat-in.

Certain kinds of occupations are particularly characteristic of the parents of sit-in participants. In particular, their fathers tend to be professionals (college faculty, lawyers, doctors) rather than businessmen, white collar employees or blue-collar workers. Moreover, somewhat unexpectedly, activists' mothers are likely to be employed, and are more likely to have "career" types of employment, than are the mothers of nonactivists.

Also of significance, although not particularly surprising, is the fact that activists are more likely to be Jewish than are nonactivists. (For example, 45% of our SAR sample reported that they were Jewish; only about one-fourth of the non-participants were Jewish). Furthermore, a very high proportion of both Jewish and non-Jewish activists report no religious preference for themselves and their parents. Associated with the Jewish enthnicity of a large proportion of our activist samples is the fact the great majority of activists' grandparents were foreign born. Yet, despite this, data from Study One show that the grandparents of activists tended to be relatively highly educated as compared to the grandparents of non-activists. Most of the grandparents of non-activists had not completed high school; nearly half of the grandparents of activists had at least a high school education and fully one-fourth of their maternal grandmothers had attended college. These data suggest that relatively high status characterized the families of activists over several generations; this conclusion is supported by data showing that, unlike non-activist grandfathers, the grandfathers of activists tended to have white collar, professional and entrepreneurial occupations rather than blue collar jobs.

In sum, our data suggest that, at least at major Northern colleges, students involved in protest activity are characteristically from families which are urban, highly educated, Jewish or irreligious, professional and affluent. It is perhaps particularly interesting that many of their mothers are uniquely well-educated and involved in careers, and that high status and education has characterized these families over at least two generations.

Activists Are More "Radical" Than Their Parents; But Activists' Parents Are Decidedly More Liberal Than Others of Their Status. The demographic data reported above suggests that activists come from high status families, but the occupational, religious and educational characteristics of these families are unique in several important ways. The distinctiveness of these families is especially clear when we examine data from Study One on the political attitudes of students and their parents. In this study, it should be remembered, activist and nonactivist families were roughly equivalent in status, income and education because of our sampling procedures. Our data quite clearly demonstrate that the fathers of activists are disproportionately liberal. For example, whereas forty per cent of the nonactivists' fathers said that they were Republicans, only thirteen per cent of the activists' fathers were Republicans. Only six per cent of nonactivists' fathers were willing to describe themselves as "highly liberal" or "socialist," whereas sixty per cent of the activists' fathers accepted such designations. Forty per cent of the non-activists' fathers described themselves as conservative; none of the activists' fathers endorsed that position.[3]

In general, differences in the political preferences of the students paralleled these parental differences. The nonactivist sample is only slightly less conservative and Republican than their fathers; all of the activist students with Republican fathers report their own party preferences as either Democrat or independent. Thirty-two per cent of the activists regard themselves as "socialist" as compared with sixteen per cent of their fathers. In general, both nonactivists and their fathers are typically "moderate" in their politics; activists and their fathers tend to be at least "liberal," but a substantial proportion of the activists prefer a more "radical" designation.

A somewhat more detailed picture of comparative political positions emerges when we examine responses of students and their fathers to a series of 6-point scales on which respondents rated their attitudes on such issues as: US bombing of North Vietnam, US troops in the Dominican Republic, student participation in protest demonstrations, civil rights protests involving civil disobedience, Lyndon Johnson, Barry Goldwater, congressional investigations of "unAmerican activities," full socialization of all industries, socialization of the medical profession.

Table 1 presents data on activists and nonactivists and their fathers with respect to these items. This table suggests, first, wide divergence between the two groups of fathers on most issues, with activist fathers typically critical of current policies. Although activists' fathers are overwhelmingly "liberal" in their responses, for the most part, activist students tend to endorse "left-wing" positions more strongly and consistently than do their fathers. The items showing strongest divergence between activists and their fathers are interesting. Whereas activists overwhelmingly endorse civil disobedience, nearly half of their fathers do not. Whereas fathers of both activists and nonactivists tend to approve of Lyndon Johnson, activist students tend to disapprove of him. Whereas activists' fathers tend to disapprove of "full socialization of industry," this item is endorsed by the majority of activists (although fewer gave an extremely radical response on this item than any other); whereas the vast majority of activists approve of socialized medicine, the majority of their fathers do not. This table provides further support for the view that activists, though more "radical" than their fathers, come predominantly from very liberal homes. The attitudes of nonactivists and their fathers are conventional

[3] For the purposes of this report, "activists" are those students who were in the top third on our Activism index; "nonactivists" are those students who were in the bottom third—this latter group reported virtually no participation in any activity associated with the student movement. The "activists" on the other hand had taken part in at least one activity indicating high commitment to the movement (e.g. going to jail, working full-time, serving in a leadership capacity).

TABLE 1.   STUDENTS' AND FATHERS' ATTITUDES ON CURRENT ISSUES

| | Activists | | Nonactivists | |
Issue	Students	Fathers	Students	Fathers
Per cent who approve:				
Bombing of North Vietnam	9	27	73	80
American troops in Dominican Republic	6	33	65	50
Student participation in protest				
demonstrations	100	80	61	37
Civil disobedience in civil rights protests	97	57	28	23
Congressional investigations of				
"un-American activities"	3	7	73	57
Lyndon Johnson	35	77	81	83
Barry Goldwater	0	7	35	20
Full socialization of industry	62	23	5	10
Socialization of the medical profession	94	43	30	27
N	34	30	37	30

and supportive of current policies; there is a slight tendency on some items for nonactivist students to endorse more conservative positions than their fathers.

It seems fair to conclude, then, that most students who are involved in the movement (at least those one finds in a city like Chicago) are involved in neither "conversion" from nor "rebellion" against the political perspectives of their fathers. A more supportable view suggests that the great majority of these students are attempting to fulfill and renew the political traditions of their families. However, data from our research which have not yet been analyzed as of this writing, will permit a more systematic analysis of the political orientations of the two generations.

Activism Is Related to a Complex of Values, Not Ostensibly Political, Shared by Both the Students and Their Parents. Data which we have just begun to analyze suggest that the political perspectives which differentiate the families of activists from other families at the same socioeconomic level are part of a more general clustering of values and orientations. Our findings and impressions on this point may be briefly summarized by saying that, whereas nonactivists and their parents tend to express conventional orientations toward achievement, material success, sexual morality and religion, the activists and their parents tend to place greater stress on involvement in intellectual and esthetic pursuits, humanitarian concerns, opportunity for self-expression, and tend to de-emphasize or positively disvalue personal achievement, conventional morality and conventional religiosity.

When asked to rank order a list of "areas of life," nonactivist students and their parents typically indicate that marriage, career and religion are most important. Activists, on the other hand, typically rank these lower than the "world of ideas, art and music" and "work for national and international betterment"—and so, on the whole, do their parents.

When asked to indicate their vocational aspirations, nonactivist students are typically firmly decided on a career and typically mention orientations toward the professions, science and business. Activists, on the other hand, are very frequently undecided on a career; and most typically those who have decided mention college teaching, the arts or social work as aspirations.

These kinds of responses suggest, somewhat crudely, that student activists identify with life goals which are intellectual and "humanitarian" and that they reject conventional and "privatized" goals more frequently than do nonactivist students.

Four Value Patterns

More detailed analyses which we are just beginning to undertake support the view that the value-patterns expressed by activists are highly correlated with those of their parents. This analysis has involved the isolation of a number of value-patterns which emerged in the interview material, the development of systems of code categories related to each of these patterns, and the blind coding of all the interviews with respect to these categories. The kinds of data we are obtaining in this way may be illustrated by describing four of the value patterns we have observed:

ROMANTICISM: ESTHETIC AND EMOTIONAL SENSITIVITY

This variable is defined as: "sensitivity to beauty and art—appreciation of painting, literature and music, creativity in art forms—concern with esthetic experience and the development of capacities for esthetic expression—concern with emotions deriving from perception of beauty —attachment of great significance to esthetic experience. More broadly, it can be conceived of as involving explicit concern with experience as such, with feeling and passion, with immediate and inner experience; a concern for the realm of feeling rather than the rational, technological or instrumental side of life; preference for the realm of experience as against that of activity, doing or achieving." Thirteen items were coded in these terms: for each item a score of zero signified no mention of "romanticist" concerns, a score of one signified that such a concern appeared. Table 2 indicates the relationship between "romanticism" and Activism. Very few Activists received scores on Romanticism which placed them as "low"; conversely, there were very few high "romantics" among the nonactivists.

INTELLECTUALISM

This variable is defined as: "Concern with ideas—desire to realize intellectual capacities—high valuation of intellectual creativities—appreciation of theory and knowledge—participation in intellectual activity (e.g., reading, studying, teaching, writing)—broad intellectual concerns." Ten items were scored for "intellectualism." Almost no Activists are low on this variable; almost no nonactivists received a high score.

HUMANITARIANISM

This variable is defined as: "Concern with plight of others in society; desire to help others—value on compassion and sympathy—desire to alleviate suffering; value on egalitarianism in the sense of opposing privi-

TABLE 2.   SCORES ON SELECTED VALUES BY ACTIVISM (PERCENTAGES)

	Activists	Nonactivists
(a) *Romanticism*		
High	35	11
Medium	47	49
Low	18	40
(b) *Intellectualism*		
High	32	3
Medium	65	57
Low	3	40
(c) *Humanitarianism*		
High	35	0
Medium	47	22
Low	18	78
(d) *Moralism*		
High	6	54
Medium	53	35
Low	41	11
N	34	37

lege based on social and economic distinction; particular sensitivity to the deprived position of the disadvantaged." This variable was coded for ten items; an attempt was made to exclude from this index all items referring directly to participation in social action. As might be expected, "humanitarianism" is strongly related to Activism, as evidenced in Table 2.

MORALISM AND SELF CONTROL
     This variable is defined as: "Concern about the importance of strictly controlling personal impulses—opposition to impulsive or spontaneous behavior—value on keeping tight control over emotions—adherence to conventional authority; adherence to conventional morality—a high degree of moralism about sex, drugs, alcohol, etc.—reliance on a set of external and inflexible rules to govern moral behavior; emphasis on importance of hard work; concern with determination, "stick-to-itiveness"; antagonism toward idleness—value on diligence, entrepreneurship, task orientation, ambition." Twelve items were scored for this variable. As Table 2 suggests, "moralism" is also strongly related to activism; very few Activists score high on this variable, while the majority of nonactivists are high scorers.

     These values are strongly related to activism. They are also highly inter-correlated, and, most importantly, parent and student scores on these variables are strongly correlated.

     These and other value patterns will be used as the basis for studying value transmission in families, generational similarities and differences and several other problems. Our data with respect to them provide further support for the view that the unconventionality of activists flows out of and is supported by their family traditions.

Activists' Parents Are More "Permissive" Than Parents of Nonactivists. We have just begun to get some findings bearing on our hypothesis that parents of Activists will tend to have been more "permissive" in their child-rearing practices than parents of equivalent status whose children are not oriented toward activism.

One measure of parental permissiveness we have been using is a series of rating scales completed by each member of the family. A series of seven-point bipolar scales was presented in a format similar to that of the "Semantic Differential". Students were asked to indicate "how my mother (father) treated me as a child" on such scales as "warm-cold"; "stern-mild"; "hard-soft" —10 scales in all. Each parent, using the same scales, rated "how my child thinks I treated him."

Table 3 presents data on how sons and daughters rated each of their parents on each of four scales: "mild-stern"; "soft-hard"; "lenient-severe"; and "easy-strict." In general, this table shows that Activist sons and daughters tend to rate their parents as "milder," "more lenient," and "less severe" than do nonactivists. Similar data were obtained using the parents' ratings of themselves.

A different measure of permissiveness is based on the parents' response to a series of "hypothetical situations." Parents were asked, for example, what they would do if their son (daughter) "decided to drop out of school and doesn't know what he really wants to do." Responses to this open-ended question were coded as indicating "high intervention" or "low intervention." Data for fathers on this item are reported in Table 4. Another hypothetical situation presented to the parents was that their child was living with a member of the opposite sex. Responses to this item were coded as "strongly intervene, mildly intervene, not intervene." Data for this item for fathers appear in Table 5. Both tables show that fathers of Activists report themselves to be much less interventionist than fathers of nonactivists. Similar results were obtained with mothers, and for other hypothetical situations.

Clearly both types of measures just reported provide support for our hypothesis about the relationship between parental permissiveness and activ-

TABLE 3.   SONS AND DAUGHTERS RATINGS OF PARENTS BY ACTIVISM (PERCENTAGES)

| | Males | | Females | |
Trait of Parent	Hi Act	Lo Act	Hi Act	Lo Act
Mild-Stern				
Per cent rating mother "mild"	63	44	59	47
Per cent rating father "mild"	48	33	48	32
Soft-Hard				
Per cent rating mother "soft"	69	61	60	57
Per cent rating father "soft"	50	50	62	51
Lenient-Severe				
Per cent rating mother "lenient"	94	61	66	63
Per cent rating father "lenient"	60	44	47	42
Easy-Strict				
Per cent rating mother "easy"	75	50	77	52
Per cent rating father "easy"	69	44	47	37
N	23	24	27	26

TABLE 4. FATHER'S INTERVENTION—"IF CHILD DROPPED OUT OF SCHOOL"
(PERCENTAGES)

| | Activism of Child | |
Degree of Intervention	High	Low
Low	56	37
High	44	63
N	30	30

TABLE 5. FATHER'S INTERVENTION—"IF CHILD WERE LIVING WITH MEMBER
OF OPPOSITE SEX" (PERCENTAGES)

| | Activism of Child | |
Degree of Intervention	High	Low
None	20	14
Mild	50	28
Strong	30	58
N	30	30

ism. We expect these relationships to be strengthened if "activism" is combined with certain of the value-patterns described earlier.

A Concluding Note

The data reported here constitute a small but representative sampling of the material we have collected in our studies of the student movement. In general, they provide support for the impressions and expectations we had when we undertook this work. Our view of the student movement as an expression of deep discontent felt by certain types of high status youth as they confront the incongruities between the values represented by the authority and occupational structure of the larger society and the values inculcated by their families and peer culture seems to fit well with the data we have obtained.

A variety of questions remain which, we hope, can be answered, at least in part, by further analyses of our data. Although it is clear that value differences between parents of activists and nonactivists are centrally relevant for understanding value, attitudinal and behavioral cleavages among types of students on the campus, it remains to be determined whether differences in family status, on the one hand, and childrearing practices, on the other, make an independent contribution to the variance. A second issue has to do with political ideology. First impressions of our data suggest that activists vary considerably with respect to their degree of politicization and their concern with ideological issues. The problem of isolating the key determinants of this variation is one we will be paying close attention to in further analysis of our interview material. Two factors are likely to be of importance here—

first, the degree to which the student participates in radical student organizations; second, the political history of his parents.

At least two major issues are not confronted by the research we have been doing. First, we have not examined in any detail the role of campus conditions as a determinant of student discontent. The research reported here emphasizes family socialization and other antecedent experiences as determinants of student protest, and leads to the prediction that students experiencing other patterns of early socialization will be unlikely to be in revolt. This view needs to be counterbalanced by recalling instances of active student unrest on campuses where very few students are likely to have the backgrounds suggested here as critical. Is it possible that there are two components to the student protest movement—one generated to a great extent by early socialization; the second by grievances indigenous to the campus? At any rate, the inter-relationships between personal dispositions and campus conditions need further detailed elucidation.

A second set of questions unanswerable by our research has to do with the future—what lies ahead for the movement as a whole and for the individual young people who participate in it? One direction for the student movement is toward institutionalization as an expression of youth discontent. This outcome, very typical of student movements in many countries, would represent a narrowing of the movement's political and social impact, a way of functionally integrating it into an otherwise stable society. Individual participants would be expected to pass through the movement on their way to eventual absorption, often at an elite level, into the established institutional order. An alternative direction would be toward the development of a full-fledged political "left," with the student movement serving, at least initially, as a nucleus. The potential for this latter development is apparent in recent events. It was the student movement which catalyzed professors and other adults into protest with respect to the Vietnam war. Students for a Democratic Society, the main organizational expression of the student movement, has had, for several years, a program for "community organizing," in which students and ex-students work full-time at the mobilization of constituencies for independent radical political and social action. This SDS program began in poverty areas; it is now beginning to spread to "middle class" communities. These efforts, and others like them, from Berkeley to New Haven, became particularly visible during the 1966 congressional elections, as a wave of "new left" candidates emerged across the country, often supported by large and sophisticated political organizations. Moreover, in addition to attempts at political organizations, SDS, through its "Radical Education Project," has begun to seek the involvement of faculty members, professionals and other intellectuals for a program of research and education designed to lay the foundations for an intellectually substantial and ideologically developed "new left."

At its convention in September, 1966, SDS approached, but did not finally decide, the question of whether to continue to maintain its character as a campus-based, student organization or to transform itself into a "Movement for a Democratic Society." Characteristically, the young people there assembled amended the organization's constitution so that anyone regardless of status or age could join, while simultaneously they affirmed the student character of the group by projecting a more vigorous program to organize uncommitted students.

The historical significance of the student movement of the Sixties remains to be determined. Its impact on the campus and on the larger society has already been substantial. It is clearly a product of deep discontent in certain significant and rapidly growing segments of the youth population. Whether it becomes an expression of generational discontent, or the forerunner of major political realignments—or simply disintegrates—cannot really be predicted by detached social scientists. The ultimate personal and political meaning of the student movement remains a matter to be determined by those who are involved with it—as participants, as allies, as critics, as enemies.

REFERENCES

Aaron, Daniel. *Writers on the left.* New York: Avon, 1965.

Bell, Daniel. *The end of ideology.* New York: The Free Press, 1962.

Braungart, R. G. "Social stratification and political attitudes." Pennsylvania State University, 1966, (unpublished ms.).

Bronfenbrenner, U. "The changing American child: A speculative analysis." *Merrill-Palmer Quarterly*, 1961, 7, 73–85.

Coser, Lewis. *Men of ideas.* New York: The Free Press, 1965.

Erikson, Erik. "Identity and the life-cycle." *Psychological Issues*, 1959, 1, 1–171.

Erikson, Erik. *Childhood and society.* New York: Norton, 1963, 306–325.

Eisenstadt, Shmuel N. *From generation to generation.* Glencoe: The Free Press, 1956.

Flacks, R. "The liberated generation." University of Chicago, 1966. (mimeo.).

Goldsen, Rose; Rosenberg, Moris; Williams, Robin; and Suchman, Edward. *What college students think*, Princeton: Van Nostrand, 1960.

Jacob, Philip. *Changing values in college.* New York: Harper, 1957.

Keniston, Kenneth. *The uncommitted.* New York: Harcourt Brace, 1965a.

Keniston, Kenneth. "Social change and youth in America." In E. Erikson (Ed.). *The challenge of youth.* Garden City: Doubleday Anchor, 1965b.

Lasch, Christopher. *The new radicalism in America.* New York: Knopf, 1965.

Lipset, Seymour. *Political man, the social bases of politics.* Garden City: Doubleday Anchor, 1960.

Lipset, Seymour. "University students and politics in underdeveloped countries." *Comparative Education Review*, 1966, 10, 132–162.

Lipset, Seymour and Altbach, P. "Student politics and higher education in the United States." *Comparative Education Review*, 1966, 10, 320–349.

Miller, Daniel and Swanson, G. E. *The changing american parent.* New York: Wiley, 1958.

Newcomb, Theodore and Flacks, R. *Deviant subcultures on a college campus.* U.S. Office of Education, 1963.

Parsons, Talcott. "Youth in the context of American society." In E. Erikson (Ed.). *The challenge of youth.* Garden City: Doubleday Anchor, 1965.

Shils, Edward. "The intellectuals in the political development of new states. *World Politics*, 1960, 12, 329–368.

Stinchcombe, Arthur. *Rebellion in a high school.* Chicago: Quadrangle, 1964.
Trow, Martin. "Student cultures and administrative action." In Sutherland, R. *et al.* (Eds.), *Personality factors on the college campus.* Austin: Hogg Foundation for Mental Health, 1962.
Veblen, Thornstein. "The intellectual pre-eminence of Jews in modern Europe." In B. Rosenberg (Ed.), *Thorstein Veblen.* New York: Crowell, 1963.

THE OBEDIENT REBELS[*][1]

LAWRENCE F. SCHIFF

The rapidly increasing tempo of American college student activism in the past few years has included one little attended to development that sets apart the current period of resurgence from its historical predecessors. The inclusion of conservative students, and a conservative student movement as a dramatically visible part of the contemporary campus scene, marks the first time there has been noticeable activity from that quarter. This, however, does not mean any sudden appearance of student conservatism *per se*. In fact, as Goldsen et al. (9) noted, extreme political and economic conservatism characterizes the dominant political climate on the American campus.

Nevertheless, although conservatively inclined students are in the majority on American college campuses, non-party affiliated political activism has traditionally been a monopoly of the left wing. The prevailing image of the conservative student sees him as deeply satisfied and content with existing social arrangements, a posture that has remained constant during earlier periods of intense right wing and left wing protest.[2] In the current period, in contrast, attempts to organize campus right wing groups and hence create a population of *conservative activists* have met with a considerable degree of success. Political conservative groups are active on well over one hundred college campuses in all sections of the nation. The major arm of the campus conservative movement, a group known as Young Americans for Freedom, has upwards of 10,000 campus members and an additional large number of students are active in political conservative groups unaffiliated with YAF. These groups have become an integral part of the current national conservative

[*] Reprinted from Lawrence F. Schiff, "The Obedient Rebels: A Study of College Conversions to Conservatism," *Journal of Social Issues*, Vol. 20, No. 4, pp. 74–95, by permission of the publisher.
[1] An earlier version of this paper was presented at the Conference on Youth and Social Action held at Howard University, Washington, D.C., October 1, 1963. The author would like to express his appreciation to Drs. George W. Goethals, Morton J. Horwitz and Professor David Riesman for helpful suggestions and to the Social Science Research Council, The American Jewish Committee, the Society for the Psychological Study of Social Issues and the Laboratory of Social Relations, Harvard University for helpful financial support.
[2] There have beeen other attempts to organize student conservatives. A group called "Students for America" was formed in 1952 and lasted about two years. At its peak it claimed 2,500 members on 160 high school and college campuses. Except for SFA, however, and a variety of short-lived local campus groups, campus organizations for conservatives have beeen non-political.

dissent and so, for the first time, a large number of conservative students find themselves actively identified as members of a minority social protest movement.

Conservative politics in America today is, of course, directed toward massive social change. Regardless of which segments of the American Right one focuses on, the view from the Right is of a society engaged in certain tendencies, trends and directions that are pernicious and need to be altered. In its broadest sense the contemporary conservative leadership aims at establishing a new consciousness and conscientiousness in the society, an awareness of what they perceive as "eternal truths" and a commitment to do battle against forces threatening those truths. Coexistent with these broad aims are conservatism's immediate political goals, at the time of the research very much concentrated on the presidential candidacy of Barry Goldwater,[3] but which operate on more localized "direct action" fronts as well. However, even in its political strategy, the conservative movement seeks to establish new mechanisms, partially outside of the traditional two party framework, of which the campus movement is one of the chief instruments. Thus the narrower political and the broader social goals of the conservative movement are inextricable.

A movement aimed at social change will have to first work its changes on the lives of individuals. It is this active interplay of the individual and the movement, of personal experience and contemporary social, political and historical events that is of primary concern here. That is, it is the involvement of college students in the "new" conservative movement, rather than student conservatives or student conservatism as a whole that is primarily at issue. As a new force on the campus scene, it is necessary for the young conservative movement to stimulate interest, activity and especially a sense of commitment and concern among a student population which, while in many ways containing a sizeable amount of sympathy and agreement with its beliefs, has historically been inert insofar as active espousal is concerned. The social adjustment of the conservative student has usually been a rather peaceful affair, marked off by continual progress through highly organized and sanctioned institutional frameworks into the role of citizen-parent. For the politically interested, the youth groups of the national parties provided the latticework for growth. A considerable part of the movement's success will then ultimately lie in its ability to convert previously apolitical, apathetic, inactive and "moderate" conservatives to its new standard of strident and radical conservatism. The present report is directed to an analysis of those young men who were successfully recruited, the converts to the campus conservative movement.[4]

Primary material for the analysis comes from interviews and a variety of paper and pencil instruments administered to forty-seven conservatives on nine

---

[3] The research reported here was conducted in 1963; the author has no information on the impact of Goldwater's presidential defeat on student participation.

[4] For information on the movement itself, see Cain (4), Evans (7) and Forster and Epstein (8). Extensive analysis of the sociopsychological forces behind the general right wing movement will be found in the collection of essays edited by Daniel Bell (3). See especially the papers by Bell, Richard Hofstadter, Peter Vierick, Talcott Parsons and Seymour Lipset.

college campuses,[5] all but one in the New England region. The sample, while not representative of the movement nationally, provided an adequate cross section of conservative activity on most of the campuses visited, and, while small in number, it ranged over a considerable amount of demographic and political response variety. Geographically it included students from every region in the country; academically, from drop-outs to Rhodes scholars; economically, parents' incomes ranged from $5,000 to upwards of $75,000; politically, from moderate Republicans through John Birch enthusiasts to unreconstructed royalists; in religion, from avowed atheism to extreme ortho-doxy. The diversity so represented (probably due to the diversity among and within the colleges visited), while making generalizations more difficult, gives the sample more significance than if it had been more homogeneous. Further, none of the campuses included presented an overwhelmingly clear conservative environment, thus bringing to the fore the participants' own selective processes and thereby permitting more extensive analysis of the social psychological dynamics involved in the adoption of the conservative activist identity.

Our subject matter broadly speaking is the relation between youth and conservatism, the reationships that hold between the age-specific energies, conflicts and tasks associated with adolescence and the development of an affinity to conservative activism as a particular political orientation. What is it that happens during a person's adolescence that would lead him to take on a conservative-activist political identity and what is it in the conservative-activist political identity that appeals to adolescents? Thus it is those respondents whose affiliation with the movement implied some dynamic reorganization of the adolescent or late-adolescent self, the converts, who are the central concern of the present analysis.

Among the subjects in the sample, about one-third could not be consid-ered to be converts to the movement.[6] These are the young men for whom affiliation was simply based on a traditional or continuous pattern of social adaptation, whose *political beliefs* have continued more or less unchanged and are identical with the beliefs of parents and of the community of orienta-tion, and whose *political involvement* is of equally long standing, originating in an environment fostered interest in politics and developing within given imstitutional settings (e.g., high-school debating and Young Republican clubs) into personal political involvement. The motives for affiliation of these indi-viduals are irrelevant for the understanding of the dynamics of the "new con-servatism," for there is nothing new about their new behavior; theirs is simply an adjustment to a new situation (the presence or availability of a campus conservative group) employing patterns of behavior long in existence.

For most of the young men in the sample, however, participation in a conservative activist group represented a discontinuity with previous social adaptations sufficient to suggest some direct connection between the poten-

[5] Responses to the paper and pencil instruments were also obtained from ten students active in left-wing groups. The major instrument used was a 160 item adaptation of a personality inventory developed by Arthur Couch (5). See Schiff (11) for a com-plete report of the instruments and interview schedule.
[6] Such a statistic does not necessarily reflect on the actual proportion of converts and non-converts. Probably the percentage of converts in the whole movement is smaller.

tially new appeals of the campus conservative movement and the underlying developmental needs of the new recruits. The political development of these converts involved one or more of the following characteristics:

a. a sudden, discontinuous political involvement or interest that brings the individual's latent conservatism out into an activistic orientation;
b. a definite movement to the political right in the person's attitudinal or ideological stance; or
c. a "self-initiated" development of a conservative political orientation, one that occurs outside the context of the nuclear family.

Among these converts, about two-thirds of the sample, there was, of course, considerable variation—in the dynamics of their conversions, in their political orientations and political behavior and in their social and psychological orientations in general. Any attempts at thoroughly analyzing the complete range of the phenomenon in the present paper could only lead to an unsatisfactory superficiality. The following discussion is, therefore, limited to a single type of conservative convert, a type that includes those among the converting subjects who must approximate "core" participants in the movement. These converts, by and large, showed the greatest affinity to the movement; they were the most involved in it and found its general outlook, program and spirit most congenial.

The discussion is primarily oriented around the dynamics of the core participant's conversion experience, its structure, etiology and consequences. These conversions provided an illuminating entree into understanding the personal meaning of participation and, further, while far from a perfect correspondence, those converting subjects who tended to be most committed to the movement (or the local campus variation of the movement) and those whose relationship to the movement's outlook and program tended to be most regular (or orthodox) also tended to convert to conservative activism under somewhat similar or equivalent circumstances and in a somewhat similar manner. The characteristic features of this dominant conversion pattern will thus be analyzed in detail as a clue to understanding the inner dynamics of campus conservative activism.

Conservative Conversions and the Experience of Totalism

Adolescence, particularly in its later stages (when this "typical" conversion tended to take place), is, of course, a period of significant personal change, and to work a change on (or in) oneself in adolescence is not unusual. Indeed William James (10, p. 199) spoke of conversion as "in its essence a normal adolescent phenomenon, incidental to the passage from the child's small universe to the wider intellectual and spiritual life of maturity." And to Erik Erikson, the central task of adolescence, the achievement of a viable and secure ego-identity, calls for a change akin to conversion in its search for a "new and yet a reliable identity."

Adolescent conversions can thus come about in benign fashion. According to James, the "once-born" (the "naturally" healthy and harmonious individual) is converted through "suggestion and imitation" without a disturbance of his inner tranquility. The idea of harmoniousness remains central in Erikson's thinking. In the successful quest of ego-identity, a sense of "essential wholeness" will be preserved, an adaptation which requires that

> the young person must feel a progressive continuity between that which he has come to be during the long years of childhood and that which he promises to become in the anticipated future; between that which he perceives himself to be and that which he perceives others to see in him and expect of him. (6, p. 168)

But such, particularly in our times, does not always come easily, and

> when the human being, because of accidental or developmental shifts, loses an essential wholeness, he restructures himself and the world by taking recourse to what we may call totalism. . . . Where the (process of) self-definition, for personal or collective reasons, becomes too difficult, a sense of Role-Diffusion results; the youth counter-points rather than synthesizes his sexual, ethnic, occupation and typological alternatives and is often driven to decide definitely and totally for one side or the other. (6, p. 168)

Striking signs of such rigid counterpointing and totalistic commitment typified the core convert's transformation into a conservative activist. Significantly, these conversions tended to take place at a time of crucial role transition during the period between secondary school graduation and the beginning of the second year in college. Such a period accentuates the need to adapt to a new personal environment and to begin to incorporate (or refuse to begin to incorporate) adult role self-images, while simultaneously making irreversible moves out of the immediate parental orbit, physically and emotionally.

With the transitionary background setting the stage, the conservative conversion was characteristically triggered off by the convert's "shocking" discoveries about his newly widening universe. Often these discoveries were directly tinged with a primitive and totalistic morality.

> Herron's conversion took place while he was stationed abroad in the Navy. Disturbed by the "slothfulness" and "self-indulgent habits" of the local citizenry, he had a sudden realization of "the consequences of not subscribing to a strict moral code."

> Manning reacted to his college's total climate. He found himself "appalled and amazed" about some of the college newspaper editorials, particularly one espousing the "hard-core liberal" idea that Castro had brought social justice to Cuba. He was "awfully amazed and incredulous —I really didn't understand the mental processes there." He was, at the same time, also "disappointed" with the college's moral climate: "I came to college and I find so many people whom I consider to be uppercrust people . . . who, to my sense of feeling anyway, behave in a manner which is *very* unsuitable for what I think they should be doing. It bothers me a little bit to see so many people who should be virtuous and decent cheating on tests and fornicating all over the place, you know, various things which are generally considered immoral."

Robard, coming East to college, found himself "in kind of a flux" and "distressed . . . shocked (and) disillusioned" with his new peers. He recalls hearing a conservative professor hissed and booed when he was talking about patriotism, the communist Gus Hall "fervently" applauded by undergraduates and Eisenhower "disintegrated" and "split all over" by the faculty. These things "made an indelible imprint on my mind," they "started me thinking about what were the values of this generation, this group of kids I was associated with. It really surprised me. . . . I couldn't believe it, it was incomprehensible to me."

Barton, a small-town mid-westerner, traces his conversion to his "exposure" to the "undesirable types" he saw in a poor section of the city bordering on his college.

In other situations, the "shock" was more narrowly political, though no less total in its impact.

Rango had been an avowed Democrat and Kennedy supporter in the 1960 campaign. Always a "strong anti-communist," he went at the suggestion of a priest to view the right wing film "Operation Abolition." "I was very shocked and disgusted with the whole thing. I realized that many of the people who I though were on my side were trying to knock down this film. There the seed of doubt was put into my mind as to whether I could really belong to this element."

Rosa's conservative views "began to build partially out of resentment against my (college) teachers because I felt they were pushing so much stuff down my throat—I got it in every class. There wasn't one teacher I could find that had views any different."

Dorsey recalled all the "liberal indoctrination" he received during his first year at college. "I was shocked, I think, to hear some of the things I did hear."

In each of these cases the individual's relevant personal environment had taken on a new and sinister quality, one which seemed to threaten or challenge some essential and valued component of the self. The crystallization of this challenge into political terms, while sometimes partially fortuitous, was strengthened by the availability of a liberal stereotype capable of absorbing a complex variety of negative attributes.

As Wayne, a sudden convert to political activism, saw them, "rabid liberals" were "characters (who) seemed to be against any idea of God, against any sort of traditional value. They seem to reject any of the traditional concepts of America. . . . Whenever you bring up any tradition, or sort of accepted way of life, like, you know, patriotism, raising a flag, going to church or anything like that, they seem to reject it completely. I often have the impression that they just lead kind of a bare life, that they all seem to be looking for something that isn't there. (While) the members of YAF as far as I can see just seem to be a bunch of, you know, ordinary college students. Very nice kids and nothing unusual about any of them, nothing to mark them out from the rest of the crowd, like a beard. They just seem to be normal American kids."

For many, the transition from one setting to another itself produced a sense of loss of some stabilizing anchorage preserving an old equilibrium; environs that had been familiar and safe were now unfamiliar and unsafe. Often the move took place through physical and cultural space, though even the simple change of status to that of college student can have a dramatic, even licentious impact:

> Manning's parents "were pretty strict with me and didn't give me much freedom. . . . As a senior in high school I was told what my curfew was, while other kids could stay out all night." But immediately upon entering college, his situation changed radically. "They're really funny in that respect. They seemed to have chosen an age (after which) just like that I'm free. As soon as I went to college—no transition at all, just the space of a month—in that space in their eyes I grew from a child into an adult."

With the disappearance of externally imposed social controls, many of these young men seemed to perceive themselves as threatened with becoming something very different from what they were or subconsciously felt they ought to be, a loss of an "essential wholeness" that precipitated a totalistic restructuring. The conversion, which began with the perceptual accentuation of malevolent elements in the environment, was then characteristically brought rapidly to a final and definitive conclusion.

In some cases latent identity components were available to accomplish the redefining process.

> Thus Herron, for example, was able to "activate (my) established views" on politics and morality with the resulting conclusions revealing a "correspondence between what I found out on my own and my family's views."

And Barton was able to agree with the previously rejected views of his parents that the idea of "community" demanded "some exclusion."

For others the conversion involved a short period of intensive self-indoctrination (rarely mediated by any close interpersonal contacts) from which the individual emerged with a self-identifiable and settled sense of identity.

> Rosa, for whom "the views were always there in me," nevertheless "sought elsewhere for the sake of finding another view (from that of his teachers). I found it in the *Conscience of a Conservative* which I thought was a great book and still do, because it covers such a wide range of *basic* issues, *gut* issues in the great battle of ideologies in the twentieth century. I read it and reread it and reread it and reread it. It was a real bible to me. . . . Just about everything that Goldwater put forth in that book I would firmly agree with."

The conversion often took place with dramatic speed and results:

> Finestock, an upper-middle class Jew, had flunked out of college after two years and had spent a year working. At the time "I had no interest in anything, including politics. . . . In the meantime, this may sound silly, I got ahold of *Conscience of a Conservative* and it just seemed to

appeal to me . . . everything that Goldwater said seemed to have fitted in. So after I read this book I started reading Edmund Burke, Locke, and then I realized I should go back to school. . . . I never knew (before) what to call myself."

In Dorsey's freshman year YAF was founded. "I looked it over at the time and decided I wasn't conservative enough, I would not join it. . . . After reading several issues (of *National Review*) over a period of time, over the months, my views shifted and so by Spring and into the Summer at the end of my freshman year I'd become quite solidly a conservative. And during the Summer I read a lot of political things, as much as I could. . . . When I came back . . . I joined the Young Americans for Freedom."

Rango, after viewing the film "Operation Abolition," immediately contacted a member of the John Birch Society, started reading its literature and "realized I couldn't remain the way I was." After a summer of reading, it became "a very clear thing that if students, especially (Catholic) students don't begin working with the same zeal as the Communists, there's not going to be any Western civilization left as far as I can see."

The thrust of these conversions was generally to settle issues by settling on a newly found cloak of identity, to push away any lingering or uncomfortable uncertainty by achieving what might be called "identity foreclosure." In attempting to reconstruct the state of mind that prevailed at the time of these late adolescent conversions, it seems as if the most clearly felt need was to restore (or construct) as rapidly as possible a feeling of clarity and certainty about the self and its position in the new social environment. As Finestock put it, "I never knew what to call myself." Now they knew, and for most, knowing was in itself sufficient. The conservative system was seized upon totally—the response was not to this or that substantive feature of it; nor, as in the case of other types of conversions, was it a response to real or imaginative heroic and exciting individuals. Rather, the conversion seemed directed toward two immediate ends, to disconfirm what one was not (or should not be), i.e., the amoral, deviant liberal, and to confirm a desirable image of the self. In the pursuit of these ends, conservatism was taken up macroscopically, its inner content often less relevant than its outward appearance.

Background of the Conservative Conversions

While the background of these converts varied widely, some common elements are discernible which make the intensity and function of the reaction more comprehensible. The general pattern was composed of two elements, a common configuration in regard to family structure and familial experience and certain shared elements of character structure that shaped the converts' reaction to their personal backgrounds.

In examining the familial backgrounds of the totalistic converts, one is immediately impressed with the striking degree to which American families retain a capacity to generate intensive achievement and characterological demands on their children. In virtually all cases, the early experience of these young men was dominated by a parent (sometimes both parents) with extremely well delineated and ambitious expectations of their children, with the heaviest burden falling on our subjects who were, with but one exception, the eldest or only sons in their families.

Herron's father, a highly successful independent lawyer, early and ardently began to infuse his young son with the spirit of his "adherence to strict moral standards," keeping him isolated from his contemporaries in the process of inculcating high standards of achievement, character and excellence.

Rosa's immigrant parents managed, within a remarkably short time to attain complete economic and stylistic mobility into middle-class standards. Through hard work and "frugality," his father's butcher shop provided his family with a lovely home in an upper-middle class suburban community. The parents joined and were active in a variety of community social organizations and transferred their political allegiance from support of Roosevelt to "ardent" Republicans and "Truman-haters."

Finestock's immigrant father received a primary school education here and then in true Horatio Alger fashion, rose out of this background to put together a fabulously successful business. He intended that his son would actualize his success, starting him off on this path by sending him to a predominantly Protestant, highly ranked prep school.

Dorsey's childhood was dominated by the orthodox religiosity and stern morality of a father with a highly prestigeful/low income occupation. The father sought to perpetuate the symbolic perquisites of his status through the elite schooling of his son.

Manning first felt the weight of his parents' expectations while in the first grade, "when my teacher told my mother that I might be left back. My mother said she wasn't going to have anything like that, so she and my father sat down to teach me to read. . . . My father was ready to slug me (and) after the first few months of screaming 'I can't do it,' I had it impressed on me that I could." His parents "pushed me pretty hard in school. . . . Mother was always pretty proud of how far back college degrees go in her family. They had been the upper-crusts—not in money or being aristocrats—but in knowledge and virtue and education back for I don't know how many generations. . . . She was quite concerned that I not let down the family line. . . . I think my mother had the attitude that if you're going to be a scholar you have to sit in the garret and read. She told me, 'forget all those frivolous things, they'll come after you get your education.' "

Against enormous pressure to measure up to parental demands and expectations, the converts, each in his own way but always covertly and at times involuntarily, found themselves veering away from the parental blueprint. Unsuccessful at completely conforming to these expectations and unwilling to openly defy them, the converts arrived at the point of conversion bearing, to varying degrees, the weight of unacknowledged intergenerational conflict.

For Herron, dissonance was introduced early. Chafing under the isolation and low impulse gratification of his father's tutelage, he began to channel his energies into activities only marginally related to the development of intellect or character. Faced with a choice between going to a private preparatory school (his father's preference) or continuing in the local school where his newly developing interests could be furthered, he chose the latter and by implication thereby began to repudiate the social role his father had selected for him.

His activities in high school were sufficiently "aristocratic," however, to preserve the trappings of his social position, and he had intended to continue this temporizing rebellion through his selection of a "playboy's" college. Throughout his adolescence he managed to balance off his resentment against his father by avoiding overt disobedience, always by maintaining the form but not the substance of his father's preachments.

The rebellion collapsed, however, before he got to college. Because of complicated external circumstances, he found it necessary to enlist in the Navy for a standard tour of duty and without a commission. He thus suddenly found himself, lacking rank, college education and reputation, without any social prestige. It was precisely at this point that he became interested in politics and "discovered" the "correspondence" between his views and those of his father. The implicit personological shift implied was further realized in the changing of his earlier college plans and his choice instead of an intellectually elite college.

The central themes of Herron's story are found over and over again in the life situation of other converts. Sometimes the conflict between the parental plan and the youthful inclinations was introduced less voluntarily.

Rosa and Finestock were both eager participants in their parents' climb to the top of the middle. Finestock, for instance, enjoyed his Protestant prep school tremendously, strongly disagreeing with other Jewish students there who were disturbed by latent and overt anti-semitism. But both young men collapsed in their attempt to actualize their parents' plans. Finestock's father had "pulled strings" to get him into a first-rate college, but after two unhappy years there he flunked out. Rosa's parents also stressed education as the means by which their son would continue their own upward mobility. However, by the end of his high school years, Rosa's lack of academic accomplishment was apparent and while other students from his fine suburban high school were going to the better schools throughout the nation, Rosa had to settle for the school of general studies in a second rate urban institution. It was in the immediate context of the manifestation of their academic failures that both young men discovered and enthusiastically embraced conservative activism.

Dorsey's experience further illuminates the relation of the conversion to the parental relationship.

In his five year stay at prep school, he felt stultified by the "monastic" setting, unable to get along with the "New England preppie types" and was consistently unhappy. He began to crack the mold when, after a particularly unpleasant summer experience, he returned to his last year of school and decided against following in the footsteps of his father's career. This decision was not made without unarticulated misgivings. "It was no great revolution against (it) or anything like that. You might say that that now is my second choice."

Nevertheless, the decision presaged a more generalized feeling of emancipation experienced by Dorsey when he entered college. Capitalizing on the heady sense of freedom he now felt, he threw himself into college power politics. Operating under the lingering realization that his politicking displeased his parents, Dorsey's conversion, by implicitly corresponding with certain parentally induced themes (religiosity and status aspiration) served at least in part to mitigate the appearance of disobedience.

As these cases illustrate, the turn to conservatism often played a crucial role in resolving the dissonance between the child and his parents. The pattern of such crisis resolutions differed from case to case, but generally resembled one of "obedient rebellion," a repudiation of repudiation that either served to disguise any overt intergenerational rebellion or transform it. This configuration of two seemingly discordant tendencies, obedience and rebellion, is more intricate than it may at first appear. For one thing we cannot assume that the dissonance introduced into the parent-child relationship was accidental or unintentional in the broadest sense of that word which includes unconscious intentions. Psychodynamically, there was within these subjects a rebellious or hostile tendency, one that led adequately bright young men like Rosa or Finestock to function poorly academically. Clinically we know that such abrasive encounters do not in any real sense dissolve, but we also know that there is usually no simplified one-for-one displacement of conflicts from one level to another.

In the simplest sense the conversion betokened a fairly straightforward displacement wherein obedience to parents was enhanced through rebellion against potentially disobedient youthful inclinations projected out into the peer or nonparental social environment. Rosa's conversion of his college faculty into a "negative reference group" is a clear example of the political conversion's use as a defensive mechanism to accomplish the ends of continued parental obedience (while still keeping the rebellious inclinations alive).

> Manning provides a somewhat convoluted example of the same processes. Though overtly critical of both his parents, his resentment is strongest against his mother. Since entering college he has, while remaining verbally critical, moved much closer to his father, taking an interest in and participating with his father in the latter's active hobbies. His conservatism, which he traces to parental and particularly paternal influences, would seem at least in part to be serving the same ends as the other behavior, i.e., moving himself back into his father's good graces.
>
> At the same time it allowed him to bring out a long suppressed expressive-activist mode while continuing to feel obedient. That the latter need was still operative and important was revealed at one point in the interview when, in a plaintive aside as he was criticizing his mother, he said, "I'm not going to let down the family tradition."

The desire to appear as the dutiful son is extremely pronounced in many of the young conservatives. More than half of the college-age converts with siblings (and two of the more deeply involved non-converting conservative activists) appeared in this role in their families. Some of the siblings in question actively defied their parents, adopting religious, political or career lines that directly conflicted with parental wishes. Other siblings were chronic failures or playboys, disobedient types. In every instance where there was sharp contrast or complementarity between siblings, the totalistic convert emerged as the "good boy."

Disobedient inclinations are often most effectively disguised (from both the actor and his targets) by over-obedience. Sometimes this is carried out by a kind of hair-splitting in which any repudiational implication that becoming a conservative activist might imply (as, for example, when the individual appears to be becoming more completely assimilated than his parents) is maneuvered by the individual, sometimes genuinely and sometimes through rationalization, so as to have it appear as a highly sanctioned *extension* of parental precepts. Thus Rango assuaged any ill effects of his "being more accepted in the community" than his first-generation parents by an espousal of a narrow and rigid orthodox Catholicism that exceeded the religiosity of his parents (who did not want him to go to a parochial high school). By over-obeying on one end, he was thereby freed to move away from his parents on another.

On another level, the obedience and rebellion are fused to an even greater degree. The adoption of a "conservative" political position serves to so thoroughly align the child with the implicit and explicit values of his parents, even to the degree represented by Dorsey and others where the conservatism is almost a caricature of the parents' status-seeking propensities, that the young person is able to use the political identity as a wrap within which he is able to carry on some marginal hell-raising that otherwise might have been subject to disapprobation. The result has the flavor of Herron's adolescent obedience to the form but not the substance of his father's preachments. It seems to be true that whenever the political behavior of the young conservatives displays cantankerous tendencies, it is firmly shored up by a high degree of parent-child correspondence in the realm of moral values, or ironically, with a feeling that parents had not been strict enough, one of the few "complaints" raised by the conservatives against their parents' way of bringing them up.

The Choice of Conservatism

The choice of any particular ideological system and social behavioral orientation emerges out of extremely complex and multiple causes. Given the relatively severe late adolescent crises of the present group, their choice of conservative activism as (part of) a way out of the storm can only receive a series of partial explanations, any one of which (and even all of which taken together) can only make the choice plausible and perhaps probable, but certainly not necessary.

We start with the observed fact that the new conservative program satisfied the needs and was in harmony with the personal characteristics of this group of late-adolescent converts. Drawing on the interviews with them and on "outside" a priori interpretations of that program, we can present an admittedly circular and post-dictive analysis of the bases of the "connections" between person and ideology. It is our feeling, however, that, in contrast with other conversions, the obedient rebellions had a more necessary connection to the essence of conservatism, i.e., that they are, to a large degree, "natural" conservatives for whom no other ideological orientation could nearly so well have served.

The most striking of what we will call the appeals of the conservative package (its "demand" character, those characteristics of conservatism that made it attractive) is its *high symbolic prestige value*. Conservatives today present their position as the "true American" one, as the incarnation of genuine, traditional American values. Further, all segments of the American community generally identify conservatism with the well-born and highly placed in our society.

In coping with the self-definitional difficulties that for one reason or another were of particular concern to them, the obedient rebels' readjustments were invariably directed either toward the American "core" or to status slots consensually defined attractive because of their "highness" in the social structure. In other words, the direction of these converts is inward and upward and involves a total acceptance of the American mainstream's evaluation of "the good."

Thus:

Herron's conversion served to recapture in his own mind and probably in the image of the self projected to his colleagues, his prestigeful status, which had disappeared from view when he entered the Navy without benefit of any of the ascriptive symbols of his former station in life.

Rosa's conversion served directly and indirectly to maintain the up-wardly mobile and assimiliationist movement so aggressively begun by his parents.

Finestock's conversion corresponded with his previous experience at a predominantly Protestant prep school where he, in contrast to most of his Jewish classmates, felt and wanted acceptance.

Rango's conversion served similarly "inwardly mobile" aims, but in a more complex way, by enabling him to over-lay his hard-core orthodox Catholicism with a virulent nationalism and permitting the adoption of an economic philosophy amenable to the "third generation," one that contrasts with "the appeal of money and paternalism to immigrant groups" and "goes with being accepted in the community."

Barton's conversion returned him to the cultural *zeitgeist* of his small, mid-western hometown, where there existed a real "sense of community" thanks to its having "very few poor, foreign or non-white people."

Nile's conversion allowed him, to use his own words, to be one of those "conservatives who come from lower income backgrounds and iden-tify with the 'higher orders.' "

Hudson's conversion allowed him to fully identify with the proud and prestigeful family tradition of his mother's side, as embodied in the person of his still living grandfather, a college-educated and highly successful businessman who is also an extreme and active conservative. This identity element contrasted sharply with that provided by his stepfather, a poorly educated proletarian.

Behind these status seeking propensities lies, of course, the obedient rebels' psychological acceptance of their parents' values and frames of reference as their own. This obedience characteristic suggests another of the sociopsychological bases of attraction to the new conservatism. Through *its espousal of deference to legitimate authority and the sanctity of traditional morality*, the new conservatism presents a stimulus totally congruent with deep-rooted psychological inclinations of its adherents. Above and beyond the ideological agreement involved, it is able to justify, in an otherwise youthfully attractive package, a parental obedience streak that is somewhat out of place in our contemporary peer-oriented culture. The trait of obedience is probably strongly present in large "pockets" of our society; the New Conservatism would seem to be eminently capable of offering a service for those in whom the trait is especially deeply ingrained and for those in whom the trait is strong while simultaneously being a subject of intra-psychic conflict (the converts being the latter).

The most striking difference that emerged from the administration of personality scales to a group of ten liberals along with the conservatives was that between the groups' scores on an Authoritarian Conformity scale. This scale was designed to assess an orientation to the demands of the social environment as revealed in the *mode* of conformity (authoritarian v. nonauthoritarian) adopted by the individual. In contrast to the significant difference between the groups on this dimension, a short scale designed by Allport (2) to indirectly tap prejudice (through the scale items, perception of "the world as a jungle"), along with two of the original F scale items (1) failed completely to differentiate the groups. These data tend to support our feeling derived from the interviews:

that *conventionality is* and *ethnocentrism is not* a salient distinguishing characteristic of the young conservatives;

that the political judgments and perceptions of the young conservatives are based on *social identification factors* but *not ethnic prejudice*;

that the young conservatives' view of social desirability is essentially *open*, i.e., that *anyone can be a member* of the club of good Americans if they are willing to accept the membership requirements; and

that the impelling thrust involved here is the individuals' own sense of marginality or confusion about "belonging," not necessarily the need to exclude others.

As a concomitant of their parental deference tendencies, the young conservatives often find themselves out of step with the prestigeful persons and values on their campuses. (This varies widely from school to school but is somewhat true throughout, as is implicitly conceded in the conservative contention that the "liberal establishment" is everywhere in control.) Here perhaps is the most singularly new contribution of the new conservatism, its presentation of *an intellectual apparatus* with which young collegiates may identify without finding it necessary to change what they feel they "instinctively" are. The personnel (epitomized by Ivy-League educated and scholarly-sounding William Buckley) and wide ranging publications of the movement (particularly Buckley's *National Review*) have provided a means by and through which the young conservatives can come out in the open on the campus and, more significantly, the embrace of the conservative ideology can come out in the open from within the individual.

There is, of course, a wide range in the degree to which the intellectual rationale is taken seriously. At one extreme was Manning, a voracious reader in general and currently deeply involved in conservative writings. At the other is a remark overheard by the author as he left a particularly obscure and convoluted "academic" speech by Buckley: "I didn't understand a word he said, but I'm glad he's on our side." Between these extremes, and most characteristic of the preponderance of young conservatives (especially of the participants on Eastern campuses), was a low-level attempt to keep this identity element ("young intellectual") accessible, yet secondary.

Another element of appeal in the conservative program brought out by the obedient rebellion conversions is the program's ideological emphasis on *risk-taking* and *romanticization of achievement-oriented* behavior. These young men, though accepting these traditional values as right and proper, are for the most part unwilling or unable to act on them in shaping their own futures. In contrast, their career-plans emerge out of and are eminently compatible with the low-risk, high-security atmosphere that actually prevails for contemporary American college educated youths. This "split" was visible in the frequent references made by the young conservatives to the nobility of risk-taking and profit-seeking behavior, which references were accompanied by personal disclaimers of materialism.

Seen in this light, the conservative program becomes a convenient arena for "acting on" these values in a displaced sense, for example, substituting national risk-taking behavior for unacceptable personal risk-taking. On occasion the entrepreneurial dream edged close to the young conservatives' aspirations in the attenuated form of a political career. But even here, heroic individual accomplishment and ambition were hedged behind the safety of a successful law practice. Security and solvency came first.

The conservative program, by its *intellectual simplicity*, by its *closed and deductive format*, by its *pessimistic outlook* on human perfectibility and by its self-consciously *hard-line* posture was able to provide comforting assurance for the many among the late adolescent converts whose self-esteem had been transitorily disturbed, those for whom "identity foreclosure" rather than genuine personal change was the way out of a developmental crisis. The precious and difficult balancing of tentative possibilities during youth's optional psychosocial moratorium, a necessary step in achieving a genuine change of the self, requires a characterological capacity to tolerate anxiety and ambiguity.

By providing a way out of this period, the new conservatism reveals another of its functions. In a subtle way it legitimates and hardens a sense of resignation; and, by allowing the growth tendencies of youth to find other outlets, albeit more sober, "realistic" ones, it institutionalizes a compromising attitude toward human possibility that is congruent with the experience of some young people.

The opposite of tolerating anxiety was found to be the second conservative personality trait that emerged as significantly different from the small group of left-wingers also given the personality scales. The conservative group was heavily oriented to the "ego control" end of an Ego Control v. Manifest Anxiety scale. Since the theoretical assumption underlying the scales was that the "amount" of anxiety was not differentially distributed according to outcome on this nuclear issue; and since the conservatives were also found to be significantly higher on the Repression scale (the third and last statistically significant difference between the groups); and, finally, since, as we have seen, the young conservatives were involved in their fair share of anxiety-producing (and revealing) situations, it would seem probable that the exercising of a tight control over personal anxiety is both a very strong psychodynamic tendency of the group and one that would reveal itself in social behavior.

When we pause to examine the nature of the contemporary political world waiting to be apperceived by politically conscious young men, the young conservatives' pattern becomes even more comprehensible. Consider the bombardment of negative stimuli that nowadays confronts our well-advantaged youth: Americans are, to most of the world, the fattest, most affluent, self-indulgent people; Americans are the perpetrators of that most heinous of crimes, atomic aggression; white Americans are the systematic exploiters of their black brothers; that most prized American value, making money by making things work, is now regarded with disdain.

Consider these messages and the fact that every socially aware young person is exposed unceasingly to them. Some self-preservative means must be found of coping with these in the course of the young person's development of an ideology. Our young conservatives, because of their own peculiar inner-dynamics and character structures, could do naught but repudiate these collective assaults on their persons.

In doing so, they consciously become "hard" (the oft-repeated, "I go along with the hard line foreign policy") and pessimistically "realistic" (frequently addressing themselves against the liberals' so-called utopianism and naive optimism), and wind up justifying hardness as a valued element of the self—for some at least, this self-denying twist is the only recourse. (We would hazard a guess that young men on the left today have, to a great degree, coped with the "negative stimuli" in a quite different manner, by internalizing it and carrying the guilt within.)

Looked at another way, the need to defend against anxiety involves a need to maintain a high level of self-esteem. Taken together with the heavy emphasis on definitions of the self compatible with those formed in childhood, this would result in a tendency toward preserving a rather narrow concept of the self and of what other social symbols are made a part of the self-system. In this respect the conservative program's *ideological legitimation of self-interest* as a basis for political evaluations and judgments (as in its espousal of national self-interest over concern for the whole of mankind and of the need to maintain [middle-class, white] "individual" freedoms and traditions over the need [of lower class and non-white groups] to achieve equality of access and opportunity) is a powerful buttress to the personal inclinations of the program's adherents.

Observers have often puzzled over the seeming anachronism of the prejudiced person who is at the same time unqualifiedly warm and friendly to those who come within his orbit, the phenomenon of white "southern hospitality" epitomizing this situation. Though our young conservatives are, for the most part, not consciously prejudiced (some are actively anti-prejudicial), the mechanisms by which they arrive at their moderately xenophobic positions probably enters into the non-expressive component involved in all prejudice.

Our material would suggest, first, that the young conservatives are not lower in "empathy" than non-conservatives (though this proposition was not tested directly, the virtually identical scores of both groups on the emotionality and aggressivity scales point in this direction, as does also the general openness and cordiality that we encountered in the interviews), second, that they are no more hostile, or, indeed, power-oriented in their social perceptions (although some individual scale items give some support to the last possibility), but that their chief contrast with equivalently middle-class left-wing thinkers is their more parochial, narrower, self-oriented frames of reference in determining what and with whom they will identify.

Of course, most young conservatives sincerely do not see their political positions as motivated by self-interest (many counterposed their concern for "what was good for the nation," against "materialistic" liberal groups who were concerned only with their own good). That the "national" interest happens to coincide, sometimes indirectly, with their own middle-class positions was lost to many of them. What is true, of course, is that all political ideologies conform to an individual's self-interest; what varies is how the self is defined, and the young conservatives' definition of self proceeds from the various psychological and social traits and forces that we have been discussing.

We have left to the end the new conservatism's function as a vehicle for the *displacement of otherwise inexpressable hostility.* This demand quality is really in evidence in all political programs, particularly those with an extreme and totalistic ideology. As we have seen, this "function" of the ideology appears to be neither more nor less important for the right wing than for the left wing systems, and of varying significance to different individuals within either group. There is, however, some evidence (from the personality scales and from the interview impressions) that the "need" to express aggression as a general trait or the need to displace any internal aggressive impulses onto socially approved objects is more characteristic of the right wing converts than of the group of conservatives whose political orientation has evolved toward the center. (This centrist: extremist relationship could hold equally well for the left.) What evidence there is to suggest this comes mainly from the observation that centrist-evolvers as opposed to rightist converts tend to present more emotionally open, warm personalities and seem to be more involved in "positive affective" and non-goal oriented relationships with peers.

Concluding Remarks

In the new conservative program, the late-adolescent converts appear to have come upon an ideology that fits exceptionally well with their character structures, backgrounds and developmental conflicts. On the basis of the multiple points of coincidence between personalities and personal experiences on the one hand and the substance and format of the ideology on the other, it would seem a certainty that no other modern political ideology could have been as harmoniously adopted by the late adolescent converts in our sample. However, any ideology that was capable of exercising a wide-spread appeal to young men like those we have been discussing, would have to have been very much in and of this world, since the obedient rebels have basically secular outlooks. This would pretty much rule out the possibility that religious ideologies could be as fundamentally satisfying as political conservatism, though there is an overlap. Purely technocratic (non-ideological) ideology was, for the reasons enumerated above, not fully adequate to carry these young men into adulthood, though, again, they do not in fact reject technocracy as a guide to conduct.

In this report attention has been limited to a particular type of participant in the campus conservative movement. While most typical of the core member in the present sample, a reminder is warranted about the sample's limited range. It is quite possible, even probable, that its limitation solely to New England colleges has led to an overemphasis on the importance of conventionalizing and self-restricting traits and tendencies and deemphasis on the activist/expressive side of the conservative posture. Further, in spite of the highlighting of totalism in the original conversion, it should be clear that the young men reported on here are not of a totalitarian bent, that in fact they have, for the most part, a well-internalized orientation to democratic modes of thinking and acting. This was, to be sure not true of all the young conservatives encountered in the investigation. The extremist zealot, the racist and the anti-democratic reactionary did turn up in the course of the inquiry, but what is most significant here is that these types were neither attracted to the underlying spirit of the campus conservative movement nor were they particularly welcome or influential in the conservative groups on their campuses. The same tendency is, however, equally true of the small number of truly creative and innovative young conservatives. By and large this side of youthful conservatism, which usually is manifested in a rampant individualism and a surprisingly high degree of psychological-mindedness, also was unsympathetic with the campus movement and largely unrecognized by it.[7]

The emphasis placed on the conventionally minded obedient rebel corresponds with the weakness of autonomous overt political action demonstrated both by the most active campus groups in the sample and by the participants at a national YAF convention attended by the author. Keynoting the style of the movement "in action" was a passive, though frequently enthusiastic, obedience to duly constituted leaders, strict hierarchical social organization and a general dependence on adult figures to provide both programs and direction. Self-initiated activity was rare and active participation in any setting by the "rank and file" was even rarer. One is reminded in this respect of the strange ambivalences of the movement's leading hero, Barry Goldwater. Goldwater's reluctance to take the initiative in the national conservative movement, his apparently genuine disavowals of personal ambition,

---

[7] For a detailed discussion of these "minor" characters in the movement, see Schiff (9, chap. 4).

his self-defeating political strategies—all speak to a largely unrecognized proclivity toward posturing rather than program that constitutes one important quality of the complex current conservative impulse in America.

REFERENCES

1. Adorno, T. W., et al., *The Authoritarian Personality*, New York: Harper, 1950.
2. Allport, G. W. "Inquiry concerning social and religious views," Unpublished questionnaire, Harvard University, 1963.
3. Bell, D. (Ed.) *The Radical Right*. Garden City: Doubleday, 1963.
4. Cain, E. *They'd Rather Be Right: Youth and the Conservative Movement*. New York: Macmillan, 1963.
5. Couch, A. "Personality Determinants of Interpersonal Behavior," Unpublished doctoral dissertation. Harvard University, 1960.
6. Erikson, E. H. "Wholeness and Totality;" in *Totalitarianism* (Friedrich, C. J. Ed.). Cambridge: Harvard University Press, 1953.
7. Evans, M. S. *Revolt on the Campus*. Chicago: Regnery, 1961.
8. Forster, A. and B. R. Epstein. *Danger on the Right*. Random House: New York, 1964.
9. Goldsen, R. K. et al., *What College Students Think*. Princeton: Van Nostrand, 1960.
10. James, W. *Varieties of Religious Experience*. New York: Longmans, Green, 1902.
11. Schiff, L. F. "The Conservative Movement on American College Campuses," Unpublished doctoral dissertation. Harvard University, 1964.

CAMPUS PROTEST:
AN INSIDE PERSPECTIVE*

JAMES SIMON KUNEN

Columbia used to be called King's College. They changed the name in 1784 because they wanted to be patriotic and *Columbia* means *America*. This week we've been finding out what America means.

Every morning now when I wake up I have to run through the whole thing in my mind. I have to do that because I wake up in a familiar place that isn't what it was. I wake up and I see blue coats and brass buttons all over the campus. ("Brass buttons, blue coat, can't catch a nanny goat" goes the Harlem nursery rhyme.) I start to go off the campus but then remember to turn and walk two blocks uptown to get to the only open gate. There I squeeze through the three-foot "out" opening in the police barricade, and I feel for my wallet to be sure I've got the two I.D.'s necessary to get back into my college. I stare at the cops. They stare back and see a red armband and long hair and they perhaps tap their night sticks on the barricade. They're looking at a radical leftist.

I wasn't always a radical leftist. Although not altogether straight, I'm not a hair person either, and ten days ago I was writing letters to Kokomo, Indiana, for Senator McCarthy; my principal association with the left was that I rowed port on crew. But then I got involved in this movement and one thing led to another. I am not a leader, you understand. But leaders cannot seize and occupy buildings. It takes great numbers of people to do that. I am one of those great numbers. What follows is the chronicle of a single revolutionary digit.

Monday, April 22: A mimeograph has appeared around the campus charging SDS with using coercion to gain its political ends. SDS is for free speech for itself only, it is charged. SDS physically threatens the administration. SDS breaks rules with impunity while we (undefined) are subject to dismissal for tossing a paper airplane out a dorm window. Aren't you TIRED, TIRED, TIRED of this? Will Mark Rudd be our next dean? Do something about it. Come to the SDS rally tomorrow and *be prepared*. At first anonymous, the leaflet reappears in a second edition signed Students for a Free Campus. The jocks have done it again. As with the demonstrations against Marine campus recruiting in the spring of '67, threats of violence from the right will bring hundreds of the usually moderate to the SDS ranks just to align themselves against jock vio-

* Reprinted from *The Strawberry Statement*, pp. 19–37, by James Simon Kunen. Copyright © 1968, 1969 by James Simon Kunen. Reprinted by permission of Random House, Inc., and the Sterling Lord Agency.

lence. I personally plan to be there, but I'm not up tight about it. At the boat house, a guy says he's for the jock position. Don't get me wrong, I say, I'm not against beating up on a few pukes, I just don't think you should stoop to their level by mineographing stuff. We both go out and kill ourselves trying to row a boat faster than eight students from MIT will be able to.

Tuesday, April 23: Noon. At the sundial are 500 people ready to follow Mark Rudd (whom they don't particularly like because he always refers to President Kirk as "that shithead") into the Low Library administration building to demand severance from IDA, an end to gym construction, and to defy Kirk's recent edict prohibiting indoor demonstrations. There are around 100 counter-demonstrators. They are what Trustee Arthur Ochs Sulzberger's newspaper refers to as "burly white youths" or "students of considerable athletic attainment"—jocks. Various deans and other father surrogates separate the two factions. Low Library is locked. For lack of a better place to go we head for the site of the gym in Morningside Park, chanting "Gym Crow must go." I do not chant because I don't like chanting.

I have been noncommittal to vaguely against the gym, but now I see the site for the first time. There is excavation cutting across the whole park. It's really ugly. And there's a chain link fence all around the hole. I don't like fences anyway so I am one of the first to jump on it and tear it down. Enter the New York Police Department. One of them grabs the fence gate and tries to shut it. Some demonstrators grab him. I yell "Let that cop go," partly because I feel sorry for the cop and partly because I know that the night sticks will start to flagellate on our heads, which they proceed to do. One of my friends goes down and I pull him out. He's on adrenaline now and tries to get back at the cops but I hold him, because I hit a cop at Whitehall and I wished I hadn't very shortly thereafter.[1] After the usual hassle, order is restored and the cops let Rudd mount a dirt pile to address us. As soon as he starts to talk he is drowned out by jackhammers but, at the request of the police, they are turned off. Rudd suggests we go back to the sundial and join with 300 demonstrators there, but we know that he couldn't possibly know whether there are 300 demonstrators there and we don't want to leave. He persists and we defer.

Back at the sundial there is a large crowd. It's clear we've got something going. An offer comes from Vice-President Truman to talk with us in McMillin Theatre but Rudd, after some indecision, refuses. It seems we have the initiative and Truman just wants to get us in some room and bullshit till we all go back to sleep. Someone suggests we go sit down for awhile in Hamilton, the main college classroom building, and we go there. Sitting down turns to sitting-in, although we do not block classes. Rudd asks, "Is this a demonstration?" "Yes!" we answer, all together. "Is it indoors?" "Yes!"

---

[1] *In October of 1967, there was a series of "Stop the Draft Week" demonstrations at Whitehall, the Army Induction Center for Manhattan. At about 6 A.M. on a Thursday morning a blue cossack rode his lumbering steed at me on the sidewalk. It was just too early in the morning to get run over by a horse. I slugged him (the cop) in the thigh, which was as high as I could reach, and was immediately brought to bay and apprehended by a detective, who smashed me in the knee with a movie camera, and later let me go when he deduced from my name that I was Irish, which I'm not.*

An immediate demand is the release of the one student arrested at the park, Mike Smith, who might as well be named John Everyman, because nobody knows him. To reciprocate for Mike's detention, Dean Coleman is detained.

At four o'clock, like Pavlov's dog, I go to crew, assuring a long-hair at the door that I'll be back. At practice it is pointed out to me that the crew does not have as many WASPS as it should have according to the population percentage of WASPS in the nation, so don't I think that crew should be shut down? I answer no, I don't think crew should be shut down.

Back at school at eight I prepared to spend the night at Hamilton. My friend Rock is there. We decide that we are absolutely bound to meet some girls or at least boys since there are 300 of them in the lobby. Every ten minutes he yells to me, "Hey, did you make any friends yet?" I say no each time, and he says that he hasn't either, but he's bound to soon.

I go upstairs to reconnoiter and there is none other than Peter Behr of Linda LeClair fame chalking on the wall, " 'Up against the wall, mother-fucker, . . .' from a poem by LeRoi Jones." I get some chalk and write "I am sorry about defacing the walls, but babies are being burned and men are dying, and this University is at fault quite directly." Also I draw some SANE symbols and then at 2:30 A.M. go to sleep.

Wednesday, April 24, 5:30 A.M. Someone just won't stop yelling that we've got to get up, that we're leaving, that the blacks occupying Hamilton with us have asked us to leave. I get up and leave. The column of evicted whites shuffles over to Low Library. A guy in front rams a wooden sign through the security office side doors and about 200 of us rush in. Another 150 hang around outside because the breaking glass was such a bad sound. They become the first "sundial people." Inside we rush up to Kirk's office and someone breaks the lock. I am not at all enthusiastic about this and suggest that perhaps we ought to break up all the Ming Dynasty art that's on display while we're at it. A kid turns on me and says in a really ugly way that the exit is right over there. I reply that I am staying, but that I am not a sheep and he is.

Rudd calls us all together. He looks very strained. He elicits promises from the *Spectator* reporters in the crowd not to report what he is about to say. Then he says that the blacks told us to leave Hamilton because they do not feel that we are willing to make the sacrifices they are willing to make. He says that they have carbines and grenades and that they're not leaving. I think that's really quite amazing.

We all go into Kirk's office and divide into three groups, one in each room. We expect the cops to come any moment. After an hour's discussion my room votes 29–16 to refuse to leave, to make the cops carry us out. The losing alternative is to escape through the windows and then go organize a strike. The feeling is that if we get busted, *then* there will be something to organize a strike about. The man chairing the discussion is standing on a small wooden table and I am very concerned lest he break it. We collect water in wastebaskets in case of tear gas. Some of it gets spilled and I spend my time trying to wipe it up. I don't want to leave somebody else's office all messy.

We check to see what other rooms have decided. One room is embroiled in a political discussion, and in the other everyone is busy playing with the office machines.

At about 8:30 A.M. we hear that the cops are coming. One hundred seventy-three people jump out the window. (I don't jump because I've been reading *Lord Jim*.) That leaves twenty-seven of us sitting on the floor, waiting to be arrested. In stroll an inspector and two cops. We link arms and grit our teeth. After about five minutes of gritting our teeth it dawns on us that the cops aren't doing anything. We relax a little and they tell us they have neither the desire nor the orders to arrest us. In answer to a question they say they haven't got MACE, either.

In through the window like Batman climbs Professor Orest Ranum, liberal, his academic robes billowing in the wind. We laugh at his appearance. He tells us that our action will precipitate a massive right-wing reaction in the faculty. He confides that the faculty had been nudging Kirk toward resignation, but now we've blown everything, the faculty will flock to support the President. We'll all be arrested, he says, and we'll all be expelled. He urges us to leave. We say no. One of us points out that Sorel said only violent action changes things. Ranum says that Sorel is dead. He gets on the phone to Truman and offers us trial by a tripartite committee if we'll leave. We discuss it and vote no. Enter Mark Rudd, through the window. He says that twenty-seven people can't exert any pressure, and the best thing we could do would be to leave and join a big sit-in in front of Hamilton. We say no, we're not leaving until our demands on the gym, IDA, and amnesty for demonstrators are met. Rudd goes out and comes back and asks us to leave again, and we say no again. He leaves to get reinforcements. Ranum leaves. Someone comes in to take pictures. We all cover our faces with different photographs of Grayson Kirk.

It's raining out, and the people who are climbing back in are marked by their wetness. Offered a towel by one of the new people, a girl pointedly says "No, thank you, I haven't been out." Rationally, we twenty-seven are glad that there are now 150 people in the office, but emotionally we resent them. As people dry out, the old and new become less easily differentiable, and I am trying for a field promotion in the movement so that I will not fade into the masses who jumped and might jump again.

The phone continues to ring and we inform the callers that we are sorry, but Dr. Kirk will not be in today because Columbia is under new management. After noon, all the phones are cut off by the administration.

At 3:45 I smoke my first cigarette in four months and wonder if Lenin smoked. I don't go to crew. I grab a typewriter and, though preoccupied by its electricness, manage to write:

> The time has come to pass the time.
> I am not having good times here. I do not know many people who are here, and I have doubts about why they are here. Worse, I have doubts about why I am here. (Note the frequency of the word *here*. The place I am is the salient characteristic of my situation.) It's possible that I'm here to be cool or to meet people or to meet girls (as distinct from people) or to get out of crew or to be arrested. Of course the possibility exists that I am here to precipitate some change at the Uni-

versity. I am willing to accept the latter as true or, rather, I am willing, even anxious, not to think about it any more. If you think too much on the second tier (think about why you are thinking what you think) you can be paraylzed.

I really made the conflicting-imperative scene today. I have never let down the crew before, I think. Let down seven guys. I am one-eighth of the crew. I am one-fiftieth of this demonstration. And I am not even sure that this demonstration is right. But I multiplied these figures by an absolute importance constant. I hate to hamper the hobby of my friends (and maybe screw, *probably* screw, my own future in it), I am sorry about that, but death is being done by this University and I would rather fight it than row a boat.

But then I may, they say, be causing a right-wing reaction and hurting the cause. Certainly it isn't conscionable to hold Dean Coleman captive. But attention is being gotten. Steps will be taken in one direction or another. The polls will fluctuate and the market quiver. Our being here is the cause of an effect. We're trying to make it good; I don't know what else to say or do. That is, I have no further statement to make at this time, gentlemen.

The news comes in that Avery Hall, the architecture school, has been liberated. We mark it as such on Grayson's map. At about 8 p.m. we break back into Kirk's inner office, which had been relocked by security when we gathered into one room when the cops came in the morning. The $450,000 Rembrandt and the TV have gone with the cops.

We explore. The temptation to loot is tremendous, middle-class morality notwithstanding, but there is no looting. I am particularly attracted by a framed diploma from American Airlines declaring Grayson Kirk a V.I.P., but I restrict myself to a few Grayson Kirk introduction cards. Someone finds a book on masochism behind a book on government. Someone else finds what he claims is Grayson's draft card and preparations are made to mail it back to the Selective Service. On his desk is an American Airlines jigsaw puzzle which has apparently been much played with.

We have a meeting to discuss politics and defense, but I sit at the door as a guard. A campus guard appears and, before I can do anything, surprises me by saying, "As long as you think you're right, fuck 'em." He hopes something good for him might come out of the whole thing. He makes eighty-six dollars a week after twenty years at the job.

I go down to the basement of Low, where the New York City Police have set up shop. There are approximately forty of them; there is precisely one of me. I ask one for the score of the Red Sox game. He seems stunned that a hippie faggot could be interested in such things, but he looks it up for me. Rained out.

I use the pay phone to call a girl at Sarah Lawrence. I tell her how isolated I feel and how lonely I am and hungry and tired and she says oh. I explain that I'll be busted any minute and she says she knows that.

I return upstairs. One of these people who knows how to do things has reconnected a phone, but he needs someone to hold the two wires together while he talks. I do it. I'll do anything to feel like I'm doing something.

Thursday, April 25: I get up and shave with Grayson Kirk's razor, use his toothpaste, splash on his after-shave, grooving on it all. I need something morale-building like this, because my revolutionary fervor takes about half an hour longer than the rest of me to wake up.

Someone asks if anyone knows how to fix a Xerox 3000, and I say yes, lying through my teeth. Another man and I proceed to take it apart and put it back together. To test it I draw a pierced heart with "Mother" in the middle and feed it to the machine. The machine gives back three of the same. Much rejoicing. Now we can get to work on Kirk's files. My favorite documents are a gym letter which ends with the sentence "Bring on the bulldozers!" and a note to a Columbia representative to the land negotiations telling him to be careful *not* to mention to Parks Commissioner Hoving that the date for digging has been moved up. ("We don't want him to know that we decided on this over a year ago," the note explains.)

Since a bust does not seem imminent, I climb out the window and go to crew at four. I talk to the coach and we agree that I will sleep in Low but will show up for the bus to Cambridge the next morning if I'm not in jail.

When I get back from crew I have to run a police cordon and leap for the second-story ledge. A cop, much to my surprise, bothers to grab me and tries to pull me down, but some people inside grab me and pull me up.

A meeting is going on discussing defense. J.J. wants to pile art treasures on the windows so the cops will have to break them to get in. I'm for that. But he also wants to take poles and push cops off the ledge. When this is criticized he tries to make it clear that it will be done in a nonviolent way. A friend whispers to me that J.J. is SDS's answer to the jock. A guy in a red crash helmet begins to say that maybe we won't fight because we're not as manly as the blacks, but it is well known that he is loony as hell and he is shouted down in a rare violation of the democratic process. After two hours' debate it is decided to man the barricades until they start to fall, then gather in groups with locked arms and resist passively. A motion to take off all our clothes when the police arrive is passed, with most girls abstaining.

I get back to the Xerox and copy seventy-three documents, including clippings from *The New York Times*. I hear over the radio that Charles 37X Kenyatta and the Mau Maus are on campus. This does not surprise me.

J.J. is recruiting volunteers to liberate another building. He has thirty, male and female, and at 2 A.M. he's ready to move. I go out on the ledge to check for cops. There are only three, so we climb down and sprint to Mathematics Hall. There we are joined by twenty radicals who could no longer stand the Establishment-liberal atmosphere of the previously liberated Fayerweather Hall. We get inside and immediately pile up about 2000 pounds of furniture at the front door. Only then do we discover two housekeepers still in the building. They are quite scared but only say "Why didn't you tell us you were coming?" and laugh. We help them out a window and along a ledge with the aid of the just-arrived-press movie lights.

We hold the standard two-hour meeting to decide how to deal with the cops, whom we understand to be on their way. The meeting is chaired by Tom Hayden, who is an Outside Agitator. Reverend Starr, the Protestant counselor, tells us the best positions for firehoses and so on. Dean Alexander

B. Platt is allowed in through the window. He looks completely dead. We consider capturing him, but no one has the energy, so we let him go after thanking him for coming. Professor Allen Westin, liberal, comes and offers us a tripartite committee which he has no authority to constitute and which we don't want. He is thanked and escorted to the window.

At 6 A.M. I go to sleep.

Friday, April 26: I wake up at 8:55 and run to the crew bus and leave for MIT. From Cambridge I call my home in Marlboro. My mother asks me, "Are you on the side of the law-breakers in this thing?" For ten minutes we exchange mother talk and revolutionary rhetoric. She points out that neither Gandhi nor Thoreau would have asked for amnesty. I admit I haven't read them. But Gandhi had no Gandhi to read and Thoreau hadn't read Thoreau. They had to reach their own conclusions and so will I.

Saturday, April 27: I row a boat race and split. That wraps up the crew season —for me. On the MTA to Logan Airport a middle-aged man starts winking and smiling and gesticulating at my right lapel. Looking down, I see that I am wearing a broken rifle pin, symbol of the War Resisters' League. I tell him that it so happens I am on my way back to Columbia right now to carry on a Revolution. He thinks that's fine.

I get back to Math around 4:30 and sit down on the public-relations ledge over Broadway. People from a peace demonstration downtown are depositing money and food in a bucket at the bottom of a rope. Each time we haul it up and re-lower it we include I.D.'s for people who want to get into the campus. A remarkable number of cars toot their support, and when a bus driver pulls over to wave us a victory sign, ten people nearly fall off the ledge.

In the evening I discover that the electricity to the kitchen is cut off. I run downstairs and almost call for "someone important" but somehow I am unwilling to accept that kind of status relation. I tell several of my peers and one of them finds the fuse box and sets things right.

I volunteer for shopping. We buy twenty dollars of food for eighteen dollars (the merchants earlier had contributed food outright) and on the way back meet a gentleman who seems to belong to Drunken Faculty to Forget the Whole Mess. Someone whom I think of as a friend threatens to punch me because I am carrying food.

As the evening wears on I feel less useful and more alienated, so I assign myself the task of keeping the mayonnaise covered. After covering it twelve times I give up and decide to write home. I wonder whether the Paris Commune was this boring.

In the letter I try to justify rebelling on my father's money. I point out that one of the dangers of going to college is that you learn things, and that my present actions are much influenced by my Contemporary Civilization (C1001y) readings. After sealing the letter I realize that my conception of the philosophy of law comes not so much from Rousseau as from Fess Parker as Davy Crockett. I remember his saying that you should decide what you think is right and then go ahead and do it. Walt Disney really bagged that one; the old fascist inadvertently created a whole generation of radicals.

I discover a phone which has not been cut off and call my brother. As I am talking someone puts a piece of paper beside me and writes "This . . . phone . . . is . . . tapped." I address myself briefly to the third party and go on talking. It feels good to talk to someone on the outside, although it is disappointing to find out that the outside world is going on as usual.

Sunday, April 28: Four hours of meetings about tactical matters, politics, and reports from Strike Central. I begin to long for a benevolent dictator. It is announced that we are spending as much money on cigarettes as food. I wonder, as I look about me, whether Lenin was as concerned with the breast size of his revolutionary cohorts as I am. It is now daylight-saving time; under all the clocks are signs saying "It's later than you think."

I spend the day sunning and reading *Lord Jim* on the ledge. At 3 P.M. four fire trucks scream up and men go running onto the campus with axes. Some people think this is the bust, but it seems like the wrong public agency to me. It turns out to be a false alarm.

The neighborhood little kids are anxious and able to squeeze through the fences. I talk to some of them and they are all conversant with the issues and on our side. I conduct an informal class in peace graffiti and distribute chalk.

The older brothers of these same kids are in the middle of Broadway throwing eggs at us. This action—one of them tells me later—is completely apolitical.

We have red flags flying from the roof. I explain to a cop on the sidewalk below that these stand for revolution, not for communism. He says yes, he remembers reading something about that. I hope he is not referring to the *Daily News*. The *News* charges us with vandalism and alcoholism. (Actually we voted to bar both grass and liquor, and there was only one dissident, named Melvin.) One cartoon, titled "Dancing to the Red Tune," shows a beatnik and some sort of cave girl dancing as a band sings "Louse up the campuses, yeah, yeah, yeah."

In the evening I walk into a room where there is a poetry reading. I don't want to be rude so I stay. A med student who looks like Dr. Kildare reads a poem entitled "Ode to Mickey Mantle's Five-hundredth HR."

Mutiny on the Bounty (Gable) is on TV and I find it inspirational, or at least amusing.

The student radio station, WKCR, announces that a clergyman is wanted in Fayerweather; a couple wants to get married. This does not surprise me. Reverend Starr performs the ceremony and says, "I pronounce you children of the new age." Shortly after we hear it, we see a candlelight procession approaching. The bride is carrying roses. She hands them to me and I pass them inside. The demonstration peaks for me as I touch the roses—I am stoned on revolutionary zeal. The newlyweds call themselves Mr. and Mrs. Fayerweather.

I volunteer for jock-watch from 2:00 to 3:00 but do not wake up the next man and stay out on the entrance window ledge until five. I am to let no one in as we now have a population of 150 and we want a stable commune—no tourists. We even consider a Stalinist purge to reduce the mouths to feed. Only tonight does my roommate decide to occupy a building. I have about seven degrees of disdain and contempt for him, but he got in before my watch. I stamp "Rush" on the hand of anyone who leaves. This allows them to get back in.

During my watch five guys in black cowls come by dragging a coffin and murmuring in Latin.

Monday, April 29: The Majority Coalition (read: jocks) have cordoned off Low and are trying to starve the demonstrators out. We decide to break the blockade. We plan tactics on a blackboard and go, shaking hands with those staying behind as though we might not be back. There are thirty of us with three cartons of food. We march around Low, making our presence known. Spontaneously, and at the wrong tactical place, the blacks in front jump into the jock line. I go charging through the gap with my box of grapefruit and quickly fall upon the ground or, more accurately, on top of two layers of people and beneath two. I manage to throw three grapefruit, two of which make it. Then I come back to where I started. Some blood is visible on both sides. Back at Math, some of our people say that the jocks they were fighting had handcuffs on their belts. Band-Aided noses abound and are a mark of distinction. We discuss alternative plans for feeding Low and someone suggests blockading the jocks—"If they run out of beer they're through." In the meantime, we can see hundreds of green armbands (for amnesty) throwing food up to the Low windows. We decide on a rope-and-pulley system between a tree and the Low windows, but there is some question about how to get the line up to the people in Low without the jocks grabbing it. When one kid suggests tying an end to a broom handle and throwing it like a harpoon, John (Outside Agitator) suggests we train a bird. A helicopter has already been looked into by Strike Central, but the FAA won't allow it. Finally we agree on shooting in a leader line with a bow and arrow.

A girl and myself are dispatched to get a bow. We go to the roof of the Barnard Library where the phys. ed. archery range is. We are in the midst of discovering how incredibly locked the cabinet is when a guard comes out on the roof. We crouch. He walks right past us. It would be just like TV were I not so preoccupied with it being just like TV. After ten minutes he finds us. The girl laughs coyly and alleges that oh, we just came up to spend the night. I am rather taken with the idea, but the guard is unmoved and demands our I.D.'s. This is our first bust.

Our second bust, the real one, begins to take shape at 2:30 A.M. We hear over WBAI that there are busloads of TPF (Tactical Police Force, Gestapo) at 156th and 125th and that patrol cars are arriving from all precincts with four helmeted cops per auto. I am unimpressed. So many times now we've been going to be busted. It just doesn't touch me anymore. I assume that the cops are there to keep the Mau Maus out.

A girl comes up to me with some paper towels. Take these, she says, so you can wipe the vaseline (slows tear-gas penetration) off your face when you're in jail. I haven't got vaseline on my face. I am thinking that vaseline is a big petroleum interest, probably makes napalm, and anyway it's too greasy. I hear over the walky-talky that Hamilton has been busted and that the sundial people are moving to Low and Fayerweather to obstruct the police. I put vaseline on my face. I also put vaseline on my hands and arms and legs above the socks and a cigarette filter in each nostril and carefully refold my plastic-bag gas mask so I'll be able to put it on quickly with the holes at the back of my head so my hair will absorb the gas and I'll be able to breathe long enough to cool the cannister with a CO_2 fire extinguisher and pick it up with my asbestos gloves and throw it back at the cops. Someone tells me that he can't get busted or he'll miss his shrink again.

I take my place with seven others at the front barricade. All along the stairs our people are lined up, ready to hole up in the many lockable-from-within rooms on the three floors above me. We sing "We Shall Not Be Moved" and realize that something is ending. The cops arrive. The officer bullhorns us: "On behalf of the Trustees of Columbia University and with the authority vested in me . . . ." That's as far as he is able to get, as we answer his question and all others with out commune motto—"Up against the wall, motherfuckers." We can't hold the barricade because the doors open out and the cops simply pull the stuff out. They have to cut through ropes and hoses and it takes them fifteen minutes before they can come through. All the while they're not more than thirty feet from me, but all I can do is watch their green-helmeted heads working. I shine a light in their eyes but Tom tells me not to and he's head of the defense committee so I stop.

At 4:00 A.M. the cops come in. The eight of us sit down on the stairs (which we've made slippery with green soap and water) and lock arms. The big cop says "Don't make it hard for us or you're gonna get hurt." We do not move. We want to make it clear that the police have to step over more than chairs to get our people out. They pull us apart and carry us out, stacking us like cord wood under a tree. The press is here so we are not beaten. As I sit under the tree I can see kids looking down at us from every window in the building. We exchange the "V" sign. The police will have to ax every door to get them out of those offices. They do. Tom Hayden is out now. He yells "Keep the radio on! Peking will instruct you!" When they have sixty of us out they take us to the paddy wagons at mid-campus. I want to make them carry us, but the consensus is that it's a long, dark walk and we'll be killed if we don't cooperate, so I walk. At the paddy wagons there are at least a thousand people cheering us and chanting "Strike! Strike! Strike!" We are loaded in a wagon and the doors shut. John tells a story about how a cop grabbed the cop that grabbed him and then said "Excuse me." We all laugh raucously to show an indomitable spirit and freak out the cops outside.

We are taken to the 24th precinct to be booked. "Up against the wall," we are told. I can't get over how they really do use the term. We turn and lean on the wall with our hands high, because that's what we've seen in the movies. We are told to can that shit and sit down. Booking takes two hours. Lieutenant Dave Bender is the plainclothesman in charge. He seems sternly unhappy that college turns out people like us. He asks John if he thinks he could be a policeman and John says no; he doesn't think he's cut out for it.

We are allowed three calls each. A fat officer makes them for us and he is a really funny and good man. He is only mildly displeased when he is duped into calling Dial-a-Demonstration. He expresses interest in meeting a girl named Janice when three of us give him her number, one as his sister, one as his girl friend, and one as his ex-wife.

We go downstairs to await transportation to court. A TPF man comes in escorting Angus Davis, who was on the sixth floor of Math and refused to walk down. He has been dragged down four flights of marble stairs and kicked and clubbed all the way. A two-inch square patch on his hair has been pulled out. Ben, Outside Agitator, yells, "You're pretty brave when you've got that club." The officer comes over and dares him to say that again. He says it again. The cop kicks for Ben's groin, but Ben knows karate and blocks it. John says to the cop, "Thank you, you have just proved Ben's point." This is sufficiently subtle not to further arouse the cop, and he leaves. A caged bus takes us all the way downtown to the tombs (the courthouse). The kid beside me keeps asking me what bridge is this and what building is that. Finally he recognizes something and declares that we are going to pass his grandmother's house. I am busy trying to work a cigarette butt through the window grate so that I can litter from a police bus. Arriving, we drive right into the building; a garage door clamps down behind us.

Our combs and keys are confiscated so that we won't be able to commit suicide. In the elevator to the cells a white cop tells us we look like a fine bunch of men—we ought to be put on the front lines in Vietnam. Someone says that Vietnam is here, now. As we get out I look at the black cop running the elevator for some sort of reaction. He says "Keep the faith."

He said "Keep the faith," I say, and everyone is pleased. We walk by five empty cells and then are jammed into one, thirty-four of us in a 12×15 room. We haven't slept in twenty-four hours and there isn't even space for all of us to sit down at one time.

Some of our cellmates are from Avery. They tell us how they were handcuffed and dragged downstairs on their stomachs. Their shirts are bloody.

After a couple of hours we start to perk up. We bang and shout until a guard comes, and then tell him that the door seems to be stuck. Someone screams "All right, all right, I'll talk." It is pointed out that you don't need tickets to get to policemen's balls. We sing folk songs and "The Star-Spangled Banner." They allowed one of us to bring in a recorder and he plays Israeli folk music.

A court officer comes and calls a name. "He left," we say. Finally he finds the right list.

We are arraigned before a judge. The Outsiders are afraid they will be held for bail, but they are released on their own recognizance, like the rest of us, except they have some form of loitering charge tacked on the standard second-degree criminal trespassing.

Back at school I eat in a restaurant full of police. As audibly as possible I compose a poem entitled "Ode to the TPF." It extolls the beauty of rich wood billies, the sheen of handcuffs, the feel of a boot on your face.

Meeting a cellmate, I extend my hand to him and he slaps it. I have to remember that—handslaps, not shakes, in the Revolution.

Tom Hayden is in Chicago now. As an Outside Agitator, he has a lot of outsides to agitate in. Like the Lone Ranger, he didn't even wave good-bye, but quietly slipped away, taking his silver protest buttons to another beleaguered campus.

Everyone is organizing now—moderates, independent radicals, Liberated

Artists, librarians. And the Yippies are trying to sue the University for evicting us from our homes which we owned by virtue of squatters' rights. You can hardly move for the leaflets here. Except at Barnard. The Barnard girls are typing their papers and getting ready to go to Yale for the weekend.

We are on strike, of course. There are "liberation classes" but the scene is essentially no more pencils, no more books.

I saw a cellist math major in Chock Full O' Nuts looking alone. Liberation classes won't help him. He is screwed. Every Revolution leaves a trail of screwed drifting in its wake.

The campus is still locked, although I think you could get in with a Raleigh coupon as an I.D. today. That's our latest issue; a liberated campus should be open. We want free access by June so we can open the summer school under our own aegis.

A particularly thick swatch of air pollution drifted by today and a lot of people thought the gym site was burning. That did not surprise me. Nothing surprises me any more.

CHAPTER 7

Youth
and Organized
Religion

To facilitate exploration of the religious attitudes of American youth, we must provide some background on the nature of religion in American culture. The covert philosophy of secularism which dominates American life and thought is so pervasive that it affects thinking about religion as well as thinking about other matters in life. American religion is said to be closely interrelated with the development of American society to the point that an understanding of one is essential to an understanding of the other.[1] We are said to be a contemporary paradox—at once a most religious and a most secular of nations. For Americans are active in establishing church memberships, in patterned participation, and in building new churches. But religious thought seems to have lost some of its authentic Christian or Jewish content as it has been moderated by the national democratic life-style which marks Americans.

As religious groups have "lost authenticity" they have become more ecumenical. According to Talcott Parsons, we have "moved from largely negative toleration of non-Protestants to their inclusion in a denominationally pluralistic community, the pluralism of which comprises all the most important religious groups of Western history."[2] The nature of this pluralism is expanded to mean not only the toleration of other religious groups than one's own, but the acceptance that other groups have a *moral right* to flourish. This development in the American religious area has been closely linked to the ecumenical movement in the whole Christian world, coinciding with the election and mourning of John F. Kennedy and the brief leadership of Pope John XXIII.

We have thus far characterized American religious behavior as influenced by secularism and by ecumenism. It is also influenced by tendencies toward privatism. We have "privatised" religious affiliation by law

---

[1] Will Herberg, *Protestant, Catholic, Jew*, Garden City, N. Y.: Anchor Books, Doubleday and Company, Inc., 1960, Chap. I.
[2] Talcott Parsons, "The Nature of American Pluralism," in Theodore R. Sizer (ed.), *Religion and Public Education*, Boston: Houghton Mifflin Company, 1967, p. 250.

and in practice. Whether one wishes to join a religious group is voluntary. And furthermore, we have established in the law an individual's right of choice in religious matters. Religious behavior is not ascriptively determined although it is conditioned or influenced by family background. Thus it is likely or predictable that one born of Catholic, or Jewish, or Protestant parents will worship as Catholic, Jew, or Protestant when adult, but there is no compulsion of a lawful sort to do so.

America was not always so religiously pluralistic as described in the preceding paragraphs. It was necessary to adopt the First Amendment to the United States Constitution to insure that the Federal Government could not violate religious freedom and could not establish a national religion. Whatever the intent of those who framed the First Amendment, it functioned to prohibit sectarian instruction in the public schools. In the 1960s, the United States Supreme Court came to terms with religion and the Constitution and decided that Bible reading and prayers in public schools were illegal. The school prayer issue is not dead for the question continues to animate citizens. (When the crew of Frank Borman in Apollo VIII circumnavigated the moon and read portions of the book of Genesis at Christmas in 1968, they were stoutly defended by many thousands of Americans who judged that act beautiful and appropriate.) Schools have not been enjoined to suppress the cultural understanding of religion, but public criticism ignores the delicate difference between religious indoctrination and teaching about religions objectively.

This brief exposition of social history is necessary to an understanding of the context in which American young people are socialized toward religious beliefs, concerns, interests, and values. It is difficult to locate materials written from a sociological perspective on the subject of youth and religion, hence we have included only two selections for presentation. One examines high school populations; the other is concerned with the effects on religious participation of the transition into college. In the first selection Bealer and Willits have surveyed the empirical literature based on adolescent religious interests. They have organized the ways in which a person can be religious according to certain dimensions: ritualistic, experiential, ideological, intellectual, and consequential. As to how religious American high school youth are, the answer is that they, like adults, take a "hedging stance." There is tremendous diversity in religious interests on the continuum of no religiosity to deep religiosity.

The second selection by Hadden and Evans is specifically concerned with the extent of religious participation of college freshmen and the correlates of this participation pattern which may be found in the educational levels and participation frequencies of parents. The findings are suggestive but not conclusive, and many important questions linking the transitional experience of college and adolescent autonomy from the family to religious behavior are raised for the reader's serious consideration.

Having turned to the religious orientations of college youth, we find an abundance of research literature on the religious change and stability of undergraduate students. From this literature, some tentative general conclusions may be drawn relative to the importance of religious values among freshmen and senior populations: (1) scores of religious values scales decrease toward the senior year; (2) there is a tendency toward less orthodoxy and fundamentalism in the beliefs of seniors; (3) church attendance is reportedly lower among seniors; and (4) upperclassmen are less moralistic, more liberal, and more flexible than freshmen.[3]

While one might assume that such changes are attributable to the college experience *per se*, it may be that analogous influences operate on non-college populations. Little research bears on this important question of causality though available data hint of a "facilitative effect" of colleges toward attitudinal change. For general education at the university level has become greatly rationalized or secularized. The graduate programs which are at the apex of the American university system concentrate on secular intellectual disciplines. The modern university's structure is incompatible with higher education's remaining under denominational auspices. College after college has faced the compulsory chapel issue and has removed itself further from denominational control. The grand system of Catholic universities is tending to invite and accept students and faculty of non-Catholic origins.

Not everyone evaluates the secularizing of the universities in a positive fashion. In the words of philosopher-writer Michael Novak, the objectivity or, more strongly, the agnosticism of the classroom encourages a blandly tolerant style among students—stay close to the facts, don't offend, avoid a personal commitment.[4] His observation is that the secularization of everything moves students away from the personal confrontation and growth which are as much a part of the process of education as the transfer of information from faculty minds to student notebooks. Is the university dehumanized by our rejection of a religious orientation? Or are we hindering the search for truth with a universally applied objective scholarship model in all fields? Is this objectivity productive of the facilitation of attitudinal change toward religious matters?

[3] Kenneth A. Feldman, "Change and Stability of Religious Orientations During College," Part I, *Review of Religious Research*, XI (Fall 1969), pp. 40–60.
[4] Michael Novak, "God in the Colleges: The Dehumanization of the University," *Harpers*, CCXXXIII (October 1961), pp. 173–178.

THE RELIGIOUS INTERESTS OF AMERICAN
HIGH SCHOOL YOUTH*

ROBERT C. BEALER
FERN K. WILLITS[1]

Introduction

Knowledge of one's clientele is a prerequisite to any effective action program. Without adequate information about the interests, attitudes, and related social dimensions of an intended audience, even the best conceived programs can fail. Today's young people are the target of many efforts in religious education. Nonetheless, very little organized information about adolescent religious interests is available to people concerned with reaching our youth. Another writer has noted in this regard that:

> With each year we know more about when the adolescent enters cliques, whom he admires among his peers, what affects his performance in school, which occupations he aspires to, why he becomes delinquent . . . to name just a few areas in which research has been undertaken. But what he thinks about his religion and the degree to which he observes its rules, and why, is possibly one of the least researched areas in contemporary American life (28, p. 2).

But this does not mean that the research record is completely bare.[2] Some few studies have been done. Their conclusions, unfortunately, are neither systematic nor unitary. It is the task of this paper to try and bring some order

* Reprinted from Robert C. Bealer and Fern K. Willits, "The Religious Interests of American High School Youth," in *Religious Education*, Vol. 62 (September–October 1967), pp. 435–464, by permission of the publisher, The Religious Education Association, New York City.

[1] The authors wish to acknowledge the aid of Orville E. Lanham in helping compile the research information on which this paper is based. The paper was prepared for a conference on "Religion in the Public Domain" sponsored by the Penn State University Department of Religious Studies and held at University Park, Pennsylvania, May 1–3, 1966.

[2] Because the paper is concerned with summarizing the scientific evidence regarding the religious interests of adolescents, we have excluded from consideration the large number of tracts which have commented on the presumed state of affairs or presented simply the author's intuitions or personal perceptions of the religious scene. We have also limited our attention to those studies which have been conducted in the last decade or so, feeling that the fervor and possible flux of recent activity in American religious institutions casts doubt on the current descriptive relevancy of studies conducted prior to the early 1950's. Furthermore, as sociologists, we have tended to most thoroughly explore the sociological literature, although we have not confined our efforts here. Even so, significant omissions may have occurred.

to the diversity of ideas that have been addressed and, hopefully, to draw some tentative conclusions regarding the religious concerns and interests of American high school youth.[3]

In addressing the relevant research, we need, first of all, to establish what we mean by religiousness and delineate the different ways in which individuals *can* be religious. It is not a startling matter to note that there are different aspects to religious orientations. Yet past research, in general, has curiously avoided this recognition.

One noteworthy exception is the conceptualization of religious commitment offered by Charles Glock and Rodney Stark in their recent book *Religion and Society in Tension*. They distinguish the following five dimensions of religion:

1. The *ritualistic dimension* encompasses the specifically religious practices expected of religious adherents. It comprises such activities as worship, prayer, participation in special sacraments, fasting, and the like.
2. The *experiential dimension* gives recognition to the fact that all religions have certain expectations, however imprecisely they may be stated, that the religious person will at one time or another [and in one way or another] achieve direct knowledge of ultimate reality or will experience religious emotion. . . . Every religion places some value on subjective religious experience as a sign of individual religiosity.
3. The *ideological dimension* is constituted . . . by expectations that the religious person will hold to certain beliefs. The content and scope of beliefs will vary not only between religions but often within the same religious tradition. However, every religion sets forth some set of beliefs to which its followers are expected to adhere.
4. The *intellectual dimension* has to do with the expectation that the religious person will be informed and knowledgeable about the basic tenets of his faith and its sacred scriptures.
5. The *consequential dimension* . . . encompasses the secular effects of religious belief, experience, and knowledge on the individual (14, pp. 20–21, *passim*).

Glock and Stark suggest that persons who are highly religious in regard to one dimension are not necessarily equally religious in regard to the other aspects and any consideration of the nature of religious commitment needs to consider each of the various dimensions.[4] In addressing the question of the religiousness of youth this paper uses the Glock and Stark conceptualization as a framework for organizing some of the research materials that have been reported.

[3] We have excluded research studies of college students because it is quite clear that such persons are a rather select element and probably not representative of the more general population of adolescents. The exclusion is, of course, not made without cost. College students are an extremely well researched grouping in our society. As captive, readily cooperative respondents, they are the subjects of a large part of the research literature. And, what is true for social science inquiry generally is no less so for studies of religion (see particularly, 37).

[4] For systematic research supporting this suggestion see (7, 17). These studies did not, however, use adolescent subjects.

I. The Ritualistic Dimension

Undoubtedly the most studied facet of adolescent religious behavior is religious practice—what Glock and Stark have termed the *ritualistic* dimension. In a sample of approximately 1300 high school students surveyed in 1961 by George Gallup, more than 85% indicated that they were members of a church or temple, and more than 60% of the boys and almost ¾ of the girls indicated that they attended religious services "regularly" (10). Information derived from the Purdue University Opinion Polls in 1957 and 1962 is more precise concerning the frequency of attendance. In both time periods, almost 70% of the youngsters indicated that they attended religious services once a week or oftener. In fact, ¼ reported that they attended *more* than once a week. Catholics were most likely to attend once a week or oftener, with more than 80% of the youth reporting in this way compared with slightly less than 70% of the Protestants and fewer than 40% of the Jews (24, 25).

In addition, more than half of the respondents indicated that they prayed one or more times a day. Only 20% said that they never or only occasionally prayed (25, p. 174). These figures are about the same as those found in national samples of Lutheran youth (35) and Presbyterian adolescents (39). As with church attendance, girls were more "religious" in regard to frequency of prayer than were boys.

Over-all, if we consider the question of religious commitment only in terms of frequency of participation in or attendance of ritualistic services, we must conclude that American youth are not irreligious. However, this dimension focuses "on what people do rather than on the meaning of the activity to them" (14, p. 28). This information is of limited utility for in itself it says nothing about the *reasons* for participation.[5] Some adolescents go to church for "non-religious" reasons. They may go out of a secular deference to or an identification with either parents' or peers' wishes, or for a number of other reasons taken singly or in combination.[6]

The notion that attendance at religious services is not always identical

[5] Even with the limited data so far collected, most published studies *could* provide more insight into the meaning of ritual behavior than they have so far done by using only slightly altered analysis techniques. That is, if one has answers to how often a young person prays and data also on whether or not he feels that his prayers have been answered—as for example in the Purdue studies—the answer to the second question could be used to see whether rates of prayers being perceived as harkened is related, at least, to the rate of praying. In this limited way, the possible meaning of ritual behavior could be extended. Incidentally, we should point out that, while extant studies could give us more insights along this line, one cannot make such comparisons from the published data. One would need access to the distributions upon which the published tables are based in order to make the necessary cross-tabulations.

[6] Rosen's study (28) found all of these factors operating. His study is the rare exception in that he has tried to get at the motives involved in religious practices. However, there are sufficient belief and faith differences between the Christian majority and the Jewish minority to suggest that it would be hazardous to try and generalize Rosen's findings to Catholics and Protestants. Nonetheless, note particularly pp. 73–80; 92–104; 125–137; 152–160.

with other facets of religious orientation is to emphasize the need to look beyond the "ritualistic." Unfortunately, the other dimensions have not been as extensively assessed by research studies. However, some questions bearing on most of the dimensions have been utilized in various investigations, and it is from these items that we can hopefully gain some additional insights into the religiousness of youth.

II. The Experiential Dimension

The experiential variable refers to "religious feeling" or the experiencing of religious emotion. At least two types of such religious experiences can be differentiated: (1) simple concern, a seeking after a purpose in life or a wish to believe in a transcendentally based ideology; and (2) a subjective awareness of a divine presence and "interpersonal" encounters with God.

1. CONCERN

The degree to which youth are subjectively concerned about religion and the transcendental is unclear. One of the Purdue studies asked their respondents whether they "would like to know more about religion." If we can assume that one cares to have more knowledge about a phenomenon only if there is at least some interest in it, their responses are revealing. Youth gave an overwhelming "yes" reply to the question. Over-all, 89% of the young people responded in this way and the figure was approximately the same regardless of the person's age, sex, place of residence, family income, region of the country or degree of parental education. The only exception to the extremely high "yes" response rate was for Jewish children where only 68% answered affirmatively (25, p. 168). This may reflect the fact that the question taps an intellectual as well as an experiential aspect and that, with the traditional tendency of Jewish children to be schooled in their cultural and religious heritage, these respondents were merely saying that they were already knowledgeable and felt less of a need for further information. The same confounding of personal religious concern and simple interest in obtaining more knowledge may be present in the answers of other respondents and this probably results in an *overstatement* of the level of concern of the average adolescent.

A somewhat different means of assessing concern was utilized in a national poll conducted by Elmo Roper. A sample of adolescents and young adults was asked: "Try to think back to a couple of years ago. What was your most important problem or thing you were most worried about then—the thing that bothered you most *then*, whether you'd call it important or unimportant today?" The same question was repeated to get at "the most important problem or thing worried about *now*" and, again, as "what in the *next* couple of years ahead" would be a worry. The responses centered largely on education, job aspirations, sex, and interpersonal relationships generally. Concern over religious matters was evidenced by only 1% or 2% of the respondents (27, p. 145). This figure, however, may considerably *underestimate* the level of concern because the question appeared at the very end of the interview following a battery of items specifically eliciting the respondent's information and worry about education, jobs, social relationships, and sex.

Some insight into the apparently conflicting findings regarding the level of youthful "concern" over religion can perhaps be gained by turning to several other empirical studies. Unfortunately, none of these utilized representative cross-sectional samples of American adolescents. Consequently, the data cannot be directly generalized to the total teenage population. However, the findings may be at least suggestive.

A nationwide sample of nearly 3,000 Lutheran adolescents was asked to indicate their level of concern over 240 different "problem items." Factor analysis reduced the 240 items to seven families or areas of highly intercorrelated concern items. Here religious matters, called in the study "personal faith," clearly emerged as a topic of youth's interest. Sixty-six per cent of the sample marked items of personal faith as being at least to some degree "disturbing." Like the Roper study, interpersonal relations, sex, and education were found to be significant areas of concern (35, pp. 90–93).

It is also instructive to note the kinds of items in the Lutheran "personal faith" measure. The most prominent one was the register of "much" or "quite a bit" of worry over an inability to "find a deep faith in God." Fully 60% of the Lutheran youth expressed this response; 24% expressed "some" concern. Only 16% registered no misgivings about their orientation. Similarly, 86% of the youngsters had "much" or "some" concern over their feelings that they were not living up to their professed Christian convictions; 14% were unconcerned over this matter (35, p. 328). Furthermore, when those youth who participated most in the ritualistic aspects of religion were compared with those who participated least, more than half of *both* groupings indicated that they desired help regarding matters of personal faith (35, p. 193).

Another study, using a national (but again probably non-representative) sample of pre-adolescents and adolescents found that, in response to a request to indicate things about which they "wondered," there was considerable interest expressed in religious items. Over half of the sample "wondered" about religion, and this form of wonder increased as the youngsters grew older. Furthermore, the wondering about matters classed as "religion and philosophy" shared the number one rank with items classed as "science and technology" (9).

In yet another study, this one utilizing high school students in Lexington, Kentucky, religious values, as measured by the Allport, Vernon, and Lindzey scale ranked first with all the respondents. This was true irrespective of sex, race, and whether or not the person was college bound or noncollege oriented in plans (18, p. 39).

If we can generalize from these studies, it appears that, while American adolescents may see other problem areas as more pressing or crucial, they are not religiously unconcerned. While we do not have the data to precisely gauge this aspect of the experiential dimension, and while it may not be uniform for all types of adolescents, it does seem safe to assert a level of religious concern clearly above that which one might garner from the more popular notions that teenage interests are somehow limited to cars; pizza, pimples, and personality; or sex, sports, songs, and school (4, 15, 31, 33, 36).

2. FAITH

Thus, American adolescents appear to have some religious concerns. To what extent does this concern find expression in *faith*, the second aspect of the experiential dimension?

Faith, as an aspect of the experiential dimension of religion is taken here to refer to a feeling of closeness, and of personal interaction with the divine. This interpersonal encounter between man and God, has been suggested by Glock and Stark as having an ordered progression of intimacy:

> By conceiving of the divinity and the individual undergoing the religious experience as a pair of actors involved in a social encounter, we may specify some general configurations of relations between them which can be ordered in terms of social distance. . . . We may sketch four such possible configurations of inter-actor relations:
> 1. The human actor simply notes . . . the existence or presence of the divine actor;
> 2. Mutual presence is acknowledged, the divine actor is perceived as noting the presence of the human actor;
> 3. The awareness of mutual presence is replaced by an affective relationship akin to love or friendship;
> 4. The human actor perceives himself as a confidant of or a fellow participant in action with the divine actor (14, pp. 42–43).

While we have no data that systematically assesses the degree of religious commitment in terms of the level of intimacy of the relationship between youth and God, some information drawn from the Gallup study and the Purdue Polls allows some insight here. To acknowledge the presence of God is the least intimate and least entangling of the man-God relationships. Nearly all teenagers do report that they believe in God. Less than 5% indicated that they "have some doubts" or don't believe at all (10). The next level of intimacy is to admit that God knows one's behavior. Somewhat over 80% of the respondents in the Purdue Polls said they believed that "God knows our every thought and movement." However, while the respondents may have a sense of being *watched*, they were considerably less certain of being *cared for* by the Divine. Just 60% fully agreed that "God controls everything that happens everywhere." To act *in trust* on the control of the other is to admit the highest level of entwinement and faith. Asked if they believed religious faith was better than logic for solving life's important problems, only 38% responded "yes" in 1962 (24, pp. 4–5). It should be noted that, the proportion of the over-all adolescent population that expressed agreement with the reality of the varying levels of religious commitment *decreased* as the level of commitment or intimacy increased, with more than 95% acknowledging the existence of God, but less than 40% willing to entrust their lives completely to divine power.[7]

[7] Based only on the availability of table marginals we cannot be certain that Glock and Stark's model of intimacy with the Transcendental is accurate. They suggest that persons at more intimate levels of involvement should have gone through earlier, less intimate stages. For this to be demonstrated in our data the 38% of youth in 1962 who answered "yes" to a willingness to take faith over logic in solving life's important problems should also have said "yes" to the two earlier questions about a knowing and a controlling God. We do not know whether, in fact, they did.

Jewish youth were less likely to report that they felt on "intimate" terms with God than was the Christian adolescent. Only 38% of the Jewish young people agreed that God knows one's every thought and action; 31% agreed that God controls everything, and but 23% agreed that religion is better than logic for solving the important problems of life (25, pp. 171–172).

Catholic students in this study answered approximately like the Protestants with a somewhat greater tendency to affirm God as controlling the universe and a somewhat greater willingness to agree that life's important problems are best solved on the basis of faith (24, pp. 171–172).

From these data, it would seem that unswerving trust and faith is *not* the norm for American adolescents. The overwhelming majority are quite willing to agree that the Almighty exists, watches, and perhaps controls the world. But there is marked reluctance to really trust this control and count solely upon it. They are not at all sure that "God will take care of them." One gets the impression that many youth are "playing it cool"—unwilling to fully accept the implications of divine control but also unwilling to deny its existence. In this regard, it is interesting to note that a lack of faith in others is not taken as villainous. Over 60% of the teenagers polled in the Purdue Study disagreed with the statement that: "Most people who don't believe in God are bad people." Another 20% indicated that they were uncertain (25, p. 172). Thus, for most teenagers, rejection of the Almighty is not seen as catastrophic. But, the youth were not quite willing to leave God out either. Asked whether "Men working and thinking together can build a good society without any divine or supernatural help," only one-third of the sample could agree to this (25, p. 172). Uncertain whether God is necessary or not, the American teenager apparently "hedges" the matter.[8] He seems to be saying: we cannot have a good society without God but people who deny God are not bad. What is true for the whole, does not hold for the parts!

III. *The Ideological Dimension*

The third dimension of religiousness, ideology or "belief," addresses the extent to which individuals differ in regard to their acceptance of church doctrine. Every religion sets forth some set of beliefs to which its followers are expected to adhere. Of course, there is a vast array of such beliefs associated with the Judaeo-Christian heritage that might conceivably be examined here. We have neither the space, nor, more important, the data to do this. Therefore, we shall examine only those beliefs on which some information is available and which seem to be common to the dominant religious groups in American society.

Some beliefs, warranting the existence of the divine and defining its character have already been noted in the previous discussion in terms of the nature of man's relationship with God. Let it suffice to recall here that almost all teenagers acknowledged the existence of God, and conceptualize the

---

[8] This kind of hedging does not appear to diminish with age. While high school seniors were more accepting of non-believer than were freshmen, the percentage seeing divine help as necessary *increased* with increasing age from 37% for the ninth graders to 51% for seniors. (25, p. 172).

Almighty as all-knowing. In addition, more than 80% (in the Gallup Poll) reported that they believed God to be their judge who observes their actions and will reward or punish them for what they do. These are all highly traditional and "orthodox" views.

Moreover, more than 80% of the adolescents surveyed indicated that they believed that there is a life after death (10). The Lutheran study, cited earlier, found a slightly higher percentage (90%) who asserted belief in life after death.

Going beyond belief in after-life, the Purdue study also asked whether our fate in the hereafter depends upon how we behave on earth. Sixty-nine per cent of the total sample affirmed a belief that such was the case. Only 9% registered a negative response. The remainder (22%) failed to answer the question or recorded a "don't know" reply. Catholic youth were somewhat more convinced, with 77% answering "yes." Jewish youth were more skeptical, with only 23% saying "yes," and 46% registering a doubting "don't know" answer (25, p. 172).

A similar tendency for a clustering of "don't know" answers was found when the youth were asked about the sacredness of the scriptures. While the majority (57%) of young people indicated they agreed that "the first writing of the Bible was done under the guidance of God," fully ¼ of the sample indicated a "don't know" response. As on most of the other belief items, Catholics had the highest rate of agreement (64%) and Jews the lowest (42%) (25, p. 173). Finally, we can note the Gallup data showed that, although roughly 90% of American youth felt the Bible to be "true," about ⅓ of the adolescents qualified their response and indicated that it was "mostly" rather than "completely" true. However, less than 2 of the sample was willing to answer that the Bible is "just a fable" (10).

What can be concluded from these data? Strommen has nicely summarized the overall picture of youth's beliefs when he writes of his Lutheran adolescents:

> Searching minds and disquieted hearts often doubt what is taught.
> . . . A few upwards to many doubters are seen for every belief [surveyed]
> . . . Yet the percentage of these doubters is less than might be expected
> for this scientific age. Only 17 per cent, for example, doubt that "miracles
> take place today" . . . only one-third disbelieve in the existence of a
> devil . . . and only one-third doubt that the Bible is historically accurate
> (35, p. 54).

Whatever may be said, then, of the quality of today's adolescents, the evidence presented here certainly suggests that they are not untraditional. At least in the basic ideological factors assessed here, American teenagers either overwhelmingly accept the orthodox point of view or, at the very most, they express some doubts about it. Almost none, however, *reject* the traditional positions.

IV. The Intellectual Dimension

The fourth dimension of religion delineated by Glock and Stark refers to the degree of knowledge that the individual possesses of church dogma, doctrine, and history. This is a cognitive aspect. It asks not what the individual feels, or believes, but what he "knows" intellectually. As with the ideological dimension a wide range of ideas could be assessed to determine the level of knowledge of adolescents concerning their religious heritage. Unfortunately, while there is evidence that at least some such studies have been carried out, the results have not found their way into published literature readily available to the general reader. A study dealing with college sophomores may be suggestive (20). However, if such persons were at least as knowledgeable as the average adolescent, then the typical teenager in American society is quite ignorant of basic church tenets. In a test of 100 items (50 questions covering various aspects of the Old Testament and 50 dealing with the New Testament), the range of scores was between 0 and 80—but, the *median* score was only 17! Thus, while the adolescent overtly supports both the established church *and* the basic tenets of Judaeo-Christian belief, he may very well know little of the "factual" information concerning his religion.

V. The Consequential Dimension

The final dimension of religiousness differs from the preceding four. It refers, not to the *internal* aspects of religion, such as faith, belief, and knowledge, but rather raises the question of how religious commitment, as measured by the other dimensions, conditions or influences the behavior or feelings of the individual.

Research has not been unconcerned with this aspect. However, certain methodological shortcomings mar the work and make it of limited worth. There has been a general failure in these studies to differentiate the various dimensions of religiousness, and, unfortunately,

> research on religious effects cannot be done in isolation from [careful] research on other aspects of religiosity. How religious a person is on these other dimensions provides the warrant for asserting that a given act is, in fact, a religious effect. By definition, an act can be a religious effect only if it flows from religiosity (14, p. 35).

Most of the work done assessing the importance of religious effects, whether using adult or adolescent populations has tended to use ritualistic practices— usually church attendance or membership—as the measure of religiousness. While this is a convenient index, easily measured and readily obtainable, it is probably among the least satisfactory indicators (1). This is true if for no other reason than that it fails to differentiate within the population. The overwhelming majority of people apparently regard themselves as church members and "regular" attenders.

Even in those few instances where more adequate indicators of religious commitment have been employed, the insights gained from the research are limited because almost all of these studies are cross-sectional. "Done at one point in time, they do not allow warranted conclusions as to the causal direction of the associations they find" (14, p. 37). Simply because two factors are empirically related does *not* necessarily mean that they are causally linked, nor is the direction of cause and effect always obvious. Thus in one study, based on the observed relationship between church attendance and civil liberties, it was concluded that church attendance *leads* people to be less civil libertarian. However, the opposite conclusion could be equally plausible. That is, being less supportive of civil liberties may lead people to more church attendance. Similarly, while the research is by no means consistent and conclusive in this regard, some studies have found a negative association between religiousness (as indicated by church participation and/or beliefs) and delinquency (30, 32, 35). But, we cannot be sure that religious values are in fact the causal agent. The relationship could easily result from the linkage of both delinquency and religiousness with another causal factor such as social class. Unless one has longitudinal data to carefully trace the influence of religion, we must remain essentially ignorant of its consequences.

While we know very little about the effects of various religious orientations, this does not mean that beliefs and interests are necessarily unimportant or causally impotent. Undoubtedly they can be and sometimes are crucial conditioners of action.[9] To what extent this occurs, however, is not clear.

Some Concluding Remarks

How religious are the youth of America? We have suggested that the answer to this question is not a simple one. To arrive at any evaluation at all, we need to consider all of the various dimensions of religion. In the brief review of research just presented, we have suggested that typically the adolescent embraces both a traditional belief system and a not immodest degree of participation in the ritualistic aspects of religion. His level of knowledge has not been systematically assessed but probably is low. In terms of the experiential dimension, his concern and interest in religion, while not clearly measured, appear to be quite high. The development of concern into deep, orthodox faith is not, however, apparently typical. The American adolescent seems reluctant to deny the idea of a supernatural, but, at the same time, is unwilling or unable to yield himself with firm conviction to the hands of the Divine. Perhaps the best label we can apply to the teenager's religious orientation is "hedging." He appears to embrace neither nihilism nor firm commitment.

Of course, it should be clear that the picture we have drawn from the meager data available is for the "average" or "typical" teenager. While we have given some brief indications of diversity within the adolescent grouping, we obviously could not fully explore it within the limited scope of this paper. Yet, clearly, the recognition of the point is vital. *There are* some youth who have deep religious commitment and act upon it[10] and some few who

[9] Max Weber's analysis and documentation of the significant role of the particular religious orientations he called the Protestant Ethic in the development of Western societies is well known. (38)
[10] P. A. Riffel (26) has pointed to what he calls "scrupulosity" as one style of adolescent self identity in which there is meticulous adherence to religious and moral precepts. This pattern of rigid conformity to traditional beliefs and practices seems to occur most frequently among youth attending parochial schools and appears to be

show almost no religiosity. Moreover there is considerable variability not only in degree, but also in content. As Strommen has noted regarding his sample of Lutheran youth:

> [They] . . . are astonishingly heterogeneous in their beliefs. Some embrace concepts which identify them as distinctively Lutheran, whereas others hold beliefs that are indistinguishable from those of other Protestants. Almost half hold a mixture of beliefs which include tenets that are neither Christian nor distinctive. . . . This great variety constantly qualified any generalizations about Lutheran youth. (35, pp. 69 and 233).

When this consideration of *within* denomination variability is superimposed on the contention and research findings of Glock and Stark that the differences *among* Protestant denominations, as seen in adult members, are considerably greater than some recent ecumenical movements and desires would lead one to expect, the dangers in making sweeping generalization are high-lighted.

It also needs emphasis that, while we have limited our survey to adolescents, this should *not* be taken to mean that adolescents are unique. On the contrary, the characterization of the average American teenager may be equally applicable to the average American adult. Adults too may exhibit the same "hedging stance" as the youth—unwilling to deny the existence of God, yet reluctant to totally trust divine power to guide them. We do know, from careful analysis of the research record that, popular mythology to the contrary, the adolescent tends strongly to accept rather than reject parental values (2). What is true in other areas is probably equally true for religion. Thus, for example, in the Purdue studies, 78% of the youth felt their beliefs agreed with the orientation of both parents (25, p. 168). This supposition of generational agreement has been confirmed in other studies (22). Thus, whether one takes the religious orientations of American adolescents to be "good" or "bad," it is vital to recognize that the dispositions do not exist in a vacuum, but in a socially supporting milieu.

Is there anything then about the adolescent's beliefs and religious behavior that is distinctively "adolescent"? We do not have data to make firm conclusions in this area, but we can speculate from what we know of the "teen" years. Adolescence is typically a time in which the youth is seeking his own self identity (6, 16, 21). Unsure of the kind of person he is and wishes to be, he is often beset by a sense of insecurity in relating himself to others, and to the world in general (35). An important aspect of concern is likely to be the matter of resolving one's relationship to the supernatural. Most adolescents are unwilling to simply accept their families' faith without question (only slightly over ¼ of the youth assessed in the Purdue study indicated that one should do this). At the same time the youth is vitally concerned over the quality of his interpersonal relations with others. Given the context of Ameri-

---

a transitory (though not necessarily a short-lived) phase. In the scrupulosity pattern there can be little doubt about the importance of religious motives. However, the extent of this style of adolescent identity is not clear. David Matza has estimated that, "scrupulosity seems of roughly the same order of magnitude as that youthful style at the other end of the spectrum which nowadays attracts so much public attention— juvenile delinquency." (19, p. 200) can society where religious commitment is given at least overt endorsement as "good" by old and young alike, the individual adolescent may be unwilling to risk social rejection by making public the doubts he has over religion. Consequently, his behavior is likely to reflect, for the most part, a ritualistic performance of church attendance and an overt subscription to at least basic Judaeo-Christian dogma. In fact, this involvement in such activities may be more intense than the participation of his parents or the general adult population.[11] In a paradoxical way his concerns about the sacred gets caught in a web where to communicate about the concern becomes a sacred breach against one's self. It is perhaps revealing that, in the Purdue study, when asked if they enjoyed "arguing about religion," less than one in five of the youth said "yes" (25, p. 168). But religious doubts may still exist and the adolescent's uncertainty concerning the "correctness" of his beliefs may make him unwilling to rely wholly upon his faith to guide his actions. And so he hedges. Whether we are correct in this interpretation is, of course, an open matter and one which, like so many areas of adolescent religious behavior, obviously needs more insightful research.

BIBLIOGRAPHY

1. Altshuler, Nathan, "Religion and Mental Health: Demographic and Personal Variables," in Richard V. McCann, *The Churches and Mental Health*. New York: Basic Books, 1962, Chapter 12, pp. 209–227.
2. Bealer, Robert C., Willits, Fern K., and Maida, Peter R., "Rebellious Youth Subculture—A Myth," *Children*, Vol. 11 (1964), pp. 43-48.
3. ————, "The Myth of a Rebellious Adolescent Subculture: Its Detrimental Effects for Understanding Rural Youth," in Lee G. Burchinal, ed., *Rural Youth in Crisis: Facts, Myths, and Social Change*. Washington, D. C.: Department of Health, Education, and Welfare, 1965, pp. 45–61.
4. Bernard, Jessie, ed., "Teen-Age Culture," *The Annals*, Vol. 338 (1961).
5. Elkind, David and Sally, "Varieties of Religious Experience in Young Adolescents," *Journal for the Scientific Study of Religion*, Vol. 2 (1962), pp. 102–112.
6. Erikson, Erik H., ed., *Youth: Change and Challenge*. New York: Basic Books, Inc., 1963.
7. Faulkner, Joseph E. and DeJong, Gordon F., "Religiosity in 5-D: An Empirical Analysis," paper read at the American Sociological Association, Chicago, Illinois, September, 1965.
8. Fichter, Joseph H., *Dynamics of a City Church: Southern Parish*. Chicago: University of Chicago Press, 1951.
9. Fukuyama, Yoshio, "Wonder Letters: An Experimental Study of the Religious Sensitivities of Children," *Religious Education*, Vol. 58 (1963), pp. 377–383.

[11] Directly comparable data for youth and adults is sketchy, but suggestive. The Purdue survey found that, while 69% of the teenagers said they attend formal worship services, "about once a week" or oftener, only 40% reported that their fathers and 57% that their mothers attend at least two or more times a month (25, p. 167). Furthermore, the Gallup Poll found that both college students and young adults were less likely to be "regular" attenders than were high school students. (10)

10. Gallup, George and Hill, Evan, *Religious Beliefs of Youth*, 1961. Unpublished data.

11. ———, "Youth: The Cool Generation," *Saturday Evening Post*, Vol. 234 (1961), pp. 63–80.

12. Gesell, Arnold and Ames, L. B., *Youth: The Years From Ten to Sixteen*. New York: Harpers, 1956.

13. Glock, Charles Y. and Stark, Rodney, "Is There an American Protestantism?" *Trans-action*, Vol. 3 (1965), pp. 8–13; 48–49.

14. Glock, Charles Y., *Religion and Society in Tension*. Chicago: Rand McNally & Company, 1965.

15. Gottlieb, David and Ramsey, Charles, *The American Adolescent*. Homewood, Illinois: The Dorsey Press, 1964.

16. Jersild, Arthur T., *The Psychology of Adolescence*. New York: The Macmillan Company, 1963, 2nd ed.

17. Lenski, Gerhard, *The Religious Factor*. Garden City, New York: Doubleday, 1961.

18. Lott, Albert J. and Lott, Bernice E., *Negro and White Youth*. New York: Holt, Rinehart, and Winston, Inc., 1963.

19. Matza, David, "Position and Behavior Patterns of Youth," in Robert E. L. Faris, ed., *Handbook of Modern Sociology*. Chicago: Rand McNally and Company, 1964, pp. 191–216.

20. Payne, Raymond, "Knowledge of the Bible Among Protestant and Jewish University Students: An Exploratory Study," *Religious Education*, Vol. 58 (1963), pp. 289–294.

21. Peck, Robert F. and Havighurst, Robert J., *The Psychology of Character Development*. New York: John Wiley, 1960.

22. Putney, Snell and Middleton, Russell, "Rebellion, Conformity and Parental Religious Ideologies," *Sociometry*, Vol. 24 (1961), pp. 125–135.

23. Reisman, David, Glazer, Nathan, and Denney, Reuel, *The Lonely Crowd: A Study of the Changing American Character*. New York: Doubleday, 1953.

24. Remmers, H. H., "Teenagers' Attitudes Toward Study Habits, Vocational Plans, Religious Beliefs, and Luck," Report of Poll No. 67, The Purdue Opinion Panel. Lafayette, Indiana: Division of Educational Reference, December, 1962.

25. Remmers, H. H. and Radler, D. H., *The American Teenager*. Indianapolis: Bobbs-Merrill Company, Charter Books, 1962.

26. Riffel, P. A., "Sex and Scrupulosity," in W. C. Bier, ed., *The Adolescent: His Search for Understanding*. New York: Fordham University Press, 1963, pp. 39–51.

27. Roper, Elmo and Associates, *A Study of the Problems, Attitudes and Aspirations of Rural Youth*. Unpublished report prepared for the Rockefeller Brothers Fund, October, 1963.

28. Rosen, Bernard C., *Adolescence and Religion: The Jewish Teenager in American Society*. Cambridge, Mass.: Schenkman Publishing Company, Inc., 1965.

29. Ross, Murray, *Religious Beliefs of Youth*. New York: Association Press, 1950.

30. Scholl, Mason E. and Beker, Jerome, "A Comparison of the Religious Beliefs of Delinquent and Non-Delinquent Protestant Adolescent Boys," *Religious Education*, Vol. 59 (1964), pp. 250–253.

31. Seventeen Magazine, *The Teen-age Girl: 1960*. New York: Seventeen Magazine, 1960.

32. Shoeben, Edward J., Jr., "Moral Behavior and Moral Learning," *Religious Education*, Vol. 58 (1963), pp. 137–145.

33. Smith, Ernest A., *American Youth Culture*. Glencoe, Illinois: The Free Press, 1962.

34. Stouffer, Samuel, *Communism, Conformity, and Civil Liberties.* Garden City, New York: Doubleday and Co., 1955.
35. Strommen, Merton P., *Profiles of Church Youth.* St. Louis, Missouri: Concordia Publishing House, 1963.
36. "The Teen-agers," *Newsweek*, March 21, 1966, pp. 57–75.
37. Van Dyke, Paul, II and Pierce-Jones, John, "The Psychology of Religion of Middle and Late Adolescence: A Review of Empirical Research, 1950–1960," *Religious Education*, Vol. 58 (1963), pp. 529–537.
38. Weber, Max, *The Protestant Ethic and the Spirit of Capitalism*, trans. by Talcott Parsons. London: Allen and Unwin, 1930.
39. Whitman, Lauris B., Keating, Barry J., and Matthews, Robert W., *The Presbyterian National Education Survey*, Vol. 3. New York: Board of Christian Education of the United Presbyterian Church in the United States of America, 1965.
40. Williams, Robin M., *American Society: A Sociological Interpretation.* New York: Knopf, 1960, 2nd ed.

RELIGIOUS PARTICIPATION
AMONG COLLEGE FRESHMEN*,1

JEFFREY K. HADDEN
ROBERT R. EVANS

Introduction

The college years are an extremely important period in the lives of an increasingly large proportion of American young people. For most, it is the first extended absence from parents, and it serves as a period of transition from a high degree of dependence on parents to relative independence from them. The new college student usually finds a broader range of beliefs and outlooks on life than he has previously encountered, and there is pressure to resolve the conflicts between his own beliefs and those expressed by others. Depending on the degree of internalization of values taught by parents and early significant others in his home community, coming to grips with conflicting life philosophies may be relatively simple or it may be very traumatic. Belief systems may remain relatively intact and be reinforced, or they may be very greatly altered.

Religious belief and practice is one domain that is frequently purported to be challenged by the college milieu. Various scholars have argued that education has a secularizing influence on the population and that upgrading the educational level of the population will have the net effect of secularizing the society.[2] This argument is based at least in part on the assumption that science not only contradicts certain traditional religious dogma but represents a fundamentally different *weltanschauung*, or "world-view."[3]

In this paper we examine the extent of formal religious participation, its change during the transition from high school to college, and some of the

* Reprinted from Jeffrey K. Hadden and Robert R. Evans, "Some Correlates of Religious Participation among College Freshmen," in *Religious Education*, Vol. 60 (July–August 1965), pp. 277–285, by permission of the publisher, The Religious Education Association, New York City.
1 Revision of a paper presented at the annual meetings of the Midwest Sociological Society, Kansas City, Missouri, April, 1964. This study was made possible by a grant from The University of Wisconsin Research Committee.
2 Thomas Ford Hoult, for example, reviews a number of research findings to conclude that they "demonstrate the fact that education in secular subjects, even when supervised by sectarian groups, very often undermines traditional religious belief." *Sociology of Religion*, New York: Dryden, 1958, p. 345. For the same effect among graduate students, cf. Jan Hajda, "Alienation and Integration of Student Intellectuals," *American Journal of Sociology*, 26 (Oct. 1961), pp. 758–777, especially Table 5.
3 Cf. Rodney Stark, "On the Incompatibility of Religion and Science: A Survey of American Graduate Students," *Journal for the Scientific Study of Religion*, III (Oct. 1963), pp. 3–20.

concomitants of variations in participation patterns among three freshman college populations.

It should be emphasized at the outset that religious participation is only one kind of religious "involvement." It does not necessarily follow that an individual's infrequent participation in religious services means that he is irreligious. Furthermore, frequent participation in religious activities may be motivated by other than religious or devotional concerns. Generally, however, the relationship between religious participation and membership, belief, religiousness, commitment, and other "dimensions" of religious involvement is not very clearly understood.[4] Our own data do indicate that among college students religious participation is correlated positively with religious belief and other indicators of religious involvement.

Regardless of the relationship between religious participation and other kinds of religious involvement in the general population, participation is of fundamental importance to the understanding of the role of religion in our society. The strength and importance of our religious institutions are very much dependent upon the support the populace gives to religious organizations through participation. (It is difficult to imagine how religious institutions could maintain as influential a position in our society as they currently do if all the churches in America were empty.) In short, we would argue that religious participation is one fundamental basis for the continued strength of religion in American society, and therefore understanding the concomitants of religious participation is of fundamental importance to understanding American society. Further, a religious environment tends to lend stability to religious faith, and removal from a religious environment may shake this faith.

Sample

Respondents to our questionnaire were freshmen at three Midwestern schools: a large state university and two smaller, religiously affiliated schools.[5]

---

[4] Among the many sets of dimensions for measurement of religiousness which have been implemented in recent research: Charles Y. Glock ("The Religious Revival in America?" in Jane Zahn, ed., *Religions and the Face of America*, Berkeley: University Extension, University of California, 1959, pp. 25–42) found his experiential, ritualistic, ideological, and consequential dimensions to be "interrelated rather than independent;" Gerhard Lenski (*The Religious Factor*, Garden City, New York: Doubleday, 1961) established attitude and behavior differences between respondents classed on a doctrinal orthodoxy vs. devotional dichotomy as well as between those dichotomized on associational vs. communal involvement; Yoshio Fukuyama ("The Major Dimensions of Church Membership," *Review of Religious Research*, 2 Spring 1961, pp. 154–161) worked with a modification of the Glock (*ibid.*) dimensions called cognitive, cultic, creedal, and devotional; Nicholas J. Demerath III ("The Church-Sect Distinction Applied to Individual Participation," *Review of Religious Research*, 2 Spring 1961, pp. 146–154) applied measures of two separate dimensions, ritual observance and communal attachment. (For an extended research and broader discussion of this literature see N. J. Demerath III, *Social Class in American Protestantism*, Chicago: Rand McNally and Company, 1965.

[5] The administrations of the religiously affiliated schools asked that these not be identified. Both have enrollments of less than one thousand students. The state university is The University of Wisconsin.

The selection of schools was designed to include as broad a range of campus environments as possible within the confines of a limited research budget.

Both of the smaller schools were founded by and have maintained close ties with the same major Protestant denomination, but one of them was reported to place considerably more emphasis on religious education than the other. We shall refer to the reportedly more religiously oriented school as Midwestern College and the other denominational school as Central College.

The 588 respondents from State University were recruited from introductory sociology courses and constituted 17 percent of the freshman class in the College of Letters and Science. At the two religiously affiliated schools, freshmen volunteers were solicited via offering a modest cash incentive to the Freshman Class treasury for each respondent. At Central, 249 freshmen representing 85 percent of the class filled out questionnaires. The freshmen at Midwestern were less responsive, and we obtained only 60 per cent $(N=170)$ of the class for our sample. Since it is conceivable that non-respondents differ systematically from respondents (e.g., less religious persons may have less interest in filling out the questionnaire or may hesitate to express views that they perceive are contradictory to the dominant campus norms), we administered a shortened form to fifty initial respondents and fifty non-respondents. The respondents for the short questionnaire were randomly selected from the lists of respondents and non-respondents to the regular questionnaire. A comparison of the two groups revealed no differences between respondents and non-respondents on religious background and belief.

Extent of Participation

With participation defined here as frequency of "attendance at religious services," there appeared sharp declines between respondents' participation during their junior and senior years of high school and their initial two months behavior at college. This was true for two ways of measuring the difference.

First, we asked if the respondent was going to church less often now than when in the second half of high school. At Central and State, 44 and 46 percent respectively perceived themselves as attending less; at Midwestern, only 31 percent reported their attendance to be less.

Second, we compared their reported high school attendance with reported college attendance. Resulting proportions showing an attendance drop were: 49 percent at Central, 39 percent at Midwestern, and 35 percent at State. That State had a smaller proportion reporting a decline than either of the religiously affiliated schools may actually be the result of the regression effect. That is, if students who go to religiously affiliated schools participated in religious services with great frequency in high school, then statistically they are more likely to regress toward the mean—and, in fact, Midwestern and Central freshmen did attend with somewhat greater frequency in high school than freshmen at State.

Pressures of time and change in belief are the principle reasons given for decline in religious attendance at State and Central, but freedom from parents and laziness are also frequently cited. At Midwestern, however, almost one third of the freshmen reporting less attendance gave "freedom from parents" as the primary reason.

Parental expectations are clearly an important reason why students at all three schools participated in religious services in high school, but it is a much more important factor for Midwestern students. This should not be interpreted to mean, however, that a large number of Midwestern students are rebelling against a cloister pattern of their parents, since by far the majority of the students are maintaining a pattern of regular participation similar to their participation in high school.

The categories that we have used to classify reasons for decline in attendance are not necessarily independent. For example, the reason one finds it preferable to sleep on Sunday rather than go to church may be a manifestation of the fact that parents are no longer around to make him attend church, or it may reflect a change in belief, or it may be a physiological response to the heavy time commitments of college life during the week, or it may be for several or even all these reasons.

The question of whether church attendance has declined masks a broad range of variation in participation patterns. For example, two students may have reported that they attended church every week in high school, but on arriving at college one may never attend and the other attend "almost every week." Both are attending religious services less now than in high school. One might be inclined to think that something drastic has happened to the former, but there is probably little reason to suspect that there has been any significant change in the religious involvement of the latter.

To account for this, we grouped students according to the extent to which their patterns of religious participation remained stable. Students who reported attending religious services almost every week or more often in high school and only a few times or less in college were classified as *sliders*. Also included as *sliders* were those who reported attending church a couple of times a month in high school who had never attended religious services in college. Those who reported attending religious services almost every week or more in high school and maintained that frequency during the first two months of college were classified as *faithfuls*. A third group consists of those who reported that they never attended religious services or attended only a few times in high school and showed no signs of change in college. We dub this group the *uninvolved*.[6]

The proportion of students who became *sliders* during their first two months at college varies considerably among colleges and by sex, as seen in Table 1. At Midwestern, 22 percent of those who had been regular church attenders in high school became *sliders*; at State, 37 percent; at Central, 45 percent.

The proportion of females who became *sliders* is less at each school than the proportion of males. However, in each case, the female attendance more nearly resembles the male pattern at that school than the pattern of females at other schools. There is less than a ten percent *slider* differential between males and females within any school, but there are more than twenty percentage points separating Central and Midwestern.

---

[6] A fourth logical possibility would be those who seldom or never participated in religious services in high school who began attending almost every week or more in college. There are only eleven such *converts* among the thousand respondents in the three samples. This is an insufficient number of cases to deal with statistically, but it does illustrate the fact that initial college life does not "drive" students to religion.

TABLE 1. PERCENTAGE OF STUDENTS WHO ATTENDED RELIGIOUS SERVICES
REGULARLY WHILE IN HIGH SCHOOL AND REMAIN FAITHFUL OR
LET ATTENDANCE SLIDE AT COLLEGE

Frequency of Attendance in High School	State University			Central College			Midwestern College		
	Total	Male	Female	Total	Male	Female	Total	Male	Female
Almost every week and each week or more (combined)	61.4	58.1	67.5	64.6	62.5	57.3	82.2	73.5	95.5
Each week or more	42.2	32.8	46.8	45.3	43.4	74.8	61.5	51.0	77.6
Practically never or less	7.4	10.8	6.0	10.0	12.5	7.1	3.5	5.9	0.0

There probably are fewer *sliders* at Midwestern than at Central because "religiousness" is an important criterion in choosing to attend Midwestern. What is more difficult to explain is the greater "sliding" at Central than at State. Some possible reasons are: (1) State students may have expressed their religious doubts and disinterest while still in high school; (2) church attendance may actually be contrary to the informal norms at Central as much as it is a part of the norms at Midwestern; and (3) there is an overrepresentation of females at State, which tends to depress the proportion who become *sliders*.

CONCOMITANTS OF RELIGIOUS PARTICIPATION

While there is a substantial literature on the concomitants of religious participation and beliefs in the general population, the findings are hardly conclusive.[7] Some further evidence, taken from our three student samples, is presented here: relationships between the students' attendance patterns and their parents' educational levels and frequency of religious participation. Other concomitants such as social class, community, background, etc., are to be reported elsewhere.

Education. That education has a secularizing influence on religious values is not a new thought. Just before the turn of the century, Starbuck found that

[7] A review and analysis of these studies is not feasible within the limitations of this paper, but our hypotheses are based on a large body of literature including the following: Louis Bultens, "Church Membership and Church Attendance in Madison, Wisconsin," *American Sociological Review*, 14 (June 1949), pp. 384–389; Lee G. Burchinal, "Some Social Status Criteria and Church Membership and Church Attendance," *Journal of Social Psychology*, 49 (1959), pp. 53–64; Otis Dudley Duncan and Jay W. Artis, "Social Stratification in a Pennsylvania Rural Community," *Bulletin 543,* Agricultural Experimental Station, The Pennsylvania State College School of Agriculture, State College, Pa.: October, 1951; August B. Hollingshead, *Elmstown's Youth,* New York: Wiley, 1949 (republished, New York: Science Editions, 1961); Bernard Lazerwitz, "Some Factors Associated with Variations in Church Attendance," *Social Forces,* 39 (October 1961), pp. 301–309; Gerhard E. Lenski, "Social Correlates of Religious Interest," *American Sociological Review,* 18 (August 1953), pp. 533–544; *The Religious Factor,* Garden City, New York: Doubleday, 1961 (republished, New York: Doubleday Anchor, 1963); and John D. Photiadis and Jeanne Biggar, "Religiosity, Education, and Ethnic Distance," *The American Journal of Sociology,* 67 (May 1962), pp. 666–672.

education tended to create doubts about religious beliefs.[8] In another pioneering study in 1920, Katz and Allport found that almost two-thirds of the students in their sample at Syracuse expressed a change in religious belief in college.[9] However, the change was not from belief to non-belief, but rather from traditional personal concepts of God to more liberal and non-personal orientations. Again in 1948, Allport, Gillespie, and Young reported that more than three-fifths of Catholic and almost three-fourths of non-Catholic students at Harvard acknowledged having reacted against their religious training.[10] A number of other studies have indicated that education does have a secularizing influence on religious beliefs and religious involvement. One of the most recent and carefully documented studies is that of Stark who shows with a national sample that graduate education is negatively associated with religious involvement.[11] In another recent study, Hadden found that University of Wisconsin seniors who were attending religious services less than when they entered college were more likely to have fathers who attended college than those whose pattern of religious participation had not changed since entering college, suggesting that education has an intergenerational secularizing influence.[12]

If education does have an intergenerational secularizing influence, then we would predict that the greater the educational achievement of one's parents, the lower his rate of religious participation in high school and the greater the probability that he will become a *slider* in college.

At State and Central there is a tendency for the rate of religious participation to decline as parent's level of education increases, although the relationship is not perfect (Table 2). This hypothesis, however, does not hold at Midwestern, where, in fact, there is a positive relationship between the student's rate of participation and mother's educational level. At Central the rate of attendance drops with each increasing level of father's education until professional and graduate school, and then increases sharply.[13]

There is a tendency for the educational level of parents to be positively associated with becoming a *slider* in college (Table 3). There is also a tendency for children of parents with high educational achievement to be uninvolved in religious activities prior to entering college. Therefore, if the *sliders* and *uninvolved* are grouped, we should see a clearer picture of the relationship

[8] Edwin D. Starbuck, *The Psychology of Religion*, London: Walter Scott, 1899. Starbuck found that 53 percent of the females and 79 percent of the males in this study experienced a "distinct period of doubt," and among the males who doubted, 73 percent attributed this doubt to educational influences.

[9] Daniel Katz and Floyd H. Allport, *Students' Attitudes*, Syracuse, New York: Craftsman Press, 1931.

[10] Gordon W. Allport, James M. Gillespie, and Jacqueline Young, "The Religion of the Post-War College Student," *Journal of Psychology*, 25 (1948), p. 11. John Kosa and Cyril O. Schommer, S.J., "Religious Participation, Religious Knowledge, and Scholastic Aptitude: An Empirical Study," *Journal for the Scientific Study of Religion*, I (October 1961), p. 96.

[11] Rodney Stark, *op. cit.*

[12] Jeffrey K. Hadden, "An Analysis of Some Factors Associated with Religious and Political Affiliation in a College Population," *Journal for the Scientific Study of Religion*, II (Spring 1963), pp. 209–216.

[13] This relationship can probably be accounted for by a large number of students whose fathers are in the ministry. Unfortunately, the occupational category "professional" on the questionnaire was not further subdivided to permit checking this speculation.

TABLE 2.   APPROXIMATE MEAN ANNUAL ATTENDANCE[1] AT RELIGIOUS SERV-
ICES DURING LAST HALF OF HIGH SCHOOL, BY PARENTAL EDUCA-
TION AND ATTENDANCE

	State	Central	Midwestern
Father's education			
Less than 8 years	39.2	43.5	50.2
High school	38.5	35.0	51.3
College	36.7	34.8	53.7
Professional or graduate school	32.0	41.1	51.1
Mother's education			
Less than 8 years	41.1	63.3	33.1
High school	37.8	37.4	50.5
College	43.8	38.1	52.5
Professional or graduate school	27.1	35.3	61.3
Father's religious attendance			
Never or practically never	27.5	24.9	34.4
Few times per year—Couple times each month	27.3	27.9	40.1
Almost every week or more	47.7	48.0	61.5
Mother's religious attendance			
Never or practically never	14.0	19.9	27.0
Few times per year—Couple times each month	23.2	25.8	35.4
Almost every week or more	46.9	46.1	58.9

[1] "Approximate mean attendance" is estimated by weighing responses to the question, "About how often did *you* attend religious services during your junior and senior years in *high school?*" as follows: Daily or several times a week, 100; Each week, 50; Almost every week, 40; A couple of times each month, 25; About once a month, 12; A few times each year, 4; Practically never, 1; and Never, 0.

between parent's educational level and ego's participation. At State the relationship becomes dramatically clear; the greater the educational level of both mother and father, the greater the probability of being *uninvolved* or a *slider* in college. However, at Central and Midwestern the relationship is less clear.

We further reasoned that if education does have an intergenerational secularizing influence, it should be more marked if both parents, rather than only one, had achieved a high educational level. This hypothesis is empirically incorrect for our samples, both in terms of high school attendance and college sliding.

Parents' Religious Participation.   It is generally assumed that a child's religious participation closely parallels that of his parents, but by the time a person reaches adolescence he may be given considerable liberty, and just how closely his religious participation does in fact parallel his parents' has been neither extensively investigated nor clearly established.[14]

We would hypothesize that the greater the participation of parents in

[14] Allport, Gillespie and Young, *op. cit.*, is one of the few studies to consider this common assumption; the relevant finding here is that Harvard and Radcliffe students *"trained* in religion find that they *need* religion more often than do others" (p. 11).

TABLE 3. PERCENTAGE OF HIGH CHURCH ATTENDERS DURING FINAL HIGH
SCHOOL YEARS WHO LET ATTENDANCE "SLIDE" AT COLLEGE, AND
"SLIDERS" COMBINED WITH THOSE CONTINUING TO BE "UNIN-
VOLVED," BY PARENTAL EDUCATION AND ATTENDANCE

	"Sliders"			"Sliders" plus "Uninvolved"		
	State	Mid-Central	western	State	Mid-Central	western
Father's Education						
Less than 8 years	14.9	37.5	15.4	23.1	44.4	21.4
High school	35.2	26.9	23.2	48.1	47.2	28.4
College	43.9	55.0	19.6	56.3	64.2	21.2
Professional or graduate school	40.0	45.3	29.2	63.3	53.9	39.3
Mother's Education						
Less than 8 years	13.8	33.3	16.7	21.9	33.3	23.1
High school	32.4	44.7	29.2	46.3	57.4	33.8
College	45.2	46.3	10.6	59.0	54.8	17.6
Professional or graduate school	42.1	45.8	37.5	66.6	60.6	37.5
Father's religious attendance						
Never or practically never	27.0	26.8	50.0	70.3	73.2	75.0
Few times per year—						
Couple times each month	32.9	40.4	15.2	70.6	71.9	30.3
Almost every week or more	26.3	38.4	18.8	32.7	42.0	19.8
Mother's religious attendance						
Never or practically never	19.7	23.5	25.0	90.2	70.8	62.5
Few times per year—						
Couple times each month	36.3	36.3	11.4	89.3	80.0	27.7
Almost every week or more	28.0	28.0	21.6	33.0	46.1	23.3

religious services, the higher a student's participation while in high school, and
the lower the probability of becoming a *slider* in college. If both parents
participate in religious services regularly, we would expect the student to
participate more than if only one parent participates regularly; and similarly,
the probability that he will become a *slider* is less if both parents participate
regularly in religious services.

Religious participation is strongly related to both mother's and father's
religious participation in all three samples: the greater the religious participation of parents, the greater that of the students (See Table 2). Also, when the
mother never or practically never participated in religious services, the student's
rate of participation is substantially lower than when the father never or
practically never attended.

The probability of becoming a *slider* in college is not related to parental
participation patterns (Table 3). The reason for this, obviously, is that parental behavior has already had its greatest impact prior to college entry. However, when we combine those who are *uninvolved* and those who became
sliders in college, we see the dramatic influence of parents' attendance patterns
on their children. Unless parents attend church "almost every week or more,"
the probability that their children will be *sliders* or else *uninvolved* is very

great. The exception to this conclusion is Midwestern. But even here, the probability that the student will be *uninvolved* in a religious organization is rather great unless parents participate at least occasionally.

We may probe one step further and ask to what extent, if any, attendance is influenced by the joint participation of parents. In Table 4, we see that the student's participation is higher when both parents attend religious services regularly than when only one parent does so. This holds for both high school and the first months in college. Also, the frequency of religious participation tends to be lower if both parents are inactive than if only one parent is inactive (cf: Tables 2 and 4). However, the obverse does not hold: i.e., our data do not support the proposition that the mother's regular attendance is as good a predictor of the student's attendance as the regular attendance of both parents.

SUMMARY AND CONCLUSIONS

The primary focus of this paper has been on the relationships between the changes in religious participation patterns during the transition from high school to college and parental participation and education, among three fresh-

TABLE 4.   FOUR INDICES OF STUDENT ATTENDANCE AT RELIGIOUS SERVICES ACCORDING TO PARENTAL ATTENDANCE

	State	Central	Midwestern
I. *Mean annual frequency of attendance in high school*[1] *when:*			
Both parents attend regularly[2]	49.2	49.5	61.3
Only one parent attends regularly	40.8	36.5	54.1
Both parents never or practically never attend	12.3	20.8	24.1
II. *Mean frequency of attendance during first two months of college*[3] *when:*			
Both parents attend regularly	6.2	5.4	8.0
Only one parent attends regularly	4.7	4.2	8.0
Both parents never or practically never attend	1.2	3.8	3.7
III. *Percent*[4] *letting attendance "slide" in college when:*			
Both parents attend regularly	26.8	36.3	20.2
Only one parent attends regularly	34.4	49.0	20.6
IV. *Percent*[4] *becoming "sliders" or continuing "uninvolved" when:*			
Both parents attend regularly	29.8	39.2	21.3
Only one parent attends regularly	47.9	65.3	23.5

[1] "Approximate mean attendance in high school," is estimated by weighting responses to the question, "About how often did *you* attend religious services during your junior and senior years in high school?" as follows: Daily or several times a week, 100; Each week, 50; Almost every week, 40; A couple of times each month, 25; About once a month, 12; A few times a year, 4; Practically never, 1; and Never, 0.
[2] Regular attendance is defined as almost every week or more.
[3] "Approximately mean attendance during first two months at college" is a direct interpolation for the eight-week period.
[4] Computed from base of "faithfuls" plus "sliders" plus "uninvolved."

man college populations. It was found that religious participation in high school had been considerable, but that a sizeable proportion of those who had attended regularly in high school showed marked declines in this pattern during the first two months of college.

While these conclusions hold for all three schools, there are, nevertheless, substantial differences. Of the two religiously affiliated schools, the freshmen entering Midwestern had attended religious services during high school with greater frequency and they began a pattern of greater frequency in college. Central freshmen had attended religious services only slightly more often than State students during the first two months at college, and actually became *sliders* in greater proportion.

Two possible concomitants of religious participation—parents' participation and education—were examined. The hypothesis that education has an intergenerational secularizing effect led to the prediction of an inverse relationship between the educational level of the parents and the attendance pattern of the student. This found support at State and Central, but not at Midwestern. However, religious participation in college was not lower when both parents had reached a high level of educational attainment than when only one parent had done so.

The extent of students' religious attendance was closely associated with their parents' pattern of attendance. Participation was greater if both parents participated regularly than if only one parent participated regularly. The rate of participation was lower among students reporting that their mothers never or practically never attended religious services than for those reporting their fathers never or practically never attended (though the difference was not great). When the joint effect of both parents' inactivity was taken into account, the rate of participation was only slightly lower than when the mother was inactive, suggesting that the mother's inactivity had a greater impact on the student than the father's inactivity.

In short, the students' religious participation did decline substantially when they entered college, but the extent to which this decline occurred among the campuses in this investigation varied considerably.

Limitations to the data pointed out along the way disallow taking of the evidence presented here as conclusive. However, our data do lead to some important observations. One is that caution must be exercised in generalizing findings from a single case study. If the present investigation had included only students from State, the findings would have been very clear-cut, and the inclination might have been to overgeneralize. Inclusion of data from the two additional campuses, however, demonstrated the fact that the empirical concomitants of religious participation are, in fact, not that clear at all.

Religion obviously occupies a position of varying prominence on different college campuses, and its prominence on a given campus seems to be an important determinant of the role that religion will play in the life of the students there. In some cases, in fact, this level of prominence may become a factor in college selection by the student and/or his parents. Clearly, generalizations regarding the impact of campus life on student religion cannot appropriately be made until not only the range in types of campus milieus has been established but the proportion of campuses fitting each type, as well.

Further, methodological cautions should be emphasized. For one, this study tells us nothing about changes that may take place in the religious participation patterns of that great majority of youth who leave home to take a job or enter the service rather than going to college.

The data reported here are cross-sectional: they tell us something about what happened to religious participation during the first two months of college. We don't know what will happen to these people's participation habits between that time and the time they are seniors, no less what will happen after college.

We have focused on only one kind of religious involvement, namely participation, or attendance. While we have noted that participation is positively related to other kinds of religious involvement, we have fallen far short of controlling all the predictable variance, and thus, other measures of religious involvement may be related to the other variables considered in this study in quite different ways.

There are, too, other speculative interpretations of the effects of higher education on religion in American society. Some argue that decline in religious participation in college is only another phase of adolescent rebellion against parents and adult society, and that when young people marry and begin their families, they return to regular participation in religious organizations. But if they do return, does the regularity of their participation change? Are the motives for their participation the same? Do they hold different views regarding the teachings of the church? If they reject some of the principal premises of their faith, but participate in religious activities for the moral or social benefits of the church, what effect does this religious perspective have on their offspring? Are the children of people who reject the teachings of the church in part more likely to reject the teaching of the church in toto? If the religious views of the people and their leaders are becoming more secular, what implications does this have for the role of religion and the church in contemporary society, and for society two generations hence?

For all the concern with the role of the church and religion in contemporary society, there are no empirical answers to these very important questions. Our contribution to an understanding of these complex problems is at best a small piece in a large puzzle. We have focused on the religious participation of college students because we believe that if significant changes are occurring in the texture of religion in America, a great share of these changes have their genesis on the college campus.

CHAPTER 8

The Social Problem
Status of Youth

It may be that the status of youth in all societies is problematic. There is evidence that adults have been concerned about the offensive behavior of juveniles at least since recorded history began. Of course, much of this concern is associated with the "natural" imperfection of behavior in the earlier stages of socialization, the threat to the adult ego by less-than-satisfactory behavior of progeny, the inaccurate recall of adults as to how well they behaved when they were young, and the inappropriateness of the current adult generations' behavioral standards for those maturing in somewhat different circumstances.

It seems, however, that in modern industrial societies the problematic status of youth is both quantitatively and qualitatively different. Exact explanations for the difference are not available. Previous readings in this volume have alluded to some relevant variables, e.g., the prolonged preparatory stage prior to full adult social citizenship, the high value placed on the fresh approaches and the flexibility of youth in a technological society, the "future orientation" of modern adult generations, etc. Other factors, such as the rapidly spreading belief that societal forces can be successfully harnessed and directed toward specific goals, are undoubtedly important also for explaining the unequaled concern of modern industrial societies for the condition of their youth.

Whatever has propelled the problems of youth into social consciousness, they are there in such profusion and prominence that adults in modern industrial societies tend to imbue the total youth status with a problematic character. That is to say, beyond the response to individuals and categories of youths who evidence specific problem behavior, the social position which lies between childhood and adulthood is itself perceived to be problematic. Being among the adolescent or youthful *means* occupying a social position whose role enactments are likely to be perceived as problems by significant portions of the society—both young and adult. In a sense we are describing a social structural condition somewhat analogous to the "storm and stress" which has been seen as part of the normal personality development of adolescents by many psychologists and psychiatrists. From the unsophisticated and agonizing question, "What's wrong with youth today?" to the aura pervading the preceding selections in this anthology, it is abundantly clear that in highly industrialized societies as they are currently configured, the status of youth is unclear, poorly integrated, conflictual—in other words, problematic.

An amazingly small volume of literature has been devoted to analyses of the problematic nature of the position or status of youth. Most efforts focus upon problem individuals and the possible explanations of their errant behavior. In more recent writings an occasional reference is made to the notions of position problems rather than personality problems. It is not that a focus on behavioral problems as personality inadequacies is an unproductive perspective, but there is obvious merit to the analysis of the social origins of personality problems which might reflect social structural conditions and to an analysis of the social process of differentiating problem from non-problem behavior by a society's diverse membership.

The four selections which follow have been chosen to illustrate the growing awareness of the status of youth itself presenting a social problem to the established adult order.

In the first selection Bordua traces the development of major perspectives from which juvenile delinquency has been explained. It is interesting to note that all approaches are compatible with the spirit of the other selections in this chapter, i.e., that the position of youth in modern industrial societies is in itself problematic.

After reading of Michael Brown's fears that modern America is becoming less tolerant of the unique behaviors of youths, you may not be surprised to find academic explanations for delinquency swerving toward definitional or labeling concerns at the time delinquency steadily increases. Brown provides an insightful description of "hippies" and their near universal condemnation by the established order. Their extreme behavior aside, Brown's major point is that in the instance of "hippies" persecution has become institutionalized rather than the rite of accommodation as suggested by the next writer. Thomas Smith's case study of teen-age beach resort riots catches the essence of an institutionalized problems-oriented relationship between youth and the adult world. Youths on vacation looked for clashes with authority and the Authorities busily prepared for what they knew would come. Those in both camps walked through their roles of preparation, instigation, conflict, and disengagement and planning for the next time. Appropriate labels were attached routinely, newspaper editorials appeared which mildly chastized all participants, and tactics were nudged into greater sophistication. But then "boys will be boys" and "youths will be youthful" and that *means* rowdy crowd behavior and the attendant problems.

Probably only in an advanced technological society in which youth is affluent, congregated, self-confident, unsure of its identity, and unencumbered with critical responsibilities could it engage in such time consuming and personally low-yielding activities. Likewise only in such societies is the established order likely to engage in a dialogue of accommodation, treatment, repression, and negotiation. The two selections end, therefore, on different notes: The first on the point that dramatic and persistent difference is met with condemnation and repression which then spreads to broader social application with fearful dimensions and consequences, the second that the Establishment and Youth engage in a game of mutual influence and adjustment.

The last selection deals less with the dialogue between youth engaged in socially disapproved activities and the agencies responding to this behavior and more with the process of attempting to develop explanations via social research methodologies for involvement or non-involvement in socially disapproved behavior. The behavior under study is illegal drug use. There is a societal paranoia over the alleged wide-spread use of marihuana among youth of high-school and college age. State and federal laws and the parental generation are not as tolerant of drug use as are the young themselves. The legitimacy of norms governing drug use is being questioned by the adolescents as a whole in this study. However, the likelihood of marihuana involvement is impressively associated in a positive direction with a variety of family variables: broken homes, parental use of liquor and "legal" drugs, parental indifference and coolness. Planful inquiries such as this one by Nechama Tec increase our understanding of adolescent behavior through systematic study. Indeed, the contradictory and emotionally based attitudes toward drug use emphasize the value of social research.

SOCIOLOGICAL PERSPECTIVES
ON DEVIANCE AMONG JUVENILES*

DAVID J. BORDUA

Since juvenile delinquency and other forms of socially deviant conduct are largely the product of social forces, both our understanding of such phenomena and our efforts to cope with them must of necessity be largely influenced by sociological theory. It is the purpose of the present chapter to review realistically the present status of sociological thought.

The present period is one in which there is considerable theory-building in progress. To understand the significance of this, we shall first deal with what we shall term "the received tradition," the accepted thinking which had developed by the close of the 1940's. Then, we shall examine current theories, which stress the nature and effects of subcultures. Lastly, we shall deal with the key questions concerning how the several theories can be tested, the bearing of alternative explanations, and the significant facts which challenge the theories.

The Received Tradition

By the end of World War II, sociological theory of delinquency had developed into a loose body of doctrine centering around a few basic organizing concepts and approaches: the area approach, social disorganization, differential association, and culture conflict. Of these, the last was the least well formulated, although it was at times treated as the master concept which somehow included the others. While most of the developments underlying these basic orienting ideas are now ancient intellectual history, probably familiar to everyone, there is still some gain in reviewing the core of these perspectives as background for some of the more recent theoretical developments. The most interesting use of these ideas was in the so-called area approach which we may take as our starting point.

THE AREA APPROACH

As is still true, the "received tradition" was an attempt to make sense of both a major social change and a set of observations about delinquency. The social change was the combination of urbanization and immigration; the

* Reprinted from David J. Bordua, "Sociological Perspectives," in William Wattenberg, ed., *Social Deviance among Youth*, The Sixty-Fifth Yearbook of the National Society for the Study of Education (Chicago: University of Chicago Press), 1966, pp. 78–101, by permission of the author and the publisher.

observations were the facts that rates of recorded delinquency varied from place to place in the city, that these variations were appreciable, and that variations in recidivism rates parallel variations in rates of initial delinquency.[1] A subsidiary observation, which was to constitute in the long run a more important one, was that delinquent acts were generally committed in group situations. The reasons for the significance of this observation—so commonplace now but so fateful then—lay more in what interpretations it seemed to preclude than in its positive contributions. It served as the major weapon in the struggle against abnormal psychology, which characterized so much sociological thought.

The approach to the theoretical explanation of these facts was on several levels, which we may designate as the ecological, the demographic, the area organization, the delinquent organization, and the individual levels. On the ecological level, Shaw and McKay attempted to relate the spatial variations in the incidence of delinquency to the functional development of the city as it was reflected in the economic and social differentiation of spatial areas. The processes of ecological location and land use were seen as creating distinguishable areas within the city. Such areas were characterized by specialized types of land use and bore a predictable, functional relationship to the center of urban dominance—the central business district. At this level, Shaw and McKay were attempting to show that the "delinquency area," like the "roomer's underworld" or the other "natural areas," could be derived from fundamental urban locational processes. Much effort was expended showing that high delinquency rates were found in areas adjacent to sectors of business and industrial land use and that rates declined systematically as one proceeded outward from the city center.

On the demographic level, the area approach attempted to discover what populations were attracted to these "delinquency areas." These are the places where those who find themselves in a poor competitive position must locate (and from which they move, given improvements in their competitive positions). Such areas become populated by recent immigrants, Negro and white migrants, adult criminals, and so on. The population heterogeneity and instability and the presence of recent immigrant and migrant groups, unaccustomed to urban life, set the stage for the development of the social structure of the delinquency area as a community.

In 1931, Shaw and McKay referred to these areas as areas of social disorganization—areas in which the lack of community consensus on values, the shifts in population, and the lack of organized agencies to express the conventional sentiments of the local populace all combine to produce a "community" which is one in name only and which cannot function as an effective agency of social control. Thus, the urban ecological process as a way of "organizing" the larger community results in the "disorganization" of some of the subcommunities. The term "social disorganization" antedated the work of Shaw and McKay, and, since their use of it, it has had a checkered

---

[1] Clifford R. Shaw and Henry D. McKay, *Social Factors in Juvenile Delinquency*, Vol. II of National Commission on Law Observance and Enforcement, *Report on the Causes of Crime*. Washington: U.S. Government Printing Office, 1931. See especially chap. xii.

theoretical history. It was in much favor in the 1920's and '30's, went out of favor in the 1940's and '50's and shows signs of returning to favor in altered form in the 1960's.

At the level of delinquent organization, the condition of social disorganization enables delinquency to become a tradition: an organized, persistent competitor of the moral values of conventional society. In their discussion of the social structure of delinquency itself, Shaw and McKay emphasize that it is a group phenomenon, that the delinquent group possesses a differentiated and well-integrated cultural system or code of behavior, and that this system is handed down from generation to generation by personal contacts between older and younger boys.

Finally, from this discussion of the socially structured nature of delinquent activities, Shaw and McKay proceeded to the level of the individual delinquent. The individual boy becomes a delinquent by becoming a member of a group and participating in the delinquent cultural system. The desires and motives that are satisfied by this membership and participation are the same desires that in other social contexts lead to participation in conventional youth activities and are rewarded with recognition, esteem, companionship, thrills, and adventure.

DIFFERENTIAL-ASSOCIATION THEORY

The area approach and its attending core concepts of culture conflict and social disorganization came under heavy fire from other sociologists and, indeed, much of the recent theorizing is still a reaction to perceived inadequacies of the "Chicago synthesis." Before considering the currently popular subcultural theories as both criticisms and extensions of the received tradition, it is fruitful to carry the historical development further in the work of Sutherland.

Probably no theorist has been less well appreciated than Sutherland nor any theory less well understood than his "differential-association" theory. The theory was conceived by Sutherland as an attempt to do two things. First, he wanted a theory that would be general within its claimed sphere of application, and, second, he wanted a theory that would better link the broader social structural elements of the social disorganization approach to the level of individual behavior.

In this search Sutherland was led to make three major contributions. In describing his own theoretical attempts, Sutherland made the following statements in 1942:

> This culture conflict was interpreted as referring specifically to law and crime and as not including conflicts in relation to religion, politics, standard of living or other things. At an earlier date I had used the concept of culture conflict in this broader sense on the assumption that any kind of culture conflict caused crime. . . . The second concept, differential association, is a statement of culture conflict from the point of view of the person who commits the crime.
>
> The third concept, social disorganization, was borrowed from Shaw and McKay. I had used it but had not been satisfied with it because the organization of the delinquent group, which is very complex is social

disorganization only from an ethical or some other particularistic point of view . . . this concept has been changed to differential group organization, with organization for criminal activities on one side and organization against criminal activities on the other. . . . Differential group organization therefore should explain the crime rate, while differential association should explain the criminal behavior of a person.[2]

In many ways the most controversial and least well understood of these three contributions was the theory of differential association. As Cressey recently pointed out in an exhaustive review of the literature on the theory, criticism has often proceeded without much evidence of careful reading.[3] It seems appropriate, therefore, to reproduce the nine basic statements of the theory not only for their own sake but to illustrate the fact that the Sutherland formulation, taken in its entirety, illustrates one of the two basic modes of theorizing about delinquency—an approach through the efficacy of social control as compared with an approach through theories about deviant motivation. The propositions of the theory follow:

1. Criminal behavior is learned. . . .
2. Criminal behavior is learned in interaction with other persons in a process of communication. . . .
3. The principal part of the learning of criminal behavior occurs within intimate personal groups. . . .
4. When criminal behavior is learned, . . . the learning includes (*a*) techniques, of committing the crime, which are sometimes very complicated, sometimes very simple; (*b*) the specific direction of motives, drives, rationalizations, and attiudes. . . .
5. The specific direction of motives and drives is learned from definitions of legal codes as favorable and unfavorable. . . .
6. A person becomes delinquent because of an excess of definitions favorable to violation of law over definitions unfavorable to violation of law. . . .
7. Differential associations may vary in frequency, duration, priority and intensity. . . .
8. The process of learning criminal behavior by association with criminal and anti-criminal patterns involves all of the mechanisms that are involved in any other learning. . . .
9. Though criminal behavior is an expression of general needs and values, it is not explained by those general needs and values since non-criminal behavior is an expression of the same needs and values. . . .[4]

By 1942, proponents of the area approach had responded to many criticisms of the social disorganization concept. Social disorganization as an orienting concept is replaced by "differential social organization."[5] In addition

[2] Albert K. Cohen, Alfred R. Lindesmith, and Karl Schuessler, *The Sutherland Papers*, pp. 20–21. Bloomington, Indiana: University of Indiana Press, 1956.
[3] Donald R. Cressey, "Epidemiology and Child Conduct: A Case from Criminology," *Pacific Sociological Review*, III (Fall 1960), 47–58.
[4] Edwin H. Sutherland, *Principles of Criminology*. New York: J. B. Lippincott & Co., 1947 (fourth edition).
[5] Clifford R. Shaw and Henry D. McKay, *Juvenile Delinquency and Urban Areas*, esp. chap. vii. Chicago: University of Chicago Press, 1942.

to stressing subcommunity differences in social values and social structure rather than the blanket term "social disorganization," the authors of *Juvenile Delinquency and Urban Areas* made a brief excursion in a direction that was to provide the basic line of argument for the soon-to-appear subculture theories. Again a quotation seems appropriate.

> It is recognized that in a free society the struggle to improve one's status in terms of accepted values is common to all persons in all social strata. And it is a well-known fact that attempts are made by some persons in all economic classes to improve their positions by violating the rules and laws designed to regulate economic activity. However, it is assumed that these violations with reference to property are most frequent where the prospect of thus enhancing one's social status outweighs the chances for loss of position and prestige in the competitive struggle. It is in this connection that the existence of a system of values supporting criminal behavior becomes important as a factor in shaping individual life-patterns, since it is only where such a system exists that the person through criminal activity may acquire the material goods so essential for status in our society and at the same time increase, rather than lose, his prestige in the smaller group system of which he has become an integral part.[6]

Before discussing the subculture theories, however, it is appropriate to try to draw out some of the basic themes underlying the material which we have so far presented. The most fundamental is the idea that delinquency is a consequence of the failure of social control. Thus, attempts at theoretical generalization, at least within the body of material which we have so far discussed, tend to be either at the level of the social structural conditions for effective social control or, as with differential-association theory, of the conditions whereby the individual is effectively governed by social control processes. This basic—and often unstated—presumption is at least as significant for what it tends to leave out as for what it includes. On the negative side, it means that this type of theorizing tends to scant development of theory of the motivation for delinquency.

The second theme concerns the several broad and often implicit presumptions with respect to the motivation underlying the "received tradition." First, some vague list of basic motives is assumed as the general equipment of the individual—delinquent and nondelinquent alike. The universality of these "motives" rules them out as an explanation of either deviance or conformity. The best example of this universality assumption in the older work is in the use of the famous four wishes of W. I. Thomas by Thrasher in his book, *The Gang.*[7] Thrasher posits that gang behavior responds to the same "needs" as does other behavior. The basic thrust of the analysis in Thrasher is that of normal boys satisfying normal needs in deviant (not "abnormal") ways. The same presupposition is restated in the ninth "proposition" of differential-association theory as cited above.

The second presumption regarding motivation is one which sees "motives" as deriving not from universal human "needs" but from participa-

[6] *Ibid.*, p. 183.
[7] Frederick M. Thrasher, *The Gang*. Edited by James F. Short, Jr. Chicago: University of Chicago Press, 1964 (revised edition).

tion in a specific society. An example of this formulation is given in the above quotation from *Juvenile Delinquency and Urban Areas*. In the earlier formulations, these motives, too, were "universal" within a given society and, therefore, as such, could not account for the differential frequency of delinquency as among individuals or subpopulations.

Finally, we may mention a subtheme concerning motivation that was especially visible in the first great study of what we have come to call "delinquent subcultures." Thrasher, while never offering a sophisticated theory of motivation, does describe in detail the social contexts within which gangs develop, and he does describe the seeming sources of satisfaction in gang membership and delinquent activities. Both explicitly and implicitly, Thrasher describes gang and delinquent activities as attractive to boys because of a variety of "situational payoffs," ranging from close companionship to monetary return from theft. This idea that gang activity exerts "pulls" on boys as well as being a response to "pushes" in the environment has not been systematically followed up.

Perhaps at the most fundamental level, what all these perspectives have in common—whether oriented to societal structure, to local community structure, or to a delinquency-supporting group or individual—is the idea that conformity, not deviance, requires explanation. *Deviance occurs in the absence of effective devices for producing conformity.* Thus, theft as a device for acquiring goods is a natural technique which occurs in the absence of effective prohibition. Violence is an equally natural technique for the achievement of individual or group ends. It is, indeed, a technique of considerable generality in that, like buying and selling, it can be adapted to a variety of purposes.

In the broader context of intellectual history, these theorists were Hobbesian in their basic perspective on man and society. The more modern theorists seem to have given up this basic proposition, partly because it does not account satisfactorily for the questions of motivation and partly because of more subtle shifts in the sociological *Zeitgeist* away from the Hobbesian perspective to analyses based on assumptions of social equilibrium.

The third basic theme of these theorists is that the collective nature of delinquency serves two major functions. The delinquency-bearing group simultaneously serves as a barrier to effective social control and serves to relate a whole series of otherwise "neutral" gratifications to the continued participation in delinquency. In short, through the mechanism of the group, the individual delinquent is able to secure the rewards of companionship, recreation, prestige, et cetera, which otherwise he would have to forfeit. He is able to garner many or most of the rewards of conformity by adhering to a "deviant" group and its norms. The group nature of delinquency, then, is a key factor in lowering the costs of deviance to tolerable levels while it simultaneously raises the gains attached to deviance.

THE PROBLEM OF GENERALITY

Among the most severe criticisms of the received tradition has been the pointing out of its weaknesses as a general theory of crime or delinquency. There are several aspects to this criticism, and the sociological perspectives we have been considering are varyingly vulnerable to the different aspects. The first criticism was that, in their focus on certain segments of the social structure, the sociological theorists neglected crime and delinquency occurring in other segments. Most pointedly, they tended to neglect the problem of delinquency in high-status areas in which the usual battery of slum-oriented analytic techniques was hard to use. Secondly, they tended to ignore the problem of individual differences in whatever segments of the social structure they were found.

In many ways, these two are the same problem—or at least have been considered so. In fact, with some notable exceptions, the problem of generalizing from the slum to the suburbs has been seen as a problem in moving from the "social" to the "individual" level of analysis. This has been partly due to the observation that delinquency tends to be more "individualized" in higher-status areas—an observation which may not be sound.

Sutherland's differential-association theory is perhaps the major American attempt to formulate a general theory of delinquency or crime that would apply both across social environments and across individuals. Such attempts are few in the more recent literature. The formulation of a "differential-identification" approach by Glaser and the work using reference-group theory by Haskell are among the recent attempts, as is the development of containment theory by Reckless.[8]

The concern for generality led naturally and, indeed, was a response to the problem of individual differences in delinquency. The question was often raised by psychological critics. Broadly speaking, some version or other of differential association or allied approaches was the answer. The individual becomes delinquent by associating with delinquent "patterns." But what was the source of these patterns? And could it not be just as legitimate to say that the delinquent patterns are simply the result of boys, already delinquent joining together?

Thus, the Gluecks could make the rather embarassing rejoinder:

> So far as delinquency is concerned, then, "birds of a feather flock together." This tendency is a much more fundamental fact than the theory that accidental differential association of non-delinquents with delinquents is the basic cause of crime.[9]

These criticisms called for a theory of the origins of the delinquent patterns stressed by Sutherland. The first attempt to formulate one comes close to reorienting the whole problem of individual differences and, indeed, to rephrasing the problem of motivation.

Theories of Subcultural Origins

It is not clear when such terms as delinquent patterns, delinquent traditions, and the like became theoretically formalized under the label "subcul

[8] Daniel Glaser, "Criminality Theories and Behavioral Images," *American Journal of Sociology*, LXI (March 1951), 433–44; Martin Haskell, "Toward a Reference Group Theory of Juvenile Delinquency," *Social Problems*, VIII, No. 3 (Winter 1960–61) 220–30; Walter C. Reckless, "A New Theory of Delinquency and Crime," *Federal Probation*, XXV (December 1961), 42–46.
[9] Sheldon and Eleanor Glueck, *Unravelling Juvenile Delinquency*, p. 164. Cambridge Massachusetts: Harvard University Press, 1950.

ture." It is clear, however, that the first major theorist to develop a theory of delinquent subcultures was Cohen, in his now classic book, *Delinquent Boys*. Since that time several other treatments of gang delinquency, broadly or specifically in the subcultural vein, have appeared. For contemporary theoretical purposes the most significant later development is the opportunity theory of subcultural delinquency associated with the work of Cloward and Ohlin. Contemporaneous with these two approaches and focused on the same problem of lower-class, urban, male, gang delinquency, but proceeding from a quite different perspective, is the work of Miller, which we may characterize as the "lower-class-culture" approach.[10]

STATUS-DEPRIVATION APPROACH

The status-deprivation approach, first stated by Cohen in 1955, can be briefly summarized as follows: Individuals are sensitive to the evaluations of others in their social milieus, especially of those in positions of authority or prestige. This concern for positive evaluations from others is reflected in the taking on by individuals of these same evaluations as aspects of self-regard. Such evaluations in social groups become differentiated and unevenly distributed and, thus, constitute systems of differential *status*. The concern to maintain or increase such evaluations may motivate a variety of behaviors, depending mainly on the status-ranking criteria used in a group. Loss of or inability to gain status may be an adjustment problem for individuals. In a now classic statement, Cohen says:

> The crucial condition for the emergence of new cultural forms is the existence, *in effective interaction with one another, of a number of actors with similar problems of adjustment*.[11]

When interpreting the development of delinquent subcultures in urban, male, working-class populations, Cohen goes beyond the general theory of subcultures as enunciated in the quotation to specify (*a*) the content of delinquent subcultures, (*b*) the social structural sources of the problem of adjustment, and (*c*) the mechanisms whereby the problem of adjustment gives rise to the particular collective resolution contained in the delinquent subculture.

Cohen describes the subculture as malicious, negativistic, versatile, hedonistic, nonutilitarian, and oriented toward group autonomy from adult controls. By contrast, the "middle-class measuring rod" used by the formal

---

[10] Albert K. Cohen, *Delinquent Boys: The Culture of the Gang* (Glencoe, Illinois: Free Press, 1955); Albert K. Cohen and James F. Short, Jr., "Research in Delinquent Subcultures," *Journal of Social Issues*, XIV (1958), 20–36; Richard A. Cloward, "Illegitimate Means, Anomie and Deviant Behavior," *American Sociological Review*, XXIV (April 1959), 164–76; Richard A. Cloward and Lloyd E. Ohlin, *Delinquency and Opportunity* (Glencoe, Illinois: Free Press, 1960). The following papers are all by Walter B. Miller, "Lower Class Culture as a Generating Milieu of Gang Delinquency," *Journal of Social Issues*, XIV (1958), 5–19; "Preventive Work with Street-Corner Groups: Boston Delinquency Project," *The Annals*, CCCXXII (March 1959), 97–196; "Implications of Urban Lower-Class Culture for Social Work," *Social Service Review*, XXXIII (September 1959), 219–36.

[11] Cohen, *Delinquent Boys, op. cit.*, p. 59.

child-rating institutions of the society emphasizes ambition, individual responsibility, the cultivation of skill, postponement of gratification, manners and courtesy, constructive use of leisure, and respect for property.

The value themes of the delinquent subculture and of the middle-class measuring rod are diametrically opposed. The delinquent culture stands the middle-class measuring rod on its head. It is not only an evasion culture or a subcultural variant but a specifically oppositional culture or "contraculture."[12]

The problem of adjustment to which this culture is a solution is produced by the fact that the middle-class measuring rod is applied to all comers in the society in accordance with what Cohen calls the "democratic status universe" which characterizes American society. All boys are not, however, equally prepared to measure up. Cultural differences associated with social class position and residential distribution assure, simultaneously, that the urban, lower-class (Cohen says "working-class," a source of much ambiguity) population will contain more ill-prepared youngsters and that they will be in "effective interaction." Because the less well-prepared boys are sensitive to the evaluations of teachers, et cetera, the problem of social esteem becomes one, simultaneously, of self-esteem. The subculture then must deal with both, the enemy without and the enemy within.

Because the problem is one of social evaluation, the solution must be collective. Because the boys suffer from ambivalence about the middle-class measuring rod, the collective solution must defend against self-recognition of the validity of the middle-class judgment. Because the delinquent subculture begins to exacerbate conflict between the boys and the surrounding community, it also comes to contain definitions of conventional persons as hostile, et cetera. Thus, the subculture has a developmental cycle which—other things being equal—drives it more and more into opposition.

Cohen's description of the subculture as malicious, et cetera, and especially as nonutilitarian, led him to reject a closely related formulation—a formulation which, in its modern version, is associated with the work of Robert Merton. According to Cohen, Merton's theory of anomie (anomie is a technical term referring to normlessness, lack of accepted standards of value) cannot account for the nonrational features of the subculture and is more appropriate as an interpretation of more utilitarian, economically oriented adult crime.[13]

OPPORTUNITY-STRUCTURE THEORY

Anomie theory, however, became the basis of the second of the major theories of the origins of delinquent subcultures. In their work, Cloward and Ohlin emphasize the disjuncture between cultural goals and socially struc-

---

[12] For elaborations on the distinctions between subculture and contraculture, see J. Milton Yinger, "Contraculture and Subculture," *American Sociological Review*, XXV (1960), 625–35; and Ruth Shonle Cavan, *Juvenile Delinquency*, especially chap. ii. (New York: J. B. Lippincott Co., 1962).

[13] Robert K. Merton, "Social Structure and Anomie," in *Social Theory and Social Structure*. New York: Free Press of Glencoe, 1957 (revised edition). The Merton formulation originally appeared in 1938. For an extremely valuable exploration of this entire area of theory, see *Anomie and Deviant Behavior* (edited by Marshall B. Clinard. New York: Free Press of Glencoe, 1964).

tured means so central to the Merton formulation. They derive from this starting point a theory of the origins of delinquent subcultures that stresses not the differential ability to measure up according to the middle-class standards but, rather, the *unjust* distributions of opportunity among the social classes.

Cloward and Ohlin take a much more objectivist and structural position and assume that it is those boys who want only higher incomes and not status mobility (and who are therefore presumably insensitive to the middle-class measuring rod), who respond to the limitation of opportunity by directing hostility against the social order rather than against themselves. They do so because the barriers to opportunity are, in a sense, themselves deviant— opportunity is not distributed according to the formally announced criteria.

Blaming the system leads to alienation and the withdrawal of sentiments of legitimacy from the established norms. The subcultural outcome of the alienation will depend on the particular neighborhood. Where *illegitimate* opportunities are present and promise satisfying careers, i.e., where crime is stable and linked to the young through some age-graded relational system, alienation will result in criminal subcultures oriented to economic gain. Where both the controlling influence and the anticipatory gratifications of stable crime are not present, subcultures leading to combat are a more likely resolution. With those boys who are "double failures," i.e., who cannot anticipate gratifying opportunities in either legitimate or illegitimate opportunity systems, retreatist or drug-use subcultures are more likely.

ALTERNATIVE THEORIES

There are a variety of alternative theories which differ in one or more ways from the "status-deprivation" and "opportunity-structure" approaches. Yablonsky in *The Violent Gang* differs, primarily on the descriptive level, in arguing that the conflict subculture serves essentially as a public myth to legitimate private pathology. He argues that the primary recruits for the violent gang are suffering from basic social rejection in interpersonal relations, especially in the family, far more than from rejections visited upon them by the formal institutional system or by anticipations of low income and blocked aspirations in the labor market.[14]

Bloch and Niederhoffer in their book, *The Gang*, question the empirical limitation of group delinquency to lower-class populations and emphasize not class but adolescence as the major social structural root of delinquent gangs.[15]

Two other theorists, Miller and Matza, have dealt with delinquent subcultures in ways which are more significant for our concern with delinquency theory in sociology. Their perspectives are quite different, but both challenge the kind of formulation found in the work of Cohen and of Cloward and Ohlin. They do so in different ways, however, and in the process raise significant general issues. Miller challenges what may be called the reactive nature of gang culture; Matza calls into question the at-least-implicit reification of the delinquent subculture.

[14] Lewis Yablonsky, *The Violent Gang*. New York: Macmillan Co., 1962.
[15] Herbert Bloch and Arthur Niederhoffer, *The Gang*. New York: Philosophical Library, 1958.

Miller has challenged not only the factual premises of the Cohen and Cloward-Ohlin arguments but, more fundamentally, the entire style of theorizing. Where they are concerned with the delinquent subculture as a reaction to real or anticipated deprivations at the hands of the dominant society, Miller sees the life style of gang delinquency as an expression of lower-class culture. Miller claims that the common conditions of life at the bottom of the economic heap in large American cities give rise, on the adult level, to a culture built around transient and insecure employment, the female-based household, and a series of crucial focal concerns.

> It is the thesis of this paper that from these extremely diverse and heterogeneous origins (with, however, certain common features), there is emerging a relatively homogeneous and stabilized native-American lower class culture; however, in many communities the process of fusion is as yet in its earlier phases, and evidences of the original ethnic or locality culture are still strong.[16]
>
> In the case of "gang" delinquency, the cultural system which exerts the most direct influences on behavior is that of the lower class community itself—a long established, distinctively patterned tradition with an integrity of its own—rather than a so-called "delinquent subculture" which has arisen through conflict with middle class culture and is oriented to the deliberate violation of middle class norms.[17]

Miller's conception of lower-class culture includes a series of "focal concerns"—a conceptualization that seems to have won a secure place in the literature along with Cohen's general theory of subcultures and Cloward's concept of illegitimate opportunities. These focal concerns are trouble, toughness, smartness, excitement, fate, and autonomy.[18] Miller sees gang delinquency as mainly the adolescent form of lower-class culture rather than as a reaction to middle-class culture or as the result of alienation from dominant norms.

In this all-too-brief excursion through the twisting byways of subculture theory we shall consider only one more perspective. The latest of the "little books" on group delinquency is by Matza.[19] *Delinquency and Drift* is concerned with several topics other than those of the delinquent subculture. It is basically a critique of positivistic criminology—critical of it on two general grounds. First, the positivists overstress determinism as a property of social reality rather than as a property of scientific models. A scientific perspective becomes reified and imputed to the empirical world. Second, due partly to the methodological commitments of positivism, the object of study becomes reified and inaccurately differentiated. The psychological positivists tend to reify the criminal or delinquent "personality"; the sociological positivists tend to reify the delinquent "subculture."

The critique of positivism leads to an attempt to view delinquency in the theoretical perspective provided by classical criminology and, therefore, in a

---

[16] Miller, "Implications of Urban Lower Class Culture for Social Work," *op. cit.*, p. 225.
[17] Miller, "Lower Class Culture as a Generating Milieu of Gang Delinquency," *op. cit.*, pp. 5–6.
[18] *Ibid.*, p. 7.
[19] David Matza, *Delinquency and Drift*. New York: John Wiley & Sons, Inc., 1964.

legal context. The Matza perspective is characterized by a strong emphasis on a quasi-legal vocabulary in describing the content and functions of delinquent subcultures and also on contacts with the legal order as a source of delinquents' beliefs. Indeed, Matza says that he is concerned with the consequences of injustice suffered at the hands of the legal system, just as Cloward and Ohlin are concerned with injustice at the hands of the economic system. Matza's book, however, deals less with the origins of delinquent subcultures than with the functions of subcultural beliefs. Indeed, he says, "there is a subculture of delinquency but it is not a delinquent subculture."[20] The basic function of these beliefs is to neutralize the moral bind of law—to create the condition of *drift*. Thus, the subculture of delinquency serves not to compel but to enable delinquency.

Matza's approach to the delinquent subculture contains, then, the following major elements. First, it is a theory of the functions rather than of the origins of the subculture. Second, it strongly emphasizes the partial nature of the delinquent's commitment to the norms of the subcultural system. Thirdly, the empirical data drawn upon emphasize the same thing, i.e., the fact that the commitment to delinquency is partial and sporadic and may not reflect very closely the "private" values of the participants. Thus, Matza challenges severely the implicit or explicit conception of the subcultural delinquents as "separated brethren" deeply committed to deviant values. He stresses especially that the beliefs of the subculture are most strongly expressed in what he calls the "situation of company" and, indeed, even goes so far as to state that the reason why delinquents are convinced that their friends are committed to delinquent values is essentially pluralistic ignorance. At one point, he interprets the subculture of delinquency as essentially a cognitive mistake on a collective basis.

In addition to calling into question the solidity of the delinquent subculture, Matza—perhaps even more significantly—calls into question the oversimplistic concepts of central American values. In his concept of subterranean traditions, he points to the fact that in a pluralistic society many value traditions persist which are partially submerged but nevertheless fairly readily visible—especially to the young. The central significance of this criticism is that the use of a middle-class measuring rod or the ethic of universal success goals as a defining starting point in the analysis of deviant behavior may be inappropriate and is certainly an oversimplification of the value complexity of American society. Most crucial of Matza's points in this connection is the assertion that the same middle-class value-carriers who seek to impose the "middle-class measuring rod" also carry and display other values which may be contradictory. Thus, the instrumental activism imagery of Cohen's measuring rod competes with the expressive or consummatory activism of the "Pepsi generation." The plurality of displayed value patterns becomes of especial significance in understanding delinquency because so many delinquent offenses are "status offenses," i.e., forbidden only to the young. Thus, prohibitions against drink, driving, sex, and school truancy require only the passage of time or other change in status before they become inoperative.

[20] *Ibid.*, p. 33.

In the specific case of lower-class boys, we might point out that "middle-class values" are likely to be communicated by professional value-presenters, such as teachers, social workers, and the like, who probably present them in a rather formalized and systematized way as adjuncts of specialized role requirements. Thus, the middle-class values presented to lower-class boys are not likely to be, either in content or contextual support and flexibility, identical to the "same" values presented to "middle-class" boys. As another observation, we might point out that the vaunted ability of middle-class children to "defer gratification" is assisted by a massive input of immediate supportive gratification. Such is far less likely to be the case with lower-class boys. Indeed, the increasingly widespread image of the middle-class boy in his private bedroom studying hard as a precondition to driving his car to a party in a friend's "family room" where he and his peers will practice gratification deferral by consuming food and drink, playing records, and dancing the "frug" to display emotional restraint indicates that middle-class *adolescent* culture constitutes a major "subterranean tradition" with respect to the value preferences of the children of the poor.

It is increasingly clear in our society that middle-class status enables adolescents to have a far greater share of both immediate and delayed gratifications than is the case for lower-class boys. To ask lower-class boys to measure up to the middle-class measuring rod is to ask them to be not *like* but *unlike* middle-class adolescents—like in the costly ways, and unlike in the gratifying ways.

If we assume that class-linked styles of adolescent life are an important reference structure for lower-class boys—and not just class-linked adult roles or mobility chances—then the legitimating nexus between achievement and reward breaks down completely. Neither lower-class nor middle-class adolescents "deserve" what they get. The sumptuous life style of the middle-class adolescent and the sparse life style of his lower-class counterpart are purely gratuitous consequences of class position.

Problems of Proof

To the educator who has been reading these pages with an eye to finding material on the basis of which to decide what schools can do, whether or not to participate in some community endeavor, or how to react to suggestions, the existence of theories so widely divergent in their implications is a problem. That this uncertainty also afflicts public officials, social welfare organizations, and the general public offers little comfort.

Readers are bound to wonder how to judge which theories are "right," or how to decide which offer greatest promise. Hence, we must now turn to the question of how the several theories stand up under test.

It is not our aim here to review in detail the empirical findings of recent research on delinquency. However, it does seem appropriate to extend the discussion of the subcultural theories by dealing with some of the problems of proof posed by those theories and then to take up a few empirical findings that illustrate some of the problems.

The most fundamental problem of proof posed by the subcultural theories is that they are simply not stated in a propositional form. The statements in the theories vary from assumptions of fact to semipropositional statements of relationships between variables and to complex narrative interpretations. Thus, the theories are open to varied interpretations, and it is rarely clear what tests —if any are indeed possible—would be crucial for the theories.

DIFFICULTIES

Especially significant is the large role played by dubious factual assertions. Thus, Cohen's "description" of the delinquent subculture is presumably central to his theoretical formulation. If the description is false, then presumably the theory is invalid—or at least some parts of it are. Presumably, also, if the description is true, some alternative explanations are ruled out. Cohen, thus, specifically rules out Merton's theory of "anomie" because of the supposedly "nonutilitarian" features of the delinquent subculture. Yet, Cloward and Ohlin have no difficulty in using the Merton formulation as a basic underpinning, though at least two of their subcultural types—the conflict and drug-use types—would seem to fall within the "nonutilitarian" rubric.

Even a concept like "nonutilitarian" illustrates a third difficulty in the theories—the use of very high-level abstractions as descriptive terms. I have elsewhere pointed out that the supposed nonutilitarianism of the delinquent subculture in Cohen's formulation neglects the fact that acts may "make sense" when the focus is on the delinquent group and its conditions of maintenance rather than on its "subculture." Cohen's analysis also neglects the fact that it is the behavior of children and adolescents with which theory is concerned.[21] Recently, Short and Strodtbeck have attacked another of the Cohen characterizations—short-run hedonism—by showing how delinquent acts can flow from reasonable adaptations to situational exigencies which arise much more frequently in the lives of gang members. These exigencies are, however, consequences and not sources of gang membership.[22]

A similar problem arises with Cloward and Ohlin's use of the term "retreatist" to refer to the drug-use subculture. The concept of retreatism is itself ambiguous, and the *factual* justification for applying it to drug use is not clear.[23] In short, many of the "descriptive" assumptions of the theories are themselves better thought of as complex bundles of cryptohypotheses.

A fourth aspect of the problems of proof posed by these theories in one degree or another is their varied relations to temporal flow. This is a particularly difficult problem with opportunity-structure theory, since neither social history nor personal biography is dealt with systematically. The theory has

---

[21] David J. Bordua, "Delinquent Subcultures: Sociological Interpretations of Gang Delinquency," *The Annals of the American Academy of Political and Social Science,* CCCXXXVIII (November 1961), 121–22.

[22] Fred L. Strodtbeck and James F. Short, Jr., "Aleatory Risks versus Short-Run Hedonism in Explanation of Gang Action," *Social Problems,* XII, No. 2 (Fall 1964), 127–40.

[23] Alfred R. Lindesmith and John Gagnon, "Anomie and Drug Addiction" in *Anomie and Deviant Behavior.* Edited by Marshall B. Clinard. New York: Free Press of Glencoe, 1964.

both explicit and implicit ordering in a kind of flow chart, but the linkages between the theoretical flow and actual temporal succession of events are not clear.

Especially in the Cloward and Ohlin book, the time problem has several serious implications. One of them is the fact that the origins of subcultures and the origins of delinquency can be confused. Of more general significance is the fact that, as part of its atemporal character, opportunity theory has great difficulty specifying the "givens," to use Homans' phrase. Indeed, from some points of view, the theory has no "givens" at all but only cultureless structures and personalityless people. To specify givens or empirical parameters in a theory is tantamount to specifying what pasts the objects of analysis have had and, therefore, what variations among them exist at any time. When a theory is intended to be tested in the social world rather than in the laboratory, this specification is especially necessary, since ways of controlling for or systematically varying pasts are scarce.

ILLUSTRATIVE STUDIES

In addition to these matters of form which make testing difficult, there are also matters of content. Even where hypotheses can be derived which are in principle testable, it is often very difficult to do so in practice, as with the emphasis both of Cohen and of Cloward and Ohlin on aspirations and expectations of success. If delinquent boys are found to have larger gaps between aspiration and expectation than do nondelinquent boys, the theories presumably are borne out. But the size of the gap can be produced by several combinations of aspiration and expectation. Just as importantly, both aspirations and expectations can change over time. Because of the significance of the research problems associated with these questions, it is worthwhile to report the results of two studies for illustrative purposes.

The first is the study of delinquency in Flint, Michigan, by Gold.[24] The study compared 93 repeatedly delinquent boys (two or more serious crimes recorded by the police within a three-year period) with 93 nondelinquent boys. The boys were all white, in the normal I.Q. range, and over twelve years of age. Delinquents and nondelinquents were, in addition, individually matched for I.Q., age, school level (junior or senior high), and father's occupation.

Gold's data show that, as compared to the nondelinquents, the delinquent boys had lower job *aspirations*, the same perception of their chances to get the jobs they *did* want, a superior assessment of their chances of realizing the "American Dream," lower school grades in the fifth and sixth grades, an equal general belief in the American dream of equal opportunity, and similar general ratings of the relative desirability of a list of occupations.

Gold found further that school performance was positively correlated with boys' and parents' occupational aspirations and boys' occupational expectations. School performance was also positively correlated with attitude toward school. This complex network of data typifies the problem associated with test

[24] Martin Gold, *Status Forces in Delinquent Boys.* Ann Arbor, Michigan: Institute for Social Research, University of Michigan, 1963.

of the "status-deprivation" approach. On the face of it, the delinquents seem less likely than nondelinquents to be experiencing "status deprivation." They want less occupationally but are equally or more sure of getting it than are the nondelinquents. However, Gold interprets the lack of disparity between aspiration and expectation as "defensive" and indicative of felt personal failure. He supports his interpretation with the material on school performance, aspiration, expectations, and school adjustment. Gold argues that school failure leads to defensive lowering of aspirations and an accompanying sense of personal failure. He acknowledges that lower aspirations may lead to school failure rather than the reverse.

Whatever the plausibility of the interpretation, it is clearly a *post hoc* attempt to rationalize the failure of the initial hypothesis and, indeed, except for the replies to specific questions on occupational futures, the data simply replicate the large body of material indicating that school failure is involved in delinquency *somehow!* Sociologists have traditionally attacked psychoanalytic theories of delinquency because of the unresearchability of defensive processes. Gold's interpretation indicates that the shoe may now be on the other foot. Indeed, the ironic thing about theory and research in the subcultural vein is that, as the general thrust of the theories has grown more "sociological," the empirical controversies have, in many ways, grown more "psychological." Gold's work indicates also that presumptive reconstructions of life histories play an important part in research in the subcultural tradition even though the theories themselves are extremely vague on the subject.

Short reports more results bearing on the same questions of aspiration and delinquency from a study directly comparing gang and nongang boys in Chicago.[25] Six populations of boys were studied: Negro lower-class gang, Negro lower-class nongang, white lower-class gang, white lower-class nongang, Negro middle-class, and white middle-class. Gang and nongang lower-class boys of each race were selected from the same neighborhoods.

Two points from the Short-Strodtbeck material that bear on the general subcultural perspective should be mentioned before we tackle some of the data on aspiration. In the Chicago study the pure types of subcultures were hard to find. There were many conflict groups, especially among Negroes, but the members also did much stealing. It took the project a whole year to locate a retreatist, i.e., drug-using, group. The second point is that commitment to delinquent norms is quite tenuous, except in situations which involve the group, such as a threat from another group. Gang membership may include "corner boys" and even "college boys." In some ways the relationship of public and private, deviant and conventional norms seem reversed. Boys would express conventional attitudes toward work, school, and marriage in private but not in "public"—i.e., when with other gang members. Indeed, as

[25] James F. Short, Jr., "Gang Delinquency and Anomie," in *Anomie and Deviant Behavior op. cit.* The study was jointly conducted by Short and Fred L. Strodtbeck. It is the most promising of the current studies of delinquent "subcultures." The report by Short discussed here is especially germane to the issues of this chapter but is only one of many from the study. Many of these are cited in the above discussion by Short and in *Group Process and Gang Delinquency* by Short and Strodtbeck (Chicago: University of Chicago Press, 1965).

measured by semantic differential responses, lower-class gang boys are different from middle-class and nongang boys, not in what they believe but in what they do not disbelieve—the values supporting delinquency.

The findings reported by Short with respect to aspiration, expectation, school success, et cetera, are even more complex than those reported by Gold. In general the outcome for this part of subculture theories seems doubtful at best. Moreover, some of the research translations of theory are themselves doubtful.

Perhaps the most telling criticism from the theoretical point of view is Short's conclusion that commitment to conventional values should stress commitment to "means" norms rather than just to "goal" values, such as success. Thus, in the crucial case of educational aspiration and adjustment, he reports that unsuccessful school adjustment is related to high delinquency regardless of educational aspiration, while high aspiration reduces delinquency regardless of actual school success and race or gang status. On the question of perceived closure of educational opportunity, gang boys of both races reduce aspirations when closure is perceived, whereas nongang boys do so little or not at all.

Thus, the argument that subcultural delinquency should flourish among those whose high aspirations are unreduced either by school failure or perceived educational closure is not borne out. Persistent aspiration even in the face of poor performance and perceived closure seems to act as an insulator against delinquency. Perhaps high aspiration indexes a sensitivity to rewards borne by respectable primary groups and, therefore, a relative unwillingness to settle for the rewards of deviant groups emphasized in the earlier quotation from Shaw and McKay.

The most dramatic evidence of the effects of the aspiration variables as well as of the variability *within* gangs are the variations among Negro lower-class gang boys. In this category, those who had high educational aspirations and successful school adaptation had an average of 0.9 recorded offenses, while those who had low aspirations and poor adaptations had an average of 3.4 recorded offenses.[26]

Short interprets some of the findings as supportive of opportunity theory and some as not supportive. However, the difficulties presented by such a theory seem even more manifest in this sort of "test." At least some of the derivations from theory seem arguable. Thus, Cloward and Ohlin hypothesize (as mentioned earlier) that those boys who want monetary success without status change should be the main originators of delinquent subcultures. These boys will *not* aspire to higher status nor do well in school because they are deaf to the status-mobility message of the educational system. Nor, presumably, will they aspire to middle-class jobs for the same reason.[27] Indeed, one of the few derivable differences between the Cloward and Ohlin approach and

---

[26] Short, Jr., "Gang Delinquency and Anomie," *op. cit.*, Table 4, p. 110.
[27] Cloward and Ohlin, *Delinquency and Opportunity, op. cit.*, p. 95. I have already referred to this formulation as positing prealienated boys. They seem to have no aspirations—only greeds. Indeed, like many gang delinquents, they seem to *start out* theoretically as poor workers and bad learners but great spenders. Cf. also Bordua, "Some Comments on Theories of Group Delinquency," *op. cit.*, p. 257.

that of Cohen lies in this area. The data reported by Short seem to support the opportunity-structure approach and to disconfirm the status-deprivation approach.

Of greater interest, however, is the question of why the opportunity-structure approach was not taken on its own terms—at least where it seems possible to do so. Rather than asking to what jobs or educational levels the boys aspired, the researcher should inquire as to what income level they aspire and whether they see income achievement is linked to the conventional means, such as status upgrading via a job or education.

Short concludes his discussion by pointing out that, "It is quite possible, of course, for aspirations to reflect commitment to culturally approved means as well as goals."[28] He hints, however, that commitment to means is at least partially a function of the degree to which these means are articulated with the achievement of long-range goals of occupational and economic success. The formulation by Cloward and Ohlin is premised on such a disarticulation between means and goals. The boys in the Cloward and Ohlin study seem to have decided in some way prior to actual experience that striving and conformity are not worth the effort, either because they do not want the non-economic changes implicit in conventional mobility or do not believe that the *economic* payoffs they seek will, in fact, be forthcoming as a result of playing the education game.

Indeed, at times, it seems as though Cloward and Ohlin have *defined* a type of boy for whom theft is the only logically possible way out. Moreover, in one crucial sense, their boys seem the victims of a truly monumental failure of socialization. If they aspire to large (how large?) incomes *within* the style of the lower-class life they clearly aspire to the impossible and, indeed—except through some type of crime—the almost unimaginable. They seem to be as much the victims of misinformation as of injustice.

Finally, in all this welter of means and ends, aspirations raised and lowered, anticipatory pasts, and retroactive presents, two major points are in danger of being lost. The first is the significance of close-in relationships as sources of personal status, and the second is the importance of primary group socialization as providing the characterological equipment for achievement in the larger institutional order. The development of theories of the origins of delinquent subcultures which ignore these key points makes for severely truncated theoretical perspectives. Not all research on delinquent subcultures excludes considerations of status in the "close-in" world of primary relations and the interpersonal creation of capacity. The study by Short and Strodtbeck, to which we have referred, includes considerable attention to the social elaboration and satisfaction of needs other than those of social and/or economic mobility. Indeed, in some of their work the concept of social disorganization, or something very much like it, has been reintroduced to account for the seeming social disability of lower-class Negro gang boys. The disordering of interpersonal relations in their lives seems so great that many are disadvantaged on the basic level of feelings of human worth and interpersonal trust quite independently of problems of economic achievement. The gang

[28] Short, "Gang Delinquency and Anomie," *op. cit.*, p. 114.

serves not simply as an alternative to upward mobility but as the only available locus of trust. Tragically, even here the human bonds seem brittle and unsatisfying.[29]

SELECTED READINGS

Cohen, Albert K. *Delinquent Boys: The Culture of the Gang.* Glencoe, Illinois: The Free Press, 1955.

Matza, David. *Delinquency and Drift.* New York: John Wiley & Sons, 1964.

Shaw, Clifford R., and McKay, Henry D. *Juvenile Delinquency and Urban Areas.* Chicago: University of Chicago Press, 1942.

Sutherland, Edwin H. *Principles of Criminology.* New York: J. B. Lippincott & Co., 1947.

Yablonsky, Lewis. *The Violent Gang.* New York: Macmillan Co., 1962.

[29] James F. Short, Jr., and Fred L. Strodtbeck, *Group Process and Gang Delinquency,* *op. cit.,* chap. x (by Short and Robert A. Gordon) and chap. ii.

THE CONDEMNATION AND PERSECUTION OF HIPPIES*

MICHAEL BROWN

This article is about persecution and terror. It speaks of the Hippie and the temptations of intimacy that the myth of Hippie has made poignant, and it does this to discuss the institutionalization of repression in the United States.

When people are attacked as a group, they change. Individuals in the group may or may not change, but the organization and expression of their collective life will be transformed. When the members of a gathering believe that there is a grave danger imminent and that opportunities for escape are rapidly diminishing, the group loses its organizational quality. It becomes transformed in panic. This type of change can also occur outside a situation of strict urgency: When opportunities for mobility or access to needed resources are cut off, people may engage in desperate collective actions. In both cases, the conversion of social form occurs when members of a collectivity are about to be hopelessly locked into undesired and undesirable positions.

The process is not, however, automatic. The essential ingredient for conversion is social control exercised by external agents on the collectivity itself. The result can be benign, as a panic mob can be converted into a crowd that makes an orderly exit from danger. Or it can be cruel.

The transformation of groups under pressure is of general interest; but there are special cases that are morally critical to any epoch. Such critical cases occur when pressure is persecution, and transformation is destruction. The growth of repressive mechanisms and institutions is a key concern in this time of administrative cruelty. Such is the justification for the present study.

Social Control as Terror

Four aspects of repressive social control such as that experienced by Hippies are important. First, the administration of control is suspicious. It projects a dangerous future and guards against it. It also refuses the risk of inadequate coverage by enlarging the controlled population to include all who might be active in any capacity. Control may or may not be administered with a heavy hand, but it is always a generalization applied to specific instances. It is a rule and thus ends by pulling many fringe innocents into its bailiwick; it creates as it destroys.

Second, the administration of control is a technical problem which,

* Reprinted from Michael Brown, "The Condemnation and Persecution of Hippies," in TRANS-action (September 1969), pp. 33–46, by permission of the publisher. Copyright © September 1969, by TRANS-action, Inc., New Brunswick, New Jersey.

depending on its site and object, requires the bringing together of many different agencies that are ordinarily dissociated or mutually hostile. A conglomerate of educational, legal, social welfare, and police organizations is highly efficient. The German case demonstrates that. Even more important, it is virtually impossible to oppose control administered under the auspices of such a conglomerate since it includes the countervailing institutions ordinarily available. When this happens control is not only efficient and wide-spread, but also legitimate, commanding a practical, moral and ideological realm that is truly "one-dimensional."

Third, as time passes, control is applied to a wider and wider range of details, ultimately blanketing its objects' lives. At that point, as Hilberg suggests in his *The Destruction of the European Jews*, the extermination of the forms of lives leads easily to the extermination of the lives themselves. The line between persecution and terror is thin. For the oppressed, life is purged of personal style as every act becomes inexpressive, part of the struggle for survival. The options of a life-style are eliminated at the same time that its proponents are locked into it.

Fourth, control is relentless. It develops momentum as organization accumulates, as audiences develop, and as unofficial collaborators assume the definition of tasks, expression and ideology. This, according to W. A. Westley's "The Escalation of Violence Through Legitimation," is the culture of control. It not only limits the behaviors, styles, individuals and groups toward whom it is directed, it suppresses all unsanctioned efforts. As struggle itself is destroyed, motivation vanishes or is turned inward.

These are the effects of repressive control. We may contrast them with the criminal law, which merely prohibits the performance of specific acts (with the exception, of course, of the "crime without victims"—homosexuality, abortion, and drug use). Repression converts or destroys an entire social form, whether that form is embodied in a group, a style or an idea. In this sense, it is terror.

These general principles are especially relevant to our understanding of tendencies that are ripening in the United States day by day. Stated in terms that magnify it so that it can be seen despite ourselves, this is the persecution of the Hippies, a particularly vulnerable group of people who are the cultural wing of a way of life recently emerged from its quiet and individualistic quarters. Theodore Roszak, describing the Hippies in terms of their relationship to the culture and politics of dissent, notes that "the underlying unity of youthful dissent consists . . . in the effort of beat-hip bohemianism to work out the personality structure, the total life-style that follows from New Left social criticism." This life-style is currently bearing the brunt of the assault on what Roszak calls a "counter-culture"; it is an assault that is becoming more concentrated and savage every day. There are lessons for the American future to be drawn from this story.

Persecution

Near Boulder, Colorado, a restaurant sign says "Hippies not served here." Large billboards in upstate New York carry slogans like "Keep America

Clean: Take a Bath." and "Keep America Clean: Get a Haircut." These would be as amusing as ethnic jokes if they did not represent a more systematic repression.

The street sweeps so common in San Francisco and Berkeley in 1968 and 1969 were one of the first lines of attack. People were brutally scattered by club-wielding policemen who first closed exits from the assaulted area and then began systematically to beat and arrest those who were trapped. This form of place terror, like surveillance in Negro areas and defoliation in Vietnam, curbs freedom and forces people to fight or submit to minute inspection by hostile forces. There have also been one-shot neighborhood programs, such as the police assault on the Tompkins Square Park gathering in New York's Lower East Side on Memorial Day, 1967: "Sadistic glee was written on the faces of several officers," wrote the *East Village Other*. Some women became hysterical. The police slugged Frank Wise, and dragged him off, handcuffed and bloody, crying, "My God, my God, where is this happening? Is this America?" The police also plowed into a group of Hippies, Yippies, and straights at the April, 1968, "Yip-in" at Grand Central Station. The brutality was as clear in this action as it had been in the Tompkins Square bust. In both cases, the major newspapers editorialized against the police tactics, and in the first the Mayor apologized for the "free wielding of nightsticks." But by the summer of 1968, street sweeps and busts and the continuous presence of New York's Tactical Police Force had given the Lower East Side an ominous atmosphere. Arrests were regularly accompanied by beatings and charges of "resistance to arrest." It became clear that arrests rather than subsequent procedures were the way in which control was to be exercised. The summer lost its street theaters, the relaxed circulation of people in the neighborhood and the easy park gatherings.

Official action legitimizes nonofficial action. Private citizens take up the cudgel of law and order newly freed from the boundaries of due process and respect. After Tompkins Square, rapes and assaults became common as local toughs assumed the role, with the police, of defender of the faith. In Cambridge, Massachusetts, following a virulent attack on Hippies by the Mayor, *Newsweek* reported that vigilantes attacked Hippie neighborhoods in force.

Ultimately more damaging are the attacks on centers of security. Police raids on "Hippie pads," crash pads, churches and movement centers have become daily occurrences in New York and California over the past two and a half years. The usual excuses for raids are drugs, runaways and housing violations, but many incidents of unlawful entry by police and the expressions of a more generalized hostility by the responsible officials suggests that something deeper is involved. The Chief of Police in San Francisco put it bluntly; quoted in *The New York Times* magazine in May, 1967, he said:

> Hippies are no asset to the community. These people do not have the courage to face the reality of life. They are trying to escape. Nobody should let their young children take part in this hippy thing.

The Director of Health for San Francisco gave teeth to this counsel when he sent a task force of inspectors on a door-to-door sweep of the Haight-Ashbury

—"a two-day blitz" that ended with a strange result, again according to *The Times*: Very few of the Hippies were guilty of housing violations.

Harrassment arrests and calculated degradation have been two of the most effective devices for introducing uncertainty to the day-to-day lives of the Hippies. Cambridge's Mayor's attack on the "hipbos" (the suffix stands for body odor) included, said *Newsweek* of Oct. 30, 1967, a raid on a "hippie pad" by the Mayor and "a platoon of television cameramen." They "seized a pile of diaries and personal letters and flushed a partially clad girl from the closet." In Wyoming, *The Times* reported that two "pacifists" were "jailed and shaved" for hitchhiking. This is a fairly common hazard, though Wyoming officials are perhaps more sadistic than most. A young couple whom I interviewed were also arrested in Wyoming during the summer of 1968. They were placed in solitary confinement for a week during which they were not permitted to place phone calls and were not told when or whether they would be charged or released. These are not exceptional cases. During the summer of 1968, I interviewed young hitchhikers throughout the country; most of them had similar stories to tell.

In the East Village of New York, one hears countless stories of apartment destruction by police (occasionally reported in the newspapers), insults from the police when rapes or robberies are reported, and cruel speeches and even crueler bails set by judges for arrested Hippies.

In the light of this, San Francisco writer Mark Harris' indictment of the Hippies as paranoid seems peculiar. In the September 1967 issue of *The Atlantic*, he wrote,

> The most obvious failure of perception was the hippies' failure to discriminate among elements of the Establishment, whether in the Haight-Ashbury or in San Francisco in general. Their paranoia was the paranoia of all youthful heretics. . . .

This is like the demand of some white liberals that Negroes acknowledge that they (the liberals) are not the power structure, or that black people must distinguish between the good and the bad whites despite the fact that the black experience of white people in the United States has been, as the President's Commission on Civil Disorder suggested, fairly monolithic and racist.

Most journalists reviewing the "Hippie scene" with any sympathy at all seem to agree with *Newsweek* that "the hippies do seem natural prey for publicity-hungry politicians—if not overzealous police," and that they have been subjected to varieties of cruelty that ought to be intolerable. This tactic was later elaborated in the massive para-military assault on Berkeley residents and students during a demonstration in support of Telegraph Avenue's street people and their People's Park. The terror of police violence, a constant in the lives of street people everywhere, in California carries the additional threat of martial law under a still-active state of extreme emergency. The whole structure of repression was given legitimacy and reluctant support by University of California officials. Step by step, they become allies of Reagan's "dogs of war." Roger W. Heyns, chancellor of the Berkeley campus, found himself belatedly reasserting the university's property in the lot. It was the law and the rights of university that trapped the chancellor in the network of control and performed the vital function of providing justification and legitimacy for Sheriff Madigan and the National Guard. Heyns said: "We will have to put up a fence to re-establish the conveniently forgotten fact that this field is indeed the university's, and to exclude unauthorized personnel from the site. . . . The fence will give us time to plan and consult. We tried to get this time some other way and failed—hence the fence." And hence "Bloody Thursday" and the new regime.

And what of the Hippies? They have come far since those balmy days of 1966–67, days of flowers, street-cleaning, free stores, decoration and love. Many have fled to the hills of Northern California to join their brethren who had set up camps there several years ago. Others have fled to communes outside the large cities and in the Middle West. After the Tompkins Square assault, many of the East Village Hippies refused to follow the lead of those who were more political. They refused to develop organizations of defense and to accept a hostile relationship with the police and neighborhood. Instead, they discussed at meeting after meeting, how they could show their attackers love. Many of those spirits have fled; others have been beaten or jailed too many times; and still others have modified their outlook in ways that reflect the struggle. Guerrilla theater, Up Against the Wall Mother Fucker, the Yippies, the urban communes; these are some of the more recent manifestations of the alternative culture. One could see these trends growing in the demonstrations mounted by Hippies against arrests of runaways or pot smokers, the community organizations, such as grew in Berkeley for self-defense and politics, and the beginnings of the will to fight back when trapped in street sweeps.

It is my impression that the Hippie culture is growing as it recedes from the eye of the media. As a consequence of the destruction of their urban places, there has been a redistribution of types. The flower people have left for the hills and become more communal; those who remained in the city were better adapted to terror, secretive or confrontative. The Hippie culture is one of the forms radicalism can take in this society. The youngsters, 5,000 of them, who came to Washington to counter-demonstrate against the Nixon inaugural showed the growing amalgamation of the New Left and its cultural wing. The Yippies who went to Chicago for guerrilla theater and learned about "pigs" were the multi-generational expression of the new wave. A UAWMF (Up Against the Wall Mother Fucker) drama, played at Lincoln Center during the New York City garbage strike—they carted garbage from the neglected Lower East Side and dumped it at the spic 'n' span cultural center—reflected another interpretation of the struggle, one that could include the politically militant as well as the culturally defiant. Many Hippies have gone underground—in an older sense of the word. They have shaved their beards, cut their hair, and taken straight jobs, like the secret Jews of Spain; but unlike those Jews, they are consciously an underground, a resistance.

What is most interesting and, I believe, a direct effect of the persecution, is the enormous divergence of forms that are still recognizable by the outsider as Hippie and are still experienced as a shared identity. "The Yippies," says Abbie Hoffman, "are like Hippies, only fiercer and more fun." The "hippie types" described in newspaper accounts of drug raids on colleges turn out, in many cases, to be New Leftists.

The dimensions by which these various forms are classified are quite conventional: religious-political, visible-secret, urban-hill, communal-individualistic. As their struggle intensifies, there will be more efforts for unity and more militant approaches to the society that gave birth to a real alternative only to turn against it with a mindless savagery. Yippie leader Jerry Rubin, in an "emergency letter to my brothers and sisters in the movement" summed up:

> Huey Newton is in prison.
> Eldridge Cleaver is in exile.
> Oakland Seven are accused of conspiracy.
> Tim Leary is up for 30 years and how many of our brothers are in court and jail for getting high?
> . . .
> Camp activists are expelled and arrested.
> War resisters are behind bars.
> Add it up!

Rubin preambles his summary with:

> From the Bay Area to New York, we are suffering the greatest depression in our history. People are taking bitterness in their coffee instead of sugar. The hippie-yippie-SDS movement is a "white nigger" movement. The American economy no longer needs young whites and blacks. We are waste material. We fulfill our destiny in life by rejecting a system which rejects us.

He advocates organizing "massive mobilizations for the spring, nationally coordinated and very theatrical, taking place near courts, jails, and military stockades."

An article published in a Black Panther magazine is entitled "The Hippies Are Not Our Enemies." White radicals have also overcome their initial rejection of cultural radicals. Something clearly is happening, and it is being fed, finally, by youth, the artists, the politicos and the realization, through struggle, that America is not beautiful.

Some Historical Analogies

The persecution of the Jews destroyed both a particular social form and the individuals who qualified for the Jewish fate by reason of birth. Looking at the process in the aggregate, Hilberg describes it as a gradual coming together or a multitude of loose laws, institutions, and intentions, rather than a program born mature. The control conglomerate that resulted was a refined engine "whose devices," Hilberg writes, "not only trap a larger number of victims; they also require a greater degree of specialization, and with that division of labor, the moral burden too is fragmented among the participants. The perpetrator can now kill his victims without touching them, without hearing them, without seeing them. . . . This ever growing capacity for destruction cannot be arrested anywhere." Ultimately, the persecution of the Jews was a mixture of piety, repression and mobilization directed against those who were in the society but suddenly not of it.

The early Christians were also faced with a refined and elaborate administrative structure whose harsh measures were ultimately directed at their ways of life: their social forms and their spiritual claims. The rationale was, and is, that certain deviant behaviors endanger society. Therefore, officials are obligated to use whatever means of control or persuasion they consider necessary to strike these forms from the list of human possibilities. This is the classical administrative rationale for the suppression of alternative values and world views.

As options closed and Christians found the opportunities to lead and explore Christian lives rapidly struck down, Christian life itself had to become rigid, prematurely closed and obsessed with survival.

The persecution of the early Christians presents analogies to the persecution of European Jews. The German assault affected the quality of Jewish organizations no less than it affected the lives of individual Jews, distorting communities long before it destroyed them. Hilberg documents some of the ways in which efforts to escape the oppression led on occasion to a subordination of energies to the problem of simply staying alive—of finding some social options within the racial castle. The escapist mentality that dominated the response to oppression and distorted relationships can be seen in some Jewish leaders in Vienna. They exchanged individuals for promises. This is what persecution and terror do. As options close and all parts of the life of the oppressed are touched by procedure, surveillance and control, behavior is transformed. The oppressed rarely retaliate (especially where they have internalized the very ethic that rejects them), simply because nothing is left untouched by the persecution. No energy is available for hostility, and, in any case, it is impossible to know where to begin. Bravery is stoicism. One sings to the cell or gas chamber.

The persecution of Hippies in the United States involves, regardless of the original intentions of the agencies concerned, an assault on a way of life, an assault no less concentrated for its immaturity and occasional ambivalence. Social, cultural and political resources have been mobilized to bring a group of individuals into line and to prevent others from refusing to toe the line.

The attractiveness of the Hippie forms and the pathos of their persecution have together brought into being an impressive array of defenders. Nevertheless theirs has been a defense of gestures, outside the realm of politics and social action essential to any real protection. It has been verbal, scholarly and appreciative, with occasional expressions of horror at official actions and attitudes. But unfortunately the arena of conflict within which the Hippies, willy-nilly, must try to survive is dominated not by the likes of Susan Sontag, but by the likes of Daniel Patrick Moynihan whose apparent compassion for the Hippies will probably never be translated into action. For even as he writes (in the *American Scholar*, Autumn, 1967) that these youths are "trying to tell us something" and that they are one test of our "ability to survive," he rejects them firmly, and not a little *ex cathedra*, as a "truth gone astray." The Hippie remains helpless and more affected by the repressive forces (who will probably quote Moynihan) than by his own creative capacity or the sympathizers who support him in the journals. As John Kifner reported in *The Times*, " 'This scene is not the same anymore,' said the tall, thin Negro called Gypsy. '. . . There are some very bad vibrations.' "

Social Form and Cultural Heresy

But it's just another murder. A hippie being killed is just like a housewife being killed or a career girl being killed or a hoodlum being killed. None of these people, notice, are persons; they're labels. Who cares who Groovy was; if you know he was a "hippie," then already you know more about him than he did about himself.

See, it's hard to explain to a lot of you what a hippie is because a lot of you really think a hippie IS something. You don't realize that the word is just a convenience picked up by the press to personify a social change thing beginning to happen to young people. (*Paul William, in an article entitled "Label Dies—But Not Philosophy." Open City, Los Angeles, November 17–23, 1967,*)

Because the mass media have publicized the growth of a fairly well-articulated Hippie culture, it now bears the status of a social form. Variously identified as "counter-culture," "Hippie-dom," "Youth" or "Underground," the phenomenon centers on a philosophy of the present and takes the personal and public forms appropriate to that philosophy. Its values constitute a heresy in a society that consecrates the values of competition, social manipulation and functionalism, a society that defines ethical quality by long-range and general consequences, and that honors only those attitudes and institutions that affirm the primacy of the future and large-scale over the local and immediately present. It is a heresy in a society that eschews the primary value of intimacy for the sake of impersonal service to large and enduring organizations, a society that is essentialist rather than existentialist, a society that prizes biography over interactive quality. It is a heresy in a country whose President could be praised for crying, "Ask not what your country can do for you, but what you can do for your country!" Most important, however, it is heresy in a society whose official values, principles of operation and officials themselves are threatened domestically and abroad.

For these reasons the Hippie is available for persecution. When official authority is threatened, social and political deviants are readily conjured up as demons requiring collective exorcism and thus a reaffirmation of that authority. Where exorcism is the exclusive province of government, the government's power is reinforced by the adoption of a scapegoat. Deviant style and ideals make a group vulnerable to exploitation as a scapegoat, but it is official action which translates vulnerability into actionable heresy.

By contrast, recent political developments within black communities and the accommodations reached through bargaining with various official agencies have placed the blacks alongside the Viet Cong as an official enemy, but not as a scapegoat. As an enemy, the black is not a symbol but a source of society's troubles. It is a perferable position. The Hippie's threat lies in the lure of his way of life rather than in his political potential. His vulnerability as well as his proven capacity to develop a real alternative life permits his selection as scapegoat. A threatened officialdom is all too likely to take the final step that "brings on the judge." At the same time, by defining its attack as moderate, it reaffirms its moral superiority in the very field of hate it cultivates.

A Plausible Force

We are speaking of that which claims the lives, totally or in part, of perhaps hundreds of thousands of people of all ages throughout the United States and elsewhere. The number is not inconsiderable.

The plausibility of the Hippie culture and its charisma can be argued on several grounds. Their outlook derives from a profound mobilizing idea: Quality resides in the present. Therefore, one seeks the local in all its social detail—not indulgently and alone, but openly and creatively. Vulnerability and improvisation are principles of action, repudiating the "rational" hierarchy of plans and stages that defines, for the grounded culture, all events as incidents of passage and means to an indefinitely postponable end—as transition. The allocation of reality to the past and the future is rejected in favor of the present, and a present that is known and felt immediately, not judged by external standards. The long run is the result rather than the goal of the present. "Psychical distance," the orientation of the insulated tourist to whom the environment is something forever foreign or of the administrator for whom the world is an object of administration, is repudiated as a relational principle. It is replaced by a principal of absorption. In this, relationships are more like play, dance or jazz. Intimacy derives from absorption, from spontaneous involvement, to use Erving Goffman's phrase, rather than from frequent contact or attraction, as social psychologists have long argued.

This vision of social reality makes assumptions about human nature. It sees man as only a part of a present that depends on all its parts. To be a "part" is not to play a stereotyped role or to plan one's behavior prior to entering the scene. It is to be of a momentum. Collaboration, the overt manifestation of absorption, is critical to any social arrangement because the present, as experience, is essentially social. Love and charisma are the reflected properties of the plausible whole that results from mutual absorption. "To swing" or "to groove" is to be of the scene rather than simply at or in the scene. "Rapping," an improvised, expansive, and collaborative conversational form, is an active embodiment of the more general ethos. Its craft is humor, devotion, trust, openness to events in the process of formation, and the capacity to be relevant. Identity is neither strictly personal nor something to be maintained, but something always to be discovered. The individual body is the origin of sounds and motions, but behavior, ideas, images, and reflective thought stem from interaction itself. Development is not of personalities but of situations that include many bodies but, in effect, one mind. Various activities, such as smoking marijuana, are disciplines that serve the function of bringing people together and making them deeply interesting to each other.

The development of an authentic "counter-culture," or, better, "alternative culture," has some striking implications. For one, information and stress are processed through what amounts to a new conceptual system—a culture that replaces, in the committed, the intrapersonal structures that Western personality theories have assumed to account for intrapersonal order. For example, in 1966, young Hippies often turned against their friends and their experience after a bad acid trip. But that was the year during which "the Hippie thing" was merely one constructive expression of dissent. It was not, at that point, an alternative culture. As a result, the imagery cued in by the trauma was the imagery of the superego, the distant and punitive authority of the Western family and its macrocosmic social system. Guilt, self-hatred and the rejection of experience was the result. Many youngsters returned home filled with a humiliation that could be forgotten, or converted to a seedy and defensive hatred of the dangerously deviant. By 1968 the bad trip, while still an occasion for reconversion for some, had for others become something to be guarded against and coped with in a context of care and experienced guidance. The atmosphere of trust and new language of stress-inspired dependence rather than recoil as the initial stage of cure. One could "get high with a little help from my friends." Conscience was purged of "authority."

Although the ethos depends on personal contact, it is carried by underground media (hundreds of newspapers claiming hundreds of thousands of readers), rock music, and collective activities, artistic and political, which deliver and duplicate the message; and it is processed through a generational flow. It is no longer simply a constructive expression of dissent and thus attractive because it is a vital answer to a system that destroys vitality; it is culture, and the young are growing up under the wisdom of its older generations. The ethos is realized most fully in the small communes that dot the American urbscape and constitute an important counter-institution of the Hippies.

This complex of population, culture, social form, and ideology is both a reinforcing environment for individuals and a context for the growth and elaboration of the complex itself. In it, life not only begins, it goes on; and, indeed, it must go on for those who are committed to it. Abbie Hoffman's *Revolution for the Hell of It* assumes the autonomy of this cultural frame of reference. It assumes that the individual has entered and has burned his bridges.

As the heresy takes an official definition and as the institutions of persecution form, a they-mentality emerges in the language which expresses the relationship between the oppressor and the oppressed. For the oppressed, it distinguishes life from nonlife so that living can go on. The they-mentality of the oppressed temporarily relieves them of the struggle by acknowledging the threat, identifying its agent, and compressing both into a quasi-poetic image, a cliche that can accomodate absurdity. One young man said, while coming down from an amphetamine high: "I'm simply going to continue to do what I want until they stop me."

But persecution is also structured by the they-mentality of the persecutors. This mentality draws lines around its objects as it fits them conceptually for full-scale social action. The particular uses of the term "hippie" in the mass media—like "Jew," "Communist," "Black Muslim," or "Black Panther" —cultivates not only disapproval and rejection but a climate of opinion capable of excluding Hippies from the moral order altogether. This is one phase of a subtle process that begins by locating and isolating a group, tying it to the criminal, sinful or obscene, developing and displaying referential symbols at a high level of abstraction which depersonalize and objectify the group, defining the stigmata by which members are to be known and placing the symbols in the context of ideology and readiness for action.

At this point, the symbols come to define public issues and are, consequently, sources of strength. The maintenance of power—the next phase of the story—depends less on the instruction of reading and viewing publics than on the elaboration of the persecutory institutions which demonstrate and justify power. The relationship between institution and public ceases to be one of expression or extension (of a public to an institution) and becomes one of transaction or dominance (of a public with or by an institution). The total dynamic is similar to advertising or the growth of the military as domestic powers in America.

An explosion of Hippie stories appeared in the mass media during the summer of 1967. Almost every large-circulation magazine featured articles on the Hippie "fad" or "subculture." *Life*'s "The Other Culture" set the tone. The theme was repeated in *The New York Times Magazine*, May 14, 1967, where Hunter Thompson wrote that "The 'Hashbury' (Haight-Ashbury in San Francisco) is the new capital of what is rapidly becoming a drug culture." *Time*'s "wholly new subculture" was "a cult whose mystique derives essentially from the influences of hallucinogenic drugs." By fall, while maintaining the emphasis on drugs as the cornerstone of the culture, the articles had shifted from the culturological to a "national character" approach, reminiscent of the World War II anti-Japanese propaganda, as personal traits were piled into the body of the symbol and objectification began. The Hippies were "acid heads," "generally dirty," and "visible, audible and sometimes smellable young rebels."

As "hippie" and its associated terms ("long-haired," "bearded") accumulated pejorative connotation, they began to be useful concepts and were featured regularly in news headlines: for example, "Hippie Mother Held in Slaying of Son, 2" (*The New York Times*, Nov. 22, 1967); "S Squad Hits Four Pads" (*San Francisco Chronicle*, July 27, 1967). The articles themselves solidified usage by dwelling on "hippie types," "wild drug parties" and "long-haired, bearded" youths (see, for example, *The New York Times* of Feb. 13, 1968, Sept. 16, 1968 and Nov. 3, 1967).

This is a phenomenon that R. H. Turner and S. J. Surace described in 1956 in order to account for the role of media in the development of hostile consciousness toward Mexicans. The presentation of certain symbols can remove their referents from the constraints of the conventional moral order so that extralegal and extramoral action can be used against them. Political cartoonists have used the same device with less powerful results. To call Mexican-Americans "zootsuiters" in Los Angeles, in 1943, was to free hostility from the limits of the conventional, though fragile, antiracism required by liberal ideology. The result was a wave of brutal anti-Mexican assaults. Turner and Surace hypothesized that:

> To the degree, then, to which any symbol evokes only one consistent set of connotations throughout the community, only one general course of action with respect to that object will be indicated, and the union of diverse members of the community into an acting crowd will be facilitated . . . or it will be an audience prepared to accept novel forms of official action.

First the symbol, then the accumulation of hostile connotations, and finally the action-issue: Such a sequence appears in the news coverage of Hippies from the beginning of 1967 to the present. The amount of coverage has decreased in the past year, but this seems less a result of sympathy or sophistication and more one of certainty: The issue is decided and certain truths can be taken for granted. As this public consciousness finds official representation in the formation of a control conglomerate, it heralds the final and institutional stage in the growth of repressive force, persecution and terror.

The growth of this control conglomerate, the mark of any repressive system, depends on the development of new techniques and organizations. But its momentum requires an ideological head of steam. In the case of the Hippie life the ideological condemnation is based on several counts: that it is dangerous and irresponsible, subversive to authority, immoral, and psychopathological.

Commenting on the relationship between beliefs and the development of the persecutory institutions for witch-control in the 16th century, Trevor-Roper, in an essay on "Witches and Witchcraft," states:

> In a climate of fear, it is easy to see how this process could happen: how individual deviations could be associated with a central pattern. We have seen it happen in our own time. The "McCarthyite" experience of the United States in the 1950's was exactly comparable: Social fear, the fear of an incompatible system of society, was given intellectual form as a heretical ideology and suspect individuals were persecuted by reference to that heresy.

The same fear finds its ideological expression against the Hippies in the statement of Dr. Stanley F. Yolles, director of the National Institute of Mental Health, that "alienation," which he called a major underlying cause of drug abuse, "was wider, deeper and more diffuse now than it has been in any other period in American history." The rejection of dissent in the name of mental health rather than moral values or social or political interest is a modern characteristic. Dr. Yolles suggested that if urgent attention is not given the problem:

> there are serious dangers that large proportions of current and future generations will reach adulthood embittered towards the larger society, unequipped to take on parental, vocational and other citizen roles, and involved in some form of socially deviant behavior. . . .

Dr. Seymour L. Halleck, director of student psychiatry at the University of Wisconsin, also tied the heresy to various sources of sin: affluence, lack of contact with adults, and an excess of freedom. Dr. Henry Brill, director of Pilgrim State Hospital on Long Island and a consultant on drug use to federal and state agencies, is quoted in *The New York Times*, Sept. 26, 1967:

> It is my opinion that the unrestricted use of marijuana type substances produces a significant amount of vagabondage, dependency, and psychiatric disability.

Drs. Yolles, Halleck, and Brill are probably fairly representative of psychiatric opinion. Psychiatry has long defined normality and health in terms of each other in a "scientific" avoidance of serious value questions. Psychiatrists agree in principle on several related points which could constitute a medical rational foundation for the persecution of Hippies: They define the normal and healthy individual as patient and instrumental. He plans for the long range and pursues his goals temperately and economically. He is an individual with a need for privacy and his contacts are moderate and respectful. He is stable in style and identity, reasonably competitive and optimistic. Finally, he accepts reality and participates in the social forms which constitute the givens of his life. Drug use, sexual pleasure, a repudiation of clear long-range goals, the insistence on intimacy and self-affirmation, distrust of official authority and radical dissent are all part of the abnormality that colors the Hippies "alienated" or "disturbed" or "neurotic."

This ideology characterizes the heresy in technical terms. Mental illness is a scientific and medical problem, and isolation and treatment are recommended. Youth, alienation and drug use are the discrediting characteristics of those who are unqualified for due process, discussion or conflict. The genius of the ideology has been to separate the phenomenon under review from consideration of law and value. In this way the mutual hostilities that ordinarily divide the various agencies of control are bypassed and the issue endowed with ethical and political neutrality. Haurek and Clark, in their "Variants of Integration of Social Control Agencies," described two opposing orientations among social control agencies, the authoritarian-punitive (the police, the courts) and the humanitarian-welfare (private agencies, social workers), with the latter holding the former in low esteem. The Hippies have brought them together.

The designation of the Hippie impulse as heresy on the grounds of psychopathology not only bypasses traditional enmity among various agencies of social control, but its corollaries activate each agency. It is the eventual coordination of their efforts that constitutes the control conglomerate. We will briefly discuss several of these corollaries before examining the impact of the conglomerate. Youth, danger and disobedience are the major themes.

Dominating the study of adolescence is a general theory which holds that the adolescent is a psychosexual type. Due to an awakening of the instincts after a time of relative quiescence, he is readily overwhelmed by them. Consequently, his behavior may be viewed as the working out of intense intrapsychic conflict—it is symptomatic or expressive rather than rational and realistic. He is idealistic, easily influenced, and magical. The idealism is the expression of a threatened superego; the susceptibility to influence is an attempt to find support for an identity in danger of diffusion; the magic, reflected in adolescent romance and its rituals, is an attempt to get a grip on a reality that shifts and turns too much for comfort. By virtue of his entrance into the youth culture, he joins in the collective expression of emotional immaturity. At heart, he is the youth of Golding's *Lord of the Flies*, a fledgling adult living out a transitional status. His idealism may be sentimentally touching, but in truth he is morally irresponsible and dangerous.

Youth

As the idealism of the young is processed through the youth culture, it becomes radical ideology, and even radical practice. The attempts by parents and educators to break the youth culture by rejecting its symbols and limiting the opportunities for its expression (ranging from dress regulations in school to the censorship of youth music on the air) are justified as a response to the dangerous political implications of the ideology of developed and ingrown immaturity. That these same parents and educators find their efforts to conventionalize the youth culture (through moderate imitations of youthful dress and attempts to "get together with the kids") rejected encourages them further to see the young as hostile, unreasonable and intransigent. The danger of extremism (the New Left and the Hippies) animates their criticism, and all intrusions on the normal are read as pointing in that direction. The ensuing conflict between the wise and the unreasonable is called (largely by the wise) the "generation gap."

From this it follows that radicalism is the peculiar propensity of the young and, as Christopher Jencks and David Riesman have pointed out in *The Academic Revolution,* of those who identify with the young. At its best it is not considered serious; at its worst it is the "counter-culture." The myth of the generation gap, a myth that is all the more strongly held as we find less and less evidence for it, reinforces this view by holding that radicalism ends, or should end, when the gap is bridged—when the young grow older and wiser. While this lays the groundwork for tolerance or more likely, forbearance, it is a tolerance limited to youthful radicalism. It also lays the groundwork for a more thorough rejection of the radicalism of the not-so-young and the "extreme."

Thus, the theory of youth classifies radicalism as immature and, when cultivated, dangerous or pathological. Alienation is the explanation used to account for the extension of youthful idealism and paranoia into the realm of the politically and culturally adult. Its wrongness is temporary and trivial. If it persists, it becomes a structural defect requiring capture and treatment rather than due process and argument.

Danger

Once a life-style and its practices are declared illegal, its proponents are by definition criminal and subversive. On the one hand, the very dangers presupposed by the legal proscriptions immediately become clear and present. The illegal life-style becomes the living demonstration of its alleged dangers. The ragged vagabondage of the Hippie is proof that drugs and promiscuity are alienating, and the attempts to sleep in parks, gather and roam are the new "violence" of which we have been reading. Crime certainly is crime, and the Hippies commit crime by their very existence. The dangers are: (1) crime and the temptation to commit crime; (2) alienation and the temptation to drop out. The behaviors that, if unchecked, become imbedded in the personality of the suspectible are, among others, drug use (in particular marijuana), apparel deviance, dropping out (usually of school), sexual promiscuity, communal living, nudity, hair deviance, draft resistance, demonstrating against the feudal oligarchies in cities and colleges, gathering, roaming, doing strange art and being psychedelic. Many of these are defused by campaigns of definition; they become topical and in fashion. To wear bell-bottom pants, long side-burns, flowers on your car and beads, is, if done with taste and among the right people, stylish and eccentric rather than another step toward the brink or a way of lending aid and comfort to the enemy. The disintegration of a form by co-opting only its parts is a familiar phenomenon. It is tearing an argument apart by confronting each proposition as if it had no context, treating a message like an intellectual game.

Drugs, communalism, gathering, roaming, resisting and demonstrating, and certain styles of hair have not been defused. In fact, the drug scene is the site of the greatest concentration of justificatory energy and the banner under which the agencies of the control conglomerate unite. That their use is so widespread through the straight society indicates the role of drugs as temptation. That drugs have been pinned so clearly (despite the fact that many Hippies are nonusers) and so gladly to the Hippies, engages the institutions of persecution in the task of destroying the Hippie thing.

The antimarijuana lobby has postulated a complex of violence, mental illness, genetic damage, apathy and alienation, all arising out of the ashes of smoked pot. The hypothesis justifies a set of laws and practices of great harshness and discrimination, and the President recently recommended that they be made even more so. The number of arrests for use, possession or sale of marijuana has soared in recent years: Between 1964 and 1966 yearly arrests doubled, from 7,000 to 15,000. The United States Narcotics Commissioner attributed the problem to "certain groups" which give marijuana to young people, and to "false information" about the danger of the drug.

Drug raids ordinarily net "hippie-type youths" although lately news reports refer to "youths from good homes." The use of spies on campuses, one of the bases for the original protest demonstrations at Nanterre prior to the May revolution, has become common, with all its socially destructive implications. Extensive spy operations were behind many of the police raids of college campuses during 1967, 1968 and 1969. Among those hit were Long Island University's Southampton College (twice), State University College at Oswego, New York, the Hun School of Princeton, Bard College, Syracuse University, Stony Brook College and Franconia College in New Hampshire; the list could go on.

It is the "certain groups" that the Commissioner spoke of who bear the brunt of the condemnation and the harshest penalties. The laws themselves are peculiar enough, having been strengthened largely since the Hippies became visible, but they are enforced with obvious discrimination. Teenagers arrested in a "good residential section" of Naugatuck, Connecticut, were treated gently by the circuit court judge:

> I suspect that many of these youngsters should not have been arrested. . . . I'm not going to have these youngsters bouncing around with these charges hanging over them.

They were later released and the charges dismissed. In contrast, after a "mass arrest" in which 15 of the 25 arrested were charged with being in a place where they knew that others were smoking marijuana, Washington's Judge Halleck underscored his determination "to show these long-haired ne'er-do-wells that society will not tolerate their conduct" (*Washington Post*, May 21, 1967).

The incidents of arrest and the exuberance with which the laws are discriminatorily enforced are justified, although not explained, by the magnifying judgment of "danger." At a meeting of agents from 74 police departments in Connecticut and New York, Westchester County Sheriff John E. Hoy, "in a dramatic stage whisper," said, "It is a frightening situation, my friends . . . marijuana is creeping up on us."

One assistant district attorney stated that "the problem is staggering." A county executive agreed that "the use of marijuana is vicious," while a school superintendent argued that "marijuana is a plague-like disease, slowly but surely strangling our young people." Harvard freshmen were warned against the "social influences" that surround drugs and one chief of police attributed drug use and social deviance to permissiveness in a slogan which has since become more common (*St. Louis Post-Dispatch*, Aug. 22, 1968).

Bennett Berger has pointed out that the issue of danger is an ideological ploy (*Denver Post*, April 19, 1968): "The real issue of marijuana is ethical and political, touching the 'core of cultural values.' " *The New York Times* of Jan. 11, 1968, reports "Students and high school and college officials agree that 'drug use has increased sharply since the intensive coverage given to drugs and the Hippies last summer by the mass media.' " It is also supported by other attempts to tie drugs to heresy: *The New York Times* of Nov. 17, 1968, notes a Veterans Administration course for doctors on the Hippies which ties Hippies, drugs, and alienation together and suggests that the search for potential victims might begin in the seventh or eighth grades.

The dynamic relationship between ideology, organization and practice is revealed both in President Johnson's "Message on Crime to Insure Public Safety" (delivered to Congress on February 7, 1968) and in the gradual internationalizing of the persecution. The President recommended "strong new laws," an increase in the number of enforcement agents, and the centralization of federal enforcement machinery. At the same time, the United Nations Economic and Social Council considered a resolution asking that governments "deal effectively with publicity which advocates legalization or tolerance of the non-medical use of cannabis as a harmless drug." The resolution was consistent with President Johnson's plan to have the Federal Government of the United States "maintain world-wide operations . . . to suppress the trade in illicit narcotics and marijuana." The reasons for the international campaign were clarified by a World Health Organization panel's affirmation of its intent to prevent the use or sale of marijuana because it is "a drug of dependence, producing health and social problems." At the same time that scientific researchers at Harvard and Boston University were exonerating the substance, the penalties increased and the efforts to proscribe it reached international proportions. A number of countries, including Laos and Thailand, have barred Hippies, and Mexico has made it difficult for those with long hair and serious eyes to cross its border.

Disobedience

The assumption that society is held together by formal law and authority implies in principle that the habit of obedience must be reinforced. The details of the Hippie culture are, in relation to the grounded culture, disobedient. From that perspective, too, their values and ideology are also explicitly disobedient. The disobedience goes far beyond the forms of social organization and personal presentation to the conventional systems of healing, dietary practice and environmental use. There is virtually no system of authority that is not thrown into question. Methodologically, the situationalism of pornography, guerrilla theater and place conversion is not only profoundly subversive in itself; it turns the grounded culture around. By coating conventional behavioral norms with ridicule and obscenity, by tying radically different meanings to old routines, it challenges our sentiments. By raising the level of our self-consciousness it allows us to become moral in the areas we had allowed to degenerate into habit (apathy or gluttony). When the rock group, the Fugs, sings and dances "Group Grope" or any of their other songs devoted brutally to "love" and "taste," they pin our tender routines to a humiliating obscenity. We can no longer take our behavior and our intentions for granted. The confrontation enables us to disobey or to reconsider or to choose simply by forcing into consciousness the patterns of behavior and belief of which we have become victims. The confrontation is manly because it exposes both sides in an arena of conflict.

When questions are posed in ways that permit us to disengage ourselves from their meaning to our lives, we tolerate the questions as a moderate and decent form of dissent. And we congratulate ourselves for our tolerance. But when people refuse to know their place, and, what is worse, our place, and they insist on themselves openly and demand that we re-decide our own lives, we are willing to have them knocked down. Consciousness permits disobedience. As a result, systems threatened from within often begin the work of reassertion by an attack on consciousness and chosen forms of life.

Youth, danger and disobedience define the heresy in terms that activate the host of agencies that, together, comprise the control conglomerate. Each agency, wrote Trevor-Roper, was ready: "The engine of persecution was set up before its future victims were legally subject to it." The conglomerate has its target. But it is a potential of the social system as much as it is an actor. Trevor-Roper comments further that:

> once we see the persecution of heresy as social intolerance, the intellectual difference between one heresy and another becomes less significant.

And the difference, one might add, between one persecutor and another becomes less significant. Someone it does not matter who tells Mr. Blue (in Tom Paxton's song): "What will it take to whip you into line?"

How have I ended here? The article is an analysis of the institutionalization of persecution and the relationship between the control conglomerate which is the advanced form of official persecution and the Hippies as an alternative culture, the target of control. But an analysis must work within a vision if it is to move beyond analysis into action. The tragedy of America may be that it completed the technology of control before it developed compassion and tolerance. It never learned to tolerate history, and now it is finally capable of ending history by ending the change that political sociologists and undergroups understand. The struggle has always gone on in the mind. Only now, for this society, it is going on in the open among people. Only now is it beginning to shape lives rather than simply shaping individuals.

Whether it is too late or not will be worked out in the attempts to transcend the one-dimensionality that Marcuse described. That the alternative culture is here seems difficult to doubt. Whether it becomes revolutionary fast enough to supersede an officialdom bent on its destruction may be an important part of the story of America.

As an exercise in over-estimation, this essay proposes a methodological tool for going from analysis to action in areas which are too easily absorbed by a larger picture but which are at the same time too critical to be viewed outside the context of political action.

The analysis suggests several conclusions:

Control usually transcends itself both in its selection of targets and in its organization.

At some point in its development, control is readily institutionalized and finally institutional. The control conglomerate represents a new stage in social organization and is an authentic change-inducing force for social systems.

The hallmark of an advanced system of control (and the key to its beginning) is an ideology that unites otherwise highly differing agencies.

Persecution and terror go together in our society. The Hippies, as a genuine heresy, have engaged official opposition to a growing cultural-social-political tendency. The organization of control has both eliminated counter-vailing official forces and begun to place all deviance in the category of heresy. This pattern may soon become endemic to the society.

CONVENTIONALIZATION AND CONTROL
OF ADOLESCENT CROWDS*

THOMAS S. SMITH[1]

Several types of collective phenomena are regular, expected parts of the social landscape without being "routine" in any consistent theoretical sense. Parties, festivals, ceremonials, commemorative gatherings, and similar events are appropriately studied as part of the field of collective behavior. Rather than being routine, they are gatherings which have been characterized as "conventional." That is, they are regular and periodic; they have some attributes of control, and they are recurrent. While some social scientists have been led to remark upon the functions of such conventional events, there has been no systematic effort to describe and explain the processes through which they emerge and endure.

"Conventionalization"—a term derived by Ralph Turner and Lewis Killian[2] from Herbert Blumer's distinction among "casual," "expressive," "active," and "conventional" crowds[3]—is an appropriate name for these processes. It denotes a transformation in the attributes of a crowd toward those defining Blumer's "conventional" type, namely, crowds which are "regularized" or have patterned and anticipated attributes and which also display characteristics of control facilitating and disposing their recurrence.

This paper examines a form of crowd conventionalization illustrated by an intensive case study of repeated adolescent beach riots. The pattern of these events is quite familiar, since accounts of similar events have appeared in the news media for a number of years. Their patterning and recurrence, and the changes they have undergone, suggest some of the neglected properties of crowd situations. It is in terms of some of these properties that a preliminary model of conventionalization may be constructed. The analysis will attempt to

* Reprinted from Thomas S. Smith, "Conventionalization and Control: An Examination of Adolescent Crowds," in *American Journal of Sociology*, Vol. LXXIV (September 1968), pp. 172–183, by permission of author and University of Chicago Press. Copyright 1968 by the University of Chicago.
1 The author wishes to acknowledge the perceptive criticism of earlier drafts of this paper by Jan Hajda of the Department of Sociology, Portland State College; Morris Janowitz, David Street, and Donald Levine of the Department of Sociology, University of Chicago; and Max Heirich of the Department of Sociology, University of Michigan.
2 Ralph Turner and Lewis Killian, *Collective Behavior* (Englewood Cliffs, N.J.: Prentice-Hall, Inc., 1957), pp. 143–61, 527–29; cf. Ralph Turner, "Collective Behavior," in Robert E. L. Faris (ed.), *Handbook of Modern Sociology* (Chicago: Rand McNally, Inc., 1964), pp. 382–425.
3 Herbert Blumer, "Collective Behavior," in Alfred McClung Lee (ed.), *Principles of Sociology* (rev. ed.; New York: Barnes & Noble, 1951), pp. 178 ff.

show: (*a*) that the repetition of these crowd actions can be explained partially by examining their cultural significance, their meaning as symbolic dramas, in the experience of the participants, police control agencies, and wider public audiences; (*b*) that the salience of the events can be understood through tracing their social impact upon relevant social structures; and (*c*) that the crowd action became regularized as a symbolic activity within adolescent culture by influencing, through its "status threat" potential, the stability of adolescent peer group leadership. What we believe we have observed in these crowd actions is a development here called "ceremonialization," which we treat as a type of conventionalization. Preliminary explanation of these developments is proposed later in this paper through an analysis of changes and emergent tendencies in the repeated encounters between the adolescent crowds and an adjacent authority system.

Case materials.   The events recounted here are the product of personal observations, interviews with participants and the police, a review of newspaper accounts, and access to tactical reports of state police. Detailed field notes, made after the first outburst, led to the collection of the rest of the data, including further observational materials from similar disturbances occurring over the following five years. Altogether, the materials cover the period between the Labor Day weekend in 1959, when the first outburst occurred, and the Labor Day weekend in 1964, when the last observations were made. The events occurred in Ocean City, Maryland.

On Labor Day eve in 1959 there were some 75,000 vacationers in Ocean City, most of them from Baltimore, Washington, and Philadelphia. It was not a quiet night; the bars and nightclubs were filled, and the Boardwalk was congested with people in all states of celebration. The police were busy, as was normal for the last big weekend of the summer season.

An hour before midnight one of the local policemen arrested a youth for disorderliness and intoxication, while a group of the boy's friends looked on. The arrest was clumsy, the policeman using his nightstick to stun the boy and prod him from the gathering of spectators. Before the officer was out of sight, the episode had become a focus for bystanders, and a mood of discontent had begun to spread.

State police records indicate that the first alert was received at their Salisbury barracks just before midnight. A teletype message requesting assistance had been sent from the chief of police in Ocean City. In the very center of the resort, on the Boardwalk at Ninth Street, in a location where they had traditionally congregated for the preceding half-decade, a crowd of about one thousand teen-agers had begun to riot and was out of control. Of the score of police in Ocean City, all but the chief and one of his assistants were temporary summer employees without training or police experience. Sharing a local enthusiasm for maintaining an image of their town as a relaxed family resort, they had never been very successful in managing the town's growing teen-age clientele. On successive weekends, for several seasons, they had watched their town being transformed by the influx of adolescents, who were attracted to the resort by the prospects of "cutting up," partying, and by the ease of buying liquor from among the large number of marginal businesses opened only for the summer. The 1,700 natives of the town dubbed these Friday-through-Sunday immigrants "weekend warriors," an appellation the teen-agers enthusiastically adopted into their own argot and which, at last, the riot had chilled with the tincture of reality.

By the time the state police could establish a command post in Ocean City, the rioting crowd of youths had swollen in size and intensity. The police estimated the crowd at about two thousand. The noise and the prospect of excitement attracted most latecomers, who joined earlier arrivals in milling about the scene of the arrest. They protested, intensifying the unrest which their earlier experiences with the resort authorities had already made explicit. There were a number of rallying cries, but one—"On to City Hall!" the spot to which the arrested youth had been transported—was finally adopted by a succession of spontaneous leaders, who used it to generate movement in the crowd. The city hall became its target.

Massed together, the members of the crowd forced a path through the streets, over police cars and fire engines and through manicured gardens and miniature golf courses, toward the inlet between the ocean and the bay at the southern edge of the narrow barrier reef where the city had originated. Fire engines, ambulances, and police cars hastily retreated to a point in advance of the moving crowd, where they were deployed across streets that led to the target, a few blocks behind them. In the street along which the crowd advanced, fifty state policemen formed a phalanx to arrest its progress and otherwise intimidate its participants with the regalia of riot control: gas masks, tear-gas rifles, clubs, assorted guns, flares, megaphones, and walkie-talkies. Behind the barrier and on the tops of adjacent vehicles, local officials and state police considered alternative strategies for control should the one behind which they stood prove ineffective. The mayor declared a curfew; the field force commander of the state police read the ordinance into a megaphone and otherwise attempted to reason with the crowd periphery; and the fire chief threatened to play a stream of water into the path of the advance.

When the motion of the oncoming crowd stopped, 25 yards separated the two sets of faces, by then confronting one another fully aware of the probable outcome of their encounter. For a full quarter of an hour, the two sides stood poised in a tense equilibrium. On the part of the teen-agers, there seemed to be an unsurrendering but defeated defiance, exploring, in assorted individual acts and shouts (which in retrospect would seem irresponsible to their authors) the extent to which the authorities, appropriately equipped to suppress their challenge, could be innocuously provoked while preoccupied with an inactive but larger threat.

The police were well aware of their capacity to control the situation. They sought only to restore public order by dispersing the crowd. But to do so implied the tactic of decomposing it, fragmenting it into smaller collectivities less resistant to control and, ultimately, into the personalities that made it up. Then it would be not simply legally rational and clearly legitimate but also an incumbent duty upon them to treat the youths as individuals whose rebellious actions, however understandable in the mass, were explicitly defined within the law in terms of repressive legal consequences. To do less, they felt, would be to discredit their own competence; yet to do anything at all before fragmenting the crowd, before depressing the emotional transport that held its members, created dilemmas in a different order of significance than that urging the control of the situation upon them.

As the crowd pressed toward the barrier, it moved unknowingly into a pocket of control. Only to the north, in the direction from which it had come, was additional movement still possible. To the police, concerned with preserving property and preventing injuries, the best possible outcome in the situation was for the crowd to disperse spontaneously, just as it seemed to have arisen. It seemed rational to make arrests only for their symbolic value and, indeed, somewhat futile and unjust to make them in order to punish individuals. They sought, not to apply the law, but to restore the order within which the law functioned.[4]

When they observed the crowd of teen-agers confining itself before them, and watched its forward motion stop, the police began to assert their control. The crowd, whose actions had been somewhat unpredictable, was now "in hand," its possible courses of action anticipated and inhibited. Though decomposing, the crowd necessitated a few symbolic arrests, the larger strategy involved simply "cooling off" the participants. Knowing the crowd to be in hand, the police thus stood firmly about it, absorbing minor acts of aggression, waiting for the mood to dissolve and for its participants to retire for the night.

Ten blocks from the point of its inception, the movement of the crowd of teen-agers had fitfully ended. The noise that had enveloped it all along reached a higher level. The chanting continued and then abated, supplanted now by a focus half inside itself and half still externalized toward the barrier ahead of it. A few voices toward the forward edge of a pod that extended into a side street unsuccessfully tried to redefine the path of movement, and yet others, to whom the majority refused to listen, insisted that the barrier should be confronted. Immobility threatened the mood maintained until then, brought on still further attempts to redefine the situation, and resulted in the ambivalent equilibrium foreshadowing the end of the encounter. Activeness gave way to an overwhelming passivity, to an excited form of collective introspection that sought expressive symbols of resistance to the authorities. For a few minutes then—and again the next day, when another crowd formed at Ninth Street—the subdued rioters enacted minor aggression against the varieties of authority then confronting them (local politicians, local police, state police officers and patrolmen, and a few unidentified elders in the entourage of the town's mayor). Some rioters shouted curses and standard insults and screams; others audibly degraded the competence of the mayor and struck at the toadying of those about him; and a few destroyed minor bits of property, where unnoticed, and defied ordinances against the wearing (and non-wearing) of certain kinds of apparel. A few at the front of the crowd bowed to and

---

[4] Indeed, because riots like this one have structures unamenable to describing a locus of legally defined responsibility, the acts they promote, both within themselves and directed against them, occur in a distinctly impersonal matrix. Police control in such situations assumes a quasi-military ethic: the allocation of repression proceeds according to a set of tactical principles which randomizes the distribution of targets for sanctions, with respect to personalities, and systematizes its allocation, with respect to unconquered (uncontrolled) territory.

"mooned"[5] the fire chief, mayor, and chief of local police. But almost as if consciously attempting to maintain a protective control over their members, the majority of the participants, suddenly having become more aware of their vulnerability or at least that the police were beginning to show signs of meaning business, began again to mill about, to shuffle uneasily amidst their peers. Toward those whose excitement seemed to have transported them to near frenzy were directed calming remarks, muffled suggestions that they, among all the rest, because of their extraordinary loudness or whatever, seemed to have attracted special attention from the observing police cadre. As the authorities had gambled, the crowd seemed to be cooling itself off, reasserting its own rationality, spontaneously decomposing.

Shortly thereafter, small groups began to break away, retreating slowly back into the city to join the others lost along the way in the march toward the city hall. As the crowd dwindled, the police moved forward to coax the others along, making arrests here and there among the most resistant stragglers. Where just moments earlier an enthusiastic curse would have been submerged in the anonymous barrage, it now exposed its source as the last "warrior" in the streets. A few small groups lingered about even as the last arrest was made, disappearing with the rest only as it became clear that they, too, however innocently curious they wanted to appear, were no less immune from the jurisdiction of the curfew than those already marked for a night in jail. In a few moments the streets were again quiet; the extra police patrols during the night proved to be a superfluous precaution.

Once having happened, having been discussed and partially evaluated, the riot seemed to gather significance. Almost as soon as it was over, it had a name: the "Labor Day Riot." And sometimes, though most people seemed to leave it implicit, the qualification "teen-age" was inserted, as if to color the images provoked by the name with associations connected to popular sterotypes of adolescence—itself an implicit way of excusing the riot, rationalizing it, making it seem less than a threat to public order and more one of its expected concomitants. Even during the day after the first riot, when another teen-age crowd came up from the adjacent beach and assembled in the afternoon at Ninth Street (this time to voice displeasure at the arrest of one of their members who defied a city ordinance requiring the wearing of a shirt by a person walking on the Boardwalk), a transformation in the nature of their crowd activity became apparent. The police, who had foreseen the possibility of another outburst during the weekend, deployed a strengthened contingent of men in the area where the teenagers generally congregated. Without threatening the crowd, they cordoned off the area as inconspicuously as possible, readying themselves should another march begin, but refusing to stimulate or provoke the crowd by providing it with too great an appearance of their

[5] The verb "moon," as it is used by teen-agers and some college students, refers to the act (generally confined to males) of "dropping trow" (dropping one's trousers) so as to expose the nude hindquarters contemptuously to unexpecting on-lookers, usually adults or prissy peers. Its origins seem to be in archaic ceremonies which involved ritual defecation upon figures of authority. In the context of the riot, it preserved this gestive significance.

concern with the situation. Surrounded by the array of police, aware of them, and yet disinterested in anything but their control, the teen-agers stood their own ground. Again, but this time more cautiously, they used the apparent anonymity provided by the crowd situation to shout insults and to express contempt for the local authorities. The crowd situation, far from again being a medium of active aggression and mobile rebellion, nevertheless generated a high degree of excitement and involvement. Rather than involving thoughtless movement and activity, however, it seemed to have become a predominantly expressive crowd, its members caught up in a mood that seemed to embody their discontent, collectively symbolizing what they now acknowledged as rebellion against the authority system. And again, as on the night before, the crowd slowly began to cool off. Battered by little more than minor verbal abuse, the police again arrested a few of the more apparent leaders and then removed all but a token patrol from the area. As a number of the participants phrased it, this last day's events "capped off" the season. By degrees, they slowly gathered up their friends and belongings and headed out of the resort, back to their homes and to another year of school.

The reaction to the teen-agers' riot was curiously mixed. In the metropolitan newspapers there was the expected factual reportage, but in addition there appeared a number of quick editorial reactions and feature stories. Somehow, what had happened was felt to involve a kind of sympathetic "human interest" angle; the riot was not simply another riot, another disturbance in some closed population or asylum. It involved youth, and that made a difference. There was no condoning what had happened; public order had been disrupted, and that was deplorable. But the reasons for the riots troubled people. The crowd was not a drunken mob, its participants not juvenile delinquents.

Instead of blaming the teen-agers, the papers in fact displaced the responsibility to parents and to local officials in the resort, reserving praise for the state police for having handled the situation so efficiently. The two principal groups of participants, the teen-agers and the police, got off with sympathetic slaps, on the wrist and on the back, respectively, in the end making both feel rather good about the whole thing, and with the public, in its own turn, left to ponder the situation vicariously.

However ill-defined and ambivalently responded to, the affair was not quickly forgotten, either by the teen-agers and state police, or the public, the media, or the local officials in Ocean City. Because of its location, its participants, its timing, its general temper, the riot retained an element of fascination for all. The "Labor Day Riot" stood out symbolically in the consciences of the various groups responding to it, as if awareness of it satisfied expressive needs originating in sources common to all. The lasting response was not loud and clamorously persistent among any of the groups; yet, in a muted way, its strength perhaps growing out of the simple ambiguity of information about the facts, the response became infused with a sort of populism. Among the participants and the public, at least, the riot seemed to appear as an exemplary prototype of small-scale rebelliousness against the recalcitrance of local authorities.

The riot in fact had sufficiently powerful consequences and seemed to have arisen from such sufficiently intractable sources that another one was expected to occur on the following Labor Day. The police expected it to recur; the local officials in Ocean City expected it; the press expected it (in fact several metropolitan newspapers sent reporters and photographers); and, most significantly, the teen-agers, beyond expecting it, hoped that it would recur. In fact, another riot, or near-riot, did occur at the end of the next summer; and another one happened the year after that. For the following five summers, in fact, crowds of teen-agers congregated in Ocean City on Labor Day eve. The crowd situation had become periodic and regularized. The state police routinely deployed riot control squads in the city during each Labor Day weekend. And each year the press sent reporters, photographers, and feature writers to cover the events. They were treated annually to much the same spectacle: A crowd would form at Ninth Street; the police would instantly surround and capture it; a few arrests would be made, and the police, in the process of cooling off the crowd, would get "dumped-on" to the delight of onlookers and retreating participants. The newspapers would feature the story the next day and grind subsequent features out of it for weeks after that. The police would get a slap on the back, and for the following year the teen-agers would talk excitedly about what had happened.

Analysis. Proportionally, of course, only a small number of teen-agers, compared with the total size of the larger adolescent society, were active participants in any one of the Labor Day Crowds. But Ocean City, the town itself, was a place to which the vast majority looked for the kinds of outlets valued in teen-age culture. Over the years preceding the first riot, it had acquired a reputation for indulging their activities; and it had only been during the preceding two summers, after the election of a new mayor, that greater and greater numbers of constraints on their freedom in the resort had been put into operation, their "indulgency pattern" abrogated. The occurrence of the first riot triggered a response, therefore, for which the basis had earlier been laid down in a vague culture of discontent. Most of the youth seemed to feel that what had happened was not only proper, in the sense that the precipitating event (the arrest) justified the riot, but that the riot was one way of making the resort officials miserable for having dealt with the teen-agers so objectionably. The town, they felt, deserved to be disrupted by the riot. It seemed a great way to "cap off" their summer. And besides that, so it was argued, teen-agers had legitimate grievances; some argued, for instance, that the curfew declared by the mayor was unconstitutional, a clear violation of their citizens' rights. And others alleged police brutality from the local cops. The riot seemed to right the wrongs apparently so unjustly pushed upon them; it was a matter of fun and justice.

Though perhaps the principled response was to have been expected on the basis of recent changes in the resort itself, it involved more than simple pleasure in getting back at the local authorities. The disposition to react favorably to the first and subsequent riots also had sources in several other quarters, among them being a tendency to value occasions that provided "thrills." Engaging in disorderly crowds and illegal sorts of activities were prominent types. The teen-agers were restless, bored by the activities open to them in the resort. The riot was their own special creation. It certainly departed from the humdrum temper of the usual things to do and places to go.

To the teen-agers, part of the importance of going to Ocean City was that it put them "on their own," away from parents and familiar authorities, with the chance to exercise their growing sense of autonomy. In the absence of parental controls, one expression of their youthful quest for independence was the desire to incorporate the spirit of rebellion into the activities which they pursued. It is quite clear, for example, that Ocean City, by any objective yardstick, would appear to be a rather deadly dull sort of resort; from the points of view of the teen-agers, about the only things to its credit were the beach, the absence of parents, and the presence of a large number of peers, some of whom looked old enough to buy beer.

Yet they came to the ocean with exaggerated expectations of fun. Confronted with a rather restricted structure of opportunities, the desire to milk every drop of fun from the available possibilities made it imperative to take a few risks, for example, being caught drinking, swimming at night, or "necking" on the beach. In other words, each of the things that seemed harmless enough in itself as a type of fun, had to be taken underground. The result, one might argue, seemed to be the development of a tendency within their peer culture to provide what they called "thrills" with a sort of valued functional autonomy. Rebellion for the sake of excitement, at first implicit, became a reward in itself, a thrill that augmented the cruder creature pleasures or intrinsic fun inhering in the acts involved.

The riot intruded into this atmosphere as a super-thrill, and the response to it made out of it a compelling symbol of the short-run orientation to risk taking—and through that, to anti-authoritarianism—that surrounded the significance of Ocean City in the teen-age culture. It was a perfect inflection of the short-run orientation of teenage culture, an orientation exaggerated in Ocean City, yet also pervasively rooted in more routine contexts because of the legal status of the teen-age pursuit of fun. Subsequent to the first riot, whenever a teen-ager talked about Ocean City, conjuring up memories associated with the place, the most arresting image available was that provided by the riot itself.

The association of the riot imagery with that of Ocean City shared another connection through the dynamics of status within the adolescent society. For example, it became a mark of some status to associate oneself with the riots whenever summer activities were dug up for review. In particular, in the course of our interviews with participants, they frequently remarked that those most preoccupied with the significance of the riots were younger members of various peer groups. Since considerable attention came to be focused on the riots, those who were maneuvering to gain the acceptance of their peers, especially these younger teen-agers, in associating themselves with attention-gathering events, tended to exaggerate their importance and to maintain them as focuses for conversation. In this way the riots did gain significance; they became attention-gathering events which were looked forward to as an exciting way to end the summer with a climax that had status-conferring potential.

The connection of participation—and, in particular, the mode of participation—in the riot and the status system of the adolescent society was important in another respect, too. A peculiar fact about the composition of the crowds that rioted was that they had emerged from a pre-existing milling process set up quite normally at Ninth Street among naturally formed cliques. The teen-agers, in migrating to Ocean City, had come predominantly in small groups of friends, a large proportion in fact with their high school fraternities and sororities. They had, in other words, transported their status systems with them, and in the city they tended to carry out the majority of their activities within these peer groups. In consequence, pre-existing status differentiations were a part of the group process within which the riotous moods had emerged and been cultivated. Leaders who exemplified the status qualities rewarded in the routine functioning of their peer groups, confronted with the riot situation, did not instantly cease to be aware of their status or to be looked up to. The riots, in fact, by providing a forum for challenges to their ascendancy from spontaneous leaders, provoked status threats.[6] It became clear during the interviews that many of the "established elites" of adolescent society felt that they themselves had to co-opt the functions of spontaneous leaders in the riot situation, to demonstrate that their worthiness of deference did not break down under pressure, that they had leadership skills in aggressive crowd situations as well as in stable peer competitions. The interesting result was that spontaneous leaders, and those fomenting the mood of the riots, as well as those who set up precipitating routines to generate the subsequent crowd situations and rumor processes, were not really so spontaneous as might be expected. In effect, a large number of them were high status teen-agers who, recognizing threats to their status in the crowd dynamics, had adopted leadership roles for the larger crowd. They became the ritual leaders among their peers, augmenting the security of their own status by helping to precipitate the outburst of later summers, outbursts in which they were experienced participants.

The question of the amount of "turnover" in participation in the yearly Labor Day crowds also has an interesting bearing on factors contributing to the events. Quite clearly, there was both considerable turnover in the crowd membership and yet also a significant number of hard-core repeaters, with the leaders and sociometric stars of peer culture being especially visible. The rate of turnover seemed, in fact, to give each annual crowd an interesting balance between enthusiastically curious younger newcomers and the older repeaters. The balanced seemed to contribute to the fact that each year the crowd situation could maintain a high degree of fascination for those assembling to participte in it. Over all, the strength of the riot imagery was doubtlessly tied to the fact that it was an age-graded phenomenon, with new cohorts of teen-agers continuously entering into the peer group milieu.

In the years that followed the first riot, the crowds that formed at Ninth Street on Labor Day even changed somewhat, however. In the first place,

[6] Compare the description of status-threat dynamics given by James F. Short and Fred Strodtbeck, *Group Process and Gang Delinquency* (Chicago: University of Chicago Press, 1965), chap. viii.

everyone came expecting to get another riot going and also holding a somewhat more realistic cognitive map of the likely consequences of the crowd involvement. Also, the police never really allowed another full-fledged riot to get underway. Interestingly, although they would allow the crowd to form and allow its moods to grow somewhat excited, they would maintain it in captivity. And sometimes, recognizing a repeater or trouble maker, they would call him aside and attempt to meditate their hopes for order to the crowd. The repeaters, the ritual leaders singled out by the police, had become genuine intermediaries with the authorities.

Each annual crowd had become, in addition, a cultured crowd, expressing its grievances against local authorities. Participation was fun; it was exciting and thrilling. But it was also principled. Any of the teen-agers could rationalize the significance of the crowd formation in terms of higher values and belief systems. They talked of constitutional rights, of the injustice of treatment accorded to teen-agers; they placed their action within the context of larger, sometimes philosophical issues like freedom. And, most interestingly, they invoked a kind of creolized sociology to explain the social sources of their discontent. There were few teen-agers who could not, either by themselves or through a buddy, speak in glittering generalities provided by such catch phrases as "rebellion against authority." Most of their principles of explanation on the sociological level, naturally, were self-fulfilling ones. In the end, their interpretation both explained what was going on while justifying it and simultaneously named what had happened so as to program it, to re-induce it.

Conventionalization. The significance of these crowd actions filters through three rather gross perspectives, namely, those of the police, the teen-agers, and the larger critical public. It is partly through understanding the convergence of these three outlooks, their mutual influence and compromise, and their meeting in a commonly shared higher outlook, that the partial formalization, the patterned repetition and conventionalization of this collective behavior can be explained. The following remarks attempt to show how the three outlooks tend to interact in patterned ways, permitting a sort of de facto conventionalization that produces crowd behavior resembling ceremonial.

Police action in most contexts—but vividly so during encounters with such disorderly publics—is conditioned by a constabulary ethos, and in particular by an operational rule that might be called the "principle of minimum violence." In a large proportion of cases, for instance, the police do not feel justified or compelled to gun down participants in crowd actions; rather, they seek to "capture" them—to get them back "in hand"—and then to prod such assemblages into a process of decomposition. Principles of minimum violence for crowd control minimize not only injury but also the ordinary feedback of public outrage arising from allegations of illegitimate brutality or coercion. Such a standard set of control strategies also imparts a regularity to the process of crowd decomposition. Viewed more holistically, the result is an interchange[7] with latently *ritual* properties (i.e., a sequence of actions patterned to return a disrupted social equilibrium to its stable condition).

[7] The notion of "interchange" in the sense used here is developed by Erving Goffman, who uses the concept to denote the sequence of acts precipitated by threats to "face"

The police casually call this phase in crowd control "cooling off." In effect, it functions as a special sort of communication structure. Using the example of the beach riots, one can roughly conceptualize the notion in terms of a set of interdependent multiple exchanges. In the encounter between the crowd and the police, crowd members put up expressive resistance and call insults to the police, who in turn accept them in exchange for the minimally coercive re-establishment of public order. Between the police and the public audience, a sort of professionalized degradation tolerance is exchanged with audiences for augmented informal authority and legitimacy. And between the public and the crowd, the interchange passes a sort of sympathetic indulgency for a spectacle that functions indirectly as a public drama. In the loose analogy, the rates of exchange in these transactions are biased in favor of the most disinterested parties, namely, the police in the crowd-police interchange, the public in the police-public interchange, and the crowd in their interchange with the public.

One can phrase a proposition about the conventionalization of this three-fold interchange matrix by holding the bias of two interchanges relatively constant and allowing the third to vary. For purposes of exposition, we shall assume that the interaction of crowds and police cadres follows a fairly standard pattern (as argued above) and that the interaction of police organizations and critical publics also takes place in a relatively fixed pattern (also a reasonable assumption for our purposes, given the fairly constant quantum of police anxiety to public criticism). The third variable interchange, that between critical publics and disorderly crowds, is less constant. The bias favors crowd members only when public sympathy is on their side, something that does not always happen, for example, when crowd members are an ethnic minority, a revolutionary movement, etc. This conceptualization produces several interesting consequences. In unsympathetic cases, such as in the case of the minority riot, the antipathy of the public to disorderly crowds, or its indifference to them (for example, when they are not visible or are selectively unperceived), renders the attitude of the audience to the use of public authority congruent with that of the police. The crowd confronts a monolith of opposition, with police and public being perceived similarly, the police acting in behalf of the public, representing it, and even molding part of the public response. On the other hand, when public sympathy resides with a crowd action, the opposite pattern of influence operates. The crowd and the public attitudes to the police are balanced, and the crowd is then acting in a way representative of the public, expressive of public values. In this case, the crowd-police interchange becomes a kind of symbolic drama, with the public audience participating vicariously in the action of the crowd, its own reactions to authority in this case being influenced by the posture of the restless public.

Propositions about the likely course of development of the expression of crowd unrest follow from these notions. When the crowd action provokes a public reaction, that reaction is likely to have an *evaluative* quality; the crowd action is thought to be more or less understandable, reasonable, good or bad.

---

and terminating with the return of the encounter to a condition of ritual equilibrium; see, "On Face-Work: An Analysis of Ritual Elements in Social Interaction," *Psychiatry*, XVIII (August 1955), 213–31.

When public reaction is indifference, the *moral* issues implicit in the crowd-police interchange fail to become explicit. When the reaction is antipathetic, the expression of collective unrest confronts a hostile audience and is likely (if it does not simply die out) to be taken underground, to become the basis for transformations of collective energies into formal private developments, such as sectarian or revolutionary groups. When it is sympathetic, a public development, something like a conventionalized or a ceremonialized interchange, is more likely to occur. The general proposition, therefore, is that a process of conventionalization is most probable when (*a*) there is a strong positive public reaction to the expression of unrest in captured crowd behavior, and (*b*) the unrest underlying the collective action has very generalized sources (i.e., is constantly replaced, as in the continuously present quantum of unrest among adolescents).

A ritual interchange which dramatizes the expression of unrest and gains a sympathetic climate of public reaction sets the stage for transformations in subsequent interchanges. How this is accomplished is illustrated in part by the case of the beach riots. Active crowd aggression was controlled by the police cadre by capturing the crowd and allowing it to "cool off." The process of cooling off, latently shaped by the permissive police tactics, provoked a predictable transformation in crowd action. The "cooling off" phase of crowd captivity left open an avenue in the development of crowd life that permitted a more sublimated order of collective behavior. The transformations parallel those accompanying the shift from an active to an expressive mood, in this case the decentralization of the collectively aggressive mood into one decreasingly sustained by expressive individual acts thrown up in opposition to control. Police, in managing the cooling off, tolerate abusive demonstrations of contempt for authority by crowd members, viewing such acts as necessary concomitants of their ultimate goal of restoring order. For the crowd participants, such acts are not rationally goal-directed; they are somewhat capriciously constructed, bizarre and extravagant devices of rationalizing impunity.

Just as the cooling off phase allows crowd members to disinvolve themselves, to take an objective view of the crowd mood and the impending fate of the encounter, and then to reassert the rationality of departure, so it spontaneously provokes "evaluative" reactions among them which objectify the essentially dramatic-symbolic dimensions of the encounter. The central dimension, a sort of ordered anarchy or bounded excess, involves reference to precisely the pattern of values from which such interchanges with authorities as that embodied in the cooling off could have been deduced; and from these values, the acts of the crowd members acquire their own belated rationale. Cooling off permits the rationalization of impunity in acts that go unsanctioned; it thereby enables a rebellious mood to express itself in minor, ritually rebellious acts.[8] Occurring inside the ritual interchange, rebellious expressions

---

[8] This formulation derives from Max Gluckman, "Les rites de passage," in Max Gluckman (ed.), *Essays on the Ritual of Social Relations* (Manchester: Manchester University Press, 1962), pp. 1–52. Also, V. M. Turner, "Symbols in Ndembu Ritual," in Max Gluckman (ed.), *Closed Systems and Open Minds* (Chicago: Aldine Publishing Co., 1964), pp. 20–51. We have also adopted the notion, developed by Gluckman, of "rituals of rebellion," in conceptualizing our observations; see his *Order and Rebellion in Tribal Africa* (New York: Free Press, 1963), pp. 1–49, 110–36.

remain controlled. But the acts themselves, nevertheless, stand in stark contrast to routine, accentuating its ordered properties and the values it embodies, thereby centralizing those values into the public conscience. The interchange becomes a public stage on which the drama of legitimately ordering central values is enacted.

On the part of crowd participants, a latent consequence of expressing unrest inside the ritual boundary is the *naming* of that unrest: individual acts are focused against a structure of control which absorbs them meaningfully, and the interchange becomes a vehicle for the expression of very generalized rebellion. The individual acts of crowd participants come to *name* the dispositions and moods and, hence, to acquire the symbolic capacity to re-induce these moods and dispositions, out of which the more excited collection behavior was built. Once having been so infused with meaning—on the one hand, objectively externalizing formerly ill-defined restlessness and, on the other, directing it onto a target that imposes definition upon it—such expressions gradually become understandable. The ritual action shapes the symbolic development and in the process becomes a drive-object itself.

Not only does the ritual action gratify its participants, but it also serves functions for the agents of control and the audience. Three outlooks converge in a balanced perspective of expectations. Authorities augment their informal status, their legitimacy, by tolerating innocuous derogating gestures from retreating crowd members. Subjecting themselves to degradation for the more urgent purpose of restoring control permits them to maintain an image of the public performance of their functions that is connected with the notion of their approachability, their discretionary flexibility in tempering authority. The public reward of their indulgence of symbolic attacks also serves to crystallize the manner in which they will handle similar interchanges in the future; they become disposed to permit the conventionalized recurrence of similarly rewarded degradations. And the public, sympathetic with the control of it in tempered encounters, likewise becomes disposed to assimilate its conventionalized recurrence.

The case of the beach riots is an illustration of the convergence of these general factors. The annual reconstitution of the interchanges is similar to the conventionalized ceremonial tone of more formalized collective symbolic dramas. We have used the term "ceremonialization" to denote the elevation into *public* awareness of the symbolic dimensions of the ritual interchanges and thereby the explicit definition of such otherwise latent interchanges as structures of action capable of reifying the legitimate ordering of important collective values. Processes of ceremonialization, like the one expressed by the crowd of teen-agers, depend upon deeply rooted restlessness that externalizes itself initially in sacrilegious or anti-authoritarian collective disorder; the process of "cooling off" inside an interchange with agents of control infuses collective action with a condensed structure of significance, much like a metaphor. This significance is only partly a product of the compulsion to express discontent. It arises gradually through stratifying meaning and emotion in an intense collective action which itself becomes symbolic of the functional ordering, rationalization, and maintenance of central values. The ceremonialization of such interchanges, in other words, is the process of intermittently publicizing a framework of meaning that is composed of beliefs and issues and conceptions which, except through the intensity of such inherently symbolic and deeply motivated acts as those in rituals of rebellion, are otherwise rarely subjected to meaningful consideration in routinized every-day contexts. For participants in a crowd, the larger issues may be quite different from those initially raised for police or for wider audiences; but for all persons made aware of the enduring sources of these recurrent interchanges, some principles of general explanation are invoked, some discontinuously explicit beliefs and values recentralized into the public conscience.

Conclusions. Hopefully, this analysis will serve to qualify the mortal image of collective behavior prevalent among sociologists. Our imagery of most crowd behavior ends when the police arrive, for it is then that crowds are made more securely moribund. Yet it is then, too, as we have attempted to suggest, that some of the more important developments of crowd action take place.

The analysis of the adolescent crowds and of their control by the police has led us to suggest, in a very approximate way, some of the processes involved in crowd conventionalization, but there is a clear need for further research in this area. The social control of crowd action, the management of collective unrest, is an ordinary occurrence in many stable organizations; schools, churches, and asylums, for example, are notoriously inhospitable to mass action; yet, as complex organizations, they frequently set up controlled environments in which the management of sponsored crowds is made possible by transforming them, if only temporarily, into audiences, repenters, electorates, and so on. Crowds are gullible things, baited and then captured for numerous special purposes, often as sources of support for many of the most central social institutions. Clues to further understanding the dynamics of such crowd situations, we believe, are to be uncovered in explorations of symbolic dimensions imparted to crowd action by institutional controls.

FAMILY AND DIFFERENTIAL INVOLVEMENT WITH MARIHUANA: A STUDY OF SUBURBAN TEENAGERS*[,1]

NECHAMA TEC

Despite the general interest in and numerous publications about illicit drug use by the younger generation, there is a lack of systematic knowledge in this area of behavior. Indeed, the many disagreements and contradictory views which permeate most current discussions on the subject only emphasize the need for systematic analysis based on empirical research (Blum and Associates, 1969). The present study, by relying on systematically collected empirical data, is an attempt to increase the knowledge of illicit drug use by the younger generation. As such, it is guided by two broad assumptions.

First, illicit drug use by the younger generation constitutes a complex area of behavior for which no simple explanations are readily available. It is imperative, therefore, that any systematic study should consider a multiplicity of variables as possible explanations. Secondly, in view of the complexity and relatively little clarity surrounding the subject, any systematic analysis should carefully specify the dependent and independent variables involved. Such specification should apply both at the empirical and theoretical levels.

Sample and Method

Empirical data for the present study are based on a social survey conducted in February 1969 in a well-to-do-Eastern suburban community. The sample consisted of 1704 teenage boys and girls, all enrolled in high school. This is over 90 percent of the community's population between the ages of 15 and 18, with 52 percent females and 48 percent males. Only five percent of the sample reported father's occupation as blue-collar.

A self-administered questionnaire was handed out to students on the school premises. This questionnaire was answered in the presence of a teacher. Prior to the actual data collection it was made clear that the sponsors of the study had no affiliation with the school. The anonymity of each respondent

* Reprinted from Nechama Tec, "Family and Differential Involvement With Marihuana: A Study of Suburban Teenagers" in *Journal of Marriage and the Family*, Vol. 32 (November 1970), pp. 656, 664. An enlarged version of this paper is to appear as part of a book to be published by Markham Press in 1972.
[1] I am very grateful to Herbert H. Hyman for his continuous and extensive help so generously extended at all stages of this study. I also wish to thank Esther Mallach, Executive Director Mental Health Association of Westchester County for enabling us to conduct a small pilot study in a separate high school. My thanks go to the Mid-Fairfield Child Guidance Center, Norwalk, Connecticut for financing and sponsoring this study.

was emphasized, and students were asked not to sign their names. Since the questions were precoded, a respondent had only to place a check mark next to the most appropriate answer. Once completed, the schedule was placed on a pile in any order desired by the subject. These precautionary measures might have had an effect, for despite the fact that participation in the project was voluntary, approximately 94 percent present completed the questionnaires.

Information collected included answers to 75 items covering a variety of areas. A large proportion of these concerned the degree of involvement with various drugs: marihuana, LSD, "speed," heroin, and glue sniffing. Space limitations, plus the complexity of the information obtained, dictated that only a selected number of variables be analyzed.

DIFFERENTIAL INVOLVEMENT WITH DRUGS

Turning to the dependent variables—differential involvement with illegal drugs—the present analysis is confined to involvement with marihuana alone. This decision was prompted by the fact that of all the illegal drugs used, marihuana is most popular, both among American youths and among the sample studied. Indeed, while almost a third of the sample had direct experience with marihuana, only about 10 percent of them had direct experiences with any other drug.

To ascertain the extent of marihuana use, three distinct questions were asked, each yielding essentially similar information. These questions were dispersed in the schedule as a precautionary measure to assure greater reliability of responses. Subsequently, an index of exposure to marihuana was constructed which combined responses to all three questions.

The specific procedure was as follows: when answers to a given question were close, for example: "took it once" and "use it occasionally," this respondent was defined in terms of the higher degree of involvement stated. In cases where responses skipped a degree of involvement, for example, "never took it" to "take it with regularity," to "never took it," this particular questionnaire was set aside.

There was an extremely high consistency of answers. Of the 1704 questionnaires, only four had contradictory responses. According to the index of marihuana use, the following distribution was derived: regular users—12 percent, occasional users—12 percent, tried it once—eight percent, never tried it but would like to—eight percent, never wanted to and never did try it—60 percent. The usefulness of this categorization varies with the specific questions studied. In the present context, it was found that the extreme categories rather than the moderate ones followed a definite pattern. For the sake of simplicity, some categories were collapsed. Subsequently the following groupings were set up.

1. Non users or abstainers. This includes both those who never tried marihuana but would like to try it and those who never did and never want to try it.
2. Moderate users include those who tried marihuana once and those who use it occasionally.
3. Regular users consisted of those who used marihuana once a week (30

percent), more often than once a week (49 percent), once or more a day (18 percent), miscellaneous use (3 percent).

LEGITIMACY OF NORMS REGARDING MARIHUANA

Marihuana for the youths studied constitutes a tolerated type of activity. That is, while not prescribed, neither does marihuana refer to behavior to which they themselves or their peers would apply strong negative sanctions. Specifically, it was found that slightly over 10 percent of the sample believed that they or their friends would discontinue a friendship because of marihuana use. In addition, a majority of non-marihuana users consistently expressed tolerant attitudes towards this drug.

In contrast, it is known that such tolerant views are neither reflected in the societal laws, nor in the opinions of the older generation with whom the young come into direct contact. Indeed, the possession and use of marihuana is prohibited on the state and federal level and is defined by representatives of the older generation, school authorities and parents, as deviant behavior. According to a recent national poll of parents, 85 percent of them said that they would apply severe negative sanctions if their children used marihuana. The remaining 15 percent said they would disapprove but in a less severe fashion (Philadelphia Inquirer, 1968). In the present sample, only two percent believed that their parents would not care if they smoked marihuana, while 98 percent anticipated a variety of negative sanctions.

However, knowledge about the existence of a given norm does not necessarily lead to its legitimation and/or conformity. Indeed, theoretically as well as empirically, the legitimacy attributed to a given norm and behavior which corresponds to the same norm may vary independently. Logically four types of relationships obtain between these two variables.

1. One may define a norm as legitimate and behave in a way which conforms to it.
2. One may define a norm as legitimate but still for many reasons fail to conform to it.
3. One may define a norm as illegitimate and nevertheless engage in behavior which conforms to the given norm.
4. Finally, one may define a norm as illegitimate and engage in behavior which constitutes a deviation from the norm.

The overall tolerance towards marihuana among the young suggests an area of behavior in which the definitions of the older and younger generations diverge. Thus, the legitimacy of the norms, particularly as these apply to marihuana, are being questioned by the young. In effect the attitude of the adolescents studied can be summarized as follows: "You may smoke marihuana if you want to, there is nothing wrong with it." In contrast, the position of the older generation is: "You ought not to smoke marihuana, if you do you will be punished." From the point of view of society and its representatives, marihuana use is defined as deviant behavior. Although some members of the older generation are opposed to the severe marihuana laws, this definition is still appropriate (Cholst, 1968; Kurtz, 1969; Leary, 1968; McGlothlin,

1968; Taylor, 1966; New York Times, 1969a, 1969b, 1969c; American Medical News, 1969).

Given this conceptualization, the rather broad question to be examined is under what conditions those who question the legitimacy of a given norm will or will not deviate from it.

DIFFERENTIAL INVOLVEMENT WITH FAMILY

The independent variables must be clarified, variables capable of explaining the variations in the level of this deviant behavior. The basic interactions of an adolescent revolve around the family, school, and peer group. It is primarily through role relationships in each of these units that the teenager is attached to society at large. All three spheres of activity are interdependent, and all have an impact upon an adolescent's attitudes, values and behaviors. To the extent that family, school and peer group are the most important interaction systems, the appropriate strategy for explanations of adolescent behavioral patterns should be sought in terms of all three statuses. Since simultaneous analysis of all of these statuses constituted a formidable task, each of them will be focused upon separately.

In comparing the saliency of these three spheres of behavior, the familial status and roles emerged as the most important. Despite the possible conflicts and problems which an adolescent may experience as a member of his family, the fact still remains that the kind of family he comes from and the decisions reached by it will mold and modify his life. It is indeed the family which determines the geographic and social location, the schools attended and in large measure the kind of peers.

Viewing the family of orientation as a social unit, it is important to know what kind of properties and/or conditions of this unit are associated with what levels of deviancy (Eisenstadt, 1956:305–210; Nye, 1958). To reiterate, the family of orientation is the independent variable which may be expected to explain differential involvement with marihuana. It is thus hypothesized that differential involvement with marihuana will vary with:

1. Availability of parental models for behavior, parental behaviors, controls and pressures, evaluations and attitudes.
2. Subjectively derived satisfactions and meanings from the family as a unit.

A methodological note about the independent variables—those referring to different aspects of family life is in order here. Prior to any actual examination of their impact upon the dependent variables, all questions referring to family life were cross tabulated. Results of these cross tabulations showed consistent associations in the direction expected. For example, those who reported that their families demanded the impossible were less likely to feel that the family was the most important unit in their lives, and those who did not enjoy being with the family were less likely to turn to the family when in trouble. However, while the direction of these associations was consistently predictable, none of them was sufficiently strong to warrant the conclusion that these variables measured the same aspects of reality. Although related, each of them seemed to reflect a distinct aspect of family life. Also, it should be pointed out that whatever the consistent patterns found, they refer mainly to extreme categories of marihuana involvement or non-involvement. That is, the relationships seem to be most consistent for those who abstain from marihuana use, the regular users, and less frequently the moderate users.

Chi-square tests of significance were performed on all associations with the level of significance for each being .001. This is true for tables included in the text as well as—with one exception—other findings discussed but not appearing in table form. The exception refers to the two questions which dealt with mothers' and fathers' use of a number of legal drugs. In both cases the criteria necessary for significance were not fulfilled.

Findings and Discussion

The importance of both parents as behavioral models for their children has been recognized by sociologists and psychologists. Accordingly, the absence of one parent is said to impede the process of identification, resulting in problems of adjustment. Sociological, as well as psychological literature, provides many examples of the detrimental effects of broken homes. With respect to illegal drug use, specifically hard drugs such as heroin, a high positive correlation between broken homes and heroin use has been demonstrated (Charen and Perelman, 1946; Chein *et al.*, 1964; Gerard *et al.*, 1964; Clausen, 1957; Hill, 1962). With respect to marihuana use, however, this association has not as yet been sufficiently explored.

Turning to the sample studied, it was found that there was a significantly higher proportion of marihuana users among those from broken families than among those from unbroken families (see Table 1). Interesting here are the 19 adoptive youths (one percent of the sample) who do not appear in Table 1 because of the small number. Among them there were 16 percent regular marihuana users and 65 percent non-users. In terms of regular marihuana use, they seem to resemble those who come from broken homes. The problem of adopted adolescents in general and those within the area studied in particular, are discussed in Tec and Gordon (1967) and Tec (1969).

DRUG USE AND DRINKING AMONG PARENTS

The point is sometimes made that ours is a drug consuming culture. This is reflected in the staggering amounts of drugs produced and consumed, as well as the attitude that every ill can be solved through a pill. Indeed, some argue that the difference between the consumption of drugs by the older and younger generation lies only in the type of drugs used. Drugs favored by the older generation are alcohol, tranquilizers, barbiturates and other (DeRopp, 1961; Eddy *et al.*, 1965). The source of supply is legal for adults and illegal for the young (Goddard and Barnard, 1969:124; Nowlis, 1969:24; Parry, 1968).

Those interested in this problem further assert that a positive association may exist between parental involvement with legal drugs and their children's involvement with illegal drugs. With the present data, however, this assumption can only partially be tested. Thus, the subjects were presented with a list

TABLE 1. LIVING ARRANGEMENT BY DEGREE OF INVOLVEMENT WITH
          MARIHUANA[a]

| Involvement with Marihuana | Living Arrangement | |
| | Living with Both Parents | Do Not Live with Both Parents |
	%	%
Non users	71	54
Moderate users	19	29
Regular users	10	17
N[b]	1425	251
	$x^2 = 27.67$ d.f. $= 2$	$p < .001$

[a] 19 individuals are adopted and live with both adoptive parents. Because of their small number they are not included in this table.
[b] In this and the rest of the tables the total number of cases is less than 1700, because the "no answer" respondents are not included. In none of the tables the "no answer" exceed one percent.

of behaviors and were required to place check marks next to those which applied to mother and father separately. Among the behaviors were: use of tranquilizers, sleeping pills, and hard liquor, the last refers to "drinking more than just cocktails." An individual could place as many checks as he wished. Unfortunately, however, those who failed to check any answers might have been those whose parents do not engage in any of the behaviors, or those who simply refused to answer, for no provisions were made for the distinction between "no answer" and "does not apply." Clearly this is a methodological shortcoming, since a large number of subjects left this question unanswered, 17 percent in the case of the father and 14 percent in the case of the mother.

Despite this shortcoming, when answers from the preceding two questions are related to involvement with marihuana the results are most suggestive. Thus, focusing on the answers referring to the mother, among those whose mothers take sleeping pills there were 18 percent regular users of marihuana, 20 percent among those whose mothers took tranquilizers and 23 percent among those whose mothers "drink more than just cocktails." In contrast, among respondents who left the question unanswered only eight percent were regular marihuana users. Results from responses referring to these behaviors as they are exhibited by the father point in the same direction. Briefly, then, it can be tentatively concluded that children whose parents use legal drugs show a higher level of involvement with an illegal drug such as marihuana.

PARENTAL ACCEPTANCE/REJECTION
It was anticipated that there would be a negative association between positive evaluations and attitudes of the family and involvement with marihuana. It must be emphasized that the data collected about parental pressures, controls and evaluations as well as the respondent's satisfaction with and meaning of the family, are all based on subjective reports. The extent to

which these reports reflect reality cannot be ascertained. In a sense, then, the data at hand represent reality as perceived by these youths. This brings to mind the famous theorem of W. I. Thomas: "If men define situations as real, they are real in their consequences." If the marginals in all but the first table are observed, it can be noted that responses to questions concerning positive evaluations and attitudes of the family are neither extreme nor stereotyped. Indeed, there was a great deal of variation with overall moderate and rather positive views of the family. The last point is especially interesting because of the general ideas about rebelliousness of the young and the existence of a generation gap. These marginals point out that despite the existence of a generation gap, the family not only objectively is a salient unit for teenagers but is even subjectively perceived and evaluated as such by a substantial proportion of these young people.

Probing into this problem, subjects were asked if their family was proud and pleased, disappointed and displeased, or indifferent of them as a person. Relating these responses to marihuana use, it was found that young people who felt that their family was proud and pleased with them were less likely to smoke marihuana. Some interesting differences emerged from a comparison of the "disappointed and displeased" and "indifferent" groups (see Table 2). Those whose parents were displeased and disappointed comprised a higher proportion of marihuana users than those whose parents were merely indifferent.

Subjects were asked if they "get enough recognition" from their families. Implied here is not only the evaluative aspect, but also degree of fairness. As

TABLE 2.   FAMILY'S ATTITUDE TOWARD RESPONDENT BY DEGREE OF INVOLVE-MENT WITH MARIHUANA

Involvement with Marihuana	Family's Attitude		
	Proud and Pleased %	Disappointed and Displeased %	Indifferent to You as a Person %
Non users	75	42	49
Moderate users	18	26	31
Regular users	7	32	20
N	1295	232	139
	$x^2 = 169.44$	d.f. $= 4$	p $< .001$

	Amount of Recognition and Respect Received from Family		
	Definitely Enough %	On the Whole Enough %	Some but Not Enough %	No, Not at All %
Non users	88	70	57	49
Moderate users	16	20	24	21
Regular users	6	10	19	30
N	482	768	346	99
		$x^2 = 85.86$	d.f. $= 6$	p $< .001$

in the preceding case, a consistently negative association between the amount of recognition received from parents and the degree of involvement with marihuana emerged (see Table 2).

A strategic variable affecting adolescent behavior is the amount and type of control or pressure applied by parents. Although this variable is thought to be of significance, very little about its specific direction is known. Indeed, one could argue with equal plausibility that parental control is conducive to conformist as well as deviant behavior. The problem is by no means simple depending on kind of control, strength, and a variety of other conditions and circumstances under which it is employed. Clearly then, the variable is complex, requiring a great deal of refinement (Cohen, 1966; Ney, 1958; Parsons, 1951).

In describing their families the respondents were provided with the following choices: "easy going and warm," demanding but warm," "demanding and cold," and "indifferent." In Table 3 which relates responses from this question to marihuana use, it can be observed that among those who said that their family was warm, and regardless of whether it was also said to be demanding or easy going, the proportion of marihuana users was the same. Since "easy going" and "demanding" have the same percentage of marihuana users, this tentatively suggests that to be demanding seems to have no effect on the degree of involvement with marihuana, when accompanied by warmth.

TABLE 3. DESCRIPTION AND EVALUATION OF FAMILY BY DEGREE OF INVOLVE-
MENT WITH MARIHUANA

Involvement with Marihuana	Type of Family			
	Easy-going and Warm	Demanding but Warm	Demanding and Cold	Indifferent
	%	%	%	%
Non users	71	71	53	54
Moderate users	19	19	20	27
Regular users	10	10	27	19
N	752	683	113	134
		$x^2 = 42.70$	d.f. $= 6$	p $< .001$

Parents Ask the Impossible as Far as School Work Is Concerned

	Yes Definitely	Yes Sometimes	No, They Never Demand Too Much	No, They Don't Really Care How I Do in School
	%	%	%	%
Non users	52	67	72	41
Moderate users	22	20	20	26
Regular users	26	13	8	33
N	89	683	896	27
		$x^2 = 45.03$	d.f. $= 6$	p $< .001$

The groups whose families are "demanding and cold" and those whose families are "indifferent" contain a higher proportion of marihuana users. Thus, in contrasting these two groups with the preceding two, the level of marihuana use differs rather substantially. The difference, however, does not seem to be related to presence or absence of demands but rather to presence or absence of "warmth."

Finally, a certain similarity with the results obtained can be noted in Tables 2 and 3. That is, the indifferent parents contain a smaller percentage of regular users than parents who exhibited a purely negative attitude—parents who were "demanding and cold."

Another indicator of parental pressure was sought through the following query: "Do you feel that your parents ask the impossible as far as your school grades are concerned"? As in the preceding case, it was found that the more "impossible" parental demands, the greater the likelihood to use marihuana with regularity (see Table 3).

An exception are those who said that their parents did not care how they do in school. Unlike the data in Tables 2 and 3, the "indifferent" parents contained the highest percentage of regular marihuana users. This contradiction, or lack of consistency, is rather intriguing, suggesting at least tentatively that both extremes, total indifference and rigid controls bear a similarly positive association to marihuana use, particularly when compared to warm and involved parents.

With respect to the variable of social control, as operationally defined here, it does not by itself result in conformist behavior involving the use of an illegal drug such as marihuana. For the young, pressures—particularly those emanating from parents—might have a negative connotation. It is possible when pressures are applied in subtle ways, they may produce the desired effects.

Having dealt with the ways in which adolescents perceive their families' reactions and evaluations toward themselves and how these are related to marihuana use, their own reactions to the family and how these are related to involvement with marihuana will be examined.

SIGNIFICANCE AND ENJOYMENT OF FAMILY

An earlier assumption may be recalled that in the life of a teenager the most strategic status is the familial one. While in reality the family is the most salient group; a teenager may not agree with this. Actually this very dependence upon the family unit may create resentment and opposition in an adolescent. A certain amount of opposition and rebellion during adolescence is a universal and expected pattern. Because of this potentiality for rebellion, when an adolescent says that he derives a great deal of satisfaction from family life, such a response suggests not only an appreciation of the family but also involvement.

The question was asked: "do you enjoy being with your family?" Responses ranged from "yes, definitely" to "no, definitely not." Comparing these answers in terms of involvement with marihuana, it was found that the more the subjects enjoyed being with the family the less likely they were to indulge in marihuana use (see Table 4).

TABLE 4. EXTENT TO WHICH ENJOY BEING WITH FAMILY BY DEGREE OF
           INVOLVEMENT WITH MARIHUANA

Involvement with Marihuana	Enjoy Being with Family			
	Yes Definitely %	Sometimes %	No Hardly Ever %	No Definitely Not %
Non users	85	67	45	38
Moderate users	11	23	27	24
Regular users	4	10	28	38
N	440	1000	193	58
		$x^2 = 168.54$	d.f. $= 6$	p $< .001$

Another question reflecting involvement plus relative importance of the family was included. Here an individual was asked to rate the most important aspect of his life; the family, friends, themselves, school, or nothing. In relating these answers to marihuana use, it was found that among those who said that the family was most important, five percent were regular marihuana users as compared to 16 percent among those who said that friends were most important, and 19 percent among those who said that they themselves were most important.

Another significant aspect of the relation to one's family is the extent to which a person can talk to any or all of the family members when in trouble, for the ability to talk to a family when faced with problems implies a feeling of trust and security as well as involvement. Among those who said that they would turn to the entire family when in trouble, eight percent were regular users, as compared to 21 percent regular users among those who would turn to only friends when in trouble. Recalling the overall tolerance among teenagers towards marihuana, this finding is not surprising. Far from applying negative sanctions, the tolerant views about this activity may even encourage direct experimentation. Furthermore, the percentage of regular marihuana users remains the lowest for those who rely on the family when in trouble compared to those who rely on no one and those who rely on siblings only.

Summary and Conclusions

It has been shown that the likelihood of conformity to the norm studied (prohibitions against use of marihuana) varies directly with:

1. The presence and quality of parental models for behavior. Youths who come from broken homes and/or do not live with both parents are more likely to use marihuana than youths who come from intact families. It has also been tentatively concluded that adolescents whose parents, particularly mothers, drink hard liquor or use tranquilizers and sleeping pills, are more likely to be involved with marihuana than those who do not report such parental behaviors.

2. The extent to which associations within the family unit are defined as rewarding and meaningful by its members. Thus, the more rewarding the family is in terms of recognition and respect obtained within it, and the more personally satisfactory the relationships are within it, the lesser the likelihood to smoke marihuana. Similarly, the likelihood of turning to the family when in trouble, and the subjective definition of the family as the most important unit both show a negative association to regular involvement with marihuana.

3. The presence of parental controls and/or indifference. That is, the likelihood of marihuana use increases when demands made by the family are perceived as unfair and excessive and are not accompanied by "warmth." Similarily, those who perceive their families as indifferent are also more likely to use marihuana than those who see it as undemanding and/or warm. Thus, sheer strong control and/or complete indifference as measured by the questionnaire bear a positive association to marihuana use. According to broad sociological thinking, conformity within a given unit is achieved by its system of rewards as well as direct controls.

The unit under scrutiny, the family, is by definition a primary group. Therefore, in terms of the cultural expectations as they pertain to this unit the associations are seen as typically of an intimate and personally satisfactory nature. Where those expectations are not fulfilled lack of compliance with some of its norms might be the outcome. In a sense then, rigid controls which are experienced as reality by members of such a unit might be less tolerated than within a less intimate and more formal environment. Furthermore, the age of the sample implies a certain resistance and even resentment toward parental controls.

To what extent this association would have appeared in other units is hard to determine. Many studies conducted in the field of formal organization have shown that the level of personal satisfaction as experienced by its members, rather than rigid controls, is indeed positively associated with a high level of conformity. The present findings, therefore, should be viewed as a mere beginning in what promises to be a complicated but fascinating task.

REFERENCES

American Medical News, 1969, "Marihuana law challenged." September 15, p. 3.

Blum, Richard H. and Associates, 1969, *Drugs and Society*. San Francisco: Jossey and Bass Inc.

Charen, Sol and Luis Perelman, 1946, "Personality studies of marihuana addicts." *American Journal of Psychiatry* 102 (March):674–682.

Chein, Isidor, Donald L. Gerard, Robert S. Lee, and Eva Rosenfeld, 1964, *The Road to H.* New York: Basic Books.

Cholst, Sheldon, 1968, "Notes on the use of hashish." Pp. 266–274 in David Solomon (ed.), *The Marihuana Papers*. New York: Signet Books.

Clausen, John A., 1957, "Social patterns personality and adolescent drug use." Pp. 230–277 in A. Leighton (ed.), *Explorations in Social Psychiatry*. New York: Basic Books.
Cohen, Albert K., 1966, *Deviancy and Control*. Englewood Cliffs: Prentice Hall, Inc.
DeRopp, Robert, 1961, *Drugs and the Mind*. New York: Grove Press.
Eddy, Nathan B., H. Halbach, Harris Isabell, and Maurice H. Seevers, 1965, "Drug dependence its significance and characteristics." *Bulletin World Health Organization* 32: 721–733.
Eisenstadt, S. N., 1956, *From Generation to Generation*. Glencoe, Ill.: The Free Press.
Goddard, James L. and Alfred Barnard, 1969, "The high school drug problem." Pp. 121–129 in Erich Goode (ed.), *Marihuana*. New York: Atherton Press.
Hill, Harris, 1962, "The social deviant and initial addiction to narcotics and alcohol." *Quarterly Journal of Studies on Alcohol* 23:562–582.
Kurtz, Ronald S., 1969, "Marihuana and LSD on the campus." Pp. 113–120 in Erich Goode (ed.), *Marihuana*. New York: Atherton Press.
Leary, Timothy, 1968, "The politics ethics and meaning of marihuana." Pp. 121–142 in David Solomon (ed.), *The Marihuana Papers*. New York: Signet Books.
McGlothlin, William H., 1968, "Cannabis a reference." Pp. 455–471 in David Solomon (ed.), *The Marihuana Papers*. New York: Signet Books.
New York Times, 1969a, "Administration asks softer penalty for drug abuse." October 20, p. 24. 1969b, "Marihuana curbs endorsed in poll." October 23, p. 56. 1969c, "Dr. Mead calls marihuana ban worse than drug." October 28, p. 35.
Nowlis, Helen H., 1969, *Drugs on the College Campus*. New York: Doubleday and Co., Inc.
Nye, F. Ivan, 1958, *Family Relationships and Delinquent Behavior*. New York: John Wiley and Sons, Inc.
Parry, Hugh J., 1963, "Use of psychotropic drugs by U.S. adults." *Public Health Reports* 83:799–810.
Parsons, Talcott, 1951, *The Social System*. Glencoe, Ill.: The Free Press.
Philadelphia Inquirer, 1968, "Parents draw line on teenagers using drugs." March 4.
Taylor, Norman, 1966, *Narcotics: Nature's Dangerous Gifts*. New York: Dell Publishing Co.
Tec, Leon, 1969, "On adoption." Paper presented at the Argentine Psychiatric Society Meeting, Buenos Aires.
Tec, Leon and Susanne Gordon, 1967, "The adopted child's adaptation to adolescence." Paper presented at the 44th Annual Meeting of the American Orthopsychiatric Association, Washington, D.C.

Name Index

Subject Index

Adolescence, and bodily development, 11
  as distinctive life stage, 180
  effects of maternal employment on, 123–142
  language of, 192–211
  and socialization, 104
  See also Youth
Adolescent culture, existence of, 40, 41, 172
  status systems of, 41–51, 201–206
  as subculture, 179, 192
  as transitional life stage, 178, 183
  See also Education; Youth culture
Age, as criterion for role allocation, 7
  cultural definitions of, 3–5
  of marriage, 29–34
  segregation, 37
  and youthfulness, 180
Athletics, and social status, 38, 41, 42, 48–51, 217

Birth order, 108–111
Blacks, attitudes toward integration and black consciousness, 143–152
  racial separatism, 149

Children, and apprenticeship system, 21, 22, 29
  demographic influences on, 18–21, 23–27, 30
  economic and industrial influences on, 17, 21–29, 31, 33
  as economic insurance, 25, 26
  in the eighteenth century, 19–21, 23–26, 30, 31
  and factory legislation, 23, 27, 30
  in the nineteenth century, 18–33
  as part of the labor force, 21–29, 33–35
  special status of, 17–35
  in the twentieth century, 32–35
College faculty, encounters with students, 91, 92
  roles of, 86
Colleges, two-year, 99, 102
Consumer patterns, 35
Conventionalization, 439

Dating behavior, of college students, 155
  reasons for dating, 163–166

and dating roles, 158
and stages of courtship, 154, 156–169
Disadvantaged youth, behavior problems and work failure, 263–265
  counseling and work adjustment of, 249–253
  jobseeking patterns of, 245–249
  work adjustment training of, 253–263
Drug use, and family factors, 456–462
  and marihuana involvement, 453–464
  and usage norms, 455, 456

Education, and adolescent culture, 38, 40–51
  and compulsory attendance, 27–29
  formalization of, 36
  and social mobility, 37
Educational aspirations, and peer group, 38, 223–224
  sources of, 54
  among working-class youth, 38, 52

Family, and achievement, 11
  and discipline, 115–118
  and parent-child attitude differences, 143–152
  size of, 108–111
  and social class differences, 108–122
  and socialization for activism, 330
  and socialization of children, 36, 104–105
  See also Father; Mother
Father, educational status of, 57, 59
  occupational status of, 61
Free speech, 70–83

Generational problems, 84, 102, 103

Hippies, as counter-cultural force, 437
  cultural characteristics of, 429, 430
  persecution of, 422–425

"In loco parentis," 102

Mexican Americans, acculturation process of, 237
  adolescent migration research on, 231
  child-rearing practices of, 231
  of east Los Angeles, 229–231

469